FEDERAL RULES OF EVIDENCE

2003–2004 Edition

Including
Notes by the Federal Judicial Center
Pertinent Advisory Committee Notes
Relevant Legislative History
References to McCormick on Evidence, 5th
Deleted and Superseded Materials
also

CALIFORNIA EVIDENCE CODE
(With Selected Comments)

UNIFORM RULES OF EVIDENCE

ELECTRONIC RESEARCH IN EVIDENCE

NOTES ON CASE LAW DIVERGENCE FROM THE FEDERAL RULES OF EVIDENCE

THOMSON
WEST

Material #40151011

ISBN 0-314-14666-0

TEXT IS PRINTED ON 10% POST CONSUMER RECYCLED PAPER

INTRODUCTION[1]

This Pamphlet consists of the Federal Rules of Evidence and materials designed to aid in understanding, construing, and applying them.

Chief Justice Warren in 1965 appointed an advisory committee to draft rules of evidence for the federal courts. The committee's preliminary Draft was published and circulated for comment in 1969. 46 F.R.D. 161. A Revised Draft was circulated in 1971. 51 F.R.D. 315. In 1972, the Supreme Court prescribed Federal Rules of Evidence, to be effective July 1, 1973. 56 F.R.D. 183. Justice Douglas dissented. Pursuant to the various enabling acts, Chief Justice Burger transmitted the rules to the Congress, which suspended the rules pending further study by the Congress. P.L. 93–12. After extensive study, the Congress enacted the rules into law with various amendments, to become effective July 1, 1975. P.L. 93–595, approved January 2, 1975, 88 Stat. 1926. The occasional amendments and additions that have since been made are reflected in the rules as here presented.

Thus the Federal Rules of Evidence are the product of both the rulemaking process established by the Supreme Court and the legislative process of the Congress. Of at least equal importance is the vast collection of common law precedents, with occasional statutes, that constituted the background against which the rules were evolved. It can be seen that each of these sources must be taken into consideration in reaching understanding of the rules.

The rules are in final analysis legislative in nature, and problems of their effect are problems of statutory interpretation. Questions whether interpretive inquiry should be directed to ascertaining the intent of the legislature or the meaning to its audience tend to be minimal, since the rules are directed to a skilled professional audience in the main, in contrast to, say, a criminal statute directed to the public generally. With the rules, intent and meaning tend to come together, with the same interpretive materials relevant to both. The basic relevant interpretive materials are the common law background and the legislative history, with the most significant aspects of the latter consisting of the Advisory Committee's Notes and various congressional reports and debates, briefly described below. To help a reader working sequentially through the legislative background of any given rule, if a rule was commented upon by reference to subdivisions within that rule, the Advisory Committee Notes and Reports of House/Senate Committees have been segmented and arranged to display those comments in descending order, by subdivision.

1. This introductory material was prepared by the late Professor Edward W. Cleary, Reporter to the Advisory Committee for the Federal Rules of Evidence. For a more detailed discussion, see Cleary, Preliminary Notes on Reading the Rules of Evidence, 57 Neb.L.Rev. 908 (1978).

INTRODUCTION

References to McCormick Text. The first item after each federal rule in the Pamphlet is a heading "Section References, McCormick 5th ed." [It should be noted that these references will differ somewhat from those of McCormick 1st Edition utilized in the Advisory Committee Notes following each rule.] Under it are the numbers of the text sections where the rule is mentioned or discussed, with the discussions more in depth shown in italics. Judicial decisions and other authorities construing the rule will be found in the listed sections. Any differences between the federal rule and the revised Uniform rule are pointed out in the text. Sections where the background and current posture of the common law are set forth and evaluated will be found near, usually preceding, sections discussing the rule.

Rules Prescribed by the Supreme Court. These rules were transmitted by the Court to the Congress, carried the prestige of the Court, and were the Court's exercise of the rulemaking powers granted by the various enabling acts. They constitute the framework and to a large extent also the particulars of the rules enacted by the Congress. Whether and how a Court's rule was amended by the Congress is described in the *Note by Federal Judicial Center* following each rule in the Pamphlet.

Advisory Committee's Notes. The Notes supported and explained the rules, were circulated with them, and were transmitted to the Congress with the rules. The involved congressional committees and subcommittees were thoroughly familiar with the Notes, and except where changes were made in the rules the Notes should be taken as the equivalent of a congressional committee report as representing the thinking of the Congress. The pertinent Note, or portion thereof, is set forth in the Pamphlet for each rule. Where the Congress returned to an earlier version of the rule, the Note is the one that corresponds to that version. Portions no longer relevant because of congressional changes in the rule are omitted.

Congressional Materials. The House took the lead in congressional consideration of the rules. Accordingly, in the Pamphlet any pertinent portion of the *Report of the House Committee on the Judiciary* is the first of the congressional materials under each rule. Senate consideration of the rules chronologically followed that of the House, and as a result any pertinent portion of the *Report of the Senate Committee on the Judiciary* is located under each rule in the Pamphlet after that of the House committee. Where House and Senate passed differing versions of a rule, the difference was resolved by conference, and the *Conference Report* generally concludes the congressional materials. In some instances other congressional materials which are authoritative and helpful are, however, also included.

Some General Observations

Questions as to what a rule really means present probable the most basic problem of interpretation. The language of the rule itself should be taken as the prime source of meaning, read in the light of such context as may be relevant. The most relevant context will often be legislative history, which on occasion may even override an apparently plain and unmistakable meaning of the words of the rule.[2] The result may be startling, as when the Court of Appeals for the District of Columbia Circuit concluded that a conviction for attempted burglary used for impeachment under Rule 609(a) did not involve dishonesty as the language was used in the rule.[3] Yet the opposite conclusion would have been most difficult to reach in view of the legislative history of the rule.[4]

No common law of evidence in principle remains under the rules. "All relevant evidence is admissible except as otherwise provided. . . ."[5] In reality, of course, the common law remains as a source of guidance in identifying problems and suggesting solutions, within the confines of the rules.

A recurring question is that of the extent to which the application of the rules may be extended beyond their express provisions. Some explicit authorizations to courts to invent and create are found, as for example the provision of Rule 501 that privileges "shall be governed by the principles of the common law as they may be interpreted by the courts of the United States in the light of reason and experience," and the provisions of Rules 803(24) and 804(b)(5) for the restricted admission of hearsay statements not falling within an enumerated exception. A somewhat tighter rein is kept on the judiciary by the rules that obviously contemplate a measure of invention but only within the confines of a stated principle, as in Rule 404(b) where illustrations are given of purposes for which evidence of other crimes may be admitted.

With regard to the more particularized rules, how should parallel situations be treated? Should the rule be regarded as occupying the field exclusively, or should it be extended by analogy to related situations? The answer lies in the purpose of the rule: if the additional situation presents the same problem as that with which the rule was designed to deal, application of the rule is appropriate. For example, under Rule 801(d)(1)(C) an out-of-court identification statement made after viewing a photograph has been held to be governed by the nonhearsay rule specifically applicable to statements made after viewing the accused in person.[6] Or again, the prohibition against testimony by the judge in the trial over which he is presiding, in Rule 605, was extended to preclude testimony by his clerk.[7]

2. The manner of exercise of its legislative powers by the Congress as spelled out in the Constitution is the passing of bills and obtaining the President's approval or overriding his veto. U.S. Const. art. 1 § 7. While this may suggest the irrelevance of legislative history, in the British tradition, the American commitment is contrary, and it can scarcely be denied that the reasoning of those involved is a helpful source of illumination, without having the authority of law.

3. United States v. Smith, 551 F.2d 348 (D.C.Cir.1976).

4. Id. at 362.

5. Fed.R.Evid. 402.

6. United States v. Lewis, 565 F.2d 1248 (2d Cir.1977), cert. denied 435 U.S. 973.

7. Kennedy v. Great Atlantic & Pacific Tea Co., 551 F.2d 593 (5th Cir.1977), rehearing denied 554 F.2d 475.

Not to be confused with the foregoing is the judicial engrafting onto a rule of a requirement not set forth in the rule and not supported by legislative history or other relevant context. An example is the engrafting of a requirement that other crimes as proof of intent under Rule 404(b) be proved by clear and convincing evidence, although no such provision is found in the rule.[8]

Rule 102 provides:

> These rules shall be construed to secure fairness in administration, elimination of unjustifiable expense and delay, and promotion of growth and development of the law of evidence to the end that the truth may be ascertained and proceedings justly determined.

Entitled "Purpose and Construction," the rule sets a high standard for approaching problems of application and meaning but furnishes small guidance to solving particular questions. The most important aspect of the rule may well be its implicit recognition that the rules do not, and cannot, resolve in specific terms a very large proportion of evidentiary uncertainties that may arise, and that solutions must be reached through application of accepted principles of statutory construction.

8. United States v. Beechum, 555 F.2d 487 (5th Cir.1977). The panel decision was overturned in banc. 582 F.2d 898, cert. denied 440 U.S. 920.

Summary of Contents

FEDERAL RULES OF EVIDENCE FOR UNITED STATES COURTS

ARTICLE I. GENERAL PROVISIONS

ARTICLE II. JUDICIAL NOTICE

ARTICLE III. PRESUMPTIONS IN CIVIL ACTIONS AND PROCEEDINGS

ARTICLE IV. RELEVANCY AND ITS LIMITS

SUMMARY OF CONTENTS

ARTICLE V. PRIVILEGES

ARTICLE VI. WITNESSES

ARTICLE VII. OPINIONS AND EXPERT TESTIMONY

ARTICLE VIII. HEARSAY

SUMMARY OF CONTENTS

SUMMARY OF CONTENTS

FEDERAL RULES OF EVIDENCE FOR UNITED STATES COURTS *

PUBLIC LAW 93–595; 88 STAT. 1926

Approved Jan. 2, 1975

[H.R. 5463]

An Act to establish rules of evidence for certain courts and proceedings.

Be it enacted by the Senate and House of Representatives of the United States of America in Congress assembled, That:

The following rules shall take effect on the one hundred and eightieth day beginning after the date of the enactment of this Act. These rules apply to actions, cases, and proceedings brought after the rules take effect. These rules also apply to further procedure in actions, cases, and proceedings then pending, except to the extent that application of the rules would not be feasible, or would work injustice, in which event former evidentiary principles apply.

ORDER OF APRIL 30, 1979

1. That Rule 410 of the Federal Rules of Evidence be, and it hereby is, amended to read as follows:

[See amendment made thereby following Rule 410, post.]

2. That the foregoing amendment to the Federal Rules of Evidence shall take effect on November 1, 1979, and shall be applicable to all proceedings then pending except to the extent that in the opinion of the court the application of the amended rule in a particular proceeding would not be feasible or would work injustice.

3. That THE CHIEF JUSTICE be, and he hereby is, authorized to transmit to the Congress the foregoing amendment to the Federal Rules of Evidence in accordance with the provisions of 28 U.S.C. § 2076.

CONGRESSIONAL ACTION ON AMENDMENT PROPOSED APRIL 30, 1979

Pub.L. 96–42, July 31, 1979, 93 Stat. 326, provided that the amendment proposed and transmitted to the Federal Rules of Evidence affecting rule 410, shall not take effect until Dec. 1, 1980, or until and then only to the extent approved by Act of Congress, whichever is earlier.

* References to sections of *McCormick on Evidence*, 5th ed. follow the text of each Rule. The more important section references are printed in italic.

ORDER OF MARCH 2, 1987

1. That the Federal Rules of Evidence be, and they hereby are, amended by including therein amendments to Rules 101, 104, 106, 404, 405, 411, 602, 603, 604, 606, 607, 608, 609, 610, 611, 612, 613, 615, 701, 703, 705, 706, 801, 803, 804, 806, 902, 1004, 1007 and 1101, as hereinafter set forth:

[See amendments made thereby under respective rules, post.]

2. That the foregoing changes in the Federal Rules of Evidence shall take effect on October 1, 1987.

3. That THE CHIEF JUSTICE be, and he hereby is, authorized to transmit to the Congress the foregoing changes in the rules of evidence in accordance with the provisions of Section 2076 of Title 28, United States Code.

ORDER OF APRIL 25, 1988

1. That the Federal Rules of Evidence be, and they hereby are, amended by including therein amendments to Rules 101, 602, 608, 613, 615, 902, and 1101, as hereinafter set forth:

[See amendments made thereby under respective rules, post.]

2. That the foregoing changes in the Federal Rules of Evidence shall take effect on November 1, 1988.

3. That THE CHIEF JUSTICE be, and he hereby is, authorized to transmit to the Congress the foregoing changes in the rules of evidence in accordance with the provisions of Section 2076 of Title 28, United States Code.

ORDER OF JANUARY 26, 1990

1. That the Federal Rules of Evidence be, and they hereby are, amended by including therein amendments to Rule 609(a)(1) and (2), as hereinafter set forth:

[See amendment made thereby, post].

2. That the foregoing changes in the Federal Rules of Evidence shall take effect on December 1, 1990.

3. That THE CHIEF JUSTICE be, and he hereby is, authorized to transmit to the Congress the foregoing changes in the rules of evidence in accordance with the provisions of Section 2074 of Title 28, United States Code.

ORDER OF APRIL 30, 1991

1. That the Federal Rules of Evidence for the United States District Courts be, and they hereby are, amended by including therein amendments to Evidence Rules 404(b) and 1102.

[See amendments made thereby under respective rules, post.]

2. That the foregoing amendments to the Federal Rules of Evidence shall take effect on December 1, 1991, and shall govern in all proceedings thereafter commenced and, insofar as just and practicable, all proceedings then pending.

3. That THE CHIEF JUSTICE be, and he hereby is, authorized to transmit to the Congress the foregoing amendments to the Federal Rules of Evidence in accordance with the provisions of Section 2072 of Title 28, United States Code.

ORDER OF APRIL 22, 1993

1. That the Federal Rules of Evidence for the United States District Courts be, and they hereby are, amended by including therein amendments to Evidence Rules 101, 705, and 1101.

[See amendments made thereby under respective rules, post.]

2. That the foregoing amendments to the Federal Rules of Evidence shall take effect on December 1, 1993, and shall govern in all proceedings thereafter commenced and, insofar as just and practicable, all proceedings then pending.

3. That THE CHIEF JUSTICE be, and he hereby is, authorized to transmit to the Congress the foregoing amendments to the Federal Rules of Evidence in accordance with the provisions of Section 2072 of Title 28, United States Code.

ORDER OF APRIL 29, 1994

1. That the Federal Rules of Evidence for the United States District Courts be, and they hereby are, amended by including therein amendments to Evidence Rule 412.

[See amendments made thereby under respective rules, post.]

2. That the foregoing amendments to the Federal Rules of Evidence shall take effect on December 1, 1994, and shall govern in all proceedings thereafter commenced and, insofar as just and practicable, all proceedings then pending.

3. That THE CHIEF JUSTICE be, and he hereby is, authorized to transmit to the Congress the foregoing amendments to the Federal Rules of Evidence in accordance with the provisions of Section 2072 of Title 28, United States Code.

ORDER OF APRIL 11, 1997

ORDERED:

1. That the Federal Rules of Evidence be, and they hereby are, amended by including therein amendments to Evidence Rules 407, 801, 803(24), 804(b)(5), and 806, and new Rules 804(b)(6) and 807.

2. That the foregoing amendments to the Federal Rules of Evidence shall take effect on December 1, 1997, and shall govern in all proceedings thereafter commenced and, insofar as just and practicable, all proceedings then pending.

3. That THE CHIEF JUSTICE be, and hereby is, authorized to transmit to the Congress the foregoing amendments to the Federal Rules of Evidence in accordance with the provisions of Section 2072 of Title 28, United States Code.

ORDER OF APRIL 24, 1998

ORDERED:

1. That the Federal Rules of Evidence be, and they hereby are, amended by including therein amendments to Evidence Rules 615.

2. That the foregoing amendments to the Federal Rules of Evidence shall take effect on December 1, 1998, and shall govern in all proceedings thereafter commenced and, insofar as just and practicable, all proceedings then pending.

3. That THE CHIEF JUSTICE be, and hereby is, authorized to transmit to the Congress the foregoing amendments to the Federal Rules of Evidence in accordance with the provisions of Section 2072 of Title 28, United States Code.

ORDER OF APRIL 17, 2000

ORDERED:

1. That the Federal Rules of Evidence for the United States District Courts be, and they hereby are, amended by including therein amendments to Evidence Rules 103, 404, 702, 703, 803(b) and 902.

2. That the foregoing amendments to the Federal Rules of Evidence shall take effect on December 1, 2000, and shall govern in all proceedings thereafter commenced and, insofar as just and practicable, all proceedings then pending.

3. That THE CHIEF JUSTICE be, and hereby is, authorized to transmit to the Congress the foregoing amendments to the Federal Rules of Evidence in accordance with the provisions of Section 2072 of Title 28, United States Code.

ORDER OF MARCH 27, 2003

ORDERED:

1. That the Federal Rules of Evidence be, and they hereby are, amended by including therein the amendments to Evidence Rule 608(b).

2. That the foregoing amendments to the Federal Rules of Evidence shall take effect on December 1, 2003, and shall govern in all

proceedings thereafter commenced and insofar as just and practicable, all proceedings then pending.

3. That THE CHIEF JUSTICE be, and hereby is, authorized to transmit to the Congress the foregoing amendments to the Federal Rules of Evidence in accordance with the provisions of Section 2072 of Title 28, United States Code.

ARTICLE I. GENERAL PROVISIONS

Rule

Rule 101. Scope

These rules govern proceedings in the courts of the United States and before the United States bankruptcy judges and United States magistrate judges, to the extent and with the exceptions stated in rule 1101.

(As amended Mar. 2, 1987, eff. Oct. 1, 1987; Apr. 25, 1988, eff. Nov. 1, 1988; Apr. 22, 1993, eff. Dec. 1, 1993.)

Note by Federal Judicial Center

The rule enacted by the Congress is the rule prescribed by the Supreme Court without change.

Advisory Committee's Note

56 F.R.D. 183, 194

Rule 1101 specifies in detail the courts, proceedings, questions, and stages of proceedings to which the rules apply in whole or in part.

1987 Amendment

United States bankruptcy judges are added to conform this rule with Rule 1101(b) and Bankruptcy Rule 9017.

1988 Amendment

The amendment is technical. No substantive change is intended.

1993 Amendment

This revision is made to conform the rule to changes made by the Judicial Improvements Act of 1990.

Rule 102. Purpose and Construction

These rules shall be construed to secure fairness in administration, elimination of unjustifiable expense and delay, and promotion of growth and development of the law of evidence to the end that the truth may be ascertained and proceedings justly determined.

Section references, McCormick 5th ed.

§ 60

Note by Federal Judicial Center

The rule enacted by the Congress is the rule prescribed by the Supreme Court without change.

Advisory Committee's Note

56 F.R.D. 183, 194

For similar provisions see Rule 2 of the Federal Rules of Criminal Procedure, Rule 1 of the Federal Rules of Civil Procedure, California Evidence Code § 2, and New Jersey Evidence Rule 5.

Rule 103. Rulings on Evidence

(a) Effect of erroneous ruling. Error may not be predicated upon a ruling which admits or excludes evidence unless a substantial right of the party is affected, and

(1) Objection. In case the ruling is one admitting evidence, a timely objection or motion to strike appears of record, stating the specific ground of objection, if the specific ground was not apparent from the context; or

(2) Offer of proof. In case the ruling is one excluding evidence, the substance of the evidence was made known to the court by offer or was apparent from the context within which questions were asked.

Once the court makes a definitive ruling on the record admitting or excluding evidence, either at or before trial, a party need not renew an objection or offer of proof to preserve a claim of error for appeal.

(b) Record of offer and ruling. The court may add any other or further statement which shows the character of the evidence, the form in which it was offered, the objection made, and the ruling thereon. It may direct the making of an offer in question and answer form.

(c) Hearing of jury. In jury cases, proceedings shall be conducted, to the extent practicable, so as to prevent inadmissible evidence from being suggested to the jury by any means, such as making statements or offers of proof or asking questions in the hearing of the jury.

(d) Plain error. Nothing in this rule precludes taking notice of plain errors affecting substantial rights although they were not brought to the attention of the court.

(As amended Apr. 17, 2000, eff. Dec. 1, 2000.)

Section references, McCormick 5th ed.

Generally § 51, § 52, § 58

(a). § 58

(1). § 52, § 55, § 73

(2). § 51, § 52

(b). § 51, § 58

(c). § 51, § 52, § 190

(d). § 52, § 55

Note by Federal Judicial Center

The rule enacted by the Congress is the rule prescribed by the Supreme Court, amended by substituting "court" in place of "judge," with appropriate pronominal change.

Advisory Committee's Note

56 F.R.D. 183, 195

Subdivision (a) states the law as generally accepted today. Rulings on evidence cannot be assigned as error unless (1) a substantial right is affected, and (2) the nature of the error was called to the attention of the judge, so as to alert him to the proper course of action and enable opposing counsel to take proper corrective measures. The objection and the offer of proof are the techniques for accomplishing these objectives. For similar provisions see Uniform Rules 4 and 5; California Evidence Code §§ 353 and 354; Kansas Code of Civil Procedure §§ 60–404 and 60–405. The rule does not purport to change the law with respect to harmless error. See 28 USC § 2111, F.R.Civ.P. 61, F.R.Crim.P. 52, and decisions construing them. The status of constitutional error as harmless or not is treated in Chapman v. California, 386 U.S. 18, 87 S.Ct. 824, 17 L.Ed.2d 705 (1967), reh. denied id. 987, 87 S.Ct. 1283, 18 L.Ed.2d 241.

Subdivision (b). The first sentence is the third sentence of Rule 43(c) of the Federal Rules of Civil Procedure[1] virtually verbatim. Its purpose is to reproduce for an appellate court, insofar as possible, a true reflection of what occurred in the trial court. The second sentence is in part derived from the final sentence of Rule 43(c).[1] It is designed to resolve doubts as to what testimony the witness would have in fact given, and, in nonjury cases, to provide the appellate court with material for a possible final disposition of the case in the event of reversal of a ruling which excluded evidence. See 5 Moore's Federal Practice § 43.11 (2d ed. 1968). Application is made discretionary in view of the practical impossibility of formulating a satisfactory rule in mandatory terms.

Subdivision (c). This subdivision proceeds on the supposition that a ruling which excludes evidence in a jury case is likely to be a pointless procedure if the excluded evidence nevertheless comes to the attention of the jury. Bruton v. United States, 389 U.S. 818, 88 S.Ct. 126, 19 L.Ed.2d 70 (1968). Rule 43(c) of

1. Rule 43(c) of the Federal Rules of Civil Procedure was deleted by order of the Supreme Court entered on November 20, 1972, 93 S.Ct. 3073, 3075, 3076, 3077, 34 L.Ed.2d lxv, ccv, ccviii, which action was affirmed by the Congress in P.L. 93–595 § 3 (January 2, 1975).—Federal Judicial Center.

the Federal Rules of Civil Procedure[1] provides: "The court may require the offer to be made out of the hearing of the jury." In re McConnell, 370 U.S. 230, 82 S.Ct. 1288, 8 L.Ed.2d 434 (1962), left some doubt whether questions on which an offer is based must first be asked in the presence of the jury. The subdivision answers in the negative. The judge can foreclose a particular line of testimony and counsel can protect his record without a series of questions before the jury, designed at best to waste time and at worst "to waft into the jury box" the very matter sought to be excluded.

Subdivision (d). This wording of the plain error principle is from Rule 52(b) of the Federal Rules of Criminal Procedure. While judicial unwillingness to be constricted by mechanical breakdowns of the adversary system has been more pronounced in criminal cases, there is no scarcity of decisions to the same effect in civil cases. In general, see Campbell, Extent to Which Courts of Review Will Consider Questions Not Properly Raised and Preserved, 7 Wis.L.Rev. 91, 160 (1932); Vestal, Sua Sponte Consideration in Appellate Review, 27 Fordham L.Rev. 477 (1958–59); 64 Harv.L.Rev. 652 (1951). In the nature of things the application of the plain error rule will be more likely with respect to the admission of evidence than to exclusion, since failure to comply with normal requirements of offers of proof is likely to produce a record which simply does not disclose the error.

2000 Amendment

The amendment applies to all rulings on evidence whether they occur at or before trial, including so-called "*in limine*" rulings. One of the most difficult questions arising from *in limine* and other evidentiary rulings is whether a losing party must renew an objection or offer of proof when the evidence is or would be offered at trial, in order to preserve a claim of error on appeal. Courts have taken differing approaches to this question. Some courts have held that a renewal at the time the evidence is to be offered at trial is always required. *See, e.g., Collins v. Wayne Corp.*, 621 F.2d 777 (5th Cir. 1980). Some courts have taken a more flexible approach, holding that renewal is not required if the issue decided is one that (1) was fairly presented to the trial court for an initial ruling, (2) may be decided as a final matter before the evidence is actually offered, and (3) was ruled on definitively by the trial judge, *See, e.g., Rosenfeld v. Basquiat*, 78 F.3d 84 (2d Cir. 1996) (admissibility of former testimony under the Dead Man's Statute; renewal not required). Other courts have distinguished between objections to evidence, which must be renewed when evidence is offered, and offers of proof, which need not be renewed after a definitive determination is made that the evidence is inadmissible. *See, e.g., Fusco v. General Motors Corp.*, 11 F.3d 259 (1st Cir. 1993). Another court, aware of this Committee's proposed amendment, has adopted its approach. *Wilson v. Williams*, 182 F. 3d 562 (7th Cir.1999) (en banc). Differing views on this question create uncertainty for litigants and unnecessary work for the appellate courts.

The amendment provides that a claim of error with respect to a definitive ruling is preserved for review when the party has otherwise satisfied the objection or offer of proof requirements of Rule 103(a). When the ruling is definitive, a renewed objection or offer of proof at the time the evidence is to be offered is more a formalism than a necessity. *See* Fed.R.Civ.P. 46 (formal exceptions unnecessary); Fed.R.Cr.P. 51 (same); *United States v. Mejia–Alarcon*, 995 F.2d 982, 986 (10th Cir. 1993) ("Requiring a party to renew an objection when the district court has issued a definitive ruling on a matter that can be fairly decided before trial would be in the nature of a formal exception and therefore unnecessary."). On the other hand, when the trial court appears to have reserved its ruling or to have indicated that the ruling is provisional, it makes sense to require the party to bring the issue to the court's attention subsequently. *See, e.g., United States v. Vest*, 116 F.3d 1179, 1188 (7th Cir. 1997) (where the trial court ruled *n limine* that testimony from defense witnesses could not be admitted, but allowed the defendant to seek leave at trial to call the witnesses should their testimony turn out to be relevant, the defendant's failure to seek such leave at trial meant that it was "too late to reopen the issue now on appeal"); *United States v. Valenti*, 60 F.3d 941 (2d Cir. 1995) (failure to proffer evidence at trial waives any claim of error where the trial judge had stated that he would reserve judgment on the *in limine* motion until he had heard the trial evidence).

The amendment imposes the obligation on counsel to clarify whether an *in limine* or other evidentiary ruling is definitive when there is doubt on that point. *See, e.g., Walden v. Georgia–Pacific Corp.*, 126 F.3d 506, 520 (3d Cir. 1997) (although "the district court told plaintiffs' counsel not to reargue every ruling, it did not countermand its clear opening statement that all of its rulings were tentative, and counsel never requested clarification, as he might have done.").

Even where the court's ruling is definitive, nothing in the amendment prohibits the court from revisiting its decision when the evidence is to be offered. If the court changes its initial ruling, or if the opposing party violates the terms of the initial ruling, objection must be made when the evidence is offered to preserve the claim of error for appeal. The error, if any, in such a situation occurs only when the evidence is offered and admitted. *United States Aviation Underwriters, Inc. v. Olympia Wings, Inc.*, 896 F.2d 949, 956 (5th Cir. 1990) ("objection is required to preserve error when an opponent, or the court itself, violates a motion *in limine* that was granted"); *United States v. Roenigk*, 810 F.2d 809 (8th Cir. 1987) (claim of error was not preserved where the defendant failed to object at trial to secure the benefit of a favorable advance ruling).

A definitive advance ruling is reviewed in light of the facts and circumstances before the trial court at the time of the ruling. If the relevant facts and circumstances change materially after the advance ruling has been made, those facts and circumstances cannot be relied upon on appeal unless they have been brought to the attention of the trial court by way of a renewed, and timely, objection, offer of proof, or motion to strike. *See Old Chief v. United States*, 519 U.S. 172, 182, n.6 (1997) ("It is important that a reviewing court evaluate the trial court's decision from its perspective when it had to rule and not indulge in review by hindsight."). Similarly, if the court decides in an advance ruling that proffered evidence is admissible subject to the eventual introduction by the proponent of a foundation for the evidence, and that foundation is never provided, the opponent cannot claim error based on the failure to establish the foundation unless the opponent calls that failure to the court's attention by a timely motion to strike or other suitable motion. *See Huddleston v. United States*, 485 U.S. 681, 690, n.7 (1988) ("It is, of course, not the responsibility of the judge *sua sponte* to ensure that the foundation evidence is offered; the objector must move to strike the evidence if at the close of the trial the offeror has failed to satisfy the condition.").

Nothing in the amendment is intended to affect the provisions of Fed. R.Civ.P. 72(a) or 28 U.S.C. § 636(b)(1) pertaining to nondispositive pretrial rulings by magistrate judges in proceedings that are not before a magistrate judge by consent of the parties. Fed.R.Civ.P. 72(a) provides that a party who fails to file a written objection to a magistrate judge's nondispositive order within ten days of receiving a copy "may not thereafter assign as error a defect" in the order. 28 U.S.C. § 636(b)(1) provides that any party "may serve and file written objections to such proposed findings and recommendations as provided by rules of court" within ten days of receiving a copy of the order. Several courts have held that a party must comply with this statutory provision in order to preserve a claim of error. *See, e.g., Wells v. Shriners Hospital*, 109 F.3d 198, 200 (4th Cir. 1997)("[i]n this circuit, as in others, a party 'may' file objections within ten days or he may not, as he chooses, but he 'shall' do so if he wishes further consideration."). When Fed.R.Civ.P. 72(a) or 28 U.S.C. § 636(b)(1) is operative, its requirement must be satisfied in order for a party to preserve a claim of error on appeal, even where Evidence Rule 103(a) would not require a subsequent objection or offer of proof.

Nothing in the amendment is intended to affect the rule set forth in *Luce v. United States*, 469 U.S. 38 (1984), and its progeny. The amendment provides that an objection or offer of proof need not be renewed to preserve a claim of error with respect to a definitive pretrial ruling. *Luce* answers affirmatively a separate question: whether a criminal defendant must testify at trial in order to preserve a claim of error predicated upon a trial court's decision to admit the defendant's prior convictions for impeachment. The *Luce* principle has been extended by many lower courts to other situations. *See United States v. DiMatteo*, 759 F.2d 831 (11th Cir. 1985) (applying *Luce* where the defendant's witness would be impeached with evidence offered under Rule 608). *See also United States v. Goldman*, 41 F.3d 785, 788 (1st Cir. 1994) ("Although *Luce* involved impeachment by conviction under Rule 609, the reasons given by the Supreme Court for requiring the defendant to testify apply with full force to the kind of Rule 403 and 404 objections that are advanced by Goldman in this case."); *Palmieri v. DeFaria*, 88 F.3d 136 (2d Cir. 1996) (where the plaintiff decided to take an adverse judgment rather than challenge an advance ruling by putting on evidence at trial, the *in limine* ruling would not be reviewed on appeal); *United States v. Ortiz*, 857 F.2d 900 (2d Cir. 1988) (where uncharged misconduct is ruled admissible if the defendant pursues a certain defense, the defendant must actually pursue that defense at trial in order to preserve a claim of error on appeal); *United States v. Bond*, 87 F.3d 695 (5th Cir. 1996) (where the trial court rules *in limine* that the defendant would waive his fifth amendment privilege were he to testify, the defendant must take the stand and testify in order to challenge that ruling on appeal).

The amendment does not purport to answer whether a party who objects to evidence that the court finds admissible in a definitive ruling, and who then offers the evidence to "remove the sting" of its anticipated prejudicial effect, thereby waives the right to appeal the trial court's ruling. *See, e.g., United States v. Fisher*, 106 F.3d 622 (5th Cir. 1997) (where the trial judge ruled *in limine* that the government could use a prior conviction to impeach the defendant if he testified, the defendant did not waive his right to appeal by introducing the conviction on direct examination); *Judd v. Rodman*, 105 F.3d 1339 (11th Cir. 1997) (an objection made *in limine* is sufficient to preserve a claim of error when the movant, as a matter of trial strategy, presents the objectionable evidence herself on direct examination to minimize its prejudicial effect); *Gill v. Thomas*, 83 F.3d 537, 540 (1st Cir. 1996) ("by offering the misdemeanor evidence himself, Gill waived his opportunity to object and thus did not preserve the issue for appeal"); *United States v. Williams*, 939 F.2d 721 (9th Cir. 1991) (objection to impeachment evidence was waived where the defendant was impeached on direct examination).

Rule 104. Preliminary Questions

(a) Questions of admissibility generally. Preliminary questions concerning the qualification of a person to be a witness, the existence of a privilege, or the admissibility of evidence shall be determined by the court, subject to the provisions of subdivision (b). In making its determination it is not bound by the rules of evidence except those with respect to privileges.

(b) Relevancy conditioned on fact. When the relevancy of evidence depends upon the fulfillment of a condition of fact, the court shall admit it upon, or subject to, the introduction of evidence sufficient to support a finding of the fulfillment of the condition.

(c) Hearing of jury. Hearings on the admissibility of confessions shall in all cases be conducted out of the hearing of the jury. Hearings on other preliminary matters shall be so conducted when the interests of justice require, or when an accused is a witness and so requests.

(d) Testimony by accused. The accused does not, by testifying upon a preliminary matter, become subject to cross-examination as to other issues in the case.

(e) Weight and credibility. This rule does not limit the right of a party to introduce before the jury evidence relevant to weight or credibility.

(As amended Mar. 2, 1987, eff. Oct. 1, 1987.)

Section references, McCormick 5th ed.

Generally § 15, § 53

(a). § 53, § 68, § 70, § 227

(b). § 10, § 53, § 54, § 58, § 227

(c). § 52, § 53, § 162

(d). § 53

(e). § 53

Note by Federal Judicial Center

The rule enacted by the Congress is the rule prescribed by the Supreme Court, amended by substituting "court" in place of "judge," with appropriate pronominal change, and by adding to subdivision (c) the concluding phrase, "or when an accused is a witness, if he so requests."[1]

Advisory Committee's Note

56 F.R.D. 183, 196

Subdivision (a). The applicability of a particular rule of evidence often depends upon the existence of a condition. Is the alleged expert a qualified physician? Is a witness whose former testimony is offered unavailable? Was a stranger present during a conversation between attorney and client? In each instance the admissibility of evidence will turn upon the answer to the question of the existence of the condition. Accepted practice, incorporated in the rule, places on the judge the responsibility for these determinations. McCormick § 53; Morgan, Basic Problems of Evidence 45–50 (1962).

To the extent that these inquiries are factual, the judge acts as a trier of fact. Often, however, rulings on evidence call for an evaluation in terms of a legally set standard. Thus when a hearsay statement is offered as a declaration against interest, a decision must be made whether it possesses the required against-interest characteristics. These decisions, too, are made by the judge.

In view of these considerations, this subdivision refers to preliminary requirements generally by the broad term "questions," without attempt at specification.

This subdivision is of general application. It must, however, be read as subject to the special provisions for "conditional relevancy" in subdivision (b) and those for confessions in subdivision (c)

If the question is factual in nature, the judge will of necessity receive evidence pro and con on the issue. The rule provides that the rules of evidence in general do not apply to this process. McCormick § 53, p. 123, n. 8, points out that the authorities are "scattered and inconclusive," and observes:

> "Should the exclusionary law of evidence, 'the child of the jury system' in Thayer's phrase, be applied to this hearing before the judge? Sound sense backs the view that it should not, and that the judge should be empowered to hear any relevant evidence, such as affidavits or other reliable hearsay."

This view is reinforced by practical necessity in certain situations. An item, offered and objected to, may itself be considered in ruling on admissibility, though not yet admitted in evidence. Thus the content of an asserted declaration against interest must be considered in ruling whether it is against interest. Again, common practice calls for considering the testimony of a witness, particularly a child, in determining competency. Another example is the requirement of Rule 602 dealing with personal knowledge. In the case of hearsay, it is enough, if the declarant "so far as appears [has] had an opportunity to observe the fact declared." McCormick, § 10, p. 19.

If concern is felt over the use of affidavits by the judge in preliminary hearings on admissibility, attention is directed to the many important judicial determinations made on the basis of affidavits. Rule 47 of the Federal Rules of Criminal Procedure provides:

1. The effect of the amendment was to restore language included in the 1971 Revised Draft of the Proposed Rules but deleted before the rules were presented to and prescribed by the Supreme Court.—Federal Judicial Center.

> "An application to the court for an order shall be by motion. . . . It may be supported by affidavit."

The Rules of Civil Procedure are more detailed. Rule 43(e), dealing with motions generally, provides:

> "When a motion is based on facts not appearing of record the court may hear the matter on affidavits presented by the respective parties, but the court may direct that the matter be heard wholly or partly on oral testimony or depositions."

Rule 4(g) provides for proof of service by affidavit. Rule 56 provides in detail for the entry of summary judgment based on affidavits. Affidavits may supply the foundation for temporary restraining orders under Rule 65(b).

The study made for the California Law Revision Commission recommended an amendment to Uniform Rule 2 as follows:

"In the determination of the issue aforesaid [preliminary determination], exclusionary rules shall not apply, subject, however, to Rule 45 and any valid claim of privilege." Tentative Recommendation and a Study Relating to the Uniform Rules of Evidence (Article VIII, Hearsay), Cal.Law Revision Comm'n, Rep., Rec. & Studies, 470 (1962). The proposal was not adopted in the California Evidence Code. The Uniform Rules are likewise silent on the subject. However, New Jersey Evidence Rule 8(1), dealing with preliminary inquiry by the judge, provides:

"In his determination the rules of evidence shall not apply except for Rule 4 [exclusion on grounds of confusion, etc.] or a valid claim of privilege."

Subdivision (b). In some situations, the relevancy of an item of evidence, in the large sense, depends upon the existence of a particular preliminary fact. Thus when a spoken statement is relied upon to prove notice to X, it is without probative value unless X heard it. Or if a letter purporting to be from Y is relied upon to establish an admission by him, it has no probative value unless Y wrote or authorized it. Relevance in this sense has been labelled "conditional relevancy." Morgan, Basic Problems of Evidence 45–46 (1962). Problems arising in connection with it are to be distinguished from problems of logical relevancy, e.g. evidence in a murder case that accused on the day before purchased a weapon of the kind used in the killing, treated in Rule 401.

If preliminary questions of conditional relevancy were determined solely by the judge, as provided in subdivision (a), the functioning of the jury as a trier of fact would be greatly restricted and in some cases virtually destroyed. These are appropriate questions for juries. Accepted treatment, as provided in the rule, is consistent with that given fact questions generally. The judge makes a preliminary determination whether the foundation evidence is sufficient to support a finding of fulfillment of the condition. If so, the item is admitted. If after all the evidence on the issue is in, pro and con, the jury could reasonably conclude that fulfillment of the condition is not established, the issue is for them. If the evidence is not such as to allow a finding, the judge withdraws the matter from their consideration. Morgan, supra; California Evidence Code § 403; New Jersey Rule 8(2). See also Uniform Rules 19 and 67.

The order of proof here, as generally, is subject to the control of the judge.

Subdivision (c). Preliminary hearings on the admissibility of confessions must be conducted outside the hearing of the jury. See Jackson v. Denno, 378

U.S. 368, 84 S.Ct. 1774, 12 L.Ed.2d 908 (1964).[2] Otherwise, detailed treatment of when preliminary matters should be heard outside the hearing of the jury is not feasible. The procedure is time consuming. Not infrequently the same evidence which is relevant to the issue of establishment of fulfillment of a condition precedent to admissibility is also relevant to weight or credibility, and time is saved by taking foundation proof in the presence of the jury. Much evidence on preliminary questions, though not relevant to jury issues, may be heard by the jury with no adverse effect. A great deal must be left to the discretion of the judge who will act as the interests of justice require.

Report of the House Committee on the Judiciary

House Comm. on Judiciary, Fed. Rules of Evidence, H.R.Rep. No. 650, 93d Cong., 1st Sess., p. 15 (1973); 1974 U.S.Code Cong. & Ad. News 7075, 7080

Rule 104(c) as submitted to the Congress provided that hearings on the admissibility of confessions shall be conducted outside the presence of the jury and hearings on all other preliminary matters should be so conducted when the interests of justice require. The Committee amended the Rule to provide that where an accused is a witness as to a preliminary matter, he has the right, upon his request, to be heard outside the jury's presence. Although recognizing that in some cases duplication of evidence would occur and that the procedure could be subject to abuse, the Committee believed that a proper regard for the right of an accused not to testify generally in the case dictates that he be given an option to testify out of the presence of the jury on preliminary matters.

The Committee construes the second sentence of subdivision (c) as applying to civil actions and proceedings as well as to criminal cases, and on this assumption has left the sentence unamended.

Advisory Committee's Note

56 F.R.D. 183, 199

Subdivision (d). The limitation upon cross-examination is designed to encourage participation by the accused in the determination of preliminary matters. He may testify concerning them without exposing himself to cross-examination generally. The provision is necessary because of the breadth of cross-examination [possible] under Rule 611(b).

The rule does not address itself to questions of the subsequent use of testimony given by an accused at a hearing on a preliminary matter. See Walder v. United States, 347 U.S. 62 (1954); Simmons v. United States, 390 U.S. 377 (1968); Harris v. New York, 401 U.S. 222 (1971).

Report of Senate Committee on the Judiciary

Senate Comm. on Judiciary, Fed. Rules of Evidence, S.Rep. No. 1277, 93d Cong., 2d Sess., p. 24 (1974); 1974 U.S.Code Cong. & Ad. News 7051, 7070

2. At this point the Advisory Committee's Note to the 1971 Revised Draft contained the sentence, "Also, due regard for the right of an accused not to testify generally in the case requires that he be given an option to testify out of the presence of the jury upon preliminary matters." The statement was deleted in view of the deletion from the rule, mentioned in the preceding footnote.—Federal Judicial Center.

Under Rule 104(c) the hearing on a preliminary matter may at times be conducted in front of the jury. Should an accused testify in such a hearing, waiving his privilege against self-incrimination as to the preliminary issue, Rule 104(d) provides that he will not generally be subject to cross-examination as to any other issue. This rule is not, however, intended to immunize the accused from cross-examination where, in testifying about a preliminary issue, he injects other issues into the hearing. If he could not be cross-examined about any issues gratuitously raised by him beyond the scope of the preliminary matters, injustice might result. Accordingly, in order to prevent any such unjust result, the committee intends the rule to be construed to provide that the accused may subject himself to cross-examination as to issues raised by his own testimony upon a preliminary matter before a jury.

Advisory Committee's Note

56 F.R.D. 183, 199

Subdivision (e). For similar provisions see Uniform Rule 8; California Evidence Code § 406; Kansas Code of Civil Procedure § 60–408; New Jersey Evidence Rule 8(1).

1987 Amendment

The amendments are technical. No substantive change is intended.

Rule 105. Limited Admissibility

When evidence which is admissible as to one party or for one purpose but not admissible as to another party or for another purpose is admitted, the court, upon request, shall restrict the evidence to its proper scope and instruct the jury accordingly.

Section references, McCormick 5th ed.

§ 59

Note by Federal Judicial Center

The rule enacted by the Congress is the rule prescribed by the Supreme Court as Rule 106, amended by substituting "court" in place of "judge." Rule 105 as prescribed by the Court, which was deleted from the rules enacted by the Congress, is set forth in the Appendix hereto, together with a statement of the reasons for the deletion.

Advisory Committee's Note

56 F.R.D. 183, 200

A close relationship exists between this rule and Rule 403 which ... [provides for] exclusion when "probative value is substantially outweighed by the danger of unfair prejudice, confusion of the issues, or misleading the jury." The present rule recognizes the practice of admitting evidence for a limited purpose and instructing the jury accordingly. The availability and effectiveness of this practice must be taken into consideration in reaching a decision whether to exclude for unfair prejudice under Rule 403. In Bruton v. United States, 389 U.S. 818, 88 S.Ct. 126, 19 L.Ed.2d 70 (1968), the Court ruled that a limiting instruction did not effectively protect the accused against the prejudicial effect of admitting in evidence the confession of a codefendant which implicated him. The decision does not, however, bar the use of limited admissibility with an instruction where the risk of prejudice is less serious.

Similar provisions are found in Uniform Rule 6; California Evidence Code § 355; Kansas Code of Civil Procedure § 60–406; New Jersey Evidence Rule 6. The wording of the present rule differs, however, in repelling any implication that limiting or curative instructions are sufficient in all situations.

Report of House Committee on the Judiciary

House Comm. on Judiciary, Fed. Rules of Evidence, H.R.Rep. No. 650, 93d Cong., 1st Sess., p. 6 (1973); 1974 U.S.Code Cong. & Ad. News 7075, 7080

Rule 106 as submitted by the Supreme Court (now Rule 105 in the bill) dealt with the subject of evidence which is admissible as to one party or for one purpose but is not admissible against another party or for another purpose. The Committee adopted this Rule without change on the understanding that it does not affect the authority of a court to order a severance in a multi-defendant case.

Rule 106. Remainder of or Related Writings or Recorded Statements

When a writing or recorded statement or part thereof is introduced by a party, an adverse party may require the introduction at that time of any other part or any other writing or recorded statement which ought in fairness to be considered contemporaneously with it.

(As amended Mar. 2, 1987, eff. Oct. 1, 1987.)

Section references, McCormick 5th ed.

§ 21, § 32, § 47, § 56, § 57, § 59, § 307

Note by Federal Judicial Center

The rule enacted by the Congress is the rule prescribed by the Supreme Court as Rule 107 without change.

Advisory Committee's Note

56 F.R.D. 183, 201

The rule is an expression of the rule of completeness. McCormick § 56. It is manifested as to depositions in Rule 32(a)(4) of the Federal Rules of Civil Procedure, of which the proposed rule is substantially a restatement.

The rule is based on two considerations. The first is the misleading impression created by taking matters out of context. The second is the inadequacy of repair work when delayed to a point later in the trial. See McCormick § 56; California Evidence Code § 356. The rule does not in any way circumscribe the right of the adversary to develop the matter on cross-examination or as part of his own case.

For practical reasons, the rule is limited to writings and recorded statements and does not apply to conversations.

1987 Amendment

The amendments are technical. No substantive change is intended.

ARTICLE II. JUDICIAL NOTICE

Rule 201. Judicial Notice of Adjudicative Facts

(a) Scope of rule. This rule governs only judicial notice of adjudicative facts.

(b) Kinds of facts. A judicially noticed fact must be one not subject to reasonable dispute in that it is either (1) generally known within the territorial jurisdiction of the trial court or (2) capable of accurate and ready determination by resort to sources whose accuracy cannot reasonably be questioned.

(c) When discretionary. A court may take judicial notice, whether requested or not.

(d) When mandatory. A court shall take judicial notice if requested by a party and supplied with the necessary information.

(e) Opportunity to be heard. A party is entitled upon timely request to an opportunity to be heard as to the propriety of taking judicial notice and the tenor of the matter noticed. In the absence of prior notification, the request may be made after judicial notice has been taken.

(f) Time of taking notice. Judicial notice may be taken at any stage of the proceeding.

(g) Instructing jury. In a civil action or proceeding, the court shall instruct the jury to accept as conclusive any fact judicially noticed. In a criminal case, the court shall instruct the jury that it may, but is not required to, accept as conclusive any fact judicially noticed.

Section references, McCormick 5th ed.

Generally § 328, § 332, § 333

(a). § 331, § 332, § 334

(b)(1). § 328, § 329

(2). § 329, § 330

(c). § 333

(d). § 333

(e). § 334

(f). § 333

(g). § 332

Note by Federal Judicial Center

The rule enacted by the Congress is the rule prescribed by the Supreme Court with the following changes:

In subdivisions (c) and (d) the words "judge or" before "court" were deleted.

Subdivision (g) as it is shown was substituted in place of, "The judge shall instruct the jury to accept as established any facts judicially noticed." The substituted language is from the 1969 Preliminary Draft. 46 F.R.D. 161, 195.

Advisory Committee's Note

56 F.R.D. 183, 201

Subdivision (a). This is the only evidence rule on the subject of judicial notice. It deals only with judicial notice of "adjudicative" facts. No rule deals with judicial notice of "legislative" facts. Judicial notice of matters of foreign law is treated in Rule 44.1 of the Federal Rules of Civil Procedure and Rule 26.1 of the Federal Rules of Criminal Procedure.

The omission of any treatment of legislative facts results from fundamental differences between adjudicative facts and legislative facts. Adjudicative facts are simply the facts of the particular case. Legislative facts, on the other hand, are those which have relevance to legal reasoning and the lawmaking process, whether in the formulation of a legal principle or ruling by a judge or court or in the enactment of a legislative body. The terminology was coined by Professor Kenneth Davis in his article An Approach to Problems of Evidence in the Administrative Process, 55 Harv.L.Rev. 364, 404–407 (1942). The following discussion draws extensively upon his writings. In addition, see the same author's Judicial Notice, 55 Colum.L.Rev. 945 (1955); Administrative Law Treatise, ch. 15 (1958); A System of Judicial Notice Based on Fairness and Convenience, in Perspectives of Law 69 (1964).

The usual method of establishing adjudicative facts is through the introduction of evidence, ordinarily consisting of the testimony of witnesses. If particular facts are outside the area of reasonable controversy, this process is dispensed with as unnecessary. A high degree of indisputability is the essential prerequisite.

Legislative facts are quite different. As Professor Davis says:

> "My opinion is that judge-made law would stop growing if judges, in thinking about questions of law and policy, were forbidden to take into account the facts they believe, as distinguished from facts which are 'clearly . . . within the domain of the indisputable.' Facts most needed in thinking about difficult problems of law and policy have a way of being outside the domain of the clearly indisputable." A System of Judicial Notice Based on Fairness and Convenience, supra, at 82.

An illustration is Hawkins v. United States, 358 U.S. 74, 79 S.Ct. 136, 3 L.Ed.2d 125 (1958), in which the Court refused to discard the common law rule that one spouse could not testify against the other, saying, "Adverse testimony given in criminal proceedings would, we think, be likely to destroy almost any marriage."

This conclusion has a large intermixture of fact, but the factual aspect is scarcely "indisputable." See Hutchins and Slesinger, Some Observations on the Law of Evidence—Family Relations, 13 Minn.L.Rev. 675 (1929). If the destructive effect of the giving of adverse testimony by a spouse is not indisputable, should the Court have refrained from considering it in the absence of supporting evidence?

"If the Model Code or the Uniform Rules had been applicable, the Court would have been barred from thinking about the essential factual ingredient of the problems before it, and such a result would be obviously intolerable. What the law needs at its growing points is more, not less, judicial thinking about the factual ingredients of problems of what the law ought to be, and the needed facts are seldom 'clearly' indisputable." Davis, supra, at 83.

Professor Morgan gave the following description of the methodology of determining domestic law:

> "In determining the content or applicability of a rule of domestic law, the judge is unrestricted in his investigation and conclusion. He may reject the propositions of either party or of both parties. He may consult the sources of pertinent data to which they refer, or he may refuse to do so. He may make an independent search for persuasive data or rest content with what he has or what the parties present. ... [T]he parties do no more than to assist; they control no part of the process." Morgan, Judicial Notice, 57 Harv.L.Rev. 269, 270–271 (1944).

This is the view which should govern judicial access to legislative facts. It renders inappropriate any limitation in the form of indisputability, any formal requirements of notice other than those already inherent in affording opportunity to hear and be heard and exchanging briefs, and any requirement of formal findings at any level. It should, however, leave open the possibility of introducing evidence through regular channels in appropriate situations. See Borden's Farm Products Co. v. Baldwin, 293 U.S. 194, 55 S.Ct. 187, 79 L.Ed. 281 (1934), where the cause was remanded for the taking of evidence as to the economic conditions and trade practices underlying the New York Milk Control Law.

Similar considerations govern the judicial use of non-adjudicative facts in ways other than formulating laws and rules. Thayer described them as a part of the judicial reasoning process.

> "In conducting a process of judicial reasoning, as of other reasoning, not a step can be taken without assuming something which has not been proved; and the capacity to do this with competent judgment and efficiency, is imputed to judges and juries as part of their necessary mental outfit." Thayer, Preliminary Treatise on Evidence 279–280 (1898).

As Professor Davis points out, A System of Judicial Notice Based on Fairness and Convenience, in Perspectives of Law 69, 73 (1964), every case involves the use of hundreds or thousands of non-evidence facts. When a witness in an automobile accident case says "car," everyone, judge and jury included, furnishes, from non-evidence sources within himself, the supplementing information that the "car" is an automobile, not a railroad car, that it is self-propelled, probably by an internal combustion engine, that it may be assumed to have four wheels with pneumatic rubber tires, and so on. The judicial process cannot construct every case from scratch, like Descartes creating a world based on the postulate *Cogito, ergo sum.* These items could not possibly be introduced into evidence, and no one suggests that they be. Nor are they appropriate subjects for any formalized treatment of judicial notice of facts. See Levin and Levy, Persuading the Jury with Facts Not in Evidence: The Fiction-Science Spectrum, 105 U.Pa.L.Rev. 139 (1956).

Another aspect of what Thayer had in mind is the use of non-evidence facts to appraise or assess the adjudicative facts of the case. Pairs of cases from two jurisdictions illustrate this use and also the difference between non-evidence facts thus used and adjudicative facts. In People v. Strook, 347 Ill. 460, 179 N.E. 821 (1932), venue in Cook County had been held not established by testimony that the crime was committed at 7956 South Chicago Avenue, since judicial notice would not be taken that the address was in Chicago. However, the same court subsequently ruled that venue in Cook County was established by testimony that a crime occurred at 8900 South Anthony Avenue, since notice would be taken of the common practice of omitting the name of the city when speaking of local addresses, and the witness was testifying in Chicago. People v. Pride, 16 Ill.2d 82, 156 N.E.2d 551 (1951). And in Hughes v. Vestal, 264 N.C. 500, 142 S.E.2d 361 (1965), the Supreme Court of North Carolina disapproved the trial judge's admission in evidence of a state-published table of automobile stopping distances on the basis of judicial notice, though the court itself had referred to the same table in an earlier case in a "rhetorical and illustrative" way in determining that the defendant could not have stopped her car in time to avoid striking a child who suddenly appeared in the highway and that a nonsuit was properly granted. Ennis v. Dupree, 262 N.C. 224, 136 S.E.2d 702 (1964). See also Brown v. Hale, 263 N.C. 176, 139 S.E.2d 210 (1964); Clayton v. Rimmer, 262 N.C. 302, 136 S.E.2d 562 (1964). It is apparent that this use of non-evidence facts in evaluating the adjudicative facts of the case is not an appropriate subject for a formalized judicial notice treatment.

In view of these considerations, the regulation of judicial notice of facts by the present rule extends only to adjudicative facts.

What, then, are "adjudicative" facts? Davis refers to them as those "which relate to the parties," or more fully:

> "When a court or an agency finds facts concerning the immediate parties—who did what, where, when, how, and with what motive or intent—the court or agency is performing an adjudicative function, and the facts are conveniently called adjudicative facts . . .
>
> "Stated in other terms, the adjudicative facts are those to which the law is applied in the process of adjudication. They are the facts that normally go to the jury in a jury case. They relate to the parties, their activities, their properties, their businesses." 2 Administrative Law Treatise 353.

Subdivision (b). With respect to judicial notice of adjudicative facts, the tradition has been one of caution in requiring that the matter be beyond reasonable controversy. This tradition of circumspection appears to be soundly based, and no reason to depart from it is apparent. As Professor Davis says:

> "The reason we use trial-type procedure, I think, is that we make the practical judgment, on the basis of experience, that taking evidence, subject to cross-examination and rebuttal, is the best way to resolve controversies involving disputes of adjudicative facts, that is, facts pertaining to the parties. The reason we require a determination on the record is that we think fair procedure in resolving disputes of adjudicative facts calls for giving

> each party a chance to meet in the appropriate fashion the facts that come to the tribunal's attention, and the appropriate fashion for meeting disputed adjudicative facts includes rebuttal evidence, cross-examination, usually confrontation, and argument (either written or oral or both). The key to a fair trial is opportunity to use the appropriate weapons (rebuttal evidence, cross-examination, and argument) to meet adverse materials that come to the tribunal's attention." A System of Judicial Notice Based on Fairness and Convenience, in Perspectives of Law 69, 93 (1964).

The rule proceeds upon the theory that these considerations call for dispensing with traditional methods of proof only in clear cases. Compare Professor Davis' conclusion that judicial notice should be a matter of convenience, subject to requirements of procedural fairness. Id., 94.

This rule is consistent with Uniform Rule 9(1) and (2) which limit judicial notice of facts to those "so universally known that they cannot reasonably be the subject of dispute," those "so generally known or of such common notoriety within the territorial jurisdiction of the court that they cannot reasonably be the subject of dispute," and those "capable of immediate and accurate determination by resort to easily accessible sources of indisputable accuracy." The traditional textbook treatment has included these general categories (matters of common knowledge, facts capable of verification), McCormick §§ 324, 325, and then has passed on into detailed treatment of such specific topics as facts relating to the personnel and records of the court, id. § 327, and other governmental facts, id. § 328. The California draftsmen, with a background of detailed statutory regulation of judicial notice, followed a somewhat similar pattern. California Evidence Code §§ 451, 452. The Uniform Rules, however, were drafted on the theory that these particular matters are included within the general categories and need no specific mention. This approach is followed in the present rule.

The phrase "propositions of generalized knowledge," found in Uniform Rule 9(1) and (2) is not included in the present rule. It was, it is believed, originally included in Model Code Rules 801 and 802 primarily in order to afford some minimum recognition to the right of the judge in his "legislative" capacity (not acting as the trier of fact) to take judicial notice of very limited categories of generalized knowledge. The limitations thus imposed have been discarded herein as undesirable, unworkable, and contrary to existing practice. What is left, then, to be considered, is the status of a "proposition of generalized knowledge" as an "adjudicative" fact to be noticed judicially and communicated by the judge to the jury. Thus viewed, it is considered to be lacking practical significance. While judges used judicial notice of "propositions of generalized knowledge" in a variety of situations: determining the validity and meaning of statutes, formulating common law rules, deciding whether evidence should be admitted, assessing the sufficiency and effect of evidence, all are essentially nonadjudicative in nature. When judicial notice is seen as a significant vehicle for progress in the law, these are the areas involved, particularly in developing fields of scientific knowledge. See McCormick 712. It is not believed that judges now instruct juries as to "propositions of generalized knowledge" derived from encyclopedias or other sources, or that they are likely to do so, or, indeed, that it is desirable that they do so. There is a vast difference between ruling on the basis of judicial notice that radar evidence of speed is admissible and explaining to the jury its principles and degree of accuracy, or between using a table of stopping distances of automobiles at various speeds in a judicial evaluation of testimony and telling the jury its precise application in the case. For cases raising doubt as to the propriety of the use of medical texts by lay triers of fact in passing on disability claims in administrative proceedings, see Sayers v. Gardner, 380 F.2d 940 (6th Cir.1967); Ross v. Gardner, 365 F.2d 554 (6th Cir.1966); Sosna v. Celebrezze, 234 F.Supp. 289 (E.D.Pa.1964); Glendenning v. Ribicoff, 213 F.Supp. 301 (W.D.Mo.1962).

Subdivisions (c) and (d). Under subdivision (c) the judge has a discretionary authority to take judicial notice, regardless of whether he is so requested by a party. The taking of judicial notice is mandatory, under subdivision (d), only when a party requests it and the necessary information is supplied. This scheme is believed to reflect existing practice. It is simple and workable. It avoids troublesome distinctions in the many situations in which the process of taking judicial notice is not recognized as such.

Compare Uniform Rule 9 making judicial notice of facts universally known mandatory without request, and making judicial notice of facts generally known in the jurisdiction or capable of determination by resort to accurate sources discretionary in the absence of request but mandatory if request is made and the information furnished. But see Uniform Rule 10(3), which directs the judge to decline to take judicial notice if available information fails to convince him that the matter falls clearly within Uniform Rule 9 or is insufficient to enable him to notice it judicially. Substantially the same approach is found in California Evidence Code §§ 451–453 and in New Jersey Evidence Rule 9. In contrast, the present rule treats alike all adjudicative facts which are subject to judicial notice.

Subdivision (e). Basic considerations of procedural fairness demand an opportunity to be heard on the propriety of taking judicial notice and the tenor of the matter noticed. The rule requires the granting of that opportunity upon request. No formal scheme of giving notice is provided. An adversely affected party may learn in advance that judicial notice is in contemplation, either by virtue of being served with a copy of a request by another party under subdivision (d) that judicial notice be taken, or through an advance indication by the judge. Or he may have no advance notice at all. The likelihood of the latter is enhanced by the frequent failure to recognize judicial notice as such. And in the absence of advance notice, a request made after the fact could not in fairness be considered untimely. See the provision for hearing on timely request in the Administrative Procedure Act, 5 U.S.C. § 556(e). See also Revised Model State Administrative Procedure Act (1961), 9C U.L.A. § 10(4) (Supp.1967).

Subdivision (f). In accord with the usual view, judicial notice may be taken at any stage of the proceedings, whether in the trial court or on appeal. Uniform Rule 12; California Evidence Code § 459; Kansas Rules of Evidence § 60–412; New Jersey Evidence Rule 12; McCormick § 330, p. 712.

Subdivision (g). Much of the controversy about judicial notice has centered upon the question whether evidence should be admitted in disproof of facts of which judicial notice is taken.

The writers have been divided. Favoring admissibility are Thayer, Preliminary Treatise on Evidence 308 (1898); 9 Wigmore § 2567; Davis, A System of Judicial Notice Based on Fairness and Convenience, in Perspectives of Law, 69, 76–77 (1964). Opposing admissibility are Keeffe, Landis and Shaad, Sense and Nonsense about Judicial Notice, 2 Stan.L.Rev. 664, 668 (1950); McNaughton, Judicial Notice—Excerpts Relating to the Morgan-Whitmore Controversy, 14

Vand.L.Rev. 779 (1961); Morgan, Judicial Notice, 57 Harv.L.Rev. 269, 279 (1944); McCormick 710–711. The Model Code and the Uniform Rules are predicated upon indisputability of judicially noticed facts.

The proponents of admitting evidence in disproof have concentrated largely upon legislative facts. Since the present rule deals only with judicial notice of adjudicative facts, arguments directed to legislative facts lose their relevancy.

Report of House Committee on the Judiciary

House Comm. on Judiciary, Fed. Rules of Evidence, H.R.Rep. No. 650, 93d Cong., 1st Sess., p. 6 (1973); 1974 U.S.Code Cong. & Ad.News 7075, 7080

Rule 201(g) as received from the Supreme Court provided that when judicial notice of a fact is taken, the court shall instruct the jury to accept that fact as established. Being of the view that mandatory instruction to a jury in a criminal case to accept as conclusive any fact judicially noticed is inappropriate because contrary to the spirit of the Sixth Amendment right to a jury trial, the Committee adopted the 1969 Advisory Committee draft of this subsection, allowing a mandatory instruction in civil actions and proceedings and a discretionary instruction in criminal cases.

Advisory Committee's Note (Continued)

[The following portion of the Advisory Committee's Note is from the 1969 Preliminary Draft. 46 F.R.D. 161, 204.]

Within its relatively narrow area of adjudicative facts, the rule contemplates there is to be no evidence before the jury in disproof in civil cases. The judge instructs the jury to take judicially noticed facts as conclusive. This position is justified by the undesirable effects of the opposite rule in limiting the rebutting party, though not his opponent, to admissible evidence, in defeating the reasons for judicial notice, and in affecting the substantive law to an extent and in ways largely unforeseeable. Ample protection and flexibility are afforded by the broad provision for opportunity to be heard on request, set forth in subdivision (e).

Criminal cases are treated somewhat differently in the rule. While matters falling within the common fund of information supposed to be possessed by jurors need not be proved, State v. Dunn, 221 Mo. 530, 120 S.W. 1179 (1909), these are not, properly speaking, adjudicative facts but an aspect of legal reasoning. The considerations which underlie the general rule that a verdict cannot be directed against the accused in a criminal case seem to foreclose the judge's directing the jury on the basis of judicial notice to accept as conclusive any adjudicative facts in the case. State v. Main, 91 R.I. 338, 180 A.2d 814 (1962); State v. Lawrence, 120 Utah 323, 234 P.2d 600 (1951). Cf. People v. Mayes, 113 Cal. 618, 45 P. 860 (1896); Ross v. United States, 374 F.2d 97 (8th Cir.1967). However, this view presents no obstacle to the judge's advising the jury as to a matter judicially noticed, if he instructs them that it need not be taken as conclusive.

Note on Judicial Notice of Law (by the Advisory Committee)

56 F.R.D. 183, 207

By rules effective July 1, 1966, the method of invoking the law of a foreign country is covered elsewhere. Rule 44.1 of the Federal Rules of Civil Procedure; Rule 26.1 of the Federal Rules of Criminal Procedure. These two new admirably designed rules are founded upon the assumption that the manner in which law is fed into the judicial process is never a proper concern of the rules of evidence but rather of the rules of procedure. The Advisory Committee on Evidence, believing that this assumption is entirely correct, proposes no evidence rule with respect to judicial notice of law, and suggests that those matters of law which, in addition to foreign-country law, have traditionally been treated as requiring pleading and proof and more recently as the subject of judicial notice be left to the Rules of Civil and Criminal Procedure.

ARTICLE III. PRESUMPTIONS IN CIVIL ACTIONS AND PROCEEDINGS

Rule 301. Presumptions in General in Civil Actions and Proceedings

In all civil actions and proceedings not otherwise provided for by Act of Congress or by these rules, a presumption imposes on the party against whom it is directed the burden of going forward with evidence to rebut or meet the presumption, but does not shift to such party the burden of proof in the sense of the risk of nonpersuasion, which remains throughout the trial upon the party on whom it was originally cast.

Section references, McCormick 5th ed.

§ 336, § 342, § 344

Note by Federal Judicial Center

The bill passed by the House substituted a substantially different rule in place of that prescribed by the Supreme Court. The Senate bill substituted yet a further version, which was accepted by the House, was enacted by the Congress, and is the rule shown above. . . .

Report of Senate Committee on the Judiciary

Senate Comm. on Judiciary, Fed. Rules of Evidence, S.Rep. No. 1277, 93d Cong., 2d Sess., p. 9 (1974); 1974 U.S.Code Cong. & Ad. News 7051, 7055

This rule governs presumptions in civil cases generally. Rule 302 provides for presumptions in cases controlled by State law.

As submitted by the Supreme Court, presumptions governed by this rule were given the effect of placing upon the opposing party the burden of establishing the nonexistence of the presumed fact, once the party invoking the presumption established the basic facts giving rise to it.

Instead of imposing a burden of persuasion on the party against whom the presumption is directed, the House adopted a provision which shifted the burden of going forward with the evidence. They further provided that "even though met with contradicting evidence, a presumption is sufficient evidence of the fact presumed, to be considered by the trier of fact." The effect of the amendment is that presumptions are to be treated as evidence.

The committee feels the House amendment is ill-advised. As the joint committees (the Standing Committee on Practice and Procedure of the Judicial Conference and the Advisory Committee on the Rules of Evidence) stated: "Presumptions are not evidence, but ways of dealing with evidence."[1] This treatment requires juries to perform the task of considering "as evidence" facts upon which they have no direct evidence and which may confuse them in performance of their duties. California had a rule much like that contained in the House amendment. It was sharply criticized by Justice Traynor in Speck v. Sarver [2] and was repealed after 93 troublesome years.[3]

Professor McCormick gives a concise and compelling critique of the presumption as evidence rule:

* * *

"Another solution, formerly more popular than now, is to instruct the jury that the presumption is 'evidence', to be weighed and considered with the testimony in the case. This avoids the danger that the jury may infer that the presumption is conclusive, but it probably means little to the jury, and certainly runs counter to accepted theories of the nature of evidence.[4]"

For these reasons the committee has deleted that provision of the House-passed rule that treats presumptions as evidence. The effect of the rule as adopted by the committee is to make clear that while evidence of facts giving rise to a presumption shifts the burden of coming forward with evidence to rebut or meet the presumption, it does not shift the burden of persuasion on the existence of the presumed facts. The burden of persuasion remains on the party to whom it is allocated under the rules governing the allocation in the first instance.

The court may instruct the jury that they may infer the existence of the presumed fact from proof of the basic facts giving rise to the presumption. However, it would be inappropriate under this rule to instruct the jury that the inference they are to draw is conclusive.

Conference Report

H.R., Fed. Rules of Evidence, Conf.Rep. No. 1597, 93d Cong., 2d Sess., p. 5 (1974); 1974 U.S. Code Cong. & Ad. News 7098, 7099

The House bill provides that a presumption in civil actions and proceedings shifts to the party against whom it is directed the burden of going forward with evidence to meet or rebut it. Even though evidence contradicting the presumption is offered, a presumption is considered sufficient evidence of the presumed fact to be considered by the jury. The Senate amendment provides that a presumption shifts to the party against whom it is directed the burden of going

1. Hearings Before the Committee on the Judiciary, United States Senate, H.R. 5463, p. 56.

2. 20 Cal.2d 585, 594, 128 P.2d 16, 21 (1942).

3. Cal.Ev.Code 1965, § 600.

4. McCormick, Evidence, 669 (1954); id. 825 (2d ed. 1972).

forward with evidence to meet or rebut the presumption, but it does not shift to that party the burden of persuasion on the existence of the presumed fact.

Under the Senate amendment, a presumption is sufficient to get a party past an adverse party's motion to dismiss made at the end of his case-in-chief. If the adverse party offers no evidence contradicting the presumed fact, the court will instruct the jury that if it finds the basic facts, it may presume the existence of the presumed fact. If the adverse party does offer evidence contradicting the presumed fact, the court cannot instruct the jury that it may *presume* the existence of the presumed fact from proof of the basic facts. The court may, however, instruct the jury that it may infer the existence of the presumed fact from proof of the basic facts.

The Conference adopts the Senate amendment.

Rule 302. Applicability of State Law in Civil Actions and Proceedings

In civil actions and proceedings, the effect of a presumption respecting a fact which is an element of a claim or defense as to which State law supplies the rule of decision is determined in accordance with State law.

Section references, McCormick 5th ed.

§ 336, § 344, § 349

Note by Federal Judicial Center

The rule enacted by the Congress is the rule prescribed by the Supreme Court, amended by adding "and proceedings" after "actions."

Advisory Committee's Note

56 F.R.D. 183, 211

A series of Supreme Court decisions in diversity cases leaves no doubt of the relevance of Erie Railroad Co. v. Tompkins, 304 U.S. 64, 58 S.Ct. 817, 82 L.Ed. 1188 (1938), to questions of burden of proof. These decisions are Cities Service Oil Co. v. Dunlap, 308 U.S. 208, 60 S.Ct. 201, 84 L.Ed. 196 (1939), Palmer v. Hoffman, 318 U.S. 109, 63 S.Ct. 477, 87 L.Ed. 645 (1943), and Dick v. New York Life Ins. Co., 359 U.S. 437, 79 S.Ct. 921, 3 L.Ed.2d 935 (1959). They involved burden of proof, respectively, as to status as bona fide purchaser, contributory negligence, and nonaccidental death (suicide) of an insured. In each instance the state rule was held to be applicable. It does not follow, however, that all presumptions in diversity cases are governed by state law. In each case cited, the burden of proof question had to do with a substantive element of the claim or defense. Application of the state law is called for only when the presumption operates upon such an element. Accordingly the rule does not apply state law when the presumption operates upon a lesser aspect of the case, i.e. "tactical" presumptions.

The situations in which the state law is applied have been tagged for convenience in the preceding discussion as "diversity cases." The designation is not a completely accurate one since *Erie* applies to any claim or issue having its source in state law, regardless of the basis of federal jurisdiction, and does not apply to a federal claim or issue, even though jurisdiction is based on diversity. Vestal, Erie R.R. v. Tompkins: A Projection, 48 Iowa L.Rev. 248, 257 (1963);

Hart and Wechsler, The Federal Courts and the Federal System, 697 (1953); 1A Moore, Federal Practice ¶ 0.305[3] (2d ed. 1965); Wright, Federal Courts, 217–218 (1963). Hence the rule employs, as appropriately descriptive, the phrase "as to which state law supplies the rule of decision." See A.L.I. Study of the Division of Jurisdiction Between State and Federal Courts, § 2344(c), p. 40, P.F.D. No. 1 (1965).

Presumptions in Criminal Cases

Note by Federal Judicial Center

The rules prescribed by the Supreme Court included Rule 303, Presumptions in Criminal Cases. The rule was not included in the rules enacted by the Congress. . . .

ARTICLE IV. RELEVANCY AND ITS LIMITS

Rule

Rule 401. Definition of "Relevant Evidence"

"Relevant evidence" means evidence having any tendency to make the existence of any fact that is of consequence to the determination of the action more probable or less probable than it would be without the evidence.

Section references, McCormick 5th ed.

§ 39, § 44, § 45, § 47, § 52, § 185, § 196, § 197, § 199, § 200, § 202

Note by Federal Judicial Center

The rule enacted by the Congress is the rule prescribed by the Supreme Court without change.

Advisory Committee's Note

56 F.R.D. 183, 215

Problems of relevancy call for an answer to the question whether an item of evidence, when tested by the processes of legal reasoning, possesses sufficient probative value to justify receiving it in evidence. Thus, assessment of the probative value of evidence that a person purchased a revolver shortly prior to a fatal shooting with which he is charged is a matter of analysis and reasoning.

The variety of relevancy problems is coextensive with the ingenuity of counsel in using circumstantial evidence as a means of proof. An enormous number of cases fall in no set pattern, and this rule is designed as a guide for handling them. On the other hand, some situations recur with sufficient frequency to create patterns susceptible of treatment by specific rules. Rule 404 and those following it are of that variety; they also serve as illustrations of the application of the present rule as limited by the exclusionary principles of Rule 403.

Passing mention should be made of so-called "conditional" relevancy. Morgan, Basic Problems of Evidence 45–46 (1962). In this situation, probative value depends not only upon satisfying the basic requirement of relevancy as described above but also upon the existence of some matter of fact. For example, if evidence of a spoken statement is relied upon to prove notice, probative value is lacking unless the person sought to be charged heard the statement. The problem is one of fact, and the only rules needed are for the purpose of determining the respective functions of judge and jury. See Rules 104(b) and 901. The discussion which follows in the present note is concerned with relevancy generally, not with any particular problem of conditional relevancy.

Relevancy is not an inherent characteristic of any item of evidence but exists only as a relation between an item of evidence and a matter properly provable in the case. Does the item of evidence tend to prove the matter sought to be proved? Whether the relationship exists depends upon principles evolved by experience or science, applied logically to the situation at hand. James, Relevancy, Probability and the Law, 29 Calif.L.Rev. 689, 696, n. 15 (1941), in Selected Writings on Evidence and Trial 610, 615, n. 15 (Fryer ed. 1957). The rule summarizes this relationship as a "tendency to make the existence" of the fact to be proved "more probable or less probable." Compare Uniform Rule 1(2) which states the crux of relevancy as "a tendency in reason," thus perhaps emphasizing unduly the logical process and ignoring the need to draw upon experience or science to validate the general principle upon which relevancy in a particular situation depends.

The standard of probability under the rule is "more ... probable than it would be without the evidence." Any more stringent requirement is unworkable and unrealistic. As McCormick § 152, p. 317, says, "A brick is not a wall," or, as Falknor, Extrinsic Policies Affecting Admissibility, 10 Rutgers L.Rev. 574, 576

(1956), quotes Professor McBaine, "... [I]t is not to be supposed that every witness can make a home run." Dealing with probability in the language of the rule has the added virtue of avoiding confusion between questions of admissibility and questions of the sufficiency of the evidence.

The rule uses the phrase "fact that is of consequence to the determination of the action" to describe the kind of fact to which proof may properly be directed. The language is that of California Evidence Code § 210; it has the advantage of avoiding the loosely used and ambiguous word "material." Tentative Recommendation and a Study Relating to the Uniform Rules of Evidence (Art. I. General Provisions), Cal. Law Revision Comm'n, Rep., Rec. & Studies, 10–11 (1964). The fact to be proved may be ultimate, intermediate, or evidentiary; it matters not, so long as it is of consequence in the determination of the action. Cf. Uniform Rule 1(2) which requires that the evidence relate to a "material" fact.

The fact to which the evidence is directed need not be in dispute. While situations will arise which call for the exclusion of evidence offered to prove a point conceded by the opponent, the ruling should be made on the basis of such considerations as waste of time and undue prejudice (see Rule 403), rather than under any general requirement that evidence is admissible only if directed to matters in dispute. Evidence which is essentially background in nature can scarcely be said to involve disputed matter, yet it is universally offered and admitted as an aid to understanding. Charts, photographs, views of real estate, murder weapons, and many other items of evidence fall in this category. A rule limiting admissibility to evidence directed to a controversial point would invite the exclusion of this helpful evidence, or at least the raising of endless questions over its admission. Cf. California Evidence Code § 210, defining relevant evidence in terms of tendency to prove a disputed fact.

Rule 402. Relevant Evidence Generally Admissible; Irrelevant Evidence Inadmissible

All relevant evidence is admissible, except as otherwise provided by the Constitution of the United States, by Act of Congress, by these rules, or by other rules prescribed by the Supreme Court pursuant to statutory authority. Evidence which is not relevant is not admissible.

Section references, McCormick 5th ed.

§ 44, § 45, § 47, § 184, § 196, § 197, § 199, § 200, § 202, § 212

Note by Federal Judicial Center

The rule enacted by the Congress is the rule prescribed by the Supreme Court, with the first sentence amended by substituting "prescribed" in place of "adopted", and by adding at the end thereof the phrase "pursuant to statutory authority."

Advisory Committee's Note

56 F.R.D. 183, 216

The provisions that all relevant evidence is admissible, with certain exceptions, and that evidence which is not relevant is not admissible are "a presupposition involved in the very conception of a rational system of evidence." Thayer,

Preliminary Treatise on Evidence 264 (1898). They constitute the foundation upon which the structure of admission and exclusion rests. For similar provisions see California Evidence Code §§ 350, 351. Provisions that all relevant evidence is admissible are found in Uniform Rule 7(f); Kansas Code of Civil Procedure § 60–407(f); and New Jersey Evidence Rule 7(f); but the exclusion of evidence which is not relevant is left to implication.

Not all relevant evidence is admissible. The exclusion of relevant evidence occurs in a variety of situations and may be called for by these rules, by the Rules of Civil and Criminal Procedure, by Bankruptcy Rules, by Act of Congress, or by constitutional considerations.

Succeeding rules in the present article, in response to the demands of particular policies, require the exclusion of evidence despite its relevancy. In addition, Article V recognizes a number of privileges; Article VI imposes limitations upon witnesses and the manner of dealing with them; Article VII specifies requirements with respect to opinions and expert testimony; Article VIII excludes hearsay not falling within an exception; Article IX spells out the handling of authentication and identification; and Article X restricts the manner of proving the contents of writings and recordings.

The Rules of Civil and Criminal Procedure in some instances require the exclusion of relevant evidence. For example, Rules 30(b) and 32(a) (3) of the Rules of Civil Procedure, by imposing requirements of notice and unavailability of the deponent, place limits on the use of relevant depositions. Similarly, Rule 15 of the Rules of Criminal Procedure restricts the use of depositions in criminal cases, even though relevant. And the effective enforcement of the command, originally statutory and now found in Rule 5(a) of the Rules of Criminal Procedure, that an arrested person be taken without unnecessary delay before a commissioner or other similar officer is held to require the exclusion of statements elicited during detention in violation thereof. Mallory v. United States, 354 U.S. 449, 77 S.Ct. 1356, 1 L.Ed.2d 1479 (1957); 18 U.S.C. § 3501(c).

While congressional enactments in the field of evidence have generally tended to expand admissibility beyond the scope of the common law rules, in some particular situations they have restricted the admissibility of relevant evidence. Most of this legislation has consisted of the formulation of a privilege or of a prohibition against disclosure. 8 U.S.C. § 1202(f), records of refusal of visas or permits to enter United States confidential, subject to discretion of Secretary of State to make available to court upon certification of need; 10 U.S.C. § 3693, replacement certificate of honorable discharge from Army not admissible in evidence; 10 U.S.C. § 8693, same as to Air Force; 11 U.S.C. § 25(a)(10), testimony given by bankrupt on his examination not admissible in criminal proceedings against him, except that given in hearing upon objection to discharge; 11 U.S.C. § 205(a), railroad reorganization petition, if dismissed, not admissible in evidence; 11 U.S.C. § 403(a), list of creditors filed with municipal composition plan not an admission; 13 U.S.C. § 9(a), census information confidential, retained copies of reports privileged; 47 U.S.C. § 605, interception and divulgence of wire or radio communications prohibited unless authorized by sender. These statutory provisions would remain undisturbed by the rules.

The rule recognizes but makes no attempt to spell out the constitutional considerations which impose basic limitations upon the admissibility of relevant evidence. Examples are evidence obtained by unlawful search and seizure,

Weeks v. United States, 232 U.S. 383, 34 S.Ct. 341, 58 L.Ed. 652 (1914); Katz v. United States, 389 U.S. 347, 88 S.Ct. 507, 19 L.Ed.2d 576 (1967); incriminating statement elicited from an accused in violation of right to counsel, Massiah v. United States, 377 U.S. 201, 84 S.Ct. 1199, 12 L.Ed.2d 246 (1964).

Report of House Committee on the Judiciary

House Comm. on Judiciary, Fed Rules of Evidence, H.R. Rep. No. 650, 93d Cong., 1st Sess., p. 7 (1973); 1974 U.S. Code Cong. & Ad. News 7075, 7081

Rule 402 as submitted to the Congress contained the phrase "or by other rules adopted by the Supreme Court". To accommodate the view that the Congress should not appear to acquiesce in the Court's judgment that it has authority under the existing Rules Enabling Acts to promulgate Rules of Evidence, the Committee amended the above phrase to read "or by other rules prescribed by the Supreme Court pursuant to statutory authority" in this and other Rules where the reference appears.

Rule 403. Exclusion of Relevant Evidence on Grounds of Prejudice, Confusion, or Waste of Time

Although relevant, evidence may be excluded if its probative value is substantially outweighed by the danger of unfair prejudice, confusion of the issues, or misleading the jury, or by considerations of undue delay, waste of time, or needless presentation of cumulative evidence.

Section references, McCormick 5th ed.

§ 7, § 11, § 12, § 13, § 16, § 19, § 26, § 30, § 35, § 36, § 39, § 41, § 42, § 44, § 45, § 47, § 52, § 56, § 57, § 58, § 59, § 185, § 193, § 196, § 197, § 199, § 200, § 202, § 212, § 250, § 255, § 293, § 322

Note by Federal Judicial Center

The rule enacted by the Congress is the rule prescribed by the Supreme Court without change.

Advisory Committee's Note

56 F.R.D. 183, 218

The case law recognizes that certain circumstances call for the exclusion of evidence which is of unquestioned relevance. These circumstances entail risks which range all the way from inducing decision on a purely emotional basis, at one extreme, to nothing more harmful than merely wasting time, at the other extreme. Situations in this area call for balancing the probative value of and need for the evidence against the harm likely to result from its admission. Slough, Relevancy Unraveled, 5 Kan.L.Rev. 1, 12–15 (1956); Trautman, Logical or Legal Relevancy—A Conflict in Theory, 5 Van.L.Rev. 385, 392 (1952); McCormick § 152, pp. 319–321. The rules which follow in this Article are concrete applications evolved for particular situations. However, they reflect the policies underlying the present rule, which is designed as a guide for the handling of situations for which no specific rules have been formulated.

Exclusion for risk of unfair prejudice, confusion of issues, misleading the jury, or waste of time, all find ample support in the authorities. "Unfair prejudice" within its context means an undue tendency to suggest decision on an improper basis, commonly, though not necessarily, an emotional one.

The rule does not enumerate surprise as a ground for exclusion, in this respect following Wigmore's view of the common law. 6 Wigmore § 1849. Cf. McCormick § 152, p. 320, n. 29, listing unfair surprise as a ground for exclusion but stating that it is usually "coupled with the danger of prejudice and confusion of issues." While Uniform Rule 45 incorporates surprise as a ground and is followed in Kansas Code of Civil Procedure § 60–445, surprise is not included in California Evidence Code § 352 or New Jersey Rule 4, though both the latter otherwise substantially embody Uniform Rule 45. While it can scarcely be doubted that claims of unfair surprise may still be justified despite procedural requirements of notice and instrumentalities of discovery, the granting of a continuance is a more appropriate remedy than exclusion of the evidence. Tentative Recommendation and a Study Relating to the Uniform Rules of Evidence (Art. VI. Extrinsic Policies Affecting Admissibility), Cal. Law Revision Comm'n, Rep., Rec. & Studies, 612 (1964). Moreover, the impact of a rule excluding evidence on the ground of surprise would be difficult to estimate.

In reaching a decision whether to exclude on grounds of unfair prejudice, consideration should be given to the probable effectiveness or lack of effectiveness of a limiting instruction. See Rule 106 [105] and Advisory Committee's Note thereunder. The availability of other means of proof may also be an appropriate factor.

Rule 404. Character Evidence Not Admissible to Prove Conduct; Exceptions; Other Crimes

(a) Character evidence generally. Evidence of a person's character or a trait of character is not admissible for the purpose of proving action in conformity therewith on a particular occasion, except:

(1) Character of accused. Evidence of a pertinent trait of character offered by an accused, or by the prosecution to rebut the same, or if evidence of a trait of character of the alleged victim of the crime is offered by an accused and admitted under Rule 404 (a) (2), evidence of the same trait of character of the accused offered by the prosecution;

(2) Character of alleged victim. Evidence of a pertinent trait of character of the alleged victim of the crime offered by an accused, or by the prosecution to rebut the same, or evidence of a character trait of peacefulness of the alleged victim offered by the prosecution in a homicide case to rebut evidence that the alleged victim was the first aggressor;

(3) Character of witness. Evidence of the character of a witness, as provided in rules 607, 608, and 609.

(b) Other crimes, wrongs, or acts. Evidence of other crimes, wrongs, or acts is not admissible to prove the character of a person in order to show action in conformity therewith. It may, however, be admissible for other purposes, such as proof of motive, opportunity, intent, preparation, plan, knowledge, identity, or absence of mistake or accident, provided that upon request by the accused, the prosecution in a criminal case shall provide reasonable notice in advance of trial, or during trial if the court excuses pretrial notice on good cause shown, of the general nature of any such evidence it intends to introduce at trial.

(As amended Mar. 2, 1987, eff. Oct. 1, 1987; Apr. 30, 1991, eff. Dec. 1, 1991; Apr. 17, 2000, eff. Dec. 1, 2000.)

Section references, McCormick 5th ed.

Generally, § 189, § 192, § 196, § 197, § 200

(a). § 186, § 187, § 192

(1). § 186, § 187, § 191

(2). § 186, § 193

(3). § 186, § 191

(b). § 59, § 186, § 187, § 190, § 193

Note by Federal Judicial Center

The rule enacted by the Congress is the rule prescribed by the Supreme Court, with the second sentence of subdivision (b) amended by substituting "It may, however, be admissible" in place of "This subdivision does not exclude the evidence when offered."

Advisory Committee's Note

56 F.R.D. 183, 219

Subdivision (a). This subdivision deals with the basic question whether character evidence should be admitted. Once the admissibility of character evidence in some form is established under this rule, reference must then be made to Rule 405, which follows, in order to determine the appropriate method of proof. If the character is that of a witness, see Rules 608 and 609 for methods of proof.

Character questions arise in two fundamentally different ways. (1) Character may itself be an element of a crime, claim, or defense. A situation of this kind is commonly referred to as "character in issue." Illustrations are: the chastity of the victim under a statute specifying her chastity as an element of the crime of seduction, or the competency of the driver in an action for negligently entrusting a motor vehicle to an incompetent driver. No problem of the general relevancy of character evidence is involved, and the present rule therefore has no provision on the subject. The only question relates to allowable methods of proof, as to which see Rule 405, immediately following. (2) Character evidence is susceptible of being used for the purpose of suggesting an inference that the person acted on the occasion in question consistently with his character. This use of character is often described as "circumstantial." Illustrations are: evidence of a violent disposition to prove that person was the aggressor in an affray, or evidence of honesty in disproof of a charge of theft. This circumstantial use of character evidence raises questions of relevancy as well as questions of allowable methods of proof.

In most jurisdictions today, the circumstantial use of character is rejected but with important exceptions: (1) an accused may introduce pertinent evidence of good character (often misleadingly described as "putting his character in issue"), in which event the prosecution may rebut with evidence of bad character; (2) an accused may introduce pertinent evidence of the character of the victim, as in support of a claim of self-defense to a charge of homicide or consent in a case of rape,[2] and the prosecution may introduce similar evidence in rebuttal of the character evidence, or, in a homicide case, to rebut a claim that deceased was the first aggressor, however proved; and (3) the character of a witness may be gone into as bearing on his credibility. McCormick §§ 155–161. This pattern is incorporated in the rule. While its basis lies more in history and experience than in logic an underlying justification can fairly be found in terms of the relative presence and absence of prejudice in the various situations. Falknor, Extrinsic Policies Affecting Admissibility, 10 Rutgers L.Rev. 574, 584 (1956); McCormick § 157. In any event, the criminal rule is so deeply imbedded in our jurisprudence as to assume almost constitutional proportions and to override doubts of the basic relevancy of the evidence.

The limitation to pertinent traits of character, rather than character generally, in paragraphs (1) and (2) is in accordance with the prevailing view. McCormick § 158, p. 334. A similar provision in Rule 608, to which reference is made in paragraph (3), limits character evidence respecting witnesses to the trait of truthfulness or untruthfulness.

The argument is made that circumstantial use of character ought to be allowed in civil cases to the same extent as in criminal cases, i.e. evidence of good (nonprejudicial) character would be admissible in the first instance, subject to rebuttal by evidence of bad character. Falknor, Extrinsic Policies Affecting Admissibility, 10 Rutgers L.Rev. 574, 581–583 (1956); Tentative Recommendation and a Study Relating to the Uniform Rules of Evidence (Art. VI. Extrinsic Policies Affecting Admissibility), Cal Law Revision Comm'n, Rep., Rec. & Studies, 657–658 (1964). Uniform Rule 47 goes farther, in that it assumes that character evidence in general satisfies the conditions of relevancy, except as provided in Uniform Rule 48. The difficulty with expanding the use of character evidence in civil cases is set forth by the California Law Revision Commission in its ultimate rejection of Uniform Rule 47, id., 615:

> "Character evidence is of slight probative value and may be very prejudicial. It tends to distract the trier of fact from the main question of what actually happened on the particular occasion. It subtly permits the trier of fact to reward the good man and to punish the bad man because of their respective characters despite what the evidence in the case shows actually happened."

Much of the force of the position of those favoring greater use of character evidence in civil cases is dissipated by their support of Uniform Rule 48 which excludes the evidence in negligence cases, where it could be expected to achieve its maximum usefulness. Moreover, expanding concepts of "character," which seem of necessity to extend into such areas as psychiatric evaluation and psychological testing, coupled with expanded admissibility, would open up such vistas of mental examinations as caused the Court concern in Schlagenhauf v. Holder, 379 U.S. 104, 85 S.Ct. 234, 13 L.Ed.2d 152 (1964). It is believed that those espousing change have not met the burden of persuasion.

Subdivision (b) deals with a specialized but important application of the general rule excluding circumstantial use of character evidence. Consistently

2. But see Rule 412, infra, added by Act of Congress in 1978.—Ed.

with that rule, evidence of other crimes, wrongs, or acts is not admissible to prove character as a basis for suggesting the inference that conduct on a particular occasion was in conformity with it. However, the evidence may be offered for another purpose, such as proof of motive, opportunity, and so on, which does not fall within the prohibition. In this situation the rule does not require that the evidence be excluded. No mechanical solution is offered. The determination must be made whether the danger of undue prejudice outweighs the probative value of the evidence in view of the availability of other means of proof and other factors appropriate for making decisions of this kind under Rule 403. Slough and Knightly, Other Vices, Other Crimes, 41 Iowa L.Rev. 325 (1956).

Report of House Committee on the Judiciary

House Comm. on Judiciary, Fed. Rules of Evidence, H.R. Rep. No. 650, 93d Cong., 1st Sess., p. 7 (1973); 1974 U.S.Code Cong. & Ad. News 7075, 7081

The second sentence of Rule 404(b) as submitted to the Congress began with the words "This subdivision does not exclude the evidence when offered". The Committee amended this language to read "It may, however, be admissible", the words used in the 1971 Advisory Committee draft, on the ground that this formulation properly placed greater emphasis on admissibility than did the final Court version.

Report of Senate Committee on the Judiciary

Senate Comm. on Judiciary, Fed. Rules of Evidence, S. Rep. No. 1277, 93d Cong., 2d Sess., p. 24 (1974); 1974 U.S.Code Cong. & Ad. News 7051, 7071

This rule provides that evidence of other crimes, wrongs, or acts is not admissible to prove character but may be admissible for other specified purposes such as proof of motive.

Although your committee sees no necessity in amending the rule itself, it anticipates that the use of the discretionary word "may" with respect to the admissibility of evidence of crimes, wrongs, or acts is not intended to confer any arbitrary discretion on the trial judge. Rather, it is anticipated that with respect to permissible uses for such evidence, the trial judge may exclude it only on the basis of those considerations set forth in Rule 403, i.e. prejudice, confusion or waste of time.

1987 Amendment

The amendments are technical. No substantive change is intended.

1991 Amendment

Rule 404(b) has emerged as one of the most cited Rules in the Rules of Evidence.

And in many criminal cases evidence of an accused's extrinsic acts is viewed as an important asset in the prosecution's case against an accused. Although there are a few reported decisions on use of such evidence by the defense, *see, e.g., United States v. McClure,* 546 F.2d 670 (5th Cir.1990) (acts of informant offered in entrapment defense), the overwhelming number of cases involve introduction of that evidence by the prosecution.

The amendment to Rule 404(b) adds a pretrial notice requirement in criminal cases and is intended to reduce surprise and promote early resolution on the issue of admissibility. The notice requirement thus places Rule 404(b) in the mainstream with notice and disclosure provisions in other rules of evidence. *See, e.g.,* Rule 412 (written motion of intent to offer evidence under rule), Rule 609 (written notice of intent to offer conviction older than 10 years), Rule 803(24) and 804(b)(5) (notice of intent to use residual hearsay exceptions).

The Rule expects that counsel for both the defense and the prosecution will submit the necessary request and information in a reasonable and timely fashion. Other than requiring pretrial notice, no specific time limits are stated in recognition that what constitutes a reasonable request or disclosure will depend largely on the circumstances of each case. *Compare* Fla.Stat.Ann. § 90.404(2)(b) (notice must be given at least 10 days before trial) *with* Tex. R.Evid. 404(b) (no time limit).

Likewise, no specific form of notice is required. The Committee considered and rejected a requirement that the notice satisfy the particularity requirements normally required of language used in a charging instrument. *Cf.* Fla.Stat.Ann. § 90.404(2)(b) (written disclosure must describe uncharged misconduct with particularity required of an indictment or information). Instead, the Committee opted for a generalized notice provision which requires the prosecution to apprise the defense of the general nature of the evidence of extrinsic acts. The Committee does not intend that the amendment will supercede other rules of admissibility or disclosure, such as the Jencks Act, 18 U.S.C. § 3500, et seq. nor require the prosecution to disclose directly or indirectly the names and addresses of its witnesses, something it is currently not required to do under Federal Rule of Criminal Procedure 16.

The amendment requires the prosecution to provide notice, regardless of how it intends to use the extrinsic act evidence at trial, i.e., during its case-in-chief, for impeachment, or for possible rebuttal. The court in its discretion may, under the facts, decide that the particular request or notice was not reasonable, either because of the lack of timeliness or completeness. Because the notice requirement serves as condition precedent to admissibility of 404(b) evidence, the offered evidence is inadmissible if the court decides that the notice requirement has not been met.

Nothing in the amendment precludes the court from requiring the government to provide it with an opportunity to rule *in limine* on 404(b) evidence before it is offered or even mentioned during trial. When ruling *in limine,* the court may require the government to disclose to it the specifics of such evidence which the court must consider in determining admissibility.

The amendment does not extend to evidence of acts which are "intrinsic" to the charged offense, *see United States v. Williams,* 900 F.2d 823 (5th Cir.1990) (noting distinction between 404(b) evidence and intrinsic offense evidence). Nor is the amendment intended to redefine what evidence would otherwise be admissible under Rule 404(b). Finally, the Committee does not intend through the amendment to affect the role of the court and the jury in considering such evidence. *See United States v. Huddleston,* ___ U.S. ___, 108 S.Ct. 1496 (1988).

2000 Amendment

Rule 404(a)(1) has been amended to provide that when the accused attacks the character of an alleged victim under subdivision (a)(2) of this Rule, the door is opened to an attack on the same character trait of the accused. Current law does not allow the government to introduce negative character evidence as to the accused unless the accused introduces evidence of good character. *See, e.g., United States v. Fountain*, 768 F.2d 790 (7th Cir. 1985) (when the accused offers proof of self-defense, this permits proof of the alleged victim's character trait for peacefulness, but it does not permit proof of the accused's character trait for violence).

The amendment makes clear that the accused cannot attack the alleged victim's character and yet remain shielded from the disclosure of equally relevant evidence concerning the same character trait of the accused. For example, in a murder case with a claim of self-defense, the accused, to bolster this defense, might offer evidence of the alleged victim's violent disposition. If the government has evidence that the accused has a violent character, but is not allowed to offer this evidence as part of its rebuttal, the jury has only part of the information it needs for an informed assessment of the probabilities as to who was the initial aggressor. This may be the case even if evidence of the accused's prior violent acts is admitted under Rule 404(b), because such evidence can be admitted only for limited purposes and not to show action in conformity with the accused's character on a specific occasion. Thus, the amendment is designed to permit a more balanced presentation of character evidence when an accused chooses to attack the character of the alleged victim.

The amendment does not affect the admissibility of evidence of specific acts of uncharged misconduct offered for a purpose other than proving character under Rule 404(b). Nor does it affect the standards for proof of character by evidence of other sexual behavior or sexual offenses under Rules 412–415. By its placement in Rule 404(a)(1), the amendment covers only proof of character by way of reputation or opinion.

The amendment does not permit proof of the accused's character if the accused merely uses character evidence for a purpose other than to prove the alleged victim's propensity to act in a certain way. *See United States v. Burks*, 470 F.2d 432, 434–5 (D.C.Cir. 1972) (evidence of the alleged victim's violent character, when known by the accused, was admissible "on the issue of whether or not the defendant reasonably feared he was in danger of imminent great bodily harm"). Finally, the amendment does not permit proof of the accused's character when the accused attacks the alleged victim's character as a witness under Rule 608 or 609.

The term "alleged" is inserted before each reference to "victim" in the Rule, in order to provide consistency with Evidence Rule 412.

Rule 405. Methods of Proving Character

(a) Reputation or opinion. In all cases in which evidence of character or a trait of character of a person is admissible, proof may be made by testimony as to reputation or by testimony in the form of an opinion. On cross-examination, inquiry is allowable into relevant specific instances of conduct.

(b) Specific instances of conduct. In cases in which character or a trait of character of a person is an essential element of a charge, claim, or defense, proof may also be made of specific instances of that person's conduct.

(As amended Mar. 2, 1987, eff. Oct. 1, 1987.)

Section references, McCormick 5th ed.

Generally § 186, § 189, § 191, § 196, § 197, § 206

(a). § 191

(b). § 187

Note by Federal Judicial Center

The rule enacted by the Congress is the rule prescribed by the Supreme Court without change. The bill reported by the House Committee on the Judiciary deleted the provision in subdivision (a) for making proof by testimony in the form of an opinion, but the provision was reinstated on the floor of the House. [120 Cong.Rec. 2370–73 (1974)].

Advisory Committee's Note

56 F.R.D. 183 222

The rule deals only with allowable methods of proving character, not with the admissibility of character evidence, which is covered in Rule 404.

Of the three methods of proving character provided by the rule, evidence of specific instances of conduct is the most convincing. At the same time it possesses the greatest capacity to arouse prejudice, to confuse, to surprise, and to consume time. Consequently the rule confines the use of evidence of this kind to cases in which character is, in the strict sense, in issue and hence deserving of a searching inquiry. When character is used circumstantially and hence occupies a lesser status in the case, proof may be only by reputation and opinion. These latter methods are also available when character is in issue. This treatment is, with respect to specific instances of conduct and reputation, conventional contemporary common law doctrine. McCormick § 153.

In recognizing opinion as a means of proving character, the rule departs from usual contemporary practice in favor of that of an earlier day. See 7 Wigmore § 1986, pointing out that the earlier practice permitted opinion and arguing strongly for evidence based on personal knowledge and belief as contrasted with "the secondhand, irresponsible product of multiplied guesses and gossip which we term 'reputation'." It seems likely that the persistence of reputation evidence is due to its largely being opinion in disguise. Traditionally character has been regarded primarily in moral overtones of good and bad: chaste, peaceable, truthful, honest. Nevertheless, on occasion nonmoral considerations crop up, as in the case of the incompetent driver, and this seems bound to happen increasingly. If character is defined as the kind of person one is, then account must be taken of varying ways of arriving at the estimate. These may range from the opinion of the employer who has found the man honest to the opinion of the psychiatrist based upon examination and testing. No effective dividing line exists between character and mental capacity, and the latter traditionally has been provable by opinion.

According to the great majority of cases, on cross-examination inquiry is allowable as to whether the reputation witness has heard of particular instances of conduct pertinent to the trait in question. Michelson v. United States, 335 U.S. 469, 69 S.Ct. 213, 93 L.Ed. 168 (1948); Annot., 47 A.L.R.2d 1258. The theory is that, since the reputation witness relates what he has heard, the inquiry tends to shed light on the accuracy of his hearing and reporting. Accordingly, the opinion witness would be asked whether he knew, as well as whether he had heard. The fact is, of course, that these distinctions are of slight if any practical significance, and the second sentence of subdivision (a) eliminates them as a factor in formulating questions. This recognition of the propriety of inquiring into specific instances of conduct does not circumscribe inquiry otherwise into the bases of opinion and reputation testimony.

The express allowance of inquiry into specific instances of conduct on cross-examination in subdivision (a) and the express allowance of it as part of a case in chief when character is actually in issue in subdivision (b) contemplate that testimony of specific instances is not generally permissible on the direct examination of an ordinary opinion witness to character. Similarly as to witnesses to the character of witnesses under Rule 608(b). Opinion testimony on direct in these situations ought in general to correspond to reputation testimony as now given, i.e., be confined to the nature and extent of observation and acquaintance upon which the opinion is based. See Rule 701.

1987 Amendment

The amendment is technical. No substantive change is intended.

Rule 406. Habit; Routine Practice

Evidence of the habit of a person or of the routine practice of an organization, whether corroborated or not and regardless of the presence of eyewitnesses, is relevant to prove that the conduct of the person or organization on a particular occasion was in conformity with the habit or routine practice.

Section references, McCormick 5th ed.

§ 195, § 271

Note by Federal Judicial Center

The rule enacted by the Congress is subdivision (a) of the rule prescribed by the Supreme Court. Subdivision (b) of the Court's rule was deleted for reasons stated in the Report of the House Committee on the Judiciary set forth below. ***

Advisory Committee's Note

56 F.R.D. 183, 223

An oft-quoted paragraph, McCormick, § 162, p. 340, describes habit in terms effectively contrasting it with character:

> "Character and habit are close akin. Character is a generalized description of one's disposition, or of one's disposition in respect to a general trait, such as honesty, temperance, or peacefulness. 'Habit,' in modern usage, both lay and psychological, is more specific. It describes one's regular

> response to a repeated specific situation. If we speak of character for care, we think of the person's tendency to act prudently in all the varying situations of life, in business, family life, in handling automobiles and in walking across the street. A habit, on the other hand, is the person's regular practice of meeting a particular kind of situation with a specific type of conduct, such as the habit of going down a particular stairway two stairs at a time, or of giving the hand-signal for a left turn, or of alighting from railway cars while they are moving. The doing of the habitual acts may become semi-automatic."

Equivalent behavior on the part of a group is designated "routine practice of an organization" in the rule.

Agreement is general that habit evidence is highly persuasive as proof of conduct on a particular occasion. Again quoting McCormick § 162, p. 341:

> "Character may be thought of as the sum of one's habits though doubtless it is more than this. But unquestionably the uniformity of one's response to habit is far greater than the consistency with which one's conduct conforms to character or disposition. Even though character comes in only exceptionally as evidence of an act, surely any sensible man in investigating whether X did a particular act would be greatly helped in his inquiry by evidence as to whether he was in the habit of doing it."

When disagreement has appeared, its focus has been upon the question what constitutes habit, and the reason for this is readily apparent. The extent to which instances must be multiplied and consistency of behavior maintained in order to rise to the status of habit inevitably gives rise to differences of opinion. Lewan, Rationale of Habit Evidence, 16 Syracuse L.Rev. 39, 49 (1964). While adequacy of sampling and uniformity of response are key factors, precise standards for measuring their sufficiency for evidence purposes cannot be formulated.

The rule is consistent with prevailing views. Much evidence is excluded simply because of failure to achieve the status of habit. Thus, evidence of intemperate "habits" is generally excluded when offered as proof of drunkenness in accident cases, Annot., 46 A.L.R.2d 103, and evidence of other assaults is inadmissible to prove the instant one in a civil assault action, Annot., 66 A.L.R.2d 806. In Levin v. United States, 119 U.S.App.D.C. 156, 338 F.2d 265 (1964), testimony as to the religious "habits" of the accused, offered as tending to prove that he was at home observing the Sabbath rather than out obtaining money through larceny by trick, was held properly excluded:

> "It seems apparent to us that an individual's religious practices would not be the type of activities which would lend themselves to the characterization of 'invariable regularity.' [1 Wigmore 520.] Certainly the very volitional basis of the activity raises serious questions as to its invariable nature, and hence its probative value." Id. at 272.

These rulings are not inconsistent with the trend towards admitting evidence of business transactions between one of the parties and a third person as tending to prove that he made the same bargain or proposal in the litigated situation. Slough, Relevancy Unraveled, 6 Kan.L.Rev. 38–41 (1957). Nor are they inconsistent with such cases as Whittemore v. Lockheed Aircraft Corp., 65 Cal.App.2d 737, 151 P.2d 670 (1944), upholding the admission of evidence that plaintiff's intestate had on four other occasions flown planes from defendant's factory for delivery to his employer airline, offered to prove that he was piloting rather than a guest on a plane which crashed and killed all on board while en route for delivery.

A considerable body of authority has required that evidence of the routine practice of an organization be corroborated as a condition precedent to its admission in evidence. Slough, Relevancy Unraveled, 5 Kan.L.Rev. 404, 449 (1957). This requirement is specifically rejected by the rule on the ground that it relates to the sufficiency of the evidence rather than admissibility. A similar position is taken in New Jersey Rule 49. The rule also rejects the requirement of the absence of eyewitnesses, sometimes encountered with respect to admitting habit evidence to prove freedom from contributory negligence in wrongful death cases. For comment critical of the requirements see Frank, J., in Cereste v. New York, N.H. & H.R. Co., 231 F.2d 50 (2d Cir.1956), cert. denied 351 U.S. 951, 76 S.Ct. 848, 100 L.Ed. 1475, 10 Vand.L.Rev. 447 (1957); McCormick § 162, p. 342. The omission of the requirement from the California Evidence Code is said to have effected its elimination. Comment, Cal.Ev.Code § 1105.

Report of House Committee on the Judiciary

House Comm. on Judiciary, Fed. Rules of Evidence, H.R. Rep. No. 650, 93d Cong., 1st Sess., p. 5 (1973); 1974 U.S.Code Cong. & Ad. News 7075, 7079

Rule 406 as submitted to Congress contained a subdivision (b) providing that the method of proof of habit or routine practice could be "in the form of an opinion or by specific instances of conduct sufficient in number to warrant a finding that the habit existed or that the practice was routine." The Committee deleted this subdivision believing that the method of proof of habit and routine practice should be left to the courts to deal with on a case-by-case basis. At the same time, the Committee does not intend that its action be construed as sanctioning a general authorization of opinion evidence in this area.

Rule 407. Subsequent Remedial Measures

When, after an injury or harm allegedly caused by an event, measures are taken that, if taken previously, would have made the injury or harm less likely to occur, evidence of the subsequent measures is not admissible to prove negligence, culpable conduct, a defect in a product, a defect in a product's design, or a need for a warning or instruction. This rule does not require the exclusion of evidence of subsequent measures when offered for another purpose, such as proving ownership, control, or feasibility of precautionary measures, if controverted, or impeachment.

(As Amended Apr. 11, 1997, eff. Dec. 1, 1997.)

Section references, McCormick 5th ed.

§ 267

Note by Federal Judicial Center

The rule enacted by the Congress is the rule prescribed by the Supreme Court without change.

Advisory Committee's Note

56 F.R.D. 183, 225

The rule incorporates conventional doctrine which excludes evidence of subsequent remedial measures as proof of an admission of fault. The rule rests on two grounds. (1) The conduct is not in fact an admission, since the conduct is equally consistent with injury by mere accident or through contributory negligence. Or, as Baron Bramwell put it, the rule rejects the notion that "because the world gets wiser as it gets older, therefore it was foolish before." Hart v. Lancashire & Yorkshire Ry. Co., 21 L.T.R. N.S. 261, 263 (1869). Under a liberal theory of relevancy this ground alone would not support exclusion as the inference is still a possible one. (2) The other, and more impressive, ground for exclusion rests on a social policy of encouraging people to take, or at least not discouraging them from taking, steps in furtherance of added safety. The courts have applied this principle to exclude evidence of subsequent repairs, installation of safety devices, changes in company rules, and discharge of employees, and the language of the present rule is broad enough to encompass all of them. See Falknor, Extrinsic Policies Affecting Admissibility, 10 Rutgers L.Rev. 574, 590 (1956).

The second sentence of the rule directs attention to the limitations of the rule. Exclusion is called for only when the evidence of subsequent remedial measures is offered as proof of negligence or culpable conduct. In effect it rejects the suggested inference that fault is admitted. Other purposes are, however, allowable, including ownership or control, existence of duty, and feasibility of precautionary measures, if controverted, and impeachment. 2 Wigmore § 283; Annot., 64 A.L.R.2d 1296. Two recent federal cases are illustrative. Boeing Airplane Co. v. Brown, 291 F.2d 310 (9th Cir.1961), an action against an airplane manufacturer for using an allegedly defectively designed alternator shaft which caused a plane crash, upheld the admission of evidence of subsequent design modification for the purpose of showing that design changes and safeguards were feasible. And Powers v. J.B. Michael & Co., 329 F.2d 674 (6th Cir.1964), an action against a road contractor for negligent failure to put out warning signs, sustained the admission of evidence that defendant subsequently put out signs to show that the portion of the road in question was under defendant's control. The requirement that the other purpose be controverted calls for automatic exclusion unless a genuine issue be present and allows the opposing party to lay the groundwork for exclusion by making an admission. Otherwise the factors of undue prejudice, confusion of issues, misleading the jury, and waste of time remain for consideration under Rule 403.

For comparable rules, see Uniform Rule 51; California Evidence Code § 1151; Kansas Code of Civil Procedure § 60–451; New Jersey Evidence Rule 51.

1997 Amendment

The amendment to Rule 407 makes two changes in the rule. First, the words "an injury or harm allegedly caused by" were added to clarify that the rule applies only to changes made after the occurrence that produced the damages giving rise to the action. Evidence of measures taken by the defendant prior to the "event" causing "injury or harm" do not fall within the exclusionary scope of Rule 407 even if they occurred after the manufacture or design of the product. See *Chase v. General Motors Corp.*, 856 F.2d 17, 21–22 (4th Cir. 1988).

Second, Rule 407 has been amended to provide that evidence of subsequent remedial measures may not be used to prove "a defect in a product or its design, or that a warning or instruction should have accompanied a product." This amendment adopts the view of a majority of the circuits that have interpreted Rule 407 to apply to products liability actions. See *Raymond v. Raymond Corp.*, 938 F.2d 1518, 1522 (1st Cir. 1991); *In re Joint Eastern District and Southern District Asbestos Litigation v. Armstrong World Industries, Inc.*, 995 F.2d 343 (2d Cir. 1993); *Cann v. Ford Motor Co.*, 658 F.2d 54, 60 (2d Cir. 1981), *cert. denied*, 456 U.S. 960 (1982); *Kelly v. Crown Equipment Co.*, 970 F.2d 1273, 1275 (3d Cir. 1992); *Werner v. Upjohn, Inc.*, 628 F.2d 848 (4th Cir. 1980), *cert. denied*, 449 U.S. 1080 (1981); *Grenada Steel Industries, Inc. v. Alabama Oxygen Co., Inc.*, 695 F.2d 883 (5th Cir. 1983); *Bauman v. Volkswagenwerk Aktiengesellschaft*, 621 F.2d 230, 232 (6th Cir. 1980); *Flaminio v. Honda Motor Company, Ltd.*, 733 F.2d 463, 469 (7th Cir. 1984); *Gauthier v. AMF, Inc.*, 788 F.2d 634, 636–37 (9th Cir. 1986).

Although this amendment adopts a uniform federal rule, it should be noted that evidence of subsequent remedial measures may be admissible pursuant to the second sentence of Rule 407. Evidence of subsequent measures that is not barred by Rule 407 may still be subject to exclusion on Rule 403 grounds when the dangers of prejudice or confusion substantially outweigh the probative value of the evidence.

Rule 408. Compromise and Offers to Compromise

Evidence of (1) furnishing or offering or promising to furnish, or (2) accepting or offering or promising to accept, a valuable consideration in compromising or attempting to compromise a claim which was disputed as to either validity or amount, is not admissible to prove liability for or invalidity of the claim or its amount. Evidence of conduct or statements made in compromise negotiations is likewise not admissible. This rule does not require the exclusion of any evidence otherwise discoverable merely because it is presented in the course of compromise negotiations. This rule also does not require exclusion when the evidence is offered for another purpose, such as proving bias or prejudice of a witness, negativing a contention of undue delay, or proving an effort to obstruct a criminal investigation or prosecution.

Section references, McCormick 5th ed.

§ 267

Note by Federal Judicial Center

The rule enacted by the Congress is the rule prescribed by the Supreme Court, amended by the insertion of the third sentence. Other amendments, proposed by the House bill, were not enacted, for reasons stated in the Report of the Senate Committee on the Judiciary and in the Conference Report, set forth below.

Advisory Committee's Note

56 F.R.D. 183, 226

As a matter of general agreement, evidence of an offer to compromise a claim is not receivable in evidence as an admission of, as the case may be, the validity or invalidity of the claim. As with evidence of subsequent remedial measures, dealt with in Rule 407, exclusion may be based on two grounds. (1) The evidence is irrelevant, since the offer may be motivated by a desire for peace rather than from any concession of weakness of position. The validity of this position will vary as the amount of the offer varies in relation to the size of the claim and may also be influenced by other circumstances. (2) A more consistently impressive ground is promotion of the public policy favoring the compromise and settlement of disputes. McCormick §§ 76, 251. While the rule is ordinarily phrased in terms of offers of compromise, it is apparent that a similar attitude must be taken with respect to completed compromises when offered against a party thereto. This latter situation will not, of course, ordinarily occur except when a party to the present litigation has compromised with a third person.

The same policy underlies the provision of Rule 68 of the Federal Rules of Civil Procedure that evidence of an unaccepted offer of judgment is not admissible except in a proceeding to determine costs.

The practical value of the common law rule has been greatly diminished by its inapplicability to admissions of fact, even though made in the course of compromise negotiations, unless hypothetical, stated to be "without prejudice," or so connected with the offer as to be inseparable from it. McCormick § 251, pp. 540–541. An inevitable effect is to inhibit freedom of communication with respect to compromise, even among lawyers. Another effect is the generation of controversy over whether a given statement falls within or without the protected area. These considerations account for the expansion of the rule herewith to include evidence of conduct or statements made in compromise negotiations, as well as the offer or completed compromise itself. For similar provisions see California Evidence Code §§ 1152, 1154.

The policy considerations which underlie the rule do not come into play when the effort is to induce a creditor to settle an admittedly due amount for a lesser sum. McCormick § 251, p. 540. Hence the rule requires that the claim be disputed as to either validity or amount.

The final sentence of the rule serves to point out some limitations upon its applicability. Since the rule excludes only when the purpose is proving the validity or invalidity of the claim or its amount, an offer for another purpose is not within the rule. The illustrative situations mentioned in the rule are supported by the authorities. As to proving bias or prejudice of a witness, see Annot., 161 A.L.R. 395, contra, Fenberg v. Rosenthal, 348 Ill.App. 510, 109 N.E.2d 402 (1952), and negativing a contention of lack of due diligence in presenting a claim, 4 Wigmore § 1061. An effort to "buy off" the prosecution or a prosecuting witness in a criminal case is not within the policy of the rule of exclusion. McCormick § 251, p. 542.

For other rules of similar import, see Uniform Rules 52 and 53; California Evidence Code §§ 1152, 1154; Kansas Code of Civil Procedure §§ 60–452, 60–453; New Jersey Evidence Rules 52 and 53.

Report of House Committee on the Judiciary

House Comm. on Judiciary, Fed.Rules of Evidence, H.R.Rep. No. 650, 93d Cong., 1st Sess., p. 8 (1973); 1974 U.S.Code Cong. & Ad. News 7075, 7081

Under existing federal law evidence of conduct and statements made in compromise negotiations is admissible in subsequent litigation between the parties. The second sentence of Rule 408 as submitted by the Supreme Court proposed to reverse that doctrine in the interest of further promoting non-judicial settlement of disputes. Some agencies of government expressed the view that the Court formulation was likely to impede rather than assist efforts to achieve settlement of disputes. For one thing, it is not always easy to tell when compromise negotiations begin, and informal dealings end. Also, parties dealing with government agencies would be reluctant to furnish factual information at preliminary meetings; they would wait until "compromise negotiations" began and thus hopefully effect an immunity for themselves with respect to the evidence supplied. In light of these considerations, the Committee recast the Rule so that admissions of liability or opinions given during compromise negotiations continue inadmissible, but evidence of unqualified factual assertions is admissible. The latter aspect of the Rule is drafted, however, so as to preserve other possible objections to the introduction of such evidence. The Committee intends no modification of current law whereby a party may protect himself from future use of his statements by couching them in hypothetical conditional form.

Report of Senate Committee on the Judiciary

Senate Comm. on Judiciary, Fed. Rules of Evidence, S.Rep. No. 1277, 93d Cong., 2d Sess., p. 10 (1974); 1974 U.S.Code Cong. & Ad. News 7051, 7056

This rule as reported makes evidence of settlement or attempted settlement of a disputed claim inadmissible when offered as an admission of liability or the amount of liability. The purpose of this rule is to encourage settlements which would be discouraged if such evidence were admissible.

Under present law, in most jurisdictions, statements of fact made during settlement negotiations, however, are excepted from this ban and are admissible. The only escape from admissibility of statements of fact made in a settlement negotiation is if the declarant or his representative expressly states that the statement is hypothetical in nature or is made without prejudice. Rule 408 as submitted by the Court reversed the traditional rule. It would have brought statements of fact within the ban and made them, as well as an offer of settlement, inadmissible.

The House amended the rule and would continue to make evidence of facts disclosed during compromise negotiations admissible. It thus reverted to the traditional rule. The House committee report states that the committee intends to preserve current law under which a party may protect himself by couching his statements in hypothetical form.[1] The real impact of this amendment, however, is to deprive the rule of much of its salutary effect. The exception for factual admissions was believed by the Advisory Committee to hamper free communication between parties and thus to constitute an unjustifiable restraint upon efforts to negotiate settlements—the encouragement of which is the purpose of

1. See Report No. 93–650, dated November 15, 1973.

the rule. Further, by protecting hypothetically phrased statements, it constituted a preference for the sophisticated, and a trap for the unwary.

Three States which had adopted rules of evidence patterned after the proposed rules prescribed by the Supreme Court opted for versions of rule 408 identical with the Supreme Court draft with respect to the inadmissibility of conduct or statements made in compromise negotiations.[2]

For these reasons, the committee has deleted the House amendment and restored the rule to the version submitted by the Supreme Court with one additional amendment. This amendment adds a sentence to insure that evidence, such as documents, is not rendered inadmissible merely because it is presented in the course of compromise negotiations if the evidence is otherwise discoverable. A party should not be able to immunize from admissibility documents otherwise discoverable merely by offering them in a compromise negotiation.

Conference Report

H.R., Fed. Rules of Evidence, Conf. Rep. No. 1597, 93d Cong., 2d Sess., p. 6 (1974); 1974 U.S.Code Cong. & Ad. News 7098, 7099

The House bill provides that evidence of admissions of liability or opinions given during compromise negotiations is not admissible, but that evidence of facts disclosed during compromise negotiations is not inadmissible by virtue of having been first disclosed in the compromise negotiations. The Senate amendment provides that evidence of conduct or statements made in compromise negotiations is not admissible. The Senate amendment also provides that the rule does not require the exclusion of any evidence otherwise discoverable merely because it is presented in the course of compromise negotiations.

The House bill was drafted to meet the objection of executive agencies that under the rule as proposed by the Supreme Court, a party could present a fact during compromise negotiations and thereby prevent an opposing party from offering evidence of that fact at trial even though such evidence was obtained from independent sources. The Senate amendment expressly precludes this result.

The Conference adopts the Senate amendment.

Rule 409. Payment of Medical and Similar Expenses

Evidence of furnishing or offering or promising to pay medical, hospital, or similar expenses occasioned by an injury is not admissible to prove liability for the injury.

Section references, McCormick 5th ed.

§ 267

Note by Federal Judicial Center

The rule enacted by the Congress is the rule prescribed by the Supreme Court without change.

2. Nev.Rev.Stats. § 48.105; N.Mex.Stats.Anno. (1973 Supp.) § 20–4–408; West's Wis. Stats.Anno. (1973 Supp.) § 904.08.

Advisory Committee's Note

56 F.R.D. 183, 228

The considerations underlying this rule parallel those underlying Rules 407 and 408, which deal respectively with subsequent remedial measures and offers of compromise. As stated in Annot., 20 A.L.R.2d 291, 293:

> "[G]enerally, evidence of payment of medical, hospital, or similar expenses of an injured party by the opposing party, is not admissible, the reason often given being that such payment or offer is usually made from humane impulses and not from an admission of liability, and that to hold otherwise would tend to discourage assistance to the injured person."

Contrary to Rule 408, dealing with offers of compromise, the present rule does not extend to conduct or statements not a part of the act of furnishing or offering or promising to pay. This difference in treatment arises from fundamental differences in nature. Communication is essential if compromises are to be effected, and consequently broad protection of statements is needed. This is not so in cases of payments or offers or promises to pay medical expenses, where factual statements may be expected to be incidental in nature.

For rules on the same subject, but phrased in terms of "humanitarian motives," see Uniform Rule 52; California Evidence Code § 1152; Kansas Code of Civil Procedure § 60–452; New Jersey Evidence Rule 52.

Rule 410. Inadmissibility of Pleas, Plea Discussions, and Related Statements

Except as otherwise provided in this rule, evidence of the following is not, in any civil or criminal proceeding, admissible against the defendant who made the plea or was a participant in the plea discussions:

(1) a plea of guilty which was later withdrawn;

(2) a plea of nolo contendere;

(3) any statement made in the course of any proceedings under Rule 11 of the Federal Rules of Criminal Procedure or comparable state procedure regarding either of the foregoing pleas; or

(4) any statement made in the course of plea discussions with an attorney for the prosecuting authority which do not result in a plea of guilty or which result in a plea of guilty later withdrawn.

However, such a statement is admissible (i) in any proceeding wherein another statement made in the course of the same plea or plea discussions has been introduced and the statement ought in fairness be considered contemporaneously with it, or (ii) in a criminal proceeding for perjury or false statement if the statement was made by the defendant under oath, on the record and in the presence of counsel.

(As amended by P.L. 94–149, § 1(9), Dec. 12, 1975, 89 Stat. 805; Apr. 30, 1979, eff. Dec. 1, 1980.)

Section references, McCormick 5th ed.

§ 42, § 159, § 257, § 266

Rule 410 as originally enacted

Editorial Note

When first enacted together with the other Federal Rules of Evidence, Rule 410 read as follows:

> Except as otherwise provided by Act of Congress, evidence of a plea of guilty, later withdrawn, or a plea of nolo contendere, or of an offer to plead guilty or nolo contendere to the crime charged or any other crime, or of statements made in connection with any of the foregoing pleas or offers, is not admissible in any civil or criminal action, case, or proceeding against the person who made the plea or offer. This rule shall not apply to the introduction of voluntary and reliable statements made in court on the record in connection with any of the foregoing pleas or offers where offered for impeachment purposes or in a subsequent prosecution of the declarant for perjury or false statement.
>
> This rule shall not take effect until August 1, 1975, and shall be superseded by any amendment to the Federal Rules of Criminal Procedure which is inconsistent with this rule, and which takes effect after the date of the enactment of the Act establishing these Federal Rules of Evidence.

As prescribed by the Supreme Court, the rule had consisted only of the first sentence, without the clause "Except as otherwise provided by Act of Congress". That clause and the remaining language were added by congressional amendment. The theory of the Supreme Court's rule is explained in the Advisory Committee's Note set forth immediately below, and the reasons for the amendments are stated in the congressional reports which follow it. In addition to these latter reports, see Chairman Hungate's explanation. 120 Cong.Rec. 40890 (1974); 1975 U.S.Code Cong. & Ad.News 7108, 7109.

Advisory Committee's Note

56 F.R.D. 183, 228

Withdrawn pleas of guilty were held inadmissible in federal prosecutions in Kercheval v. United States, 274 U.S. 220, 47 S.Ct. 582, 71 L.Ed. 1009 (1927). The Court pointed out that to admit the withdrawn plea would effectively set at naught the allowance of withdrawal and place the accused in a dilemma utterly inconsistent with the decision to award him a trial. The New York Court of Appeals, in People v. Spitaleri, 9 N.Y.2d 168, 212 N.Y.S.2d 53, 173 N.E.2d 35 (1961), reexamined and overturned its earlier decisions which had allowed admission. In addition to the reasons set forth in Kercheval, which was quoted at length, the court pointed out that the effect of admitting the plea was to compel defendant to take the stand by way of explanation and to open the way for the prosecution to call the lawyer who had represented him at the time of entering the plea. State court decisions for and against admissibility are collected in Annot., 86 A.L.R.2d 326.

Pleas of *nolo contendere* are recognized by Rule 11 of the Rules of Criminal Procedure, although the law of numerous States is to the contrary. The present rule gives effect to the principal traditional characteristic of the *nolo* plea, i.e.

avoiding the admission of guilt which is inherent in pleas of guilty. This position is consistent with the construction of Section 5 of the Clayton Act, 15 U.S.C. § 16(a), recognizing the inconclusive and compromise nature of judgments based on *nolo* pleas. General Electric Co. v. City of San Antonio, 334 F.2d 480 (5th Cir.1964); Commonwealth Edison Co. v. Allis-Chalmers Mfg. Co., 323 F.2d 412 (7th Cir.1963), cert. denied 376 U.S. 939, 84 S.Ct. 794, 11 L.Ed.2d 659; Armco Steel Corp. v. North Dakota, 376 F.2d 206 (8th Cir.1967); City of Burbank v. General Electric Co., 329 F.2d 825 (9th Cir.1964). See also state court decisions in Annot., 18 A.L.R.2d 1287, 1314.

Exclusion of offers to plead guilty or *nolo* has as its purpose the promotion of disposition of criminal cases by compromise. As pointed out in McCormick § 251, p. 543.

> "Effective criminal law administration in many localities would hardly be possible if a large proportion of the charges were not disposed of by such compromises."

See also People v. Hamilton, 60 Cal.2d 105, 32 Cal.Rptr. 4, 383 P.2d 412 (1963), discussing legislation designed to achieve this result. As with compromise offers generally, Rule 408, free communication is needed, and security against having an offer of compromise or related statement admitted in evidence effectively encourages it.[1]

Limiting the exclusionary rule to use against the accused is consistent with the purpose of the rule, since the possibility of use for or against other persons will not impair the effectiveness of withdrawing pleas or the freedom of discussion which the rule is designed to foster. See A.B.A. Standards Relating to Pleas of Guilty § 2.2 (1968). See also the narrower provisions of New Jersey Evidence Rule 52(2) and the unlimited exclusion provided in California Evidence Code § 1153.

Report of House Committee on the Judiciary

House Comm. on Judiciary, Fed. Rules of Evidence, H.R.Rep. No. 650, 93d Cong., 1st Sess., p. 8 (1973); 1974 U.S.Code Cong. & Ad. News 7075, 7082

The Committee added the phrase "Except as otherwise provided by Act of Congress" to Rule 410 as submitted by the Court in order to preserve particular congressional policy judgments as to the effect of a plea of guilty or of nolo contendere. See 15 U.S.C. 16(a). The Committee intends that its amendment refers to both present statutes and statutes subsequently enacted.

Report of Senate Committee on the Judiciary

Senate Comm. on Judiciary, Fed. Rules of Evidence, S. Rep. No. 1277, 93d Cong., 2d Sess., p. 10 (1974); 1974 U.S.Code Cong. & Ad. News 7051, 7057

As adopted by the House, rule 410 would make inadmissible pleas of guilty or nolo contendere subsequently withdrawn as well as offers to make such pleas. Such a rule is clearly justified as a means of encouraging pleading. However, the House rule would then go on to render inadmissible for any purpose statements made in connection with these pleas or offers as well.

1. The rule as enacted, it should be noted, allows use of the statements for impeachment or in a subsequent prosecution for perjury or false statement.

The committee finds this aspect of the House rule unjustified. Of course, in certain circumstances such statements should be excluded. If, for example, a plea is vitiated because of coercion, statements made in connection with the plea may also have been coerced and should be inadmissible on that basis. In other cases, however, voluntary statements of an accused made in court on the record, in connection with a plea, and determined by a court to be reliable should be admissible even though the plea is subsequently withdrawn. This is particularly true in those cases where, if the House rule were in effect, a defendant would be able to contradict his previous statements and thereby lie with impunity.[2] To prevent such an injustice, the rule has been modified to permit the use of such statements for the limited purposes of impeachment and in subsequent perjury or false statement prosecutions.

Conference Report

H.R., Fed. Rules of Evidence, Conf. Rep. No. 1597, 93d
Cong., 2d Sess., p. 6 (1974); 1974 U.S.Code
Cong. & Ad. News 7098, 7100

The House bill provides that evidence of a guilty or nolo contendere plea, of an offer of either plea, or of statements made in connection with such pleas or offers of such pleas, is inadmissible in any civil or criminal action, case or proceeding against the person making such plea or offer. The Senate amendment makes the rule inapplicable to a voluntary and reliable statement made in court on the record where the statement is offered in a subsequent prosecution of the declarant for perjury or false statement.

The issues raised by Rule 410 are also raised by proposed Rule 11(e)(6) of the Federal Rules of Criminal Procedure presently pending before Congress. This proposed rule, which deals with the admissibility of pleas of guilty or nolo contendere, offers to make such pleas, and statements made in connection with such pleas, was promulgated by the Supreme Court on April 22, 1974, and in the absence of congressional action will become effective on August 1, 1975. The conferees intend to make no change in the presently-existing case law until that date, leaving the courts free to develop rules in this area on a case-by-case basis.

The Conferees further determined that the issues presented by the use of guilty and nolo contendere pleas, offers of such pleas, and statements made in connection with such pleas or offers, can be explored in greater detail during Congressional consideration of Rule 11(e)(6) of the Federal Rules of Criminal Procedure. The Conferees believe, therefore, that it is best to defer its effective date until August 1, 1975. The Conferees intend that Rule 410 would be superseded by any subsequent Federal Rule of Criminal Procedure or Act of Congress with which it is inconsistent, if the Federal Rule of Criminal Procedure or Act of Congress takes effect or becomes law after the date of the enactment of the act establishing the rules of evidence.

The conference adopts the Senate amendment with an amendment that expresses the above intentions.

Rule 410 as amended in 1975

Editorial Note

In 1975 the Congress amended Rule 11(e)(6) of the Federal Rules of Criminal Procedure, P.L. 94–64, July 31, 1975, 89 Stat. 371, and then amended Evidence Rule 410 to conform to it. Amended Rule 410 read:

2. See Harris v. New York, 401 U.S. 222 (1971).

Except as otherwise provided in this rule, evidence of a plea of guilty, later withdrawn, or a plea of nolo contendere, or of an offer to plead guilty or nolo contendere to the crime charged or any other crime, or of statements made in connection with, and relevant to, any of the foregoing pleas or offers, is not admissible in any civil or criminal proceeding against the person who made the plea or offer. However, evidence of a statement made in connection with, and relevant to, a plea of guilty, later withdrawn, a plea of nolo contendere, or an offer to plead guilty or nolo contendere to the crime charged or any other crime, is admissible in a criminal proceeding for perjury or false statement if the statement was made by the defendant under oath, on the record, and in the presence of counsel. P.L. 94–149, Dec. 12, 1975, 89 Stat. 805.

Report of House Committee on the Judiciary

House Comm. on Judiciary, Fed. Rules of Criminal Procedure, H.R. Rep. No. 247, 94th Cong., 1st Sess. (1975); 1975 U.S.Code Cong. & Ad.News 674, 679

The Committee added an exception to subdivision (e)(6). That subdivision provides:[1]

Evidence of a plea of guilty, later withdrawn, or a plea of nolo contendere, or of an offer to plead guilty or nolo contendere to the crime charged or any other crime, or of statements made in connection with any of the foregoing pleas or offers, is not admissible in any civil or criminal proceeding against the person who made the plea or offer.

The Committee's exception permits the use of such evidence in a perjury or false statement prosecution where the plea, offer, or related statement was made by the defendant on the record, under oath and in the presence of counsel. The Committee recognizes that even this limited exception may discourage defendants from being completely candid and open during plea negotiations and may even result in discouraging the reaching of plea agreements. However, the Committee believes that, on balance, it is more important to protect the integrity of the judicial process from willful deceit and untruthfulness. [The Committee does not intend its language to be construed as mandating or encouraging the swearing-in of the defendant during proceedings in connection with the disclosure and acceptance or rejection of a plea agreement.] The Committee recast the language of Rule 11(c), which deals with the advice given to a defendant before the court can accept his plea of guilty or nolo contendere. The Committee acted in part because it believed that the warnings given to the defendant ought to include those that Boykin v. Alabama, 395 U.S. 238 (1969), said were constitutionally required. In addition, and as a result of its change in subdivision (e)(6), the Committee thought it only fair that the defendant be warned that his plea of guilty (later withdrawn) or nolo contendere, or his offer of either plea, or his statements made in connection with such pleas or offers, could later be used against him in a perjury trial if made under oath, on the record, and in the presence of counsel.

Conference Report

H.R., Fed. Rules of Criminal Procedure, Conf. Rep. No. 414, 94th Cong., 1st Sess., (1975); 1976 U.S.Code Cong. & Ad.News 713, 714

1. As prescribed by the Supreme Court and transmitted to the Congress.

Rule 11(e)(6) deals with the use of statements made in connection with plea agreements. The House version permits a limited use of pleas of guilty, later withdrawn, or nolo contendere, offers of such pleas, and statements made in connection with such pleas or offers. Such evidence can be used in a perjury or false statement prosecution if the plea, offer, or related statement was made under oath, on the record, and in the presence of counsel. The Senate version permits evidence of voluntary and reliable statements made in court on the record to be used for the purpose of impeaching the credibility of the declarant or in a perjury or false statement prosecution.

The Conference adopts the House version with changes. The Conference agrees that neither a plea nor the offer of a plea ought to be admissible for any purpose. The Conference-adopted provision, therefore, like the Senate provision, permits only the use of statements made in connection with a plea of guilty, later withdrawn, or a plea of nolo contendere, or in connection with an offer of a guilty or nolo contendere plea.

Rule 410 as revised in 1980

Editorial Note

The Supreme Court adopted and on April 30, 1979, transmitted to the Congress a revision of Rule 11(e)(6) of the Federal Rules of Criminal Procedure, which was to operate also as a revision of Evidence Rule 410. The Congress suspended the effective date of the revision to December 1, 1980, absent congressional action otherwise. P.L. 96–42, July 31, 1979, 93 Stat. 326. Congress having taken no action, the rule as revised became effective on December 1, 1980, and is the present Rule 410, printed at the beginning of these comments.

Advisory Committee's Note

77 F.R.D. 507, 533

The major objective of the amendment to rule 11(e)(6) transmitted by the Supreme Court on April 30, 1979 is to describe more precisely, consistent with the original purpose of the provision, what evidence relating to pleas or plea discussions is inadmissible. The present language is susceptible to interpretation which would make it applicable to a wide variety of statements made under various circumstances other than within the context of those plea discussions authorized by rule 11(e) and intended to be protected by subdivision (e)(6) of the rule. See United States v. Herman, 544 F.2d 791 (5th Cir.1977), discussed herein.

Fed.R.Ev. 410, as originally adopted by Pub.L. 93–595, provided in part that "evidence of a plea of guilty, later withdrawn, or a plea of nolo contendere, or of an offer to plead guilty or nolo contendere to the crime charged or any other crime, or of statements made in connection with any of the foregoing pleas or offers, is not admissible in any civil or criminal action, case, or proceeding against the person who made the plea or offer." (This rule was adopted with the proviso that it "shall be superseded by any amendment to the Federal Rules of Criminal Procedure which is inconsistent with this rule.") As the Advisory Committee Note explained: "Exclusion of offers to plead guilty or nolo has as its purpose the promotion of disposition of criminal cases by compromise." The amendment of Fed.R.Crim.P. 11, transmitted to Congress by the Supreme Court in April 1974, contained a subdivision (e)(6) essentially identical to the rule 410 language quoted above, as a part of a substantial revision of rule 11. The most significant feature of this revision was the express recognition given to the fact that the "attorney for the government and the attorney for the defendant or the defendant when acting pro se may engage in discussions with a view toward reaching" a plea agreement. Subdivision (e)(6) was intended to encourage such discussions. As noted in H.R.Rep. No. 94–247, 94th Cong., 1st Sess. 7 (1975), the purpose of subdivision (e)(6) is to not "discourage defendants from being completely candid and open during plea negotiations." Similarly, H.R.Rep. No. 94–414, 94th Cong., 1st Sess. 10 (1975), states that "Rule 11(e)(6) deals with the use of statements made in connection with plea agreements." (Rule 11(e)(6) was thereafter enacted, with the addition of the proviso allowing use of statements in a prosecution for perjury, and with the qualification that the inadmissible statements must also be "relevant to" the inadmissible pleas or offers. Pub.L. 94–64; Fed.R.Ev. 410 was then amended to conform. Pub.L. 94–149.)

While this history shows that the purpose of Fed.R.Ev. 410 and Fed. R.Crim.P. 11(e)(6) is to permit the unrestrained candor which produces effective plea discussions between the "attorney for the government and the attorney for the defendant or the defendant when acting pro se," given visibility and sanction in rule 11(e), a literal reading of the language of these two rules could reasonably lead to the conclusion that a broader rule of inadmissibility obtains. That is, because "statements" are generally inadmissible if "made in connection with, and relevant to" an "offer to plead guilty," it might be thought that an otherwise voluntary admission to law enforcement officials is rendered inadmissible merely because it was made in the hope of obtaining leniency by a plea. Some decisions interpreting rule 11(e)(6) point in this direction. See United States v. Herman, 544 F.2d 791 (5th Cir.1977) (defendant in custody of two postal inspectors during continuance of removal hearing instigated conversation with them and at some point said he would plead guilty to armed robbery if the murder charge was dropped; one inspector stated they were not "in position" to make any deals in this regard; held, defendant's statement inadmissible under rule 11(e)(6) because the defendant "made the statements during the course of a conversation in which he sought concessions from the government in return for a guilty plea"); United States v. Brooks, 536 F.2d 1137 (6th Cir.1976) (defendant telephoned postal inspector and offered to plead guilty if he got 2-year maximum; statement inadmissible).

The amendment makes inadmissible statements made "in the course of any proceedings under this rule regarding" either a plea of guilty later withdrawn or a plea of nolo contendere, and also statements "made in the course of plea discussions with an attorney for the government which do not result in a plea of guilty or which result in a plea of guilty later withdrawn." It is not limited to statements by the defendant himself, and thus would cover statements by defense counsel regarding defendant's incriminating admissions to him. It thus fully protects the plea discussion process authorized by rule 11 without attempting to deal with confrontations between suspects and law enforcement agents, which involve problems of quite different dimensions. See, e.g., ALI Model Code of Pre-Arraignment Procedure, art. 140 and § 150.2(8) (Proposed Official Draft, 1975) (latter section requires exclusion if "a law enforcement officer induces any person to make a statement by promising leniency"). This change, it must be emphasized, does not compel the conclusion that statements made to law enforcement agents, especially when the agents purport to have authority to bargain, are inevitably admissible. Rather, the point is that such cases are not covered by the per se rule of 11(e)(6) and thus must be resolved by that body of law dealing with police interrogations.

If there has been a plea of guilty later withdrawn or a plea of nolo contendere, subdivision (e)(6)(C) makes inadmissible statements made "in the course of any proceedings under this rule" regarding such pleas. This includes, for example, admissions by the defendant when he makes his plea in court pursuant to rule 11 and also admissions made to provide the factual basis pursuant to subdivision (f). However, subdivision (e)(6)(C) is not limited to statements made in court. If the court were to defer its decision on a plea agreement pending examination of the presentence report, as authorized by subdivision (e)(2), statements made to the probation officer in connection with the preparation of that report would come within this provision.

This amendment is fully consistent with all recent and major law reform efforts on this subject. ALI Model Code of Pre-Arraignment Procedure § 350.7 (Proposed Official Draft, 1975), and ABA Standards Relating to Pleas of Guilty § 3.4 (Approved Draft, 1968) both provide:

> Unless the defendant subsequently enters a plea of guilty or nolo contendere which is not withdrawn, the fact that the defendant or his counsel and the prosecuting attorney engaged in plea discussions or made a plea agreement should not be received in evidence against or in favor of the defendant in any criminal or civil action or administrative proceedings.

The Commentary to the latter states:

> The above standard is limited to discussions and agreements with the prosecuting attorney. Sometimes defendants will indicate to the police their willingness to bargain, and in such instances these statements are sometimes admitted in court against the defendant. State v. Christian, 245 S.W.2d 895 (Mo.1952). If the police initiate this kind of discussion, this may have some bearing on the admissibility of the defendant's statement. However, the policy considerations relevant to this issue are better dealt with in the context of standards governing in-custody interrogation by the police.

Similarly, Unif.R.Crim.P. 441(d) (Approved Draft, 1974), provides that except under limited circumstances "no discussion between the parties or statement by the defendant or his lawyer under this Rule," i.e., the rule providing "the parties may meet to discuss the possibility of pretrial diversion ... or of a plea agreement," are admissible. The amendment is likewise consistent with the typical state provision on this subject; see, e.g., Ill.S.Ct. Rule 402(f).

The language of the amendment identifies with more precision than the present language the necessary relationship between the statements and the plea or discussion. See the dispute between the majority and concurring opinions in United States v. Herman, 544 F.2d 791 (5th Cir.1977), concerning the meanings and effect of the phrases "connection to" and "relevant to" in the present rule. Moreover, by relating the statements to "plea discussions" rather than "an offer to plead," the amendment ensures "that even an attempt to open plea bargaining [is] covered under the same rule of inadmissibility." United States v. Brooks, 536 F.2d 1137 (6th Cir.1976).

The last sentence of Rule 11(e)(6) is amended to provide a second exception to the general rule of nonadmissibility of the described statements. Under the amendment, such a statement is also admissible "in any proceeding wherein another statement made in the course of the same plea or plea discussions has been introduced and the statement ought in fairness be considered contemporaneously with it." This change is necessary so that, when evidence of statements made in the course of or as a consequence of a certain plea or plea discussions are introduced under circumstances not prohibited by this rule (e.g., not "against" the person who made the plea), other statements relating to the same plea or plea discussions may also be admitted when relevant to the matter at issue. For example, if a defendant upon a motion to dismiss a prosecution on some ground were able to admit certain statements made in aborted plea discussions in his favor, then other relevant statements made in the same plea discussions should be admissible against the defendant in the interest of determining the truth of the matter at issue. The language of the amendment follows closely that in Fed.R.Evid. 106, as the considerations involved are very similar.

The phrase "in any civil or criminal proceeding" has been moved from its present position, following the word "against" for purposes of clarity. An ambiguity presently exists because the word "against" may be read as referring either to the kind of proceeding in which the evidence is offered or the purpose for which it is offered. The change makes it clear that the latter construction is correct. No change is intended with respect to provisions making evidence rules inapplicable in certain situations. See, e.g., Fed.R.Evid. 104(a) and 1101(d).

Unlike ABA Standards Relating to Pleas of Guilty § 3.4 (Approved Draft, 1968), and ALI Model Code of Pre-Arraignment Procedure § 350.7 (Proposed Official Draft, 1975), rule 11(e)(6) does not also provide that the described evidence is inadmissible "in favor of" the defendant. This is not intended to suggest, however, that such evidence will inevitably be admissible in the defendant's favor. Specifically, no disapproval is intended of such decisions as United States v. Verdoorn, 528 F.2d 103 (8th Cir.1976), holding that the trial judge properly refused to permit the defendants to put into evidence at their trial the fact the prosecution had attempted to plea bargain with them, as "meaningful dialogue between the parties would, as a practical matter, be impossible if either party had to assume the risk that plea offers would be admissible in evidence."

Rule 411. Liability Insurance

Evidence that a person was or was not insured against liability is not admissible upon the issue whether the person acted negligently or otherwise wrongfully. This rule does not require the exclusion of evidence of insurance against liability when offered for another purpose, such as proof of agency, ownership, or control, or bias or prejudice of a witness.

(As amended Mar. 2, 1987, eff. Oct. 1, 1987.)

Section references, McCormick 5th ed.

§ 201

Note by Federal Judicial Center

The rule enacted by the Congress is the rule prescribed by the Supreme Court without change.

Advisory Committee's Note

56 F.R.D. 183, 230

The courts have with substantial unanimity rejected evidence of liability insurance for the purpose of proving fault, and absence of liability insurance as proof of lack of fault. At best the inference of fault from the fact of insurance coverage is a tenuous one, as is its converse. More important, no doubt, has been the feeling that knowledge of the presence or absence of liability insurance would induce juries to decide cases on improper grounds. McCormick § 168; Annot., 4 A.L.R.2d 761. The rule is drafted in broad terms so as to include contributory negligence or other fault of a plaintiff as well as fault of a defendant.

The second sentence points out the limits of the rule, using well established illustrations. Id.

For similar rules see Uniform Rule 54; California Evidence Code § 1155; Kansas Code of Civil Procedure § 60–454; New Jersey Evidence Rule 54.

1987 Amendment

The amendment is technical. No substantive change is intended.

Rule 412. Sex Offense Cases; Relevance of Alleged Victim's Past Sexual Behavior or Alleged Sexual Predisposition

(a) Evidence generally inadmissible. The following evidence is not admissible in any civil or criminal proceeding involving alleged sexual misconduct except as provided in subdivisions (b) and (c):

(1) Evidence offered to prove that any alleged victim engaged in other sexual behavior.

(2) Evidence offered to prove any alleged victim's sexual predisposition.

(b) Exceptions.

(1) In a criminal case, the following evidence is admissible, if otherwise admissible under these rules:

(A) evidence of specific instances of sexual behavior by the alleged victim offered to prove that a person other than the accused was the source of semen, injury or other physical evidence;

(B) evidence of specific instances of sexual behavior by the alleged victim with respect to the person accused of the sexual misconduct offered by the accused to prove consent or by the prosecution; and

(C) evidence the exclusion of which would violate the constitutional rights of the defendant.

(2) In a civil case, evidence offered to prove the sexual behavior or sexual predisposition of any alleged victim is admissible if it is otherwise admissible under these rules and its probative value substantially outweighs the danger of harm to any victim and of unfair prejudice to any party. Evidence of an alleged victim's reputation is admissible only if it has been placed in controversy by the alleged victim.

(c) Procedure to determine admissibility.

(1) A party intending to offer evidence under subdivision (b) must:

(A) file a written motion at least 14 days before trial specifically describing the evidence and stating the purpose for which it is offered unless the court, for good cause requires a different time for filing or permits filing during trial; and

(B) serve the motion on all parties and notify the alleged victim or, when appropriate, the alleged victim's guardian or representative.

(2) Before admitting evidence under this rule the court must conduct a hearing in camera and afford the victim and parties a right to attend and be heard. The motion, related papers, and the record of the hearing must be sealed and remain under seal unless the court orders otherwise.

(Added Pub.L. 95–540, § 2(a), Oct. 28, 1978, 92 Stat. 2046, and amended Nov. 18, 1988, Pub.L. 100–690, Title VII, § 7046(a), 102 Stat. 4400; Apr. 29, 1994, eff. Dec. 1, 1994; Sept. 13, 1994, Pub.L. 103–322, Title IV, § 40141(b), 108 Stat. 1919.)

Section references, McCormick 5th ed.

§ 43, § 44, § 193.

Notes of Advisory Committee

1994 Amendment

Rule 412 has been revised to diminish some of the confusion engendered by the original rule and to expand the protection afforded alleged victims of sexual misconduct. Rule 412 applies to both civil and criminal proceedings. The rule aims to safeguard the alleged victim against the invasion of privacy, potential embarrassment and sexual stereotyping that is associated with public disclosure of intimate sexual details and the infusion of sexual innuendo into the factfinding process. By affording victims protection in most instances, the rule also encourages victims of sexual misconduct to institute and to participate in legal proceedings against alleged offenders.

Rule 412 seeks to achieve these objectives by barring evidence relating to the alleged victim's sexual behavior or alleged sexual predisposition, whether offered as substantive evidence or for impeachment, except in designated circumstances in which the probative value of the evidence significantly outweighs possible harm to the victim.

The revised rule applies in all cases involving sexual misconduct without regard to whether the alleged victim or person accused is a party to the litigation. Rule 412 extends to "pattern" witnesses in both criminal and civil cases whose testimony about other instances of sexual misconduct by the person accused is otherwise admissible. When the case does not involve alleged sexual misconduct, evidence relating to a third-party witness' alleged sexual activities is not within the ambit of Rule 412. The witness will, however, be protected by other rules such as Rules 404 and 608, as well as Rule 403.

The terminology "alleged victim" is used because there will frequently be a factual dispute as to whether sexual misconduct occurred. It does not connote any requirement that the misconduct be alleged in the pleadings. Rule 412 does not, however, apply unless the person against whom the evidence is offered can reasonably be characterized as a "victim of alleged sexual misconduct." When this is not the case, as for instance in a defamation action involving statements concerning sexual misconduct in which the evidence is offered to show that the alleged defamatory statements were true or did not damage the plaintiff's reputation, neither Rule 404 nor this rule will operate to bar the evidence; Rule [sic] 401 and 403 will continue to control. Rule 412 will, however, apply in a Title VII action in which the plaintiff has alleged sexual harassment.

The reference to a person "accused" is also used in a non-technical sense. There is no requirement that there be a criminal charge pending against the person or even that the misconduct would constitute a criminal offense. Evidence offered to prove allegedly false prior claims by the victim is not barred by Rule 412. However, this evidence is subject to the requirements of Rule 404.

Subdivision (a). As amended, Rule 412 bars evidence offered to prove the victim's sexual behavior and alleged sexual predisposition. Evidence, which might otherwise be admissible under Rules 402, 404(b), 405, 607, 608, 609, or some other evidence rule, must be excluded if Rule 412 so requires. The word "other" is used to suggest some flexibility in admitting evidence "intrinsic" to the alleged sexual misconduct. *Cf.* Committee Note to 1991 amendment to Rule 404(b).

Past sexual behavior connotes all activities that involve actual physical conduct, i.e. sexual intercourse and sexual contact, or that imply sexual intercourse or sexual contact. *See, e.g., United States v. Galloway,* 937 F.2d 542 (10th Cir.1991), *cert. denied,* 113 S.Ct. 418 (1992) (use of contraceptives inadmissible since use implies sexual activity); *United States v. One Feather,* 702 F.2d 736 (8th Cir.1983) (birth of an illegitimate child inadmissible); *State v. Carmichael,* 727 P.2d 918, 925 (Kan.1986) (evidence of venereal disease inadmissible). In addition, the word "behavior" should be construed to include activities of the mind, such as fantasies or dreams. *See* 23 C. Wright & K. Graham, Jr., *Federal Practice and Procedure,* § 5384 at p. 548 (1980) ("While there may be some doubt under statutes that require 'conduct,' it would seem that the language of Rule 412 is broad enough to encompass the behavior of the mind.").

The rule has been amended to also exclude all other evidence relating to an alleged victim of sexual misconduct that is offered to prove a sexual predisposition. This amendment is designed to exclude evidence that does not directly refer to sexual activities or thoughts but that the proponent believes may have a sexual connotation for the factfinder. Admission of such evidence would contravene Rule 412's objectives of shielding the alleged victim from potential embarrassment and safeguarding the victim against stereotypical thinking. Consequently, unless the (b)(2) exception is satisfied, evidence such as that relating to the alleged victim's mode of dress, speech, or life-style will not be admissible.

The introductory phrase in subdivision (a) was deleted because it lacked clarity and contained no explicit reference to the other provisions of law that were intended to be overridden. The conditional clause, "except as provided in subdivisions (b) and (c)" is intended to make clear that evidence of the types described in subdivision (a) is admissible only under the strictures of those sections.

The reason for extending the rule to all criminal cases is obvious. The strong social policy of protecting a victim's privacy and encouraging victims to come forward to report criminal acts is not confined to cases that involve a charge of sexual assault. The need to protect the victim is equally great when a defendant is charged with kidnapping, and evidence is offered, either to prove motive or as background, that the defendant sexually assaulted the victim.

The reason for extending Rule 412 to civil cases is equally obvious. The need to protect alleged victims against invasions of privacy, potential embarrassment, and unwarranted sexual stereotyping, and the wish to encourage victims to come forward when they have been sexually molested do not disappear because the context has shifted from a criminal prosecution to a claim for damages or injunctive relief. There is a strong social policy in not only punishing those who engage in sexual misconduct, but in also providing relief to the victim. Thus, Rule 412 applies in any civil case in which a person claims to be the victim of sexual misconduct, such as actions for sexual battery or sexual harassment.

Subdivision (b). Subdivision (b) spells out the specific circumstances in which some evidence may be admissible that would otherwise be barred by the general rule expressed in subdivision (a). As amended, Rule 412 will be virtually unchanged in criminal cases, but will provide protection to any person alleged to be a victim of sexual misconduct regardless of the charge actually brought against an accused. A new exception has been added for civil cases.

In a criminal case, evidence may be admitted under subdivision (b)(1) pursuant to three possible exceptions, provided the evidence also satisfies other requirements for admissibility specified in the Federal Rules of Evidence, including Rule 403. Subdivisions (b)(1)(A) and (b)(1)(B) require proof in the form of specific instances of sexual behavior in recognition of the limited probative value and dubious reliability of evidence of reputation or evidence in the form of an opinion.

Under subdivision (b)(1)(A), evidence of specific instances of sexual behavior with persons other than the person whose sexual misconduct is alleged may be admissible if it is offered to prove that another person was the source of semen, injury or other physical evidence. Where the prosecution has directly or indirectly asserted that the physical evidence originated with the accused, the defendant must be afforded an opportunity to prove that another person was responsible. *See United States v. Begay,* 937 F.2d 515, 523 n. 10 (10th Cir.1991). Evidence offered for the specific purpose identified in this subdivision may still be excluded if it does not satisfy Rules [sic] 401 or 403. *See, e.g., United States v. Azure,* 845 F.2d 1503, 1505–06 (8th Cir.1988) (10 year old victim's injuries indicated recent use of force; court excluded evidence of consensual sexual activities with witness who testified at in camera hearing that he had never hurt victim and failed to establish recent activities).

Under the exception in subdivision (b)(1)(B), evidence of specific instances of sexual behavior with respect to the person whose sexual misconduct is alleged is admissible if offered to prove consent, or offered by the prosecution. Admissible pursuant to this exception might be evidence of prior instances of sexual activities between the alleged victim and the accused, as well as statements in which the alleged victim expressed an intent to engage in sexual intercourse with the accused, or voiced sexual fantasies involving the specific accused. In a prosecution for child sexual abuse, for example, evidence of uncharged sexual activity between the accused and the alleged victim offered by the prosecution may be admissible pursuant to Rule 404(b) to show a pattern of behavior. Evidence relating to the victim's alleged sexual predisposition is not admissible pursuant to this exception.

Under subdivision (b)(1)(C), evidence of specific instances of conduct may not be excluded if the result would be to deny a criminal defendant the protections afforded by the Constitution. For example, statements in which the victim has expressed an intent to have sex with the first person encountered on a particular occasion might not be excluded without violating the due process right of a rape defendant seeking to prove consent. Recognition of this basic principle was expressed in subdivision (b)(1) of the original rule. The United States Supreme Court has recognized that in various circumstances a defendant may have a right to introduce evidence otherwise precluded by an evidence rule under the Confrontation Clause. *See, e.g., Olden v. Kentucky,* 488 U.S. 227 (1988) (defendant in rape cases had right to inquire into alleged victim's cohabitation with another man to show bias).

Subdivision (b)(2) governs the admissibility of otherwise proscribed evidence in civil cases. It employs a balancing test rather than the specific exceptions stated in subdivision (b)(1) in recognition of the difficulty of foreseeing future developments in the law. Greater flexibility is needed to accommodate evolving causes of action such as claims for sexual harassment.

The balancing test requires the proponent of the evidence, whether plaintiff or defendant, to convince the court that the probative value of the proffered evidence "substantially outweighs the danger of harm to any victim and of unfair prejudice of any party." This test for admitting evidence offered to prove sexual behavior or sexual propensity in civil cases differs in three respects from the general rule governing admissibility set forth in Rule 403. First, it reverses the usual procedure spelled out in Rule 403 by shifting the burden to the proponent to demonstrate admissibility rather than making the opponent justify exclusion of the evidence. Second, the standard expressed in subdivision (b)(2) is more stringent than in the original rule; it raises the threshold for admission by requiring that the probative value of the evidence *substantially* outweigh the specified dangers. Finally, the Rule 412 test puts "harm to the victim" on the scale in addition to prejudice to the parties.

Evidence of reputation may be received in a civil case only if the alleged victim has put his or her reputation into controversy. The victim may do so without making a specific allegation in a pleading. *Cf.* Fed.R.Civ.P. 35(a).

Subdivision (c). Amended subdivision (c) is more concise and understandable than the subdivision it replaces. The requirement of a motion before trial is continued in the amended rule, as is the provision that a late motion may be permitted for good cause shown. In deciding whether to permit late filing, the court may take into account the conditions previously included in the rule: namely whether the evidence is newly discovered and could not have been obtained earlier through the existence of due diligence, and whether the issue to which such evidence relates has newly arisen in the case. The rule recognizes that in some instances the circumstances that justify an application to introduce evidence otherwise barred by Rule 412 will not become apparent until trial.

The amended rule provides that before admitting evidence that falls within the prohibition of Rule 412(a), the court must hold a hearing in camera at which the alleged victim and any party must be afforded the right to be present and an opportunity to be heard. All papers connected with the motion and any record of a hearing on the motion must be kept and remain under seal during the course of trial and appellate proceedings unless otherwise ordered. This is to assure that the privacy of the alleged victim is preserved in all cases in which the court rules that proffered evidence is not admissible, and in which the hearing refers to matters that are not received, or are received in another form.

The procedures set forth in subdivision (c) do not apply to discovery of a victim's past sexual conduct or predisposition in civil cases, which will be continued to be governed by Fed.R.Civ.P. 26. In order not to undermine the rationale of Rule 412, however, courts should enter appropriate orders pursuant to Fed.R.Civ.P. 26(c) to protect the victim against unwarranted inquiries and to ensure confidentiality. Courts should presumptively issue protective orders barring discovery unless the party seeking discovery makes a showing that the evidence sought to be discovered would be relevant under the facts and theories of the particular case, and cannot be obtained except through discovery. In an action for sexual harassment, for instance, while some evidence of the alleged victim's sexual behavior and/or predisposition in the workplace may perhaps be relevant, non-work place conduct will usually be irrelevant. *Cf. Burns v. McGregor Electronic Industries, Inc.*, 989 F.2d 959, 962–63 (8th Cir.1993) (posing for a nude magazine outside work hours is irrelevant to issue of unwelcomeness of sexual advances at work). Confidentiality orders should be presumptively granted as well.

One substantive change made in subdivision (c) is the elimination of the following sentence: "Notwithstanding subdivision (b) of Rule 104, if the relevancy of the evidence which the accused seeks to offer in the trial depends upon the fulfillment of a condition of fact, the court, at the hearing in chambers or at a subsequent hearing in chambers scheduled for such purpose, shall accept evidence on the issue of whether such condition of fact is fulfilled and shall determine such issue." On its face, this language would appear to authorize a trial judge to exclude evidence of past sexual conduct between an alleged victim and an accused or a defendant in a civil case based upon the judge's belief that such past acts did not occur. Such an authorization raises questions of invasion of the right to a jury trial under the Sixth and Seventh Amendments. *See* 1 S. Saltzburg & M. Martin, *Federal Rules of Evidence Manual,* 396–97 (5th ed. 1990).

The Advisory Committee concluded that the amended rule provided adequate protection for all persons claiming to be the victims of sexual misconduct, and that it was inadvisable to continue to include a provision in the rule that has been confusing and that raises substantial constitutional issues.

[Advisory Committee Note adopted by Congressional Conference Report accompanying Pub.L. 103–322. See H.R.Conf.Rep. No. 103–711, 103rd Cong., 2nd Sess., 383 (1994).]

1978 Congressional Discussion

The following discussion in the House of Representatives on October 10, 1978, preceded passage of H.R. 4727, which enacted Rule 412. The discussion appears in 124 Cong. Record, at page H. 11944.

Mr. MANN. Mr. Speaker, I yield myself such time as I may consume.

Mr. Speaker, for many years in this country, evidentiary rules have permitted the introduction of evidence about a rape victim's prior sexual conduct. Defense lawyers were permitted great latitude in bringing out intimate details about a rape victim's life. Such evidence quite often serves no real purpose and only results in embarrassment to the rape victim and unwarranted public intrusion into her private life.

The evidentiary rules that permit such inquiry have in recent years come under question; and the States have taken the lead to change and modernize their evidentiary rules about evidence of a rape victim's prior sexual behavior. The bill before us similarly seeks to modernize the Federal evidentiary rules.

The present Federal Rules of Evidence reflect the traditional approach. If a defendant in a rape case raises the defense of consent, that defendant may then offer evidence about the victim's prior sexual behavior. Such evidence may be in the form of opinion evidence, evidence of reputation, or evidence of specific instances of behavior. Rule 404(a)(2) of the Federal Rules of Evidence permits the introduction of evidence of a "pertinent character trait." The advisory committee note to that rule cites, as an example of what the rule covers, the character of a rape victim when the issue is consent. Rule 405 of the Federal Rules of Evidence permits the use of opinion or reputation evidence or the use of evidence of specific behavior to show a character trait.

Thus, Federal evidentiary rules permit a wide ranging inquiry into the private conduct of a rape victim, even though that conduct may have at best a tenuous connection to the offense for which the defendant is being tried.

H.R. 4727 amends the Federal Rules of Evidence to add a new rule, applicable only in criminal cases, to spell out when, and under what conditions, evidence of a rape victim's prior sexual behavior can be admitted. The new rule provides that reputation or opinion evidence about a rape victim's prior sexual behavior is not admissible. The new rule also provides that a court cannot admit evidence of specific instances of a rape victim's prior sexual conduct except in three circumstances.

The first circumstance is where the Constitution requires that the evidence be admitted. This exception is intended to cover those infrequent instances where, because of an unusual chain of circumstances, the general rule of inadmissibility, if followed, would result in denying the defendant a constitutional right.

The second circumstance in which the defendant can offer evidence of specific instances of a rape victim's prior sexual behavior is where the defendant raises the issue of consent and the evidence is of sexual behavior with the defendant. To admit such evidence, however, the court must find that the evidence is relevant and that its probative value outweighs the danger of unfair prejudice.

The third circumstance in which a court can admit evidence of specific instances of a rape victim's prior sexual behavior is where the evidence is of behavior with someone other than the defendant and is offered by the defendant on the issue of whether or not he was the source of semen or injury. Again, such evidence will be admitted only if the court finds that the evidence is relevant and that its probative value outweighs the danger of unfair prejudice.

The new rule further provides that before evidence is admitted under any of these exceptions, there must be an in camera hearing—that is, a proceeding that takes place in the judge's chambers out of the presence of the jury and the general public. At this hearing, the defendant will present the evidence he intends to offer and be able to argue why it should be admitted. The prosecution, of course, will be able to argue against that evidence being admitted.

The purpose of the in camera hearing is twofold. It gives the defendant an opportunity to demonstrate to the court why certain evidence is admissible and ought to be presented to the jury. At the same time, it protects the privacy of the rape victim in those instances when the court finds that evidence is inadmissible. Of course, if the court finds the evidence to be admissible, the evidence will be presented to the jury in open court.

The effect of this legislation, therefore, is to preclude the routine use of evidence of specific instances of a rape victim's prior sexual behavior. Such evidence will be admitted only in clearly and narrowly defined circumstances and only after an in camera hearing. In determining the admissibility of such evidence, the court will consider all of the facts and circumstances surrounding the evidence, such as the amount of time that lapsed between the alleged prior act and the rape charged in the prosecution. The greater the lapse of time, of course, the less likely it is that such evidence will be admitted.

Mr. Speaker, the principal purpose of this legislation is to protect rape victims from the degrading and embarrassing disclosure of intimate details about their private lives. It does so by narrowly circumscribing when such evidence may be admitted. It does not do so, however, by sacrificing any constitutional right possessed by the defendant. The bill before us fairly balances the interests involved—the rape victim's interest in protecting her private life from unwarranted public exposure; the defendant's interest in being able adequately to present a defense by offering relevant and probative evidence; and society's interest in a fair trial, one where unduly prejudicial evidence is not permitted to becloud the issues before the jury.

I urge support of the bill.

Mr. WIGGINS. Mr. Speaker, I yield myself such time as I may consume.

(Mr. WIGGINS asked and was given permission to revise and extend his remarks.)

Mr. WIGGINS. Mr. Speaker, this legislation addresses itself to a subject that is certainly a proper one for our consideration. Many of us have been troubled for years about the indiscriminate and prejudicial use of testimony with respect to a victim's prior sexual behavior in rape and similar cases. This bill deals with that problem. It is not, in my opinion, Mr. Speaker, a perfect bill in the manner in which it deals with the problem, but my objections are not so fundamental as would lead me to oppose the bill.

I think, Mr. Speaker, that it is unwise to adopt a per se rule absolutely excluding evidence of reputation and opinion with respect to the victim—and this bill does that—but it is difficult for me to foresee the specific case in which such evidence might be admissible. The trouble is this, Mr. Speaker: None of us can foresee perfectly all of the various circumstances under which the propriety of evidence might be before the court. If this bill has a defect, in my view it is because it adopts a per se rule with respect to opinion and reputation evidence.

Alternatively we might have permitted that evidence to be considered in camera as we do other evidence under the bill.

I should note, however, in fairness, having expressed minor reservations, that the bill before the House at this time does improve significantly upon the bill which was presented to our committee.

I will not detail all of those improvements but simply observe that the bill upon which we shall soon vote is a superior product to that which was initially considered by our subcommittee.

Mr. Speaker, I ask my colleagues to vote for this legislation as being, on balance, worthy of their support, and urge its adoption.

I reserve the balance of my time.

Mr. MANN. Mr. Speaker, this legislation has more than 100 cosponsors, but its principal sponsor, as well as its architect is the gentlewoman from New York (Ms. Holtzman). As the drafter of the legislation she will be able to provide additional information about the probable scope and effect of the legislation.

I yield such time as she may consume to the gentlewoman from New York (Ms. Holtzman).

(Ms. HOLTZMAN asked and was given permission to revise and extend her remarks.)

Ms. HOLTZMAN. Mr. Speaker, I would like to begin first by complimenting the distinguished gentleman from South Carolina (Mr. Mann), the chairman of the subcommittee, for his understanding of the need for corrective legislation in this area and for the fairness with which he has conducted the subcommittee hearings. I would like also to compliment the other members of the subcommittee, including the gentleman from California (Mr. Wiggins).

Too often in this country victims of rape are humiliated and harassed when they report and prosecute the rape. Bullied and cross-examined about their prior sexual experiences, many find the trial almost as degrading as the rape itself. Since rape trials become inquisitions into the victim's morality, not trials of the defendant's innocence or guilt, it is not surprising that it is the least reported crime. It is estimated that as few as one in ten rapes is ever reported.

Mr. Speaker, over 30 States have taken some action to limit the vulnerability of rape victims to such humiliating cross-examination of their past sexual experiences and intimate personal histories. In federal courts, however, it is permissible still to subject rape victims to brutal cross-examination about their past sexual histories. H.R. 4727 would rectify this problem in Federal courts and I hope, also serve as a model to suggest to the remaining states that reform of existing rape laws is important to the equity of our criminal justice system.

H.R. 4727 applies only to criminal rape cases in Federal courts. The bill provides that neither the prosecution nor the defense can introduce any reputation or opinion evidence about the victim's past sexual conduct. It does permit, however, the introduction of specific evidence about the victim's past sexual conduct in three very limited circumstances.

First, this evidence can be introduced if it deals with the victim's past sexual relations with the defendant and is relevant to the issue of whether she consented. Second, when the defendant claims he had no relations with the victim, he can use evidence of the victim's past sexual relations with others if the evidence rebuts the victim's claim that the rape caused certain physical consequences, such as semen or injury. Finally, the evidence can be introduced if it is constitutionally required. This last exception, added in subcommittee, will insure that the defendant's constitutional rights are protected.

Before any such evidence can be introduced, however, the court must determine at a hearing in chambers that the evidence falls within one of the exceptions.

Furthermore, unless constitutionally required, the evidence of specific instances of prior sexual conduct cannot be introduced at all if it would be more prejudicial and inflammatory than probative.

Mr. Speaker, I urge adoption of this bill. It will protect women from both injustice and indignity.

Mr. MANN. Mr. Speaker, I have no further requests for time, and I yield back the balance of my time.

Mr. WIGGINS. Mr. Speaker, I have no further requests for time, and yield back the balance of my time.

The SPEAKER pro tempore. The question is on the motion offered by the gentleman from South Carolina (Mr. Mann) that the House suspend the rules and pass the bill H.R. 4727, as amended.

The question was taken; and (two-thirds having voted in favor thereof) the rules were suspended and the bill, as amended, was passed.

A motion to reconsider was laid on the table.

Rule 413. Evidence of Similar Crimes in Sexual Assault Cases

(a) In a criminal case in which the defendant is accused of an offense of sexual assault, evidence of the defendant's commission of another offense or offenses of sexual assault is admissible, and may be considered for its bearing on any matter to which it is relevant.

(b) In a case in which the Government intends to offer evidence under this rule, the attorney for the Government shall disclose the evidence to the defendant, including statements of witnesses or a summary of the substance of any testimony that is expected to be offered, at least fifteen days before the scheduled date of trial or at such later time as the court may allow for good cause.

(c) This rule shall not be construed to limit the admission or consideration of evidence under any other rule.

(d) For purposes of this rule and Rule 415, "offense of sexual assault" means a crime under Federal law or the law of a State (as defined in section 513 of title 18, United States Code) that involved—

(1) any conduct proscribed by chapter 109A of title 18, United States Code;

(2) contact, without consent, between any part of the defendant's body or an object and the genitals or anus of another person;

(3) contact, without consent, between the genitals or anus of the defendant and any part of another person's body;

(4) deriving sexual pleasure or gratification from the infliction of death, bodily injury, or physical pain on another person; or

(5) an attempt or conspiracy to engage in conduct described in paragraphs (1)–(4).

(Added Sept. 13, 1994, Pub.L. 103–322, Title XXXII, § 320935(a), 108 Stat. 2135, effective July 9, 1995.)

Rule 414. Evidence of Similar Crimes in Child Molestation Cases

(a) In a criminal case in which the defendant is accused of an offense of child molestation, evidence of the defendant's commission of another offense or offenses of child molestation is admissible, and may be considered for its bearing on any matter to which it is relevant.

(b) In a case in which the Government intends to offer evidence under this rule, the attorney for the Government shall disclose the evidence to the defendant, including statements of witnesses or a summary of the substance of any testimony that is expected to be offered, at least fifteen days before the scheduled date of trial or at such later time as the court may allow for good cause.

(c) This rule shall not be construed to limit the admission or consideration of evidence under any other rule.

(d) For purposes of this rule and Rule 415, "child" means a person below the age of fourteen, and "offense of child molestation" means a crime under Federal law or the law of a State (as defined in section 513 of title 18, United States Code) that involved—

(1) any conduct proscribed by chapter 109A of title 18, United States Code, that was committed in relation to a child;

(2) any conduct proscribed by chapter 110 of title 18, United States Code;

(3) contact between any part of the defendant's body or an object and the genitals or anus of a child;

(4) contact between the genitals or anus of the defendant and any part of the body of a child;

(5) deriving sexual pleasure or gratification from the infliction of death, bodily injury, or physical pain on a child; or

(6) an attempt or conspiracy to engage in conduct described in paragraphs (1)–(5).

(Added Sept. 13, 1994, Pub.L. 103–322, Title XXXII, § 320935(a), 108 Stat. 2135, effective July 9, 1995.)

Rule 415. Evidence of Similar Acts in Civil Cases Concerning Sexual Assault or Child Molestation

(a) In a civil case in which a claim for damages or other relief is predicated on a party's alleged commission of conduct constituting an offense of sexual assault or child molestation, evidence of that party's commission of another offense or offenses of sexual assault or child molestation is admissible and may be considered as provided in Rule 413 and Rule 414 of these rules.

(b) A party who intends to offer evidence under this Rule shall disclose the evidence to the party against whom it will be offered, including statements of witnesses or a summary of the substance of any testimony that is expected to be offered, at least fifteen days before the scheduled date of trial or at such later time as the court may allow for good cause.

(c) This rule shall not be construed to limit the admission or consideration of evidence under any other rule.

(Added Sept. 13, 1994, Pub.L. 103–322, Title XXXII, § 320935(a), 108 Stat. 2135, effective July 9, 1995.)

ARTICLE V. PRIVILEGES

Rule 501. General Rule

Except as otherwise required by the Constitution of the United States or provided by Act of Congress or in rules prescribed by the Supreme Court pursuant to statutory authority, the privilege of a witness, person, government, State, or political subdivision thereof shall be governed by the principles of the common law as they may be interpreted by the courts of the United States in the light of reason and experience. However, in civil actions and proceedings, with respect to an element of a claim or defense as to which State law supplies the rule of decision, the privilege of a witness, person, government, State, or political subdivision thereof shall be determined in accordance with State law.

Section references, McCormick 5th ed.

§ 9, § 53, § 66, § 75, § 76, § 78

Note by Federal Judicial Center

The rules enacted by the Congress substituted the single Rule 501 in place of the 13 rules dealing with privilege prescribed by the Supreme Court as Article V.... The reasons given in support of the congressional action are stated in the Report of the House Committee on the Judiciary, the Report of the Senate Committee on the Judiciary, and Conference Report, set forth below.

Report of House Committee on the Judiciary

House Comm. of Judiciary, Fed. Rules of Evidence, H.R.Rep. No. 650, 93d Cong., 1st Sess., p. 8 (1973); 1974 U.S.Code Cong. & Ad.News 7075, 7082

Article V as submitted to Congress contained thirteen Rules. Nine of those Rules defined specific non-constitutional privileges which the federal courts must recognize (i.e. required reports, lawyer-client, psychotherapist-patient, husband-wife, communications to clergymen, political vote, trade secrets, secrets of state and other official information, and identity of informer). Another Rule provided that only those privileges set forth in Article V or in some other Act of Congress could be recognized by the federal courts. The three remaining Rules addressed collateral problems as to waiver of privilege by voluntary disclosure, privileged matter disclosed under compulsion or without opportunity to claim privilege, comment upon or inference from a claim of privilege, and jury instruction with regard thereto.

The Committee amended Article V to eliminate all of the Court's specific Rules on privileges. Instead, the Committee, through a single Rule, 501, left the law of privileges in its present state and further provided that privileges shall continue to be developed by the courts of the United States under a uniform standard applicable both in civil and criminal cases. That standard, derived from Rule 26 of the Federal Rules of Criminal Procedure, mandates the application of the principles of the common law as interpreted by the courts of the United States in the light of reason and experience. The words "person, government, State, or political subdivision thereof" were added by the Committee to the lone term "witnesses" used in Rule 26 to make clear that, as under present law, not only witnesses may have privileges. The Committee also included in its amendment a proviso modeled after Rule 302 and similar to language added by the Committee to Rule 601 relating to the competency of witnesses. The proviso is designed to require the application of State privilege law in civil actions and proceedings governed by Erie R. Co. v. Tompkins, 304 U.S. 64 (1938), a result in accord with current federal court decisions. See Republic Gear Co. v. Borg-Warner Corp., 381 F.2d 551, 555–556 n. 2 (2nd Cir.1967). The Committee deemed the proviso to be necessary in the light of the Advisory Committee's view (see its note to Court Rule 501) that this result is not mandated under *Erie.*

The rationale underlying the proviso is that federal law should not supersede that of the States in substantive areas such as privilege absent a compelling reason. The Committee believes that in civil cases in the federal courts where an element of a claim or defense is not grounded upon a federal question, there is no federal interest strong enough to justify departure from State policy. In addition, the Committee considered that the Court's proposed Article V would have promoted forum shopping in some civil actions, depending upon differences in the privilege law applied as among the State and federal courts. The Committee's proviso, on the other hand, under which the federal courts are bound to apply the State's privilege law in actions founded upon a State-created right or defense, removes the incentive to "shop".

Report of Senate Committee on the Judiciary

Senate Comm. on Judiciary, Fed. Rules of Evidence, S.Rep. No. 1277, 93d Cong., 2d Sess., p. 11 (1974); 1974 U.S.Code Cong. & Ad.News 7051, 7058

Article V as submitted to Congress contained 13 rules. Nine of those rules defined specific nonconstitutional privileges which the Federal courts must recognize (i.e., required reports, lawyer-client, psychotherapist-patient, husband-wife, communications to clergymen, political vote, trade secrets, secrets of state and other official information, and identity of informer). Many of these rules contained controversial modifications or restrictions upon common law privileges. As noted supra, the House amended article V to eliminate all of the Court's specific rules on privileges. Through a single rule, 501, the House provided that privileges shall be governed by the principles of the common law as interpreted by the courts of the United States in the light of reason and experience (a standard derived from rule 26 of the Federal Rules of Criminal Procedure) except in the case of an element of a civil claim or defense as to which State law supplies the rule of decision in which event state privilege law was to govern.

The committee agrees with the main thrust of the House amendment: that a federally developed common law based on modern reason and experience shall apply except where the State nature of the issues renders deference to State privilege law the wiser course, as in the usual diversity case. The committee understands that thrust of the House amendment to require that State privilege law be applied in "diversity" cases (actions on questions of State law between citizens of different States arising under 28 U.S.C. § 1332). The language of the House amendment, however, goes beyond this in some respects, and falls short of it in others: State privilege law applies even in nondiversity, Federal question civil cases, where an issue governed by State substantive law is the object of the evidence (such issues do sometimes arise in such cases); and, in all instances where State privilege law is to be applied, e.g., on proof of a State issue in a diversity case, a close reading reveals that State privilege law is not to be applied unless the matter to be proved is an element of that state claim or defense, as distinguished from a step along the way in the proof of it.

The committee is concerned that the language used in the House amendment could be difficult to apply. It provides that "in civil actions . . . with respect to an element of a claim or defense as to which State law supplies the rule of decision," State law on privilege applies. The question of what is an element of a claim or defense is likely to engender considerable litigation. If the matter in question constitutes an element of a claim, State law supplies the privilege rule; whereas if it is a mere item of proof with respect to a claim, then, even though State law might supply the rule of decision, Federal law on the privilege would apply. Further, disputes will arise as to how the rule should be applied in an antitrust action or in a tax case where the Federal statute is silent as to a particular aspect of the substantive law in question, but Federal cases had incorporated State law by reference to State law.[1] Is a claim (or defense) based on such a reference a claim or defense as to which federal or State law supplies the rule of decision?

Another problem not entirely avoidable is the complexity or difficulty the rule introduces into the trial of a Federal case containing a combination of Federal and State claims and defenses, e.g. an action involving Federal antitrust and State unfair competition claims. Two different bodies of privilege law would need to be consulted. It may even develop that the same witness-testimony might be relevant on both counts and privileged as to one but not the other.[2]

The formulation adopted by the House is pregnant with litigious mischief. The committee has, therefore, adopted what we believe will be a clearer and more practical guideline for determining when courts should respect State rules of privilege. Basically, it provides that in criminal and Federal question civil cases, federally evolved rules on privilege should apply since it is Federal policy which is being enforced.[3] Conversely, in diversity cases where the litigation in question turns on a substantive question of State law, and is brought in the Federal courts because the parties reside in different States, the committee believes it is clear that State rules of privilege should apply unless the proof is directed at a claim or defense for which Federal law supplies the rule of decision (a situation which would not commonly arise.)[4] It is intended that the State rules of privilege should apply equally in original diversity actions and diversity actions removed under 28 U.S.C. § 1441(b).

Two other comments on the privilege rule should be made. The committee has received a considerable volume of correspondence from psychiatric organizations and psychiatrists concerning the deletion of rule 504 of the rule submitted by the Supreme Court. It should be clearly understood that, in approving this general rule as to privileges, the action of Congress should not be understood as disapproving any recognition of a psychiatrist-patient, or husband-wife, or any other of the enumerated privileges contained in the Supreme Court rules.

1. For a discussion of reference to State substantive law, see note on Federal Incorporation by Reference of State Law, Hart & Wechsler, The Federal Courts and the Federal System, pp. 491–94 (2d ed. 1973).

2. The problems with the House formulation are discussed in Rothstein, The Proposed Amendments to the Federal Rules of Evidence, 62 Georgetown University Law Journal 125 (1973) at notes 25, 26 and 70–74 and accompanying text.

3. It is also intended that the Federal law of privileges should be applied with respect to pendant State law claims when they arise in a Federal question case.

4. While such a situation might require use of two bodies of privilege law, federal and state, in the same case, nevertheless the occasions on which this would be required are considerably reduced as compared with the House version, and confined to situations where the Federal and State interests are such as to justify application of neither privilege law to the case as a whole. If the rule proposed here results in two conflicting bodies of privilege law applying to the same piece of evidence in the same case, it is contemplated that the rule favoring reception of the evidence should be applied. This policy is based on the present rule 43(a) of the Federal Rules of Civil Procedure which provides: In any case, the statute or rule which favors the reception of the evidence governs and the evidence shall be presented according to the most convenient method prescribed in any of the statutes or rules to which reference is herein made.

Rather, our action should be understood as reflecting the view that the recognition of a privilege based on a confidential relationship and other privileges should be determined on a case-by-case basis.

Further, we would understand that the prohibition against spouses testifying against each other is considered a rule of privilege and covered by this rule and not by rule 601 of the competency of witnesses.

Conference Report

H.R., Fed. Rules of Evidence, Conf.Rep. No. 1597, 93d Cong., 2d Sess., p. 7 (1974); 1974 U.S.Code Cong. & Ad.News 7098, 7100

Rule 501 deals with the privilege of a witness not to testify. Both the House and Senate bills provide that federal privilege law applies in criminal cases. In civil actions and proceedings, the House bill provides that state privilege law applies "to an element of a claim or defense as to which State law supplies the rule of decision." The Senate bill provides that "in civil actions and proceedings arising under 28 U.S.C. § 1332 or 28 U.S.C. § 1335, or between citizens of different States and removed under 28 U.S.C. § 1441(b) the privilege of a witness, person, government, State or political subdivision thereof is determined in accordance with State law, unless with respect to the particular claim or defense, Federal law supplies the rule of decision."

The wording of the House and Senate bills differs in the treatment of civil actions and proceedings. The rule in the House bill applies to evidence that relates to "an element of a claim or defense." If an item of proof tends to support or defeat a claim or defense, or an element of a claim or defense, and if state law supplies the rule of decision for that claim or defense, then state privilege law applies to that item of proof.

Under the provision in the House bill, therefore, state privilege law will usually apply in diversity cases. There may be diversity cases, however, where a claim or defense is based upon federal law. In such instances, federal privilege law will apply to evidence relevant to the federal claim or defense. See Sola Electric Co. v. Jefferson Electric Co., 317 U.S. 173 (1942).

In nondiversity jurisdiction civil cases, federal privilege law will generally apply. In those situations where a federal court adopts or incorporates state law to fill interstices or gaps in federal statutory phrases, the court generally will apply federal privilege law. As Justice Jackson has said:

> A federal court sitting in a non-diversity case such as this does not sit as a local tribunal. In some cases it may see fit for special reasons to give the law of a particular state highly persuasive or even controlling effect, but in the last analysis its decision turns upon the law of the United States, not that of any state.

D'Oench, Duhme & Co. v. Federal Deposit Insurance Corp., 315 U.S. 447, 471 (1942) (Jackson, J., concurring). When a federal court chooses to absorb state law, it is applying the state law as a matter of federal common law. Thus, state law does not supply the rule of decision (even though the federal court may apply a rule derived from state decisions), and state privilege law would not apply. See C.A. Wright, Federal Courts 251–252 (2d ed. 1970); Holmberg v. Armbrecht, 327 U.S. 392 (1946); DeSylva v. Ballentine, 351 U.S. 570, 581 (1956); 9 Wright & Miller, Federal Rules and Procedure § 2408.

In civil actions and proceedings, where the rule of decision as to a claim or defense or as to an element of a claim or defense is supplied by state law, the House provision requires that state privilege law apply.

The Conference adopts the House provision.

ARTICLE VI. WITNESSES

Rule 601. General Rule of Competency

Every person is competent to be a witness except as otherwise provided in these rules. However, in civil actions and proceedings, with respect to an element of a claim or defense as to which State law supplies the rule of decision, the competency of a witness shall be determined in accordance with State law.

Section references, McCormick 5th ed.

§ 9, § 44, § 53, § 62, § 63, § 65, § 66, § 68, § 70, § 71, § 253

Note by Federal Judicial Center

The first sentence of the rule enacted by the Congress is the entire rule prescribed by the Supreme Court, without change. The second sentence was added by congressional action.

Advisory Committee's Note

56 F.R.D. 183, 262

This general ground-clearing eliminates all grounds of incompetency not specifically recognized in the succeeding rules of this Article. Included among the grounds thus abolished are religious belief, conviction of crime, and connection with the litigation as a party or interested person or spouse of a party or interested person. With the exception of the so-called Dead Man's Acts, American jurisdictions generally have ceased to recognize these grounds.

The Dead Man's Acts are surviving traces of the common law disqualification of parties and interested persons. They exist in variety too great to convey conviction of their wisdom and effectiveness. These rules contain no provision of this kind. . . .

No mental or moral qualifications for testifying as a witness are specified. Standards of mental capacity have proved elusive in actual application. A leading commentator observes that few witnesses are disqualified on that ground. Weihofen, Testimonial Competence and Credibility, 34 Geo. Wash.L.Rev. 53 (1965). Discretion is regularly exercised in favor of allowing the testimony. A witness wholly without capacity is difficult to imagine. The question is one particularly suited to the jury as one of weight and credibility, subject to judicial authority to review the sufficiency of the evidence. 2 Wigmore §§ 501, 509. Standards of moral qualification in practice consist essentially of evaluating a person's truthfulness in terms of his own answers about it. Their principal utility is in affording an opportunity on voir dire examination to impress upon the witness his moral duty. This result may, however, be accomplished more directly, and without haggling in terms of legal standards, by the manner of administering the oath or affirmation under Rule 603.

Admissibility of religious belief as a ground of impeachment is treated in Rule 610. Conviction of crime as a ground of impeachment is the subject of Rule 609. Marital relationship is the basis for privilege under Rule 505. Interest in the outcome of litigation and mental capacity are, of course, highly relevant to credibility and require no special treatment to render them admissible along with other matters bearing upon the perception, memory, and narration of witnesses.

Report of House Committee on the Judiciary

House Comm. on Judiciary, Fed. Rules of Evidence, H.R.Rep. No. 650, 93d Cong., 1st Sess., p. 9 (1973); 1974 U.S.Code Cong. & Ad.News 7075, 7083

Rule 601 as submitted to the Congress provided that "Every person is competent to be a witness except as otherwise provided in these rules." One effect of the Rule as proposed would have been to abolish age, mental capacity, and other grounds recognized in some State jurisdictions as making a person incompetent as a witness. The greatest controversy centered around the Rule's rendering inapplicable in the federal courts the so-called Dead Man's Statutes which exist in some States. Acknowledging that there is substantial disagreement as to the merit of Dead Man's Statutes, the Committee nevertheless believed that where such statutes have been enacted they represent State policy which should not be overturned in the absence of a compelling federal interest. The Committee therefore amended the Rule to make competency in civil actions determinable in accordance with State law with respect to elements of claims or defenses as to which State law supplies the rule of decision. Cf. Courtland v. Walston & Co., Inc., 340 F.Supp. 1076, 1087–1092 (S.D.N.Y.1972).

Report of Senate Committee on the Judiciary

Senate Comm. on Judiciary, Fed. Rules of Evidence, S.Rep. No. 1277, 2d Sess., p. 3 (1974); 1974 U.S.Code Cong. & Ad.News 7051, 7059

The amendment to rule 601 parallels the treatment accorded rule 501 discussed immediately above.

Conference Report

H.R., Fed. Rules of Evidence, Conf.Rep. No. 1597, 93d Cong., 2d Sess., p 8 (1974); 1975 U.S.Code Cong. & Ad.News 7098, 7101

Rule 601 deals with competency of witnesses. Both the House and Senate bills provide that federal competency law applies in criminal cases. In civil actions and proceedings, the House bill provides that state competency law applies "to an element of a claim or defense as to which State law supplies the rule of decision." The Senate bill provides that "in civil actions and proceedings arising under 28 U.S.C. § 1332 or 28 U.S.C. § 1335, or between citizens of different States and removed under 28 U.S.C. § 1441(b) the competency of a witness, person, government, State or political subdivision thereof is determined in accordance with State law, unless with respect to the particular claim or defense, Federal law supplies the rule of decision."

The wording of the House and Senate bills differs in the treatment of civil actions and proceedings. The rule in the House bill applies to evidence that relates to "an element of a claim or defense." If an item of proof tends to support or defeat a claim or defense, or an element of a claim or defense, and if state law supplies the rule of decision for that claim or defense, then state competency law applies to that item of proof.

For reasons similar to those underlying its action on Rule 501, the Conference adopts the House provision.

Rule 602. Lack of Personal Knowledge

A witness may not testify to a matter unless evidence is introduced sufficient to support a finding that the witness has personal knowledge of the matter. Evidence to prove personal knowledge may, but need not, consist of the witness' own testimony. This rule is subject to the provisions of rule 703, relating to opinion testimony by expert witnesses.

(As amended Mar. 2, 1987, eff. Oct. 1, 1987; Apr. 25, 1988, eff. Nov. 1, 1988.)

Section references, McCormick 5th ed.

§ 10, § 11, § 43, § 44, § 71

Note by Federal Judicial Center

The rule enacted by the Congress is the rule prescribed by the Supreme Court without change.

Advisory Committee's Note

56 F.R.D. 183, 263

"... [T]he rule requiring that a witness who testifies to a fact which can be perceived by the senses must have had an opportunity to observe, and must have actually observed the fact" is a "most pervasive manifestation" of the common law insistence upon "the most reliable sources of information." McCormick § 10, p. 19. These foundation requirements may, of course, be furnished by the testimony of the witness himself; hence personal knowledge is not an absolute but may consist of what the witness thinks he knows from personal perception. 2 Wigmore § 650. It will be observed that the rule is in fact a specialized application of the provisions of Rule 104(b) on conditional relevancy.

This rule does not govern the situation of a witness who testifies to a hearsay statement as such, if he has personal knowledge of the making of the statement. Rules 801 and 805 would be applicable. This rule would, however, prevent him from testifying to the subject matter of the hearsay statement, as he has no personal knowledge of it.

The reference to Rule 703 is designed to avoid any question of conflict between the present rule and the provisions of that rule allowing an expert to express opinions based on facts of which he does not have personal knowledge.

1987 Amendment

The amendments are technical. No substantive change is intended.

1988 Amendment

The amendment is technical. No substantive change is intended.

Rule 603. Oath or Affirmation

Before testifying, every witness shall be required to declare that the witness will testify truthfully, by oath or affirmation administered in a form calculated to awaken the witness' conscience and impress the witness' mind with the duty to do so.

(As amended Mar. 2, 1987, eff. Oct. 1, 1987.)

Section references, McCormick 5th ed.

§ 44, § 46, § 63, § 71, § 245

Note by Federal Judicial Center

The rule enacted by the Congress is the rule prescribed by the Supreme Court without change.

Advisory Committee's Note

56 F.R.D. 183, 263

The rule is designed to afford the flexibility required in dealing with religious adults, atheists, conscientious objectors, mental defectives, and children. Affirmation is simply a solemn undertaking to tell the truth; no special verbal formula is required. As is true generally, affirmation is recognized by federal law. "Oath" includes affirmation, 1 U.S.C. § 1; judges and clerks may administer oaths and affirmations, 28 U.S.C §§ 459, 953; and affirmations are acceptable in lieu of oaths under Rule 43(d) of the Federal Rules of Civil Procedure. Perjury by a witness is a crime, 18 U.S.C. § 1621.

1987 Amendment

The amendments are technical. No substantive change is intended.

Rule 604. Interpreters

An interpreter is subject to the provisions of these rules relating to qualification as an expert and the administration of an oath or affirmation to make a true translation.

(As amended Mar. 2, 1987, eff. Oct. 1, 1987.)

Section references, McCormick 5th ed.

None

Note by Federal Judicial Center

The rule enacted by the Congress is the rule prescribed by the Supreme Court without change.

Advisory Committee's Note

56 F.R.D. 183, 264

The rule implements Rule 43(f) of the Federal Rules of Civil Procedure and Rule 28(b) of the Federal Rules of Criminal Procedure, both of which contain provisions for the appointment and compensation of interpreters.

1987 Amendment

The amendment is technical. No substantive change is intended.

Rule 605. Competency of Judge as Witness

The judge presiding at the trial may not testify in that trial as a witness. No objection need be made in order to preserve the point.

Section references, McCormick 5th ed.

§ 62, § 68, § 70, § 71

Note by Federal Judicial Center

The rule enacted by the Congress is the rule prescribed by the Supreme Court without change.

Advisory Committee's Note

56 F.R.D. 183, 264

In view of the mandate of 28 U.S.C. § 455 that a judge disqualify himself in "any case in which he . . . is or has been a material witness," the likelihood that the presiding judge in a federal court might be called to testify in the trial over which he is presiding is slight. Nevertheless the possibility is not totally eliminated.

The solution here presented is a broad rule of incompetency, rather than such alternatives as incompetency only as to material matters, leaving the matter to the discretion of the judge, or recognizing no incompetency. The choice is the result of inability to evolve satisfactory answers to questions which arise when the judge abandons the bench for the witness stand. Who rules on objections? Who compels him to answer? Can he rule impartially on the weight and admissibility of his own testimony? Can he be impeached or cross-examined effectively? Can he, in a jury trial, avoid conferring his seal of approval on one side in the eyes of the jury? Can he, in a bench trial, avoid an involvement destructive of impartiality? The rule of general incompetency has substantial support. See Report of the Special Committee on the Propriety of Judges Appearing as Witnesses, 36 A.B.A.J. 630 (1950); cases collected in Annot. 157 A.L.R. 311; McCormick § 68, p. 147; Uniform Rule 42; California Evidence Code § 703; Kansas Code of Civil Procedure § 60–442; New Jersey Evidence Rule 42. Cf. 6 Wigmore § 1909, which advocates leaving the matter to the discretion of the judge, and statutes to that effect collected in Annot., 157 A.L.R. 311.

The rule provides an "automatic" objection. To require an actual objection would confront the opponent with a choice between not objecting, with the result of allowing the testimony, and objecting, with the probable result of excluding the testimony but at the price of continuing the trial before a judge likely to feel that his integrity had been attacked by the objector.

Rule 606. Competency of Juror as Witness

(a) At the trial. A member of the jury may not testify as a witness before that jury in the trial of the case in which the juror is sitting. If the juror is called so to testify, the opposing party shall be afforded an opportunity to object out of the presence of the jury.

(b) Inquiry into validity of verdict or indictment. Upon an inquiry into the validity of a verdict or indictment, a juror may not testify as to any matter or statement occurring during the course of the jury's deliberations or to the effect of anything upon that or any other juror's mind or emotions as influencing the juror to assent to or dissent from the verdict or indictment or concerning the juror's mental processes in connection therewith, except that a juror may testify on the question whether extraneous prejudicial information was improperly brought to the jury's attention or whether any outside influence was improperly brought to bear upon any juror. Nor may a juror's affidavit or evidence of any statement by the juror concerning a matter about which the juror would be precluded from testifying be received for these purposes.

(As amended P.L. 94–149, § 1(10), Dec. 12, 1975, 89 Stat. 805; Mar. 2, 1987, eff. Oct. 1, 1987.)

Section references, McCormick 5th ed.

Generally § 71

(a). § 62, § 68, § 70

(b). § 68

Note by Federal Judicial Center

The rule enacted by the Congress is the rule prescribed by the Supreme Court, amended only by the addition of the concluding phrase "for these purposes." The bill originally passed by the House did not contain in the first sentence the prohibition as to matters or statements during the deliberations or the clause beginning "except."

Advisory Committee's Note

56 F.R.D. 183, 265

Subdivision (a). The considerations which bear upon the permissibility of testimony by a juror in the trial in which he is sitting as juror bear an obvious similarity to those evoked when the judge is called as a witness. See Advisory Committee's Note to Rule 605. The judge is not, however in this instance so involved as to call for departure from usual principles requiring objection to be made; hence the only provision on objection is that opportunity be afforded for its making out of the presence of the jury. Compare Rule 605.

Subdivision (b). Whether testimony, affidavits, or statements of jurors should be received for the purpose of invalidating or supporting a verdict or indictment, and if so, under what circumstances, has given rise to substantial differences of opinion. The familiar rubric that a juror may not impeach his own verdict, dating from Lord Mansfield's time, is a gross oversimplification. The values sought to be promoted by excluding the evidence include freedom of deliberation, stability and finality of verdicts, and protection of jurors against annoyance and embarrassment. McDonald v. Pless, 238 U.S. 264, 35 S.Ct. 785, 59 L.Ed. 1300 (1915). On the other hand, simply putting verdicts beyond effective reach can only promote irregularity and injustice. The rule offers an accommodation between these competing considerations.

The mental operations and emotional reactions of jurors in arriving at a given result would, if allowed as a subject of inquiry, place every verdict at the mercy of jurors and invite tampering and harassment. See Grenz v. Werre, 129 N.W.2d 681 (N.D.1964). The authorities are in virtually complete accord in excluding the evidence. Fryer, Note on Disqualification of Witnesses, Selected Writings on Evidence and Trial 345, 347 (Fryer ed. 1957); Maguire, Weinstein, et al., Cases on Evidence 887 (5th ed. 1965); 8 Wigmore § 2349 (McNaughton Rev.1961). As to matters other than mental operations and emotional reactions of jurors, substantial authority refuses to allow a juror to disclose irregularities which occur in the jury room, but allows his testimony as to irregularities occurring outside and allows outsiders to testify as to occurrences both inside and out. 8 Wigmore § 2354 (McNaughton Rev.1961). However, the door of the jury room is not necessarily a satisfactory dividing point, and the Supreme Court has refused to accept it for every situation. Mattox v. United States, 146 U.S. 140, 13 S.Ct. 50, 36 L.Ed. 917 (1892).

Under the federal decisions the central focus has been upon insulation of the manner in which the jury reached its verdict, and this protection extends to each of the components of deliberation, including arguments, statements, discussions, mental and emotional reactions, votes, and any other feature of the process. Thus testimony or affidavits of jurors have been held incompetent to show a compromise verdict, Hyde v. United States, 225 U.S. 347, 382 (1912); a quotient verdict, McDonald v. Pless, 238 U.S. 264 (1915); speculation as to insurance coverage, Holden v. Porter, 405 F.2d 878 (10th Cir. 1969), Farmers Coop. Elev. Ass'n v. Strand, 382 F.2d 224, 230 (8th Cir. 1967), cert. denied 389 U.S. 1014; misinterpretation of instructions, Farmers Coop. Elev. Ass'n v. Strand, supra; mistake in returning verdict, United States v. Chereton, 309 F.2d 197 (6th Cir. 1962); interpretation of guilty plea by one defendant as implicating others, United States v. Crosby, 294 F.2d 928, 949 (2d Cir. 1961). The policy does not, however, foreclose testimony by jurors as to prejudicial extraneous information or influences injected into or brought to bear upon the deliberative process. Thus a juror is recognized as competent to testify to statements by the bailiff or the introduction of a prejudicial newspaper account into the jury room, Mattox v. United States, 146 U.S. 140 (1892). See also Parker v. Gladden, 385 U.S. 363 (1966).

This rule does not purport to specify the substantive grounds for setting aside verdicts for irregularity; it deals only with the competency of jurors to testify concerning those grounds.

See also Rule 6(e) of the Federal Rules of Criminal Procedure and 18 U.S.C. § 3500, governing the secrecy of grand jury proceedings. The present rule does not relate to secrecy and disclosure but to the competency of certain witnesses and evidence.

Report of House Judiciary Committee

House Comm. on Judiciary, Fed. Rules of Evidence, H.R.Rep. No. 650, 93d Cong., 1st Sess., p. 9 (1973); 1974 U.S.Code Cong. & Ad.News 7075, 7083

As proposed by the Court, Rule 606(b) limited testimony by a juror in the course of an inquiry into the validity of a verdict or indictment. He could testify as to the influence of extraneous prejudicial information brought to the jury's attention (e.g. a radio newscast or a newspaper account) or an outside influence which improperly had been brought to bear upon a juror (e.g. a threat to the safety of a member of his family), but he could not testify as to other irregularities which occurred in the jury room. Under this formulation a quotient verdict could not be attacked through the testimony of a juror, nor could a juror testify to the drunken condition of a fellow juror which so disabled him that he could not participate in the jury's deliberations.

The 1969 and 1971 Advisory Committee drafts would have permitted a member of the jury to testify concerning these kinds of irregularities in the jury room. The Advisory Committee note in the 1971 draft stated that "... the door of the jury room is not a satisfactory dividing point, and the Supreme Court has refused to accept it." The Advisory Committee further commented that—

> The trend has been to draw the dividing line between testimony as to mental processes, on the one hand, and as to the existence of conditions or occurrences of events calculated improperly to influence the verdict, on the other hand, without regard to whether the happening is within or without the jury room.... The jurors are the persons who know what really happened. Allowing them to testify as to matters other than their own reactions involves no particular hazard to the values sought to be protected. The rule is based upon this conclusion. It makes no attempt to specify the substantive grounds for setting aside verdicts for irregularity.

Objective jury misconduct may be testified to in California, Florida, Iowa, Kansas, Nebraska, New Jersey, North Dakota, Ohio, Oregon, Tennessee, Texas, and Washington.

Persuaded that the better practice is that provided for in the earlier drafts, the Committee amended subdivision (b) to read in the text of those drafts.

Report of Senate Judiciary Committee

Senate Comm. on Judiciary, Fed. Rules of Evidence, S.Rep. No. 1277, 93d Cong., 2d Sess., p. 13 (1974); 1974 U.S.Code Cong. & Ad.News 7051, 7060

As adopted by the House, this rule would permit the impeachment of verdicts by inquiry into, not the mental processes of the jurors, but what happened in terms of conduct in the jury room. This extension of the ability to impeach a verdict is felt to be unwarranted and ill-advised.

The rule passed by the House embodies a suggestion by the Advisory Committee of the Judicial Conference that is considerably broader than the final version adopted by the Supreme Court, which embodied long-accepted Federal law. Although forbidding the impeachment of verdicts by inquiry into the jurors' mental processes, it deletes from the Supreme Court version the proscription against testimony "as to any matter or statement occurring during the course of the jury's deliberations." This deletion would have the effect of opening verdicts up to challenge on the basis of what happened during the jury's internal deliberations, for example, where a juror alleged that the jury refused to follow the trial judge's instructions or that some of the jurors did not take part in deliberations.

Permitting an individual to attack a jury verdict based upon the jury's internal deliberations has long been recognized as unwise by the Supreme Court. In McDonald v. Pless, the Court stated:

> . . .
>
> [L]et it once be established that verdicts solemnly made and publicly returned into court can be attacked and set aside on the testimony of those who took part in their publication and all verdicts could be, and many would be, followed by an inquiry in the hope of discovering something which might invalidate the finding. Jurors would be harassed and beset by the defeated party in an effort to secure from them evidence of facts which might establish misconduct sufficient to set aside a verdict. If evidence thus secured could be thus used, the result would be to make what was intended to be a private deliberation, the constant subject of public investigation—to

the destruction of all frankness and freedom of discussion and conference.[2]

. . .

As it stands then, the rule would permit the harassment of former jurors by losing parties as well as the possible exploitation of disgruntled or otherwise badly-motivated ex-jurors.

Public policy requires a finality to litigation. And common fairness requires that absolute privacy be preserved for jurors to engage in the full and free debate necessary to the attainment of just verdicts. Jurors will not be able to function effectively if their deliberations are to be scrutinized in post-trial litigation. In the interest of protecting the jury system and the citizens who make it work, rule 606 should not permit any inquiry into the internal deliberations of the jurors.

Conference Report

H.R., Fed.Rules of Evidence, Conf.Rep. No. 1597, 93d
Cong., 2d Sess., p. 8 (1974); 1974 U.S.Code
Cong. & Ad.News 7098, 7102

Rule 606(b) deals with juror testimony in an inquiry into the validity of a verdict or indictment. The House bill provides that a juror cannot testify about his mental processes or about the effect of anything upon his or another juror's mind as influencing him to assent to or dissent from a verdict or indictment. Thus, the House bill allows a juror to testify about objective matters occurring during the jury's deliberation, such as the misconduct of another juror or the reaching of a quotient verdict. The Senate bill does not permit juror testimony about any matter or statement occurring during the course of the jury's deliberations. The Senate bill does provide, however, that a juror may testify on the question whether extraneous prejudicial information was improperly brought to the jury's attention and on the question whether any outside influence was improperly brought to bear on any juror.

The Conference adopts the Senate amendment. The Conferees believe that jurors should be encouraged to be conscientious in promptly reporting to the court misconduct that occurs during jury deliberations.

1987 Amendment

The amendments are technical. No substantive change is intended.

Rule 607. Who May Impeach

The credibility of a witness may be attacked by any party, including the party calling the witness.

(As amended Mar. 2, 1987, eff. Oct. 1, 1987.)

Section references, McCormick 5th ed.

§ 23, § 38, § 39

Note by Federal Judicial Center

The rule enacted by the Congress is the rule prescribed by the Supreme Court without change.

2. 238 U.S. 264, at 267 (1914).

Advisory Committee's Note

56 F.R.D. 183, 266

The traditional rule against impeaching one's own witness is abandoned as based on false premises. A party does not hold out his witnesses as worthy of belief, since he rarely has a free choice in selecting them. Denial of the right leaves the party at the mercy of the witness and the adversary. If the impeachment is by a prior statement, it is free from hearsay dangers and is excluded from the category of hearsay under Rule 801(d)(1). Ladd, Impeachment of One's Own Witness—New Developments, 4 U.Chi.L.Rev. 69 (1936); McCormick § 38; 3 Wigmore §§ 896–918. The substantial inroads into the old rule made over the years by decisions, rules, and statutes are evidence of doubts as to its basic soundness and workability. Cases are collected in 3 Wigmore § 905. Revised Rule 32(a)(1) of the Federal Rules of Civil Procedure allows any party to impeach a witness by means of his deposition, and Rule 43(b) has allowed the calling and impeachment of an adverse party or person identified with him. Illustrative statutes allowing a party to impeach his own witness under varying circumstances are Ill.Rev.Stats.1967, c. 110, § 60; Mass.Laws Annot. 1959, c. 233 § 23; 20 N.M.Stats. Annot. 1953, § 20–2–4; N.Y. CPLR § 4514 (McKinney 1963); 12 Vt.Stats. Annot. 1959, §§ 1641a, 1642. Complete judicial rejection of the old rule is found in United States v. Freeman, 302 F.2d 347 (2d Cir.1962). The same result is reached in Uniform Rule 20; California Evidence Code § 785; Kansas Code of Civil Procedure § 60–420. See also New Jersey Evidence Rule 20.

1987 Amendment

The amendment is technical. No substantive change is intended.

Rule 608. Evidence of Character and Conduct of Witness

[*Effective until December 1, 2003*]

(a) Opinion and reputation evidence of character. The credibility of a witness may be attacked or supported by evidence in the form of opinion or reputation, but subject to these limitations: (1) the evidence may refer only to character for truthfulness or untruthfulness, and (2) evidence of truthful character is admissible only after the character of the witness for truthfulness has been attacked by opinion or reputation evidence or otherwise.

(b) Specific instances of conduct. Specific instances of the conduct of a witness, for the purpose of attacking or supporting the witness' credibility, other than conviction of crime as provided in rule 609, may not be proved by extrinsic evidence. They may, however, in the discretion of the court, if probative of truthfulness or untruthfulness, be inquired into on cross-examination of the witness (1) concerning the witness' character for truthfulness or untruthfulness, or (2) concerning the character for truthfulness or untruthfulness of another witness as to which character the witness being cross-examined has testified.

The giving of testimony, whether by an accused or by any other witness, does not operate as a waiver of the accused's or the witness' privilege against self-incrimination when examined with respect to matters which relate only to credibility.

[*Effective December 1, 2003*]

Rule 608. Evidence of Character and Conduct of Witness

(a) Opinion and reputation evidence of character. The credibility of a witness may be attacked or supported by evidence in the form of opinion or reputation, but subject to these limitations: (1) the evidence may refer only to character for truthfulness or untruthfulness, and (2) evidence of truthful character is admissible only after the character of the witness for truthfulness has been attacked by opinion or reputation evidence or otherwise.

(b) Specific instances of conduct. Specific instances of the conduct of a witness, for the purpose of attacking or supporting the witness' character for truthfulness, other than conviction of crime as provided in rule 609, may not be proved by extrinsic evidence. They may, however, in the discretion of the court, if probative of truthfulness or untruthfulness, be inquired into on cross-examination of the witness (1) concerning the witness' character for truthfulness or untruthfulness, or (2) concerning the character for truthfulness or untruthfulness of another witness as to which character the witness being cross-examined has testified.

The giving of testimony, whether by an accused or by any other witness, does not operate as a waiver of the accused's or the witness' privilege against self-incrimination when examined with respect to matters that relate only to character for truthfulness.

(As amended Mar. 2, 1987, eff. Oct. 1, 1987; Apr. 25, 1988, eff. Nov. 1, 1988; March 27, 2003, eff. Dec. 1, 2003.)

Section references, McCormick 5th ed.

Generally § 25

(a). § 43, § 44, § 47

(b). § 41, § 45, § 47

Note by Federal Judicial Center

The rule enacted by the Congress is the rule prescribed by the Supreme Court, changed only by amending the second sentence of subdivision (b). The sentence as prescribed by the Court read: "They may, however, if probative of truthfulness or untruthfulness and not remote in time, be inquired into on cross-examination of the witness himself or on cross-examination of a witness who testifies to his character for truthfulness or untruthfulness." The effect of the amendments was to delete the phrase "and not remote in time," to add the phrase "in the discretion of the court," and otherwise only to clarify the meaning of the sentence. The reasons for the amendments are stated in the Report of the

House Committee on the Judiciary, set forth below. See also Note to Rule 405(a) by Federal Judicial Center, supra.

Advisory Committee's Note

56 F.R.D. 183 268

Subdivision (a). In Rule 404(a) the general position is taken that character evidence is not admissible for the purpose of proving that the person acted in conformity therewith, subject, however, to several exceptions, one of which is character evidence of a witness as bearing upon his credibility. The present rule develops that exception.

In accordance with the bulk of judicial authority, the inquiry is strictly limited to character for veracity, rather than allowing evidence as to character generally. The result is to sharpen relevancy, to reduce surprise, waste of time, and confusion, and to make the lot of the witness somewhat less unattractive. McCormick § 44.

The use of opinion and reputation evidence as means of proving the character of witnesses is consistent with Rule 405(a). While the modern practice has purported to exclude opinion, witnesses who testify to reputation seem in fact often to be giving their opinions, disguised somewhat misleadingly as reputation. See McCormick § 44. And even under the modern practice, a common relaxation has allowed inquiry as to whether the witnesses would believe the principal witness under oath. United States v. Walker, 313 F.2d 236 (6th Cir.1963), and cases cited therein; McCormick § 44, pp. 94–95, n. 3.

Character evidence in support of credibility is admissible under the rule only after the witness' character has first been attacked, as has been the case at common law. Maguire, Weinstein, et al., Cases on Evidence 295 (5th ed. 1965); McCormick § 49, p. 105; 4 Wigmore § 1104. The enormous needless consumption of time which a contrary practice would entail justifies the limitation. Opinion or reputation that the witness is untruthful specifically qualifies as an attack under the rule, and evidence of misconduct, including conviction of crime, and of corruption also fall within this category. Evidence of bias or interest does not. McCormick § 49; 4 Wigmore §§ 1106, 1107. Whether evidence in the form of contradiction is an attack upon the character of the witness must depend upon the circumstances. McCormick § 49. Cf. 4 Wigmore §§ 1108, 1109.

As to the use of specific instances on direct by an opinion witness, see the Advisory Committee's Note to Rule 405, supra.

Subdivision (b). In conformity with Rule 405, which forecloses use of evidence of specific incidents as proof in chief of character unless character is an issue in the case, the present rule generally bars evidence of specific instances of conduct of a witness for the purpose of attacking or supporting his credibility. There are, however, two exceptions: (1) specific instances are provable when they have been the subject of criminal conviction, and (2) specific instances may be inquired into on cross-examination of the principal witness or of a witness giving an opinion of his character for truthfulness.

(1) Conviction of crime as a technique of impeachment is treated in detail in Rule 609, and here is merely recognized as an exception to the general rule excluding evidence of specific incidents for impeachment purposes.

(2) Particular instances of conduct, though not the subject of criminal conviction, may be inquired into on cross-examination of the principal witness himself or of a witness who testifies concerning his character for truthfulness. Effective cross-examination demands that some allowance be made for going into matters of this kind, but the possibilities of abuse are substantial. Consequently safeguards are erected in the form of specific requirements that the instances inquired into be probative of truthfulness or its opposite . . . . Also, the overriding protection of Rule 403 requires that probative value not be outweighed by danger of unfair prejudice, confusion of issues or misleading the jury, and that of Rule 611 bars harassment and undue embarrassment.

The final sentence constitutes a rejection of the doctrine of such cases as People v. Sorge, 301 N.Y. 198, 93 N.E.2d 637 (1950), that any past criminal act relevant to credibility may be inquired into on cross-examination, in apparent disregard of the privilege against self-incrimination. While it is clear that an ordinary witness cannot make a partial disclosure of incriminating matter and then invoke the privilege on cross-examination, no tenable contention can be made that merely by testifying he waives his right to foreclose inquiry on cross-examination into criminal activities for the purpose of attacking his credibility. So to hold would reduce the privilege to a nullity. While it is true that an accused, unlike an ordinary witness, has an option whether to testify, if the option can be exercised only at the price of opening up inquiry as to any and all criminal acts committed during his lifetime, the right to testify could scarcely be said to possess much vitality. In Griffin v. California, 380 U.S. 609, 85 S.Ct. 1229, 14 L.Ed.2d 106 (1965), the Court held that allowing comment on the election of an accused not to testify exacted a constitutionally impermissible price, and so here. While no specific provision in terms confers constitutional status on the right of an accused to take the stand in his own defense, the existence of the right is so completely recognized that a denial of it or substantial infringement upon it would surely be of due process dimensions. See Ferguson v. Georgia, 365 U.S. 570, 81 S.Ct. 756, 5 L.Ed.2d 783 (1961); McCormick § 131; 8 Wigmore § 2276 (McNaughton Rev.1961). In any event, wholly aside from constitutional considerations, the provision represents a sound policy.

Report of House Committee on the Judiciary

House Comm. on Judiciary, Fed.Rules of Evidence, H.R.Rep. No. 650, 93d Cong., 1st Sess., p. 10 (1973); 1974 U.S.Code Cong. & Ad.News 7075, 7084

The second sentence of Rule 608(b) as submitted by the Court permitted specific instances of misconduct of a witness to be inquired into on cross-examination for the purpose of attacking his credibility, if probative of truthfulness or untruthfulness, "and not remote in time." Such cross-examination could be of the witness himself or of another witness who testifies as to "his" character for truthfulness or untruthfulness.

The Committee amended the Rule to emphasize the discretionary power of the court in permitting such testimony and deleted the reference to remoteness in time as being unnecessary and confusing (remoteness from time of trial or remoteness from the incident involved?). As recast, the Committee amendment also makes clear the antecedent of "his" in the original Court proposal.

1987 Amendment

The amendments are technical. No substantive change is intended.

1988 Amendment

The amendment is technical. No substantive change is intended.

2003 Amendment

The Rule has been amended to clarify that the absolute prohibition on extrinsic evidence applies only when the sole reason for proffering that evidence is to attack or support the witness' character for truthfulness. *See United States v. Abel*, 469 U.S. 45 (1984); *United States v. Fusco*, 748 F.2d 996 (5th Cir.1984) (Rule 608(b) limits the use of evidence "designed to show that the witness has done things, unrelated to the suit being tried, that make him more or less believable per se"); Ohio R.Evid. 608(b). On occasion the Rule's use of the overbroad term "credibility" has been read "to bar extrinsic evidence for bias, competency and contradiction impeachment since they too deal with credibility." American Bar Association Section of Litigation, *Emerging Problems Under the Federal Rules of Evidence* at 161 (3d ed. 1998). The amendment conforms the language of the Rule to its original intent, which was to impose an absolute bar on extrinsic evidence only if the sole purpose for offering the evidence was to prove the witness' character for veracity. *See* Advisory Committee Note to Rule 608(b) (stating that the Rule is "[i]n conformity with Rule 405, which forecloses use of evidence of specific incidents as proof in chief of character unless character is an issue in the case . . . ").

By limiting the application of the Rule to proof of a witness' character for truthfulness, the amendment leaves the admissibility of extrinsic evidence offered for other grounds of impeachment (such as contradiction, prior inconsistent statement, bias and mental capacity) to Rules 402 and 403. *See, e.g., United States v. Winchenbach*, 197 F.3d 548 (1st Cir.1999) (admissibility of a prior inconsistent statement offered for impeachment is governed by Rules 402 and 403, not Rule 608(b)); *United States v. Tarantino*, 846 F.2d 1384 (D.C.Cir.1988) (admissibility of extrinsic evidence offered to contradict a witness is governed by Rules 402 and 403); *United States v. Lindemann*, 85 F.3d 1232 (7th Cir.1996) (admissibility of extrinsic evidence of bias is governed by Rules 402 and 403).

It should be noted that the extrinsic evidence prohibition of Rule 608(b) bars any reference to the consequences that a witness might have suffered as a result of an alleged bad act. For example, Rule 608(b) prohibits counsel from mentioning that a witness was suspended or disciplined for the conduct that is the subject of impeachment, when that conduct is offered only to prove the character of the witness. *See United States v. Davis*, 183 F.3d 231, 257 n. 12 (3d Cir.1999) (emphasizing that in attacking the defendant's character for truthfulness "the government cannot make reference to Davis's forty-four day suspension or that Internal Affairs found that he lied about" an incident because "[s]uch evidence would not only be hearsay to the extent it contains assertion of fact, it would be inadmissible extrinsic evidence under Rule 608(b)"). *See also* Stephen A. Saltzburg, *Impeaching the Witness: Prior Bad Acts and Extrinsic Evidence*, 7 Crim. Just. 28, 31 (Winter 1993) ("counsel should not be permitted to circumvent the no-extrinsic-evidence provision by tucking a third person's opinion about prior acts into a question asked of the witness who has denied the act").

For purposes of consistency the term "credibility" has been replaced by the term "character for truthfulness" in the last sentence of subdivision (b). The term "credibility" is also used in subdivision (a). But the Committee found it unnecessary to substitute "character for truthfulness" for "credibility" in Rule 608(a), because subdivision (a)(1) already serves to limit impeachment to proof of such character.

Rules 609(a) and 610 also use the term "credibility" when the intent of those Rules is to regulate impeachment of a witness' character for truthfulness. No inference should be derived from the fact that the Committee proposed an amendment to Rule 608(b) but not to Rules 609 and 610.

Changes Made After Publication and Comments. The last sentence of Rule 608(b) was changed to substitute the term "character for truthfulness" for the existing term "credibility." This change was made in accordance with public comment suggesting that it would be helpful to provide uniform terminology throughout Rule 608(b). A stylistic change was also made to the last sentence of Rule 608(b).

Rule 609. Impeachment by Evidence of Conviction of Crime

(a) General rule. For the purpose of attacking the credibility of a witness,

(1) evidence that a witness other than an accused has been convicted of a crime shall be admitted, subject to Rule 403, if the crime was punishable by death or imprisonment in excess of one year under the law under which the witness was convicted, and evidence that an accused has been convicted of such a crime shall be admitted if the court determines that the probative value of admitting this evidence outweighs its prejudicial effect to the accused; and

(2) evidence that any witness has been convicted of a crime shall be admitted if it involved dishonesty or false statement, regardless of the punishment.

(b) Time limit. Evidence of a conviction under this rule is not admissible if a period of more than ten years has elapsed since the date of the conviction or of the release of the witness from the confinement imposed for that conviction, whichever is the later date, unless the court determines, in the interests of justice, that the probative value of the conviction supported by specific facts and circumstances substantially outweighs its prejudicial effect. However, evidence of a conviction more than 10 years old as calculated herein, is not admissible unless the proponent gives to the adverse party sufficient advance written notice of intent to use such evidence to provide the adverse party with a fair opportunity to contest the use of such evidence.

(c) Effect of pardon, annulment, or certificate of rehabilitation. Evidence of a conviction is not admissible under this rule if (1) the conviction has been the subject of a pardon, annulment, certificate of rehabilitation, or other equivalent procedure based on a finding of the rehabilitation of the person convicted, and that person has not been convicted of a subsequent crime which was punishable by death or imprisonment in excess of one year, or (2) the conviction has been the subject of a pardon, annulment, or other equivalent procedure based on a finding of innocence.

(d) Juvenile adjudications. Evidence of juvenile adjudications is generally not admissible under this rule. The court may, however, in a criminal case allow evidence of a juvenile adjudication of a witness other than the accused if conviction of the offense would be admissible to attack the credibility of an adult and the court is satisfied that admission in evidence is necessary for a fair determination of the issue of guilt or innocence.

(e) Pendency of appeal. The pendency of an appeal therefrom does not render evidence of a conviction inadmissible. Evidence of the pendency of an appeal is admissible.

(As amended Mar. 2, 1987, eff. Oct. 1, 1987; Jan. 26, 1990, eff. Dec. 1, 1990.)

Section references, McCormick 5th ed.

Generally § 42

(a). § 42

(b). § 42

(c). § 42

(d). § 42

(e). § 42

Note by Federal Judicial Center

Subdivision (a) of the rule prescribed by the Supreme Court was revised successively in the House, in the Senate, and in the Conference. The nature of the rule prescribed by the Court, the various amendments, and the reasons therefor are stated in the Report of the House Committee on the Judiciary, the Report of the Senate Committee on the Judiciary, and the Conference Report, set forth below.

Subdivision (b) of the rule prescribed by the Supreme Court was also revised successively in the House, in the Senate, and in the Conference. The nature of the rule prescribed by the Court, those amendments and the reasons therefor are likewise stated in the Report of the House Committee on the Judiciary, the Report of the Senate Committee on the Judiciary, and the Conference Report, set forth below.

Subdivision (c) enacted by the Congress is the subdivision prescribed by the Supreme Court, with amendments and reasons therefor stated in the Report of the House Committee on the Judiciary, set forth below.

Subdivision (d) enacted by the Congress is the subdivision prescribed by the Supreme Court, amended in the second sentence by substituting "court" in place of "judge" and by adding the phrase "in a criminal case."

Subdivision (e) enacted by the Congress is the subdivision prescribed by the Supreme Court without change.

Advisory Committee's Note

56 F.R.D. 183, 270

As a means of impeachment, evidence of conviction of crime is significant only because it stands as proof of the commission of the underlying criminal act. There is little dissent from the general proposition that at least some crimes are relevant to credibility but much disagreement among the cases and commentators about which crimes are usable for this purpose. See McCormick § 43; 2 Wright, Federal Practice and Procedure: Criminal § 416 (1969). The weight of traditional authority has been to allow use of felonies generally, without regard to the nature of the particular offense, and of *crimen falsi* without regard to the grade of the offense. This is the view accepted by Congress in the 1970 amendment of § 14–305 of the District of Columbia Code, P.L. 91–358, 84 Stat. 473. Uniform Rule 21 and Model Code Rule 106 permit only crimes involving "dishonesty or false statement." Others have thought that the trial judge should have discretion to exclude convictions if the probative value of the evidence of the crime is substantially outweighed by the danger of unfair prejudice. Luck v. United States, 121 U.S.App.D.C. 151, 348 F.2d 763 (1965); McGowan, Impeachment of Criminal Defendants by Prior Convictions, 1970 Law & Soc. Order 1. . . .

The proposed rule incorporates certain basic safeguards, in terms applicable to all witnesses but of particular significance to an accused who elects to testify. These protections include the imposition of definite time limitations, giving effect to demonstrated rehabilitation, and generally excluding juvenile adjudications.

Subdivision (a). For purposes of impeachment, crimes are divided into two categories by the rule: (1) those of what is generally regarded as felony grade, without particular regard to the nature of the offense, and (2) those involving dishonesty or false statement, without regard to the grade of the offense. Provable convictions are not limited to violations of federal law. By reason of our constitutional structure, the federal catalog of crimes is far from being a complete one, and resort must be had to the laws of the states for the specification of many crimes. For example, simple theft as compared with theft from interstate commerce. Other instances of borrowing are the Assimilative Crimes Act, making the state law of crimes applicable to the special territorial and maritime jurisdiction of the United States, 18 U.S.C. § 13, and the provision of the Judicial Code disqualifying persons as jurors on the grounds of state as well as federal convictions, 28 U.S.C. § 1865. For evaluation of the crime in terms of seriousness, reference is made to the congressional measurement of felony (subject to imprisonment in excess of one year) rather than adopting state definitions which vary considerably. See 28 U.S.C. § 1865, supra, disqualifying jurors for conviction in state or federal court of crime punishable by imprisonment for more than one year.

Report of House Committee on the Judiciary

House Comm. on Judiciary, Fed.Rules of Evidence, H.R.Rep. No. 650, 93d Cong., 1st Sess., p. 11 (1973); 1974 U.S.Code Cong. & Ad.News 7075, 7084

Rule 609(a) as submitted by the Court was modeled after Section 133(a) of Public Law 91–358, 14 D.C.Code 305(b)(1), enacted in 1970. The Rule provided that:

> For the purpose of attacking the credibility of a witness, evidence that he has been convicted of a crime is admissible but only if the crime (1) was

punishable by death or imprisonment in excess of one year under the law under which he was convicted or (2) involved dishonesty or false statement regardless of the punishment.

As reported to the Committee by the Subcommittee, Rule 609(a) was amended to read as follows:

> For the purpose of attacking the credibility of a witness, evidence that he has been convicted of a crime is admissible only if the crime (1) was punishable by death or imprisonment in excess of one year, unless the court determines that the danger of unfair prejudice outweighs the probative value of the evidence of the conviction, or (2) involved dishonesty or false statement.

In full committee, the provision was amended to permit attack upon the credibility of a witness by prior conviction only if the prior crime involved dishonesty or false statement. While recognizing that the prevailing doctrine in the federal courts and in most States allows a witness to be impeached by evidence of prior felony convictions without restriction as to type, the Committee was of the view that, because of the danger of unfair prejudice in such practice and the deterrent effect upon an accused who might wish to testify, and even upon a witness who was not the accused, cross-examination by evidence of prior conviction should be limited to those kinds of convictions bearing directly on credibility, i.e., crimes involving dishonesty or false statement.

Report of Senate Committee on the Judiciary

Senate Comm. on Judiciary, Fed.Rules of Evidence, S.Rep. No. 1277, 93d Cong., 2d Sess., p. 14 (1974); 1974 U.S.Code Cong. & Ad.News 7051, 7060

As proposed by the Supreme Court, the rule would allow the use of prior convictions to impeach if the crime was a felony or a misdemeanor if the misdemeanor involved dishonesty or false statement. As modified by the House, the rule would admit prior convictions for impeachment purposes only if the offense, whether felony or misdemeanor, involved dishonesty or false statement.

The committee has adopted a modified version of the House-passed rule. In your committee's view, the danger of unfair prejudice is far greater when the accused, as opposed to other witnesses, testifies, because the jury may be prejudiced not merely on the question of credibility but also on the ultimate question of guilt or innocence. Therefore, with respect to defendants, the committee agreed with the House limitation that only offenses involving false statement or dishonesty may be used. By that phrase, the committee means crimes such as perjury or subornation of perjury, false statement, criminal fraud, embezzlement or false pretense, or any other offense, in the nature of crimen falsi the commission of which involves some element of untruthfulness, deceit or falsification bearing on the accused's propensity to testify truthfully.

With respect to other witnesses, in addition to any prior conviction involving false statement or dishonesty, any other felony may be used to impeach if, and only if, the court finds that the probative value of such evidence outweighs its prejudicial effect against the party offering that witness.

Notwithstanding this provision, proof of any prior offense otherwise admissible under rule 404 could still be offered for the purposes sanctioned by that rule. Furthermore, the committee intends that notwithstanding this rule, a defendant's misrepresentation regarding the existence or nature of prior convictions may be met by rebuttal evidence, including the record of such prior convictions. Similarly, such records may be offered to rebut representations made by the defendant regarding his attitude toward or willingness to commit a general category of offense, although denials or other representations by the defendant regarding the specific conduct which forms the basis of the charge against him shall not make prior convictions admissible to rebut such statement.

In regard to either type of representation, of course, prior convictions may be offered in rebuttal only if the defendant's statement is made in response to defense counsel's questions or is made gratuitously in the course of cross-examination. Prior convictions may not be offered as rebuttal evidence if the prosecution has sought to circumvent the purpose of this rule by asking questions which elicit such representations from the defendant.

One other clarifying amendment has been added to this subsection, that is, to provide that the admissibility of evidence of a prior conviction is permitted only upon cross-examination of a witness. It is not admissible if a person does not testify. It is to be understood, however, that a court record of a prior conviction is admissible to prove that conviction if the witness has forgotten or denies its existence.

Conference Report

H.R., Fed.Rules of Evidence, Conf.Rep. No. 1597, 93d Cong., 2d Sess., p. 9 (1974); 1974 U.S.Code Cong. & Ad.News 7098, 7102

The House bill provides that the credibility of a witness can be attacked by proof of prior conviction of a crime only if the crime involves dishonesty or false statement. The Senate amendment provides that a witness' credibility may be attacked if the crime (1) was punishable by death or imprisonment in excess of one year under the law under which he was convicted or (2) involves dishonesty or false statement, regardless of the punishment.

The Conference adopts the Senate amendment with an amendment. The Conference amendment provides that the credibility of a witness, whether a defendant or someone else, may be attacked by proof of a prior conviction but only if the crime: (1) was punishable by death or imprisonment in excess of one year under the law under which he was convicted and the court determines that the probative value of the conviction outweighs its prejudicial effect to the defendant; or (2) involved dishonesty or false statement regardless of the punishment.

By the phrase "dishonesty and false statement" the Conference means crimes such as perjury or subornation of perjury, false statement, criminal fraud, embezzlement, or false pretense, or any other offense in the nature of crimen falsi, the commission of which involves some element of deceit, untruthfulness, or falsification bearing on the accused's propensity to testify truthfully.

The admission of prior convictions involving dishonesty and false statement is not within the discretion of the Court. Such convictions are peculiarly probative of credibility and, under this rule, are always to be admitted. Thus, judicial discretion granted with respect to the admissibility of other prior convictions is not applicable to those involving dishonesty or false statement.

With regard to the discretionary standard established by paragraph (1) of rule 609(a), the Conference determined that the prejudicial effect to be weighed against the probative value of the conviction is specifically the prejudicial effect *to the defendant.* The danger of prejudice to a witness other than the defendant (such as injury to the witness' reputation in his community) was considered and rejected by the Conference as an element to be weighed in determining admissibility. It was the judgment of the Conference that the danger of prejudice to a nondefendant witness is outweighed by the need for the trier of fact to have as much relevant evidence on the issue of credibility as possible. Such evidence should only be excluded where it presents a danger of improperly influencing the outcome of the trial by persuading the trier of fact to convict the defendant on the basis of his prior criminal record.

Advisory Committee's Note

56 F.R.D. 183, 271

Subdivision (b). Few statutes recognize a time limit on impeachment by evidence of conviction. However, practical considerations of fairness and relevancy demand that some boundary be recognized. See Ladd, Credibility Tests—Current Trends, 89 U.Pa.L.Rev. 166, 176–177 (1940). This portion of the rule is derived from the proposal advanced in Recommendation Proposing an Evidence Code, § 788(5), p. 142, Cal.Law Rev.Comm'n (1965), though not adopted. See California Evidence Code § 788.

Report of House Committee on the Judiciary

House Comm. on Judiciary, Fed.Rules of Evidence, H.R.Rep. No. 650, 93d Cong., 1st Sess., p. 11 (1973); 1974 U.S.Code Cong. & Ad.News 7075, 7085

Rule 609(b) as submitted by the Court was modeled after Section 133(a) of Public Law 91–358, 14 D.C.Code 305(b)(2)(B), enacted in 1970. The Rule provided:

> Evidence of a conviction under this rule is not admissible if a period of more than ten years has elapsed since the date of the release of the witness from confinement imposed for his most recent conviction, or the expiration of the period of his parole, probation, or sentence granted or imposed with respect to his most recent conviction, whichever is the later date.

Under this formulation, a witness' entire past record of criminal convictions could be used for impeachment (provided the conviction met the standard of subdivision (a)), if the witness had been most recently released from confinement, or the period of his parole or probation had expired, within ten years of the conviction.

The Committee amended the Rule to read in the text of the 1971 Advisory Committee version to provide that upon the expiration of ten years from the date of a conviction of a witness, or of his release from confinement for that offense, that conviction may no longer be used for impeachment. The Committee was of the view that after ten years following a person's release from confinement (or from the date of his conviction) the probative value of the conviction with respect to that person's credibility diminished to a point where it should no longer be admissible.

Report of Senate Committee on the Judiciary

Senate Comm. on Judiciary, Fed.Rules of Evidence, S.Rep. No. 1277, 93d Cong., 2d Sess., p. 15 (1974); 1974 U.S.Code Cong. & Ad.News 7051, 7061

Although convictions over ten years old generally do not have much probative value, there may be exceptional circumstances under which the conviction substantially bears on the credibility of the witness. Rather than exclude all convictions over 10 years old, the committee adopted an amendment in the form of a final clause to the section granting the court discretion to admit convictions over 10 years old, but only upon a determination by the court that the probative value of the convictions supported by specific facts and circumstances, substantially outweighs its prejudicial effect.

It is intended that convictions over 10 years old will be admitted very rarely and only in exceptional circumstances. The rules provide that the decision be supported by specific facts and circumstances thus requiring the court to make specific findings on the record as to the particular facts and circumstances it has considered in determining that the probative value of the conviction substantially outweighs its prejudicial impact. It is expected that, in fairness, the court will give the party against whom the conviction is introduced a full and adequate opportunity to contest its admission.

Conference Report

H.R., Fed.Rules of Evidence, Conf.Rep. No. 1597, 93d Cong., 2d Sess., p. 10 (1974); 1974 U.S.Code Cong. & Ad.News 7098, 7103

The House bill provides in subsection (b) that evidence of conviction of a crime may not be used for impeachment purposes under subsection (a) if more than ten years have elapsed since the date of the conviction or the date the witness was released from confinement imposed for the conviction, whichever is later. The Senate amendment permits the use of convictions older than ten years, if the court determines, in the interests of justice, that the probative value of the conviction, supported by specific facts and circumstances, substantially outweighs its prejudicial effect.

The Conference adopts the Senate amendment with an amendment requiring notice by a party that he intends to request that the court allow him to use a conviction older than ten years. The Conferees anticipate that a written notice, in order to give the adversary a fair opportunity to contest the use of the evidence, will ordinarily include such information as the date of the conviction, the jurisdiction, and the offense or statute involved. In order to eliminate the possibility that the flexibility of this provision may impair the ability of a party-opponent to prepare for trial, the Conferees intend that the notice provision operate to avoid surprise.

Advisory Committee's Note

56 F.R.D. 183, 271

Subdivision (c). A pardon or its equivalent granted solely for the purpose of restoring civil rights lost by virtue of a conviction has no relevance to an inquiry into character. If, however, the pardon or other proceeding is hinged upon a showing of rehabilitation the situation is otherwise. The result under the rule is to render the conviction inadmissible. The alternative of allowing in evidence both the conviction and the rehabilitation has not been adopted for reasons of policy, economy of time, and difficulties of evaluation.

A similar provision is contained in California Evidence Code § 788. Cf. A.L.I. Model Penal Code, Proposed Official Draft § 306.6(3)(e) (1962), and discussion in A.L.I. Proceedings 310 (1961).

Pardons based on innocence have the effect, of course, of nullifying the conviction *ab initio.*

Report of House Committee on the Judiciary

House Comm. on Judiciary, Fed.Rules of Evidence, H.R.Rep. No. 650, 93d Cong., 1st Sess., p. 12 (1973); 1974 U.S.Code Cong. & Ad.News 7075, 7085

Rule 609(c) as submitted by the Court provided in part that evidence of a witness' prior conviction is not admissible to attack his credibility if the conviction was the subject of a pardon, annulment, or other equivalent procedure, based on a showing of rehabilitation, and the witness has not been convicted of a subsequent crime. The Committee amended the Rule to provide that the "subsequent crime" must have been "punishable by death or imprisonment in excess of one year", on the ground that a subsequent conviction of an offense not a felony is insufficient to rebut the finding that the witness has been rehabilitated. The Committee also intends that the words "based on a finding of the rehabilitation of the person convicted" apply not only to "certificate of rehabilitation, or other equivalent procedure", but also to "pardon" and "annulment."

Advisory Committee's Note

56 F.R.D. 183, 271

Subdivision (d). The prevailing view has been that a juvenile adjudication is not usable for impeachment. Thomas v. United States, 74 App.D.C. 167, 121 F.2d 905 (1941); Cotton v. United States, 355 F.2d 480 (10th Cir.1966). This conclusion was based upon a variety of circumstances. By virtue of its informality, frequently diminished quantum of required proof, and other departures from accepted standards for criminal trials under the theory of *parens patriae,* the juvenile adjudication was considered to lack the precision and general probative value of the criminal conviction. While In re Gault, 387 U.S. 1, 87 S.Ct. 1428, 18 L.Ed.2d 527 (1967), no doubt eliminates these characteristics insofar as objectionable, other obstacles remain. Practical problems of administration are raised by the common provisions in juvenile legislation that records be kept confidential and that they be destroyed after a short time. While *Gault* was skeptical as to the realities of confidentiality of juvenile records, it also saw no constitutional obstacles to improvement. 387 U.S. at 25, 87 S.Ct. 1428. See also Note, Rights and Rehabilitation in the Juvenile Courts, 67 Colum.L.Rev. 281, 289 (1967). In addition, policy considerations much akin to those which dictate exclusion of adult convictions after rehabilitation has been established strongly suggest a rule of excluding juvenile adjudications. Admittedly, however, the rehabilitative process may in a given case be a demonstrated failure, or the strategic importance of a given witness may be so great as to require the overriding of general policy in the interests of particular justice. See Giles v. Maryland, 386 U.S. 66, 87 S.Ct. 793, 17 L.Ed.2d 737 (1967). Wigmore was outspoken in his condemnation of the disallowance of juvenile adjudications to impeach, especially when the witness is the complainant in a case of molesting a minor. 1 Wigmore § 196; 3

id. §§ 924a, 980. The rule recognizes discretion in the judge to effect an accommodation among these various factors by departing from the general principle of exclusion. In deference to the general pattern and policy of juvenile statutes, however, no discretion is accorded when the witness is the accused in a criminal case.

Subdivision (e). The presumption of correctness which ought to attend judicial proceedings supports the position that pendency of an appeal does not preclude use of a conviction for impeachment. United States v. Empire Packing Co., 174 F.2d 16 (7th Cir.1949), cert. denied 337 U.S. 959, 69 S.Ct. 1534, 93 L.Ed. 1758; Bloch v. United States, 226 F.2d 185 (9th Cir.1955), cert. denied 350 U.S. 948, 76 S.Ct. 323, 100 L.Ed. 826 and 353 U.S. 959, 77 S.Ct. 868, 1 L.Ed.2d 910; and see Newman v. United States, 331 F.2d 968 (8th Cir.1964). Contra, Campbell v. United States, 85 U.S.App.D.C. 133, 176 F.2d 45 (1949). The pendency of an appeal is, however, a qualifying circumstance properly considerable.

1987 Amendment

The amendments are technical. No substantive change is intended.

1990 Amendment

The amendment to Rule 609(a) makes two changes in the rule. The first change removes from the rule the limitation that the conviction may only be elicited during cross-examination, a limitation that virtually every circuit has found to be inapplicable. It is common for witnesses to reveal on direct examination their convictions to "remove the sting" of the impeachment. See e.g., United States v. Bad Cob, 560 F.2d 877 (8th Cir.1977). The amendment does not contemplate that a court will necessarily permit proof of prior convictions through testimony, which might be time-consuming and more prejudicial than proof through a written record. Rules 403 and 611(a) provide sufficient authority for the court to protect against unfair or disruptive methods of proof.

The second change effected by the amendment resolves an ambiguity as to the relationship of Rules 609 and 403 with respect to impeachment of witnesses other than the criminal defendant. See, Green v. Bock Laundry Machine Co., 109 S.Ct. ___, ___ U.S. ___ (1989). The amendment does not disturb the special balancing test for the criminal defendant who chooses to testify. Thus, the rule recognizes that, in virtually every case in which prior convictions are used to impeach the testifying defendant, the defendant faces a unique risk of prejudice—i.e., the danger that convictions that would be excluded under Fed.R.Evid. 404 will be misused by a jury as propensity evidence despite their introduction solely for impeachment purposes. Although the rule does not forbid all use of convictions to impeach a defendant, it requires that the government show that the probative value of convictions as impeachment evidence outweighs their prejudicial effect.

Prior to the amendment, the rule appeared to give the defendant the benefit of the special balancing test when defense witnesses other than the defendant were called to testify. In practice, however, the concern about unfairness to the defendant is most acute when the defendant's own convictions are offered as evidence. Almost all of the decided cases concern this type of impeachment, and the amendment does not deprive the defendant of any meaningful protection, since Rule 403 now clearly protects against unfair impeachment of any defense witness other than the defendant. There are cases in which a defendant might be prejudiced when a defense witness is impeached. Such cases may arise, for example, when the witness bears a special relationship to the defendant such that the defendant is likely to suffer some spill-over effect from impeachment of the witness.

The amendment also protects other litigants from unfair impeachment of their witnesses. The danger of prejudice from the use of prior convictions is not confined to criminal defendants. Although the danger that prior convictions will be misused as character evidence is particularly acute when the defendant is impeached, the danger exists in other situations as well. The amendment reflects the view that it is desirable to protect all litigants from the unfair use of prior convictions, and that the ordinary balancing test of Rule 403, which provides that evidence shall not be excluded unless its prejudicial effect substantially outweighs its probative value, is appropriate for assessing the admissibility of prior convictions for impeachment of any witness other than a criminal defendant.

The amendment reflects a judgment that decisions interpreting Rule 609(a) as requiring a trial court to admit convictions in civil cases that have little, if anything, to do with credibility reach undesirable results. See, e.g., Diggs v. Lyons, 741 F.2d 577 (3d Cir.1984), cert. denied, 105 S.Ct. 2157 (1985). The amendment provides the same protection against unfair prejudice arising from prior convictions used for impeachment purposes as the rules provide for other evidence. The amendment finds support in decided cases. See, e.g., Petty v. Ideco, 761 F.2d 1146 (5th Cir.1985); Czaka v. Hickman, 703 F.2d 317 (8th Cir.1983).

Fewer decided cases address the question whether Rule 609(a) provides any protection against unduly prejudicial prior convictions used to impeach government witnesses. Some courts have read Rule 609(a) as giving the government no protection for its witnesses. See, e.g., United States v. Thorne, 547 F.2d 56 (8th Cir.1976); United States v. Nevitt, 563 F.2d 406 (9th Cir.1977), cert. denied, 444 U.S. 847 (1979). This approach also is rejected by the amendment. There are cases in which impeachment of government witnesses with prior convictions that have little, if anything, to do with credibility may result in unfair prejudice to the government's interest in a fair trial and unnecessary embarrassment to a witness. Fed.R.Evid. 412 already recognizes this and excluded certain evidence of past sexual behavior in the context of prosecutions for sexual assaults.

The amendment applies the general balancing test of Rule 403 to protect all litigants against unfair impeachment of witnesses. The balancing test protects civil litigants, the government in criminal cases, and the defendant in a criminal case who calls other witnesses. The amendment addresses prior convictions offered under Rule 609, not for other purposes, and does not run afoul, therefore, of Davis v. Alaska, 415 U.S. 308 (1974). Davis involved the use of a prior juvenile adjudication not to prove a past law violation, but to prove bias. The defendant in a criminal case has the right to demonstrate the bias of a witness and to be assured a fair trial, but not to unduly prejudice a trier of fact. See generally Rule 412. In any case in which the trial court believes that confrontation rights require admission of impeachment evidence, obviously the Constitution would take precedence over the rule.

The probability that prior convictions of an ordinary government witness will be unduly prejudicial is low in most criminal cases. Since the behavior of the witness is not the issue in dispute in most cases, there is little chance that the trier of fact will misuse the convictions offered as impeachment evidence as propensity evidence. Thus, trial courts will be skeptical when the government objects to impeachment of its witnesses with prior convictions. Only when the government is able to point to a real danger of prejudice that is sufficient to outweigh substantially the probative value of the conviction for impeachment purposes will the conviction be excluded.

The amendment continues to divide subdivision (a) into subsections (1) and (2) thus facilitating retrieval under current computerized research programs which distinguish the two provisions. The Committee recommended no substantive change in subdivision (a)(2), even though some cases raise a concern about the proper interpretation of the words "dishonesty or false statement." These words were used but not explained in the original Advisory Committee Note accompanying Rule 609. Congress extensively debated the rule, and the Report of the House and Senate Conference Committee states that "[b]y the phrase 'dishonesty and false statement,' the Conference means crimes such as perjury, subornation of perjury, false statement, criminal fraud, embezzlement, or false pretense, or any other offense in the nature of *crimen falsi*, commission of which involves some element of deceit, untruthfulness, or falsification bearing on the accused's propensity to testify truthfully." The Advisory Committee concluded that the Conference Report provides sufficient guidance to trial courts and that no amendment is necessary, notwithstanding some decisions that take an unduly broad view of "dishonesty," admitting convictions such as for bank robbery or bank larceny. Subsection (a)(2) continues to apply to any witness, including a criminal defendant.

Finally, the Committee determined that it was unnecessary to add to the rule language stating that, when a prior conviction is offered under Rule 609, the trial court is to consider the probative value of the prior conviction *for impeachment*, not for other purposes. The Committee concluded that the title of the rule, its first sentence, and its placement among the impeachment rules clearly establish that evidence offered under Rule 609 is offered only for purposes of impeachment.

Rule 610. Religious Beliefs or Opinions

Evidence of the beliefs or opinions of a witness on matters of religion is not admissible for the purpose of showing that by reason of their nature the witness' credibility is impaired or enhanced.

(As amended Mar. 2, 1987, eff. Oct. 1, 1987.)

Section references, McCormick 5th ed.

§ 46

Note by Federal Judicial Center

The rule enacted by the Congress is the rule prescribed by the Supreme Court without change.

Advisory Committee's Note

56 F.R.D. 183, 272

While the rule forecloses inquiry into the religious beliefs or opinions of a witness for the purpose of showing that his character for truthfulness is affected by their nature, an inquiry for the purpose of showing interest or bias because of them is not within the prohibition. Thus disclosure of affiliation with a church which is a party to the litigation would be allowable under the rule. Cf. Tucker v. Reil, 51 Ariz. 357, 77 P.2d 203 (1938). To the same effect, though less specifically worded, is California Evidence Code § 789. See 3 Wigmore § 936.

1987 Amendment

The amendment is technical. No substantive change is intended.

Rule 611. Mode and Order of Interrogation and Presentation

(a) Control by court. The court shall exercise reasonable control over the mode and order of interrogating witnesses and presenting evidence so as to (1) make the interrogation and presentation effective for the ascertainment of the truth, (2) avoid needless consumption of time, and (3) protect witnesses from harassment or undue embarrassment.

(b) Scope of cross-examination. Cross-examination should be limited to the subject matter of the direct examination and matters affecting the credibility of the witness. The court may, in the exercise of discretion, permit inquiry into additional matters as if on direct examination.

(c) Leading questions. Leading questions should not be used on the direct examination of a witness except as may be necessary to develop the witness' testimony. Ordinarily leading questions should be permitted on cross-examination. When a party calls a hostile witness, an adverse party, or a witness identified with an adverse party, interrogation may be by leading questions.

(As amended Mar. 2, 1987, eff. Oct. 1, 1987.)

Section references, McCormick 5th ed.

Generally § 4, § 5, § 16, § 25, § 36, § 56, § 57, § 60

(a). § 4, § 5, § 6, § 7, § 16, § 29, § 32, § 40, § 41, § 42, § 44, § 51, § 52, § 55, § 56, § 58

(b). § 20, § 21, § 22, § 23, § 24, § 25, § 26, § 27, § 29, § 33, § 40, § 134

(c). § 6, § 20, § 25, § 26

Note by Federal Judicial Center

Subdivision (a) of the rule enacted by the Congress is the subdivision prescribed by the Supreme Court, amended only by substituting "court" in place of "judge."

Subdivision (b) of the rule enacted by the Congress is substantially different from the subdivision prescribed by the Supreme Court. The nature of the changes and the reasons therefor are stated in the Report of the House Committee on the Judiciary, set forth below.

The first two sentences of subdivision (c) of the rule enacted by the Congress are the same as prescribed by the Supreme Court. The third sentence has been amended in the manner and for the reasons stated in the Report of the House Committee on the Judiciary, set forth below.

Advisory Committee's Note

56 F.R.D. 183, 273

Subdivision (a). Spelling out detailed rules to govern the mode and order of interrogating witnesses and presenting evidence is neither desirable nor feasible. The ultimate responsibility for the effective working of the adversary system rests with the judge. The rule sets forth the objectives which he should seek to attain.

Item (1) restates in broad terms the power and obligation of the judge as developed under common law principles. It covers such concerns as whether testimony shall be in the form of a free narrative or responses to specific questions, McCormick § 5, the order of calling witnesses and presenting evidence, 6 Wigmore § 1867, the use of demonstrative evidence, McCormick § 179, and the many other questions arising during the course of a trial which can be solved only by the judge's common sense and fairness in view of the particular circumstances.

Item (2) is addressed to avoidance of needless consumption of time, a matter of daily concern in the disposition of cases. A companion piece is found in the discretion vested in the judge to exclude evidence as a waste of time in Rule 403(b).

Item (3) calls for a judgment under the particular circumstances whether interrogation tactics entail harassment or undue embarrassment. Pertinent circumstances include the importance of the testimony, the nature of the inquiry, its relevance to credibility, waste of time, and confusion. McCormick § 42. In Alford v. United States, 282 U.S. 687, 694, 51 S.Ct. 218, 75 L.Ed. 624 (1931), the Court pointed out that, while the trial judge should protect the witness from questions which "go beyond the bounds of proper cross-examination merely to harass, annoy or humiliate," this protection by no means forecloses efforts to discredit the witness. Reference to the transcript of the prosecutor's cross-examination in Berger v. United States, 295 U.S. 78, 55 S.Ct. 629, 79 L.Ed. 1314 (1935), serves to lay at rest any doubts as to the need for judicial control in this area.

The inquiry into specific instances of conduct of a witness allowed under Rule 608(b) is, of course, subject to this rule.

Subdivision (b) *. The tradition in the federal courts and in numerous state courts has been to limit the scope of cross-examination to matters testified to on direct, plus matters bearing upon the credibility of the witness. Various reasons have been advanced to justify the rule of limited cross-examination. (1) A party vouches for his own witness but only to the extent of matters elicited on direct. Resurrection Gold Mining Co. v. Fortune Gold Mining Co., 129 Fed. 668,

* The Advisory Committee's Note to subdivision (b) is from the 1969 Preliminary Draft. 46 F.R.D. 161, 304.—Federal Judicial Center.

675 (8th Cir.1904), quoted in Maguire, Weinstein, et al., Cases on Evidence 277, n. 38 (5th ed. 1965). But the concept of vouching is discredited, and Rule 6–07[607] rejects it. (2) A party cannot ask his own witness leading questions. This is a problem properly solved in terms of what is necessary for a proper development of the testimony rather than by a mechanistic formula similar to the vouching concept. See discussion under subdivision (c). (3) A practice of limited cross-examination promotes orderly presentation of the case. Finch v. Weiner, 109 Conn. 616, 145 Atl. 31 (1929). In the opinion of the Advisory Committee this latter reason has merit. It is apparent, however, that the rule of limited cross-examination thus viewed becomes an aspect of the judge's general control over the mode and order of interrogating witnesses and presenting evidence, to be administered as such. The matter is not one in which involvement at the appellate level is likely to prove fruitful. See, for example, Moyer v. Aetna Life Ins. Co., 126 F.2d 141 (3rd Cir.1942); Butler v. New York Central R. Co., 253 F.2d 281 (7th Cir.1958); United States v. Johnson, 285 F.2d 35 (9th Cir.1960); Union Automobile Indemnity Ass'n v. Capitol Indemnity Ins. Co., 310 F.2d 318 (7th Cir.1962). In view of these considerations, the rule is phrased in terms of a suggestion rather than a mandate to the trial judge.

The qualification "as if on direct examination," applicable when inquiry into additional matters is allowed is designed to terminate at that point the asking of leading questions as a matter of right and to bring into operation subdivision (c) of the rule.

The rule does not purport to determine the extent to which an accused who elects to testify thereby waives his privilege against self-incrimination. The question is a constitutional one, rather than a mere matter of administering the trial. Under United States v. Simmons, 390 U.S. 377 (1968), no general waiver occurs when the accused testifies on such preliminary matters as the validity of a search and seizure or the admissibility of a confession. Rule 1–04(d) [104(d)], supra. When he testifies on the merits, however, can he foreclose inquiry into an aspect or element of the crime by avoiding it on direct? The affirmative answer given in Tucker v. United States, 5 F.2d 818 (8th Cir.1925), is inconsistent with the description of the waiver as extending to "all other relevant facts" in Johnson v. United States, 318 U.S. 189, 195 (1943). See also Brown v. United States, 356 U.S. 148 (1958). The situation of an accused who desires to testify on some but not all counts of a multiple-count indictment is one to be approached, in the first instance at least, as a problem of severance under Rule 14 of the Federal Rules of Criminal Procedure. Cross v. United States, 335 F.2d 987 (D.C.Cir.1964). Cf. United States v. Baker, 262 F.Supp. 657, 686 (D.D.C. 1966). In all events, the extent of the waiver of the privilege against self-incrimination ought not to be determined as a by-product of a rule on scope of cross-examination.

Report of House Committee on the Judiciary

House Comm. on Judiciary, Fed.Rules of Evidence, H.R.Rep. No. 650, 93d Cong., 1st Sess., p. 12 (1973); 1974 U.S.Code Cong. & Ad.News 7075, 7085

As submitted by the Court, Rule 611(b) provided:

> A witness may be cross-examined on any matter relevant to any issue in the case, including credibility. In the interests of justice, the judge may limit cross-examination with respect to matters not testified to on direct examination.

The Committee amended this provision to return to the rule which prevails in the federal courts and thirty-nine State jurisdictions. As amended, the Rule is in the text of the 1969 Advisory Committee draft. It limits cross-examination to credibility and to matters testified to on direct examination, unless the judge permits more, in which event the cross-examiner must proceed as if on direct examination. This traditional rule facilitates orderly presentation by each party at trial. Further, in light of existing discovery procedures, there appears to be no need to abandon the traditional rule.

Report of Senate Committee on the Judiciary

Senate Comm. on Judiciary, Fed.Rules of Evidence, S.Rep. No. 1277, 93d Cong., 2d Sess., p. 25 (1974); 1974 U.S.Code Cong. & Ad.News 7051, 7071

Rule 611(b) as submitted by the Supreme Court permitted a broad scope of cross-examination: "cross-examination on any matter relevant to any issue in the case" unless the judge, in the interests of justice, limited the scope of cross-examination.

The House narrowed the Rule to the more traditional practice of limiting cross-examination to the subject matter of direct examination (and credibility), but with discretion in the judge to permit inquiry into additional matters in situations where that would aid in the development of the evidence or otherwise facilitate the conduct of the trial.

The committee agrees with the House amendment. Although there are good arguments in support of broad cross-examination from perspectives of developing all relevant evidence, we believe the factors of insuring an orderly and predictable development of the evidence weigh in favor of the narrower rule, especially when discretion is given to the trial judge to permit inquiry into additional matters. The committee expressly approves this discretion and believes it will permit sufficient flexibility allowing a broader scope of cross-examination whenever appropriate.

The House amendment providing broader discretionary cross-examination permitted inquiry into additional matters only as if on direct examination. As a general rule, we concur with this limitation, however, we would understand that this limitation would not preclude the utilization of leading questions if the conditions of subsection (c) of this rule were met, bearing in mind the judge's discretion in any case to limit the scope of cross-examination.[1]

Further, the committee has received correspondence from Federal judges commenting on the applicability of this rule to section 1407 of title 28. It is the committee's judgment that this rule as reported by the House is flexible enough to provide sufficiently broad cross-examination in appropriate situations in multidistrict litigation.

Advisory Committee's Note

56 F.R.D. 183, 275

Subdivision (c). The rule continues the traditional view that the suggestive powers of the leading question are as a general proposition undesirable. Within this tradition, however, numerous exceptions have achieved recognition: The witness who is hostile, unwilling, or biased; the child witness or the adult

1. See McCormick on Evidence, §§ 24–26 (especially 24) (2d ed. 1972).

with communication problems; the witness whose recollection is exhausted; and undisputed preliminary matters. 3 Wigmore §§ 774–778. An almost total unwillingness to reverse for infractions has been manifested by appellate courts. See cases cited in 3 Wigmore § 770. The matter clearly falls within the area of control by the judge over the mode and order of interrogation and presentation and accordingly is phrased in words of suggestion rather than command.

The rule also conforms to tradition in making the use of leading questions on cross-examination a matter of right. The purpose of the qualification "ordinarily" is to furnish a basis for denying the use of leading questions when the cross-examination is cross-examination in form only and not in fact, as for example the "cross-examination" of a party by his own counsel after being called by the opponent (savoring more of re-direct) or of an insured defendant who proves to be friendly to the plaintiff.

The final sentence deals with categories of witnesses automatically regarded and treated as hostile. Rule 43(b) of the Federal Rules of Civil Procedure has included only "an adverse party or an officer, director, or managing agent of a public or private corporation or of a partnership or association which is an adverse party." This limitation virtually to persons whose statements would stand as admissions is believed to be an unduly narrow concept of those who may safely be regarded as hostile without further demonstration. See, for example, Maryland Casualty Co. v. Kador, 225 F.2d 120 (5th Cir.1955), and Degelos v. Fidelity and Casualty Co., 313 F.2d 809 (5th Cir.1963), holding despite the language of Rule 43(b) that an insured fell within it, though not a party in an action under the Louisiana direct action statute. The phrase of the rule, "witness identified with" an adverse party, is designed to enlarge the category of persons thus callable.

Report of House Committee on the Judiciary

House Comm. on Judiciary, Fed.Rules of Evidence, H.R.Rep. No. 650, 93d Cong., 1st Sess., p. 12 (1973); 1974 U.S.Code Cong. & Ad.News 7075, 7086

The third sentence of Rule 611(c) as submitted by the Court provided that:

> In civil cases, a party is entitled to call an adverse party or witness identified with him and interrogate by leading questions.

The Committee amended this Rule to permit leading questions to be used with respect to any hostile witness, not only an adverse party or person identified with such adverse party. The Committee also substituted the word "When" for the phrase "In civil cases" to reflect the possibility that in criminal cases a defendant may be entitled to call witnesses identified with the government, in which event the Committee believed the defendant should be permitted to inquire with leading questions.

Report of Senate Committee on the Judiciary

Senate Comm. on Judiciary, Fed.Rules of Evidence, S.Rep. No. 1277, 93d Cong., 2d Sess., p. 25 (1974); 1974 U.S.Code Cong. & Ad.News 7051, 7072

As submitted by the Supreme Court, the rule provided: "In civil cases, a party is entitled to call an adverse party or witness identified with him and interrogate by leading questions."

The final sentence of subsection (c) was amended by the House for the purpose of clarifying the fact that a "hostile witness"—that is a witness who is hostile in fact—could be subject to interrogation by leading questions. The rule as submitted by the Supreme Court declared certain witnesses hostile as a matter of law and thus subject to interrogation by leading questions without any showing of hostility in fact. These were adverse parties or witnesses identified with adverse parties. However, the wording of the first sentence of subsection (c) while generally prohibiting the use of leading questions on direct examination, also provides "except as may be necessary to develop his testimony." Further, the first paragraph of the Advisory Committee note explaining the subsection makes clear that they intended that leading questions could be asked of a hostile witness or a witness who was unwilling or biased and even though that witness was not associated with an adverse party. Thus, we question whether the House amendment was necessary.

However, concluding that it was not intended to affect the meaning of the first sentence of the subsection and was intended solely to clarify the fact that leading questions are permissible in the interrogation of a witness, who is hostile in fact, the committee accepts that House amendment.

The final sentence of this subsection was also amended by the House to cover criminal as well as civil cases. The committee accepts this amendment, but notes that it may be difficult in criminal cases to determine when a witness is "identified with an adverse party," and thus the rule should be applied with caution.

1987 Amendment

The amendment is technical. No substantive change is intended.

Rule 612. Writing Used to Refresh Memory

Except as otherwise provided in criminal proceedings by section 3500 of title 18, United States Code, if a witness uses a writing to refresh memory for the purpose of testifying, either—

(1) while testifying, or

(2) before testifying, if the court in its discretion determines it is necessary in the interests of justice,

an adverse party is entitled to have the writing produced at the hearing, to inspect it, to cross-examine the witness thereon, and to introduce in evidence those portions which relate to the testimony of the witness. If it is claimed that the writing contains matters not related to the subject matter of the testimony the court shall examine the writing in camera, excise any portions not so related, and order delivery of the remainder to the party entitled thereto. Any portion withheld over objections shall be preserved and made available to the appellate court in the event of an appeal. If a writing is not produced or delivered pursuant to order under this rule, the court shall make any order justice requires, except that in criminal cases when the prosecution elects not to comply, the order shall be one striking the testimony or, if the court in its discretion determines that the interests of justice so require, declaring a mistrial.

(As amended Mar. 2, 1987, eff. Oct. 1, 1987.)

Section references, McCormick 5th ed.

§ 9, § 93, § 97

Note by Federal Judicial Center

The rule enacted by the Congress is the rule prescribed by the Supreme Court, amended by substituting "court" in place of "judge," with appropriate pronominal change, and in the first sentence, by substituting "the writing" in place of "it" before "produced," and by substituting the phrase "(1) while testifying, or (2) before testifying if the court in its discretion determines it is necessary in the interests of justice" in place of "before or while testifying." The reasons for the latter amendment are stated in the Report of the House Committee on the Judiciary, set forth below.

Advisory Committee's Note

56 F.R.D. 183, 277

The treatment of writings used to refresh recollection while on the stand is in accord with settled doctrine. McCormick § 9, p. 15. The bulk of the case law has, however, denied the existence of any right to access by the opponent when the writing is used prior to taking the stand, though the judge may have discretion in the matter. Goldman v. United States, 316 U.S. 129, 62 S.Ct. 993, 86 L.Ed. 1322 (1942); Needelman v. United States, 261 F.2d 802 (5th Cir.1958), cert. dismissed 362 U.S. 600, 80 S.Ct. 960, 4 L.Ed.2d 980, rehearing denied 363 U.S. 858, 80 S.Ct. 1606, 4 L.Ed.2d 1739, Annot., 82 A.L.R.2d 473, 562 and 7 A.L.R.3d 181, 247. An increasing group of cases has repudiated the distinction, People v. Scott, 29 Ill.2d 97, 193 N.E.2d 814 (1963); State v. Mucci, 25 N.J. 423, 136 A.2d 761 (1957); State v. Hunt, 25 N.J. 514, 138 A.2d 1 (1958); State v. Deslovers, 40 R.I. 89, 100 A. 64 (1917), and this position is believed to be correct. As Wigmore put it, "the risk of imposition and the need of safeguard is just as great" in both situations. 3 Wigmore § 762, p. 111. To the same effect is McCormick § 9, p. 17.

The purpose of the phrase "for the purpose of testifying" is to safeguard against using the rule as a pretext for wholesale exploration of an opposing party's files and to insure that access is limited only to those writings which may fairly be said in fact to have an impact upon the testimony of the witness.

The purpose of the rule is the same as that of the *Jencks* statute, 18 U.S.C. § 3500: to promote the search of credibility and memory. The same sensitivity to disclosure of government files may be involved; hence the rule is expressly made subject to the statute, subdivision (a) of which provides: "In any criminal prosecution brought by the United States, no statement or report in the possession of the United States which was made by a Government witness or prospective Government witness (other than the defendant) shall be the subject of subpena, discovery, or inspection until said witness has testified on direct examination in the trial of the case." Items falling within the purview of the statute are producible only as provided by its terms, Palermo v. United States, 360 U.S. 343, 351 (1959), and disclosure under the rule is limited similarly by the statutory conditions. With this limitation in mind, some differences of application may be noted. The *Jencks* statute applies only to statements of witnesses; the rule is not so limited. The statute applies only to criminal cases; the rule applies to all cases. The statute applies only to government witnesses; the rule applies to all witnesses. The statute contains no requirement that the statement be consulted for purposes of refreshment before or while testifying; the rule so requires. Since many writings would qualify under either statute or rule, a substantial overlap exists, but the identity of procedures makes this of no importance.

The consequences of nonproduction by the government in a criminal case are those of the *Jencks* statute, striking the testimony or in exceptional cases a mistrial. 18 U.S.C. § 3500(d). In other cases these alternatives are unduly limited, and such possibilities as contempt, dismissal, finding issues against the offender, and the like are available. See Rule 16(g) of the Federal Rules of Criminal Procedure and Rule 37(b) of the Federal Rules of Civil Procedure for appropriate sanctions.

Report of House Committee on the Judiciary

House Comm. on Judiciary, Fed.Rules of Evidence, H.R.Rep. No. 650, 93d Cong., 1st Sess., p. 13 (1973); 1974 U.S.Code Cong. & Ad.News 7075, 7086

As submitted to Congress, Rule 612 provided that except as set forth in 18 U.S.C. § 3500, if a witness uses a writing to refresh his memory for the purpose of testifying, "either before or while testifying," an adverse party is entitled to have the writing produced at the hearing, to inspect it, to cross-examine the witness on it, and to introduce in evidence those portions relating to the witness' testimony. The Committee amended the Rule so as still to require the production of writings used by a witness while testifying, but to render the production of writings used by a witness to refresh his memory before testifying discretionary with the court in the interests of justice, as is the case under existing federal law. See Goldman v. United States, 316 U.S. 129 (1942). The Committee considered that permitting an adverse party to require the production of writings used before testifying could result in fishing expeditions among a multitude of papers which a witness may have used in preparing for trial.

The Committee intends that nothing in the Rule be construed as barring the assertion of a privilege with respect to writings used by a witness to refresh his memory.

1987 Amendment

The amendment is technical. No substantive change is intended.

Rule 613. Prior Statements of Witnesses

(a) Examining witness concerning prior statement. In examining a witness concerning a prior statement made by the witness, whether written or not, the statement need not be shown nor its contents disclosed to the witness at that time, but on request the same shall be shown or disclosed to opposing counsel.

(b) Extrinsic evidence of prior inconsistent statement of witness. Extrinsic evidence of a prior inconsistent statement by a witness is not admissible unless the witness is afforded an opportunity to explain or deny the same and the opposite party is afforded an opportunity to interrogate the witness thereon, or the interests of justice otherwise require. This provision does not apply to admissions of a party-opponent as defined in rule 801(d)(2).

(As amended Mar. 2, 1987, eff. Oct. 1, 1987; Apr. 25, 1988, eff. Nov. 1, 1988.)

Section references, McCormick 5th ed.

Generally § 34, § 37, § 39

(a). § 28, § 37, § 39

(b). § 37

Note by Federal Judicial Center

The rule enacted by the Congress is the rule prescribed by the Supreme Court, amended only by substituting "nor" in the place of "or" in subdivision (a).

Advisory Committee's Note

56 F.R.D. 183, 278

Subdivision (a). The Queen's Case, 2 Br. & B. 284, 129 Eng.Rep. 976 (1820), laid down the requirement that a cross-examiner, prior to questioning the witness about his own prior statement in writing, must first show it to the witness. Abolished by statute in the country of its origin, the requirement nevertheless gained currency in the United States. The rule abolishes this useless impediment, to cross-examination. Ladd, Some Observations on Credibility: Impeachment of Witnesses, 52 Cornell L.Q. 239, 246–247 (1967); McCormick § 28; 4 Wigmore §§ 1259–1260. Both oral and written statements are included.

The provision for disclosure to counsel is designed to protect against unwarranted insinuations that a statement has been made when the fact is to the contrary.

The rule does not defeat the application of Rule 1002 relating to production of the original when the contents of a writing are sought to be proved. Nor does it defeat the application of Rule 26(b)(3) of the Rules of Civil Procedure, as revised, entitling a person on request to a copy of his own statement, though the operation of the latter may be suspended temporarily.

Subdivision (b). The familiar foundation requirement that an impeaching statement first be shown to the witness before it can be proved by extrinsic evidence is preserved but with some modifications. See Ladd, Some Observations on Credibility: Impeachment of Witnesses, 52 Cornell L.Q. 239, 247 (1967). The traditional insistence that the attention of the witness be directed to the statement on cross-examination is relaxed in favor of simply providing the witness an opportunity to explain and the opposite party an opportunity to examine on the statement, with no specification of any particular time or sequence. Under this procedure, several collusive witnesses can be examined before disclosure of a joint prior inconsistent statement. See Comment to California Evidence Code § 770. Also, dangers of oversight are reduced. See McCormick § 37, p. 68.

In order to allow for such eventualities as the witness becoming unavailable by the time the statement is discovered, a measure of discretion is conferred upon the judge. Similar provisions are found in California Evidence Code § 770 and New Jersey Evidence Rule 22(b).

Under principles of *expression unius* the rule does not apply to impeachment by evidence of prior inconsistent conduct. The use of inconsistent statements to impeach a hearsay declaration is treated in Rule 806.

1987 Amendment

The amendments are technical. No substantive change is intended.

1988 Amendment

The amendment is technical. No substantive change is intended.

Rule 614. Calling and Interrogation of Witnesses by Court

(a) Calling by court. The court may, on its own motion or at the suggestion of a party, call witnesses, and all parties are entitled to cross-examine witnesses thus called.

(b) Interrogation by court. The court may interrogate witnesses, whether called by itself or by a party.

(c) Objections. Objections to the calling of witnesses by the court or to interrogation by it may be made at the time or at the next available opportunity when the jury is not present.

Section references, McCormick 5th ed.

§ 8

Note by Federal Judicial Center

The rule enacted by the Congress is the rule prescribed by the Supreme Court, amended only by substituting "court" in place of "judge," with conforming pronominal changes.

Advisory Committee's Note

56 F.R.D. 183, 279

Subdivision (a). While exercised more frequently in criminal than in civil cases, the authority of the judge to call witnesses is well established. McCormick § 8, p. 14; Maguire, Weinstein, et al., Cases on Evidence 303–304 (5th ed. 1965); 9 Wigmore § 2484. One reason for the practice, the old rule against impeaching one's own witness, no longer exists by virtue of Rule 607, supra. Other reasons remain, however, to justify the continuation of the practice of calling court's witnesses. The right to cross-examine, with all it implies, is assured. The tendency of juries to associate a witness with the party calling him, regardless of technical aspects of vouching, is avoided. And the judge is not imprisoned within the case as made by the parties.

Subdivision (b). The authority of the judge to question witnesses is also well established. McCormick § 8, pp. 12–13; Maguire, Weinstein, et al., Cases on Evidence 737–739 (5th ed. 1965); 3 Wigmore § 784. The authority is, of course, abused when the judge abandons his proper role and assumes that of advocate, but the manner in which interrogation should be conducted and the proper extent of its exercise are not susceptible of formulation in a rule. The omission in no sense precludes courts of review from continuing to reverse for abuse.

Subdivision (c). The provision relating to objections is designed to relieve counsel of the embarrassment attendant upon objecting to questions by the judge in the presence of the jury, while at the same time assuring that objections are made in apt time to afford the opportunity to take possible corrective measures. Compare the "automatic" objection feature of Rule 605 when the judge is called as a witness.

Rule 615. Exclusion of Witnesses

At the request of a party the court shall order witnesses excluded so that they cannot hear the testimony of other witnesses, and it may make the order of its own motion. This rule does not authorize exclusion of (1) a party who is a natural person, or (2) an officer or employee of a party which is not a natural person designated as its representative by its attorney, or (3) a person whose presence is shown by a party to be essential to the presentation of the party's cause, or (4) a person authorized by statute to be present.

(As amended Mar. 2, 1987, eff. Oct. 1, 1987; Apr. 25, 1988, eff. Nov. 1, 1988; Nov. 18, 1988, Pub.L. 100–690, Title VII, § 7075(a), 102 Stat. 4405; Apr. 24, 1998, eff. Dec. 1, 1998.)

Section references, McCormick 5th ed.

§ 50

Note by Federal Judicial Center

The rule enacted by the Congress is the rule prescribed by the Supreme Court, amended only by substituting "court," in place of "judge," with conforming pronominal changes.

Advisory Committee's Note

56 F.R.D. 183, 280

The efficacy of excluding or sequestering witnesses has long been recognized as a means of discouraging and exposing fabrication, inaccuracy, and collusion. 6 Wigmore §§ 1837–1838. The authority of the judge is admitted, the only question being whether the matter is committed to his discretion or one of right. The rule takes the latter position. No time is specified for making the request.

Several categories of persons are excepted. (1) Exclusion of persons who are parties would raise serious problems of confrontation and due process. Under accepted practice they are not subject to exclusion. 6 Wigmore § 1841. (2) As the equivalent of the right of a natural-person party to be present, a party which is not a natural person is entitled to have a representative present. Most of the cases have involved allowing a police officer who has been in charge of an investigation to remain in court despite the fact that he will be a witness. United States v. Infanzon, 235 F.2d 318 (2d Cir.1956); Portomene v. United States, 221 F.2d 582 (5th Cir.1955); Powell v. United States, 208 F.2d 618 (6th Cir.1953); Jones v. United States, 252 F.Supp. 781 (W.D.Okl.1966). Designation of the representative by the attorney rather than by the client may at first glance appear to be an inversion of the attorney-client relationship, but it may be assumed that the attorney will follow the wishes of the client, and the solution is simple and workable. See California Evidence Code § 777. (3) The category contemplates such persons as an agent who handled the transaction being litigated or an expert needed to advise counsel in the management of the litigation. See 6 Wigmore § 1841, n. 4.

Report of Senate Committee on the Judiciary

Senate Comm. on Judiciary, Fed.Rules of Evidence, S.Rep. No. 1277, 93d Cong., 2d Sess., p. 26 (1974); 1974 U.S.Code Cong. & Ad.News 7051, 7072

Many district courts permit government counsel to have an investigative agent at counsel table throughout the trial although the agent is or may be a witness. The practice is permitted as an exception to the rule of exclusion and compares with the situation defense counsel finds himself in—he always has the client with him to consult during the trial. The investigative agent's presence may be extremely important to government counsel, especially when the case is complex or involves some specialized subject matter. The agent, too, having lived with the case for a long time, may be able to assist in meeting trial surprises where the best-prepared counsel would otherwise have difficulty. Yet, it would not seem the Government could often meet the burden under rule 615 of showing that the agent's presence is essential. Furthermore, it could be dangerous to use the agent as a witness as early in the case as possible, so that he might then help counsel as a nonwitness, since the agent's testimony could be needed in rebuttal. Using another, nonwitness agent from the same investigative agency would not generally meet government counsel's needs.

This problem is solved if it is clear that investigative agents are within the group specified under the second exception made in the rule, for "an officer or employee of a party which is not a natural person designated as its representative by its attorney." It is our understanding that this was the intention of the House committee. It is certainly this committee's construction of the rule.

1987 Amendment

The amendment is technical. No substantive change is intended.

1988 Amendment

The amendment is technical. No substantive change is intended.

1998 Amendment

The amendment is in response to: (1) the Victim's Rights and Restitution Act of 1990, 42 U.S.C. § 10606, which guarantees, within certain limits, the right of a crime victim to attend the trial; and (2) the Victim Rights Clarification Act of 1997 (18 U.S.C. § 3510).

ARTICLE VII. OPINIONS AND EXPERT TESTIMONY

Rule

Rule 701. Opinion Testimony by Lay Witnesses

If the witness is not testifying as an expert, the witness' testimony in the form of opinions or inferences is limited to those opinions or inferences which are (a) rationally based on the perception of the witness, and (b) helpful to a clear understanding of the witness' testimony or the determination of a fact in issue, and (c) not based on scientific, technical, or other specialized knowledge within the scope of Rule 702.

(As amended Mar. 2, 1987, eff. Oct. 1, 1987; Apr. 17, 2000, eff. Dec. 1, 2000.)

Section references, McCormick 5th ed.

§ 11, § 12, § 14, § 35, § 43, § 313

Note by Federal Judicial Center

The rule enacted by the Congress is the rule prescribed by the Supreme Court without change.

Advisory Committee's Note

56 F.R.D. 183, 281

The rule retains the traditional objective of putting the trier of fact in possession of an accurate reproduction of the event.

Limitation (a) is the familiar requirement of first-hand knowledge or observation.

Limitation (b) is phrased in terms of requiring testimony to be helpful in resolving issues. Witnesses often find difficulty in expressing themselves in language which is not that of an opinion or conclusion. While the courts have made concessions in certain recurring situations, necessity as a standard for permitting opinions and conclusions has proved too elusive and too unadaptable to particular situations for purposes of satisfactory judicial administration. McCormick § 11. Moreover, the practical impossibility of determining by rule what is a "fact," demonstrated by a century of litigation of the question of what is a fact for purposes of pleading under the Field Code, extends into evidence also. 7 Wigmore § 1919. The rule assumes that the natural characteristics of the adversary system will generally lead to an acceptable result, since the detailed account carries more conviction than the broad assertion, and a lawyer can be expected to display his witness to the best advantage. If he fails to do so, cross-examination and argument will point up the weakness. See Ladd, Expert

Testimony, 5 Vand.L.Rev. 414, 415–417 (1952). If, despite these considerations, attempts are made to introduce meaningless assertions which amount to little more than choosing up sides, exclusion for lack of helpfulness is called for by the rule.

The language of the rule is substantially that of Uniform Rule 56(1). Similar provisions are California Evidence Code § 800; Kansas Code of Civil Procedure § 60–456(a); New Jersey Evidence Rule 56(1).

1987 Amendment

The amendments are technical. No substantive change is intended.

2000 Amendment

Rule 701 has been amended to eliminate the risk that the reliability requirements set forth in Rule 702 will be evaded through the simple expedient of proffering an expert in lay witness clothing. Under the amendment, a witness' testimony must be scrutinized under the rules regulating expert opinion to the extent that the witness is providing testimony based on scientific, technical, or other specialized knowledge within the scope of Rule 702. *See generally Asplundh Mfg. Div. v. Benton Harbor Eng'g*, 57 F.3d 1190 (3d Cir. 1995). By channeling testimony that is actually expert testimony to Rule 702, the amendment also ensures that a party will not evade the expert witness disclosure requirements set forth in Fed.R.Civ.P. 26 and Fed.R.Crim.P.16 by simply calling an expert witness in the guise of a layperson. *See Joseph. Emerging Expert Issues Under the 1993 Disclosure Amendments to the Federal Rules of Civil Procedure*, 164 F.R.D. 97, 108 (1996) (noting that "there is no good reason to allow what is essentially surprise expert testimony." and that "the Court should be vigilant to preclude manipulative conduct designed to thwart the expert disclosure and discovery process") *See also United States v. Figueroa–Lopez*, 125 F.3d 1241, 1246 (9th Cir. 1997) (law enforcement agents testifying that the defendant's conduct was consistent with that of a drug trafficker could not testify as lay witnesses: to permit such testimony under Rule 701 "subverts the requirements of Federal Rule of Criminal Procedure 16(a)(1)(E)").

The amendment does not distinguish between expert and lay *witnesses*, but rather between expert and lay *testimony*. Certainly it is possible for the same witness to provide both lay and expert testimony in a single case. *See, e.g, United States v. Figueroa–Lopez*, 125 F.3d 1241, 1246 (9th Cir. 1997) (law enforcement agents could testify that the defendant was acting suspiciously, without being qualified as experts; however, the rules on experts were applicable where the agents testified on the basis of extensive experience that the defendant was using code words to refer to drug quantities and prices). The amendment makes clear that any part of a witness' testimony that is based upon scientific, technical, or other specialized knowledge within the scope of Rule 702 is governed by the standards of Rule 702 and the corresponding disclosure requirements of the Civil and Criminal Rules.

The amendment is not intended to affect the "prototypical example[s] of the type of evidence contemplated by the adoption of Rule 701 relat[ing] to the appearance of persons or things, identity, the manner of conduct, competency of a person, degrees of light or darkness, sound, size, weight, distance, and an endless number of items that cannot be described factually in words apart from inferences." *Asplundh Mfg. Div. v. Benton Harbor Eng'g*, 57 F.3d 1190, 1196 (3d Cir. 1995).

For example, most courts have permitted the owner or officer of a business to testify to the value or projected profits of the business. without the necessity of qualifying the witness as an accountant, appraiser, or similar expert. *See, e.g., Lightning Lube, Inc. v. Witco Corp.* 4 F.3d 1153 (3d Cir. 1993) (no abuse of discretion in permitting the plaintiff's owner to give lay opinion testimony as to damages, as it was based on his knowledge and participation in the day-to-day affairs of the business). Such opinion testimony is admitted not because of experience, training or specialized knowledge within the realm of an expert, but because of the particularized knowledge that the witness has by virtue of his or her position in the business. The amendment does not purport to change this analysis. Similarly, courts have permitted lay witnesses to testify that a substance appeared to be a narcotic, so long as a foundation of familiarity with the substance is established. *See, e.g., United States v. Westbrook*, 896 F.2d 330 (8th Cir. 1990) (two lay witnesses who were heavy amphetamine users were properly permitted to testify that a substance was amphetamine; but it was error to permit another witness to make such an identification where she had no experience with amphetamines). Such testimony is not based on specialized knowledge within the scope of Rule 702, but rather is based upon a layperson's personal knowledge. If, however, that witness were to describe how a narcotic was manufactured, or to describe the intricate workings of a narcotic distribution network, then the witness would have to qualify as an expert under Rule 702. *United States v. Figueroa–Lopez, supra.*

The amendment incorporates the distinctions set forth in *State v. Brown*. 836 S.W.2d 530, 549 (1992), a case involving former Tennessee Rule of Evidence 701, a rule that precluded lay witness testimony based on "special knowledge." In *Brown*, the court declared that the distinction between lay and expert witness testimony is that lay testimony "results from a process of reasoning familiar in everyday life," while expert testimony "results from a process of reasoning which can be mastered only by specialists in the field." The court in *Brown* noted that a lay witness with experience could testify that a substance appeared to be blood, but that a witness would have to qualify as an expert before he could testify that bruising around the eyes is indicative of skull trauma. That is the kind of distinction made by the amendment to this Rule.

Rule 702. Testimony by Experts

If scientific, technical, or other specialized knowledge will assist the trier of fact to understand the evidence or to determine a fact in issue, a witness qualified as an expert by knowledge, skill, experience, training, or education, may testify thereto in the form of an opinion or otherwise, if (1) the testimony is based upon sufficient facts or data, (2) the testimony is the product of reliable principles and methods, and (3) the witness has applied the principles and methods reliably to the facts of the case.

(As amended Apr. 17, 2000, eff. Dec. 1, 2000.)

Section references, McCormick 5th ed.

§ 12, § 13, § 14, § 202, § 203

Note by Federal Judicial Center

The rule enacted by the Congress is the rule prescribed by the Supreme Court without change.

Advisory Committee's Note

56 F.R.D. 183, 282

An intelligent evaluation of facts is often difficult or impossible without the application of some scientific, technical, or other specialized knowledge. The most common source of this knowledge is the expert witness, although there are other techniques for supplying it.

Most of the literature assumes that experts testify only in the form of opinions. The assumption is logically unfounded. The rule accordingly recognizes that an expert on the stand may give a dissertation or exposition of scientific or other principles relevant to the case, leaving the trier of fact to apply them to the facts. Since much of the criticism of expert testimony has centered upon the hypothetical question, it seems wise to recognize that opinions are not indispensable and to encourage the use of expert testimony in nonopinion form when counsel believes the trier can itself draw the requisite inference. The use of opinions is not abolished by the rule, however. It will continue to be permissible for the expert to take the further step of suggesting the inference which should be drawn from applying the specialized knowledge to the facts. See Rules 703 to 705.

Whether the situation is a proper one for the use of expert testimony is to be determined on the basis of assisting the trier. "There is no more certain test for determining when experts may be used than the common sense inquiry whether the untrained layman would be qualified to determine intelligently and to the best possible degree the particular issue without enlightenment from those having a specialized understanding of the subject involved in the dispute." Ladd, Expert Testimony, 5 Vand.L.Rev. 414, 418 (1952). When opinions are excluded, it is because they are unhelpful and therefore superfluous and a waste of time. 7 Wigmore § 1918.

The rule is broadly phrased. The fields of knowledge which may be drawn upon are not limited merely to the "scientific" and "technical" but extend to all "specialized" knowledge. Similarly, the expert is viewed, not in a narrow sense, but as a person qualified by "knowledge, skill, experience, training, or education." Thus within the scope of the rule are not only experts in the strictest sense of the word, e.g. physicians, physicists, and architects, but also the large group sometimes called "skilled" witnesses, such as bankers or landowners testifying to land values.

2000 Amendment

Rule 702 has been amended in response to *Daubert v. Merrell Dow Pharmaceuticals, Inc.*, 509 U.S. 579 (1993), and to the many cases applying *Daubert*, including *Kumho Tire Co. v. Carmichael*, 119 S.Ct. 1167 (1999). In *Daubert* the Court charged trial judges with the responsibility of acting as gatekeepers to exclude unreliable expert testimony, and the Court in *Kumho* clarified that this gatekeeper function applies to all expert testimony, not just testimony based in science. *See also Kumho*, 119 S.Ct. at 1178 (citing the Committee Note to the proposed amendment to Rule 702, which had been released for public comment before the date of the *Kumho* decision). The amendment affirms the trial court's role as gatekeeper and provides some general standards that the trial court must use to assess the reliability and helpfulness of proffered expert testimony. Consistently with *Kumho*, the Rule as amended provides that all types of expert testimony present questions of admissibility for the trial court in deciding whether the evidence is reliable and helpful. Consequently, the admissibility of all expert testimony is governed by the principles of Rule 104(a). Under that Rule, the proponent has the burden of establishing that the pertinent admissibility requirements are met by a preponderance of the evidence. *See Bourjaily v. United States*, 483 U.S. 171 (1987).

Daubert set forth a non-exclusive checklist for trial courts to use in assessing the reliability of scientific expert testimony. The specific factors explicated by the *Daubert* Court are (1) whether the expert's technique or theory can be or has been tested—that is, whether the expert's theory can be challenged in some objective sense, or whether it is instead simply a subjective, conclusory approach that cannot reasonably be assessed for reliability; (2) whether the technique or theory has been subject to peer review and publication; (3) the known or potential rate of error of the technique or theory when applied; (4) the existence and maintenance of standards and controls; and (5) whether the technique or theory has been generally accepted in the scientific community. The Court in Kumho held that these factors might also be applicable in assessing the reliability of non-scientific expert testimony, depending upon "the particular circumstances of the particular case at issue." 119 S.Ct. at 1175.

No attempt has been made to "codify" these specific factors. *Daubert* itself emphasized that the factors were neither exclusive nor dispositive. Other cases have recognized that not all of the specific *Daubert* factors can apply to every type of expert testimony. In addition to *Kumho*, 119 S.Ct. at 1175, *see Tyus v. Urban Search Management*. 102 F.3d 256 (7th Cir. 1996) (noting that the factors mentioned by the Court in *Daubert* do not neatly apply to expert testimony from a sociologist). *See also Kannankeril v. Terminix Int'l. Inc.*, 128 F.3d 802, 809 (3d Cir. 1997) (holding that lack of peer review or publication was not dispositive where the expert's opinion was supported by "widely accepted scientific knowledge"). The standards set forth in the amendment are broad enough to require consideration of any or all of the specific *Daubert* factors where appropriate.

Courts both before and after *Daubert* have found other factors relevant in determining whether expert testimony is sufficiently reliable to be considered by the trier of fact. These factors include:

(1) Whether experts are "proposing to testify about matters growing naturally and directly out of research they have conducted independent of the litigation, or whether they have developed their opinions expressly for purposes of testifying." *Daubert v. Merrell Dow Pharmaceuticals, Inc.*, 43 F.3d 1311. 1317 (9th Cir. 1995).

(2) Whether the expert has unjustifiably extrapolated from an accepted premise to an unfounded conclusion. *See General Elec. Co. v. Joiner*, 522 U.S. 136, 146 (1997) (noting that in some cases a trial court "may conclude that there is simply too great an analytical gap between the data and the opinion proffered").

(3) Whether the expert has adequately accounted for obvious alternative explanations. *See Claar v. Burlington N.R.R.*, 29 F.3d 499 (9th Cir. 1994)

(testimony excluded where the expert failed to consider other obvious causes for the plaintiff's condition). *Compare Ambrosini v. Labarraque*, 101 F.3d 129 (D.C. Cir. 1996) (the possibility of some uneliminated causes presents a question of weight, so long as the most obvious causes have been considered and reasonably ruled out by the expert).

(4) Whether the expert "is being as careful as he would be in his regular professional work outside his paid litigation consulting." *Sheehan v. Daily Racing Form, Inc.*, 104 F.3d 940, 942 (7th Cir. 1997). *See Kumho Tire Co. v. Carmichael*, 119 S.Ct. 1167, 1176 (1999) (*Daubert* requires the trial court to assure itself that the expert "employs in the courtroom the same level of intellectual rigor that characterizes the practice of an expert in the relevant field").

(5) Whether the field of expertise claimed by the expert is known to reach reliable results for the type of opinion the expert would give. *See Kumho Tire Co. v. Carmichael*, 119 S.Ct.1167, 1175 (1999) (*Daubert's* general acceptance factor does not "help show that an expert's testimony is reliable where the discipline itself lacks reliability, as for example, do theories grounded in any so-called generally accepted principles of astrology or necromancy."), *Moore v. Ashland Chemical, Inc.*, 151 F.3d 269 (5th Cir. 1998) (en banc) (clinical doctor was properly precluded from testifying to the toxicological cause of the plaintiff's respiratory problem, where the opinion was not sufficiently grounded in scientific methodology); *Sterling v. Velsicol Chem. Corp.*, 855 F.2d 1188 (6th Cir. 1988) (rejecting testimony based on "clinical ecology" as unfounded and unreliable).

All of these factors remain relevant to the determination of the reliability of expert testimony under the Rule as amended. Other factors may also be relevant. *See Kumho*, 119 S.Ct. 1167, 1176 ("[W]e conclude that the trial judge must have considerable leeway in deciding in a particular case how to go about determining whether particular expert testimony is reliable."). Yet no single factor is necessarily dispositive of the reliability of a particular expert's testimony. *See, e.g., Heller v. Shaw Industries, Inc.*, 167 F.3d 146, 155 (3d Cir. 1999) ("not only must each stage of the expert's testimony be reliable, but each stage must be evaluated practically and flexibly without bright-line exclusionary (or inclusionary) rules."); *Daubert v. Merrell Dow Pharmaceuticals, Inc.*, 43 F.3d 1311, 1317, n.5 (9th Cir. 1995) (noting that some expert disciplines "have the courtroom as a principal theatre of operations" and as to these disciplines "the fact that the expert has developed an expertise principally for purposes of litigation will obviously not be a substantial consideration.").

A review of the caselaw after *Daubert* shows that the rejection of expert testimony is the exception rather than the rule. *Daubert* did not work a "seachange over federal evidence law," and "the trial court's role as gatekeeper is not intended to serve as a replacement for the adversary system." *United States v. 14.38 Acres of Land Situated in Leflore County, Mississippi*, 80 F.3d 1074, 1078 (5th Cir. 1996). As the Court in *Daubert* stated: "Vigorous cross-examination, presentation of contrary evidence, and careful instruction on the burden of proof are the traditional and appropriate means of attacking shaky but admissible evidence." 509 U.S. at 595. Likewise, this amendment is not intended to provide an excuse for an automatic challenge to the testimony of every expert. *See Kumho Tire Co. v. Carmichael*, 119 S.Ct.1167, 1176 (1999) (noting that the trial judge has the discretion "both to avoid unnecessary 'reliability' proceedings in ordinary cases where the reliability of an expert's methods is properly taken for granted, and to require appropriate proceedings in the less usual or more complex cases where cause for questioning the expert's reliability arises.'').

When a trial court, applying this amendment, rules that an expert's testimony is reliable, this does not necessarily mean that contradictory expert testimony is unreliable. The amendment is broad enough to permit testimony that is the product of competing principles or methods in the same field of expertise. *See, e.g., Heller v. Shaw Industries, Inc.*, 167 F.3d 146, 160 (3d Cir. 1999) (expert testimony cannot be excluded simply because the expert uses one test rather than another, when both tests are accepted in the field and both reach reliable results). As the court stated in *In re Paoli R.R. Yard PCB Litigation*, 35 F.3d 717, 744 (3d Cir. 1994), proponents "do not have to demonstrate to the judge by a preponderance of the evidence that the assessments of their experts are correct, they only have to demonstrate by a preponderance of evidence that their opinions are reliable.... The evidentiary requirement of reliability is lower than the merits standard of correctness." *See also Daubert v. Merrell Dow Pharmaceuticals, Inc.*, 43 F.3d 1311, 1318 (9th Cir. 1995) (scientific experts might be permitted to testify if they could show that the methods they used were also employed by "a recognized minority of scientists in their field."); *Ruiz-Troche v. Pepsi Cola*, 161 F.3d 77, 85 (1st Cir. 1998) ("*Daubert* neither requires nor empowers trial courts to determine which of several competing scientific theories has the best provenance.").

The Court in *Daubert* declared that the "focus, of course, must be solely on principles and methodology, not on the conclusions they generate." 509 U.S. at 595. Yet as the Court later recognized, "conclusions and methodology are not entirely distinct from one another." *General Elec. Co. v. Joiner*, 522 U.S. 136, 146 (1997). Under the amendment, as under *Daubert*, when an expert purports to apply principles and methods in accordance with professional standards, and yet reaches a conclusion that other experts in the field would not reach, the trial court may fairly suspect that the principles and methods have not been faithfully applied. *See Lust v. Merrell Dow Pharmaceuticals, Inc.*, 89 F.3d 594, 598 (9th Cir. 1996). The amendment specifically provides that the trial court must scrutinize not only the principles and methods used by the expert, but also whether those principles and methods have been properly applied to the facts of the case. As the court noted in *In re Paoli R.R. Yard PCB Litig.*, 35 F.3d 717, 745 (3d Cir. 1994), "*any* step that renders the analysis unreliable ... renders the expert's testimony inadmissible. *This is true whether the step completely changes a reliable methodology or merely misapplies that methodology.*"

If the expert purports to apply principles and methods to the facts of the case, it is important that this application be conducted reliably. Yet it might also be important in some cases for an expert to educate the factfinder about general principles, without ever attempting to apply these principles to the specific facts of the case. For example, experts might instruct the factfinder on the principles of thermodynamics, or bloodclotting, or on how financial markets respond to corporate reports, without ever knowing about or trying to tie their testimony into the facts of the case. The amendment does not alter the venerable practice of using expert testimony to educate the factfinder on general principles. For this kind of generalized testimony, Rule 702 simply requires that: (1) the expert be qualified; (2) the testimony address a subject matter on which the factfinder can be assisted by an expert; (3) the testimony be reliable; and (4) the testimony "fit" the facts of the case.

As stated earlier, the amendment does not distinguish between scientific and other forms of expert testimony. The trial court's gatekeeping function applies to testimony by any expert. *See Kumho Tire Co. v. Carmichael*, 119 S.Ct. 1167, 1171 (1999) ("We conclude that *Daubert's* general holding—setting forth the trial judge's general 'gatekeeping' obligation—applies not only to testimony based on 'scientific' knowledge, but also to testimony based on 'technical' and 'other specialized' knowledge."). While the relevant factors for determining reliability will vary from expertise to expertise, the amendment rejects the premise that an expert's testimony should be treated more permissively simply because it is outside the realm of science. An opinion from an expert who is not a scientist should receive the same degree of scrutiny for reliability as an opinion from an expert who purports to be a scientist. *See Watkins v. Telsmith, Inc.*, 121 F.3d 984, 991 (5th Cir. 1997) ("[I]t seems exactly backwards that experts who purport to rely on general engineering principles and practical experience might escape screening by the district court simply by stating that their conclusions were not reached by any particular method or technique."). Some types of expert testimony will be more objectively verifiable, and subject to the expectations of falsifiability, peer review, and publication, than others. Some types of expert testimony will not rely on anything like a scientific method, and so will have to be evaluated by reference to other standard principles attendant to the particular area of expertise. The trial judge in all cases of proffered expert testimony must find that it is properly grounded, well-reasoned, and not speculative before it can be admitted. The expert's testimony must be grounded in an accepted body of learning or experience in the expert's field, and the expert must explain how the conclusion is so grounded. *See, e.g.*, American College of Trial Lawyers, *Standards and Procedures for Determining the Admissibility of Expert Testimony after Daubert*, 157 F.R.D. 571, 579 (1994) ("[W]hether the testimony concerns economic principles, accounting standards, property valuation or other non-scientific subjects, it should be evaluated by reference to the 'knowledge and experience' of that particular field.").

The amendment requires that the testimony must be the product of reliable principles and methods that are reliably applied to the facts of the case. While the terms "principles" and "methods" may convey a certain impression when applied to scientific knowledge, they remain relevant when applied to testimony based on technical or other specialized knowledge. For example, when a law enforcement agent testifies regarding the use of code words in a drug transaction, the principle used by the agent is that participants in such transactions regularly use code words to conceal the nature of their activities. The method used by the agent is the application of extensive experience to analyze the meaning of the conversations. So long as the principles and methods are reliable and applied reliably to the facts of the case, this type of testimony should be admitted.

Nothing in this amendment is intended to suggest that experience alone—or experience in conjunction with other knowledge, skill, training or education—may not provide a sufficient foundation for expert testimony. To the contrary, the text of Rule 702 expressly contemplates that an expert may be qualified on the basis of experience. In certain fields, experience is the predominant, if not sole, basis for a great deal of reliable expert testimony. *See, e.g., United States v.*

Jones, 107 F.3d 1147 (6th Cir. 1997) (no abuse of discretion in admitting the testimony of a handwriting examiner who had years of practical experience and extensive training, and who explained his methodology in detail); *Tassin v. Sears Roebuck*, 946 F.Supp. 1241, 1248 (M.D.La. 1996) (design engineer's testimony can be admissible when the expert's opinions "are based on facts, a reasonable investigation, and traditional technical/mechanical expertise, and he provides a reasonable link between the information and procedures he uses and the conclusions he reaches"). *See also Kumho Tire Co. v. Carmichael*, 119 S.Ct. 1167, 1178 (1999) (stating that "no one denies that an expert might draw a conclusion from a set of observations based on extensive and specialized experience.").

If the witness is relying solely or primarily on experience, then the witness must explain how that experience leads to the conclusion reached, why that experience is a sufficient basis for the opinion, and how that experience is reliably applied to the facts. The trial court's gatekeeping function requires more than simply "taking the expert's word for it." *See Daubert v. Merrell Dow Pharmaceuticals, Inc.*, 43 F.3d 1311, 1319 (9th Cir. 1995) ("We've been presented with only the experts' qualifications, their conclusions and their assurances of reliability. Under *Daubert*, that's not enough."). The more subjective and controversial the expert's inquiry, the more likely the testimony should be excluded as unreliable. *See O'Conner v. Commonwealth Edison Co.*, 13 F.3d 1090 (7th Cir. 1994) (expert testimony based on a completely subjective methodology held properly excluded). *See also Kumho Tire Co. v. Carmichael*, 119 S.Ct. 1167, 1176 (1999) ("[I]t will at times be useful to ask even of a witness whose expertise is based purely on experience, say, a perfume tester able to distinguish among 140 odors at a sniff, whether his preparation is of a kind that others in the field would recognize as acceptable.").

Subpart (1) of Rule 702 calls for a quantitative rather than qualitative analysis. The amendment requires that expert testimony be based on sufficient underlying "facts or data." The term "data" is intended to encompass the reliable opinions of other experts. See the original Advisory Committee Note to Rule 703. The language "facts or data" is broad enough to allow an expert to rely on hypothetical facts that are supported by the evidence. *Id.*

When facts are in dispute, experts sometimes reach different conclusions based on competing versions of the facts. The emphasis in the amendment on "sufficient facts or data" is not intended to authorize a trial court to exclude an expert's testimony on the ground that the court believes one version of the facts and not the other.

There has been some confusion over the relationship between Rules 702 and 703. The amendment makes clear that the sufficiency of the basis of an expert's testimony is to be decided under Rule 702. Rule 702 sets forth the overarching requirement of reliability, and an analysis of the sufficiency of the expert's basis cannot be divorced from the ultimate reliability of the expert's opinion. In contrast, the "reasonable reliance" requirement of Rule 703 is a relatively narrow inquiry. When an expert relies on inadmissible information, Rule 703 requires the trial court to determine whether that information is of a type reasonably relied on by other experts in the field. If so, the expert can rely on the information in reaching an opinion. However, the question whether the expert is relying on a *sufficient* basis of information—whether admissible information or not—is governed by the requirements of Rule 702.

The amendment makes no attempt to set forth procedural requirements for exercising the trial court's gatekeeping function over expert testimony. *See* Daniel J. Capra, *The Daubert Puzzle*, 38 Ga.L.Rev. 699, 766 (1998) ("Trial courts should be allowed substantial discretion in dealing with *Daubert* questions; any attempt to codify procedures will likely give rise to unnecessary changes in practice and create difficult questions for appellate review."). Courts have shown considerable ingenuity and flexibility in considering challenges to expert testimony under *Daubert*, and it is contemplated that this will continue under the amended Rule. *See, e.g., Cortes-Irizarry v. Corporacion Insular*, 111 F.3d 184 (1st Cir. 1997) (discussing the application of *Daubert* in ruling on a motion for summary judgment); *In re Paoli R.R. Yard PCB Litig.*, 35 F.3d 717, 736, 739 (3d Cir. 1994) (discussing the use of *in limine* hearings); *Claar v. Burlington N.R.R.*, 29 F.3d 499, 502–05 (9th Cir. 1994) (discussing the trial court's technique of ordering experts to submit serial affidavits explaining the reasoning and methods underlying their conclusions).

The amendment continues the practice of the original Rule in referring to a qualified witness as an "expert." This was done to provide continuity and to minimize change. The use of the term "expert" in the Rule does not, however, mean that a jury should actually be informed that a qualified witness is testifying as an "expert." Indeed, there is much to be said for a practice that prohibits the use of the term "expert" by both the parties and the court at trial. Such a practice "ensures that trial courts do not inadvertently put their stamp of authority" on a witness's opinion, and protects against the jury's being "overwhelmed by the so-called 'experts'." Hon. Charles Richey, *Proposals to Eliminate the Prejudicial Effect of the Use of the Word "Expert" Under the Federal Rules of Evidence in Criminal and Civil Jury Trials*, 154 F.R.D. 537, 559 (1994) (setting forth limiting instructions and a standing order employed to prohibit the use of the term "expert" injury trials).

Rule 703. Bases of Opinion Testimony by Experts

The facts or data in the particular case upon which an expert bases an opinion or inference may be those perceived by or made known to the expert at or before the hearing. If of a type reasonably relied upon by experts in the particular field in forming opinions or inferences upon the subject, the facts or data need not be admissible in evidence in order for the opinion or inference to be admitted. Facts or data that are otherwise inadmissible shall not be disclosed to the jury by the proponent of the opinion or inference unless the court determines that their probative value in assisting the jury to evaluate the expert's opinion substantially outweighs their prejudicial effect.

(As amended Mar. 2, 1987, eff. Oct. 1, 1987; Apr. 17, 2000, eff. Dec. 1, 2000.)

Section references, McCormick 5th ed.

§ 10, § 13, § 14, § 15, § 203, § 208, § 324.3

Note by Federal Judicial Center

The rule enacted by the Congress is the rule prescribed by the Supreme Court without change.

Advisory Committee's Note

56 F.R.D. 183, 283

Facts or data upon which expert opinions are based may, under the rule, be derived from three possible sources. The first is the firsthand observation of the witness, with opinions based thereon traditionally allowed. A treating physician affords an example. Rheingold, The Basis of Medical Testimony, 15 Vand.L.Rev. 473, 489 (1962). Whether he must first relate his observations is treated in Rule 705. The second source, presentation at the trial, also reflects existing practice. The technique may be the familiar hypothetical question or having the expert attend the trial and hear the testimony establishing the facts. Problems of determining what testimony the expert relied upon, when the latter technique is employed and the testimony is in conflict, may be resolved by resort to Rule 705. The third source contemplated by the rule consists of presentation of data to the expert outside of court and other than by his own perception. In this respect the rule is designed to broaden the basis for expert opinions beyond that current in many jurisdictions and to bring the judicial practice into line with the practice of the experts themselves when not in court. Thus a physician in his own practice bases his diagnosis on information from numerous sources and of considerable variety, including statements by patients and relatives, reports and opinions from nurses, technicians and other doctors, hospital records, and X rays. Most of them are admissible in evidence, but only with the expenditure of substantial time in producing and examining various authenticating witnesses. The physician makes life-and-death decisions in reliance upon them. His validation, expertly performed and subject to cross-examination, ought to suffice for judicial purposes. Rheingold, supra, at 531; McCormick § 15. A similar provision is California Evidence Code § 801(b).

The rule also offers a more satisfactory basis for ruling upon the admissibility of public opinion poll evidence. Attention is directed to the validity of the techniques employed rather than to relatively fruitless inquiries whether hearsay is involved. See Judge Feinberg's careful analysis in Zippo Mfg. Co. v. Rogers Imports, Inc., 216 F.Supp. 670 (S.D.N.Y.1963). See also Blum et al., The Art of Opinion Research: A Lawyer's Appraisal of an Emerging Service, 24 U.Chi. L.Rev. 1 (1956); Bonynge, Trademark Surveys and Techniques and Their Use in Litigation, 48 A.B.A.J. 329 (1962); Zeisel, The Uniqueness of Survey Evidence, 45 Cornell L.Q. 322 (1960); Annot., 76 A.L.R.2d 919.

If it be feared that enlargement of permissible data may tend to break down the rules of exclusion unduly, notice should be taken that the rule requires that the facts or data "be of a type reasonably relied upon by experts in the particular field." The language would not warrant admitting in evidence the opinion of an "accidentologist" as to the point of impact in an automobile collision based on statements of bystanders, since this requirement is not satisfied. See Comment, Cal.Law Rev.Comm'n, Recommendation Proposing an Evidence Code 148–150 (1965).

1987 Amendment

The amendment is technical. No substantive change is intended.

2000 Amendment

Rule 703 has been amended to emphasize that when an expert reasonably relies on inadmissible information to form an opinion or inference, the underlying information is not admissible simply because the opinion or inference is admitted. Courts have reached different results on how to treat inadmissible information when it is reasonably relied upon by an expert in forming an opinion or drawing an inference. *Compare United States v. Rollins*, 862 F.2d 1282 (7th Cir. 1988) (admitting, as part of the basis of an FBI agent's expert opinion on the meaning of code language, the hearsay statements of an informant), *with United States v. 0.59 Acres of Land*. 109 F.3d 1493 (9th Cir. 1997) (error to admit hearsay offered as the basis of an expert opinion, without a limiting instruction). Commentators have also taken differing views. *See e.g.*, Ronald Carlson, *Policing the Bases of Modern Expert Testimony*, 39 Vand.L.Rev. 577 (1986) (advocating limits on the jury's consideration of otherwise inadmissible evidence used as the basis for an expert opinion); Paul Rice, *Inadmissible Evidence as a Basis for Expert Testimony: A Response to Professor Carlson*, 40 Vand.L.Rev. 583 (1987) (advocating unrestricted use of information reasonably relied upon by an expert).

When information is reasonably relied upon by an expert and yet is admissible only for the purpose of assisting the jury in evaluating an expert's opinion, a trial court applying this Rule must consider the information's probative value in assisting the jury to weigh the expert's opinion on the one hand, and the risk of prejudice resulting from the jury's potential misuse of the information for substantive purposes on the other. The information may be disclosed to the jury, upon objection, only if the trial court finds that the probative value of the information in assisting the jury to evaluate the expert's opinion substantially outweighs its prejudicial effect. If the otherwise inadmissible information is admitted under this balancing test, the trial judge must give a limiting instruction upon request, informing the jury that the underlying information must not be used for substantive purposes. *See* Rule 105. In determining the appropriate course, the trial court should consider the probable effectiveness or lack of effectiveness of a limiting instruction under the particular circumstances.

The amendment governs only the disclosure to the jury of information that is reasonably relied on by an expert, when that information is not admissible for substantive purposes. It is not intended to affect the admissibility of an expert's testimony. Nor does the amendment prevent an expert from relying on information that is inadmissible for substantive purposes.

Nothing in this Rule restricts the presentation of underlying expert facts or data when offered by an adverse party. *See* Rule 705. Of course, an adversary's attack on an expert's basis will often open the door to a proponent's rebuttal with information that was reasonably relied upon by the expert, even if that information would not have been discloseable initially under the balancing test provided by this amendment. Moreover, in some circumstances the proponent might wish to disclose information that is relied upon by the expert in order to "remove the sting" from the opponent's anticipated attack, and thereby prevent the jury from drawing an unfair negative inference. The trial court should take this consideration into account in applying the balancing test provided by this amendment.

This amendment covers facts or data that cannot be admitted for any purpose other than to assist the jury to evaluate the expert's opinion. The balancing test provided in this amendment is not applicable to facts or data that are admissible for any other purpose but have not yet been offered for such a purpose at the time the expert testifies.

The amendment provides a presumption against disclosure to the jury of information used as the basis of an expert's opinion and not admissible for any substantive purpose, when that information is offered by the proponent of the expert. In a multi-party case, where one party proffers an expert whose testimony is also beneficial to other parties, each such party should be deemed a "proponent" within the meaning of the amendment.

Rule 704. Opinion on Ultimate Issue

(a) Except as provided in subdivision (b), testimony in the form of an opinion or inference otherwise admissible is not objectionable because it embraces an ultimate issue to be decided by the trier of fact.

(b) No expert witness testifying with respect to the mental state or condition of a defendant in a criminal case may state an opinion or inference as to whether the defendant did or did not have the mental state or condition constituting an element of the crime charged or of a defense thereto. Such ultimate issues are matters for the trier of fact alone.

(As amended Pub.L. 98–473, Title II, § 406, Oct. 12, 1984, 98 Stat. 2067.)

Section references, McCormick 5th ed.

§ 12, § 14, § 206, § 313

Editorial Note

Subdivision (a) is the entire rule prescribed by the Supreme Court and enacted without change by the Congress when it enacted the Rules of Evidence in 1974, except for the addition of the matter preceding the comma, which was added by the Congress in 1984.

Subdivision (b) was added by the Congress in 1984 as a part of the Insanity Defense Reform Act of 1984. P.L. 98–473, Title II, ch. IV, § 406.

Advisory Committee's Note

56 F.R.D. 183, 284

Subdivision (a).

The basic approach to opinions, lay and expert, in these rules is to admit them when helpful to the trier of fact. In order to render this approach fully effective and to allay any doubt on the subject, the so-called "ultimate issue" rule is specifically abolished by the instant rule.

The older cases often contained strictures against allowing witnesses to express opinions upon ultimate issues, as a particular aspect of the rule against opinions. The rule was unduly restrictive, difficult of application, and generally served only to deprive the trier of fact of useful information. 7 Wigmore §§ 1920, 1921; McCormick § 12. The basis usually assigned for the rule, to prevent the witness from "usurping the province of the jury," is aptly characterized as "empty rhetoric." 7 Wigmore § 1920, p. 17. Efforts to meet the felt needs of particular situations led to odd verbal circumlocutions which were said not to violate the rule. Thus a witness could express his estimate of the criminal responsibility of an accused in terms of sanity or insanity, but not in terms of ability to tell right from wrong or other more modern standard. And in cases of medical causation, witnesses were sometimes required to couch their opinions in cautious phrases of "might or could," rather than "did," though the result was to deprive many opinions of the positiveness to which they were entitled, accompanied by the hazard of a ruling of insufficiency to support a verdict. In other instances the rule was simply disregarded, and, as concessions to need, opinions were allowed upon such matters as intoxication, speed, handwriting, and value, although more precise coincidence with an ultimate issue would scarcely be possible.

Many modern decisions illustrate the trend to abandon the rule completely. People v. Wilson, 25 Cal.2d 341, 153 P.2d 720 (1944), whether abortion necessary to save life of patient; Clifford-Jacobs Forging Co. v. Industrial Comm., 19 Ill.2d 236, 166 N.E.2d 582 (1960), medical causation; Dowling v. L.H. Shattuck, Inc., 91 N.H. 234, 17 A.2d 529 (1941), proper method of shoring ditch; Schweiger v. Solbeck, 191 Or. 454, 230 P.2d 195 (1951), cause of landslide. In each instance the opinion was allowed.

The abolition of the ultimate issue rule does not lower the bars so as to admit all opinions. Under Rules 701 and 702, opinions must be helpful to the trier of fact, and Rule 403 provides for exclusion of evidence which wastes time. These provisions afford ample assurances against the admission of opinions which would merely tell the jury what result to reach, somewhat in the manner of the oath-helpers of an earlier day. They also stand ready to exclude opinions phrased in terms of inadequately explored legal criteria. Thus the question, "Did T have capacity to make a will?" would be excluded, while the question, "Did T have sufficient mental capacity to know the nature and extent of his property and the natural objects of his bounty and to formulate a rational scheme of distribution?" would be allowed. McCormick § 12.

For similar provisions see Uniform Rule 56(4); California Evidence Code § 805; Kansas Code of Civil Procedure § 60–456(d); New Jersey Evidence Rule 56(3).

Report of House Committee on the Judiciary

H.R. Report 98–1030, 98th Cong., 2d Sess., p. 230; 1984 U.S.Code Cong. & Ad.News 232 (Legislative History)

Subdivision (b).

The purpose of this amendment is to eliminate the confusing spectacle of competing expert witnesses testifying to directly contradictory conclusions as to the ultimate legal issue to be found by the trier of fact. Under this proposal, expert psychiatric testimony would be limited to presenting and explaining their diagnosis, such as whether the defendant had a severe mental disease or defect and what the characteristics of such a disease or defect, if any, may have been. ***

Rule 705. Disclosure of Facts or Data Underlying Expert Opinion

The expert may testify in terms of opinion or inference and give reasons therefor without first testifying to the underlying facts or data, unless the court requires otherwise. The expert may in any event be required to disclose the underlying facts or data on cross-examination.

(As amended Mar. 2, 1987, eff. Oct. 1, 1987; Apr. 22, 1993, eff. Dec. 1, 1993.)

Section references, McCormick 5th ed.

§ 13, § 14, § 15, § 16, § 31, § 324.3

Note by Federal Judicial Center

The rule enacted by the Congress is the rule prescribed by the Supreme Court, amended only by substituting "court" in place of "judge."

Advisory Committee's Note

56 F.R.D. 183, 285

The hypothetical question has been the target of a great deal of criticism as encouraging partisan bias, affording an opportunity for summing up in the middle of the case, and as complex and time consuming. Ladd, Expert Testimony, 5 Vand.L.Rev. 414, 426–427 (1952). While the rule allows counsel to make disclosure of the underlying facts or data as a preliminary to the giving of an expert opinion, if he chooses, the instances in which he is required to do so are reduced. This is true whether the expert bases his opinion on data furnished him at secondhand or observed by him at firsthand.

The elimination of the requirement of preliminary disclosure at the trial of underlying facts or data has a long background of support. In 1937 the Commissioners on Uniform State Laws incorporated a provision to this effect in their Model Expert Testimony Act, which furnished the basis for Uniform Rules 57 and 58. Rule 4515, N.Y.CPLR (McKinney 1963), provides:

> "Unless the court orders otherwise, questions calling for the opinion of an expert witness need not be hypothetical in form, and the witness may state his opinion and reasons without first specifying the data upon which it is based. Upon cross-examination, he may be required to specify the data . . . ."

See also California Evidence Code § 802; Kansas Code of Civil Procedure §§ 60–456, 60–457; New Jersey Evidence Rules 57, 58.

If the objection is made that leaving it to the cross-examiner to bring out the supporting data is essentially unfair, the answer is that he is under no compulsion to bring out any facts or data except those unfavorable to the opinion. The answer assumes that the cross-examiner has the advance knowledge which is essential for effective cross-examination. This advance knowledge has been afforded, though imperfectly, by the traditional foundation requirement. Rule 26(b)(4) of the Rules of Civil Procedure, as revised, provides for substantial discovery in this area, obviating in large measure the obstacles which have been raised in some instances to discovery of findings, underlying data, and even the identity of the experts. Friedenthal, Discovery and Use of an Adverse Party's Expert Information, 14 Stan.L.Rev. 455 (1962).

These safeguards are reinforced by the discretionary power of the judge to require preliminary disclosure in any event.

1987 Amendment

The amendment is technical. No substantive change is intended.

1993 Amendment

This rule, which relates to the manner of presenting testimony at trial, is revised to avoid an arguable conflict with revised Rules 26(a)(2)(B) and 26(e)(1) of the Federal Rules of Civil Procedure or with revised Rule 16 of the Federal Rules of Criminal Procedure, which require disclosure in advance of trial of the basis and reasons for an expert's opinions.

If a serious question is raised under Rule 702 or 703 as to the admissibility of expert testimony, disclosure of the underlying facts or data on which opinions are based may, of course, be needed by the court before deciding whether, and to what extent, the person should be allowed to testify. This rule does not preclude such an inquiry.

Rule 706. Court Appointed Experts

(a) Appointment. The court may on its own motion or on the motion of any party enter an order to show cause why expert witnesses should not be appointed, and may request the parties to submit nominations. The court may appoint any expert witnesses agreed upon by the parties, and may appoint expert witnesses of its own selection. An expert witness shall not be appointed by the court unless the witness consents to act. A witness so appointed shall be informed of the witness' duties by the court in writing, a copy of which shall be filed with the clerk, or at a conference in which the parties shall have opportunity to participate. A witness so appointed shall advise the parties of the witness' findings, if any; the witness' deposition may be taken by any party; and the witness may be called to testify by the court or any party. The witness shall be subject to cross-examination by each party, including a party calling the witness.

(b) Compensation. Expert witnesses so appointed are entitled to reasonable compensation in whatever sum the court may allow. The compensation thus fixed is payable from funds which may be provided by law in criminal cases and civil actions and proceedings involving just compensation under the fifth amendment. In other civil actions and proceedings the compensation shall be paid by the parties in such proportion and at such time as the court directs, and thereafter charged in like manner as other costs.

(c) Disclosure of appointment. In the exercise of its discretion, the court may authorize disclosure to the jury of the fact that the court appointed the expert witness.

(d) Parties' experts of own selection. Nothing in this rule limits the parties in calling expert witnesses of their own selection.

(As amended Mar. 2, 1987, eff. Oct. 1, 1987.)

Section references, McCormick 5th ed.

§ 8, § 17

Note by Federal Judicial Center

The rule enacted by the Congress is the rule prescribed by the Supreme Court, amended by substituting "court" in place of "judge," with conforming pronominal changes, and, in subdivision (b), by substituting the phrase "and civil actions and proceedings" in place of "and cases" before "involving" in the second sentence.

Advisory Committee's Note

56 F.R.D. 183, 286

The practice of shopping for experts, the venality of some experts, and the reluctance of many reputable experts to involve themselves in litigation, have been matters of deep concern. Though the contention is made that court appointed experts acquire an aura of infallibility to which they are not entitled, Levy, Impartial Medical Testimony—Revisited, 34 Temple L.Q. 416 (1961), the trend is increasingly to provide for their use. While experience indicates that actual appointment is a relatively infrequent occurrence, the assumption may be made that the availability of the procedure in itself decreases the need for resorting to it. The ever-present possibility that the judge *may* appoint an expert in a given case must inevitably exert a sobering effect on the expert witness of a party and upon the person utilizing his services.

The inherent power of a trial judge to appoint an expert of his own choosing is virtually unquestioned. Scott v. Spanjer Bros., Inc., 298 F.2d 928 (2d Cir. 1962); Danville Tobacco Assn. v. Bryant-Buckner Associates, Inc., 333 F.2d 202 (4th Cir.1964); Sink, The Unused Power of a Federal Judge to Call His Own Expert Witnesses, 29 S.Cal.L.Rev. 195 (1956); 2 Wigmore § 563, 9 id. § 2484; Annot., 95 A.L.R.2d 383. Hence the problem becomes largely one of detail.

The New York plan is well known and is described in Report by Special Committee of the Association of the Bar of the City of New York: Impartial Medical Testimony (1956). On recommendation of the Section of Judicial Administration, local adoption of an impartial medical plan was endorsed by the American Bar Association. 82 A.B.A.Rep. 184–185 (1957). Descriptions and analyses of plans in effect in various parts of the country are found in Van Dusen, A United States District Judge's View of the Impartial Medical Expert System, 32 F.R.D. 498 (1963); Wick and Kightlinger, Impartial Medical Testimony Under the Federal Civil Rules: A Tale of Three Doctors, 34 Ins. Counsel J. 115 (1967); and numerous articles collected in Klein, Judicial Administration and the Legal Profession 393 (1963). Statutes and rules include California Evidence Code §§ 730–733; Illinois Supreme Court Rule 215(d), Ill.Rev.Stat. 1969, c. 110A, § 215(d); Burns Indiana Stats.1956, § 9–1702; Wisconsin Stats.Annot.1958, § 957.27.

In the federal practice, a comprehensive scheme for court appointed experts was initiated with the adoption of Rule 28 of the Federal Rules of Criminal Procedure in 1946. The Judicial Conference of the United States in 1953 considered court appointed experts in civil cases, but only with respect to whether they should be compensated from public funds, a proposal which was rejected. Report of the Judicial Conference of the United States 23 (1953). The present rule expands the practice to include civil cases.

Subdivision (a) is based on Rule 28 of the Federal Rules of Criminal Procedure, with a few changes, mainly in the interest of clarity. Language has been added to provide specifically for the appointment either on motion of a party or on the judge's own motion. A provision subjecting the court appointed expert to deposition procedures has been incorporated. The rule has been revised to make definite the right of any party, including the party calling him, to cross-examine.

Subdivision (b) combines the present provision for compensation in criminal cases with what seems to be a fair and feasible handling of civil cases, originally found in the Model Act and carried from there into Uniform Rule 60. See also California Evidence Code §§ 730–731. The special provision for Fifth Amendment compensation cases is designed to guard against reducing constitutionally guaranteed just compensation by requiring the recipient to pay costs. See Rule 71A(*l*) of the Rules of Civil Procedure.

Subdivision (c) seems to be essential if the use of court appointed experts is to be fully effective. Uniform Rule 61 so provides.

Subdivision (d) is in essence the last sentence of Rule 28(a) of the Federal Rules of Criminal Procedure.

1987 Amendment

The amendments are technical. No substantive change is intended.

ARTICLE VIII. HEARSAY

Advisory Committee's Note

INTRODUCTORY NOTE: THE HEARSAY PROBLEM

The factors to be considered in evaluating the testimony of a witness are perception, memory, and narration. Morgan, Hearsay Dangers and the Application of the Hearsay Concept, 62 Harv.L.Rev. 177 (1948), Selected Writings on Evidence and Trial 764, 765 (Fryer ed. 1957); Shientag, Cross-Examination—A Judge's Viewpoint, 3 Record 12 (1948); Strahorn, A Reconsideration of the Hearsay Rule and Admissions, 85 U.Pa.L.Rev. 484, 485 (1937), Selected Writings, supra, 756, 757; Weinstein, Probative Force of Hearsay, 46 Iowa L.Rev. 331 (1961). Sometimes a fourth is added, sincerity, but in fact it seems merely to be an aspect of the three already mentioned.

In order to encourage the witness to do his best with respect to each of these factors, and to expose any inaccuracies which may enter in, the Anglo-American tradition has evolved three conditions under which witnesses will ideally be required to testify: (1) under oath, (2) in the personal presence of the trier of fact, (3) subject to cross-examination.

(1) Standard procedure calls for the swearing of witnesses. While the practice is perhaps less effective than in an earlier time, no disposition to relax the requirement is apparent, other than to allow affirmation by persons with scruples against taking oaths.

(2) The demeanor of the witness traditionally has been believed to furnish trier and opponent with valuable clues. Universal Camera Corp. v. N.L.R.B., 340 U.S. 474, 495–496, 71 S.Ct. 456, 95 L.Ed. 456 (1951); Sahm, Demeanor Evidence: Elusive and Intangible Imponderables, 47 A.B.A.J. 580 (1961), quoting numerous authorities. The witness himself will probably be impressed with the solemnity of the occasion and the possibility of public disgrace. Willingness to falsify may reasonably become more difficult in the presence of the person against whom directed. Rules 26 and 43(a) of the Federal Rules of Criminal and Civil Procedure, respectively, include the general requirement that testimony be taken orally in open court. The Sixth Amendment right of confrontation is a manifestation of these beliefs and attitudes.

(3) Emphasis on the basis of the hearsay rule today tends to center upon the condition of cross-examination. All may not agree with Wigmore that cross-

examination is "beyond doubt the greatest legal engine ever invented for the discovery of truth," but all will agree with his statement that it has become a "vital feature" of the Anglo-American system. 5 Wigmore, § 1367, p. 29. The belief, or perhaps hope, that cross-examination, is effective in exposing imperfections of perception, memory, and narration is fundamental. Morgan, Foreword to Model Code of Evidence 37 (1942).

The logic of the preceding discussion might suggest that no testimony be received unless in full compliance with the three ideal conditions. No one advocates this position. Common sense tells that much evidence which is not given under the three conditions may be inherently superior to much that is. Moreover, when the choice is between evidence which is less than best and no evidence at all, only clear folly would dictate an across-the-board policy of doing without. The problem thus resolves itself into effecting a sensible accommodation between these considerations and the desirability of giving testimony under the ideal conditions.

The solution evolved by the common law has been a general rule excluding hearsay but subject to numerous exceptions under circumstances supposed to furnish guarantees of trustworthiness. Criticisms of this scheme are that it is bulky and complex, fails to screen good from bad hearsay realistically, and inhibits the growth of the law of evidence.

Since no one advocates excluding all hearsay, three possible solutions may be considered: (1) abolish the rule against hearsay and admit all hearsay; (2) admit hearsay possessing sufficient probative force, but with procedural safeguards; (3) revise the present system of class exceptions.

(1) Abolition of the hearsay rule would be the simplest solution. The effect would not be automatically to abolish the giving of testimony under ideal conditions. If the declarant were available, compliance with the ideal conditions would be optional with either party. Thus the proponent could call the declarant as a witness as a form of presentation more impressive than his hearsay statement. Or the opponent could call the declarant to be cross-examined upon his statement. This is the tenor of Uniform Rule 63(1), admitting the hearsay declaration of a person "who is present at the hearing and available for cross-examination." Compare the treatment of declarations of available declarants in Rule 801(d)(1) of the instant rules. If the declarant were unavailable, a rule of free admissibility would make no distinctions in terms of degrees of noncompliance with the ideal conditions and would exact no quid pro quo in the form of assurances of trustworthiness. Rule 503 of the Model Code did exactly that, providing for the admissibility of any hearsay declaration by an unavailable declarant, finding support in the Massachusetts act of 1898, enacted at the instance of Thayer, Mass.Gen.L.1932, c. 233 § 65, and in the English act of 1938, St.1938, c. 28, Evidence. Both are limited to civil cases. The draftsmen of the Uniform Rules chose a less advanced and more conventional position. Comment, Uniform Rule 63. The present Advisory Committee has been unconvinced of the wisdom of abandoning the traditional requirement of some particular assurance of credibility as a condition precedent to admitting the hearsay declaration of an unavailable declarant.

In criminal cases, the Sixth Amendment requirement of confrontation would no doubt move into a large part of the area presently occupied by the hearsay rule in the event of the abolition of the latter. The resultant split between civil and criminal evidence is regarded as an undesirable development.

(2) Abandonment of the system of class exceptions in favor of individual treatment in the setting of the particular case, accompanied by procedural safeguards, has been impressively advocated. Weinstein, The Probative Force of Hearsay, 46 Iowa L.Rev. 331 (1961). Admissibility would be determined by weighing the probative force of the evidence against the possibility of prejudice, waste of time, and the availability of more satisfactory evidence. The bases of the traditional hearsay exceptions would be helpful in assessing probative force. Ladd, The Relationship of the Principles of Exclusionary Rules of Evidence to the Problem of Proof, 18 Minn.L.Rev. 506 (1934). Procedural safeguards would consist of notice of intention to use hearsay, free comment by the judge on the weight of the evidence, and a greater measure of authority in both trial and appellate judges to deal with evidence on the basis of weight. The Advisory Committee has rejected this approach to hearsay as involving too great a measure of judicial discretion, minimizing the predictability of rulings, enhancing the difficulties of preparation for trial, adding a further element to the already over-complicated congeries of pretrial procedures, and requiring substantially different rules for civil and criminal cases. The only way in which the probative force of hearsay differs from the probative force of other testimony is in the absence of oath, demeanor, and cross-examination as aids in determining credibility. For a judge to exclude evidence because he does not believe it has been described as "altogether atypical, extraordinary. . . ." Chadbourn, Bentham and the Hearsay Rule—A Benthamic View of Rule 63(4)(c) of the Uniform Rules of Evidence, 75 Harv.L.Rev. 932, 947 (1962).

(3) The approach to hearsay in these rules is that of the common law, i.e., a general rule excluding hearsay, with exceptions under which evidence is not required to be excluded even though hearsay. The traditional hearsay exceptions are drawn upon for the exceptions, collected under two rules, one dealing with situations where availability of the declarant is regarded as immaterial and the other with those where unavailability is made a condition to the admission of the hearsay statement. Each of the two rules concludes with a provision for hearsay statements not within one of the specified exceptions "but having comparable [equivalent] circumstantial guarantees of trustworthiness." Rules 803(24) and 804(b)(6)[5]. This plan is submitted as calculated to encourage growth and development in this area of the law, while conserving the values and experience of the past as a guide to the future.

CONFRONTATION AND DUE PROCESS

Until very recently, decisions invoking the confrontation clause of the Sixth Amendment were surprisingly few, a fact probably explainable by the former inapplicability of the clause to the states and by the hearsay rule's occupancy of much the same ground. The pattern which emerges from the earlier cases invoking the clause is substantially that of the hearsay rule, applied to criminal cases: an accused is entitled to have the witnesses against him testify under oath, in the presence of himself and trier, subject to cross-examination; yet considerations of public policy and necessity require the recognition of such exceptions as dying declarations and former testimony of unavailable witnesses. Mattox v. United States, 156 U.S. 237, 15 S.Ct. 337, 39 L.Ed. 409 (1895); Motes v. United States, 178 U.S. 458, 20 S.Ct. 993, 44 L.Ed. 1150 (1900); Delaney v.

United States, 263 U.S. 586, 44 S.Ct. 206, 68 L.Ed. 462 (1924). Beginning with Snyder v. Massachusetts, 291 U.S. 97, 54 S.Ct. 330, 78 L.Ed. 674 (1934), the Court began to speak of confrontation as an aspect of procedural due process, thus extending its applicability to state cases and to federal cases other than criminal. The language of *Snyder* was that of an elastic concept of hearsay. The deportation case of Bridges v. Wixon, 326 U.S. 135, 65 S.Ct. 1443, 89 L.Ed. 2103 (1945), may be read broadly as imposing a strictly construed right of confrontation in all kinds of cases or narrowly as the product of a failure of the Immigration and Naturalization Service to follow its own rules. In re Oliver, 333 U.S. 257, 68 S.Ct. 499, 92 L.Ed. 682 (1948), ruled that cross-examination was essential to due process in a state contempt proceeding, but in United States v. Nugent, 346 U.S. 1, 73 S.Ct. 991, 97 L.Ed. 1417 (1953), the court held that it was not an essential aspect of a "hearing" for a conscientious objector under the Selective Service Act. Stein v. New York, 346 U.S. 156, 196, 73 S.Ct. 1077, 97 L.Ed. 1522 (1953), disclaimed any purpose to read the hearsay rule into the Fourteenth Amendment, but in Greene v. McElroy, 360 U.S. 474, 79 S.Ct. 1400, 3 L.Ed.2d 1377 (1959), revocation of security clearance without confrontation and cross-examination was held unauthorized, and a similar result was reached in Willner v. Committee on Character, 373 U.S. 96, 83 S.Ct. 1175, 10 L.Ed.2d 224 (1963). Ascertaining the constitutional dimensions of the confrontation-hearsay aggregate against the background of these cases is a matter of some difficulty, yet the general pattern is at least not inconsistent with that of the hearsay rule.

In 1965 the confrontation clause was held applicable to the states. Pointer v. Texas, 380 U.S. 400, 85 S.Ct. 1065, 13 L.Ed.2d 923 (1965). Prosecution use of former testimony given at a preliminary hearing where petitioner was not represented by counsel was a violation of the clause. The same result would have followed under conventional hearsay doctrine read in the light of a constitutional right to counsel, and nothing in the opinion suggests any difference in essential outline between the hearsay rule and the right of confrontation. In the companion case of Douglas v. Alabama, 380 U.S. 415, 85 S.Ct. 1074, 13 L.Ed.2d 934 (1965), however, the result reached by applying the confrontation clause is one reached less readily via the hearsay rule. A confession implicating petitioner was put before the jury by reading it to the witness in portions and asking if he made that statement. The witness refused to answer on grounds of self-incrimination. The result, said the Court, was to deny cross-examination, and hence confrontation. True, it could broadly be said that the confession was a hearsay statement which for all practical purposes was put in evidence. Yet a more easily accepted explanation of the opinion is that its real thrust was in the direction of curbing undesirable prosecutorial behavior, rather than merely applying rules of exclusion, and that the confrontation clause was the means selected to achieve this end. Comparable facts and a like result appeared in Brookhart v. Janis, 384 U.S. 1, 86 S.Ct. 1245, 16 L.Ed.2d 314 (1966).

The pattern suggested in *Douglas* was developed further and more distinctly in a pair of cases at the end of the 1966 term. United States v. Wade, 388 U.S. 218, 87 S.Ct. 1926, 18 L.Ed.2d 1149 (1967), and Gilbert v. California, 388 U.S. 263, 87 S.Ct. 1951, 18 L.Ed.2d 1178 (1967), hinged upon practices followed in identifying accused persons before trial. This pretrial identification was said to be so decisive an aspect of the case that accused was entitled to have counsel present; a pretrial identification made in the absence of counsel was not itself receivable in evidence and, in addition, might fatally infect a courtroom identification. The presence of counsel at the earlier identification was described as a necessary prerequisite for "a meaningful confrontation at trial." United States v. Wade, supra, 388 U.S. at p. 236, 87 S.Ct. at p. 1937. *Wade* involved no evidence of the fact of a prior identification and hence was not susceptible of being decided on hearsay grounds. In *Gilbert,* witnesses did testify to an earlier identification, readily classifiable as hearsay under a fairly strict view of what constitutes hearsay. The Court, however, carefully avoided basing the decision on the hearsay ground, choosing confrontation instead. 388 U.S. 263, 272, n. 3, 87 S.Ct. 1951. See also Parker v. Gladden, 385 U.S. 363, 87 S.Ct. 468, 17 L.Ed.2d 420 (1966), holding that the right of confrontation was violated when the bailiff made prejudicial statements to jurors, and Note, 75 Yale L.J. 1434 (1966).

Under the earlier cases, the confrontation clause may have been little more than a constitutional embodiment of the hearsay rule, even including traditional exceptions but with some room for expanding them along similar lines. But under the recent cases the impact of the clause clearly extends beyond the confines of the hearsay rule. These considerations have led the Advisory Committee to conclude that a hearsay rule can function usefully as an adjunct to the confrontation right in constitutional areas and independently in nonconstitutional areas. In recognition of the separateness of the confrontation clause and the hearsay rule, and to avoid inviting collisions between them or between the hearsay rule and other exclusionary principles, the exceptions set forth in Rules 803 and 804 are stated in terms of exemption from the general exclusionary mandate of the hearsay rule, rather than in positive terms of admissibility. See Uniform Rule 63(1) to (31) and California Evidence Code §§ 1200–1340.

Rule 801. Definitions

The following definitions apply under this article:

(a) Statement. A "statement" is (1) an oral or written assertion or (2) nonverbal conduct of a person, if it is intended by the person as an assertion.

(b) Declarant. A "declarant" is a person who makes a statement.

(c) Hearsay. "Hearsay" is a statement, other than one made by the declarant while testifying at the trial or hearing, offered in evidence to prove the truth of the matter asserted.

(d) Statements which are not hearsay. A statement is not hearsay if—

(1) Prior statement by witness. The declarant testifies at the trial or hearing and is subject to cross-examination concerning the statement, and the statement is (A) inconsistent with the declarant's testimony, and was given under oath subject to the penalty of perjury at a trial, hearing, or other proceeding, or in a deposition, or (B) consistent with the declarant's testimony and is offered to rebut an express or implied charge against the declarant of recent fabrication or improper influence or motive, or (C) one of identification of a person made after perceiving the person; or

(2) Admission by party-opponent. The statement is offered against a party and is (A) the party's own statement, in either an individual or a representative capacity or (B) a statement of which the party has manifested an adoption or belief in its truth, or (C) a statement by a person authorized by the party to make a statement concerning the subject, or (D) a statement by the party's agent or servant concerning a matter within the scope of the agency or employment, made during the existence of the relationship, or (E) a statement by a coconspirator of a party during the course and in furtherance of the conspiracy. The contents of the statement shall be considered but are not alone sufficient to establish the declarant's authority under subdivision (C), the agency or employment relationship and scope thereof under subdivision (D), or the existence of the conspiracy and the participation therein of the declarant and the party against whom the statement is offered under subdivision (E).

(As amended Pub.L. 94–113, § 1, Oct. 16, 1975, 89 Stat. 576; Mar. 2, 1987, eff. Oct. 1, 1987, April 11, 1997, eff. Dec. 1, 1997.)

Section references, McCormick 5th ed.

General. § 246

(a). § 250

(c). § 245

(d)(1). § 34, § 36, § 37, § 36, § 251, § 324.1, § 326

(A). § 50, § 324.3

(B). § 47, § 324.3

(C). § 251

(d)(2). § 35, § 144, § 160, § 254, § 255, § 256

(A). § 251, § 263, § 264, § 265

(B). § 251, § 259, § 261, § 262

(C). § 251, § 259

(D). § 255, § 259

(E). § 53, § 259

Note by Federal Judicial Center

The rule enacted by the Congress is the rule prescribed by the Supreme Court, with [an] amendment[s] to subdivision (d)(1). The amendment[s] inserted in item (A), after "testimony," [adds] the phrase "and was given under oath subject to the penalty of perjury at a trial, hearing, or other proceeding, or in a deposition." The reasons for [the] amendment[s] are stated in the Report of the House Committee on the Judiciary, the Report of the Senate Committee on the Judiciary, and the Conference Report, set forth below.

Advisory Committee's Note

56 F.R.D. 183, 293

Subdivision (a). The definition of "statement" assumes importance because the term is used in the definition of hearsay in subdivision (c). The effect of the definition of "statement" is to exclude from the operation of the hearsay rule all evidence of conduct, verbal or nonverbal, not intended as an assertion. The key to the definition is that nothing is an assertion unless intended to be one.

It can scarcely be doubted that an assertion made in words is intended by the declarant to be an assertion. Hence verbal assertions readily fall into the category of "statement." Whether nonverbal conduct should be regarded as a statement for purposes of defining hearsay requires further consideration. Some nonverbal conduct, such as the act of pointing to identify a suspect in a lineup, is clearly the equivalent of words, assertive in nature, and to be regarded as a statement. Other nonverbal conduct, however, may be offered as evidence that the person acted as he did because of his belief in the existence of the condition sought to be proved, from which belief the existence of the condition may be inferred. This sequence is, arguably, in effect an assertion of the existence of the condition and hence properly includable within the hearsay concept. See Morgan, Hearsay Dangers and the Application of the Hearsay Concept, 62 Harv. L.Rev. 177, 214, 217 (1948), and the elaboration in Finman, Implied Assertions as Hearsay: Some Criticisms of the Uniform Rules of Evidence, 14 Stan.L.Rev. 682 (1962). Admittedly evidence of this character is untested with respect to the perception, memory, and narration (or their equivalents) of the actor, but the Advisory Committee is of the view that these dangers are minimal in the absence of an intent to assert and do not justify the loss of the evidence on hearsay grounds. No class of evidence is free of the possibility of fabrication, but the likelihood is less with nonverbal than with assertive verbal conduct. The situations giving rise to the nonverbal conduct are such as virtually to eliminate questions of sincerity. Motivation, the nature of the conduct, and the presence or absence of reliance will bear heavily upon the weight to be given the evidence. Falknor, The "Hear-Say" Rule as a "See-Do" Rule: Evidence of Conduct, 33 Rocky Mt.L.Rev. 133 (1961). Similar considerations govern nonassertive verbal conduct and verbal conduct which is assertive but offered as a basis for inferring something other than the matter asserted, also excluded from the definition of hearsay by the language of subdivision (c).

When evidence of conduct is offered on the theory that it is not a statement, and hence not hearsay, a preliminary determination will be required to determine whether an assertion is intended. The rule is so worded as to place the burden upon the party claiming that the intention existed; ambiguous and doubtful cases will be resolved against him and in favor of admissibility. The determination involves no greater difficulty than many other preliminary questions of fact. Maguire, The Hearsay System: Around and Through the Thicket, 14 Vand.L.Rev. 741, 765–767 (1961).

For similar approaches, see Uniform Rule 62(1); California Evidence Code §§ 225, 1200; Kansas Code of Civil Procedure § 60–459(a); New Jersey Evidence Rule 62(1).

Subdivision (c). The definition follows along familiar lines in including only statements offered to prove the truth of the matter asserted. McCormick § 225; 5 Wigmore § 1361, 6 id. § 1766. If the significance of an offered statement lies solely in the fact that it was made, no issue is raised as to the truth of anything asserted, and the statement is not hearsay. Emich Motors Corp. v. General Motors Corp., 181 F.2d 70 (7th Cir.1950), rev'd on other grounds 340 U.S. 558, 71 S.Ct. 408, 95 L.Ed. 534, letters of complaint from customers offered as a reason for cancellation of dealer's franchise, to rebut contention that franchise was revoked for refusal to finance sales through affiliated finance company. The effect is to exclude from hearsay the entire category of "verbal acts" and "verbal parts of an act," in which the statement itself affects the legal rights of the parties or is a circumstance bearing on conduct affecting their rights.

The definition of hearsay must, of course, be read with reference to the definition of statement set forth in subdivision (a).

Testimony given by a witness in the course of court proceedings is excluded since there is compliance with all the ideal conditions for testifying.

Subdivision (d). Several types of statements which would otherwise literally fall within the definition are expressly excluded from it:

(1) *Prior statement by witness.* Considerable controversy has attended the question whether a prior out-of-court statement by a person now available for cross-examination concerning it, under oath and in the presence of the trier of fact, should be classed as hearsay. If the witness admits on the stand that he made the statement and that it was true, he adopts the statement and there is no hearsay problem. The hearsay problem arises when the witness on the stand denies having made the statement or admits having made it but denies its truth. The argument in favor of treating these latter statements as hearsay is based upon the ground that the conditions of oath, cross-examination, and demeanor observation did not prevail at the time the statement was made and cannot adequately be supplied by the later examination. The logic of the situation is troublesome. So far as concerns the oath, its mere presence has never been regarded as sufficient to remove a statement from the hearsay category, and it receives much less emphasis than cross-examination as a truth-compelling device. While strong expressions are found to the effect that no conviction can be had or important right taken away on the basis of statements not made under fear of prosecution for perjury, Bridges v. Wixon, 326 U.S. 135, 65 S.Ct. 1443, 89 L.Ed. 2103 (1945), the fact is that, of the many common law exceptions to the hearsay rule, only that for reported testimony has required the statement to have been made under oath. [It should be noted, however, that rule 801(d)(1)(A), as enacted by the Congress, requires that a prior inconsistent statement have been made under oath.] Nor is it satisfactorily explained why cross-examination cannot be conducted subsequently with success. The decisions contending most vigorously for its inadequacy in fact demonstrate quite thorough exploration of the weaknesses and doubts attending the earlier statement. State v. Saporen, 205 Minn. 358, 285 N.W. 898 (1939); Ruhala v. Roby, 379 Mich. 102, 150 N.W.2d 146 (1967); People v. Johnson, 68 Cal.2d 646, 68 Cal.Rptr. 599, 441 P.2d 111 (1968). In respect to demeanor, as Judge Learned Hand observed in Di Carlo v. United States, 6 F.2d 364 (2d Cir.1925), when the jury decides that the truth is not what the witness says now, but what he said before, they are still deciding from what they see and hear in court. The bulk of the case law nevertheless has been against allowing prior statements of witnesses to be used generally as substantive evidence. Most of the writers and Uniform Rule 63(1) have taken the opposite position.

The position taken by the Advisory Committee in formulating this part of the rule is founded upon an unwillingness to countenance the general use of prior prepared statements as substantive evidence, but with a recognition that particular circumstances call for a contrary result. The judgment is one more of experience than of logic. The rule requires in each instance, as a general safeguard, that the declarant actually testify as a witness, and it then enumerates three situations in which the statement is excepted from the category of hearsay. Compare Uniform Rule 63(1) which allows any out-of-court statement of a declarant who is present at the trial and available for cross-examination.

(A) Prior inconsistent statements traditionally have been admissible to impeach but not as substantive evidence. Under the rule they are substantive evidence. As has been said by the California Law Revision Commission with respect to a similar provision:

"Section 1235 admits inconsistent statements of witnesses because the dangers against which the hearsay rule is designed to protect are largely nonexistent. The declarant is in court and may be examined and cross-examined in regard to his statements and their subject matter. In many cases, the inconsistent statement is more likely to be true than the testimony of the witness at the trial because it was made nearer in time to the matter to which it relates and is less likely to be influenced by the controversy that gave rise to the litigation. The trier of fact has the declarant before it and can observe his demeanor and the nature of his testimony as he denies or tries to explain away the inconsistency. Hence, it is in as good a position to determine the truth or falsity of the prior statement as it is to determine the truth or falsity of the inconsistent testimony given in court. Moreover, Section 1235 will provide a party with desirable protection against the 'turncoat' witness who changes his story on the stand and deprives the party calling him of evidence essential to his case." Comment, California Evidence Code § 1235. See also McCormick § 39. The Advisory Committee finds these views more convincing than those expressed in People v. Johnson, 68 Cal.2d 646, 68 Cal.Rptr. 599, 441 P.2d 111 (1968). The constitutionality of the Advisory Committee's view was upheld in California v. Green, 399 U.S. 149, 90 S.Ct. 1930, 26 L.Ed.2d 489 (1970). Moreover, the requirement that the statement be inconsistent with the testimony given assures a thorough exploration of both versions while the witness is on the stand and bars any general and indiscriminate use of previously prepared statements. [It should be noted that the rule as enacted by the Congress also requires that the prior inconsistent statement have been made under oath.]

Report of House Committee on the Judiciary

House Comm. on Judiciary, Fed.Rules of Evidence, H.R.Rep. No. 650, 93d Cong., 1st Sess., p. 13 (1973); 1975 U.S. Code Cong. & Ad.News 7075, 7086

Present federal law, except in the Second Circuit, permits the use of prior inconsistent statements of a witness for impeachment only. Rule 801(d)(1) as proposed by the Court would have permitted all such statements to be admissible as substantive evidence, an approach followed by a small but growing number of State jurisdictions and recently held constitutional in California v. Green, 399 U.S. 149 (1970). Although there was some support expressed for the Court Rule, based largely on the need to counteract the effect of witness intimidation in criminal cases, the Committee decided to adopt a compromise version of the Rule similar to the position of the Second Circuit. The Rule as amended draws a distinction between types of prior inconsistent statements (other than statements of identification of a person made after perceiving him which are currently admissible, see United States v. Anderson, 406 F.2d 719, 720 (4th Cir.), cert. denied, 395 U.S. 967 (1969)) and allows only those made while the declarant was subject to cross-examination at a trail [trial] or hearing or in a deposition, to be admissible for their truth. Compare United States v. DeSisto, 329 F.2d 929 (2nd Cir.), cert. denied, 377 U.S. 979 (1964); United States v. Cunningham, 446 F.2d 194 (2nd Cir.1971) (restricting the admissibility of prior inconsistent statements as substantive evidence to those made under oath in a formal proceeding, but not requiring that there have been an opportunity for cross-examination). The rationale for the Committee's decision is that (1) unlike in most other situations involving unsworn or oral statements, there can be no dispute as to whether the prior statement was made; and (2) the context of a formal proceeding, an oath, and the opportunity for cross-examination provide firm additional assurances of the reliability of the prior statement.

Report of Senate Committee on the Judiciary

Senate Comm. on Judiciary, Fed.Rules of Evidence, S.Rep. No. 1277, 93d Cong., 2d Sess., p. 15 (1974); 1974 U.S. Code Cong. & Ad.News 7051, 7062

Rule 801 defines what is and what is not hearsay for the purpose of admitting a prior statement as substantive evidence. A prior statement of a witness at a trial or hearing which is inconsistent with his testimony is, of course, always admissible for the purpose of impeaching the witness' credibility.

As submitted by the Supreme Court, subdivision (d)(1)(A) made admissible as substantive evidence the prior statement of a witness inconsistent with this present testimony.

The House severely limited the admissibility of prior inconsistent statements by adding a requirement that the prior statement must have been subject to cross-examination, thus precluding even the use of grand jury statements. The requirement that the prior statement must have been subject to cross-examination appears unnecessary since this rule comes into play only when the witness testifies in the present trial. At that time, he is on the stand and can explain an earlier position and be cross-examined as to both.

The requirement that the statement be under oath also appears unnecessary. Notwithstanding the absence of an oath contemporaneous with the statement, the witness, when on the stand, qualifying or denying the prior statement, is under oath. In any event, of all the many recognized exceptions to the hearsay rule, only one (former testimony) requires that the out-of-court statement have been made under oath. With respect to the lack of evidence of the demeanor of the witness at the time of the prior statement, it would be difficult to improve upon Judge Learned Hand's observation that when the jury decides that the truth is not what the witness says now but what he said before, they are still deciding from what they see and hear in court.[1]

The rule as submitted by the Court has positive advantages. The prior statement was made nearer in time to the events, when memory was fresher and intervening influences had not been brought into play. A realistic method is provided for dealing with the turncoat witness who changes his story on the stand.[2]

1. Di Carlo v. United States, 6 F.2d 364 (2d Cir.1925).

2. See Comment, California Evidence Code § 1235; McCormick, Evidence, § 38 (2nd ed. 1972).

New Jersey, California, and Utah have adopted a rule similar to this one; and Nevada, New Mexico, and Wisconsin have adopted the identical Federal rule.

For all of these reasons, we think the House amendment should be rejected and the rule as submitted by the Supreme Court reinstated.[3]

Conference Report

H.R., Fed.Rules of Evidence, Conf.Rep. No. 1597, 93d Cong., 2d Sess., p. 10 (1974); 1974 U.S. Code Cong. & Ad.News 7098, 7104

The House bill provides that a statement is not hearsay if the declarant testifies and is subject to cross-examination concerning the statement and if the statement is inconsistent with his testimony and was given under oath subject to cross-examination and subject to the penalty of perjury at a trial or hearing or in a deposition. The Senate amendment drops the requirement that the prior statement be given under oath subject to cross-examination and subject to the penalty of perjury at a trial or hearing or in a deposition.

The Conference adopts the Senate amendment with an amendment, so that the rule now requires that the prior inconsistent statement be given under oath subject to the penalty of perjury at a trial, hearing, or other proceeding, or in a deposition. The rule as adopted covers statements before a grand jury. Prior inconsistent statements may, of course, be used for impeaching the credibility of a witness. When the prior inconsistent statement is one made by a defendant in a criminal case, it is covered by Rule 801(d)(2).

Advisory Committee's Note

56 F.R.D. 183, 296

(B) Prior consistent statements traditionally have been admissible to rebut charges of recent fabrication or improper influence or motive but not as substantive evidence. Under the rule they are substantive evidence. The prior statement is consistent with the testimony given on the stand and, if the opposite party wishes to open the door for its admission in evidence, no sound reason is apparent why it should not be received generally.

Editorial Note

Subdivision (d)(1)(C) was included in the rule as prescribed by the Supreme Court but was deleted by the Congress in enacting the rules, as indicated in the Conference Report above. However, the subdivision was restored by Act effective Oct. 31, 1975. Therefore the Advisory Committee's Note to the subdivision is now reprinted below.

Advisory Committee's Note

56 F.R.D. 183, 296

(C) The admission of evidence of identification finds substantial support, although it falls beyond a doubt in the category of prior out-of-court statements.

3. It would appear that some of the opposition to this Rule is based on a concern that a person could be convicted solely upon evidence admissible under this Rule. The Rule, however, is not addressed to the question of the sufficiency of evidence to send a case to the jury, but merely as to its admissibility. Factual circumstances could well arise where, if this were the sole evidence, dismissal would be appropriate.

Illustrative are People v. Gould, 54 Cal.2d 621, 7 Cal.Rptr. 273, 354 P.2d 865 (1960); Judy v. State, 218 Md. 168, 146 A.2d 29 (1958); State v. Simmons, 63 Wash.2d 17, 385 P.2d 389 (1963); California Evidence Code § 1238; New Jersey Evidence Rule 63(1)(c); N.Y.Code of Criminal Procedure § 393–b. Further cases are found in 4 Wigmore § 1130. The basis is the generally unsatisfactory and inconclusive nature of courtroom identifications as compared with those made at an earlier time under less suggestive conditions. The Supreme Court considered the admissibility of evidence of prior identification in Gilbert v. California, 388 U.S. 263, 87 S.Ct. 1951, 18 L.Ed.2d 1178 (1967). Exclusion of lineup identification was held to be required because the accused did not then have the assistance of counsel. Significantly, the Court carefully refrained from placing its decision on the ground that testimony as to the making of a prior out-of-court identification ("That's the man") violated either the hearsay rule or the right of confrontation because not made under oath, subject to immediate cross-examination, in the presence of the trier. Instead the Court observed:

> "There is a split among the States concerning the admissibility of prior extra-judicial identifications, as independent evidence of identity, both by the witness and third parties present at the prior identification. See 71 A.L.R.2d 449. It has been held that the prior identification is hearsay, and, when admitted through the testimony of the identifier, is merely a prior consistent statement. The recent trend, however, is to admit the prior identification under the exception that admits as substantive evidence a prior communication by a witness who is available for cross-examination at the trial. See 5 A.L.R.2d Later Case Service 1225–1228. . . ." 388 U.S. at 272, n. 3, 87 S.Ct. at 1956.[1]

(2) *Admissions.* Admissions by a party-opponent are excluded from the category of hearsay on the theory that their admissibility in evidence is the result of the adversary system rather than satisfaction of the conditions of the hearsay rule. Strahorn, A Reconsideration of the Hearsay Rule and Admissions, 85 U.Pa.L.Rev. 484, 564 (1937); Morgan, Basic Problems of Evidence 265 (1962); 4 Wigmore § 1048. No guarantee of trustworthiness is required in the case of an admission. The freedom which admissions have enjoyed from technical demands of searching for an assurance of trustworthiness in some against-interest circumstance, and from the restrictive influences of the opinion rule and the rule requiring firsthand knowledge, when taken with the apparently prevalent satisfaction with the results, calls for generous treatment of this avenue to admissibility.

The rule specifies five categories of statements for which the responsibility of a party is considered sufficient to justify reception in evidence against him:

(A) A party's own statement is the classic example of an admission. If he has a representative capacity and the statement is offered against him in that capacity, no inquiry whether he was acting in the representative capacity in making the statement is required; the statement need only be relevant to representative affairs. To the same effect is California Evidence Code § 1220. Compare Uniform Rule 63(7), requiring a statement to be made in a representative capacity to be admissible against a party in a representative capacity.

(B) Under established principles an admission may be made by adopting or acquiescing in the statement of another. While knowledge of contents would

1. See also 121 Cong.Rec. 19752 and 31866 (1975) for action reinstating item (C).

ordinarily be essential, this is not inevitably so: "X is a reliable person and knows what he is talking about." See McCormick § 246, p. 527, n. 15. Adoption or acquiescence may be manifested in any appropriate manner. When silence is relied upon, the theory is that the person would, under the circumstances, protest the statement made in his presence, if untrue. The decision in each case calls for an evaluation in terms of probable human behavior. In civil cases, the results have generally been satisfactory. In criminal cases, however, troublesome questions have been raised by decisions holding that failure to deny is an admission: the inference is a fairly weak one, to begin with; silence may be motivated by advice of counsel or realization that "anything you say may be used against you"; unusual opportunity is afforded to manufacture evidence; and encroachment upon the privilege against self-incrimination seems inescapably to be involved. However, recent decisions of the Supreme Court relating to custodial interrogation and the right to counsel appear to resolve these difficulties. Hence the rule contains no special provisions concerning failure to deny in criminal cases.

(C) No authority is required for the general proposition that a statement authorized by a party to be made should have the status of an admission by the party. However, the question arises whether only statements to third persons should be so regarded, to the exclusion of statements by the agent to the principal. The rule is phrased broadly so as to encompass both. While it may be argued that the agent authorized to make statements to his principal does not speak for him, Morgan, Basic Problems of Evidence 273 (1962), communication to an outsider has not generally been thought to be an essential characteristic of an admission. Thus a party's books or records are usable against him, without regard to any intent to disclose to third persons. 5 Wigmore § 1557. See also McCormick § 78, pp. 159–161. In accord is New Jersey Evidence Rule 63(8)(a). Cf. Uniform Rule 63(8)(a) and California Evidence Code § 1222 which limit status as an admission in this regard to statements authorized by the party to be made "for" him, which is perhaps an ambiguous limitation to statements to third persons. Falknor, Vicarious Admissions and the Uniform Rules, 14 Vand. L.Rev. 855, 860–861 (1961).

(D) The tradition has been to test the admissibility of statements by agents, as admissions, by applying the usual test of agency. Was the admission made by the agent acting in the scope of his employment? Since few principals employ agents for the purpose of making damaging statements, the usual result was exclusion of the statement. Dissatisfaction with this loss of valuable and helpful evidence has been increasing. A substantial trend favors admitting statements related to a matter within the scope of the agency or employment. Grayson v. Williams, 256 F.2d 61 (10th Cir.1958); Koninklijke Luchtvaart Maatschappij N.V. KLM Royal Dutch Airlines v. Tuller, 110 U.S.App.D.C. 282, 292 F.2d 775, 784 (1961); Martin v. Savage Truck Lines, Inc., 121 F.Supp. 417 (D.D.C.1954), and numerous state court decisions collected in 4 Wigmore, 1964 Supp., pp. 66–73, with comments by the editor that the statements should have been excluded as not within scope of agency. For the traditional view see Northern Oil Co. v. Socony Mobile [sic] Oil Co., 347 F.2d 81, 85 (2d Cir.1965) and cases cited therein. Similar provisions are found in Uniform Rule 63(9)(a), Kansas Code of Civil Procedure § 60–460(i)(1), and New Jersey Evidence Rule 63(9)(a).

(E) The limitation upon the admissibility of statements of co-conspirators to those made "during the course and in furtherance of the conspiracy" is in the accepted pattern. While the broadened view of agency taken in item (iv) might suggest wider admissibility of statements of co-conspirators, the agency theory of conspiracy is at best a fiction and ought not to serve as a basis for admissibility beyond that already established. See Levie, Hearsay and Conspiracy, 52 Mich. L.Rev. 1159 (1954); Comment, 25 U.Chi.L.Rev. 530 (1958). The rule is consistent with the position of the Supreme Court in denying admissibility to statements made after the objectives of the conspiracy have either failed or been achieved. Krulewitch v. United States, 336 U.S. 440, 69 S.Ct. 716, 93 L.Ed. 790 (1949); Wong Sun v. United States, 371 U.S. 471, 490, 83 S.Ct. 407, 9 L.Ed.2d 441 (1963). For similarly limited provisions see California Evidence Code § 1223 and New Jersey Rule 63(9)(b). Cf. Uniform Rule 63(9)(b).

Report of Senate Committee on the Judiciary

Senate Comm. on Judiciary, Fed.Rules of Evidence, S.Rep. No. 1277, 93d Cong., 2d Sess., p. 26 (1974); 1974 U.S. Code Cong. & Ad.News 7051, 7073

The House approved the long-accepted rule that "a statement by a coconspirator of a party during the course and in furtherance of the conspiracy" is not hearsay as it was submitted by the Supreme Court. While the rule refers to a coconspirator, it is this committee's understanding that the rule is meant to carry forward the universally accepted doctrine that a joint venturer is considered as a coconspirator for the purposes of this rule even though no conspiracy has been charged. United States v. Rinaldi, 393 F.2d 97, 99 (2d Cir.), cert. denied 393 U.S. 913 (1968); United States v. Spencer, 415 F.2d 1301, 1304 (7th Cir.1969).

1987 Amendment

The amendments are technical. No substantive change is intended.

1997 Amendment

Rule 801(d)(2) has been amended in order to respond to three issues raised by *Bourjaily v. United States*, 483 U.S. 171 (1987). First, the amendment codifies the holding in *Bourjaily* by stating expressly that a court shall consider the contents of a coconspirator's statement in determining "the existence of the conspiracy and the participation therein of the declarant and the party against whom the statement is offered." According to *Bourjaily,* Rule 104(a) requires these preliminary questions to be established by a preponderance of the evidence.

Second, the amendment resolves an issue on which the Court had reserved decision. It provides that the contents of the declarant's statement do not alone suffice to establish a conspiracy in which the declarant and the defendant participated. The court must consider in addition the circumstances surrounding the statement, such as the identity of the speaker, the context in which the statement was made, or evidence corroborating the contents of the statement in making its determination as to each preliminary question. This amendment is in accordance with existing practice. Every court of appeals that has resolved this issue requires some evidence in addition to the contents of the statement. *See, ex., United States v. Beckham*, 968 F.2d 47, 51 (D.C.Cir. 1992); *United States v. Sepulveda*, 15 F.3d 1161, 1181–82 (1st Cir. 1993), *cert. denied*, 114 S.Ct. 2714 (1994); *United States v. Daly*, 842 F.2d 1380, 1386 (2d Cir.), *cert. denied*, 488 U.S. 821 (1988); *United States v. Clark*, 18 F.3d 1337, 1341–42 (6th Cir.), *cert. denied*, 115 S.Ct. 152 (1994); *United States v. Zambrana*, 841 F.2d 1320, 1344–45 (7th

Cir. 1988); *United States v. Silverman*, 861 F.2d 571, 577 (9th Cir. 1988); *United States v. Gordon*, 844 F.2d 1397, 1402 (9th Cir. 1988); *United States v. Hernandez*, 829 F.2d 988, 993 (10th Cir. 1987), *cert. denied*, 485 U.S. 1013 (1988); *United States v. Byrom*, 910 F.2d 725, 736 (11th Cir. 1990).

Third, the amendment extends the reasoning of *Bourjaily* to statements offered under subdivisions (C) and (D) of Rule 801 (d)(2). In *Bourjaily*, the Court rejected treating foundational facts pursuant to the law of agency in favor of an evidentiary approach governed by Rule 104(a). The Advisory Committee believes it appropriate to treat analogously preliminary questions relating to the declarant's authority under subdivision (C), and the agency or employment relationship and scope thereof under subdivision (D).

Rule 802. Hearsay Rule

Hearsay is not admissible except as provided by these rules or by other rules prescribed by the Supreme Court pursuant to statutory authority or by Act of Congress.

Section references, McCormick 5th ed.

§ 246, § 299

Note by Federal Judicial Center

The rule enacted by the Congress is the rule prescribed by the Supreme Court, amended by substituting "prescribed" in place of "adopted" and by inserting the phrase "pursuant to statutory authority."

Advisory Committee's Note

56 F.R.D. 183 299

The provision excepting from the operation of the rule hearsay which is made admissible by other rules adopted by the Supreme Court or by Act of Congress continues the admissibility thereunder of hearsay which would not qualify under these Evidence Rules. The following examples illustrate the working of the exception:

FEDERAL RULES OF CIVIL PROCEDURE

Rule 4(g): proof of service by affidavit.

Rule 32: admissibility of depositions.

Rule 43(e): affidavits when motion based on facts not appearing of record.

Rule 56: affidavits in summary judgment proceedings.

Rule 65(b): showing by affidavit for temporary restraining order.

FEDERAL RULES OF CRIMINAL PROCEDURE

Rule 4(a): affidavits to show grounds for issuing warrants.

Rule 12(b)(4): affidavits to determine issues of fact in connection with motions.

ACTS OF CONGRESS

10 U.S.C. § 7730: affidavits of unavailable witnesses in actions for damages caused by vessel in naval service, or towage or salvage of same, when taking of testimony or bringing of action delayed or stayed on security grounds.

29 U.S.C. § 161(4): affidavit as proof of service in NLRB proceedings.

38 U.S.C. § 5206: affidavit as proof of posting notice of sale of unclaimed property by Veterans Administration.

Rule 803. Hearsay Exceptions; Availability of Declarant Immaterial

The following are not excluded by the hearsay rule, even though the declarant is available as a witness:

(1) Present sense impression. A statement describing or explaining an event or condition made while the declarant was perceiving the event or condition, or immediately thereafter.

(2) Excited utterance. A statement relating to a startling event or condition made while the declarant was under the stress of excitement caused by the event or condition.

(3) Then existing mental, emotional, or physical condition. A statement of the declarant's then existing state of mind, emotion, sensation, or physical condition (such as intent, plan, motive, design, mental feeling, pain, and bodily health), but not including a statement of memory or belief to prove the fact remembered or believed unless it relates to the execution, revocation, identification, or terms of declarant's will.

(4) Statements for purposes of medical diagnosis or treatment. Statements made for purposes of medical diagnosis or treatment and describing medical history, or past or present symptoms, pain, or sensations, or the inception or general character of the cause or external source thereof insofar as reasonably pertinent to diagnosis or treatment.

(5) Recorded recollection. A memorandum or record concerning a matter about which a witness once had knowledge but now has insufficient recollection to enable the witness to testify fully and accurately, shown to have been made or adopted by the witness when the matter was fresh in the witness' memory and to reflect that knowledge correctly. If admitted, the memorandum or record may be read into evidence but may not itself be received as an exhibit unless offered by an adverse party.

(6) Records of regularly conducted activity. A memorandum, report, record, or data compilation, in any form, of acts, events, conditions, opinions, or diagnoses, made at or near the time by, or from information transmitted by, a person with knowledge, if kept in the course of a regularly conducted business activity, and if it was the regular practice of that business activity to make the memorandum, report, record, or data compilation, all as shown by the testimony of the custodian or other qualified witness, or by certification that complies with Rule 902(11), Rule 902(12), or a statute permitting certification, unless the source of information or the method or circumstances of preparation indicate lack of trustworthiness. The term "business" as used in this paragraph includes business, institution, association, profession, occupation, and calling of every kind, whether or not conducted for profit.

(7) Absence of entry in records kept in accordance with the provisions of paragraph (6). Evidence that a matter is not included in the memoranda, reports, records, or data compilations, in any form, kept in accordance with the provisions of paragraph (6), to prove the nonoccurrence or nonexistence of the matter, if the matter was of a kind of which a memorandum, report, record, or data compilation was regularly made and preserved, unless the sources of information or other circumstances indicate lack of trustworthiness.

(8) Public records and reports. Records, reports, statements, or data compilations, in any form, of public offices or agencies, setting forth (A) the activities of the office or agency, or (B) matters observed pursuant to duty imposed by law as to which matters there was a duty to report, excluding, however, in criminal cases matters observed by police officers and other law enforcement personnel, or (C) in civil actions and proceedings and against the Government in criminal cases, factual findings resulting from an investigation made pursuant to authority granted by law, unless the sources of information or other circumstances indicate lack of trustworthiness.

(9) Records of vital statistics. Records or data compilations, in any form, of births, fetal deaths, deaths, or marriages, if the report thereof was made to a public office pursuant to requirements of law.

(10) Absence of public record or entry. To prove the absence of a record, report, statement, or data compilation, in any form, or the nonoccurrence or nonexistence of a matter of which a record, report, statement, or data compilation, in any form, was regularly made and preserved by a public office or agency, evidence in the form of a certification in accordance with rule 902, or testimony, that diligent search failed to disclose the record, report, statement, or data compilation, or entry.

(11) Records of religious organizations. Statements of births, marriages, divorces, deaths, legitimacy, ancestry, relationship by blood or marriage, or other similar facts of personal or family history, contained in a regularly kept record of a religious organization.

(12) Marriage, baptismal, and similar certificates. Statements of fact contained in a certificate that the maker performed a marriage or other ceremony or administered a sacrament, made by a clergyman, public official, or other person authorized by the rules or practices of a religious organization or by law to perform the act certified, and purporting to have been issued at the time of the act or within a reasonable time thereafter.

(13) Family records. Statements of fact concerning personal or family history contained in family Bibles, genealogies, charts, engravings on rings, inscriptions on family portraits, engravings on urns, crypts, or tombstones, or the like.

(14) Records of documents affecting an interest in property. The record of a document purporting to establish or affect an interest in property, as proof of the content of the original recorded document and its execution and delivery by each person by whom it purports to have been executed, if the record is a record of a public office and an applicable statute authorizes the recording of documents of that kind in that office.

(15) Statements in documents affecting an interest in property. A statement contained in a document purporting to establish or affect an interest in property if the matter stated was relevant to the purpose of the document, unless dealings with the property since the document was made have been inconsistent with the truth of the statement or the purport of the document.

(16) Statements in ancient documents. Statements in a document in existence twenty years or more the authenticity of which is established.

(17) Market reports, commercial publications. Market quotations, tabulations, lists, directories, or other published compilations, generally used and relied upon by the public or by persons in particular occupations.

(18) Learned treatises. To the extent called to the attention of an expert witness upon cross-examination or relied upon by the expert witness in direct examination, statements contained in published treatises, periodicals, or pamphlets on a subject of history, medicine, or other science or art, established as a reliable authority by the testimony or admission of the witness or by other expert testimony or by judicial notice. If admitted, the statements may be read into evidence but may not be received as exhibits.

(19) Reputation concerning personal or family history. Reputation among members of a person's family by blood, adoption, or marriage, or among a person's associates, or in the community, concerning a person's birth, adoption, marriage, divorce, death, legitimacy, relationship by blood, adoption, or marriage, ancestry, or other similar fact of his personal or family history.

(20) Reputation concerning boundaries or general history. Reputation in a community, arising before the controversy, as to boundaries of or customs affecting lands in the community, and reputation as to events of general history important to the community or State or nation in which located.

(21) Reputation as to character. Reputation of a person's character among associates or in the community.

(22) Judgment of previous conviction. Evidence of a final judgment, entered after a trial or upon a plea of guilty (but not upon a plea of nolo contendere), adjudging a person guilty of a crime punishable by death or imprisonment in excess of one year, to prove any fact essential to sustain the judgment, but not including, when offered by the Government in a criminal prosecution for purposes other than impeachment, judgments against persons other than the accused. The pendency of an appeal may be shown but does not affect admissibility.

(23) Judgment as to personal, family, or general history, or boundaries. Judgments as proof of matters of personal, family or general history, or boundaries, essential to the judgment, if the same would be provable by evidence of reputation.

(24) [Transferred to Rule 807]

(As amended P.L. 94–149, § 1(11), Dec. 12, 1975, 89 Stat. 805; Mar. 2, 1987, eff. Oct. 1, 1987, April 11, 1997 eff. Dec. 1, 1997, Apr. 17, 2000, eff. Dec. 1, 2000.)

Section references, McCormick 5th ed.

Generally § 253, § 326

(1). § 271

(2). § 272

(3). § 273, § 274, § 275, § 276

(4). § 277, § 278, § 324.3

(5). § 144, § 279, § 281, § 282, § 283

(6). § 250, § 286, § 287, § 288, § 289, § 290, § 291, § 292, § 293, § 294, § 296, § 324.1

(7). § 287

(8). § 288, § 295

(A). § 296

(B). § 296, § 297

(C). § 296, § 297

(9). § 297

(10). § 300

(11). § 288, § 299

(12). § 299

(13). § 322

(14). § 323

(15). § 323

(16). § 323

(17). § 321

(18). § 321

(19). § 322

(20). § 324

(21). § 191

(22). § 42, § 252, § 257, § 298

(23). § 322

(24). § 208, § 324, § 324.3, § 353

Note by Federal Judicial Center

The rule enacted by the Congress retains the 24 exceptions set forth in the rule prescribed by the Supreme Court. Three of the exceptions, numbered (6), (8), and (24) have been amended in respects that may fairly be described as substantial. Others, numbered (5), (7), (14), and (16), have been amended in lesser ways. The remaining 17 are unchanged. The amendments are, in numerical order, as follows.

Exception (5) as prescribed by the Supreme Court was amended by inserting after "made" the phrase "or adopted by the witness."

Exception (6) as prescribed by the Supreme Court was amended by substituting the phrase, "if kept in the course of a regularly conducted business activity, and if it was the regular practice of that business activity to make the memorandum, report, record, or data compilation, all," in place of "all in the course of a regularly conducted activity"; by substituting "source" in place of "sources"; by substituting the phrase, "the method or circumstances of preparation," in place of "other circumstances"; and by adding the second sentence.

Exception (7) as prescribed by the Supreme Court was amended by substituting the phrase, "kept in accordance with the provisions of paragraph (6)," in place of "of a regularly conducted activity." The exception prescribed by the Supreme Court included a comma after "memoranda," while the congressional enactment does not.

Exception (8) as prescribed by the Supreme Court was amended by inserting in item (B) after "law" the phrase, "as to which matters there was a duty to report, excluding, however, in criminal cases matters observed by police officers and other law enforcement personnel," and by substituting in item (C) the phrase "civil actions and proceedings," in place of "civil cases."

Exception (14) as prescribed by the Supreme Court was amended by substituting "authorizes" in place of "authorized."

Exception (16) as prescribed by the Supreme Court was amended by substituting the phrase, "the authenticity of which," in place of "whose authenticity."

Exception (24) as prescribed by the Supreme Court was amended by substituting "equivalent" in place of "comparable," and adding all that appears after "trustworthiness" in the exception as enacted by the Congress.

Advisory Committee's Note

56 F.R.D. 183, 303

The exceptions are phrased in terms of nonapplication of the hearsay rule, rather than in positive terms of admissibility, in order to repel any implication that other possible grounds for exclusion are eliminated from consideration.

The present rule proceeds upon the theory that under appropriate circumstances a hearsay statement may possess circumstantial guarantees of trustworthiness sufficient to justify nonproduction of the declarant in person at the trial even though he may be available. The theory finds vast support in the many exceptions to the hearsay rule developed by the common law in which unavailability of the declarant is not a relevant factor. The present rule is a synthesis of them, with revision where modern developments and conditions are believed to make that course appropriate.

In a hearsay situation, the declarant is, of course, a witness, and neither this rule nor Rule 804 dispenses with the requirement of firsthand knowledge. It may appear from his statement or be inferable from circumstances. See Rule 602.

Exceptions (1) and (2). In considerable measure these two [exceptions] overlap, though based on somewhat different theories. The most significant practical difference will lie in the time lapse allowable between event and statement.

The underlying theory of Exception (1) is that substantial contemporaneity of event and statement negative the likelihood of deliberate or conscious misrepresentation. Moreover, if the witness is the declarant, he may be examined on the statement. If the witness is not the declarant, he may be examined as to the circumstances as an aid in evaluating the statement. Morgan, Basic Problems of Evidence 340–341 (1962).

The theory of Exception (2) is simply that circumstances may produce a condition of excitement which temporarily stills the capacity of reflection and produces utterances free of conscious fabrication. 6 Wigmore § 1747, p. 135. Spontaneity is the key factor in each instance, though arrived at by somewhat different routes. Both are needed in order to avoid needless niggling.

While the theory of Exception (2) has been criticized on the ground that excitement impairs accuracy of observation as well as eliminating conscious fabrication, Hutchins and Slesinger, Some Observations on the Law of Evidence: Spontaneous Exclamations, 28 Colum.L.Rev. 432 (1928), it finds support in cases without number. See cases in 6 Wigmore § 1750; Annot., 53 A.L.R.2d 1245 (statements as to cause of or responsibility for motor vehicle accident); Annot., 4 A.L.R.3d 149 (accusatory statements by homicide victims). Since unexciting events are less likely to evoke comment, decisions involving Exception (1) are far less numerous. Illustrative are Tampa Elec. Co. v. Getrost, 151 Fla. 558, 10 So.2d 83 (1942); Houston Oxygen Co. v. Davis, 139 Tex. 1, 161 S.W.2d 474 (1942); and cases cited in McCormick § 273, p. 585, n. 4.

With respect to the *time element,* Exception (1) recognizes that in many, if not most, instances precise contemporaneity is not possible, and hence a slight lapse is allowable. Under Exception (2) the standard of measurement is the duration of the state of excitement. "How long can excitement prevail? Obviously there are no pat answers and the character of the transaction or event will largely determine the significance of the time factor." Slough, Spontaneous Statements and State of Mind, 46 Iowa L.Rev. 224, 243 (1961); McCormick § 272, p. 580.

Participation by the declarant is not required: a non-participant may be moved to describe what he perceives, and one may be startled by an event in which he is not an actor. Slough, supra; McCormick, supra; 6 Wigmore § 1755; Annot., 78 A.L.R.2d 300.

Whether *proof of the startling event* may be made by the statement itself is largely an academic question, since in most cases there is present at least circumstantial evidence that something of a startling nature must have occurred. For cases in which the evidence consists of the condition of the declarant (injuries, state of shock), see Insurance Co. v. Mosely, 75 U.S. (8 Wall.) 397, 19 L.Ed. 437 (1869); Wheeler v. United States, 93 U.S.App.D.C. 159, 211 F.2d 19 (1953), cert. denied 347 U.S. 1019, 74 S.Ct. 876, 98 L.Ed. 1140; Wetherbee v. Safety Casualty Co., 219 F.2d 274 (5th Cir.1955); Lampe v. United States, 97 U.S.App.D.C. 160, 229 F.2d 43 (1956). Nevertheless, on occasion the only evidence may be the content of the statement itself, and rulings that it may be sufficient are described as "increasing," Slough, supra at 246, and as the "prevailing practice," McCormick § 272, p. 579. Illustrative are Armour & Co. v. Industrial Commission, 78 Colo. 569, 243 P. 546 (1926); Young v. Stewart, 191 N.C. 297, 131 S.E. 735 (1926). Moreover, under Rule 104(a) the judge is not limited by the hearsay rule in passing upon preliminary questions of fact.

Proof of declarant's perception by his statement presents similar considerations when declarant is identified. People v. Poland, 22 Ill.2d 175, 174 N.E.2d 804 (1961). However, when declarant is an unidentified bystander, the cases indicate hesitancy in upholding the statement alone as sufficient, Garrett v. Howden, 73 N.M. 307, 387 P.2d 874 (1963); Beck v. Dye, 200 Wash. 1, 92 P.2d 1113 (1939), a result which would under appropriate circumstances be consistent with the rule.

Permissible *subject matter* of the statement is limited under Exception (1) to description or explanation of the event or condition, the assumption being that spontaneity, in the absence of a startling event, may extend no farther. In Exception (2), however, the statement need only "relate" to the startling event or condition, thus affording a broader scope of subject matter coverage. 6 Wigmore §§ 1750, 1754. See Sanitary Grocery Co. v. Snead, 67 App.D.C. 129, 90 F.2d 374 (1937), slip-and-fall case sustaining admissibility of clerk's statement, "That has been on the floor for a couple of hours," and Murphy Auto Parts Co., Inc. v. Ball, 101 U.S.App.D.C. 416, 249 F.2d 508 (1957), upholding admission, on issue of driver's agency, of his statement that he had to call on a customer and was in a hurry to get home. Quick, Hearsay, Excitement, Necessity and the Uniform Rules: A Reappraisal of Rule 63(4), 6 Wayne L.Rev. 204, 206–209 (1960).

Similar provisions are found in Uniform Rule 63(4)(a) and (b); California Evidence Code § 1240 (as to Exception (2) only); Kansas Code of Civil Procedure § 60–460(d)(1) and (2); New Jersey Evidence Rule 63(4).

Exception (3) is essentially a specialized application of Exception (1), presented separately to enhance its usefulness and accessibility. See McCormick §§ 265, 268.

The exclusion of "statements of memory or belief to prove the fact remembered or believed" is necessary to avoid the virtual destruction of the hearsay rule which would otherwise result from allowing state of mind, provable by a hearsay statement, to serve as the basis for an inference of the happening of the event which produced the state of mind. Shepard v. United States, 290 U.S. 96, 54 S.Ct. 22, 78 L.Ed. 196 (1933); Maguire, The Hillmon Case—Thirty-three Years After, 38 Harv.L.Rev. 709, 719–731 (1925); Hinton, States of Mind and the Hearsay Rule, 1 U.Chi.L.Rev. 394, 421–423 (1934). The rule of Mutual Life Ins.

Co. v. Hillmon, 145 U.S. 285, 12 S.Ct. 909, 36 L.Ed. 706 (1892), allowing evidence of intention as tending to prove the doing of the act intended, is, of course, left undisturbed.

The carving out, from the exclusion mentioned in the preceding paragraph, of declarations relating to the execution, revocation, identification, or terms of declarant's will represents an *ad hoc* judgment which finds ample reinforcement in the decisions, resting on practical grounds of necessity and expediency rather than logic. McCormick § 271, pp. 577–578; Annot., 34 A.L.R.2d 588, 62 A.L.R.2d 855. A similar recognition of the need for and practical value of this kind of evidence is found in California Evidence Code § 1260.

Report of House Committee on the Judiciary

House Comm on Judiciary, Fed.Rules of Evidence, H.R.Rep. No. 650, 93d Cong., 1st Sess., p. 13 (1973); 1974 U.S.Code Cong. & Ad.News 7075, 7087

Rule 803(3) was approved in the form submitted by the Court to Congress. However, the Committee intends that the Rule be construed to limit the doctrine of Mutual Life Insurance Co. v. Hillmon, 145 U.S. 285, 295–300 (1892), so as to render statements of intent by a declarant admissible only to prove his future conduct, not the future conduct of another person.

Advisory Committee's Note

56 F.R.D. 183, 306

Exception (4). Even those few jurisdictions which have shied away from generally admitting statements of present condition have allowed them if made to a physician for purposes of diagnosis and treatment in view of the patient's strong motivation to be truthful. McCormick § 266, p. 563. The same guarantee of trustworthiness extends to statements of past conditions and medical history, made for purposes of diagnosis or treatment. It also extends to statements as to causation, reasonably pertinent to the same purposes, in accord with the current trend, Shell Oil Co. v. Industrial Commission, 2 Ill.2d 590, 119 N.E.2d 224 (1954); McCormick § 266, p. 564; New Jersey Evidence Rule 63(12)(c). Statements as to fault would not ordinarily qualify under this latter language. Thus a patient's statement that he was struck by an automobile would qualify but not his statement that the car was driven through a red light. Under the exception the statement need not have been made to a physician. Statements to hospital attendants, ambulance drivers, or even members of the family might be included.

Conventional doctrine has excluded from the hearsay exception, as not within its guarantee of truthfulness, statements to a physician consulted only for the purpose of enabling him to testify. While these statements were not admissible as substantive evidence, the expert was allowed to state the basis of his opinion, including statements of this kind. The distinction thus called for was one most unlikely to be made by juries. The rule accordingly rejects the limitation. This position is consistent with the provision of Rule 703 that the facts on which expert testimony is based need not be admissible in evidence if of a kind ordinarily relied upon by experts in the field.

Report of House Committee on the Judiciary

House Comm. on Judiciary, Fed.Rules of Evidence, H.R.Rep. No. 650, 93d Cong., 1st Sess., p. 14 (1973); 1974 U.S.Code Cong. & Ad.News 7075, 7087

After giving particular attention to the question of physical examination made solely to enable a physician to testify, the Committee approved Rule 803(4) as submitted to Congress, with the understanding that it is not intended in any way to adversely affect present privilege rules or those subsequently adopted.

Report of Senate Committee on the Judiciary

Senate Comm. on Judiciary, Fed.Rules of Evidence, S.Rep. No. 1277, 93d Cong., 2d Sess., p. 27 (1974); 1974 U.S.Code Cong. & Ad.News 7051, 7073

The House approved this rule as it was submitted by the Supreme Court "with the understanding that it is not intended in any way to adversely affect present privilege rules." We also approve this rule, and we would point out with respect to the question of its relation to privileges, it must be read in conjunction with rule 35 of the Federal Rules of Civil Procedure which provides that whenever the physical or mental condition of a party (plaintiff or defendant) is in controversy, the court may require him to submit to an examination by a physician. It is these examinations which will normally be admitted under this exception.

Advisory Committee's Note

56 F.R.D. 183, 306

Exception (5). A hearsay exception for recorded recollection is generally recognized and has been described as having "long been favored by the federal and practically all the state courts that have had occasion to decide the question." United States v. Kelly, 349 F.2d 720, 770 (2d Cir.1965), citing numerous cases and sustaining the exception against a claimed denial of the right of confrontation. Many additional cases are cited in Annot., 82 A.L.R.2d 473, 520. The guarantee of trustworthiness is found in the reliability inherent in a record made while events were still fresh in mind and accurately reflecting them. Owens v. State, 67 Md. 307, 316, 10 A. 210, 212 (1887).

The principal controversy attending the exception has centered, not upon the propriety of the exception itself, but upon the question whether a preliminary requirement of impaired memory on the part of the witness should be imposed. The authorities are divided. If regard be had only to the accuracy of the evidence, admittedly impairment of the memory of the witness adds nothing to it and should not be required. McCormick § 277, p. 593; 3 Wigmore § 738, p. 76; Jordan v. People, 151 Colo. 133, 376 P.2d 699 (1962), cert. denied 373 U.S. 944, 83 S.Ct. 1553, 10 L.Ed.2d 699; Hall v. State, 223 Md. 158, 162 A.2d 751 (1960); State v. Bindhammer, 44 N.J. 372, 209 A.2d 124 (1965). Nevertheless, the absence of the requirement, it is believed, would encourage the use of statements carefully prepared for purposes of litigation under the supervision of attorneys, investigators, or claim adjusters. Hence the example includes a requirement that the witness not have "sufficient recollection to enable him to testify fully and accurately." To the same effect are California Evidence Code § 1237 and New Jersey Rule 63(1)(b), and this has been the position of the federal courts. Vicksburg & Meridian R.R. v. O'Brien, 119 U.S. 99, 7 S.Ct. 118,

30 L.Ed. 299 (1886); Ahern v. Webb, 268 F.2d 45 (10th Cir.1959); and see N.L.R.B. v. Hudson Pulp and Paper Corp., 273 F.2d 660, 665 (5th Cir.1960); N.L.R.B. v. Federal Dairy Co., 297 F.2d 487 (1st Cir.1962). But cf. United States v. Adams, 385 F.2d 548 (2d Cir.1967).

No attempt is made in the exception to spell out the method of establishing the initial knowledge or the contemporaneity and accuracy of the record, leaving them to be dealt with as the circumstances of the particular case might indicate. Multiple person involvement in the process of observing and recording, as in Rathbun v. Brancatella, 93 N.J.L. 222, 107 A. 279 (1919), is entirely consistent with the exception.

Locating the exception at this place in the scheme of the rules is a matter of choice. There were two other possibilities. The first was to regard the statement as one of the group of prior statements of a testifying witness which are excluded entirely from the category of hearsay by Rule 801(d)(1). That category, however, requires that declarant be "subject to cross-examination," as to which the impaired memory aspect of the exception raises doubts. The other possibility was to include the exception among those covered by Rule 804. Since unavailability is required by that rule and lack of memory is listed as a species of unavailability by the definition of the term in Rule 804(a)(3), that treatment at first impression would seem appropriate. The fact is, however, that the unavailability requirement of the exception is of a limited and peculiar nature. Accordingly, the exception is located at this point rather than in the context of a rule where unavailability is conceived of more broadly.

Report of House Committee on the Judiciary

House Comm. on Judiciary, Fed.Rules of Evidence, H.R.Rep. No. 650, 93d Cong., 1st Sess., p. 14 (1973); 1974 U.S.Code Cong. & Ad.News 7075, 7087

Rule 803(5) as submitted by the Court permitted the reading into evidence of a memorandum or record concerning a matter about which a witness once had knowledge but now has insufficient recollection to enable him to testify accurately and fully, "shown to have been made when the matter was fresh in his memory and to reflect that knowledge correctly." The Committee amended this Rule to add the words "or adopted by the witness" after the phrase "shown to have been made", a treatment consistent with the definition of "statement" in the Jencks Act, 18 U.S.C. 3500. Moreover, it is the Committee's understanding that a memorandum or report, although barred under this Rule, would nonetheless be admissible if it came within another hearsay exception. This last stated principle is deemed applicable to all the hearsay rules.

Report of Senate Committee on the Judiciary

Senate Comm. on Judiciary, Fed.Rules of Evidence, S.Rep. No. 1277, 93d Cong., 2d Sess., p. 27 (1974); 1974 U.S.Code Cong. & Ad.News 7051, 7073

Rule 803(5) as submitted by the Court permitted the reading into evidence of a memorandum or record concerning a matter about which a witness once had knowledge but now has insufficient recollection to enable him to testify accurately and fully, "shown to have been made when the matter was fresh in his memory and to reflect that knowledge correctly." The House amended the rule to add the words "or adopted by the witness" after the phrase "shown to have been made," language parallel to the Jencks Act.[1]

The committee accepts the House amendment with the understanding and belief that it was not intended to narrow the scope of applicability of the rule. In fact, we understand it to clarify the rule's applicability to a memorandum adopted by the witness as well as one made by him. While the rule as submitted by the Court was silent on the question of who made the memorandum, we view the House amendment as a helpful clarification, noting, however, that the Advisory Committee's note to this rule suggests that the important thing is the accuracy of the memorandum rather than who made it.

The committee does not view the House amendment as precluding admissibility in situations in which multiple participants were involved.

When the verifying witness has not prepared the report, but merely examined it and found it accurate, he has adopted the report, and it is therefore admissible. The rule should also be interpreted to cover other situations involving multiple participants, e.g., employer dictating to secretary, secretary making memorandum at direction of employer, or information being passed along a chain of persons, as in Curtis v. Bradley.[2]

The committee also accepts the understanding of the House that a memorandum or report, although barred under this rule, would nonetheless be admissible if it came within another hearsay exception. We consider this principle to be applicable to all the hearsay rules.

Advisory Committee's Note

56 F.R.D. 183, 307

Exception (6) represents an area which has received much attention from those seeking to improve the law of evidence. The Commonwealth Fund Act was the result of a study completed in 1927 by a distinguished committee under the chairmanship of Professor Morgan. Morgan et al., The Law of Evidence: Some Proposals for its Reform 63 (1927). With changes too minor to mention, it was adopted by Congress in 1936 as the rule for federal courts. 28 U.S.C. § 1732. A number of states took similar action. The Commissioners on Uniform State Laws in 1936 promulgated the Uniform Business Records as Evidence Act, 9A U.L.A. 506, which has acquired a substantial following in the states. Model Code Rule 514 and Uniform Rule 63(13) also deal with the subject. Difference of varying degrees of importance exist among these various treatments.

These reform efforts were largely within the context of business and commercial records, as the kind usually encountered, and concentrated considerable attention upon relaxing the requirement of producing as witnesses, or accounting for the nonproduction of, all participants in the process of gathering, transmitting, and recording information which the common law had evolved as a burdensome and crippling aspect of using records of this type. In their areas of primary emphasis on witnesses to be called and the general admissibility of ordinary business and commercial records, the Commonwealth Fund Act and the Uniform Act appear to have worked well. The exception seeks to preserve their advantages.

1. 18 U.S.C. § 3500.

2. 65 Conn. 99, 31 Atl. 591 (1894). See also, Rathbun v. Brancatella, 93 N.J.L. 222, 107 Atl. 279 (1919); see also McCormick on Evidence, § 303 (2d ed. 1972).

On the subject of what witnesses must be called, the Commonwealth Fund Act eliminated the common law requirement of calling or accounting for all participants by failing to mention it. United States v. Mortimer, 118 F.2d 266 (2d Cir.1941); La Porte v. United States, 300 F.2d 878 (9th Cir.1962); McCormick § 290, p. 608. Model Code Rule 514 and Uniform Rule 63(13) did likewise. The Uniform Act, however, abolished the common law requirement in express terms, providing that the requisite foundation testimony might be furnished by "the custodian or other qualified witness." Uniform Business Records as Evidence Act, § 2; 9A U.L.A. 506. The exception follows the Uniform Act in this respect.

The element of unusual reliability of business records is said variously to be supplied by systematic checking, by regularity and continuity which produce habits of precision, by actual experience of business in relying upon them, or by a duty to make an accurate record as part of a continuing job or occupation. McCormick §§ 281, 286, 287; Laughlin, Business Entries and the Like, 46 Iowa L.Rev. 276 (1961). The model statutes and rules have sought to capture these factors and to extend their impact by employing the phrase "regular course of business," in conjunction with a definition of "business" far broader than its ordinarily accepted meaning. The result is a tendency unduly to emphasize a requirement of routineness and repetitiveness and an insistence that other types of records be squeezed into the fact patterns which give rise to traditional business records....

Amplification of the kinds of activities producing admissible records has given rise to problems which conventional business records by their nature avoid. They are problems of the source of the recorded information, of entries in opinion form, of motivation, and of involvement as participant in the matters recorded.

Sources of information presented no substantial problem with ordinary business records. All participants, including the observer or participant furnishing the information to be recorded, were acting routinely, under a duty of accuracy, with employer reliance on the result, or in short "in the regular course of business." If, however, the supplier of the information does not act in the regular course, an essential link is broken; the assurance of accuracy does not extend to the information itself, and the fact that it may be recorded with scrupulous accuracy is of no avail. An illustration is the police report incorporating information obtained from a bystander: the officer qualifies as acting in the regular course but the informant does not. The leading case, Johnson v. Lutz, 253 N.Y. 124, 170 N.E. 517 (1930), held that a report thus prepared was inadmissible. Most of the authorities have agreed with the decision. Gencarella v. Fyfe, 171 F.2d 419 (1st Cir.1948); Gordon v. Robinson, 210 F.2d 192 (3d Cir.1954); Standard Oil Co. of California v. Moore, 251 F.2d 188, 214 (9th Cir.1957), cert. denied 356 U.S. 975, 78 S.Ct. 1139, 2 L.Ed.2d 1148; Yates v. Bair Transport, Inc., 249 F.Supp. 681 (S.D.N.Y.1965); Annot., 69 A.L.R.2d 1148. Cf. Hawkins v. Gorea Motor Express, Inc., 360 F.2d 933 (2d Cir.1966). Contra, 5 Wigmore § 1530a, n. 1, pp. 391–392. The point is not dealt with specifically in the Commonwealth Fund Act, the Uniform Act, or Uniform Rule 63(13). However, Model Code Rule 514 contains the requirement "that it was the regular course of that business for one with personal knowledge ... to make such a memorandum or record or to transmit information thereof to be included in such a memorandum or record ...." The rule follows this lead in requiring an informant with knowledge acting in the course of the regularly conducted activity.

Entries in the form of opinions were not encountered in traditional business records in view of the purely factual nature of the items recorded, but they are now commonly encountered with respect to medical diagnoses, prognoses, and test results, as well as occasionally in other areas. The Commonwealth Fund Act provided only for records of an "act, transaction, occurrence, or event," while the Uniform Act, Model Code Rule 514, and Uniform Rule 63(13) merely added the ambiguous term "condition." The limited phrasing of the Commonwealth Fund Act, 28 U.S.C. § 1732, may account for the reluctance of some federal decisions to admit diagnostic entries. New York Life Ins. Co. v. Taylor, 79 U.S.App.D.C. 66, 147 F.2d 297 (1945); Lyles v. United States, 103 U.S.App.D.C. 22, 254 F.2d 725 (1957), cert. denied 356 U.S. 961, 78 S.Ct. 997, 2 L.Ed.2d 1067; England v. United States, 174 F.2d 466 (5th Cir.1949); Skogen v. Dow Chemical Co., 375 F.2d 692 (8th Cir.1967). Other federal decisions, however, experienced no difficulty in freely admitting diagnostic entries. Reed v. Order of United Commercial Travelers, 123 F.2d 252 (2d Cir.1941); Buckminster's Estate v. Commissioner of Internal Revenue, 147 F.2d 331 (2d Cir.1944); Medina v. Erickson, 226 F.2d 475 (9th Cir.1955); Thomas v. Hogan, 308 F.2d 355 (4th Cir.1962); Glawe v. Rulon, 284 F.2d 495 (8th Cir.1960). In the state courts, the trend favors admissibility. Borucki v. MacKenzie Bros. Co., 125 Conn. 92, 3 A.2d 224 (1938); Allen v. St. Louis Public Service Co., 365 Mo. 677, 285 S.W.2d 663, 55 A.L.R.2d 1022 (1956); People v. Kohlmeyer, 284 N.Y. 366, 31 N.E.2d 490 (1940); Weis v. Weis, 147 Ohio St. 416, 72 N.E.2d 245 (1947). In order to make clear its adherence to the latter position, the rule specifically includes both diagnoses and opinions, in addition to acts, events, and conditions, as proper subjects of admissible entries.

Problems of the motivation of the informant have been a source of difficulty and disagreement. In Palmer v. Hoffman, 318 U.S. 109, 63 S.Ct. 477, 87 L.Ed. 645 (1943), exclusion of an accident report made by the since deceased engineer, offered by defendant railroad trustees in a grade crossing collision case, was upheld. The report was not "in the regular course of business," not a record of the systematic conduct of the business as a business, said the Court. The report was prepared for use in litigating, not railroading. While the opinion mentions the motivation of the engineer only obliquely, the emphasis on records of routine operations is significant only by virtue of impact on motivation to be accurate. Absence of routineness raises lack of motivation to be accurate. The opinion of the Court of Appeals had gone beyond mere lack of motive to be accurate: the engineer's statement was "dripping with motivations to misrepresent." Hoffman v. Palmer, 129 F.2d 976, 991 (2d Cir.1942). The direct introduction of motivation is a disturbing factor, since absence of motive to misrepresent has not traditionally been a requirement of the rule; that records might be self-serving has not been a ground for exclusion. Laughlin, Business Records and the Like, 46 Iowa L.Rev. 276, 285 (1961). As Judge Clark said in his dissent, "I submit that there is hardly a grocer's account book which could not be excluded on that basis." 129 F.2d at 1002. A physician's evaluation report of a personal injury litigant would appear to be in the routine of his business. If the report is offered by the party at whose instance it was made, however, it has been held inadmissible, Yates v. Bair Transport, Inc., 249 F.Supp. 681 (S.D.N.Y.1965), otherwise if offered by the opposite party, Korte v. New York, N.H. & H.R. Co., 191 F.2d 86 (2d Cir.1951), cert. denied 342 U.S. 868, 72 S.Ct. 108, 96 L.Ed. 652.

The decisions hinge on motivation and which party is entitled to be concerned about it. Professor McCormick believed that the doctor's report or the accident report were sufficiently routine to justify admissibility. McCormick § 287, p. 604. Yet hesitation must be experienced in admitting everything which is observed and recorded in the course of a regularly conducted activity. Efforts to set a limit are illustrated by Hartzog v. United States, 217 F.2d 706 (4th Cir.1954), error to admit worksheets made by since deceased deputy collector in preparation for the instant income tax evasion prosecution, and United States v. Ware, 247 F.2d 698 (7th Cir.1957), error to admit narcotics agents' records of purchases. See also Exception (8), infra, as to the public record aspects of records of this nature. Some decisions have been satisfied as to motivation of an accident report if made pursuant to statutory duty, United States v. New York Foreign Trade Zone Operators, 304 F.2d 792 (2d Cir.1962); Taylor v. Baltimore & O.R. Co., 344 F.2d 281 (2d Cir.1965), since the report was oriented in a direction other than the litigation which ensued. Cf. Matthews v. United States, 217 F.2d 409 (5th Cir.1954). The formulation of specific terms which would assure satisfactory results in all cases is not possible. Consequently the rule proceeds from the base that records made in the course of a regularly conducted activity will be taken as admissible but subject to authority to exclude if "the sources of information or other circumstances indicate lack of trustworthiness."

Occasional decisions have reached for enhanced accuracy by requiring involvement as a participant in matters reported. Clainos v. United States, 82 U.S.App.D.C. 278, 163 F.2d 593 (1947), error to admit police records of convictions; Standard Oil Co. of California v. Moore, 251 F.2d 188 (9th Cir.1957), cert. denied 356 U.S. 975, 78 S.Ct. 1139, 2 L.Ed.2d 1148, error to admit employees' records of observed business practices of others. The rule includes no requirement of this nature. Wholly acceptable records may involve matters merely observed, e.g. the weather.

The form which the "record" may assume under the rule is described broadly as a "memorandum, report, record, or data compilation, in any form." The expression "data compilation" is used as broadly descriptive of any means of storing information other than the conventional words and figures in written or documentary form. It includes, but is by no means limited to, electronic computer storage. The term is borrowed from revised Rule 34(a) of the Rules of Civil Procedure.

Report of House Committee on the Judiciary

House Comm. on Judiciary, Fed.Rules of Evidence, H.R.Rep. No. 650, 93d Cong., 1st Sess., p. 14 (1973); 1974 U.S.Code Cong. & Ad.News 7075, 7087

Rule 803(6) as submitted by the Court permitted a record made "in the course of a regularly conducted activity" to be admissible in certain circumstances. The Committee believed there were insufficient guarantees of reliability in records made in the course of activities falling outside the scope of "business" activities as that term is broadly defined in 28 U.S.C. 1732. Moreover, the Committee concluded that the additional requirement of Section 1732 that it must have been the regular practice of a business to make the record is a necessary further assurance of its trustworthiness. The Committee accordingly amended the Rule to incorporate these limitations.

Report of Senate Committee on the Judiciary

Senate Comm. on Judiciary, Fed.Rules of Evidence, S.Rep. No. 1277, 93d Cong., 2d Sess., p. 16 (1974); 1974 U.S.Code Cong. & Ad.News 7051, 7063

Rule 803(6) as submitted by the Supreme Court permitted a record made in the course of a regularly conducted activity to be admissible in certain circumstances. This rule constituted a broadening of the traditional business records hearsay exception which has been long advocated by scholars and judges active in the law of evidence.

The House felt there were insufficient guarantees of reliability of records not within a broadly defined business records exception. We disagree. Even under the House definition of "business" including profession, occupation, and "calling of every kind," the records of many regularly conducted activities will, or may be, excluded from evidence. Under the principle of ejusdem generis, the intent of "calling of every kind" would seem to be related to work-related endeavors—e.g., butcher, baker, artist, etc.

Thus, it appears that the records of many institutions or groups might not be admissible under the House amendments. For example, schools, churches, and hospitals will not normally be considered businesses within the definition. Yet, these are groups which keep financial and other records on a regular basis in a manner similar to business enterprises. We believe these records are of equivalent trustworthiness and should be admitted into evidence.

Three states, which have recently codified their evidence rules, have adopted the Supreme Court version of rule 803(6), providing for admission of memoranda of a "regularly conducted activity." None adopted the words "business activity" used in the House amendment.[3]

Therefore, the committee deleted the word "business" as it appears before the word "activity". The last sentence then is unnecessary and was also deleted.

It is the understanding of the committee that the use of the phrase "person with knowledge" is not intended to imply that the party seeking to introduce the memorandum, report, record, or data compilation must be able to produce, or even identify, the specific individual upon whose first-hand knowledge the memorandum, report, record or data compilation was based. A sufficient foundation for the introduction of such evidence will be laid if the party seeking to introduce the evidence is able to show that it was the regular practice of the activity to base such memorandums, reports, records, or data compilations upon a transmission from a person with knowledge, e.g., in the case of the content of a shipment of goods, upon a report from the company's receiving agent or in the case of a computer printout, upon a report from the company's computer programmer or one who has knowledge of the particular record system. In short, the scope of the phrase "person with knowledge" is meant to be coterminous with the custodian of the evidence or other qualified witness. The committee believes this represents the desired rule in light of the complex nature of modern business organizations.

Conference Report

H.R., Fed.Rules of Evidence, Conf.Rep. No. 1597, 93d Cong., 2d Sess., p. 11 (1974); 1974 U.S.Code Cong. & Ad.News 7098, 7104

3. See Nev.Rev.Stats. § 15.135; N.Mex.Stats. (1973 Supp.) § 20–4–803(6); West's Wis.Stats.Anno. (1973 Supp.) § 908.03(6).

The House bill provides in subsection (6) that records of a regularly conducted "business" activity qualify for admission into evidence as an exception to the hearsay rule. "Business" is defined as including "business, profession, occupation and calling of every kind." The Senate amendment drops the requirement that the records be those of a "business" activity and eliminates the definition of "business." The Senate amendment provides that records are admissible if they are records of a regularly conducted "activity."

The Conference adopts the House provision that the records must be those of a regularly conducted "business" activity. The Conferees changed the definition of "business" contained in the House provision in order to make it clear that the records of institutions and associations like schools, churches and hospitals are admissible under this provision. The records of public schools and hospitals are also covered by Rule 803(8), which deals with public records and reports.

Advisory Committee's Note

56 F.R.D. 183, 311

Exception (7). Failure of a record to mention a matter which would ordinarily be mentioned is satisfactory evidence of its nonexistence. Uniform Rule 63(14), Comment. While probably not hearsay as defined in Rule 801, supra, decisions may be found which class the evidence not only as hearsay but also as not within any exception. In order to set the question at rest in favor of admissibility, it is specifically treated here. McCormick § 289, p. 609; Morgan, Basic Problems of Evidence 314 (1962); 5 Wigmore § 1531; Uniform Rule 63(14); California Evidence Code § 1272; Kansas Code of Civil Procedure § 60–460(n); New Jersey Evidence Rule 63(14).

Report of House Committee on the Judiciary

House Comm. on Judiciary, Fed.Rules of Evidence, H.R.Rep. No. 650, 93d Cong., 1st Sess., p. 14 (1973); 1974 U.S.Code Cong. & Ad.News 7075, 7088

Rule 803(7) as submitted by the Court concerned the *absence* of entry in the records of a "regularly conducted activity." The Committee amended this Rule to conform with its action with respect to Rule 803(6).

Advisory Committee's Note

56 F.R.D. 183, 311

Exception (8). Public records are a recognized hearsay exception at common law and have been the subject of statutes without number. McCormick § 291. See, for example, 28 U.S.C. § 1733, the relative narrowness of which is illustrated by its nonapplicability to non-federal public agencies, thus necessitating resort to the less appropriate business record exception to the hearsay rule. Kay v. United States, 255 F.2d 476 (4th Cir.1958). The rule makes no distinction between federal and nonfederal offices and agencies.

Justification for the exception is the assumption that a public official will perform his duty properly and the unlikelihood that he will remember details independently of the record. Wong Wing Foo v. McGrath, 196 F.2d 120 (9th Cir.1952), and see Chesapeake & Delaware Canal Co. v. United States, 250 U.S. 123, 39 S.Ct. 407, 63 L.Ed. 889 (1919). As to items (A) and (B), further support is found in the reliability factors underlying records of regularly conducted activities generally. See Exception (6), supra.

(A) Cases illustrating the admissibility of records of the office's or agency's own activities are numerous. Chesapeake & Delaware Canal Co. v. United States, 250 U.S. 123, 39 S.Ct. 407, 63 L.Ed. 889 (1919), Treasury records of miscellaneous receipts and disbursements; Howard v. Perrin, 200 U.S. 71, 26 S.Ct. 195, 50 L.Ed. 374 (1906), General Land Office records; Ballew v. United States, 160 U.S. 187, 16 S.Ct. 263, 40 L.Ed. 388 (1895), Pension Office records.

(B) Cases sustaining admissibility of records of matters observed are also numerous. United States v. Van Hook, 284 F.2d 489 (7th Cir.1960), remanded for resentencing 365 U.S. 609, 81 S.Ct. 823, 5 L.Ed.2d 821, letter from induction officer to District Attorney, pursuant to army regulations, stating fact and circumstances of refusal to be inducted; T'Kach v. United States, 242 F.2d 937 (5th Cir.1957), affidavit of White House personnel officer that search of records showed no employment of accused, charged with fraudulently representing himself as an envoy of the President; Minnehaha County v. Kelley, 150 F.2d 356 (8th Cir.1945); Weather Bureau records of rainfall; United States v. Meyer, 113 F.2d 387 (7th Cir.1940), cert. denied 311 U.S. 706, 61 S.Ct. 174, 85 L.Ed. 459, map prepared by government engineer from information furnished by men working under his supervision.

(C) The more controversial area of public records is that of the so-called "evaluative" report. The disagreement among the decisions has been due in part, no doubt, to the variety of situations encountered, as well as to differences in principle. Sustaining admissibility are such cases as United States v. Dumas, 149 U.S. 278, 13 S.Ct. 872, 37 L.Ed. 734 (1893), statement of account certified by Postmaster General in action against postmaster; McCarty v. United States, 185 F.2d 520 (5th Cir.1950), reh. denied 187 F.2d 234, Certificate of Settlement of General Accounting Office showing indebtedness and letter from Army official stating Government had performed, in action on contract to purchase and remove waste food from Army camp; Moran v. Pittsburgh-Des Moines Steel Co., 183 F.2d 467 (3d Cir.1950), report of Bureau of Mines as to cause of gas tank explosion; Petition of W___, 164 F.Supp. 659 (E.D.Pa.1958), report by Immigration and Naturalization Service investigator that petitioner was known in community as wife of man to whom she was not married. To the opposite effect and denying admissibility are Franklin v. Skelly Oil Co., 141 F.2d 568 (10th Cir.1944), State Fire Marshal's report of cause of gas explosion; Lomax Transp. Co. v. United States, 183 F.2d 331 (9th Cir.1950), Certificate of Settlement from General Accounting Office in action for naval supplies lost in warehouse fire; Yung Jin Teung v. Dulles, 229 F.2d 244 (2d Cir.1956), "Status Reports" offered to justify delay in processing passport applications.... Various kinds of evaluative reports are admissible under federal statutes: 7 U.S.C. § 78, findings of Secretary of Agriculture prima facie evidence of true grade of grain; 7 U.S.C. § 210(f), findings of Secretary of Agriculture prima facie evidence in action for damages against stockyard owner; 7 U.S.C. § 292, order by Secretary of Agriculture prima facie evidence in judicial enforcement proceedings against producers association monopoly; 7 U.S.C. § 1622(h), Department of Agriculture inspection certificates of products shipped in interstate commerce prima facie evidence; 8 U.S.C. § 1440(c), separation of alien from military service on conditions other than honorable provable by certificate from department in proceedings to revoke citizenship; 18 U.S.C. § 4245, certificate of Director of Prisons that convicted person has been examined and found probably incompetent at time of trial prima facie evidence in court hearing on competency; 42 U.S.C. § 269(b), bill of health by appropriate official prima facie evidence of vessel's sanitary history and condition and compliance with regulations; 46 U.S.C. § 679, certificate of consul presumptive evidence of refusal of master to transport destitute seamen to United States. While these statutory exceptions to the hearsay rule are left undisturbed, Rule 802, the willingness of Congress to recognize a substantial measure of admissibility for evaluative reports is a helpful guide.

Factors which may be of assistance in passing upon the admissibility of evaluative reports include: (1) the timeliness of the investigation, McCormick, Can the Courts Make Wider Use of Reports of Official Investigations? 42 Iowa L.Rev. 363 (1957); (2) the special skill or experience of the official, *id.*, (3) whether a hearing was held and the level at which conducted, Franklin v. Skelly Oil Co., 141 F.2d 568 (10th Cir.1944); (4) possible motivation problems suggested by Palmer v. Hoffman, 318 U.S. 109, 63 S.Ct. 477, 87 L.Ed. 645 (1943). Others no doubt could be added.

The formulation of an approach which would give appropriate weight to all possible factors in every situation is an obvious impossibility. Hence the rule, as in Exception (6), assumes admissibility in the first instance but with ample provision for escape if sufficient negative factors are present. In one respect, however, the rule with respect to evaluative reports under item (C) is very specific: they are admissible only in civil cases and against the government in criminal cases in view of the almost certain collision with confrontation rights which would result from their use against the accused in a criminal case.

Report of House Committee on the Judiciary

House Comm. on Judiciary, Fed.Rules of Evidence, H.R.Rep. No. 650, 93d Cong., 1st Sess., p. 14 (1973); 1974 U.S.Code Cong. & Ad.News 7075, 7088

The Committee approved Rule 803(8) without substantive change from the form in which it was submitted by the Court. The Committee intends that the phrase "factual findings" be strictly construed and that evaluations or opinions contained in public reports shall not be admissible under this Rule.

House of Representatives

Feb. 6, 1974, 120 Cong.Rec 2387 (1974)

Amendment offered by Ms. Holtzman

Ms. HOLTZMAN. Mr. Chairman, I offer an amendment.

The Clerk read as follows:

> Amendment offered by Ms. Holtzman: On page 94, line 11, after the word "law" and before the comma, insert the following: "as to which matters there was a duty to report".

Ms. HOLTZMAN. Mr. Chairman, I will try to be very brief, because it is late in the day.

My amendment is offered to clarify and narrow a provision on the hearsay rule (Rule 803(8)(B)). This rule now provides that if any Government employee in the course of his duty observes something—in fact, anything—and makes a report of that observation, that report can be entered into evidence at a trial whether criminal or civil, without the opportunity to cross-examine the author of the report.

While I respect Government employees, I think we would all concede that they are fallible, exactly like every other human. We do not provide such broad exceptions to the hearsay rule for ordinary mortals.

My amendment makes it crystal clear that random observations by a Government employee cannot be introduced as an exception to the hearsay rule and be insulated from cross-examination. My amendment would allow reports of "matters observed" by a public official only if he had a duty to report about such matters. One operating under such a duty is far more likely to observe and report accurately.

I urge adoption of this amendment in order to narrow and restrict the broad exception to the hearsay rule in the bill.

Mr. HUNGATE. Mr. Chairman, I rise in opposition to the amendment.

This is a matter that was considered in the subcommittee, and we decided to stay with the language as presented to the House here, which states as follows:

> Records, reports, statements, or data compilations, in any form, of public offices or agencies, setting forth (A) the activities of the office or agency, or (B) matters observed pursuant to duty imposed by law....

Mr. Chairman, this is where the point of disagreement occurred. We stayed with that version of the bill, and I would recommend that version to the Committee of the Whole House.

Mr. DANIELSON. Mr. Chairman, I rise in support of the amendment offered by the gentlewoman from New York (Ms. Holtzman).

I think if we leave this language in the proposed bill, we are opening the door to a host of problems, the like of which we have probably never seen in a trial court.

I think the proper approach, in order to eliminate this, is simply to adopt the gentlewoman's amendment, and eliminate this provision, simply because there is absolutely no restriction on the sort of material which could come in under the language as proposed.

I urge the adoption of the gentlewoman's amendment.

Mr. DENNIS. Mr. Chairman, I rise in support of the gentlewoman's amendment.

So that the committee will know what we are talking about here, this permits the introduction in evidence as an exception to the hearsay rule of public records and reports, statements, or data compilations in any form of matters observed pursuant to duty imposed by law. The gentlewoman would add "as to which matters there was a duty to report."

Again it is a matter of judgment, but the difference would be this: Supposing you had a divorce case and you tried to put in a report of a social worker, rather than putting the social worker on the stand; under the committee's language anything she said in the report which would be observed by her pursuant to her general duties would be admissible. Under the amendment, only those things as to which she had some duty to make a report would be admissible.

If the law required her to observe and report certain things about a condition in the home, that could come in, but if she put in a lot of other stuff there, she could not put that in without calling her as a witness and giving the opposition a chance to cross-examine her.

On the whole I think the amendment improves the bill, and I support it.

The CHAIRMAN. The question is on the amendment offered by the gentlewoman from New York (Ms. Holtzman).

The amendment was agreed to.

Amendment offered by Mr. Dennis

Mr. DENNIS. Mr. Chairman, I offer an amendment.

The Clerk read as follows:

> Amendment offered by Mr. Dennis: On page 94, line 11 of the bill, after the word "law", insert the words "excluding, however, in criminal cases matters observed by police officers and other law enforcement personnel".

Mr. DENNIS. Mr. Chairman, this goes to the same subject matter as the last amendment. It deals with official statements and reports.

What I am saying here is that in a criminal case, only, we should not be able to put in the police report to prove your case without calling the policeman. I think in a criminal case you ought to have to call the policeman on the beat and give the defendant the chance to cross examine him, rather than just reading the report into evidence, that is the purpose of this amendment.

Ms. HOLTZMAN. Mr. Chairman, I rise in support of the amendment.

I will be very brief again.

I commend my colleague for raising this point. Again his purpose is to restrict the possible abuse of hearsay evidence.

I think the gentleman's amendment is very valuable and reaffirms the right of cross-examination to the accused. It also permits those engaged in civil trials the right of cross-examination. Cross-examination guarantees due process of law and a fair trial.

(Ms. HOLTZMAN asked and was given permission to revise and extend her remarks.)

Mr. SMITH of New York. Mr. Chairman, I rise in opposition to the amendment.

Mr. Chairman, in reading this amendment it seems to me that the effect of the gentleman's amendment is to treat police officers and other law enforcement officers as second-class citizens, because we have already agreed that we are going to allow in as exceptions to the hearsay rule matters observed pursuant to duty imposed by law. The gentleman from Indiana would exclude from that as follows: "Excluding however, in criminal cases, matters observed by police officers and other law enforcement personnel." This would be so even though they were matters observed pursuant to a duty imposed by law.

I just think we are treading in an area the impact of which will be very unfortunate and the effect of which is to make police officers and law enforcement officers second-class citizens and persons less trustworthy than social workers or garbage collectors.

. . .

Mr. DENNIS. Mr. Chairman, I would like to say on that point that of course that is not my idea. I think the point is that we are dealing here with criminal cases, and in a criminal case the defendant should be confronted with the accuser to give him the chance to cross-examine. This is not any reflection on the police officer, but in a criminal case that is the type of report with which, in fact, one is going to be concerned.

. . .

Mr. JOHNSON of Colorado. Mr. Chairman, as an ex-prosecutor I cannot imagine that the gentleman would be advocating that a policeman's report could come in to help convict a man, and not have the policeman himself subject to cross-examination.

Is that what the gentleman is advocating?

Mr. SMITH of New York. That is what I am advocating in that the policeman's report, if he is not available, should be admissible when it is made pursuant to a duty imposed on that law enforcement officer by law. This is the amendment we have just adopted, and for other public officers these police reports ought to be admissible, whatever their probative value might be.

Mr. JOHNSON of Colorado. Mr. Chairman, if the gentleman will yield further, as I said, I was a prosecutor in a State court, and there were so many cases where good cross-examination indicated a lack of investigative ability on the part of the man who made the report that I became more and more convinced that good cross-examination was one of the principal elements in any criminal trial. If the officer who made the investigation is not available for cross-examination, then you cannot have a fair trial.

I cannot believe the gentleman would be saying that we should be able to convict people where the police officer's statement is not subject to cross-examination.

Mr. SMITH of New York. All I am saying to the gentleman from Colorado is that—and I will concede that the gentleman has probably had greater experience in this field than I have had—all I am saying is that it seems to me that it should be allowed for the jury to consider such a report, together with all of the other aspects of the case, if this report was made by a police officer pursuant to a duty imposed upon that police officer by law.

I will have to admit to the gentleman from Colorado that it is not the best evidence.

Mr. JOHNSON of Colorado. If the gentleman will yield still further, I will have to say that in my opinion the Supreme Court would have to ultimately declare that kind of a rule unconstitutional if we did pass it, and that the present amendment is one that would have to be passed if we are going to preserve the rights and traditions of individuals that have been in existence since 1066—I think that is when it started.

Mr. BRASCO. Mr. Chairman, I move to strike the requisite number of words.

(Mr. BRASCO asked and was given permission to revise and extend his remarks.)

Mr. BRASCO. Mr. Chairman, I would like to ask the author of the amendment, the gentleman from Indiana (Mr Dennis) a question. I am deeply disturbed and troubled about these rules that have been brought out today.

It seems to me that many critical areas have been overlooked.

One of the basic tenets of our law is that one should be confronted by one's accuser and be able to cross-examine the accuser.

There are many, many exceptions to the hearsay rule here.

As I understand it the gentleman from New York (Mr. Smith) is advocating, in opposition to the amendment offered by the gentleman from Indiana (Mr. Dennis) that if a police officer made a report that he saw Mr. X with a gun on such and such an occasion, and then thereafter that police officer is unavailable that that statement could be used in a criminal trial against Mr. X without the defense attorney having the opportunity to cross-examine the officer with respect to his position with relation to Mr. X, the time of the day, whether he was under a light, or whether there was no light, how much time did he have in which to see the gun, and all other observations relevant to the case.

Mr. DENNIS. Mr. Chairman, I would say in answer to the question raised by the gentleman from New York (Mr. Brasco) that if the statements of the police officer in his report would, in the language of this bill, be "matters observed pursuant to a duty imposed by law, and as to which he was under a duty to make a report," and I rather think they might be, that then what the gentleman says is true, and would be true.

I am trying to remove that possibility, by saying that the rule will not apply in the case the gentleman is talking about.

Mr. BRASCO. I support the gentleman. I am just standing up talking, because I cannot believe that we would for one moment entertain any other rule. I would hope we would do it with all cases of hearsay.

. . .

Mr. HUNT. I had no intention of getting into this argument, but when the gentleman brings in the word "investigator," then I have to get in.

Mr. BRASCO. I did not say it.

Mr. HUNT. I know the gentleman from New York did not, but it was discussed. The only time I can recall in my 34 years of law enforcement that a report of an investigator was admissible in court was to test the credibility of an officer. We would never permit a report to come in unchallenged. We would never even think about bringing in a report in lieu of the officer being there to have that officer cross-examined; but reports were admitted as evidentiary fact for the purpose of testing the officer's credibility and perhaps to refresh his memory. That has always been the rule of law in the State of New Jersey, and I hope it will always remain that way—and even the Federal canons.

Mr. BRASCO. I do not think that the gentleman's amendment interferes with that at all. I think what he is talking about is that the prosecution could use this to prove its case in chief with the possibility of no other evidence being presented.

Mr. HUNT. He is talking about bringing the report in in lieu of an officer, and that certainly is not the case.

Mr. DENNIS. Mr. Chairman, will the gentleman yield?

Mr. BRASCO. I yield to the gentleman from Indiana.

Mr. DENNIS. I thank the gentleman for yielding. I certainly agree this amendment has nothing to do with what my friend, the gentleman from New Jersey, is talking about. This applies only to a hearsay exception, where it would be attempted to bring this report in instead of the officer to prove one's case in chief, which one could do if we do not pass this amendment; but we could still use the report to contradict him and cross-examine him.

Mr. HUNT. Certainly, but the gentleman is speaking of the best evidence available then in lieu of the direct evidence.

Mr. DENNIS. I say we should bring in the man who saw it and put him on the stand.

Mr. HUNT. Certainly, the gentleman is right.

The CHAIRMAN. The question is on the amendment offered by the gentleman from Indiana (Mr. Dennis).

The amendment was agreed to.

Report of Senate Committee on the Judiciary

Senate Comm. on Judiciary, Fed.Rules of Evidence, S.Rep. No. 1277, 93d Cong., 2d Sess., p. 17 (1974); 1974 U.S.Code Cong. & Ad.News 7051, 7064

The House approved rule 803(8), as submitted by the Supreme Court, with one substantive change. It excluded from the hearsay exception reports containing matters observed by police officers and other law enforcement personnel in criminal cases. Ostensibly, the reason for this exclusion is that observations by police officers at the scene of the crime or the apprehension of the defendant are not as reliable as observations by public officials in other cases because of the adversarial nature of the confrontation between the police and the defendant in criminal cases.

The committee accepts the House's decision to exclude such recorded observations where the police officer is available to testify in court about his observation. However, where he is unavailable as unavailability is defined in rule 804(a)(4) and (a)(5), the report should be admitted as the best available evidence. Accordingly, the committee has amended rule 803(8) to refer to the provision of rule 804(b)(5), which allows the admission of such reports, records or other statements where the police officer or other law enforcement officer is unavailable because of death, then existing physical or mental illness or infirmity, or not being successfully subject to legal process. [This version of rule 804(b)(5) was not included in the rules as enacted.]

The House Judiciary Committee report contained a statement of intent that "the phrase 'factual findings' in subdivision (c) be strictly construed and that evaluations or opinions contained in public reports shall not be admissible under this rule." The committee takes strong exception to this limiting understanding of the application of the rule. We do not think it reflects an understanding of the intended operation of the rule as explained in the Advisory Committee notes to this subsection. The Advisory Committee notes on subsection (c) of this subdivision point out that various kinds of evaluative reports are now admissible under Federal statutes. 7 U.S.C. § 78, findings of Secretary of Agriculture prima facie evidence of true grade of grain; 42 U.S.C. § 269(b), bill of health by appropriate official prima facie evidence of vessel's sanitary history and condition and compliance with regulations. These statutory exceptions to the hearsay rule are preserved. Rule 802. The willingness of Congress to recognize these and other such evaluative reports provides a helpful guide in determining the kind of reports which are intended to be admissible under this rule. We think the restrictive interpretation of the House overlooks the fact that while the Advisory Committee assumes admissibility in the first instance of evaluative reports, they are not admissible if, as the rule states, "the sources of information or other circumstances indicate lack of trustworthiness."

The Advisory Committee explains the factors to be considered:

* * *

> Factors which may be assistance in passing upon the admissibility of evaluative reports include: (1) the timeliness of the investigation, McCormick, Can the Courts Make Wider Use of Reports of Official Investigations? 42 Iowa L.Rev. 363 (1957); (2) the special skill or experience of the official, id.; (3) whether a hearing was held and the level at which conducted, Franklin v. Skelly Oil Co., 141 F.2d 568 (19th Cir.1944): (4) possible motivation problems suggested by Palmer v. Hoffman, 318 U.S. 109, 63 S.Ct. 477, 87 L.Ed. 645 (1943). Others no doubt could be added.[4]

* * *

The committee concludes that the language of the rule together with the explanation provided by the Advisory Committee furnish sufficient guidance on the admissibility of evaluative reports.

Conference Report

H.R., Fed.Rules of Evidence, Conf.Rep. No. 1597, 93d Cong., 2d Sess., p. 11 (1974); 1974 U.S.Code Cong. & Ad.News 7098, 7104

The Senate amendment adds language, not contained in the House bill, that refers to another rule that was added by the Senate in another amendment (Rule 804(b)(5)—Criminal law enforcement records and reports).

In view of its action on Rule 804(b)(5) (Criminal law enforcement records and reports), the Conference does not adopt the Senate amendment and restores the bill to the House version.

Advisory Committee's Note

56 F.R.D. 183, 313

Exception (9). Records of vital statistics are commonly the subject of particular statutes making them admissible in evidence, Uniform Vital Statistics Act, 9C U.L.A. 350 (1957). The rule is in principle narrower than Uniform Rule 63(16) which includes reports required of persons performing functions authorized by statute, yet in practical effect the two are substantially the same. Comment Uniform Rule 63(16). The exception as drafted is in the pattern of California Evidence Code § 1281.

4. Advisory Committee's notes, to rule 803(8)(c).

Exception (10). The principle of proving nonoccurrence of an event by evidence of the absence of a record which would regularly be made of its occurrence, developed in Exception (7) with respect to regularly conducted [business] activities, is here extended to public records of the kind mentioned in Exceptions (8) and (9). 5 Wigmore § 1633(6), p. 519. Some harmless duplication no doubt exists with Exception (7). For instances of federal statutes recognizing this method of proof, see 8 U.S.C. § 1284(b), proof of absence of alien crewman's name from outgoing manifest prima facie evidence of failure to detain or deport, and 42 U.S.C. § 405(c)(3), (4)(B), (4)(C), absence of HEW record prima facie evidence of no wages or self-employment income.

The rule includes situations in which absence of a record may itself be the ultimate focal point of inquiry, e.g. People v. Love, 310 Ill. 558, 142 N.E. 204 (1923), certificate of Secretary of State admitted to show failure to file documents required by Securities Law, as well as cases where the absence of a record is offered as proof of the non-occurrence of an event ordinarily recorded.

The refusal of the common law to allow proof by certificate of the lack of a record or entry has no apparent justification, 5 Wigmore § 1678(7), p. 752. The rule takes the opposite position, as do Uniform Rule 63(17); California Evidence Code § 1284; Kansas Code of Civil Procedure § 60–460(*c*); New Jersey Evidence Rule 63(17). Congress has recognized certification as evidence of the lack of a record. 8 U.S.C. § 1360(d), certificate of Attorney General or other designated officer that no record of Immigration and Naturalization Service of specified nature or entry therein is found, admissible in alien cases.

Exception (11). Records of activities of religious organizations are currently recognized as admissible at least to the extent of the business records exception to the hearsay rule, 5 Wigmore § 1523, p. 371, and Exception (6) would be applicable. However, both the business record doctrine and Exception (6) require that the person furnishing the information be one in the business or activity. The result is such decisions as Daily v. Grand Lodge, 311 Ill. 184, 142 N.E. 478 (1924), holding a church record admissible to prove fact, date, and place of baptism, but not age of child except that he had at least been born at the time. In view of the unlikelihood that false information would be furnished on occasions of this kind, the rule contains no requirement that the informant be in the course of the activity. See California Evidence Code § 1315 and Comment.

Exception (12). The principle of proof by certification is recognized as to public officials in Exceptions (8) and (10), and with respect to authentication in Rule 902. The present exception is a duplication to the extent that it deals with a certificate by a public official, as in the case of a judge who performs a marriage ceremony. The area covered by the rule is, however, substantially larger and extends the certification procedure to clergymen and the like who perform marriages and other ceremonies or administer sacraments. Thus certificates of such matters as baptism or confirmation, as well as marriage, are included. In principle they are as acceptable evidence as certificates of public officers. See 5 Wigmore § 1645, as to marriage certificates. When the person executing the certificate is not a public official, the self-authenticating character of documents purporting to emanate from public officials, see Rule 902, is lacking and proof is required that the person was authorized and did make the certificate. The time element, however, may safely be taken as supplied by the certificate, once authority and authenticity are established, particularly in view of the presumption that a document was executed on the date it bears.

For similar rules, some limited to certificates of marriage, with variations in foundation requirements, see Uniform Rule 63(18); California Evidence Code § 1316; Kansas Code of Civil Procedure § 60–460(p); New Jersey Evidence Rule 63(18).

Exception (13). Records of family history kept in family Bibles have by long tradition been received in evidence. 5 Wigmore §§ 1495, 1496, citing numerous statutes and decisions. See also Regulations, Social Security Administration, 20 C.F.R. § 404.703(c), recognizing family Bible entries as proof of age in the absence of public or church records. Opinions in the area also include inscriptions on tombstones, publicly displayed pedigrees, and engravings on rings. Wigmore, supra. The rule is substantially identical in coverage with California Evidence Code § 1312.

Report of House Committee on the Judiciary

House Comm. on Judiciary, Fed.Rules of Evidence, H.R.Rep. No. 650,
93d Cong., 1st Sess., p. 15 (1973); 1974 U.S.Code
Cong. & Ad.News 7075, 7088

The Committee approved this Rule in the form submitted by the Court, intending that the phrase "Statements of fact concerning personal or family history" be read to include the specific types of such statements enumerated in Rule 803(11).

Advisory Committee's Note

56 F.R.D. 183, 315

Exception (14). The recording of title documents is a purely statutory development. Under any theory of the admissibility of public records, the records would be receivable as evidence of the contents of the recorded document, else the recording process would be reduced to a nullity. When, however, the record is offered for the further purpose of proving execution and delivery, a problem of lack of first-hand knowledge by the recorder, not present as to contents, is presented. This problem is solved, seemingly in all jurisdictions, by qualifying for recording only those documents shown by a specified procedure, either acknowledgement or a form of probate, to have been executed and delivered. 5 Wigmore §§ 1647–1651. Thus what may appear in the rule, at first glance, as endowing the record with an effect independently of local law and inviting difficulties of an *Erie* nature under Cities Service Oil Co. v. Dunlap, 308 U.S. 208, 60 S.Ct. 201, 84 L.Ed. 196 (1939), is not present, since the local law in fact governs under the example [exception].

Exception (15). Dispositive documents often contain recitals of fact. Thus a deed purporting to have been executed by an attorney in fact may recite the existence of the power of attorney, or a deed may recite that the grantors are all the heirs of the last record owner. Under the rule, these recitals are exempted from the hearsay rule. The circumstances under which dispositive documents are executed and the requirement that the recital be germane to the purpose of the document are believed to be adequate guarantees of trustworthiness, particularly in view of the nonapplicability of the rule if dealings with the property have been inconsistent with the document. The age of the document is of no significance, though in practical application the document will most often be an ancient one. See Uniform Rule 63(29), Comment.

Similar provisions are contained in Uniform Rule 63(29); California Evidence Code § 1330; Kansas Code of Civil Procedure § 60–460(aa); New Jersey Evidence Rule 63(29).

Exception (16). Authenticating a document as ancient, essentially in the pattern of the common law, as provided in Rule 901(b)(8), leaves open as a separate question the admissibility of assertive statements contained therein as against a hearsay objection. 7 Wigmore § 2145a. Wigmore further states that the ancient document technique of authentication is universally conceded to apply to all sorts of documents, including letters, records, contracts, maps, and certificates, in addition to title documents, citing numerous decisions. Id. § 2145. Since most of these items are significant evidentially only insofar as they are assertive, their admission in evidence must be as a hearsay exception. But see 5 id. § 1573, p. 429, referring to recitals in ancient deeds as a "limited" hearsay exception. The former position is believed to be the correct one in reason and authority. As pointed out in McCormick § 298, danger of mistake is minimized by authentication requirements, and age affords assurance that the writing antedates the present controversy. See Dallas County v. Commercial Union Assurance Co., 286 F.2d 388 (5th Cir.1961), upholding admissibility of 58-year-old newspaper story. Cf. Morgan, Basic Problems of Evidence 364 (1962), but see id. 254.

For a similar provision, but with the added requirement that "the statement has since generally been acted upon as true by persons having an interest in the matter," see California Evidence Code § 1331.

Exception (17). Ample authority at common law supported the admission in evidence of items falling in this category. While Wigmore's text is narrowly oriented to lists, etc., prepared for the use of a trade or profession, 6 Wigmore § 1702, authorities are cited which include other kinds of publications, for example, newspaper market reports, telephone directories, and city directories. Id. §§ 1702–1706. The basis of trustworthiness is general reliance by the public or by a particular segment of it, and the motivation of the compiler to foster reliance by being accurate.

For similar provisions, see Uniform Rule 63(30); California Evidence Code § 1340; Kansas Code of Civil Procedure § 60–460(bb); New Jersey Evidence Rule 63(30). Uniform Commercial Code § 2–724 provides for admissibility in evidence of "reports in official publications or trade journals or in newspapers or periodicals of general circulation published as the reports of such [established commodity] market."

Exception (18). The writers have generally favored the admissibility of learned treatises, McCormick § 296, p. 621; Morgan, Basic Problems of Evidence 366 (1962); 6 Wigmore § 1692, with the support of occasional decisions and rules, City of Dothan v. Hardy, 237 Ala. 603, 188 So. 264 (1939); Lewandowski v. Preferred Risk Mut. Ins. Co., 33 Wis.2d 69, 146 N.W.2d 505 (1966), 66 Mich. L.Rev. 183 (1967); Uniform Rule 63(31); Kansas Code of Civil Procedure § 60–460(cc), but the great weight of authority has been that learned treatises are not admissible as substantive evidence though usable in the cross-examination of experts. The foundation of the minority view is that the hearsay objection must be regarded as unimpressive when directed against treatises since a high standard of accuracy is engendered by various factors: the treatise is written primarily and impartially for professionals, subject to scrutiny and exposure for inaccuracy, with the reputation of the writer at stake. 6 Wigmore § 1692. Sound as this position may be with respect to trustworthiness, there is, nevertheless, an additional difficulty in the likelihood that the treatise will be misunderstood and misapplied without expert assistance and supervision. This difficulty is recognized in the cases demonstrating unwillingness to sustain findings relative to disability on the basis of judicially noticed medical texts. Ross v. Gardner, 365 F.2d 554 (6th Cir.1966); Sayers v. Gardner, 380 F.2d 940 (6th Cir.1967); Colwell v. Gardner, 386 F.2d 56 (6th Cir.1967); Glendenning v. Ribicoff, 213 F.Supp. 301 (W.D.Mo.1962); Cook v. Celebrezze, 217 F.Supp. 366 (W.D.Mo.1963); Sosna v. Celebrezze, 234 F.Supp. 289 (E.D.Pa.1964); and see McDaniel v. Celebrezze, 331 F.2d 426 (4th Cir.1964). The rule avoids the danger of misunderstanding and misapplication by limiting the use of treatises as substantive evidence to situations in which an expert is on the stand and available to explain and assist in the application of the treatise if desired. The limitation upon receiving the publication itself physically in evidence, contained in the last sentence, is designed to further this policy.

The relevance of the use of treatises on cross-examination is evident. This use of treatises has been the subject of varied views. The most restrictive position is that the witness must have stated expressly on direct his reliance upon the treatise. A slightly more liberal approach still insists upon reliance but allows it to be developed on cross-examination. Further relaxation dispenses with reliance but requires recognition as an authority by the witness, developable on cross-examination. The greatest liberality is found in decisions allowing use of the treatise on cross-examination when its status as an authority is established by any means. Annot., 60 A.L.R.2d 77. The exception is hinged upon this last position, which is that of the Supreme Court, Reilly v. Pinkus, 338 U.S. 269, 70 S.Ct. 110, 94 L.Ed. 63 (1949), and of recent well considered state court decisions, City of St. Petersburg v. Ferguson, 193 So.2d 648 (Fla.App.1967), cert. denied Fla., 201 So.2d 556; Darling v. Charleston Memorial Community Hospital, 33 Ill.2d 326, 211 N.E.2d 253 (1965); Dabroe v. Rhodes Co., 64 Wash.2d 431, 392 P.2d 317 (1964).

In Reilly v. Pinkus, supra, the Court pointed out that testing of professional knowledge was incomplete without exploration of the witness' knowledge of and attitude toward established treatises in the field. The process works equally well in reverse and furnishes the basis of the rule.

The rule does not require that the witness rely upon or recognize the treatise as authoritative, thus avoiding the possibility that the expert may at the outset block cross-examination by refusing to concede reliance or authoritativeness. Dabroe v. Rhodes Co., supra. Moreover, the rule avoids the unreality of admitting evidence for the purpose of impeachment only, with an instruction to the jury not to consider it otherwise. The parallel to the treatment of prior inconsistent statements will be apparent. See Rules 613(b) and 801(d)(1).

Exceptions (19), (20), and (21). Trustworthiness in reputation evidence is found "when the topic is such that the facts are likely to have been inquired about and that persons having personal knowledge have disclosed facts which have thus been discussed in the community; and thus the community's conclusion, if any has been formed, is likely to be a trustworthy one." 5 Wigmore § 1580, p. 444, and see also § 1583. On this common foundation, reputation as to land boundaries, customs, general history, character, and marriage have come to be regarded as admissible. The breadth of the underlying principle suggests the formulation of an equally broad exception, but tradition has in fact been much narrower and more particularized, and this is the pattern of these exceptions in the rule.

Exception (19) is concerned with matters of personal and family history. Marriage is universally conceded to be a proper subject of proof by evidence of reputation in the community. 5 Wigmore § 1602. As to such items as legitimacy, relationship, adoption, birth, and death, the decisions are divided. Id. § 1605. All seem to be susceptible to being the subject of well founded repute. The "world" in which the reputation may exist may be family, associates, or community. This world has proved capable of expanding with changing times from the single uncomplicated neighborhood, in which all activities take place, to the multiple and unrelated worlds of work, religious affiliation, and social activity, in each of which a reputation may be generated. People v. Reeves, 360 Ill. 55, 195 N.E. 443 (1935); State v. Axilrod, 248 Minn. 204, 79 N.W.2d 677 (1956); Mass.Stat.1947, c. 410, M.G.L.A. c. 233 § 21A; 5 Wigmore § 1616. The family has often served as the point of beginning for allowing community reputation. 5 Wigmore § 1488. For comparable provisions see Uniform Rule 63(26), (27)(c); California Evidence Code §§ 1313, 1314; Kansas Code of Civil Procedure § 60–460(x), (y)(3); New Jersey Evidence Rule 63(26), (27)(c).

The first portion of Exception (20) is based upon the general admissibility of evidence of reputation as to land boundaries and land customs, expanded in this country to include private as well as public boundaries. McCormick § 299, p. 625. The reputation is required to antedate the controversy, though not to be ancient. The second portion is likewise supported by authority, id., and is designed to facilitate proof of events when judicial notice is not available. The historical character of the subject matter dispenses with any need that the reputation antedate the controversy with respect to which it is offered. For similar provisions see Uniform Rule 63(27)(a), (b); California Evidence Code §§ 1320–1322; Kansas Code of Civil Procedure § 60–460(y), (1), (2); New Jersey Evidence Rule 63(27)(a), (b).

Exception (21) recognizes the traditional acceptance of reputation evidence as a means of proving human character. McCormick §§ 44, 158. The exception deals only with the hearsay aspect of this kind of evidence. Limitations upon admissibility based on other grounds will be found in Rules 404, relevancy of character evidence generally, and 608, character of witness. The exception is in effect a reiteration, in the context of hearsay, of Rule 405(a). Similar provisions are contained in Uniform Rule 63(28); California Evidence Code § 1324; Kansas Code of Civil Procedure § 60–460(z); New Jersey Evidence Rule 63(28).

Exception (22). When the status of a former judgment is under consideration in subsequent litigation, three possibilities must be noted: (1) the former judgment is conclusive under the doctrine of res judicata, either as a bar or a collateral estoppel; or (2) it is admissible in evidence for what it is worth; or (3) it may be of no effect at all. The first situation does not involve any problem of evidence except in the way that principles of substantive law generally bear upon the relevancy and materiality of evidence. The rule does not deal with the substantive effect of the judgment as a bar or collateral estoppel. When, however, the doctrine of res judicata does not apply to make the judgment either a bar or a collateral estoppel, a choice is presented between the second and third alternatives. The rule adopts the second for judgments of criminal conviction of felony grade. This is the direction of the decisions, Annot., 18 A.L.R.2d 1287,

1299, which manifest an increasing reluctance to reject *in toto* the validity of the law's factfinding processes outside the confines of res judicata and collateral estoppel. While this may leave a jury with the evidence of conviction but without means to evaluate it, as suggested by Judge Hinton, Note 27 Ill.L.Rev. 195 (1932), it seems safe to assume that the jury will give it substantial effect unless defendant offers a satisfactory explanation, a possibility not foreclosed by the provision. But see North River Ins. Co. v. Militello, 104 Colo. 28, 88 P.2d 567 (1939), in which the jury found for plaintiff on a fire policy despite the introduction of his conviction for arson. For supporting federal decisions see Clark, J., in New York & Cuba Mail S S. Co. v. Continental Cas. Co., 117 F.2d 404, 411 (2d Cir.1941); Connecticut Fire Ins. Co. v. Farrara, 277 F.2d 388 (8th Cir.1960).

Practical considerations require exclusion of convictions of minor offenses, not because the administration of justice in its lower echelons must be inferior, but because motivation to defend at this level is often minimal or nonexistent. Cope v. Goble, 39 Cal.App.2d 448, 103 P.2d 598 (1940); Jones v. Talbot, 87 Idaho 498, 394 P.2d 316 (1964); Warren v. Marsh, 215 Minn. 615, 11 N.W.2d 528 (1943); Annot., 18 A.L.R.2d 1287, 1295–1297; 16 Brooklyn L.Rev. 286 (1950); 50 Colum.L.Rev. 529 (1950); 35 Cornell L.Q. 872 (1950). Hence the rule includes only convictions of felony grade, measured by federal standards.

Judgments of conviction based upon pleas of *nolo contendere* are not included. This position is consistent with the treatment of *nolo* pleas in Rule 410 and the authorities cited in the Advisory Committee's Note in support thereof.

While these rules do not in general purport to resolve constitutional issues, they have in general been drafted with a view to avoiding collision with constitutional principles. Consequently the exception does not include evidence of the conviction of a third person, offered against the accused in a criminal prosecution to prove any fact essential to sustain the judgment of conviction. A contrary position would seem clearly to violate the right of confrontation. Kirby v. United States, 174 U.S. 47, 19 S.Ct. 574, 43 L.Ed. 890 (1899), error to convict of possessing stolen postage stamps with the only evidence of theft being the record of conviction of the thieves. The situation is to be distinguished from cases in which conviction of another person is an element of the crime, e.g. 15 U.S.C. § 902(d), interstate shipment of firearms to a known convicted felon, and, as specifically provided, from impeachment.

For comparable provisions see Uniform Rule 63(20); California Evidence Code § 1300; Kansas Code of Civil Procedure § 60–460(r); New Jersey Evidence Rule 63(20).

Exception (23). A hearsay exception in this area was originally justified on the ground that verdicts were evidence of reputation. As trial by jury graduated from the category of neighborhood inquests, this theory lost its validity. It was never valid as to chancery decrees. Nevertheless the rule persisted, though the judges and writers shifted ground and began saying that the judgment or decree was as good evidence as reputation. See City of London v. Clerke, Carth. 181, 90 Eng.Rep. 710 (K.B. 1691); Neill v. Duke of Devonshire, 8 App.Cas. 135 (1882). The shift appears to be correct, since the process of inquiry, sifting, and scrutiny which is relied upon to render reputation reliable is present in perhaps greater measure in the process of litigation. While this might suggest a broader area of application, the affinity to reputation is strong, and paragraph (23) goes no further, not even including character.

The leading case in the United States, Patterson v. Gaines, 47 U.S. (6 How.) 550, 599, 12 L.Ed. 553 (1847), follows in the pattern of the English decisions, mentioning as illustrative matters thus provable: manorial rights, public rights of way, immemorial custom, disputed boundary, and pedigree. More recent recognition of the principle is found in Grant Bros. Construction Co. v. United States, 232 U.S. 647, 34 S.Ct. 452, 58 L.Ed. 776 (1914), in action for penalties under Alien Contract Labor Law, decision of board of inquiry of Immigration Service admissible to prove alienage of laborers, as a matter of pedigree; United States v. Mid-Continent Petroleum Corp., 67 F.2d 37 (10th Cir.1933), records of commission enrolling Indians admissible on pedigree; Jung Yen Loy v. Cahill, 81 F.2d 809 (9th Cir.1936), board decisions as to citizenship of plaintiff's father admissible in proceeding for declaration of citizenship. Contra, In re Estate of Cunha, 49 Haw. 273, 414 P.2d 925 (1966).

Exception (24). The preceding 23 exceptions of Rule 803 and the first five [four] exceptions of Rule 804(b), infra, are designed to take full advantage of the accumulated wisdom and experience of the past in dealing with hearsay. It would, however, be presumptuous to assume that all possible desirable exceptions to the hearsay rule have been catalogued and to pass the hearsay rule to oncoming generations as a closed system. Exception (24) and its companion provision in Rule 804(b)(6)[5] are accordingly included. They do not contemplate an unfettered exercise of judicial discretion, but they do provide for treating new and presently unanticipated situations which demonstrate a trustworthiness within the spirit of the specifically stated exceptions. Within this framework, room is left for growth and development of the law of evidence in the hearsay area, consistently with the broad purposes expressed in Rule 102. See Dallas County v. Commercial Union Assur. Co., 286 F.2d 388 (5th Cir.1961).

Report of House Committee on the Judiciary

House Comm. on Judiciary, Fed.Rules of Evidence, H.R.Rep. No. 650, 93d Cong., 1st Sess., p. 5 (1973); 1974 U.S.Code Cong. & Ad.News 7075, 7079

The proposed Rules of Evidence submitted to Congress contained identical provisions in Rules 803 and 804 (which set forth the various hearsay exceptions), to the effect that the federal courts could admit any hearsay statement not specifically covered by any of the stated exceptions, if the hearsay statement was found to have "comparable circumstantial guarantees of trustworthiness."

The Committee deleted these provisions (proposed Rules 803(24) and 804(b)(6)) as injecting too much uncertainty into the law of evidence and impairing the ability of practitioners to prepare for trial. It was noted that Rule 102 directs the courts to construe the Rules of Evidence so as to promote "growth and development." The Committee believed that if additional hearsay exceptions are to be created, they should be by amendments to the Rules, not on a case-by-case basis.

Report of Senate Committee on the Judiciary

Senate Comm. on Judiciary, Fed.Rules of Evidence, S.Rep. No. 1277, 93d Cong., 2d Sess., p. 18 (1974); 1974 U.S.Code Cong. & Ad.News 7051, 7065

The proposed Rules of Evidence submitted to Congress contained identical provisions in rules 803 and 804 (which set forth the various hearsay exceptions), admitting any hearsay statement not specifically covered by any of the stated exceptions, if the hearsay statement was found to have "comparable circumstantial guarantees of trustworthiness." The House deleted these provisions (proposed rules 803(24) and 804(b)(6)) as injecting "too much uncertainty" into the law of evidence and impairing the ability of practitioners to prepare for trial. The House felt that rule 102, which directs the courts to construe the Rules of Evidence so as to promote growth and development, would permit sufficient flexibility to admit hearsay evidence in appropriate cases under various factual situations that might arise.

We disagree with the total rejection of a residual hearsay exception. While we view rule 102 as being intended to provide for a broader construction and interpretation of these rules, we feel that, without a separate residual provision, the specifically enumerated exceptions could become tortured beyond any reasonable circumstances which they were intended to include (even if broadly construed). Moreover, these exceptions, while they reflect the most typical and well recognized exceptions to the hearsay rule, may not encompass every situation in which the reliability and appropriateness of a particular piece of hearsay evidence make clear that it should be heard and considered by the trier of fact.

The committee believes that there are certain exceptional circumstances where evidence which is found by a court to have guarantees of trustworthiness equivalent to or exceeding the guarantees reflected by the presently listed exceptions, and to have a high degree of probativeness and necessity could properly be admissible.

The case of Dallas County v. Commercial Union Assoc. Co., Ltd., 286 F.2d 388 (5th Cir.1961) illustrates the point. The issue in that case was whether the tower of the county courthouse collapsed because it was struck by lightning (covered by insurance) or because of structural weakness and deterioration of the structure (not covered). Investigation of the structure revealed the presence of charcoal and charred timbers. In order to show that lightning may not have been the cause of the charring, the insurer offered a copy of a local newspaper published over 50 years earlier containing an unsigned article describing a fire in the courthouse while it was under construction. The Court found that the newspaper did not qualify for admission as a business record or an ancient document and did not fit within any other recognized hearsay exception. The court concluded, however, that the article was trustworthy because it was inconceivable that a newspaper reporter in a small town would report a fire in the courthouse if none had occurred. See also United States v. Barbati, 284 F.Supp. 409 (E.D.N.Y.1968).

Because exceptional cases like the *Dallas County* case may arise in the future, the committee has decided to reinstate a residual exception for rules 803 and 804(b).

The committee, however, also agrees with those supporters of the House version who felt that an overly broad residual hearsay exception could emasculate the hearsay rule and the recognized exceptions or vitiate the rationale behind codification of the rules.

Therefore, the committee has adopted a residual exception for rules 803 and 804(b) of much narrower scope and applicability than the Supreme Court version. In order to qualify for admission, a hearsay statement not falling within one of the recognized exceptions would have to satisfy at least four conditions. First, it must have "equivalent circumstantial guarantees of trustworthiness." Second, it must be offered as evidence of a material fact. Third, the court must determine that the statement "is more probative on the point for which it is offered than any other evidence which the proponent can procure through reasonable efforts." This requirement is intended to insure that only statements which have high probative value and necessity may qualify for admission under the residual exceptions. Fourth, the court must determine that "the general purposes of these rules and the interests of justice will best be served by admission of the statement into evidence."

It is intended that the residual hearsay exceptions will be used very rarely, and only in exceptional circumstances. The committee does not intend to establish a broad license for trial judges to admit hearsay statements that do not fall within one of the other exceptions contained in rules 803 and 804(b). The residual exceptions are not meant to authorize major judicial revisions of the hearsay rule, including its present exceptions. Such major revisions are best accomplished by legislative action. It is intended that in any case in which evidence is sought to be admitted under these subsections, the trial judge will exercise no less care, reflection and caution than the courts did under the common law in establishing the now-recognized exceptions to the hearsay rule.

In order to establish a well-defined jurisprudence, the special facts and circumstances which, in the court's judgment, indicates that the statement has a sufficiently high degree of trustworthiness and necessity to justify its admission should be stated on the record. It is expected that the court will give the opposing party a full and adequate opportunity to contest the admission of any statement sought to be introduced under these subsections.

Conference Report [1]

H.R., Fed.Rules of Evidence, Conf.Rep. No. 1597, 93d
Cong., 2d Sess., p. 11 (1974); 1974 U.S.Code
Cong. & Ad.News 7098, 7105

The Senate amendment adds a new subsection, (24), which makes admissible a hearsay statement not specifically covered by any of the previous twenty-three subsections, if the statement has equivalent circumstantial guarantees of trustworthiness and if the court determines that (A) the statement is offered as evidence of a material fact; (B) the statement is more probative on the point for which it is offered than any other evidence the proponent can procure through reasonable efforts; and (C) the general purposes of these rules and the interests of justice will best be served by admission of the statement into evidence.

The House bill eliminated a similar, but broader, provision because of the conviction that such a provision injected too much uncertainty into the law of

1. The Conference Report contains a like provision with regard to Rule 804(b)(5).—Ed.

evidence regarding hearsay and impaired the ability of a litigant to prepare adequately for trial.

The Conference adopts the Senate amendment with an amendment that provides that a party intending to request the court to use a statement under this provision must notify any adverse party of this intention as well as of the particulars of the statement, including the name and address of the declarant. This notice must be given sufficiently in advance of the trial or hearing to provide any adverse party with a fair opportunity to prepare to contest the use of the statement.

1987 Amendment

The amendments are technical. No substantive change is intended.

1997 Amendment

Committee Note

The contents of Rule 803(24) and Rule 804(b)(5) have been combined and transferred to a new Rule 807. This was done to facilitate additions to Rules 803 and 804. No change in meaning is intended.

2000 Amendment

The amendment provides that the foundation requirements of Rule 803(6) can be satisfied under certain circumstances without the expense and inconvenience of producing time-consuming foundation witnesses. Under current law, courts have generally required foundation witnesses to testify. *See, e.g., Tongil Co., Ltd. v. Hyundai Merchant Marine Corp.*, 968 F.2d 999 (9th Cir. 1992) (reversing a judgment based on business records where a qualified person filed an affidavit but did not testify). Protections are provided by the authentication requirements of Rule 902(11) for domestic records, Rule 902(12) for foreign records in civil cases, and 18 U.S.C. § 3505 for foreign records in criminal cases.

Rule 804. Hearsay Exceptions; Declarant Unavailable

(a) Definition of unavailability. "Unavailability as a witness" includes situations in which the declarant—

(1) is exempted by ruling of the court on the ground of privilege from testifying concerning the subject matter of the declarant's statement; or

(2) persists in refusing to testify concerning the subject matter of the declarant's statement despite an order of the court to do so; or

(3) testifies to a lack of memory of the subject matter of the declarant's statement; or

(4) is unable to be present or to testify at the hearing because of death or then existing physical or mental illness or infirmity; or

(5) is absent from the hearing and the proponent of statement has been unable to procure the declarant's attendance (or in the case of a hearsay exception under subdivision (b)(2), (3), or (4), the

declarant's attendance or testimony) by process or other reasonable means.

A declarant is not unavailable as a witness if exemption, refusal, claim of lack of memory, inability, or absence is due to the procurement or wrongdoing of the proponent of a statement for the purpose of preventing the witness from attending or testifying.

(b) Hearsay exceptions. The following are not excluded by the hearsay rule if the declarant is unavailable as a witness:

(1) Former testimony. Testimony given as a witness at another hearing of the same or a different proceeding, or in a deposition taken in compliance with law in the course of the same or another proceeding, if the party against whom the testimony is now offered, or, in a civil action or proceeding, a predecessor in interest, had an opportunity and similar motive to develop the testimony by direct, cross, or redirect examination.

(2) Statement under belief of impending death. In a prosecution for homicide or in a civil action or proceeding, a statement made by a declarant while believing that the declarant's death was imminent, concerning the cause or circumstances of what the declarant believed to be impending death.

(3) Statement against interest. A statement which was at the time of its making so far contrary to the declarant's pecuniary or proprietary interest, or so far tended to subject the declarant to civil or criminal liability, or to render invalid a claim by the declarant against another, that a reasonable person in the declarant's position would not have made the statement unless believing it to be true. A statement tending to expose the declarant to criminal liability and offered to exculpate the accused is not admissible unless corroborating circumstances clearly indicate the trustworthiness of the statement.

(4) Statement of personal or family history. (A) A statement concerning the declarant's own birth, adoption, marriage, divorce, legitimacy, relationship by blood, adoption, or marriage, ancestry, or other similar fact of personal or family history, even though declarant had no means of acquiring personal knowledge of the matter stated; or (B) a statement concerning the foregoing matters, and death also, of another person, if the declarant was related to the other by blood, adoption, or marriage or was so intimately associated with the other's family as to be likely to have accurate information concerning the matter declared.

(5) [Transferred to Rule 807]

(6) Forfeiture by wrongdoing. A statement offered against a party that has engaged or acquiesced in wrongdoing that was intended to, and did, procure the unavailability of the declarant as a witness.

(As amended P.L. 94–149, § 1(12), (13), Dec. 12, 1975, 89 Stat. 806; Mar. 2, 1987, eff. Oct. 1, 1987; Nov. 18, 1988, P.L. 100–690, Title VII, § 7075(b), 102 Stat. 4405, Apr. 11, 1997, eff. Dec. 1, 1997.)

Section references, McCormick 5th ed.

Generally, § 253, § 326

(a). § 253

(b). § 320

(1). § 301, § 302, § 303, § 304, § 308

(2). § 310, § 311, § 312, § 313, § 315

(3). § 254, § 316, § 317, § 318, § 319, § 271

(4). § 322

(5). § 324, § 324.3, § 353

Note by Federal Judicial Center

The rule prescribed by the Supreme Court was amended by the Congress in a number of respects as follows:

Subdivision (a). Paragraphs (1) and (2) were amended by substituting "court" in place of "judge," and paragraph (5) was amended by inserting "(or in the case of a hearsay exception under subdivision (b)(2), (3), or (4), his attendance or testimony)".

Subdivision (b). Exception (1) was amended by inserting "the same or" after "course of," and by substituting the phrase "if the party against whom the testimony is now offered, or, in a civil action or proceeding, a predecessor in interest, had an opportunity and similar motive to develop the testimony by direct, cross, or redirect examination" in place of "at the instance of or against a party with an opportunity to develop the testimony by direct, cross, or redirect examination, with motive and interest similar to those of the party against whom now offered."

Exception (2) as prescribed by the Supreme Court, dealing with statements of recent perception, was deleted by the Congress.

... Exception (2) as enacted by the Congress is Exception (3) prescribed by the Supreme Court, amended by inserting at the beginning, "In a prosecution for homicide or in a civil action or proceeding".

Exception (3) as enacted by the Congress is Exception (4) prescribed by the Supreme Court, amended in the first sentence by deleting, after "another," the phrase "or to make him an object of hatred, ridicule, or disgrace," and amended in the second sentence by substituting, after "unless," the phrase, "corroborating circumstances clearly indicate the trustworthiness of the statement," in place of "corroborated."

Exception (4) as enacted by the Congress is Exception (5) prescribed by the Supreme Court without change.

Exception (5) as enacted by the Congress is Exception (6) prescribed by the Supreme Court, amended by substituting "equivalent" in place of "comparable" and by adding all after "trustworthiness."

Advisory Committee's Note

56 F.R.D. 183, 322

As to firsthand knowledge on the part of hearsay declarants, see the introductory portion of the Advisory Committee's Note to Rule 803.

Subdivision (a). The definition of unavailability implements the division of hearsay exceptions into two categories by Rules 803 and 804(b).

At common law the unavailability requirement was evolved in connection with particular hearsay exceptions rather than along general lines. For example, see the separate explications of unavailability in relation to former testimony, declarations against interest, and statements of pedigree, separately developed in McCormick §§ 234, 257, and 297. However, no reason is apparent for making distinctions as to what satisfies unavailability for the different exceptions. The treatment in the rule is therefore uniform although differences in the range of process for witnesses between civil and criminal cases will lead to a less exacting requirement under item (5). See Rule 45(e) of the Federal Rules of Civil Procedure and Rule 17(e) of the Federal Rules of Criminal Procedure.

Five instances of unavailability are specified:

(1) Substantial authority supports the position that exercise of a claim of privilege by the declarant satisfies the requirement of unavailability (usually in connection with former testimony). Wyatt v. State, 35 Ala.App. 147, 46 So.2d 837 (1950); State v. Stewart, 85 Kan. 404, 116 P. 489 (1911); Annot., 45 A.L.R.2d 1354; Uniform Rule 62(7)(a); California Evidence Code § 240(a)(1); Kansas Code of Civil Procedure § 60–459(g)(1). A ruling by the judge is required, which clearly implies that an actual claim of privilege must be made.

(2) A witness is rendered unavailable if he simply refuses to testify concerning the subject matter of his statement despite judicial pressures to do so, a position supported by similar considerations of practicality. Johnson v. People, 152 Colo. 586, 384 P.2d 454 (1963); People v. Pickett, 339 Mich. 294, 63 N.W.2d 681, 45 A.L.R.2d 1341 (1954). Contra, Pleau v. State, 255 Wis. 362, 38 N.W.2d 496 (1949).

(3) The position that a claimed lack of memory by the witness of the subject matter of his statement constitutes unavailability likewise finds support in the cases, though not without dissent. McCormick § 234, p. 494. If the claim is successful, the practical effect is to put the testimony beyond reach, as in the other instances. In this instance, however, it will be noted that the lack of memory must be established by the testimony of the witness himself, which clearly contemplates his production and subjection to cross-examination.

Report of House Committee on the Judiciary

House Comm. on Judiciary, Fed.Rules of Evidence, H.R.Rep. No. 650, 93d Cong., 1st Sess., p. 15 (1973); 1974 U.S.Code Cong. & Ad.News 7075, 7088

Rule 804(a)(3) was approved in the form submitted by the Court. However, the Committee intends no change in existing federal law under which the court may choose to disbelieve the declarant's testimony as to his lack of memory. See United States v. Insana, 423 F.2d 1165, 1169–1170 (2nd Cir.), cert. denied, 400 U.S. 841 (1970).

Advisory Committee's Note

56 F.R.D. 183, 322

(4) Death and infirmity find general recognition as grounds. McCormick §§ 234, 257, 297; Uniform Rule 62(7)(c); California Evidence Code § 240(a)(3); Kansas Code of Civil Procedure § 60–459(g)(3); New Jersey Evidence Rule

62(6)(c). See also the provisions on use of depositions in Rule 32(a)(3) of the Federal Rules of Civil Procedure and Rule 15(e) of the Federal Rules of Criminal Procedure.

(5) Absence from the hearing coupled with inability to compel attendance by process or other reasonable means also satisfies the requirement. McCormick § 234; Uniform Rule 62(7)(d) and (e); California Evidence Code § 240(a)(4) and (5); Kansas Code of Civil Procedure § 60–459(g)(4) and (5); New Jersey Rule 62(6)(b) and (d). See the discussion of procuring attendance of witnesses who are nonresidents or in custody in Barber v. Page, 390 U.S. 719, 88 S.Ct. 1318, 20 L.Ed.2d 255 (1968).

If the conditions otherwise constituting unavailability result from the procurement or wrongdoing of the proponent of the statement, the requirement is not satisfied. . . .

Report of House Committee on the Judiciary

House Comm. on Judiciary, Fed.Rules of Evidence, H.R.Rep. No. 650, 93d Cong., 1st Sess., p. 15 (1973); 1974 U.S.Code Cong. & Ad.News 7075, 7088

Rule 804(a)(5) as submitted to the Congress provided, as one type of situation in which a declarant would be deemed "unavailable", that he be "absent from the hearing and the proponent of his statement has been unable to procure his attendance by process or other reasonable means." The Committee amended the Rule to insert after the word "attendance" the parenthetical expression "(or, in the case of a hearsay exception under subdivision (b)(2), (3), or (4), his attendance or testimony)". The amendment is designed primarily to require that an attempt be made to depose a witness (as well as to seek his attendance) as a precondition to the witness being deemed unavailable. The Committee, however, recognized the propriety of an exception to this additional requirement when it is the declarant's former testimony that is sought to be admitted under subdivision (b)(1).

Report of Senate Committee on the Judiciary

Senate Comm. on Judiciary, Fed.Rules of Evidence, S.Rep. No. 1277, 93d Cong., 2d Sess., p. 20 (1974); 1974 U.S.Code Cong. & Ad.News 7051 7066

Subdivision (a) of rule 804 as submitted by the Supreme Court defined the conditions under which a witness was considered to be unavailable. It was amended in the House.

The purpose of the amendment, according to the report of the House Committee on the Judiciary, is "primarily to require that an attempt be made to depose a witness (as well as to seek his attendance) as a precondition to the witness being unavailable." [1]

Under the House amendment, before a witness is declared unavailable, a party must try to depose a witness (declarant) with respect to dying declarations, declarations against interest, and declarations of pedigree. None of these situations would seem to warrant this needless, impractical and highly restrictive complication. A good case can be made for eliminating the unavailability

1. H.Rept. 93–650, at p. 15.

requirement entirely for declarations against interest cases.[2]

In dying declaration cases, the declarant will usually, though not necessarily, be deceased at the time of trial. Pedigree statements which are admittedly and necessarily based largely on word of mouth are not greatly fortified by a deposition requirement.

Depositions are expensive and time-consuming. In any event, deposition procedures are available to those who wish to resort to them. Moreover, the deposition procedures of the Civil Rules and Criminal Rules are only imperfectly adapted to implementing the amendment. No purpose is served unless the deposition, if taken, may be used in evidence. Under Civil Rule (a)(3) and Criminal Rule 15(e), a deposition, though taken, may not be admissible, and under Criminal Rule 15(a) substantial obstacles exist in the way of even taking a deposition.

For these reasons, the committee deleted the House amendment.

The committee understands that the rule as to unavailability, as explained by the Advisory Committee "contains no requirement that an attempt be made to take the deposition of a declarant." In reflecting the committee's judgment, the statement is accurate insofar as it goes. Where, however, the proponent of the statement, with knowledge of the existence of the statement, fails to confront the declarant with the statement at the taking of the deposition, then the proponent should not, in fairness, be permitted to treat the declarant as "unavailable" simply because the declarant was not amenable to process compelling his attendance at trial. The committee does not consider it necessary to amend the rule to this effect because such a situation abuses, not conforms to, the rule. Fairness would preclude a person from introducing a hearsay statement on a particular issue if the person taking the deposition was aware of the issue at the time of the deposition but failed to depose the unavailable witness on that issue.

Conference Report

H.R., Fed.Rules of Evidence, Conf.Rep. No. 1597, 93d Cong., 2d Sess., p. 12 (1974); 1974 U.S.Code Cong. & Ad. News 7098, 7105

Subsection (a) defines the term "unavailability as a witness". The House bill provides in subsection (a)(5) that the party who desires to use the statement must be unable to procure the declarant's attendance by process or other reasonable means. In the case of dying declarations, statements against interest and statements of personal or family history, the House bill requires that the proponent must also be unable to procure the declarant's *testimony* (such as by deposition or interrogatories) by process or other reasonable means. The Senate amendment eliminates this latter provision.

The Conference adopts the provision contained in the House bill.

Advisory Committee's Note

56 F.R.D. 183, 323

Subdivision (b). Rule 803, supra, is based upon the assumption that a hearsay statement falling within one of its exceptions possesses qualities which

2. Uniform rule 63(10); Kan.Stat.Anno. 60–460(j); 2A N.J.Stats.Anno. 84–63(10).

justify the conclusion that whether the declarant is available or unavailable is not a relevant factor in determining admissibility. The instant rule proceeds upon a different theory: hearsay which admittedly is not equal in quality to testimony of the declarant on the stand may nevertheless be admitted if the declarant is unavailable and if his statement meets a specified standard. The rule expresses preferences: testimony given on the stand in person is preferred over hearsay, and hearsay, if of the specified quality, is preferred over complete loss of the evidence of the declarant. The exceptions evolved at common law with respect to declarations of unavailable declarants furnish the basis for the exceptions enumerated in the proposal. The term "unavailable" is defined in subdivision (a).

Exception [1]. Former testimony does not rely upon some set of circumstances to substitute for oath and cross-examination, since both oath and opportunity to cross-examine were present in fact. The only missing one of the ideal conditions for the giving of testimony is the presence of trier and opponent ("demeanor evidence"). This is lacking with all hearsay exceptions. Hence it may be argued that former testimony is the strongest hearsay and should be included under Rule 803, supra. However, opportunity to observe demeanor is what in a large measure confers depth and meaning upon oath and cross-examination. Thus in cases under Rule 803 demeanor lacks the significance which it possesses with respect to testimony. In any event, the tradition, founded in experience, uniformly favors production of the witness if he is available. The exception indicates continuation of the policy. This preference for the presence of the witness is apparent also in rules and statutes on the use of depositions, which deal with substantially the same problem.

Under the exception, the testimony may be offered (1) against the party *against* whom it was previously offered or (2) against the party *by* whom it was previously offered. In each instance the question resolves itself into whether fairness allows imposing, upon the party against whom now offered, the handling of the witness on the earlier occasion. (1) If the party against whom now offered is the one against whom the testimony was offered previously, no unfairness is apparent in requiring him to accept his own prior conduct of cross-examination or decision not to cross-examine. Only demeanor has been lost, and that is inherent in the situation. (2) If the party against whom now offered is the one *by* whom the testimony was offered previously, a satisfactory answer becomes somewhat more difficult. One possibility is to proceed somewhat along the line of an adoptive admission, i.e. by offering the testimony proponent in effect adopts it. However, this theory savors of discarded concepts of witnesses' belonging to a party, of litigants' ability to pick and choose witnesses, and of vouching for one's own witnesses. Cf. McCormick § 246, pp. 526–527; 4 Wigmore § 1075. A more direct and acceptable approach is simply to recognize direct and redirect examination of one's own witness as the equivalent of cross-examining an opponent's witness. Falknor, Former Testimony and the Uniform Rules: A Comment, 38 N.Y.U.L.Rev. 651, n. 1 (1963); McCormick § 231, p. 483. See also 5 Wigmore § 1389. Allowable techniques for dealing with hostile, double-crossing, forgetful, and mentally deficient witnesses leave no substance to a claim that one could not adequately develop his own witness at the former hearing. An even less appealing argument is presented when failure to develop fully was the result of a deliberate choice.

The common law did not limit the admissibility of former testimony to that given in an earlier trial of the same case, although it did require identity of issues as a means of insuring that the former handling of the witness was the equivalent of what would now be done if the opportunity were presented. Modern decisions reduce the requirement to "substantial" identity. McCormick § 233. Since identity of issues is significant only in that it bears on motive and interest in developing fully the testimony of the witness, expressing the matter in the latter terms is preferable. Id. Testimony given at a preliminary hearing was held in California v. Green, 399 U.S. 149, 90 S.Ct. 1930, 26 L.Ed.2d 489 (1970), to satisfy confrontation requirements in this respect.

As a further assurance of fairness in thrusting upon a party the prior handling of the witness, the common law also insisted upon identity of parties, deviating only to the extent of allowing substitution of successors in a narrowly construed privity. Mutuality as an aspect of identity is now generally discredited, and the requirement of identity of the offering party disappears except as it might affect motive to develop the testimony. Falknor, supra, at 652; McCormick § 232, pp. 487–488. The question remains whether strict identity, or privity, should continue as a requirement with respect to the party against whom offered. . . .

Report of House Committee on the Judiciary

House Comm. on Judiciary, Fed.Rules of Evidence, H.R.Rep. No. 650, 93d Cong., 1st Sess., p. 15 (1973); 1974 U.S.Code Cong. & Ad.News 7075, 7088

Rule 804(b)(1) as submitted by the Court allowed prior testimony of an unavailable witness to be admissible if the party against whom it is offered or a person "with motive and interest similar" to his had an opportunity to examine the witness. The Committee considered that it is generally unfair to impose upon the party against whom the hearsay evidence is being offered responsibility for the manner in which the witness was previously handled by another party. The sole exception to this, in the Committee's view, is when a party's predecessor in interest in a civil action or proceeding had an opportunity and similar motive to examine the witness. The Committee amended the Rule to reflect these policy determinations.

Advisory Committee's Note

56 F.R.D. 183, 326

Exception [2]. The exception is the familiar dying declaration of the common law, expanded somewhat beyond its traditionally narrow limits. While the original religious justification for the exception may have lost its conviction for some persons over the years, it can scarcely be doubted that powerful psychological pressures are present. See 5 Wigmore § 1443 and the classic statement of Chief Baron Eyre in Rex v. Woodcock, 1 Leach 500, 502, 168 Eng.Rep. 352, 353 (K.B.1789).

The common law required that the statement be that of the victim, offered in a prosecution for criminal homicide. Thus declarations by victims in prosecutions for other crimes, e.g. a declaration by a rape victim who dies in childbirth, and all declarations in civil cases were outside the scope of the exception. An occasional statute has removed these restrictions, as in Colo.R.S. § 52–1–20, or has expanded the area of offenses to include abortions, 5 Wigmore § 1432, p.

224, n. 4. Kansas by decision extended the exception to civil cases. Thurston v. Fritz, 91 Kan. 468, 138 P. 625 (1914). While the common law exception no doubt originated as a result of the exceptional need for the evidence in homicide cases, the theory of admissibility applies equally in civil cases .... The same considerations suggest abandonment of the limitation to circumstances attending the event in question, yet when the statement deals with matters other than the supposed death, its influence is believed to be sufficiently attenuated to justify the limitation. Unavailability is not limited to death. See subdivision (a) of this rule. Any problem as to declarations phrased in terms of opinion is laid at rest by Rule 701, and continuation of a requirement of first-hand knowledge is assured by Rule 602.

Comparable provisions are found in Uniform Rule 63(5); California Evidence Code § 1242; Kansas Code of Civil Procedure § 60–460(e); New Jersey Evidence Rule 63(5).

Report of House Committee on the Judiciary

House Comm. on Judiciary, Fed.Rules of Evidence, H.R.Rep. No. 650, 93d Cong., 1st Sess., p. 15 (1973); 1974 U.S.Code Cong. & Ad.News 7075, 7089

Rule 804(b)(3) as submitted by the Court (now Rule 804(b)(2) in the bill) proposed to expand the traditional scope of the dying declaration exception (i.e. a statement of the victim in a homicide case as to the cause or circumstances of his believed imminent death) to allow such statements in all criminal and civil cases. The Committee did not consider dying declarations as among the most reliable forms of hearsay. Consequently, it amended the provision to limit their admissibility in criminal cases to homicide prosecutions, where exceptional need for the evidence is present. This is existing law. At the same time, the Committee approved the expansion to civil actions and proceedings where the stakes do not involve possible imprisonment, although noting that this could lead to forum shopping in some instances.

Advisory Committee's Note

46 F.R.D. 183, 327

Exception [3]. The circumstantial guaranty of reliability for declarations against interest is the assumption that persons do not make statements which are damaging to themselves unless satisfied for good reason that they are true. Hileman v. Northwest Engineering Co., 346 F.2d 668 (6th Cir.1965). If the statement is that of a party, offered by his opponent, it comes in as an admission, Rule 803(d)(2), and there is no occasion to inquire whether it is against interest, this not being a condition precedent to admissibility of admissions by opponents.

The common law required that the interest declared against be pecuniary or proprietary but within this limitation demonstrated striking ingenuity in discovering an against-interest aspect. Higham v Ridgway, 10 East 109, 103 Eng.Rep. 717 (K.B.1808); Reg. v. Overseers of Birmingham, 1 B. & S. 763, 121 Eng.Rep. 897 (Q.B.1861); McCormick, § 256, p. 551, nn. 2 and 3.

The exception discards the common law limitation and expands to the full logical limit. One result is to remove doubt as to the admissibility of declarations tending to establish a tort liability against the declarant or to extinguish one which might be asserted by him, in accordance with the trend of the decisions in this country. McCormick, § 254, pp. 548–549. ... And finally, exposure to criminal liability satisfies the against-interest requirement. The refusal of the common law to concede the adequacy of a penal interest was no doubt indefensible in logic, see the dissent of Mr. Justice Holmes in Donnelly v. United States, 228 U.S. 243, 33 S.Ct. 449, 57 L.Ed. 820 (1913), but one senses in the decisions a distrust of evidence of confessions by third persons offered to exculpate the accused arising from suspicions of fabrication either of the fact of the making of the confession or in its contents, enhanced in either instance by the required unavailability of the declarant. Nevertheless, an increasing amount of decisional law recognizes exposure to punishment for crime as a sufficient stake. People v. Spriggs, 60 Cal.2d 868, 36 Cal.Rptr. 841, 389 P.2d 377 (1964); Sutter v. Easterly, 354 Mo. 282, 189 S.W.2d 284 (1945); Band's Refuse Removal, Inc. v. Fairlawn Borough, 62 N.J.Super. 522, 163 A.2d 465 (1960); Newberry v. Commonwealth, 191 Va. 445, 61 S.E.2d 318 (1950); Annot., 162 A.L.R. 446. The requirement of corroboration is included in the rule in order to effect an accommodation between these competing considerations. When the statement is offered by the accused by way of exculpation, the resulting situation is not adapted to control by rulings as to the weight of the evidence, and hence the provision is cast in terms of a requirement preliminary to admissibility. Cf. Rule 406(a). The requirement of corroboration should be construed in such a manner as to effectuate its purpose of circumventing fabrication.

Ordinarily the third-party confession is thought of in terms of exculpating the accused, but this is by no means always or necessarily the case: it may include statements implicating him, and under the general theory of declarations against interest they would be admissible as related statements. Douglas v. Alabama, 380 U.S. 415, 85 S.Ct. 1074, 13 L.Ed.2d 934 (1965), and Bruton v. United States, 389 U.S. 818, 88 S.Ct. 126, 19 L.Ed.2d 70 (1968), both involved confessions by codefendants which implicated the accused. While the confession was not actually offered in evidence in *Douglas,* the procedure followed effectively put it before the jury, which the Court ruled to be error. Whether the confession might have been admissible as a declaration against penal interest was not considered or discussed. *Bruton* assumed the inadmissibility, as against the accused, of the implicating confession of his codefendant, and centered upon the question of the effectiveness of a limiting instruction. These decisions, however, by no means require that all statements implicating another person be excluded from the category of declarations against interest. Whether a statement is in fact against interest must be determined from the circumstances of each case. Thus a statement admitting guilt and implicating another person, made while in custody, may well be motivated by a desire to curry favor with the authorities and hence fail to qualify as against interest. See the dissenting opinion of Mr. Justice White in *Bruton.* On the other hand, the same words spoken under different circumstances, e.g., to an acquaintance, would have no difficulty in qualifying. The rule does not purport to deal with questions of the right of confrontation.

The balancing of self-serving against disserving aspects of a declaration is discussed in McCormick § 256.

For comparable provisions, see Uniform Rule 63(10); California Evidence Code § 1230; Kansas Code of Civil Procedure § 60–460(j); New Jersey Evidence Rule 63(10).

Report of House Committee on the Judiciary

House Comm. on Judiciary, Fed.Rules of Evidence, H.R.Rep. No. 650, 93d Cong., 1st Sess., p. 16 (1973); 1974 U.S.Code Cong. & Ad.News 7075, 7089

Rule 804(b)(4) as submitted by the Court (now Rule 804(b)(3) in the bill) provided as follows:

> *Statement against interest.*—A statement which was at the time of its making so far contrary to the declarant's pecuniary or proprietary interest or so far tended to subject him to civil or criminal liability or to render invalid a claim by him against another or to make him an object of hatred, ridicule, or disgrace, that a reasonable man in his position would not have made the statement unless he believed it to be true. A statement tending to exculpate the accused is not admissible unless corroborated.

The Committee determined to retain the traditional hearsay exception for statements against pecuniary or proprietary interest. However, it deemed the Court's additional references to statements tending to subject a declarant to civil liability or to render invalid a claim by him against another to be redundant as included within the scope of the reference to statements against pecuniary or proprietary interest. See Gichner v. Antonio Triano Tile and Marble Co., 410 F.2d 238 (D.C.Cir.1968). Those additional references were accordingly deleted.

The Court's Rule also proposed to expand the hearsay limitation from its present federal limitation to include statements subjecting the declarant to criminal liability and statements tending to make him an object of hatred, ridicule, or disgrace. The Committee eliminated the latter category from the subdivision as lacking sufficient guarantees of reliability. See United States v. Dovico, 380 F.2d 325, 327 nn. 2, 4 (2nd Cir.), cert. denied, 389 U.S. 944 (1967). As for statements against penal interest, the Committee shared the view of the Court that some such statements do possess adequate assurances of reliability and should be admissible. It believed, however, as did the Court, that statements of this type tending to exculpate the accused are more suspect and so should have their admissibility conditioned upon some further provision insuring trustworthiness. The proposal in the Court Rule to add a requirement of simple corroboration was, however, deemed ineffective to accomplish this purpose since the accused's own testimony might suffice while not necessarily increasing the reliability of the hearsay statement. The Committee settled upon the language "unless corroborating circumstances clearly indicate the trustworthiness of the statement" as affording a proper standard and degree of discretion. It was contemplated that the result in such cases as Donnelly v. United States, 228 U.S. 243 (1912), where the circumstances plainly indicated reliability, would be changed. The Committee also added to the Rule the final sentence from the 1971 Advisory Committee draft, designed to codify the doctrine of Bruton v. United States, 391 U.S. 123 (1968). The Committee does not intend to affect the existing exception to the *Bruton* principle where the codefendant takes the stand and is subject to cross-examination, but believed there was no need to make specific provision for this situation in the Rule, since in that event the declarant would not be "unavailable".

Report of Senate Committee on the Judiciary

Senate Comm. on Judiciary, Fed.Rules of Evidence, S.Rep. No. 1277, 93d Cong., 2d Sess., p. 21 (1974); 1974 U.S.Code Cong. & Ad.News 7051, 7067

The rule defines those statements which are considered to be against interest and thus of sufficient trustworthiness to be admissible even though hearsay. With regard to the type of interest declared against, the version submitted by the Supreme Court included inter alia, statements tending to subject a declarant to civil liability or to invalidate a claim by him against another. The House struck these provisions as redundant. In view of the conflicting case law construing pecuniary or proprietary interests narrowly so as to exclude, e.g., tort cases, this deletion could be misconstrued.

Three States which have recently codified their rules of evidence have followed the Supreme Court's version of this rule, i.e., that a statement is against interest if it tends to subject a declarant to civil liability.[3]

The committee believes that the reference to statements tending to subject a person to civil liability constitutes a desirable clarification of the scope of the rule. Therefore, we have reinstated the Supreme Court language on this matter.

The Court rule also proposed to expand the hearsay limitation from its present federal limitation to include statements subjecting the declarant to statements tending to make him an object of hatred, ridicule, or disgrace. The House eliminated the latter category from the subdivision as lacking sufficient guarantees of reliability. Although there is considerable support for the admissibility of such statements (all three of the State rules referred to supra, would admit such statements), we accept the deletion by the House.

The House amended this exception to add a sentence making inadmissible a statement or confession offered against the accused in a criminal case, made by a codefendant or other person implicating both himself and the accused. The sentence was added to codify the constitutional principle announced in Bruton v. United States, 391 U.S. 123 (1968). *Bruton* held that the admission of the extrajudicial hearsay statement of one codefendant inculpating a second codefendant violated the confrontation clause of the sixth amendment.

The committee decided to delete this provision because the basic approach of the rules is to avoid codifying, or attempting to codify, constitutional evidentiary principles, such as the fifth amendment's right against self-incrimination and, here, the sixth amendment's right of confrontation. Codification of a constitutional principle is unnecessary and, where the principle is under development, often unwise. Furthermore, the House provision does not appear to recognize the exceptions to the *Bruton* rule, e.g. where the codefendant takes the stand and is subject to cross examination; where the accused confessed, see United States v. Mancusi, 404 F.2d 296 (2d Cir.1968), cert. denied 397 U.S. 942 (1907); where the accused was placed at the scene of the crime, see United States v. Zelker, 452 F.2d 1009 (2d Cir.1971). For these reasons, the committee decided to delete this provision.

Conference Report

H.R., Fed.Rules of Evidence, Conf.Rep. No. 1597, 93d Cong., 2d Sess., p. 12 (1974); 1974 U.S.Code Cong. & Ad.News 7098, 7105

3. Nev.Rev.Stats. § 51.345; N.Mex.Stats. (1973 Supp.) § 20–4–804(4); West's Wis. Stats.Anno. (1973 Supp.) § 908.045(4).

The Senate amendment to subsection (b)(3) provides that a statement is against interest and not excluded by the hearsay rule when the declarant is unavailable as a witness, if the statement tends to subject a person to civil or criminal liability or renders invalid a claim by him against another. The House bill did not refer specifically to civil liability and to rendering invalid a claim against another. The Senate amendment also deletes from the House bill the provision that subsection (b)(3) does not apply to a statement or confession, made by a codefendant or another, which implicates the accused and the person who made the statement, when that statement or confession is offered against the accused in a criminal case.

The Conference adopts the Senate amendment. The Conferees intend to include within the purview of this rule, statements subjecting a person to civil liability and statements rendering claims invalid. The Conferees agree to delete the provision regarding statements by a codefendant, thereby reflecting the general approach in the Rules of Evidence to avoid attempting to codify constitutional evidentiary principles.

Advisory Committee's Note

56 Fed.R.Evid. 183, 328

Exception [4]. The general common law requirement that a declaration in this area must have been made *ante litem motam* has been dropped, as bearing more appropriately on weight than admissibility. See 5 Wigmore § 1483. Item (i) specifically disclaims any need of firsthand knowledge respecting declarant's own personal history. In some instances it is self-evident (marriage) and in others impossible and traditionally not required (date of birth). Item (ii) deals with declarations concerning the history of another person. As at common law, declarant is qualified if related by blood or marriage. 5 Wigmore, § 1489. In addition, and contrary to the common law, declarant qualifies by virtue of intimate association with the family. Id., § 1487. The requirement sometimes encountered that when the subject of the statement is the relationship between two other persons the declarant must qualify as to both is omitted. Relationship is reciprocal. Id., § 1491.

For comparable provisions, see Uniform Rule 63(23), (24), (25); California Evidence Code §§ 1310, 1311; Kansas Code of Civil Procedure § 60–460(u), (v), (w); New Jersey Evidence Rules 63(23), 63(24), 63(25).

Exception [5]. In language and purpose, this exception is identical with Rule 803(24). See the Advisory Committee's Note to that provision.

Reports of House and Senate Committees on the Judiciary

[This exception and its companion exception in rule 803(24) are discussed together in the congressional committee reports. The reports are set forth under rule 803(24), supra.]

Conference Report [1]

The Senate amendment adds a new subsection, (b)(6),[2] which makes admissible a hearsay statement not specifically covered by any of the five [four]

1. The Conference Report contains a like provision with respect to Rule 803(24).—Ed.
2. Numbered (b)(5) as finally enacted.—Ed.

previous subsections, if the statement has equivalent circumstantial guarantees of trustworthiness and if the court determines that (A) the statement is offered as evidence of a material fact; (B) the statement is more probative on the point for which it is offered than any other evidence the proponent can procure through reasonable efforts; and (C) the general purposes of these rules and the interests of justice will best be served by admission of the statement into evidence.

The House bill eliminated a similar, but broader, provision because of the conviction that such a provision injected too much uncertainty into the law of evidence regarding hearsay and impaired the ability of a litigant to prepare adequately for trial.

The Conference adopts the Senate amendment with an amendment that renumbers this subsection and provides that a party intending to request the court to use a statement under this provision must notify any adverse party of this intention as well as of the particulars of the statement, including the name and address of the declarant. This notice must be given sufficiently in advance of the trial or hearing to provide any adverse party with a fair opportunity to prepare to contest the use of the statement.

1987 Amendment

The amendments are technical. No substantive change is intended.

1997 Amendment

Subdivision (b)(5). The contents of Rule 803(24) and Rule 804(b)(5) have been combined and transferred to a new Rule 807. This was done to facilitate additions to Rules 803 and 804. No change in meaning is intended.

Subdivision (b)(6). Rule 804(b)(6) has been added to provide that a party forfeits the right to object on hearsay grounds to the admission of a declarant's prior statement when the party's deliberate wrongdoing or acquiescence therein procured the unavailability of the declarant as a witness. This recognizes the need for a prophylactic rule to deal with abhorrent behavior "which strikes at the heart of the system of justice itself." *United States v. Mastrangelo*, 693 F.2d 269, 273 (2d Cir. 1982), *cert. denied*, 467 U.S. 1204 (1984). The wrongdoing need not consist of a criminal act. The rule applies to all parties, including the government. It applies to actions taken after the event to prevent a witness from testifying.

Every circuit that has resolved the question has recognized the principle of forfeiture by misconduct, although the tests for determining whether there is a forfeiture have varied. *See, e.g., United States v. Aguiar*, 975 F.2d 45, 47 (2d Cir. 1992); *United States v. Potamitis,* 739 F.2d 784, 789 (2d Cir.), *cert. denied*, 469 U.S. 918 (1984); *Steele v. Taylor,* 684 F.2d 1193, 1199 (6th Cir. 1982), *cert. denied*, 460 U.S. 1053 (1983); United *States v. Balano*, 618 F.2d 624, 629 (10th Cir. 1979), *cert. denied*, 449 U.S. 840 (1980); *United States v. Carlson*, 547 F.2d 1346, 1358–59 (8th Cir.), *cert. denied*, 431 U.S. 914 (1977). The foregoing cases apply a preponderance of the evidence standard. *Contra United States v. Thevis*, 665 F.2d 616, 631 (5th Cir.) (clear and convincing standard), *cert. denied*, 459 U.S. 825 (1982). The usual Rule 104(a) preponderance of the evidence standard has been adopted in light of the behavior the new Rule 804(b)(6) seeks to discourage.

Rule 805. Hearsay Within Hearsay

Hearsay included within hearsay is not excluded under the hearsay rule if each part of the combined statements conforms with an exception to the hearsay rule provided in these rules.

Section references, McCormick 5th ed.

§ 255, § 324.1

Note by Federal Judicial Center

The rule enacted by the Congress is the rule prescribed by the Supreme Court without change.

Advisory Committee's Note

56 F.R.D. 183, 329

On principle it scarcely seems open to doubt that the hearsay rule should not call for exclusion of a hearsay statement which includes a further hearsay statement when both conform to the requirements of a hearsay exception. Thus a hospital record might contain an entry of the patient's age based on information furnished by his wife. The hospital record would qualify as a regular entry except that the person who furnished the information was not acting in the routine of the business. However, her statement independently qualifies as a statement of pedigree (if she is unavailable) or as a statement made for purposes of diagnosis or treatment, and hence each link in the chain falls under sufficient assurances. Or, further to illustrate, a dying declaration may incorporate a declaration against interest by another declarant. See McCormick § 290, p. 611.

Rule 806. Attacking and Supporting Credibility of Declarant

When a hearsay statement, or a statement defined in Rule 801(d)(2)(C), (D), or (E), has been admitted in evidence, the credibility of the declarant may be attacked, and if attacked may be supported, by any evidence which would be admissible for those purposes if declarant had testified as a witness. Evidence of a statement or conduct by the declarant at any time, inconsistent with the declarant's hearsay statement, is not subject to any requirement that the declarant may have been afforded an opportunity to deny or explain. If the party against whom a hearsay statement has been admitted calls the declarant as a witness, the party is entitled to examine the declarant on the statement as if under cross-examination.

(As amended Mar. 2, 1987, eff. Oct. 1, 1987; Apr. 11, 1997, eff. Dec. 1, 1997.)

Section references, McCormick 5th ed.

§ 37, § 324.2

Note by Federal Judicial Center

The rule enacted by the Congress is the rule prescribed by the Supreme Court, amended by inserting the phrase "or a statement defined in Rule 801(d)(2), (C), (D), or (E)."

Advisory Committee's Note

56 F.R.D. 183, 329

The declarant of a hearsay statement which is admitted in evidence is in effect a witness. His credibility should in fairness be subject to impeachment and support as though he had in fact testified. See Rules 608 and 609. There are however, some special aspects of the impeaching of a hearsay declarant which require consideration. These special aspects center upon impeachment by inconsistent statement, arise from factual differences which exist between the use of hearsay and an actual witness and also between various kinds of hearsay, and involve the question of applying to declarants the general rule disallowing evidence of an inconsistent statement to impeach a witness unless he is afforded an opportunity to deny or explain. See Rule 613(b).

The principal difference between using hearsay and an actual witness is that the inconsistent statement will in the case of the witness almost inevitably of necessity in the nature of things be a *prior* statement, which it is entirely possible and feasible to call to his attention, while in the case of hearsay the inconsistent statement may well be a *subsequent* one, which practically precludes calling it to the attention of the declarant. The result of insisting upon observation of this impossible requirement in the hearsay situation is to deny the opponent, already barred from cross-examination, any benefit of this important technique of impeachment. The writers favor allowing the subsequent statement. McCormick, § 37, p. 69; 3 Wigmore § 1033. The cases, however, are divided. Cases allowing the impeachment include People v. Collup, 27 Cal.2d 829, 167 P.2d 714 (1946); People v. Rosoto, 58 Cal.2d 304, 23 Cal.Rptr. 779, 373 P.2d 867 (1962); Carver v. United States, 164 U.S. 694, 17 S.Ct. 228, 41 L.Ed. 602 (1897). Contra, Mattox v. United States, 156 U.S. 237, 15 S.Ct. 337, 39 L.Ed. 409 (1895); People v. Hines, 284 N.Y. 93, 29 N.E.2d 483 (1940). The force of *Mattox,* where the hearsay was the former testimony of a deceased witness and the denial of use of a subsequent inconsistent statement was upheld, is much diminished by *Carver*, where the hearsay was a dying declaration and denial of use of a subsequent inconsistent statement resulted in reversal. The difference in the particular brand of hearsay seems unimportant when the inconsistent statement is a *subsequent* one. True, the opponent is not totally deprived of cross-examination when the hearsay is former testimony or a deposition but he is deprived of cross-examining on the statement or along lines suggested by it. Mr. Justice Shiras, with two justices joining him, dissented vigorously in *Mattox.*

When the impeaching statement was made *prior* to the hearsay statement, differences in the kinds of hearsay appear which arguably may justify differences in treatment. If the hearsay consisted of a simple statement by the witness, e.g. a dying declaration or a declaration against interest, the feasibility of affording him an opportunity to deny or explain encounters the same practical impossibility as where the statement is a subsequent one, just discussed, although here the impossibility arises from the total absence of anything resembling a hearing at which the matter could be put to him. The courts by a large majority have ruled in favor of allowing the statement to be used under these circumstances. McCormick § 37, p. 69; 3 Wigmore § 1033. If, however, the hearsay consists of former testimony or a deposition, the possibility of calling the prior statement to the attention of the witness or deponent is not ruled out, since the opportunity to cross-examine was available. It might thus be concluded that with former testimony or depositions the conventional foundation should be insisted upon. Most of the cases involve depositions, and Wigmore describes them as divided. 3 Wigmore § 1031. Deposition procedures at best are cumbersome and expensive, and to require the laying of the foundation may impose an undue burden. Under the federal practice, there is no way of knowing with certainty at the time of taking a deposition whether it is merely for discovery or will ultimately end up in evidence. With respect to both former testimony and depositions the possibility exists that knowledge of the statement might not be acquired until after the time of the cross-examination. Moreover, the expanded admissibility of former testimony and depositions under Rule 804(b)(1) calls for a correspondingly expanded approach to impeachment. The rule dispenses with the requirement in all hearsay situations, which is readily administered and best calculated to lead to fair results.

Notice should be taken that Rule 26(f) of the Federal Rules of Civil Procedure, as originally submitted by the Advisory Committee, ended with the following:

> "... and, without having first called them to the deponent's attention, may show statements contradictory thereto made at any time by the deponent."

This language did not appear in the rule as promulgated in December, 1937. See 4 Moore's Federal Practice ¶¶ 26.01[9], 26.35 (2d ed. 1967). In 1951, Nebraska adopted a provision strongly resembling the one stricken from the federal rule:

> "Any party may impeach any adverse deponent by self-contradiction without having laid foundation for such impeachment at the time such deposition was taken." R.S.Neb. § 25–1267.07.

For similar provisions, see Uniform Rule 65; California Evidence Code § 1202; Kansas Code of Civil Procedure § 60–462; New Jersey Evidence Rule 65.

The provision for cross-examination of a declarant upon his hearsay statement is a corollary of general principles of cross-examination. A similar provision is found in California Evidence Code § 1203.

Report of Senate Committee on the Judiciary

Senate Comm. on Judiciary, Fed.Rules of Evidence, S.Rep. No. 1277, 93d Cong., 2d Sess., p. 22 (1974); 1974 U.S.Code Cong. & Ad.News 7051, 7068

Rule 906 [806], as passed by the House and as proposed by the Supreme Court provides that whenever a hearsay statement is admitted, the credibility of the declarant of the statement may be attacked, and if attacked may be supported, by any evidence which would be admissible for those purposes if the declarant had testified as a witness. Rule 801 defines what is a hearsay statement. While statements by a person authorized by a party-opponent to make a statement concerning the subject, by the party-opponent's agent or by a coconspirator of a party—see rule 801(d)(2)(c), (d) and (e)—are traditionally defined as exceptions to the hearsay rule, rule 801 defines such admission by a party-opponent as statements which are not hearsay. Consequently, rule 806 by referring exclusively to the admission of hearsay statements, does not appear to allow the credibility of the declarant to be attacked when the declarant is a coconspirator, agent or authorized spokesman. The committee is of the view that such statements should open the declarant to attacks on his credibility. Indeed, the reason such statements are excluded from the operation of rule 806 is likely attributable to the drafting technique used to codify the hearsay rule, viz. some statements, instead of being referred to as exceptions to the hearsay rule, are defined as statements which are not hearsay. The phrase "or a statement defined in rule 801(d)(2)(c), (d) and (e)" is added to the rule in order to subject the declarant of such statements, like the declarant of hearsay statements, to attacks on his credibility.[1]

Conference Report

H.R., Fed.Rules of Evidence, Conf.Rep. No. 1597, 93d Cong., 2d Sess., p. 13 (1974); 1974 U.S.Code Cong. & Ad.News 7098, 7106

The Senate amendment permits an attack upon the credibility of the declarant of a statement if the statement is one by a person authorized by a party-opponent to make a statement concerning the subject, only by an agent of a party-opponent, or one by a coconspirator of the party-opponent, as these statements are defined in Rules 801(d)(2)(C), (D) and (E). The House bill has no such provision.

The Conference adopts the Senate amendment. The Senate amendment conforms the rule to present practice.

1987 Amendment

The amendments are technical. No substantive change is intended.

1997 Amendment

The amendment is technical. No substantive change is intended.

Rule 807. Residual Exception

A statement not specifically covered by Rule 803 or 804 but having equivalent circumstantial guarantees of trustworthiness, is not excluded by the hearsay rule, if the court determines that (A) the statement is offered as evidence of a material fact; (B) the statement is more probative on the point for which it is offered than any other evidence which the proponent can procure through reasonable efforts; and (C) the general purposes of these rules and the interests of justice will best be served by admission of the statement into evidence. However, a statement may not be admitted under this exception unless the proponent of it makes known to the adverse party sufficiently in advance of the trial or hearing to provide the adverse party with a fair opportunity to prepare to meet it, the proponent's intention to offer the statement and the particulars of it, including the name and address of the declarant.

Advisory Committee's Note

1. The committee considered it unnecessary to include statements contained in rule 801(d)(2)(A) and (B)—the statement by the party-opponent himself or the statement of which he has manifested his adoption—because the credibility of the party-opponent is always subject to an attack on his credibility.

1997 Amendment

The contents of Rule 803(24) and Rule 804(b)(5) have been combined and transferred to a new Rule 807. This was done to facilitate additions to Rules 803 and 804. No change in meaning is intended.

ARTICLE IX. AUTHENTICATION AND IDENTIFICATION

Rule

Rule 901. Requirement of Authentication or Identification

(a) General provision. The requirement of authentication or identification as a condition precedent to admissibility is satisfied by evidence sufficient to support a finding that the matter in question is what its proponent claims.

(b) Illustrations. By way of illustration only, and not by way of limitation, the following are examples of authentication or identification conforming with the requirements of this rule:

(1) Testimony of witness with knowledge. Testimony that a matter is what it is claimed to be.

(2) Nonexpert opinion on handwriting. Nonexpert opinion as to the genuineness of handwriting, based upon familiarity not acquired for purposes of the litigation.

(3) Comparison by trier or expert witness. Comparison by the trier of fact or by expert witnesses with specimens which have been authenticated.

(4) Distinctive characteristics and the like. Appearance, contents, substance, internal patterns, or other distinctive characteristics, taken in conjunction with circumstances.

(5) Voice identification. Identification of a voice, whether heard firsthand or through mechanical or electronic transmission or recording, by opinion based upon hearing the voice at any time under circumstances connecting it with the alleged speaker.

(6) Telephone conversations. Telephone conversations, by evidence that a call was made to the number assigned at the time by the telephone company to a particular person or business, if (A) in the case of a person, circumstances, including self-identification, show the person answering to be the one called, or (B) in the case of a business, the call was made to a place of business and the conversation related to business reasonably transacted over the telephone.

(7) Public records or reports. Evidence that a writing authorized by law to be recorded or filed and in fact recorded or filed in a public office, or a purported public record, report, statement, or data compilation, in any form, is from the public office where items of this nature are kept.

(8) Ancient documents or data compilation. Evidence that a document or data compilation, in any form, (A) is in such condition as to create no suspicion concerning its authenticity, (B) was in a place where it, if authentic, would likely be, and (C) has been in existence 20 years or more at the time it is offered.

(9) Process or system. Evidence describing a process or system used to produce a result and showing that the process or system produces an accurate result.

(10) Methods provided by statute or rule. Any method of authentication or identification provided by Act of Congress or by other rules prescribed by the Supreme Court pursuant to statutory authority.

Section references, McCormick 5th ed.

Generally § 207, § 218

(a). § 222, § 224, § 227

(b)(1). § 214, § 219

(2). § 221

(3). § 221

(4). § 222, § 225

(5). § 226

(6). § 226

(7). § 224

(8). § 223, § 323

(9). § 214, § 293

Note by Federal Judicial Center

The rule enacted by the Congress is the rule prescribed by the Supreme Court, amended in subdivision (b)(10) by substituting "prescribed" in place of "adopted," and by adding "pursuant to statutory authority."

Advisory Committee's Note

56 F.R.D. 183, 332

Subdivision (a). Authentication and identification represent a special aspect of relevancy. Michael and Adler, Real Proof, 5 Vand.L.Rev. 344, 362 (1952); McCormick §§ 179, 185; Morgan, Basic Problems of Evidence 378 (1962). Thus a telephone conversation may be irrelevant because on an unrelated topic or because the speaker is not identified. The latter aspect is the one here involved. Wigmore describes the need for authentication as "an inherent logical necessity." 7 Wigmore § 2129, p. 564.

This requirement of showing authenticity or identity falls in the category of relevancy dependent upon fulfillment of a condition of fact and is governed by the procedure set forth in Rule 104(b).

The common law approach to authentication of documents has been criticized as an "attitude of agnosticism," McCormick, Cases on Evidence 388, n. 4 (3rd ed. 1956), as one which "departs sharply from men's customs in ordinary affairs," and as presenting only a slight obstacle to the introduction of forgeries in comparison to the time and expense devoted to proving genuine writings which correctly show their origin on their face, McCormick § 185, pp. 395, 396. Today, such available procedures as requests to admit and pretrial conference afford the means of eliminating much of the need for authentication or identification. Also, significant inroads upon the traditional insistence on authentication and identification have been made by accepting as at least prima facie genuine items of the kind treated in Rule 902, infra. However, the need for suitable methods of proof still remains, since criminal cases pose their own obstacles to the use of preliminary procedures, unforeseen contingencies may arise, and cases of genuine controversy will still occur.

Subdivision (b). The treatment of authentication and identification draws largely upon the experience embodied in the common law and in statutes to furnish illustrative applications of the general principle set forth in subdivision (a). The examples are not intended as an exclusive enumeration of allowable methods but are meant to guide and suggest, leaving room for growth and development in this area of the law.

The examples relate for the most part to documents, with some attention given to voice communications and computer print-outs. As Wigmore noted, no special rules have been developed for authenticating chattels. Wigmore, Code of Evidence § 2086 (3rd ed. 1942).

It should be observed that compliance with requirements of authentication or identification by no means assures admission of an item into evidence, as other bars, hearsay for example, may remain.

Example (1) contemplates a broad spectrum ranging from testimony of a witness who was present at the signing of a document to testimony establishing narcotics as taken from an accused and accounting for custody through the period until trial, including laboratory analysis. See California Evidence Code § 1413, eyewitness to signing.

Example (2) states conventional doctrine as to lay identification of handwriting, which recognizes that a sufficient familiarity with the handwriting of another person may be acquired by seeing him write, by exchanging correspondence, or by other means, to afford a basis for identifying it on subsequent occasions. McCormick § 189. See also California Evidence Code § 1416. Testimony based upon familiarity acquired for purposes of the litigation is reserved to the expert under the example which follows.

Example (3). The history of common law restrictions upon the technique of proving or disproving the genuineness of a disputed specimen of handwriting through comparison with a genuine specimen, by either the testimony of expert witnesses or direct viewing by the triers themselves, is detailed in 7 Wigmore

§§ 1991–1994. In breaking away, the English Common Law Procedure Act of 1854, 17 and 18 Vict., c. 125, § 27, cautiously allowed expert or trier to use exemplars "proved to the satisfaction of the judge to be genuine" for purposes of comparison. The language found its way into numerous statutes in this country, e.g., California Evidence Code §§ 1417, 1418. While explainable as a measure of prudence in the process of breaking with precedent in the handwriting situation, the reservation to the judge of the question of the genuineness of exemplars and the imposition of an unusually high standard of persuasion are at variance with the general treatment of relevancy which depends upon fulfillment of a condition of fact. Rule 104(b). No similar attitude is found in other comparison situations, e.g., ballistics comparison by jury, as in Evans v. Commonwealth, 230 Ky. 411, 19 S.W.2d 1091 (1929), or by experts, Annot., 26 A.L.R.2d 892, and no reason appears for its continued existence in handwriting cases. Consequently Example (3) sets no higher standard for handwriting specimens and treats all comparison situations alike, to be governed by Rule 104(b). This approach is consistent with 28 U.S.C. § 1731: "The admitted or proved handwriting of any person shall be admissible, for purposes of comparison, to determine genuineness of other handwriting attributed to such person."

Precedent supports the acceptance of visual comparison as sufficiently satisfying preliminary authentication requirements for admission in evidence. Brandon v. Collins, 267 F.2d 731 (2d Cir.1959); Wausau Sulphate Fibre Co. v. Commissioner of Internal Revenue, 61 F.2d 879 (7th Cir.1932); Desimone v. United States, 227 F.2d 864 (9th Cir.1955).

Example (4). The characteristics of the offered item itself, considered in the light of circumstances, afford authentication techniques in great variety. Thus a document or telephone conversation may be shown to have emanated from a particular person by virtue of its disclosing knowledge of facts known peculiarly to him; Globe Automatic Sprinkler Co. v. Braniff, 89 Okl. 105, 214 P. 127 (1923); California Evidence Code § 1421; similarly, a letter may be authenticated by content and circumstances indicating it was in reply to a duly authenticated one. McCormick § 192; California Evidence Code § 1420. Language patterns may indicate authenticity or its opposite. Magnuson v. State, 187 Wis. 122, 203 N.W. 749 (1925); Arens and Meadow, Psycholinguistics and the Confession Dilemma, 56 Colum.L.Rev. 19 (1956).

Example (5). Since aural voice identification is not a subject of expert testimony, the requisite familiarity may be acquired either before or after the particular speaking which is the subject of the identification, in this respect resembling visual identification of a person rather than identification of handwriting. Cf. Example (2), supra, People v. Nichols, 378 Ill. 487, 38 N.E.2d 766 (1942); McGuire v. State, 200 Md. 601, 92 A.2d 582 (1952); State v. McGee, 336 Mo. 1082, 83 S.W.2d 98 (1935).

Example (6). The cases are in agreement that a mere assertion of his identity by a person talking on the telephone is not sufficient evidence of the authenticity of the conversation and that additional evidence of his identity is required. The additional evidence need not fall in any set pattern. Thus the content of his statements or the reply technique, under Example (4), supra, or voice identification under Example (5), may furnish the necessary foundation. Outgoing calls made by the witness involve additional factors bearing upon authenticity. The calling of a number assigned by the telephone company reasonably supports the assumption that the listing is correct and that the number is the one reached. If the number is that of a place of business, the mass of authority allows an ensuing conversation if it relates to business reasonably transacted over the telephone, on the theory that the maintenance of the telephone connection is an invitation to do business without further identification. Matton v. Hoover Co., 350 Mo. 506, 166 S.W.2d 557 (1942); City of Pawhuska v. Crutchfield, 147 Okl. 4, 293 P. 1095 (1930); Zurich General Acc. & Liability Ins. Co. v. Baum, 159 Va. 404, 165 S.E. 518 (1932). Otherwise, some additional circumstance of identification of the speaker is required. The authorities divide on the question whether the self-identifying statement of the person answering suffices. Example (6) answers in the affirmative on the assumption that usual conduct respecting telephone calls furnish adequate assurances of regularity, bearing in mind that the entire matter is open to exploration before the trier of fact. In general, see McCormick § 193; 7 Wigmore § 2155; Annot., 71 A.L.R. 5, 105 id. 326.

Example (7). Public records are regularly authenticated by proof of custody, without more. McCormick § 191; 7 Wigmore §§ 2158, 2159. The example extends the principle to include data stored in computers and similar methods, of which increasing use in the public records area may be expected. See California Evidence Code §§ 1532, 1600.

Example (8). The familiar ancient document rule of the common law is extended to include data stored electronically or by other similar means. Since the importance of appearance diminishes in this situation, the importance of custody or place where found increases correspondingly. This expansion is necessary in view of the widespread use of methods of storing data in forms other than conventional written records.

Any time period selected is bound to be arbitrary. The common law period of 30 years is here reduced to 20 years, with some shift of emphasis from the probable unavailability of witnesses to the unlikeliness of a still viable fraud after the lapse of time. The shorter period is specified in the English Evidence Act of 1938, 1 & 2 Geo. 6, c. 28, and in Oregon R.S.1963, § 41.360(34). See also the numerous statutes prescribing periods of less than 30 years in the case of recorded documents. 7 Wigmore § 2143.

The application of Example (8) is not subject to any limitation to title documents or to any requirement that possession, in the case of a title document, has been consistent with the document. See McCormick § 190.

Example (9) is designed for situations in which the accuracy of a result is dependent upon a process or system which produces it. X rays afford a familiar instance. Among more recent developments is the computer, as to which see Transport Indemnity Co. v. Seib, 178 Neb. 253, 132 N.W.2d 871 (1965); State v. Veres, 7 Ariz.App. 117, 436 P.2d 629 (1968); Merrick v. United States Rubber Co., 7 Ariz.App. 433, 440 P.2d 314 (1968); Freed, Computer Print-Outs as Evidence, 16 Am.Jur.Proof of Facts 273; Symposium, Law and Computers in the Mid-Sixties, ALI–ABA (1966); 37 Albany L.Rev. 61 (1967). Example (9) does not, of course, foreclose taking judicial notice of the accuracy of the process or system.

Example (10). The example makes clear that methods of authentication provided by Act of Congress and by the Rules of Civil and Criminal Procedure or by Bankruptcy Rules are not intended to be superseded. Illustrative are the provisions for authentication of official records in Civil Procedure Rule 44 and

Criminal Procedure Rule 27, for authentication of records of proceedings by court reporters in 28 U.S.C. § 753(b) and Civil Procedure Rule 80(c), and for authentication of depositions in Civil Procedure Rule 30(f).

Rule 902. Self-Authentication

Extrinsic evidence of authenticity as a condition precedent to admissibility is not required with respect to the following:

(1) Domestic public documents under seal. A document bearing a seal purporting to be that of the United States, or of any State, district, Commonwealth, territory, or insular possession thereof, or the Panama Canal Zone, or the Trust Territory of the Pacific Islands, or of a political subdivision, department, officer, or agency thereof, and a signature purporting to be an attestation or execution.

(2) Domestic public documents not under seal. A document purporting to bear the signature in the official capacity of an officer or employee of any entity included in paragraph (1) hereof, having no seal, if a public officer having a seal and having official duties in the district or political subdivision of the officer or employee certifies under seal that the signer has the official capacity and that the signature is genuine.

(3) Foreign public documents. A document purporting to be executed or attested in an official capacity by a person authorized by the laws of a foreign country to make the execution or attestation, and accompanied by a final certification as to the genuineness of the signature and official position (A) of the executing or attesting person, or (B) of any foreign official whose certificate of genuineness of signature and official position relates to the execution or attestation or is in a chain of certificates of genuineness of signature and official position relating to the execution or attestation. A final certification may be made by a secretary of embassy or legation, consul general, consul, vice consul, or consular agent of the United States, or a diplomatic or consular official of the foreign country assigned or accredited to the United States. If reasonable opportunity has been given to all parties to investigate the authenticity and accuracy of official documents, the court may, for good cause shown, order that they be treated as presumptively authentic without final certification or permit them to be evidenced by an attested summary with or without final certification.

(4) Certified copies of public records. A copy of an official record or report or entry therein, or of a document authorized by law to be recorded or filed and actually recorded or filed in a public office, including data compilations in any form, certified as correct by the custodian or other person authorized to make the certification, by certificate complying with paragraph (1), (2), or (3) of this rule or complying with any Act of Congress or rule prescribed by the Supreme Court pursuant to statutory authority.

(5) Official publications. Books, pamphlets, or other publications purporting to be issued by public authority.

(6) Newspapers and periodicals. Printed materials purporting to be newspapers or periodicals.

(7) Trade inscriptions and the like. Inscriptions, signs, tags, or labels purporting to have been affixed in the course of business and indicating ownership, control, or origin.

(8) Acknowledged documents. Documents accompanied by a certificate of acknowledgment executed in the manner provided by law by a notary public or other officer authorized by law to take acknowledgments.

(9) Commercial paper and related documents. Commercial paper, signatures thereon, and documents relating thereto to the extent provided by general commercial law.

(10) Presumptions under Acts of Congress. Any signature, document, or other matter declared by Act of Congress to be presumptively or prima facie genuine or authentic.

(11) Certified domestic records of regularly conducted activity. The original or a duplicate of a domestic record of regularly conducted activity that would be admissible under Rule 803(6) if accompanied by a written declaration of its custodian or other qualified person, in a manner complying with any Act of Congress or rule prescribed by the Supreme Court pursuant to statutory authority, certifying that the record—

(A) was made at or near the time of the occurrence of the matters set forth by, or from information transmitted by, a person with knowledge of those matters;

(B) was kept in the course of the regularly conducted activity; and

(C) was made by the regularly conducted activity as a regular practice.

A party intending to offer a record into evidence under this paragraph must provide written notice of that intention to all adverse parties, and must make the record and declaration available for inspection sufficiently in advance of their offer into evidence to provide an adverse party with a fair opportunity to challenge them.

(12) Certified foreign records of regularly conducted activity. In a civil case, the original or a duplicate of a foreign record of regularly conducted activity that would be admissible under Rule 803(6) if accompanied by a written declaration by its custodian or other qualified person certifying that the record—

(A) was made at or near the time of the occurrence of the matters set forth by, or from information transmitted by, a person with knowledge of those matters;

(B) was kept in the course of the regularly conducted activity; and

(C) was made by the regularly conducted activity as a regular practice.

The declaration must be signed in a manner that, if falsely made, would subject the maker to criminal penalty under the laws of the country where the declaration is signed. A party intending to offer a record into evidence under this paragraph must provide written notice of that intention to all adverse parties, and must make the record and declaration available for inspection sufficiently in advance of their offer into evidence to provide an adverse party with a fair opportunity to challenge them.

(As amended Mar. 2, 1987, eff. Oct. 1, 1987; Apr. 25, 1988, eff. Nov. 1, 1988; Apr. 17, 2000, eff. Dec. 1, 2000.)

Section references, McCormick 5th ed.

Generally § 218

(1). § 228

(2). § 228

(3). § 228

(4). § 228, § 300

(5). § 228

(6). § 228

(7). § 218, § 228

(8). § 228

Note by Federal Judicial Center

The rule enacted by the Congress is the rule prescribed by the Supreme Court, amended as follows:

Paragraph (4) was amended by substituting "prescribed" in place of "adopted," and by adding "pursuant to statutory authority."

Paragraph (8) was amended by substituting "in the manner provided by law by" in place of "under the hand and seal of."

Advisory Committee's Note

56 F.R.D. 183, 337

Case law and statutes have, over the years, developed a substantial body of instances in which authenticity is taken as sufficiently established for purposes of admissibility without extrinsic evidence to that effect, sometimes for reasons of policy but perhaps more often because practical considerations reduce the possibility of unauthenticity to a very small dimension. The present rule collects and incorporates these situations, in some instances expanding them to occupy a larger area which their underlying considerations justify. In no instance is the opposite party foreclosed from disputing authenticity.

Paragraph (1). The acceptance of documents bearing a public seal and signature, most often encountered in practice in the form of acknowledgments or certificates authenticating copies of public records, is actually of broad application. Whether theoretically based in whole or in part upon judicial notice, the practical underlying considerations are that forgery is a crime and detection is fairly easy and certain. 7 Wigmore § 2161 p. 638; California Evidence Code § 1452. More than 50 provisions for judicial notice of official seals are contained in the United States Code.

Paragraph (2). While statutes are found which raise a presumption of genuineness of purported official signatures in the absence of an official seal, 7 Wigmore § 2167; California Evidence Code § 1453, the greater ease of effecting a forgery under these circumstances is apparent. Hence this paragraph of the rule calls for authentication by an officer who has a seal. Notarial acts by members of the armed forces and other special situations are covered in paragraph (10).

Paragraph (3) provides a method for extending the presumption of authenticity to foreign official documents by a procedure of certification. It is derived from Rule 44(a)(2) of the Rules of Civil Procedure but is broader in applying to public documents rather than being limited to public records.

Paragraph (4). The common law and innumerable statutes have recognized the procedure of authenticating copies of public records by certificate. The certificate qualifies as a public document, receivable as authentic when in conformity with paragraph (1), (2), or (3). Rule 44(a) of the Rules of Civil Procedure and Rule 27 of the Rules of Criminal Procedure have provided authentication procedures of this nature for both domestic and foreign public records. It will be observed that the certification procedure here provided extends only to public records, reports, and recorded documents, all including data compilations, and does not apply to public documents generally. Hence documents provable when presented in original form under paragraphs (1), (2), or (3) may not be provable by certified copy under paragraph (4).

Paragraph (5). Dispensing with preliminary proof of the genuineness of purportedly official publications, most commonly encountered in connection with statutes, court reports, rules, and regulations, has been greatly enlarged by statutes and decisions. 5 Wigmore § 1684. Paragraph (5), it will be noted, does not confer admissibility upon all official publications; it merely provides a means whereby their authenticity may be taken as established for purposes of admissibility. Rule 44(a) of the Rules of Civil Procedure has been to the same effect.

Paragraph (6). The likelihood of forgery of newspapers or periodicals is slight indeed. Hence no danger is apparent in receiving them. Establishing the authenticity of the publication may, of course, leave still open questions of authority and responsibility for items therein contained. See 7 Wigmore § 2150. Cf. 39 U.S.C. § 4005(b), public advertisement prima facie evidence of agency of person named, in postal fraud order proceeding; Canadian Uniform Evidence Act, Draft of 1936, printed copy of newspaper prima facie evidence that notices or advertisements were authorized.

Paragraph (7). Several factors justify dispensing with preliminary proof of genuineness of commercial and mercantile labels and the like. The risk of forgery is minimal. Trademark infringement involves serious penalties. Great efforts are devoted to inducing the public to buy in reliance on brand names, and substantial protection is given them. Hence the fairness of this treatment finds recognition in the cases. Curtiss Candy Co. v. Johnson, 163 Miss. 426, 141 So.

762 (1932), Baby Ruth candy bar; Doyle v. Continental Baking Co., 262 Mass. 516, 160 N.E. 325 (1928), loaf of bread; Weiner v. Mager & Throne, Inc., 167 Misc. 338, 3 N.Y.S.2d 918 (1938), same. And see W.Va.Code 1966, § 47–3–5, trade-mark on bottle prima facie evidence of ownership. Contra, Keegan v. Green Giant Co., 150 Me. 283, 110 A.2d 599 (1954); Murphy v. Campbell Soup Co., 62 F.2d 564 (1st Cir.1933). Cattle brands have received similar acceptance in the western states. Rev.Code Mont.1947, § 46–606; State v. Wolfley, 75 Kan. 406, 89 P. 1046 (1907); Annot., 11 L.R.A.(N.S.) 87. Inscriptions on trains and vehicles are held to be prima facie evidence of ownership or control. Pittsburgh, Ft. W. & C. Ry. v. Callaghan, 157 Ill. 406, 41 N.E. 909 (1895); 9 Wigmore § 2510a. See also the provision of 19 U.S.C. § 1615(2) that marks, labels, brands, or stamps indicating foreign origin are prima facie evidence of foreign origin of merchandise.

Paragraph (8). In virtually every state, acknowledged title documents are receivable in evidence without further proof. Statutes are collected in 5 Wigmore § 1676. If this authentication suffices for documents of the importance of those affecting titles, logic scarcely permits denying this method when other kinds of documents are involved. Instances of broadly inclusive statutes are California Evidence Code § 1451 and N.Y.CPLR 4538, McKinney's Consol.Laws 1963.

Report of House Committee on the Judiciary

House Comm. on Judiciary, Fed.Rules of Evidence, H.R.Rep. No. 650, 93d Cong., 1st Sess., p. 17 (1973); 1974 U.S.Code Cong. & Ad.News 7075, 7090

Rule 902(8) as submitted by the Court referred to certificates of acknowledgment "under the hand and seal of" a notary public or other officer authorized by law to take acknowledgments. The Committee amended the Rule to eliminate the requirement, believed to be inconsistent with the law in some States, that a notary public must affix a seal to a document acknowledged before him. As amended the Rule merely requires that the document be executed in the manner prescribed by State law.

Advisory Committee's Note

56 F.R.D. 183, 339

Paragraph (9). Issues of the authenticity of commercial paper in federal courts will usually arise in diversity cases, will involve an element of a cause of action or defense, and with respect to presumptions and burden of proof will be controlled by Erie Railroad Co. v. Tompkins, 304 U.S. 64, 58 S.Ct. 817, 82 L.Ed 1188 (1938). Rule 302, supra. There may, however, be questions of authenticity involving lesser segments of a case or the case may be one governed by federal common law. Clearfield Trust Co. v. United States, 318 U.S. 363, 63 S.Ct. 573, 87 L.Ed. 838 (1943). Cf. United States v. Yazell, 382 U.S. 341, 86 S.Ct. 500, 15 L.Ed.2d 404 (1966). In these situations, resort to the useful authentication provisions of the Uniform Commercial Code is provided for. While the phrasing is in terms of "general commercial law," in order to avoid the potential complications inherent in borrowing local statutes, today one would have difficulty in determining the general commercial law without referring to the Code. See Williams v. Walker-Thomas Furniture Co., 121 U.S.App.D.C. 315, 350 F.2d 445 (1965). Pertinent Code provisions are sections 1–202, 3–307, and 3–510, dealing with third-party documents, signatures on negotiable instruments, protests, and statements of dishonor.

Report of House Committee on the Judiciary

House Comm. on Judiciary, Fed.Rules of Evidence, H.R.Rep. No. 650, 93d Cong., 1st Sess., p. 17 (1973); 1974 U.S.Code Cong. & Ad.News 7075, 7090

The Committee approved Rule 902(9) as submitted by the Court. With respect to the meaning of the phrase "general commercial law", the Committee intends that the Uniform Commercial Code, which has been adopted in virtually every State, will be followed generally, but that federal commercial law will apply where federal commercial paper is involved. See Clearfield Trust Co. v. United States, 318 U.S. 363 (1943). Further, in those instances in which the issues are governed by Erie R. Co. v. Tompkins, 304 U.S. 64 (1938), State law will apply irrespective of whether it is the Uniform Commercial Code.

Advisory Committee's Note

56 F.R.D. 183 340

Paragraph (10). The paragraph continues in effect dispensations with preliminary proof of genuineness provided in various Acts of Congress. See, for example, 10 U.S.C. § 936, signature, without seal, together with title, prima facie evidence of authenticity of acts of certain military personnel who are given notarial powers; 15 U.S.C. § 77f(a), signature on SEC registration presumed genuine; 26 U.S.C. § 6064, signature to tax return prima facie genuine.

1987 Amendment

The amendments are technical. No substantive change is intended.

1988 Amendment

Two sentences were inadvertently eliminated from the 1987 amendment. The amendment is technical. No substantive change is intended.

2000 Amendment

The amendment adds two new paragraphs to the rule on self-authentication. It sets forth a procedure by which parties can authenticate certain records of regularly conducted activity, other than through the testimony of a foundation witness. See the amendment to Rule 803(6). 18 U.S.C. § 3505 currently provides a means for certifying foreign records of regularly conducted activity in criminal cases, and this amendment is intended to establish a similar procedure for domestic records, and for foreign records offered in civil cases.

A declaration that satisfies 28 U.S.C. § 1746 would satisfy the declaration requirement of Rule 902(11), as would any comparable certification under oath.

The notice requirement in Rules 902(11) and (12) is intended to give the opponent of the evidence a full opportunity to test the adequacy of the foundation set forth in the declaration.

Rule 903. Subscribing Witness' Testimony Unnecessary

The testimony of a subscribing witness is not necessary to authenticate a writing unless required by the laws of the jurisdiction whose laws govern the validity of the writing.

Section references, McCormick 5th ed.

§ 218, § 220

Note by Federal Judicial Center

The rule enacted by the Congress is the rule prescribed by the Supreme Court without change.

Advisory Committee's Note

56 F.R.D. 183, 340

The common law required that attesting witnesses be produced or accounted for. Today the requirement has generally been abolished except with respect to documents which must be attested to be valid, e.g. wills in some states. McCormick § 188. Uniform Rule 71; California Evidence Code § 1411; Kansas Code of Civil Procedure § 60–468; New Jersey Evidence Rule 71; New York CPLR Rule 4537.

ARTICLE X. CONTENTS OF WRITINGS, RECORDINGS, AND PHOTOGRAPHS

Rule

Rule 1001. Definitions

For purposes of this article the following definitions are applicable:

(1) Writings and recordings. "Writings" and "recordings" consist of letters, words, or numbers, or their equivalent, set down by handwriting, typewriting, printing, photostating, photographing, magnetic impulse, mechanical or electronic recording, or other form of data compilation.

(2) Photographs. "Photographs" include still photographs, X-ray films, video tapes, and motion pictures.

(3) Original. An "original" of a writing or recording is the writing or recording itself or any counterpart intended to have the same effect by a person executing or issuing it. An "original" of a photograph includes the negative or any print therefrom. If data are stored in a computer or similar device, any printout or other output readable by sight, shown to reflect the data accurately, is an "original".

(4) Duplicate. A "duplicate" is a counterpart produced by the same impression as the original, or from the same matrix, or by means of photography, including enlargements and miniatures, or by mechanical or electronic re-recording, or by chemical reproduction, or by other equivalent technique which accurately reproduces the original.

Section references, McCormick 5th ed.

Generally § 236

(1). § 232

(2). § 232

(3). § 230, § 236

(4). § 236

Note by Federal Judicial Center

The rule enacted by the Congress is the rule prescribed by the Supreme Court, amended in paragraph (2) by inserting "video tapes."

Advisory Committee's Note

56 F.R.D. 183 341

In an earlier day, when discovery and other related procedures were strictly limited, the misleading named "best evidence rule" afforded substantial guarantees against inaccuracies and fraud by its insistence upon production of original documents. The great enlargement of the scope of discovery and related procedures in recent times has measurably reduced the need for the rule. Nevertheless important areas of usefulness persist: discovery of documents outside the jurisdiction may require substantial outlay of time and money; the unanticipated document may not practically be discoverable; criminal cases have built-in limitations on discovery. Cleary and Strong, The Best Evidence Rule: An Evaluation in Context, 51 Iowa L.Rev. 825 (1966).

Paragraph (1). Traditionally the rule requiring the original centered upon accumulations of data and expressions affecting legal relations set forth in words and figures. This meant that the rule was one essentially related to writings. Present day techniques have expanded methods of storing data, yet the essential form which the information ultimately assumes for usable purposes is words and figures. Hence the considerations underlying the rule dictate its expansion to include computers, photographic systems, and other modern developments.

Paragraph (2).

Report of House Committee on the Judiciary

House Comm. on Judiciary, Fed.Rules of Evidence, H.R.Rep. No. 650, 93d Cong., 1st Sess., p. 17 (1973); 1974 U.S.Code Cong. & Ad.News 7075, 7090

The Committee amended this Rule expressly to include "video tapes" in the definition of "photographs."

Advisory Committee's Note

56 F.R.D. 183, 341

Paragraph (3). In most instances, what is an original will be self-evident and further refinement will be unnecessary. However, in some instances particularized definition is required. A carbon copy of a contract executed in duplicate becomes an original, as does a sales ticket carbon copy given to a customer. While strictly speaking the original of a photograph might be thought to be only the negative, practicality and common usage require that any print from the negative be regarded as an original. Similarly, practicality and usage confer the status of original upon any computer printout. Transport Indemnity Co. v. Seib, 178 Neb. 253, 132 N.W.2d 871 (1965).

Paragraph (4). The definition describes "copies" produced by methods possessing an accuracy which virtually eliminates the possibility of error. Copies thus produced are given the status of originals in large measure by Rule 1003, infra. Copies subsequently produced manually, whether handwritten or typed, are not within the definition. It should be noted that what is an original for some purposes may be a duplicate for others. Thus a bank's microfilm record of checks cleared is the original as a record. However, a print offered as a copy of a check whose contents are in controversy is a duplicate. This result is substantially consistent with 28 U.S.C. § 1732(b). Compare 26 U.S.C. § 7513(c), giving full status as originals to photographic reproductions of tax returns and other documents, made by authority of the Secretary of the Treasury, and 44 U.S.C. § 399(a), giving original status to photographic copies in the National Archives.

Rule 1002. Requirement of Original

To prove the content of a writing, recording, or photograph, the original writing, recording, or photograph is required, except as otherwise provided in these rules or by Act of Congress.

Note by Federal Judicial Center

The rule enacted by the Congress is the rule prescribed by the Supreme Court without change.

Section references, McCormick 5th ed.

§ 230

Advisory Committee's Note

56 F.R.D. 183, 342

The rule is the familiar one requiring production of the original of a document to prove its contents, expanded to include writings, recordings, and photographs, as defined in Rule 1001(1) and (2), supra.

Application of the rule requires a resolution of the question whether contents are sought to be proved. Thus an event may be proved by nondocumentary evidence, even though a written record of it was made. If, however, the event is sought to be proved by the written record, the rule applies. For example, payment may be proved without producing the written receipt which was given. Earnings may be proved without producing books of account in which they are entered. McCormick § 198; 4 Wigmore § 1245. Nor does the rule apply to testimony that books or records have been examined and found not to contain any reference to a designated matter.

The assumption should not be made that the rule will come into operation on every occasion when use is made of a photograph in evidence. On the contrary, the rule will seldom apply to ordinary photographs. In most instances a party *wishes* to introduce the item and the question raised is the propriety of receiving it in evidence. Cases in which an offer is made of the testimony of a witness as to what he saw in a photograph or motion picture, without producing the same, are most unusual. The usual course is for a witness on the stand to identify the photograph or motion picture as a correct representation of events which he saw or of a scene with which he is familiar. In fact he adopts the picture as his testimony, or, in common parlance, uses the picture to illustrate his testimony. Under these circumstances, no effort is made to prove the contents of the picture, and the rule is inapplicable. Paradis, The Celluloid Witness, 37 U.Colo.L.Rev. 235, 249–251 (1965).

On occasion, however, situations arise in which contents are sought to be proved. Copyright, defamation, and invasion of privacy by photograph or motion picture falls in this category. Similarly as to situations in which the picture is offered as having independent probative value, e.g. automatic photograph of bank robber. See People v. Doggett, 83 Cal.App.2d 405, 188 P.2d 792 (1948), photograph of defendants engaged in indecent act; Mouser and Philbin, Photographic Evidence—Is There a Recognized Basis for Admissibility? 8 Hastings L.J. 310 (1957). The most commonly encountered of this latter group is of course, the X-ray, with substantial authority calling for production of the original. Daniels v. Iowa City, 191 Iowa 811, 183 N.W. 415 (1921); Cellamare v. Third Ave. Transit Corp., 273 App.Div. 260, 77 N.Y.S.2d 91 (1948); Patrick & Tilman v. Matkin, 154 Okl. 232, 7 P.2d 414 (1932); Mendoza v. Rivera, 78 P.R.R. 569 (1955).

It should be noted, however, that Rule 703, supra, allows an expert to give an opinion based on matters not in evidence, and the present rule must be read as being limited accordingly in its application. Hospital records which may be admitted as business records under Rule 803(6) commonly contain reports interpreting X rays by the staff radiologist, who qualifies as an expert, and these reports need not be excluded from the records by the instant rule.

The references to Acts of Congress is made in view of such statutory provisions as 26 U.S.C. § 7513, photographic reproductions of tax returns and documents, made by authority of the Secretary of the Treasury, treated as originals, and 44 U.S.C. § 399(a), photographic copies in National Archives treated as originals.

Rule 1003. Admissibility of Duplicates

A duplicate is admissible to the same extent as an original unless (1) a genuine question is raised as to the authenticity of the original or (2) in the circumstances it would be unfair to admit the duplicate in lieu of the original.

Section references, McCormick 5th ed.

§ 231, § 236, § 243

Note by Federal Judicial Center

The rule enacted by the Congress is the rule prescribed by the 7Supreme Court without change.

Advisory Committee's Note

56 F.R.D. 183, 343

When the only concern is with getting the words or other contents before the court with accuracy and precision, then a counterpart serves equally as well as the original, if the counterpart is the product of a method which insures accuracy and genuineness. By definition in Rule 1001(4), supra, a "duplicate" possesses this character.

Therefore, if no genuine issue exists as to authenticity and no other reason exists for requiring the original, a duplicate is admissible under the rule. This position finds support in the decisions, Myrick v. United States, 332 F.2d 279 (5th Cir.1964), no error in admitting photostatic copies of checks instead of original microfilm in absence of suggestion to trial judge that photostats were incorrect; Johns v. United States, 323 F.2d 421 (5th Cir.1963), not error to admit concededly accurate tape recording made from original wire recording; Sauget v. Johnston, 315 F.2d 816 (9th Cir.1963), not error to admit copy of agreement when opponent had original and did not on appeal claim any discrepancy. Other reasons for requiring the original may be present when only a part of the original is reproduced and the remainder is needed for cross-examination or may disclose matters qualifying the part offered or otherwise useful to the opposing party. United States v. Alexander, 326 F.2d 736 (4th Cir.1964). And see Toho Bussan Kaisha, Ltd. v. American President Lines, Ltd., 265 F.2d 418, 76 A.L.R.2d 1344 (2d Cir.1959).

Report of House Committee on the Judiciary

House Comm. on Judiciary, Fed.Rules of Evidence, 93d Cong., 1st Sess., p. 17 (1973); 1974 U.S.Code Cong. & Ad.News 7075, 7090

The Committee approved this Rule in the form submitted by the Court, with the expectation that the courts would be liberal in deciding that a "genuine question is raised as to the authenticity of the original."

Rule 1004. Admissibility of Other Evidence of Contents

The original is not required, and other evidence of the contents of a writing, recording, or photograph is admissible if—

(1) Originals lost or destroyed. All originals are lost or have been destroyed, unless the proponent lost or destroyed them in bad faith; or

(2) Original not obtainable. No original can be obtained by any available judicial process or procedure; or

(3) Original in possession of opponent. At a time when an original was under the control of the party against whom offered, that party was put on notice, by the pleadings or otherwise, that the contents would be a subject of proof at the hearing, and that party does not produce the original at the hearing; or

(4) Collateral matters. The writing, recording, or photograph is not closely related to a controlling issue.

(As amended Mar. 2, 1987, eff. Oct. 1, 1987.)

Section references, McCormick 5th ed.

Generally § 236, § 241

(1). § 237

(2). § 238

(3). § 239

(4). § 234

Note by Federal Judicial Center

The rule enacted by the Congress is the rule prescribed by the Supreme Court without change.

Advisory Committee's Note

56 F.R.D. 183, 344

Basically the rule requiring the production of the original as proof of contents has developed as a rule of preference: if failure to produce the original is satisfactorily explained, secondary evidence is admissible. The instant rule specifies the circumstances under which production of the original is excused.

The rule recognizes no "degrees" of secondary evidence. While strict logic might call for extending the principle of preference beyond simply preferring the original, the formulation of a hierarchy of preferences and a procedure for making it effective is believed to involve unwarranted complexities. Most, if not all, that would be accomplished by an extended scheme of preferences will, in any event, be achieved through the normal motivation of a party to present the most convincing evidence possible and the arguments and procedures available to his opponent if he does not. Compare McCormick § 207.

Paragraph (1). Loss or destruction of the original, unless due to bad faith of the proponent, is a satisfactory explanation of nonproduction. McCormick § 201.

Report of House Committee on the Judiciary

House Comm. on Judiciary, Fed.Rules of Evidence, H.R.Rep. No. 650, 93d Cong., 1st Sess., p. 17 (1973); 1974 U.S.Code Cong. & Ad.News 7075, 7090

The Committee approved Rule 1004(1) in the form submitted to Congress. However, the Committee intends that loss or destruction of an original by another person at the instigation of the proponent should be considered as tantamount to loss or destruction in bad faith by the proponent himself.

Advisory Committee's Note

56 F.R.D. 183, 344

Paragraph (2). When the original is in the possession of a third person, inability to procure it from him by resort to process or other judicial procedure is a sufficient explanation of nonproduction. Judicial procedure includes subpoena duces tecum as an incident to the taking of a deposition in another jurisdiction. No further showing is required. See McCormick § 202.

Paragraph (3). A party who has an original in his control has no need for the protection of the rule if put on notice that proof of contents will be made. He can ward off secondary evidence by offering the original. The notice procedure here provided is not to be confused with orders to produce or other discovery procedures, as the purpose of the procedure under this rule is to afford the opposite party an opportunity to produce the original, not to compel him to do so. McCormick § 203.

Paragraph (4). While difficult to define with precision, situations arise in which no good purpose is served by production of the original. Examples are the newspaper in an action for the price of publishing defendant's advertisement, Foster-Holcomb Investment Co. v. Little Rock Publishing Co., 151 Ark. 449, 236 S.W. 597 (1922), and the streetcar transfer of plaintiff claiming status as a passenger, Chicago City Ry. Co. v. Carroll, 206 Ill. 318, 68 N.E. 1087 (1903). Numerous cases are collected in McCormick § 200, p. 412, n. 1.

1987 Amendment

The amendments are technical. No substantive change is intended.

Rule 1005. Public Records

The contents of an official record, or of a document authorized to be recorded or filed and actually recorded or filed, including data compilations in any form, if otherwise admissible, may be proved by copy, certified as correct in accordance with rule 902 or testified to be correct by a witness who has compared it with the original. If a copy which complies with the foregoing cannot be obtained by the exercise of reasonable diligence, then other evidence of the contents may be given.

Section references, McCormick 5th ed.

§ 240, § 300

Note by Federal Judicial Center

The rule enacted by the Congress is the rule prescribed by the Supreme Court without change.

Advisory Committee's Note

56 F.R.D. 183, 345

Public records call for somewhat different treatment. Removing them from their usual place of keeping would be attended by serious inconvenience to the public and to the custodian. As a consequence judicial decisions and statutes commonly hold that no explanation need be given for failure to produce the original of a public record. McCormick § 204; 4 Wigmore §§ 1215–1228. This blanket dispensation from producing or accounting for the original would open the door to the introduction of every kind of secondary evidence of contents of public records were it not for the preference given certified or compared copies. Recognition of degrees of secondary evidence in this situation is an appropriate *quid pro quo* for not applying the requirement of producing the original.

The provisions of 28 U.S.C. § 1733(b) apply only to departments or agencies of the United States. The rule, however, applies to public records generally and is comparable in scope in this respect to Rule 44(a) of the Rules of Civil Procedure.

Rule 1006. Summaries

The contents of voluminous writings, recordings, or photographs which cannot conveniently be examined in court may be presented in the form of a chart, summary, or calculation. The originals, or duplicates, shall be made available for examination or copying, or both, by other parties at reasonable time and place. The court may order that they be produced in court.

Section references, McCormick 5th ed.

§ 233

Note by Federal Judicial Center

The rule enacted by the Congress is the rule prescribed by the Supreme Court without change.

Advisory Committee's Note

56 F.R.D. 183 346

The admission of summaries of voluminous books, records, or documents offers the only practicable means of making their contents available to judge and jury. The rule recognizes this practice, with appropriate safeguards. 4 Wigmore § 1230.

Rule 1007. Testimony or Written Admission of Party

Contents of writings, recordings, or photographs may be proved by the testimony or deposition of the party against whom offered or by that party's written admission, without accounting for the nonproduction of the original.

(As amended Mar. 2, 1987, eff. Oct. 1, 1987.)

Section references, McCormick 5th ed.

§ 242

Note by Federal Judicial Center

The rule enacted by the Congress is the rule prescribed by the Supreme Court without change.

Advisory Committee's Note

56 F.R D. 183, 356

While the parent case, Slatterie v. Pooley, 6 M. & W. 664, 151 Eng.Rep. 579 (Exch.1840), allows proof of contents by evidence of an oral admission by the party against whom offered, without accounting for nonproduction of the original, the risk of inaccuracy is substantial and the decision is at odds with the purpose of the rule giving preference to the original. See 4 Wigmore § 1255.

The instant rule follows Professor McCormick's suggestion of limiting this use of admissions to those made in the course of giving testimony or in writing. McCormick § 208, p. 424. The limitation, of course, does not call for excluding evidence of an oral admission when nonproduction of the original has been accounted for and secondary evidence generally has become admissible. Rule 1004, supra.

A similar provision is contained in New Jersey Evidence Rule 70(1)(h).

1987 Amendment

The amendment is technical. No substantive change is intended.

Rule 1008. Functions of Court and Jury

When the admissibility of other evidence of contents of writings, recordings, or photographs under these rules depends upon the fulfillment of a condition of fact, the question whether the condition has been fulfilled is ordinarily for the court to determine in accordance with the provisions of rule 104. However, when an issue is raised (a) whether the asserted writing ever existed, or (b) whether another writing, recording, or photograph produced at the trial is the original, or (c) whether other evidence of contents correctly reflects the contents, the issue is for the trier of fact to determine as in the case of other issues of fact.

Section references, McCormick 5th ed.

§ 53, § 54

Note by Federal Judicial Center

The rule enacted by the Congress is the rule prescribed by the Supreme Court, amended by substituting "court" in place of "judge," and by adding at the end of the first sentence the phrase "in accordance with the provisions of rule 104."

Advisory Committee's Note

56 F.R.D. 183, 347

Most preliminary questions of fact in connection with applying the rule preferring the original as evidence of contents are for the judge, under the general principles announced in Rule 104, supra. Thus, the question whether the loss of the originals has been established, or of the fulfillment of other conditions specified in Rule 1004, supra, is for the judge. However, questions may arise which go beyond the mere administration of the rule preferring the original and into the merits of the controversy. For example, plaintiff offers secondary evidence of the contents of an alleged contract, after first introducing evidence of loss of the original, and defendant counters with evidence that no such contract was ever executed. If the judge decides that the contract was never executed and excludes the secondary evidence, the case is at an end without ever going to the jury on a central issue. Levin, Authentication and Content of Writings, 10 Rutgers L.Rev. 632, 644 (1956). The latter portion of the instant rule is designed to insure treatment of these situations as raising jury questions. The decision is not one for uncontrolled discretion of the jury but is subject to the control exercised generally by the judge over jury determinations. See Rule 104(b), supra.

For similar provisions, see Uniform Rule 70(2); Kansas Code of Civil Procedure § 60–467(b); New Jersey Evidence Rule 70(2), (3).

ARTICLE XI. MISCELLANEOUS RULES

Rule 1101. Applicability of Rules

(a) Courts and judges. These rules apply to the United States district courts, the District Court of Guam, the District Court of the Virgin Islands, the District Court for the Northern Mariana Islands, the United States courts of appeals, the United States Claims Court, and to United States bankruptcy judges and United States magistrate judges, in the actions, cases, and proceedings and to the extent hereinafter set forth. The terms "judge" and "court" in these rules include United States bankruptcy judges and United States magistrate judges.

(b) Proceedings generally. These rules apply generally to civil actions and proceedings, including admiralty and maritime cases, to criminal cases and proceedings, to contempt proceedings except those in which the court may act summarily, and to proceedings and cases under title 11, United States Code.

(c) Rule of privilege. The rule with respect to privileges applies at all stages of all actions, cases, and proceedings.

(d) Rules inapplicable. The rules (other than with respect to privileges) do not apply in the following situations:

(1) Preliminary questions of fact. The determination of questions of fact preliminary to admissibility of evidence when the issue is to be determined by the court under rule 104.

(2) Grand jury. Proceedings before grand juries.

(3) Miscellaneous proceedings. Proceedings for extradition or rendition; preliminary examinations in criminal cases; sentencing, or granting or revoking probation; issuance of warrants for arrest, criminal summonses, and search warrants; and proceedings with respect to release on bail or otherwise.

(e) Rules applicable in part. In the following proceedings these rules apply to the extent that matters of evidence are not provided for in the statutes which govern procedure therein or in other rules prescribed by the Supreme Court pursuant to statutory authority: the trial of minor and petty offenses by United States magistrates; review of agency actions when the facts are subject to trial de novo under section 706(2)(F) of title 5, United States Code; review of orders of the Secretary of Agriculture under section 2 of the Act entitled "An Act to authorize association of producers of agricultural products" approved February 18, 1922 (7 U.S.C. 292), and under sections 6 and 7(c) of the Perishable Agricultural Commodities Act, 1930 (7 U.S.C. 499f, 499g(c)); naturalization and revocation of naturalization under sections 310–318 of the Immigration and Nationality Act (8 U.S.C. 1421–1429); prize proceedings in admiralty under sections 7651–7681 of title 10, United States Code; review of orders of the Secretary of the Interior under section 2 of the Act entitled "An Act authorizing associations of producers of aquatic products" approved June 25, 1934 (15 U.S.C. 522); review of orders of petroleum control boards under section 5 of the Act entitled "An Act to regulate interstate and foreign commerce in petroleum and its products by prohibiting the shipment in such commerce of petroleum and its products produced in violation of State law, and for other purposes", approved February 22, 1935 (15 U.S.C. 715d); actions for fines, penalties, or forfeitures under part V of title IV of the Tariff Act of 1930 (19 U.S.C. 1581–1624), or under the Anti-Smuggling Act (19 U.S.C. 1701–1711); criminal libel for condemnation, exclusion of imports, or other proceedings under the Federal Food, Drug, and Cosmetic Act (21 U.S.C. 301–392); disputes between seamen under sections 4079, 4080, and 4081 of the Revised Statutes (22 U.S.C. 256–258); habeas corpus under sections 2241–2254 of title 28, United States Code; motions to vacate, set aside or correct sentence under section 2255 of title 28, United States Code; actions for penalties for refusal to transport destitute seamen under section 4578 of the Revised Statutes (46 U.S.C. 679); actions against the United States under the Act entitled "An Act authorizing suits against the United States in admiralty for damage caused by and salvage service rendered to public vessels belonging to the United States, and for other purposes", approved March 3, 1925 (46 U.S.C. 781–790), as implemented by section 7730 of title 10, United States Code.

(As amended P.L. 94–149, § 1(14), Dec. 12, 1975, 89 Stat. 806; P.L. 95–598, Title II, § 251, Nov. 6, 1978, 92 Stat. 2673; P.L. 97–164, Title I, § 142, Apr. 2, 1982, 96 Stat. 45; Mar. 2, 1987, eff. Oct. 1, 1987; Apr. 25, 1988, eff. Nov. 1, 1988; Nov. 18, 1988, Pub.L. 100–690, Title VII, § 7075(c), 102 Stat. 4405; Apr. 22, 1993, eff. Dec. 1, 1993.)

Section references, McCormick 5th ed.

None

Note by Federal Judicial Center

The rule enacted by the Congress is the rule prescribed by the Supreme Court, amended as follows:

Subdivision (a) was amended in the first sentence by inserting "the Court of Claims" and by inserting "actions, cases, and." It was amended in the second sentence by substituting "terms" in place of "word," by inserting the phrase "and 'court'," and by adding "commissioners of the Court of Claims."

Subdivision (b) was amended by substituting "civil actions and proceedings" in place of "civil actions," and by substituting "criminal cases and proceedings" in place of "criminal proceedings."

Subdivision (c) was amended by substituting "rule" in place of "rules" and by changing the verb to the singular.

Subdivision (d) was amended by deleting "those" after "other than" and by substituting "Rule 104" in place of "Rule 104(a)."

Subdivision (e) was amended by substituting "prescribed" in place of "adopted" and by adding "pursuant to statutory authority." The form of the statutory citations was also changed.

Advisory Committee's Note

56 F.R.D. 183, 348

Subdivision (a). [This portion of the Advisory Committee's Note discussed the courts for which the various enabling acts granted the Supreme Court power to prescribe rules. Congressional enactment of the rules has rendered the discussion moot. The enabling acts did not include the Court of Claims which the Congress added to Rule 1101(a)].

Report of House Committee on the Judiciary

House Comm. on Judiciary, Fed.Rules of Evidence, H.R.Rep. No. 650, 93d Cong., 1st Sess., p. 17 (1973); 1974 U.S.Code Cong. & Ad.News 7075, 7090

Subdivision (a) as submitted to the Congress, in stating the courts and judges to which the Rules of Evidence apply, omitted the Court of Claims and commissioners of that Court. At the request of the Court of Claims, the Committee amended the Rule to include the Court and its commissioners within the purview of the Rules.

Advisory Committee's Note

56 F.R.D 183, 351

Subdivision (b) is a combination of the language of the enabling acts, supra, with respect to the kinds of proceedings in which the making of rules is authorized. It is subject to the qualifications expressed in the subdivisions which follow.

Subdivision (c), singling out the rules of privilege for special treatment, is made necessary by the limited applicability of the remaining rules.

Subdivision (d). The rule is not intended as an expression as to when due process or other constitutional provisions may require an evidentiary hearing. Paragraph (1) restates, for convenience, the provisions of the second sentence of Rule 104(a), supra. See Advisory Committee's Note to that rule.

(2) While some states have statutory requirements that indictments be based on "legal evidence," and there is some case law to the effect that the rules of evidence apply to grand jury proceedings, 1 Wigmore § 4(5), the Supreme Court has not accepted this view. In Costello v. United States, 350 U.S. 359, 76 S.Ct. 406, 100 L.Ed. 397 (1965), the Court refused to allow an indictment to be attacked, for either constitutional or policy reasons, on the ground that only hearsay evidence was presented.

> "It would run counter to the whole history of the grand jury institution, in which laymen conduct their inquiries unfettered by technical rules. Neither justice nor the concept of a fair trial requires such a change." Id. at 364.

The rule as drafted does not deal with the evidence required to support an indictment.

(3) The rule exempts preliminary examinations in criminal cases. Authority as to the applicability of the rules of evidence to preliminary examinations has been meagre and conflicting. Goldstein, The State and the Accused: Balance of Advantage in Criminal Procedure, 69 Yale L.J. 1149, 1168, n. 53 (1960); Comment, Preliminary Hearings on Indictable Offenses in Philadelphia, 106 U. of Pa.L.Rev. 589, 592–593 (1958). Hearsay testimony is, however, customarily received in such examinations. Thus in a Dyer Act case, for example, an affidavit may properly be used in a preliminary examination to prove ownership of the stolen vehicle, thus saving the victim of the crime the hardship of having to travel twice to a distant district for the sole purpose of testifying as to ownership. It is believed that the extent of the applicability of the Rules of Evidence to preliminary examinations should be appropriately dealt with by the Federal Rules of Criminal Procedure which regulate those proceedings.

Extradition and rendition proceedings are governed in detail by statute. 18 U.S.C. §§ 3181–3195. They are essentially administrative in character. Traditionally the rules of evidence have not applied. 1 Wigmore § 4(6). Extradition proceedings are accepted from the operation of the Rules of Criminal Procedure. Rule 54(b)(5) of Federal Rules of Criminal Procedure.

The rules of evidence have not been regarded as applicable to sentencing or probation proceedings, where great reliance is placed upon the presentence investigation and report. Rule 32(c) of the Federal Rules of Criminal Procedure requires a presentence investigation and report in every case unless the court otherwise directs. In Williams v. New York, 337 U.S. 241, 69 S.Ct. 1079, 93 L.Ed. 1337 (1949), in which the judge overruled a jury recommendation of life imprisonment and imposed a death sentence, the Court said that due process does not require confrontation or cross-examination in sentencing or passing on probation, and that the judge has broad discretion as to the sources and types of information relied upon. Compare the recommendation that the substance of all derogatory information be disclosed to the defendant, in A.B.A. Project on Minimum Standards for Criminal Justice, Sentencing Alternatives and Procedures § 4.4, Tentative Draft (1967, Sobeloff, Chm.). Williams was adhered to in Specht v. Patterson, 386 U.S. 605, 87 S.Ct. 1209, 18 L.Ed.2d 326 (1967), but not extended to a proceeding under the Colorado Sex Offenders Act, which was said to be a new charge leading in effect to punishment, more like the recidivist statutes where opportunity must be given to be heard on the habitual criminal issue.

Warrants for arrest, criminal summonses, and search warrants are issued upon complaint or affidavit showing probable cause. Rules 4(a) and 41(c) of the Federal Rules of Criminal Procedure. The nature of the proceedings makes application of the formal rules of evidence inappropriate and impracticable.

Criminal contempts are punishable summarily if the judge certifies that he saw or heard the contempt and that it was committed in the presence of the court. Rule 42(a) of the Federal Rules of Criminal Procedure. The circumstances which preclude application of the rules of evidence in this situation are not present, however, in other cases of criminal contempt.

Proceedings with respect to release on bail or otherwise do not call for application of the rules of evidence. The governing statute specifically provides:

> "Information stated in, or offered in connection with, any order entered pursuant to this section need not conform to the rules pertaining to the admissibility of evidence in a court of law." 18 U.S.C.A. § 3146(f).

This provision is consistent with the type of inquiry contemplated in A.B.A. Project on Minimum Standards for Criminal Justice, Standards Relating to Pretrial Release, § 4.5(b), (c), p. 16 (1968). The references to the weight of the evidence against the accused, in Rule 46(a)(1), (c) of the Federal Rules of Criminal Procedure and in 18 U.S.C.A. § 3146(b), as a factor to be considered, clearly do not have in view evidence introduced at a hearing under the rules of evidence.

The rule does not exempt habeas corpus proceedings. The Supreme Court held in Walker v. Johnston, 312 U.S. 275, 61 S Ct. 574, 85 L.Ed. 830 (1941), that the practice of disposing of matters of fact on affidavit, which prevailed in some circuits, did not "satisfy the command of the statute that the judge shall proceed 'to determine the facts of the case, by hearing the testimony and arguments.' " This view accords with the emphasis in Townsend v. Sain, 372 U.S. 293, 83 S.Ct. 745, 9 L.Ed.2d 770 (1963), upon trial-type proceedings, id. 311, 83 S.Ct. 745, with demeanor evidence as a significant factor, id. 322, 83 S.Ct. 745, in applications by state prisoners aggrieved by unconstitutional detentions. Hence subdivision (e) applies the rules to habeas corpus proceedings to the extent not inconsistent with the statute.

Subdivision (e). In a substantial number of special proceedings, *ad hoc* evaluation has resulted in the promulgation of particularized evidentiary provisions, by Act of Congress or by rule adopted by the Supreme Court. Well adapted to the particular proceedings, though not apt candidates for inclusion in a set of general rules, they are left undisturbed. Otherwise, however, the rules of evidence are applicable to the proceedings enumerated in the subdivision.

Report of House Committee on the Judiciary

House Comm. on Judiciary, Fed.Rules of Evidence, H.R.Rep. No. 650, 93d Cong., 1st Sess., p. 17 (1973); 1974 U.S.Code Cong. & Ad.News 7075, 7090

Subdivision (b)[E] was amended merely to substitute positive law citations for those which were not.

1987 Amendment

Subdivision (a) is amended to delete the reference to the District Court for the District of the Canal Zone, which no longer exists, and to add the District

Court for the Northern Mariana Islands. The United States bankruptcy judges are added to conform the subdivision with Rule 1101(b) and Bankruptcy Rule 9017.

1988 Amendment

The amendment is technical. No substantive change is intended.

1993 Amendment

This revision is made to conform the rule to changes in terminology made by Rule 58 of the Federal Rules of Criminal Procedure and to the changes in the title of United States magistrates made by the Judicial Improvements Act of 1990.

Rule 1102. Amendments

Amendments to the Federal Rules of Evidence may be made as provided in section 2072 of title 28 of the United States Code.

(As amended Apr. 30, 1991, eff. Dec. 1, 1991.)

Note by Federal Judicial Center

This rule was not included among those prescribed by the Supreme Court. The rule prescribed by the Court as 1102 now appears as 1103.

Advisory Committee's Note

1991 Amendment. The amendment is technical. No substantive change is intended.

Rule 1103. Title

These rules may be known and cited as the Federal Rules of Evidence.

Note by Federal Judicial Center

The rule enacted by the Congress is the rule prescribed by the Supreme Court as Rule 1102 without change.

DELETED AND SUPERSEDED MATERIALS

EDITORIAL NOTE: *The following provisions, prescribed by the Supreme Court, were excised by the Congress from their finally enacted version of the Rules. However, they are useful in understanding the policies of the drafters, federal law on the matters involved, and the thinking underlying similar provisions in some state rules or codes.*

Rule 105. Summing Up and Comment By Judge [Not enacted.]

After the close of the evidence and arguments of counsel, the judge may fairly and impartially sum up the evidence and comment to the jury upon the weight of the evidence and the credibility of the witnesses, if he also instructs the jury that they are to determine for themselves the weight of the evidence and the credit to be given to the witnesses and that they are not bound by the judge's summation or comment.

Note by Federal Judicia Center

The foregoing rule prescribed by the Supreme Court was deleted from the rules enacted by the Congress.

Advisory Committee's Note

The rule states the present rule in the federal courts. Capital Traction Co. v. Hof, 174 U.S. 1, 13–14, 19 S.Ct. 580, 43 L.Ed. 873 (1899). The judge must, of course, confine his remarks to what is disclosed by the evidence. He cannot convey to the jury his purely personal reaction to credibility or to the merits of the case; he can be neither argumentative nor an advocate. Quercia v. United States, 289 U.S. 466, 469, 53 S.Ct. 698, 77 L.Ed. 1321 (1933); Billeci v. United States, 87 U.S.App.D.C. 274, 184 F.2d 394, 402, 24 A.L.R.2d 881 (1950). For further discussion see the series of articles by Wright, The Invasion of Jury: Temperature of the War, 27 Temp.L.Q. 137 (1953), Instructions to the Jury: Summary Without Comment, 1954 Wash.U.L.Q. 177, Adequacy of Instructions to the Jury, 53 Mich.L.Rev. 505, 813 (1955); A.L.I. Model Code of Evidence, Comment to Rule 8; Maguire, Weinstein, et al., Cases and Materials on Evidence 737–740 (5th ed. 1965); Vanderbilt, Minimum Standards of Judicial Administration 224–229 (1949).

Report of the House Committee on the Judiciary

Rule 105 as submitted by the Supreme Court concerned the issue of summing up and comment by the judge. It provided that after the close of the evidence and the arguments of counsel, the presiding judge could fairly and impartially sum up the evidence and comment to the jury upon its weight and the credibility of the witnesses, if he also instructed the jury that it was not bound thereby and must make its own determination of those matters. The Committee recognized that the Rule as submitted is consistent with long standing and current federal practice. However, the aspect of the Rule dealing with the authority of a judge to comment on the weight of the evidence and the credibility of witnesses—an authority not granted to judges in most State courts—was highly controversial. After much debate the Committee determined to delete the entire Rule, intending that its action be understood as reflecting no conclusion as to the merits of the proposed Rule and that the subject should be left for separate consideration at another time.

Report of Senate Committee on the Judiciary

This rule as submitted by the Supreme Court permitted the judge to sum up and comment on the evidence. The House struck the rule.

The committee accepts the House action with the understanding that the present Federal practice, taken from the common law, of the trial judge's discretionary authority to comment on and summarize the evidence is left undisturbed.

Rule 301. Presumptions in General [As prescribed by Supreme Court]

In all cases not otherwise provided for by Act of Congress or by these rules a presumption imposes on the party against whom it is directed the burden of proving that the nonexistence of the presumed fact is more probable than its existence.

Rule 301. Presumptions in General in Civil Actions and Proceedings [As passed by House of Representatives]

In all civil actions and proceedings not otherwise provided for by Act of Congress or by these rules, a presumption imposes on the party against whom it is directed the burden of going forward with the evidence, and, even though met with contradicting evidence, a presumption is sufficient evidence of the fact presumed, to be considered by the trier of the facts.

Note by Federal Judicial Center

Neither of the above versions of Rule 301 was enacted.

Advisory Committee's Note

This rule governs presumptions generally. See Rule 302 for presumptions controlled by state law and Rule 303 for those against an accused in a criminal case.

Presumptions governed by this rule are given the effect of placing upon the opposing party the burden of establishing the nonexistence of the presumed fact, once the party invoking the presumption establishes the basic facts giving rise to it. The same considerations of fairness, policy, and probability which dictate the allocation of the burden of the various elements of a case as between the prima facie case of a plaintiff and affirmative defenses also underlie the creation of presumptions. These considerations are not satisfied by giving a lesser effect to presumptions. Morgan and Maguire, Looking Backward and Forward at Evidence, 50 Harv.L.Rev. 909, 913 (1937); Morgan, Instructing the Jury upon Presumptions and Burden of Proof, 47 Harv.L.Rev. 59, 82 (1933); Cleary, Presuming and Pleading: An Essay on Juristic Immaturity, 12 Stan.L.Rev. 5 (1959).

The so-called "bursting bubble" theory, under which a presumption vanishes upon the introduction of evidence which would support a finding of the nonexistence of the presumed fact, even though not believed, is rejected as according presumptions too "slight and evanescent" an effect. Morgan and Maguire, *supra,* at p. 913.

In the opinion of the Advisory Committee, no constitutional infirmity attends this view of presumptions. In Mobile, J. & K.C.R. Co. v. Turnipseed, 219 U.S. 35, 31 S.Ct. 136, 55 L.Ed. 78 (1910), the Court upheld a Mississippi statute which provided that in actions against railroads proof of injury inflicted by the running of trains should be prima facie evidence of negligence by the railroad. The injury in the case had resulted from a derailment. The opinion made the points (1) that the only effect of the statute was to impose on the railroad the duty of producing some evidence to the contrary, (2) that an inference may be supplied by law if there is a rational connection between the fact proved and the fact presumed, as long as the opposite party is not precluded from presenting his evidence to the contrary, and (3) that considerations of public policy arising from the character of the business justified the application in question. Nineteen years later, in Western & Atlantic R. Co. v. Henderson, 279 U.S. 639, 49 S.Ct. 445, 73 L.Ed. 884 (1929), the Court overturned a Georgia statute making railroads liable for damages done by trains, unless the railroad made it appear that reasonable care had been used, the presumption being against the railroad. The declaration alleged the death of plaintiff's husband from a grade crossing collision, due to specified acts of negligence by defendant. The jury were instructed that proof of the injury raised a presumption of negligence; the burden shifted to the railroad to prove ordinary care; and unless it did so, they should find for plaintiff. The instruction was held erroneous in an opinion stating (1) that there was no rational connection between the mere fact of collision and negligence on the part of anyone, and (2) that the statute was different from that in *Turnipseed* in imposing a burden upon the railroad. The reader is left in a state of some confusion. Is the difference between a derailment and a grade crossing collision of no significance? Would the *Turnipseed* presumption have been bad if it had imposed a burden of persuasion on defendant, although that would in nowise have impaired its "rational connection"? If *Henderson* forbids imposing a burden of persuasion on defendants, what happens to affirmative defenses?

Two factors serve to explain *Henderson.* The first was that it was common ground that negligence was indispensable to liability. Plaintiff thought so, drafted her complaint accordingly, and relied upon the presumption. But how in logic could the same presumption establish her alternative grounds of negligence that the engineer was so blind he could not see decedent's truck and that he failed to stop after he saw it? Second, take away the basic assumption of no liability without fault, as *Turnipseed* intimated might be done ("considerations of public policy arising out of the character of the business"), and the structure of the decision in *Henderson* fails. No question of logic would have arisen if the statute had simply said: a prima facie case of liability is made by proof of injury by a train; lack of negligence is an affirmative defense, to be pleaded and proved as other affirmative defenses. The problem would be one of economic due process only. While it seems likely that the Supreme Court of 1929 would have voted that due process was denied, that result today would be unlikely. See, for example, the shift in the direction of absolute liability in the consumer cases. Prosser, The Assault upon the Citadel (Strict Liability to the Consumer), 69 Yale L.J. 1099 (1960).

Any doubt as to the constitutional permissibility of a presumption imposing a burden of persuasion of the nonexistence of the presumed fact in civil cases is laid at rest by Dick v. New York Life Ins. Co., 359 U.S. 437, 79 S.Ct. 921, 3 L.Ed.2d 935 (1959). The Court unhesitatingly applied the North Dakota rule that the presumption against suicide imposed on defendant the burden of proving that the death of insured, under an accidental death clause, was due to suicide.

"Proof of coverage and of death by gunshot wound shifts the burden to the insurer to establish that the death of the insured was due to his suicide." 359 U.S. at 443, 79 S.Ct. at 925.

"In a case like this one, North Dakota presumes that death was accidental and places on the insurer the burden of proving that death resulted from suicide." *Id.* at 446, 79 S.Ct. at 927.

The rational connection requirement survives in criminal cases, Tot v. United States, 319 U.S. 463, 63 S.Ct. 1241, 87 L.Ed. 1519 (1943), because the Court has been unwilling to extend into that area the greater-includes-the-lesser theory of Ferry v. Ramsey, 277 U.S. 88, 48 S.Ct. 443, 72 L.Ed. 796 (1928). In that case the Court sustained a Kansas statute under which bank directors were personally liable for deposits made with their assent and with knowledge of insolvency, and the fact of insolvency was prima facie evidence of assent and knowledge of insolvency. Mr. Justice Holmes pointed out that the state legislature could have made the directors personally liable to depositors in every case. Since the statute imposed a less stringent liability, "the thing to be considered is the result reached, not the possibly inartificial or clumsy way of reaching it." *Id.* at 94, 48 S.Ct. at 444. Mr. Justice Sutherland dissented: though the state could have created an absolute liability, it did not purport to do so; a rational connection was necessary, but lacking, between the liability created and the prima facie evidence of it; the result might be different if the basis of the presumption were being open for business.

The Sutherland view has prevailed in criminal cases by virtue of the higher standard of notice there required. The fiction that everyone is presumed to know the law is applied to the substantive law of crimes as an alternative to complete unenforceability. But the need does not extend to criminal evidence and procedure, and the fiction does not encompass them. "Rational connection" is not fictional or artificial, and so it is reasonable to suppose that Gainey should have known that his presence at the site of an illicit still could convict him of being connected with (carrying on) the business, United States v. Gainey, 380 U.S. 63, 85 S.Ct. 754, 13 L.Ed.2d 658 (1965), but not that Romano should have known that his presence at a still could convict him of possessing it, United States v. Romano, 382 U.S. 136, 86 S.Ct. 279, 15 L.Ed.2d 210 (1965).

In his dissent in Gainey, Mr. Justice Black put it more artistically:

"It might be argued, although the Court does not so argue or hold, that Congress if it wished could make presence at a still a crime in itself, and so Congress should be free to create crimes which are called 'possession' and 'carrying on an illegal distillery business' but which are defined in such a way that unexplained presence is sufficient and indisputable evidence in all cases to support conviction for those offenses. See Ferry v. Ramsey, 277 U.S. 88, 48 S.Ct. 443, 72 L.Ed. 796. Assuming for the sake of argument that Congress could make unexplained presence a criminal act, and ignoring also the refusal of this Court in other cases to uphold a statutory presumption on such a theory, see Heiner v. Donnan, 285 U.S. 312, 52 S.Ct. 358, 76 L.Ed. 772, there is no indication here that Congress intended to adopt such a misleading method of draftsmanship, nor in my judgment could the statutory provisions if so construed escape condemnation for vagueness, under the principles applied in Lanzetta v. New Jersey, 306 U.S. 451, 59 S.Ct. 618, 83 L.Ed. 888, and many other cases." 380 U.S. at 84, n. 12, 85 S.Ct. at 766.

And the majority opinion in *Romano* agreed with him:

> "It may be, of course, that Congress has the power to make presence at an illegal still a punishable crime, but we find no clear indication that it intended to so exercise this power. The crime remains possession, not presence, and with all due deference to the judgment of Congress, the former may not constitutionally be inferred from the latter." 382 U.S. at 144, 86 S.Ct. at 284.

The rule does not spell out the procedural aspects of its application. Questions as to when the evidence warrants submission of a presumption and what instructions are proper under varying states of fact are believed to present no particular difficulties.

Report of House Committee on the Judiciary

Rule 301 as submitted by the Supreme Court provided that in all cases a presumption imposes on the party against whom it is directed the burden of proving that the nonexistence of the presumed fact is more probable than its existence. The Committee limited the scope of Rule 301 to "civil actions and proceedings" to effectuate its decision not to deal with the question of presumptions in criminal cases. (See note on Rule 303 in discussion of Rules deleted). With respect to the weight to be given a presumption in a civil case, the Committee agreed with the judgment implicit in the Court's version that the so-called "bursting bubble" theory of presumptions, whereby a presumption vanishes upon the appearance of any contradicting evidence by the other party, gives to presumptions too slight an effect. On the other hand, the Committee believed that the Rule proposed by the Court, whereby a presumption permanently alters the burden of persuasion, no matter how much contradicting evidence is introduced—a view shared by only a few courts—lends too great a force to presumptions. Accordingly, the Committee amended the Rule to adopt an intermediate position under which a presumption does not vanish upon the introduction of contradicting evidence, and does not change the burden of persuasion; instead it is merely deemed sufficient evidence of the fact presumed, to be considered by the jury or other finder of fact.

Rule 303. Presumptions in Criminal Cases [Not enacted.]

(a) Scope. Except as otherwise provided by Act of Congress, in criminal cases, presumptions against an accused, recognized at common law or created by statute, including statutory provisions that certain facts are prima facie evidence of other facts or of guilt, are governed by this rule.

(b) Submission to jury. The judge is not authorized to direct the jury to find a presumed fact against the accused. When the presumed fact establishes guilt or is an element of the offense or negatives a defense, the judge may submit the question of guilt or of the existence of the presumed fact to the jury, if, but only if, a reasonable juror on the evidence as a whole, including the evidence of the basic facts, could find guilt or the presumed fact beyond a reasonable doubt. When the presumed fact has a lesser effect, its existence may be submitted to the jury if the basic facts are supported by substantial evidence, or are otherwise established, unless the evidence as a whole negatives the existence of the presumed fact.

(c) Instructing the jury. Whenever the existence of a presumed fact against the accused is submitted to the jury, the judge shall give an instruction that the law declares that the jury may regard the basic facts as sufficient evidence of the presumed fact but does not require it to do so. In addition, if the presumed fact establishes guilt or is an element of the offense or negatives a defense, the judge shall instruct the jury that its existence must, on all the evidence, be proved beyond a reasonable doubt.

Note by Federal Judicial Center

The foregoing rule prescribed by the Supreme Court was deleted from the rules enacted by the Congress.

Advisory Committee's Note

Subdivision (a). This rule is based largely upon A.L.I. Model Penal Code § 1.12(5) P.O.D. (1962) and United States v. Gainey, 380 U.S. 63, 85 S.Ct. 754, 13 L.Ed.2d 658 (1965). While the rule, unlike the Model Penal Code provision, spells out the effect of common law presumptions as well as those created by statute, cases involving the latter are no doubt of more frequent occurrence. Congress has enacted numerous provisions to lessen the burden of the prosecution, principally though not exclusively in the fields of narcotics control and taxation of liquor. Occasionally, in the pattern of the usual common law treatment of such matters as insanity, they take the form of assigning to the defense the responsibility of raising specified matters as affirmative defenses, which are not within the scope of these rules. See Comment, A.L.I. Model Penal Code § 1.13, T.D. No. 4 (1955). In other instances they assume a variety of forms which are the concern of this rule. The provision may be that proof of a specified fact (possession or presence) is sufficient to authorize conviction. 26 U.S.C. § 4704(a), unlawful to buy or sell opium except from original stamped package—absence of stamps from package prima facie evidence of violation by person in possession; 26 U.S.C. § 4724(c), unlawful for person who has not registered and paid special tax to possess narcotics—possession presumptive evidence of violation. Sometimes the qualification is added, "unless the defendant explains the possession [presence] to the satisfaction of the jury." 18

U.S.C. § 545, possession of unlawfully imported goods sufficient for conviction of smuggling, unless explained; 21 U.S.C. § 174, possession sufficient for conviction of buying or selling narcotics known to have been imported unlawfully, unless explained. See also 26 U.S.C. § 5601(a)(1), (a)(4), (a)(8), (b)(1), (b)(2), (b)(4), relating to distilling operations. Another somewhat different pattern makes possession evidence of a particular element of the crime. 21 U.S.C. § 176b, crime to furnish unlawfully imported heroin to juveniles—possession sufficient proof of unlawful importation, unless explained; 50 U.S.C.A.App. § 462(b), unlawful to possess draft card not lawfully issued to holder, with intent to use for purposes of false identification—possession sufficient evidence of intent, unless explained. See also 15 U.S.C. § 902(f), (i).

Differences between the permissible operation of presumptions against the accused in criminal cases and in other situations prevent the formulation of a comprehensive definition of the term "presumption," and none is attempted. Nor do these rules purport to deal with problems of the validity of presumptions except insofar as they may be found reflected in the formulation of permissible procedures.

The presumption of innocence is outside the scope of the rule and unaffected by it.

Subdivisions (b) and (c). It is axiomatic that a verdict cannot be directed against the accused in a criminal case, 9 Wigmore § 2495, p. 312, with the corollary that the judge is without authority to direct the jury to find against the accused as to any element of the crime, A.L.I. Model Penal Code § 1.12(1) P.O.D. (1962). Although arguably the judge could direct the jury to find against the accused as to a lesser fact, the tradition is against it, and this rule makes no use of presumptions to remove any matters from final determination by the jury.

The only distinction made among presumptions under this rule is with respect to the measure of proof required in order to justify submission to the jury. If the effect of the presumption is to establish guilt or an element of the crime or to negative a defense, the measure of proof is the one widely accepted by the Courts of Appeals as the standard for measuring the sufficiency of the evidence in passing on motions for directed verdict (now judgment of acquittal): an acquittal should be directed when reasonable jurymen must have a reasonable doubt. Curley v. United States, 81 U.S.App.D.C. 389, 160 F.2d 229 (1947), cert. denied 331 U.S. 837, 67 S.Ct. 1511, 91 L.Ed. 1850; United States v. Honeycutt, 311 F.2d 660 (4th Cir.1962); Stephens v. United States, 354 F.2d 999 (5th Cir.1965); Lambert v. United States, 261 F.2d 799 (5th Cir.1958); United States v. Leggett, 292 F.2d 423 (6th Cir.1961); Cape v. United States, 283 F.2d 430 (9th Cir.1960); Cartwright v. United States, 335 F.2d 919 (10th Cir.1964). Cf. United States v. Gonzales Castro, 228 F.2d 807 (2d Cir.1956); United States v. Masiello, 235 F.2d 279 (2d Cir.1956), cert. denied Stickel v. United States, 352 U.S. 882, 77 S.Ct. 100, 1 L.Ed.2d 79; United States v. Feinberg, 140 F.2d 592 (2d Cir.1944). But cf. United States v. Arcuri, 282 F.Supp. 347 (E.D.N.Y.1968), aff'd. 405 F.2d 691, cert. denied 395 U.S. 913; United States v. Melillo, 275 F.Supp. 314 (E.D.N.Y.1968). If the presumption operates upon a lesser aspect of the case than the issue of guilt itself or an element of the crime or negativing a defense, the required measure of proof is the less stringent one of substantial evidence, consistently with the attitude usually taken with respect to particular items of evidence. 9 Wigmore § 2497, p. 324.

The treatment of presumptions in the rule is consistent with United States v. Gainey, 380 U.S. 63, 85 S.Ct. 754, 13 L.Ed.2d 658 (1965), where the matter was considered in depth. After sustaining the validity of the provision of 26 U.S.C. § 5601(b)(2) that presence at the site is sufficient to convict of the offense of carrying on the business of distiller without giving bond, unless the presence is explained to the satisfaction of the jury, the Court turned to procedural considerations and reached several conclusions. The power of the judge to withdraw a case from the jury for insufficiency of evidence is left unimpaired; he may submit the case on the basis of presence alone, but he is not required to do so. Nor is he precluded from rendering judgment notwithstanding the verdict. It is proper to tell the jury about the "statutory inference," if they are told it is not conclusive. The jury may still acquit, even if it finds defendant present and his presence is unexplained. [Compare the mandatory character of the instruction condemned in Bollenbach v. United States, 326 U.S. 607, 66 S.Ct. 402, 90 L.Ed. 350 (1945).] To avoid any implication that the statutory language relative to explanation be taken as directing attention to failure of the accused to testify, the better practice, said the Court, would be to instruct the jury that they may draw the inference unless the evidence provides a satisfactory explanation of defendant's presence, omitting any explicit reference to the statute.

The Final Report of the National Commission on Reform of Federal Criminal Laws § 103(4) and (5) (1971) contains a careful formulation of the consequences of a statutory presumption with an alternative formulation set forth in the Comment thereto, and also of the effect of a prima facie case. In the criminal code there proposed, the terms "presumption" and "prima facie case" are used with precision and with reference to these meanings. In the federal criminal law as it stands today, these terms are not used with precision. Moreover, common law presumptions continue. Hence it is believed that the rule here proposed is better adapted to the present situation until such time as the Congress enacts legislation covering the subject, which the rule takes into account. If the subject of common law presumptions is not covered by legislation, the need for the rule in that regard will continue.

Report of House Committee on the Judiciary

Rule 303, as submitted by the Supreme Court was directed to the issues of when, in criminal cases, a court may submit a presumption to a jury and the type of instruction it should give. The Committee deleted this Rule since the subject of presumptions in criminal cases is addressed in detail in bills now pending before the Committee to revise the federal criminal code. The Committee determined to consider this question in the course of its study of these proposals.

Rule 406. Habit; Routine Practice [Subdivision (b) not enacted.]

(b) Method of proof. Habit or routine practice may be proved by testimony in the form of an opinion or by specific instances of conduct sufficient in number to warrant a finding that the habit existed or that the practice was routine.

Advisory Committee's Note

* * *

Subdivision (b). Permissible methods of proving habit or routine conduct include opinion and specific instances sufficient in number to warrant a finding that the habit or routine practice in fact existed. Opinion evidence must be "rationally based on the perception of the witness" and helpful, under the provisions of Rule 701. Proof by specific instances may be controlled by the overriding provisions of Rule 403 for exclusion on grounds of prejudice, confusion, misleading the jury, or waste of time. Thus the illustrations following A.L.I. Model Code of Evidence Rule 307 suggests the possibility of admitting testimony by W that on numerous occasions he had been with X when X crossed a railroad track and that on each occasion X had first stopped and looked in both directions, but discretion to exclude offers of 10 witnesses, each testifying to a different occasion.

Similar provisions for proof by opinion or specific instances are found in Uniform Rule 50 and Kansas Code of Civil Procedure § 60–450. New Jersey Rule 50 provides for proof by specific instances but is silent as to opinion. The California Evidence Code is silent as to methods of proving habit, presumably proceeding on the theory that any method is relevant and all relevant evidence is admissible unless otherwise provided. Tentative Recommendation and a Study Relating to the Uniform Rules of Evidence (Art. VI. Extrinsic Policies Affecting Admissibility), Rep., Rec. & Study, Cal.Law Rev.Comm'n, 620 (1964).

Report of House Committee on the Judiciary

[Reasons for deleting subdivision (b) are stated in the report, which is set forth in the main text under rule 406, supra.]

ARTICLE V. PRIVILEGES

Note by Federal Judicial Center

The 13 rules numbered 501–513 prescribed by the Supreme Court as Article V were replaced by a single rule 501 in the rules enacted by the Congress. The rules are included here for informational purposes only.

Rule 501. Privileges Recognized Only as Provided [Not enacted.]

Except as otherwise required by the Constitution of the United States or provided by Act of Congress, and except as provided in these rules or in other rules adopted by the Supreme Court, no person has a privilege to:

(1) Refuse to be a witness; or

(2) Refuse to disclose any matter; or

(3) Refuse to produce any object or writing; or

(4) Prevent another from being a witness or disclosing any matter of producing any object or writing.

Advisory Committee's Note

No attempt is made in these rules to incorporate the constitutional provisions which relate to the admission and exclusion of evidence, whether denominated as privileges or not. The grand design of these provisions does not readily lend itself to codification. The final reference must be the provisions themselves and the decisions construing them. Nor is formulating a rule an appropriate means of settling unresolved constitutional questions.

Similarly, privileges created by act of Congress are not within the scope of these rules. These privileges do not assume the form of broad principles; they are the product of resolving particular problems in particular terms. Among them are included such provisions as 13 U.S.C. § 9, generally prohibiting official disclosure of census information and conferring a privileged status on retained copies of census reports; 42 U.S.C. § 2000e–5(a), making inadmissible in evidence anything said or done during Equal Employment Opportunity conciliation proceeding; 42 U.S.C. § 2240, making required reports of incidents by nuclear facility licensees inadmissible in actions for damages; 45 U.S.C. §§ 33, 41, similarly as to reports of accidents by railroads; 49 U.S.C. § 1441(e), declaring C.A.B. accident investigation reports inadmissible in actions for damages. The rule leaves them undisturbed.

The reference to other rules adopted by the Supreme Court makes clear that provisions relating to privilege in those rules will continue in operation. See, for example, the "work product" immunity against discovery spelled out under the Rules of Civil Procedure in Hickman v. Taylor, 329 U.S. 495, 67 S.Ct. 385, 91 L.Ed. 451 (1947), now formalized in revised Rule 26(b)(3) of the Rules of Civil Procedure, and the secrecy of grand jury proceedings provided by Criminal Rule 6.

With respect to privileges created by state law, these rules in some instances grant them greater status than has heretofore been the case by according them recognition in federal criminal proceedings, bankruptcy, and federal question litigation. See Rules 502 and 510. There is, however, no provision generally adopting state-created privileges.

In federal criminal prosecutions the primacy of federal law as to both substance and procedure has been undoubted. See, for example, United States v. Krol, 374 F.2d 776 (7th Cir.1967), sustaining the admission in a federal prosecution of evidence obtained by electronic eavesdropping, despite a state statute declaring the use of these devices unlawful and evidence obtained therefrom inadmissible. This primacy includes matters of privilege. As stated in 4 Barron, Federal Practice and Procedure § 2151, p. 175 (1951):

"The determination of the question whether a matter is privileged is governed by federal decisions and the state statutes or rules of evidence have no application."

In Funk v. United States, 290 U.S. 371, 54 S.Ct. 212, 78 L.Ed. 369 (1933), the Court had considered the competency of a wife to testify for her husband and concluded that, absent congressional action or direction, the federal courts were to follow the common law as they saw it "in accordance with present day standards of wisdom and justice." And in Wolfle v. United States, 291 U.S. 7, 54 S.Ct. 279, 78 L.Ed. 617 (1934), the Court said with respect to the standard appropriate in determining a claim of privilege for an alleged confidential communication between spouses in a federal criminal prosecution:

"So our decision here, in the absence of Congressional legislation on the subject, is to be controlled by common law principles, not by local statute." *Id.*, 13, 54 S.Ct. at 280.

On the basis of *Funk* and *Wolfle,* the Advisory Committee on Rules of Criminal Procedure formulated Rule 26, which was adopted by the Court. The pertinent part of the rule provided:

"The ... privileges of witnesses shall be governed, except when an act of Congress or these rules otherwise provide, by the principles of the common law as they may be interpreted ... in the light of reason and experience."

As regards bankruptcy, section 21(a) of the Bankruptcy Act provides for examination of the bankrupt and his spouse concerning the acts, conduct, or property of the bankrupt. The Act limits examination of the spouse to business transacted by her or to which she is a party but provides "That the spouse may be so examined, any law of the United States or of any State to the contrary notwithstanding." 11 U.S.C. § 44(a). The effect of the quoted language is clearly to override any conflicting state rule of incompetency or privilege against spousal testimony. A fair reading would also indicate an overriding of any contrary state rule of privileged confidential spousal communications. Its validity has never been questioned and seems most unlikely to be. As to other privileges, the suggestion has been made that state law applies, though with little citation of authority, 2 Moore's Collier on Bankruptcy ¶ 21.13, p. 297 (14th ed. 1961). This position seems to be contrary to the expression of the Court in McCarthy v. Arndstein, 266 U.S. 34, 39, 45 S.Ct. 16, 69 L.Ed. 158 (1924), which speaks in the pattern of Rule 26 of the Federal Rules of Criminal Procedure:

"There is no provision [in the Bankruptcy Act] prescribing the rules by which the examination is to be governed. These are, impliedly, the general rules governing the admissibility of evidence and the competency and compellability of witnesses."

With respect to federal question litigation, the supremacy of federal law may be less clear, yet indications that state privileges are inapplicable preponderate in the circuits. In re Albert Lindley Lee Memorial Hospital, 209 F.2d 122 (2d Cir.1953), cert. denied Cincotta v. United States, 347 U.S. 960, 74 S.Ct. 709, 98 L.Ed. 1104; Colton v. United States, 306 F.2d 633 (2d Cir.1962); Falsone v. United States, 205 F.2d 734 (5th Cir.1953); Fraser v. United States, 145 F.2d 139 (6th Cir.1944), cert. denied 324 U.S. 849, 65 S.Ct. 684, 89 L.Ed. 1409; United States v. Brunner, 200 F.2d 276 (6th Cir.1952). *Contra,* Baird v. Koerner, 279 F.2d 623 (9th Cir.1960). Additional decisions of district courts are collected in Annot., 95 A.L.R.2d 320, 336. While a number of the cases arise from administrative income tax investigations, they nevertheless support the broad proposition of the inapplicability of state privileges in federal proceedings.

In view of these considerations, it is apparent that, to the extent that they accord state privileges standing in federal criminal cases, bankruptcy, and federal question cases, the rules go beyond what previously has been thought necessary or proper.

On the other hand, in diversity cases, or perhaps more accurately cases in which state law furnishes the rule of decision, the rules avoid giving state privileges the effect which substantial authority has thought necessary and proper. Regardless of what might once have been thought to be the command of Erie R. Co. v. Tompkins, 304 U.S. 64, 58 S.Ct. 817, 82 L.Ed. 1188 (1938), as to observance of state created privileges in diversity cases, Hanna v. Plumer, 380 U.S. 460, 85 S.Ct. 1136, 14 L.Ed.2d 8 (1965), is believed to locate the problem in the area of choice rather than necessity. Wright, Procedural Reform: Its Limitations and Its Future, 1 Ga.L.Rev. 563, 572–573 (1967). Contra, Republic Gear Co. v. Borg–Warner Corp., 381 F.2d 551, 555, n. 2 (2d Cir.1967), and see authorities there cited. Hence all significant policy factors need to be considered in order that the choice may be a wise one.

The arguments advanced in favor of recognizing state privileges are: a state privilege is an essential characteristic of a relationship or status created by state law and thus is substantive in the *Erie* sense; state policy ought not to be frustrated by the accident of diversity; the allowance or denial of a privilege is so likely to affect the outcome of litigation as to encourage forum selection on that basis, not a proper function of diversity jurisdiction. There are persuasive answers to these arguments.

(1) As to the question of "substance," it is true that a privilege commonly represents an aspect of a relationship created and defined by a State. For example, a confidential communications privilege is often an incident of marriage. However, in litigation involving the relationship itself, the privilege is not ordinarily one of the issues. In fact, statutes frequently make the communication privilege inapplicable in cases of divorce. McCormick § 88, p. 177. The same is true with respect to the attorney-client privilege when the parties to the relationship have a falling out. The reality of the matter is that privilege is called into operation, not when the relation giving rise to the privilege is being litigated, but when the litigation involves something substantively devoid of relation to the privilege. The appearance of privilege in the case is quite by accident, and its effect is to block off the tribunal from a source of information. Thus its real impact is on the method of proof in the case, and in comparison any substantive aspect appears tenuous.

(2) By most standards, criminal prosecutions are attended by more serious consequences than civil litigation, and it must be evident that the criminal area has the greatest sensitivity where privilege is concerned. Nevertheless, as previously noted, state privileges traditionally have given way in federal criminal prosecutions. If a privilege is denied in the area of greatest sensitivity, it tends to become illusory as a significant aspect of the relationship out of which it arises. For example, in a state having by statute an accountant's privilege, only the most imperceptible added force would be given the privilege by putting the accountant in a position to assure his client that, while he could not block disclosure in a federal criminal prosecution, he could do so in diversity cases as well as in state court proceedings. Thus viewed, state interest in privilege appears less substantial than at first glance might seem to be the case.

Moreover, federal interest is not lacking. It can scarcely be contended that once diversity is invoked the federal government no longer has a legitimate concern in the quality of judicial administration conducted under its aegis. The demise of conformity and the adoption of the Federal Rules of Civil Procedure stand as witness to the contrary.

(3) A large measure of forum shopping is recognized as legitimate in the American judicial system. Subject to the limitations of jurisdiction and the relatively modest controls imposed by venue provisions and the doctrine of forum non conveniens, plaintiffs are allowed in general a free choice of forum. Diversity jurisdiction has as its basic purpose the giving of a choice, not only to plaintiffs but, in removal situations, also to defendants. In principle, the basis of the choice is the supposed need to escape from local prejudice. If the choice were tightly confined to that basis, then complete conformity to local procedure as well as substantive law would be required. This, of course, is not the case, and the

choice may in fact be influenced by a wide range of factors. As Dean Ladd has pointed out, a litigant may select the federal court "because of the federal procedural rules, the liberal discovery provisions, the quality of jurors expected in the federal court, the respect held for federal judges, the control of federal judges over a trial, the summation and comment upon the weight of evidence by the judge, or the authority to grant a new trial if the judge regards the verdict against the weight of the evidence." Ladd, Privileges, 1969 Ariz.St.L.J. 555, 564. Present Rule 43(a) of the Civil Rules specifies a broader range of admissibility in federal than in state courts and makes no exception for diversity cases. Note should also be taken that Rule 26(b)(2) of the Rules of Civil Procedure, as revised, allows discovery to be had of liability insurance, without regard to local state law upon the subject.

When attention is directed to the practical dimensions of the problem, they are found not to be great. The privileges affected are few in number. Most states provide a physician-patient privilege; the proposed rules limit the privilege to a psychotherapist-patient relationship. See Advisory Committee's Note to Rule 504. The area of marital privilege under the proposed rules is narrower than in most states. See Rule 505. Some states recognize privileges for journalists and accountants; the proposed rules do not.

Physician-patient is the most widely recognized privilege not found in the proposed rules. As a practical matter it was largely eliminated in diversity cases when Rule 35 of the Rules of Civil Procedure became effective in 1938. Under that rule, a party physically examined pursuant to court order, by requesting and obtaining a copy of the report or by taking the deposition of the examiner, waives any privilege regarding the testimony of every other person who has examined him in respect of the same condition. While waiver may be avoided by neither requesting the report nor taking the examiner's deposition, the price is one which most litigant-patients are probably not prepared to pay.

Rule 502. Required Reports Privileged by Statute [Not enacted.]

A person, corporation, association, or other organization or entity, either public or private, making a return or report required by law to be made has a privilege to refuse to disclose and to prevent any other person from disclosing the return or report, if the law requiring it to be made so provides. A public officer or agency to whom a return or report is required by law to be made has a privilege to refuse to disclose the return or report if the law requiring it to be made so provides. No privilege exists under this rule in actions involving perjury, false statements, fraud in the return or report, or other failure to comply with the law in question.

Advisory Committee's Note

Statutes which require the making of returns or reports sometimes confer on the reporting party a privilege against disclosure, commonly coupled with a prohibition against disclosure by the officer to whom the report is made. Some of the federal statutes of this kind are mentioned in the Advisory Committee's Note to Rule 501, *supra*. See also the Note to Rule 402, *supra*. A provision against disclosure may be included in a statute for a variety of reasons, the chief of which are probably assuring the validity of the statute against claims of self-incrimination, honoring the privilege against self-incrimination, and encouraging the furnishing of the required information by assuring privacy.

These statutes, both state and federal, may generally be assumed to embody policies of significant dimension. Rule 501 insulates the federal provisions against disturbance by these rules; the present rule reiterates a result commonly specified in federal statutes and extends its application to state statutes of similar character. Illustrations of the kinds of returns and reports contemplated by the rule appear in the cases, in which a reluctance to compel disclosure is manifested. In re Reid, 155 F. 933 (E.D.Mich.1906), assessor not compelled to produce bankrupt's property tax return in view of statute forbidding disclosure; In re Valecia Condensed Milk Co., 240 F. 310 (7th Cir.1917), secretary of state tax commission not compelled to produce bankrupt's income tax returns in violation of statute; Herman Bros. Pet Supply, Inc. v. N.L.R.B., 360 F.2d 176 (6th Cir.1966), subpoena denied for production of reports to state employment security commission prohibited by statute, in proceeding for back wages. And see the discussion of motor vehicle accident reports in Krizak v. W.C. Brooks & Sons, Inc., 320 F.2d 37, 42–43 (4th Cir.1963). Cf. In re Hines, 69 F.2d 52 (2d Cir.1934).

Rule 503. Lawyer–Client Privilege [Not enacted.]

(a) Definitions. As used in this rule:

(1) A "client" is a person, public officer, or corporation, association, or other organization or entity, either public or private, who is rendered professional legal services by a lawyer, or who consults a lawyer with a view to obtaining professional legal services from him.

(2) A "lawyer" is a person authorized, or reasonably believed by the client to be authorized, to practice law in any state or nation.

(3) A "representative of the lawyer" is one employed to assist the lawyer in the rendition of professional legal services.

(4) A communication is "confidential" if not intended to be disclosed to third persons other than those to whom disclosure is in furtherance of the rendition of professional legal services to the client or those reasonably necessary for the transmission of the communication.

(b) General rule of privilege. A client has a privilege to refuse to disclose and to prevent any other person from disclosing confidential communications made for the purpose of facilitating the rendition of professional legal services to the client, (1) between himself or his representative and his lawyer or his lawyer's representative, or (2) between his lawyer and the lawyer's representative, or (3) by him or his lawyer to a lawyer representing another in a matter of common interest, (4) between representatives of the client or between the client and a ...entative of the client, or (5) between lawyers representing the

... **may claim the privilege.** The privilege may be claimed ...'s guardian or conservator, the personal representative of a deceased client, or the successor, trustee, or similar representative of a corporation, association, or other organization, whether or not in existence. The person who was the lawyer at the time of the communication may claim the privilege but only on behalf of the client. His authority to do so is presumed in the absence of evidence to the contrary.

(d) Exceptions. There is no privilege under this rule:

(1) Furtherance of crime or fraud. If the services of the lawyer were sought or obtained to enable or aid anyone to commit or plan to commit what the client knew or reasonably should have known to be a crime or fraud; or

(2) Claimants through same deceased client. As to a communication relevant to an issue between parties who claim through the same deceased client, regardless of whether the claims are by testate or intestate succession or by *inter vivos* transaction; or

(3) Breach of duty by lawyer or client. As to a communication relevant to an issue of breach of duty by the lawyer to his client or by the client to his lawyer; or

(4) Document attested by lawyer. As to a communication relevant to an issue concerning an attested document to which the lawyer is an attesting witness; or

(5) Joint clients. As to a communication relevant to a matter of common interest between two or more clients if the communication was made by any of them to a lawyer retained or consulted in common, when offered in an action between any of the clients.

Advisory Committee's Note

Subdivision (a). (1) The definition of "client" includes governmental bodies, Connecticut Mutual Life Ins. Co. v. Shields, 18 F.R.D. 448 (S.D.N.Y. 1955); People ex rel. Department of Public Works v. Glen Arms Estate, Inc., 230 Cal.App.2d 841, 41 Cal.Rptr. 303 (1965); Rowley v. Ferguson, 48 N.E.2d 243 (Ohio App.1942); and corporations, Radiant Burners, Inc. v. American Gas Assn., 320 F.2d 314 (7th Cir.1963). *Contra,* Gardner, A Personal Privilege for Communications of Corporate Clients—Paradox or Public Policy, 40 U.Det.L.J. 299, 323, 376 (1963). The definition also extends the status of client to one consulting a lawyer preliminarily with a view to retaining him, even though actual employment does not result. McCormick, § 92, p. 184. The client need not be involved in litigation; the rendition of legal service or advice under any circumstances suffices. 8 Wigmore § 2294 (McNaughton Rev.1961). The services must be professional legal services; purely business or personal matters do not qualify. McCormick § 92, p. 184.

The rule contains no definition of "representative of the client." In the opinion of the Advisory Committee, the matter is better left to resolution by decision on a case-by-case basis. The most restricted position is the "control group" test, limiting the category to persons with authority to seek and act upon legal advice for the client. See, *e.g.,* City of Philadelphia v. Westinghouse Electric Corp., 210 F.Supp. 483 (E.D.Pa.1962), mandamus and prohibition denied *sub nom.* General Electric Co. v. Kirkpatrick, 312 F.2d 742 (3d Cir.), cert. denied 372 U.S. 943; Garrison v. General Motors Corp., 213 F.Supp. 515 (S.D.Cal.1963); Hogan v. Zletz, 43 F.R.D. 308 (N.D.Okla.1967), aff'd *sub nom.* Natta v. Hogan, 392 F.2d 686 (10th Cir.1968); Day v. Illinois Power Co., 50 Ill.App.2d 52, 199 N.E.2d 802 (1964). Broader formulations are found in other decisions. See, *e.g.*, United States v. United Shoe Machinery Corp., 89 F.Supp. 357 (D.Mass.1950); Zenith Radio Corp. v. Radio Corp. of America, 121 F.Supp. 792 (D.Del.1954); Harper & Row Publishers, Inc. v. Decker, 423 F.2d 487 (7th Cir.1970), aff'd without opinion by equally divided court 400 U.S. 955 (1971), reh. denied 401 U.S. 950; D.I. Chadbourne, Inc. v. Superior Court, 60 Cal.2d 723, 36 Cal.Rptr. 468, 388 P.2d 700 (1964). Cf. Rucker v. Wabash R. Co., 418 F.2d 146 (7th Cir.1969). See generally, Simon, The Attorney–Client Privilege as Applied to Corporations, 65 Yale L.J. 953, 956–966 (1956); Note, Attorney–Client Privilege for Corporate Clients: The Control Group Test, 84 Harv.L.Rev. 424 (1970).

The status of employees who are used in the process of communicating, as distinguished from those who are parties to the communication, is treated in paragraph (4) of subdivision (a) of the rule.

(2) A "lawyer" is a person licensed to practice law in any state or nation. There is no requirement that the licensing state or nation recognize the attorney-client privilege, thus avoiding excursions into conflict of laws questions. "Lawyer" also includes a person reasonably believed to be a lawyer. For similar provisions, see California Evidence Code § 950.

(3) The definition of "representative of the lawyer" recognizes that the lawyer may, in rendering legal services, utilize the services of assistants in addition to those employed in the process of communicating. Thus the definition includes an expert employed to assist in rendering legal advice. United States v. Kovel, 296 F.2d 918 (2d Cir.1961) (accountant). Cf. Himmelfarb v. United States, 175 F.2d 924 (9th Cir.1949). It also includes an expert employed to assist in the planning and conduct of litigation, though not one employed to testify as a witness. Lalance & Grosjean Mfg. Co. v. Haberman Mfg. Co., 87 F. 563 (S.D.N.Y.1898), and see revised Civil Rule 26(b)(4). The definition does not, however, limit "representative of the lawyer" to experts. Whether his compensation is derived immediately from the lawyer or the client is not material.

(4) The requisite confidentiality of communication is defined in terms of intent. A communication made in public or meant to be relayed to outsiders or which is divulged by the client to third persons can scarcely be considered confidential. McCormick § 95. The intent is inferable from the circumstances. Unless intent to disclose is apparent, the attorney-client communication is confidential. Taking or failing to take precautions may be considered as bearing on intent.

Practicality requires that some disclosure be allowed beyond the immediate circle of lawyer-client and their representatives without impairing confidentiality. Hence the definition allows disclosure to persons "to whom disclosure is in furtherance of the rendition of professional legal services to the client," contemplating those in such relation to the client as "spouse, parent, business associate, or joint client." Comment, California Evidence Code § 952.

Disclosure may also be made to persons "reasonably necessary for the transmission of the communication," without loss of confidentiality.

Subdivision (b) sets forth the privilege, using the previously defined terms: client, lawyer, representative of the lawyer, and confidential communication.

Substantial authority has in the past allowed the eavesdropper to testify to overheard privileged conversations and has admitted intercepted privileged letters. Today, the evolution of more sophisticated techniques of eavesdropping and interception calls for abandonment of this position. The rule accordingly adopts a policy of protection against these kinds of invasion of the privilege.

The privilege extends to communications (1) between client or his representative and lawyer or his representative, (2) between lawyer and lawyer's representative, (3) by client or his lawyer to a lawyer representing another in a matter of common interest, (4) between representatives of the client or the client and a representative of the client, and (5) between lawyers representing the client. All these communications must be specifically for the purpose of obtaining legal services for the client; otherwise the privilege does not attach.

The third type of communication occurs in the "joint defense" or "pooled information" situation, where different lawyers represent clients who have some interests in common. In Chahoon v. Commonwealth, 62 Va. 822 (1871), the court said that the various clients might have retained one attorney to represent all; hence everything said at a joint conference was privileged, and one of the clients could prevent another from disclosing what the other had himself said. The result seems to be incorrect in overlooking a frequent reason for retaining different attorneys by the various clients, namely actually or potentially conflicting interests in addition to the common interest which brings them together. The needs of these cases seem better to be met by allowing each client a privilege as to his own statements. Thus if all resist disclosure, none will occur. Continental Oil Co. v. United States, 330 F.2d 347 (9th Cir.1964). But, if for reasons of his own, a client wishes to disclose his own statements made at the joint conference, he should be permitted to do so, and the rule is to that effect. The rule does not apply to situations where there is no common interest to be promoted by a joint consultation, and the parties meet on a purely adversary basis. Vance v. State, 190 Tenn. 521, 230 S.W.2d 987 (1950), cert. denied 339 U.S. 988, 70 S.Ct. 1010, 94 L.Ed. 1389. Cf. Hunydee v. United States, 355 F.2d 183 (9th Cir.1965).

Subdivision (c). The privilege is, of course, that of the client, to be claimed by him or by his personal representative. The successor of a dissolved corporate client may claim the privilege. California Evidence Code § 953; New Jersey Evidence Rule 26(1). *Contra,* Uniform Rule 26(1).

The lawyer may not claim the privilege on his own behalf. However, he may claim it on behalf of the client. It is assumed that the ethics of the profession will require him to do so except under most unusual circumstances. American Bar Association, Canons of Professional Ethics, Canon 37. His authority to make the claim is presumed unless there is evidence to the contrary, as would be the case if the client were now a party to litigation in which the question arose and were represented by other counsel. Ex parte Lipscomb, 111 Tex. 409, 239 S.W. 1101 (1922).

Subdivision (d) in general incorporates well established exceptions.

(1) The privilege does not extend to advice in aid of future wrongdoing. 8 Wigmore § 2298 (McNaughton Rev.1961) The wrongdoing need not be that of the client. The provision that the client knew or reasonably should have known

of the criminal or fraudulent nature of the act is designed to protect the client who is erroneously advised that a proposed action is within the law. No preliminary finding that sufficient evidence aside from the communication has been introduced to warrant a finding that the services were sought to enable the commission of a wrong is required. Cf. Clark v. United States, 289 U.S. 1, 15–16, 53 S.Ct. 465, 77 L.Ed. 993 (1933); Uniform Rule 26(2)(a). While any general exploration of what transpired between attorney and client would, of course, be inappropriate, it is wholly feasible, either at the discovery stage or during trial, so to focus the inquiry by specific questions as to avoid any broad inquiry into attorney-client communications. Numerous cases reflect this approach.

(2) Normally the privilege survives the death of the client and may be asserted by his representative. Subdivision (c), *supra.* When, however, the identity of the person who steps into the client's shoes is in issue, as in a will contest, the identity of the person entitled to claim the privilege remains undetermined until the conclusion of the litigation. The choice is thus between allowing both sides or neither to assert the privilege, with authority and reason favoring the latter view. McCormick § 98; Uniform Rule 26(2)(b); California Evidence Code § 957; Kansas Code of Civil Procedure § 60–426(b)(2); New Jersey Evidence Rule 26(2)(b).

(3) The exception is required by considerations of fairness and policy when questions arise out of dealings between attorney and client, as in cases of controversy over attorney's fees, claims of inadequacy of representation, or charges of professional misconduct. McCormick § 95; Uniform Rule 26(2)(c); California Evidence Code § 958; Kansas Code of Civil Procedure § 60–426(b)(3); New Jersey Evidence Rule 26(2)(c).

(4) When the lawyer acts as attesting witness, the approval of the client to his so doing may safely be assumed, and waiver of the privilege as to any relevant lawyer-client communications is a proper result. McCormick § 92, p. 184; Uniform Rule 26(2)(d); California Evidence Code § 959; Kansas Code of Civil Procedure § 60–426(b)(d) [*sic*].

(5) The subdivision states existing law. McCormick § 95, pp. 192–193. For similar provisions, see Uniform Rule 26(2)(e); California Evidence Code § 962; Kansas Code of Civil Procedure § 60–426(b)(4); New Jersey Evidence Rule 26(2). The situation with which this provision deals is to be distinguished from the case of clients with a common interest who retain different lawyers. See subdivision (b)(3) of this rule, *supra.*

Rule 504. Psychotherapist–Patient Privilege [Not enacted.]

(a) Definitions.

(1) A "patient" is a person who consults or is examined or interviewed by a psychotherapist.

(2) A "psychotherapist" is (A) a person authorized to practice medicine in any state or nation, or reasonably believed by the patient so to be, while engaged in the diagnosis or treatment of a mental or emotional condition, including drug addiction, or (B) a person licensed or certified as a psychologist under the laws of any state or nation, while similarly engaged.

(3) A communication is "confidential" if not intended to be disclosed to third persons other than those present to further the interest of the patient in the consultation, examination, or interview, or persons reasonably necessary for the transmission of the communication, or persons who are participating in the diagnosis and treatment under the direction of the psychotherapist, including members of the patient's family.

(b) General rule of privilege. A patient has a privilege to refuse to disclose and to prevent any other person from disclosing confidential communications, made for the purposes of diagnosis or treatment of his mental or emotional condition, including drug addiction, among himself, his psychotherapist, or persons who are participating in the diagnosis or treatment under the direction of the psychotherapist, including members of the patient's family.

(c) Who may claim the privilege. The privilege may be claimed by the patient, by his guardian or conservator, or by the personal representative of a deceased patient. The person who was the psychotherapist may claim the privilege but only on behalf of the patient. His authority so to do is presumed in the absence of evidence to the contrary.

(d) Exceptions.

(1) Proceedings for hospitalization. There is no privilege under this rule for communications relevant to an issue in proceedings to hospitalize the patient for mental illness, if the psychotherapist in the course of diagnosis or treatment has determined that the patient is in need of hospitalization.

(2) Examination by order of judge. If the judge orders an examination of the mental or emotional condition of the patient, communications made in the course thereof are not privileged under this rule with respect to the particular purpose for which the examination is ordered unless the judge orders otherwise.

(3) Condition an element of claim or defense. There is no privilege under this rule as to communications relevant to an issue of the mental or emotional condition of the patient in any proceeding in which he relies upon the condition as an element of his claim or defense, or, after the patient's death, in any proceeding in which any party relies upon the condition as an element of his claim or defense.

Advisory Committee's Note

The rules contain no provision for a general physician-patient privilege. While many states have by statute created the privilege, the exceptions which have been found necessary in order to obtain information required by the public interest or to avoid fraud are so numerous as to leave little if any basis for the privilege. Among the exclusions from the statutory privilege, the following may be enumerated; communications not made for purposes of diagnosis and treatment; commitment and restoration proceedings; issues as to wills or otherwise between parties claiming by succession from the patient; actions on insurance policies; required reports (venereal diseases, gunshot wounds, child abuse); communications in furtherance of crime or fraud; mental or physical condition put in issue by patient (personal injury cases); malpractice actions; and some or all criminal prosecutions. California, for example, excepts cases in which the patient puts his condition in issue, all criminal proceedings, will and similar contests, malpractice cases, and disciplinary proceedings, as well as certain other situations, thus leaving virtually nothing covered by the privilege. California Evidence Code §§ 990–1007. For other illustrative statutes see Ill.Rev.Stat. 1967, c. 51, § 5.1; N.Y.C.P.L.R. § 4504; N.C.Gen.Stat.1953, § 8–53. Moreover, the possibility of compelling gratuitous disclosure by the physician is foreclosed by his standing to raise the question of relevancy. See Note on "Official Information" Privilege following Rule 509, *infra*.

The doubts attendant upon the general physician-patient privilege are not present when the relationship is that of psychotherapist and patient. While the common law recognized no general physician-patient privilege, it had indicated a disposition to recognize a psychotherapist-patient privilege, Note, Confidential Communications to a Psychotherapist: A New Testimonial Privilege, 47 Nw. U.L.Rev. 384 (1952), when legislatures began moving into the field.

The case for the privilege is convincingly stated in Report No. 45, Group for the Advancement of Psychiatry 92 (1960):

"Among physicians, the psychiatrist has a special need to maintain confidentiality. His capacity to help his patients is completely dependent upon their willingness and ability to talk freely. This makes it difficult if not impossible for him to function without being able to assure his patients of confidentiality and, indeed, privileged communication. Where there may be exceptions to this general rule * * *, there is wide agreement that confidentiality is a *sine qua non* for successful psychiatric treatment. The relationship may well be likened to that of the priest-penitent or the lawyer-client. Psychiatrists not only explore the very depths of their patients' conscious, but their unconscious feelings and attitudes as well. Therapeutic effectiveness necessitates going beyond a patient's awareness and, in order to do this, it must be possible to communicate freely. A threat to secrecy blocks successful treatment."

A much more extended exposition of the case for the privilege is made in Slovenko, Psychiatry and a Second Look at the Medical Privilege, 6 Wayne L.Rev. 175, 184 (1960), quoted extensively in the careful Tentative Recommendation and Study Relating to the Uniform Rules of Evidence (Article V. Privileges), Cal.Law Rev.Comm'n, 417 (1964). The conclusion is reached that Wigmore's four conditions needed to justify the existence of a privilege are amply satisfied.

Illustrative statutes are Cal.Evidence Code §§ 1010–1026; Ga.Code § 38–418 (1961 Supp.); Conn.Gen.Stat., § 52–146a (1966 Supp.); Ill.Rev.Stat.1967, c. 51, § 5.2.

While many of the statutes simply place the communications on the same basis as those between attorney and client, 8 Wigmore § 2286, n. 23 (McNaughton Rev.1961), basic differences between the two relationships forbid resorting to attorney-client save as a helpful point of departure. Goldstein and Katz, Psychiatrist–Patient Privilege: The GAP Proposal and the Connecticut Statute, 36 Conn.B.J. 175, 182 (1962).

Subdivision (a). (1) The definition of patient does not include a person submitting to examination for scientific purposes. Cf. Cal.Evidence Code § 1101. Attention is directed to 42 U.S.C. 242(a)(2), as amended by the Drug Abuse and Control Act of 1970, P.L. 91–513, authorizing the Secretary of Health, Education, and Welfare to withhold the identity of persons who are the subjects of research on the use and effect of drugs. The rule would leave this provision in full force. See Rule 501.

(2) The definition of psychotherapist embraces a medical doctor while engaged in the diagnosis or treatment of mental or emotional conditions, including drug addiction, in order not to exclude the general practitioner and to avoid the making of needless refined distinctions concerning what is and what is not the practice of psychiatry. The requirement that the psychologist be in fact licensed, and not merely be believed to be so, is believed to be justified by the number of persons, other than psychiatrists, purporting to render psychotherapeutic aid and the variety of their theories. Cal.Law Rev.Comm'n, *supra,* at pp. 434–437.

The clarification of mental or emotional condition as including drug addiction is consistent with current approaches to drug abuse problems. See, *e.g.,* the definition of "drug dependent person" in 42 U.S.C. 201(q), added by the Drug Abuse Prevention and Control Act of 1970, P.L. 91–513.

(3) Confidential communication is defined in terms conformable with those of the lawyer-client privilege. Rule 503(a)(4), *supra,* with changes appropriate to the difference in circumstance.

Subdivisions (b) and (c). The lawyer-client rule is drawn upon for the phrasing of the general rule of privilege and the determination of those who may claim it. See Rule 503(b) and (c).

The specific inclusion of communications made for the diagnosis and treatment of drug addiction recognizes the continuing contemporary concern with rehabilitation of drug dependent persons and is designed to implement that policy by encouraging persons in need thereof to seek assistance. The provision is in harmony with Congressional actions in this area. See 42 U.S.C. § 260, providing for voluntary hospitalization of addicts or persons with drug dependence problems and prohibiting use of evidence of admission or treatment in any proceeding against him, and 42 U.S.C. § 3419 providing that in voluntary or involuntary commitment of addicts the results of any hearing, examination, test, or procedure used to determine addiction shall not be used against the patient in any criminal proceeding.

Subdivision (d). The exceptions differ substantially from those of the attorney-client privilege, as a result of the basic differences in the relationships. While it has been argued convincingly that the nature of the psychotherapist-patient relationship demands complete security against legally coerced disclosure in all circumstances, Louisell, The Psychologist in Today's Legal World: Part II, 41 Minn.L.Rev. 731, 746 (1957), the committee of psychiatrists and lawyers who drafted the Connecticut statute concluded that in three instances the need for disclosure was sufficiently great to justify the risk of possible impairment of the relationship. Goldstein and Katz, Psychiatrist–Patient Privilege: The GAP Proposal and the Connecticut Statute, 36 Conn.B.J. 175 (1962). These three exceptions are incorporated in the present rule.

(1) The interests of both patient and public call for a departure from confidentiality in commitment proceedings. Since disclosure is authorized only

when the psychotherapist determines that hospitalization is needed, control over disclosure is placed largely in the hands of a person in whom the patient has already manifested confidence. Hence damage to the relationship is unlikely.

(2) In a court ordered examination, the relationship is likely to be an arm's length one, though not necessarily so. In any event, an exception is necessary for the effective utilization of this important and growing procedure. The exception, it will be observed, deals with a court ordered examination rather than with a court appointed psychotherapist. Also, the exception is effective only with respect to the particular purpose for which the examination is ordered. The rule thus conforms with the provisions of 18 U.S.C. § 4244 that no statement made by the accused in the course of an examination into competency to stand trial is admissible on the issue of guilt and of 42 U.S.C. § 3420 that a physician conducting an examination in a drug addiction commitment proceeding is a competent and compellable witness.

(3) By injecting his condition into litigation, the patient must be said to waive the privilege, in fairness and to avoid abuses. Similar considerations prevail after the patient's death.

Rule 505. Husband–Wife Privilege [Not enacted.]

(a) General rule of privilege. An accused in a criminal proceeding has a privilege to prevent his spouse from testifying against him.

(b) Who may claim the privilege. The privilege may be claimed by the accused or by the spouse on his behalf. The authority of the spouse to do so is presumed in the absence of evidence to the contrary.

(c) Exceptions. There is no privilege under this rule (1) in proceedings in which one spouse is charged with a crime against the person or property of the other or of a child of either, or with a crime against the person or property of a third person committed in the course of committing a crime against the other, or (2) as to matters occurring prior to the marriage, or (3) in proceedings in which a spouse is charged with importing an alien for prostitution or other immoral purpose in violation of 8 U.S.C. § 1328, with transporting a female in interstate commerce for immoral purposes or other offense in violation of 18 U.S.C. §§ 2421–2424, or with violation of other similar statutes.

Advisory Committee's Note

Subdivision (a). Rules of evidence have evolved around the marriage relationship in four respects: (1) incompetency of one spouse to testify for the other; (2) privilege of one spouse not to testify against the other; (3) privilege of one spouse not to have the other testify against him; and (4) privilege against disclosure of confidential communications between spouses, sometimes extended to information learned by virtue of the existence of the relationship. Today these matters are largely governed by statutes.

With the disappearance of the disqualification of parties and interested persons, the basis for spousal incompetency no longer existed, and it, too, virtually disappeared in both civil and criminal actions. Usually reached by statute, this result was reached for federal courts by the process of decision.

Funk v. United States, 290 U.S. 371, 54 S.Ct. 212, 78 L.Ed. 369 (1933). These rules contain no recognition of incompetency of one spouse to testify for the other.

While some 10 jurisdictions recognize a privilege not to testify against one's spouse in a criminal case, and a much smaller number do so in civil cases, the great majority recognizes no privilege on the part of the testifying spouse, and this is the position taken by the rule. Compare Wyatt v. United States, 362 U.S. 525, 80 S.Ct. 901, 4 L.Ed.2d 931 (1960), a Mann Act prosecution in which the wife was the victim. The majority opinion held that she could not claim privilege and was compellable to testify. The holding was narrowly based: The Mann Act presupposed that the women with whom it dealt had no independent wills of their own, and this legislative judgment precluded allowing a victim-wife an option whether to testify, lest the policy of the statute be defeated. A vigorous dissent took the view that nothing in the Mann Act required departure from usual doctrine, which was conceived to be one of allowing the injured party to claim or waive privilege.

About 30 jurisdictions recognize a privilege of an accused in a criminal case to prevent his or her spouse from testifying. It is believed to represent the one aspect of marital privilege the continuation of which is warranted. In Hawkins v. United States, 358 U.S. 74, 79 S.Ct. 136, 3 L.Ed.2d 125 (1958) it was sustained. Cf. McCormick § 66; 8 Wigmore § 2228 (McNaughton Rev.1961): Comment, Uniform Rule 23(2).

The rule recognizes no privilege for confidential communications. The traditional justifications for privileges not to testify against a spouse and not to be testified against by one's spouse have been the prevention of marital dissension and the repugnancy of requiring a person to condemn or be condemned by his spouse. 8 Wigmore §§ 2228, 2241 (McNaughton Rev.1961). These considerations bear no relevancy to marital communications. Nor can it be assumed that marital conduct will be affected by a privilege for confidential communications of whose existence the parties in all likelihood are unaware. The other communication privileges, by way of contrast, have as one party a professional person who can be expected to inform the other of the existence of the privilege. Moreover, the relationships from which those privileges arise are essentially and almost exclusively verbal in nature, quite unlike marriage. See Hutchins and Slesinger, Some Observations on the Law of Evidence: Family Relations, 13 Minn.L.Rev. 675 (1929). Cf. McCormick § 90; 8 Wigmore § 2337 (McNaughton Rev.1961).

The parties are not spouses if the marriage was a sham, Lutwak v. United States, 344 U.S. 604 (1953), or they have been divorced, Barsky v. United States, 339 F.2d 180 (9th Cir.1964), and therefore the privilege is not applicable.

Subdivision (b). This provision is a counterpart of Rules 503(c), 504(c), and 506(c). Its purpose is to provide a procedure for preventing the taking of the spouse's testimony notably in grand jury proceedings, when the accused is absent and does not know that a situation appropriate for a claim of privilege is presented. If the privilege is not claimed by the spouse, the protection of Rule 512 is available.

Subdivision (c) contains three exceptions to the privilege against spousal testimony in criminal cases.

(1) The need of limitation upon the privilege in order to avoid grave injustice in cases of offenses against the other spouse or a child of either can

scarcely be denied. 8 Wigmore § 2239 (McNaughton Rev.1961). The rule therefore disallows any privilege against spousal testimony in these cases and in this respect is in accord with the result reached in Wyatt v. United States, 362 U.S. 525, 80 S.Ct. 901, 4 L.Ed.2d 931 (1960), a Mann Act prosecution, denying the accused the privilege of excluding his wife's testimony, since she was the woman who was transported for immoral purposes.

(2) The second exception renders the privilege inapplicable as to matters occurring prior to the marriage. This provision eliminates the possibility of suppressing testimony by marrying the witness.

(3) The third exception continues and expands established Congressional policy. In prosecutions for importing aliens for immoral purposes, Congress has specifically denied the accused any privilege not to have his spouse testify against him. 8 U.S.C. § 1328. No provision of this nature is included in the Mann Act, and in Hawkins v. United States, 358 U.S. 74, 79 S.Ct. 136, 3 L.Ed.2d 125 (1958), the conclusion was reached that the common law privilege continued. Consistency requires similar results in the two situations. The rule adopts the Congressional approach, as based upon a more realistic appraisal of the marriage relationship in cases of this kind, in preference to the specific result in *Hawkins*. Note the common law treatment of pimping and sexual offenses with third persons as exceptions to marital privilege. 8 Wigmore § 2239 (McNaughton Rev.1961).

With respect to bankruptcy proceedings, the smallness of the area of spousal privilege under the rule and the general inapplicability of privileges created by state law render unnecessary any special provision for examination of the spouse of the bankrupt, such as that now contained in section 21(a) of the Bankruptcy Act. 11 U.S.C. § 44(a).

For recent statutes and rules dealing with husband-wife privileges, see California Evidence Code §§ 970–973, 980–987; Kansas Code of Civil Procedure §§ 60–423(b), 60–428; New Jersey Evidence Rules 23(2), 28.

Rule 506. Communications to Clergymen [Not enacted.]

(a) Definitions. As used in this rule:

(1) A "clergyman" is a minister, priest, rabbi, or other similar functionary of a religious organization, or an individual reasonably believed so to be by the person consulting him.

(2) A communication is "confidential" if made privately and not intended for further disclosure except to other persons present in furtherance of the purpose of the communication.

(b) General rule of privilege. A person has a privilege to refuse to disclose and to prevent another from disclosing a confidential communication by the person to a clergyman in his professional character as spiritual adviser.

(c) Who may claim the privilege. The privilege may be claimed by the person, by his guardian or conservator, or by his personal representative if he is deceased. The clergyman may claim the privilege on behalf of the person. His authority so to do is presumed in the absence of evidence to the contrary.

Advisory Committee's Note

The considerations which dictate the recognition of privileges generally seem strongly to favor a privilege for confidential communications to clergymen. During the period when most of the common law privileges were taking shape, no clear-cut privilege for communications between priest and penitent emerged. 8 Wigmore § 2394 (McNaughton Rev.1961). The English political climate of the time may well furnish the explanation. In this country, however, the privilege has been recognized by statute in about two-thirds of the states and occasionally by the common law process of decision *Id.*, § 2395; Mullen v. United States, 105 U.S.App.D.C. 25, 263 F.2d 275 (1959).

Subdivision (a). Paragraph (1) defines a clergyman as a "minister, priest, rabbi, or other similar functionary of a religious organization." The concept is necessarily broader than that inherent in the ministerial exemption for purposes of Selective Service. See United States v. Jackson, 369 F.2d 936 (4th Cir.1966). However, it is not so broad as to include all self-denominated "ministers." A fair construction of the language requires that the person to whom the status is sought to be attached be regularly engaged in activities conforming at least in a general way with those of a Catholic priest, Jewish rabbi, or minister of an established Protestant denomination, though not necessarily on a full-time basis. No further specification seems possible in view of the lack of licensing and certification procedures for clergymen. However, this lack seems to have occasioned no particular difficulties in connection with the solemnization of marriages, which suggests that none may be anticipated here. For similar definitions of "clergyman" see California Evidence Code § 1030; New Jersey Evidence Rule 29.

The "reasonable belief" provision finds support in similar provisions for lawyer-client in Rule 503 and for psychotherapist-patient in Rule 504. A parallel is also found in the recognition of the validity of marriages performed by unauthorized persons if the parties reasonably believed them legally qualified. Harper and Skolnick, Problems of the Family 153 (Rev.Ed.1962).

(2) The definition of "confidential" communication is consistent with the use of the term in Rule 503(a)(5) for lawyer-client and in Rule 504(a)(3) for psychotherapist-patient, suitably adapted to communications to clergymen.

Subdivision (b). The choice between a privilege narrowly restricted to doctrinally required confessions and a privilege broadly applicable to all confidential communications with a clergyman in his professional character as spiritual adviser has been exercised in favor of the latter Many clergymen now receive training in marriage counseling and the handling of personality problems. Matters of this kind fall readily into the realm of the spirit. The same considerations which underlie the psychotherapist-patient privilege of Rule 504 suggest a broad application of the privilege for communications to clergymen.

State statutes and rules fall in both the narrow and the broad categories. A typical narrow statute proscribes disclosure of "a confession * * * made * * * in the course of discipline enjoined by the church to which he belongs." Ariz.Rev. Stats.Ann.1956, § 12–2233. See also California Evidence Code § 1032; Uniform Rule 29. Illustrative of the broader privilege are statutes applying to "information communicated to him in a confidential manner, properly entrusted to him in his professional capacity, and necessary to enable him to discharge the functions of his office according to the usual course of his practice or discipline, wherein such person so communicating * * * is seeking spiritual counsel and advice," Fla.Stats.Ann.1960, § 90.241, or to any "confidential communication properly entrusted to him in his professional capacity, and necessary and proper to enable him to discharge the functions of his office according to the usual course of practice or discipline," Iowa Code Ann.1950, § 622.10. See also Ill.Rev.Stats. 1967, c. 51, § 48.1; Minn.Stats.Ann.1945, § 595.02(3); New Jersey Evidence Rule 29.

Under the privilege as phrased, the communicating person is entitled to prevent disclosure not only by himself but also by the clergyman and by eavesdroppers. For discussion see Advisory Committee's Note under lawyer-client privilege, Rule 503(b).

The nature of what may reasonably be considered spiritual advice makes it unnecessary to include in the rule a specific exception for communications in furtherance of crime or fraud, as in Rule 503(d)(1).

Subdivision (c) makes clear that the privilege belongs to the communicating person. However, a prima facie authority on the part of the clergyman to claim the privilege on behalf of the person is recognized. The discipline of the particular church and the discreetness of the clergyman are believed to constitute sufficient safeguards for the absent communicating person. See Advisory Committee's Note to the similar provision with respect to attorney-client in Rule 503(c).

Rule 507. Political Vote [Not enacted.]

Every person has a privilege to refuse to disclose the tenor of his vote at a political election conducted by secret ballot unless the vote was cast illegally.

Advisory Committee's Note

Secrecy in voting is an essential aspect of effective democratic government, insuring free exercise of the franchise and fairness in elections. Secrecy after the ballot has been cast is as essential as secrecy in the act of voting. Nutting, Freedom of Silence: Constitutional Protection Against Governmental Intrusion in Political Affairs, 47 Mich.L.Rev. 181, 191 (1948). Consequently a privilege has long been recognized on the part of a voter to decline to disclose how he voted. Required disclosure would be the exercise of "a kind of inquisitorial power unknown to the principles of our government and constitution, and might be highly injurious to the suffrages of a free people, as well as tending to create cabals and disturbances between contending parties in popular elections." Johnston v. Charleston, 1 Bay 441, 442 (S.C.1795).

The exception for illegally cast votes is a common one under both statutes and case law, Nutting, *supra,* at p. 192; 8 Wigmore § 2214, p. 163 (McNaughton Rev.1961). The policy considerations which underlie the privilege are not applicable to the illegal voter. However, nothing in the exception purports to foreclose an illegal voter from invoking the privilege against self-incrimination under appropriate circumstances.

For similar provisions, see Uniform Rule 31; California Evidence Code § 1050; Kansas Code of Civil Procedure § 60–431; New Jersey Evidence Rule 31.

Rule 508. Trade Secrets [Not enacted.]

A person has a privilege, which may be claimed by him or his agent or employee, to refuse to disclose and to prevent other persons from disclosing a trade secret owned by him, if the allowance of the privilege will not tend to conceal fraud or otherwise work injustice. When disclosure is directed, the judge shall take such protective measure as the interests of the holder of the privilege and of the parties and the furtherance of justice may require.

Advisory Committee's Note

While sometimes said not to be a true privilege, a qualified right to protection against disclosure of trade secrets has found ample recognition, and, indeed, a denial of it would be difficult to defend. 8 Wigmore § 2212(3) (McNaughton Rev.1961). And see 4 Moore's Federal Practice ¶¶ 30.12 and 34.15 (2nd ed. 1963 and Supp.1965) and 2A Barron and Holtzoff, Federal Practice and Procedure § 715.1 (Wright ed. 1961). Congressional policy is reflected in the Securities Exchange Act of 1934, 15 U.S.C. § 78x, and the Public Utility Holding Company Act of 1933, *id.* § 79v, which deny the Securities and Exchange Commission authority to require disclosure of trade secrets or processes in applications and reports. See also Rule 26(c)(7) of the Rules of Civil Procedure, as revised, mentioned further hereinafter.

Illustrative cases raising trade-secret problems are: E.I. Du Pont de Nemours Powder Co. v. Masland, 244 U.S. 100, 37 S.Ct. 575, 61 L.Ed. 1016 (1917), suit to enjoin former employee from using plaintiff's secret processes, countered by defense that many of the processes were well known to the trade: Segal Lock & Hardware Co. v. FTC, 143 F.2d 935 (2d Cir.1944), question whether expert locksmiths employed by FTC should be required to disclose methods used by them in picking petitioner's "pick-proof" locks; Dobson v. Graham, 49 F. 17 (E.D.Pa.1889), patent infringement suit in which plaintiff sought to elicit from former employees now in the hire of defendant the respects in which defendant's machinery differed from plaintiff's patented machinery: Putney v. Du Bois Co., 240 Mo.App. 1075, 226 S.W.2d 737 (1950), action for injuries allegedly sustained from using defendant's secret formula dishwashing compound. See 8 Wigmore § 2212(3) (McNaughton Rev.1961); Annot., 17 A.L.R.2d 383; 49 Mich.L.Rev. 133 (1950). The need for accommodation between protecting trade secrets, on the one hand, and eliciting facts required for full and fair presentation of a case, on the other hand, is apparent. Whether disclosure should be required depends upon a weighing of the competing interests involved against the background of the total situation, including consideration of such factors as the dangers of abuse, good faith, adequacy of protective measures, and the availability of other means of proof.

The cases furnish examples of the bringing of judicial ingenuity to bear upon the problem of evolving protective measures which achieve a degree of control over disclosure. Perhaps the most common is simply to take testimony *in camera*. Annot., 62 A.L.R.2d 509. Other possibilities include making disclosure to opposing counsel but not to his client, E.I. Du Pont de Nemours Powder Co. v. Masland, 244 U.S. 100, 37 S.Ct. 575, 61 L.Ed. 1016 (1917); making disclosure only to the judge (hearing examiner), Segal Lock & Hardware Co. v. FTC, 143 F.2d 935 (2d Cir.1944); and placing those present under oath not to make disclosure, Paul v. Sinnott, 217 F.Supp. 84 (W.D.Pa.1963).

Rule 26(c) of the Rules of Civil Procedure, as revised, provides that the judge may make "any order which justice requires to protect a party or person from annoyance, embarrassment, oppression, or undue burden or expense, including one or more of the following: * * * (7) that a trade secret or other confidential research, development, or commercial information not be disclosed or be disclosed only in a designated way * * *." While the instant evidence rule extends this underlying policy into the trial, the difference in circumstances between discovery stage and trial may well be such as to require a different ruling at the trial.

For other rules recognizing privilege for trade secrets, see Uniform Rule 32; California Evidence Code § 1060; Kansas Code of Civil Procedure § 60–432; New Jersey Evidence Rule 32.

Rule 509. Secrets of State and Other Official Information [Not enacted.]

(a) Definitions.

(1) Secret of state. A "secret of state" is a governmental secret relating to the national defense or the international relations of the United States.

(2) Official information. "Official information" is information within the custody or control of a department or agency of the government the disclosure of which is shown to be contrary to the public interest and which consists of: (A) intragovernmental opinions or recommendations submitted for consideration in the performance of decisional or policymaking functions, or (B) subject to the provisions of 18 U.S.C. § 3500, investigatory files compiled for law enforcement purposes and not otherwise available, or (C) information within the custody or control of a governmental department or agency whether initiated within the department or agency or acquired by it in its exercise of its official responsibilities and not otherwise available to the public pursuant to 5 U.S.C. § 552.

(b) General rule of privilege. The government has a privilege to refuse to give evidence and to prevent any person from giving evidence upon a showing of reasonable likelihood of danger that the evidence will disclose a secret of state or official information, as defined in this rule.

(c) Procedures. The privilege for secrets of state may be claimed only by the chief officer of the government agency or department administering the subject matter which the secret information sought concerns, but the privilege for official information may be asserted by any attorney representing the government. The required showing may be made in whole or in part in the form of a written statement. The judge may hear the matter in chambers, but all counsel are entitled to inspect the claim and showing and to be heard thereon, except that, in the case of secrets of state, the judge upon motion of the government, may permit the government to make the required showing in the above form *in camera.* If the judge sustains the privilege upon a showing *in camera,* the entire text of the government's statements shall be sealed and preserved in the court's records in the event of appeal. In the case of privilege claimed for official information the court may require examination *in camera* of the information itself. The judge may take any protective measure which the interests of the government and the furtherance of justice may require.

(d) Notice to government. If the circumstances of the case indicate a substantial possibility that a claim of privilege would be appropriate but has not been made because of oversight or lack of knowledge, the judge shall give or cause notice to be given to the officer entitled to claim the privilege and shall stay further proceedings a reasonable time to afford opportunity to assert a claim of privilege.

(e) Effect of sustaining claim. If a claim of privilege is sustained in a proceeding to which the government is a party and it appears that another party is thereby deprived of material evidence, the judge shall make any further orders which the interests of justice require, including striking the testimony of a witness, declaring a mistrial, finding against the government upon an issue as to which the evidence is relevant, or dismissing the action.

Advisory Committee's Note

Subdivision (a). (1) The rule embodies the privilege protecting military and state secrets described as "well established in the law of evidence," United States v. Reynolds, 345 U.S. 1, 6, 73 S.Ct. 528, 97 L.Ed. 727 (1953), and as one "the existence of which has never been doubted," 8 Wigmore § 2378, p. 794 (McNaughton Rev.1961).

The use of the term "national defense," without attempt at further elucidation, finds support in the similar usage in statutory provisions relating to the crimes of gathering, transmitting, or losing defense information, and gathering or delivering defense information to aid a foreign government. 18 U.S.C. §§ 793, 794. See also 5 U.S.C. § 1002; 50 U.S.C.App. § 2152(d). In determining whether military or state secrets are involved, due regard will, of course, be given to classification pursuant to executive order.

(2) The rule also recognizes a privilege for specified types of official information and in this respect is designed primarily to resolve questions of the availability to litigants of data in the files of governmental departments and agencies. In view of the lesser danger to the public interest than in cases of military and state secrets, the official information privilege is subject to a generally overriding requirement that disclosure would be contrary to the public interest. It is applicable to three categories of information.

(A) Intergovernmental opinions or recommendations submitted for consideration in the performance of decisional or policy making functions. The policy basis of this aspect of the privilege is found in the desirability of encouraging candor in the exchange of views within the government. Kaiser Aluminum & Chemical Corp. v. United States, 141 Ct.Cl. 38, 157 F.Supp. 939 (1958); Davis v. Braswell Motor Freight Lines, Inc., 363 F.2d 600 (5th Cir.1966); Ackerly v. Ley, 420 F.2d 1336 (D.C.Cir.1969). A privilege of this character is consistent with the Freedom of Information Act, 5 U.S.C. § 552(b)(5), and with the standing of the agency to raise questions of relevancy, though not a party, recognized in such decisions as Boeing Airplane Co. v. Coggeshall, 108 U.S.App.D.C. 106, 280 F.2d 654, 659 (1960) (Renegotiation Board) and Freeman v. Seligson, 132 U.S.App. D.C. 56, 405 F.2d 1326, 1334 (1968) (Secretary of Agriculture).

(B) Investigatory files compiled for law enforcement purposes. This category is expressly made subject to the provisions of the Jencks Act, 18 U.S.C. § 3500, which insulates prior statements or reports of government witnesses in criminal cases against subpoena, discovery, or inspection until the witness has testified on direct examination at the trial but then entitles the defense to its production. Rarely will documents of this nature be relevant until the author has testified and thus placed his credibility in issue. Further protection against discovery of government files in criminal cases is found in Criminal Procedure Rule 16(a) and (b). The breadth of discovery in civil cases, however, goes beyond ordinary bounds of relevancy and raises problems calling for the exercise of judicial control, and in making provision for it the rule implements the Freedom of Information Act, 18 U.S.C. § 552(b)(7).

(C) Information exempted from disclosure under the Freedom of Information Act, 5 U.S.C. § 552. In 1958 the old "housekeeping" statute which had been relied upon as a foundation for departmental regulations curtailing disclosure was amended by adding a provision that it did not authorize withholding information from the public. In 1966 the Congress enacted the Freedom of Information Act for the purpose of making information in the files of departments and agencies, subject to certain specified exceptions, available to the mass media and to the public generally. 5 U.S.C. § 552. These enactments are significant expressions of Congressional policy. The exceptions in the Act are not framed in terms of evidentiary privilege, thus recognizing by clear implication that the needs of litigants may stand on somewhat different footing from those of the public generally. Nevertheless, the exceptions are based on values obviously entitled to weighty consideration in formulating rules of evidentiary privilege. In some instances in these rules, exceptions in the Act have been made the subject of specific privileges, *e.g.*, military and state secrets in the present rule and trade secrets in Rule 508. The purpose of the present provision is to incorporate the remaining exceptions of the Act into the qualified privilege here created, thus subjecting disclosure of the information to judicial determination with respect to the effect of disclosure on the public interest. This approach appears to afford a satisfactory resolution of the problems which may arise.

Subdivision (b). The rule vests the privileges in the government where they properly belong rather than a party or witness. See United States v. Reynolds, *supra,* p. 7, 73 S.Ct. 528. The showing required as a condition precedent to claiming the privilege represents a compromise between complete judicial control and accepting as final the decision of a departmental officer. See Machin v. Zuckert, 114 U.S.App.D.C. 335, 316 F.2d 336 (1963), rejecting in part a claim of privilege by the Secretary of the Air Force and ordering the furnishing of information for use in private litigation. This approach is consistent with *Reynolds.*

Subdivision (c). In requiring the claim of privilege for state secrets to be made by the chief departmental officer, the rule again follows *Reynolds,* insuring consideration by a high-level officer. This provision is justified by the lesser participation by the judge in cases of state secrets. The full participation by the judge in official information cases, on the contrary, warrants allowing the claim of privilege to be made by a government attorney.

Subdivision (d) spells out and emphasizes a power and responsibility on the part of the trial judge. An analogous provision is found in the requirement that the court certify to the Attorney General when the constitutionality of an act of Congress is in question in an action to which the government is not a party. 28 U.S.C. § 2403.

Subdivision (e). If privilege is successfully claimed by the government in litigation to which it is not a party, the effect is simply to make the evidence unavailable, as though a witness had died or claimed the privilege against self-incrimination, and no specification of the consequences is necessary. The rule therefore deals only with the effect of a successful claim of privilege by the government in proceedings to which it is a party. Reference to other types of cases serves to illustrate the variety of situations which may arise and the impossibility of evolving a single formula to be applied automatically to all of them. The privileged materials may be the statement of a government witness, as under the *Jencks* statute, which provides that, if the government elects not to produce the statement, the judge is to strike the testimony of the witness, or that he may declare a mistrial if the interests of justice so require. 18 U.S.C. § 3500(d). Or the privileged materials may disclose a possible basis for applying pressure upon witnesses. United States v. Beekman, 155 F.2d 580 (2d Cir.1946). Or they may bear directly upon a substantive element of a criminal case, requiring dismissal in the event of a successful claim of privilege. United States v. Andolschek, 142 F.2d 503 (2d Cir.1944); and see United States v. Reynolds, 345 U.S. 1, 73 S.Ct. 528, 97 L.Ed. 727 (1953). Or they may relate to an element of a plaintiff's claim against the government, with the decisions indicating unwillingness to allow the government's claim of privilege for secrets of state to be used as an offensive weapon against it. United States v. Reynolds, *supra;* Republic of China v. National Union Fire Ins. Co., 142 F.Supp. 551 (D.Md.1956).

Rule 510. Identity of Informer [Not enacted.]

(a) Rule of privilege. The government or a state or subdivision thereof has a privilege to refuse to disclose the identity of a person who has furnished information relating to or assisting in an investigation of a possible violation of law to a law enforcement officer or member of a legislative committee or its staff conducting an investigation.

(b) Who may claim. The privilege may be claimed by an appropriate representative of the government, regardless of whether the information was furnished to an officer of the government or of a state or subdivision thereof. The privilege may be claimed by an appropriate representative of a state or subdivision if the information was furnished to an officer thereof, except that in criminal cases the privilege shall not be allowed if the government objects.

(c) Exceptions.

(1) Voluntary disclosure; informer a witness. No privilege exists under this rule if the identity of the informer or his interest in the subject matter of his communication has been disclosed to those who would have cause to resent the communication by a holder of the privilege or by the informer's own action, or if the informer appears as a witness for the government.

(2) Testimony on merits. If it appears from the evidence in the case or from other showing by a party that an informer may be able to give testimony necessary to a fair determination of the issue of guilt or innocence in a criminal case or of a material issue on the merits in a civil case to which the government is a party, and the government invokes the privilege, the judge shall give the government an opportunity to show *in camera* facts relevant to determining whether the informer can, in fact, supply that testimony. The showing will ordinarily be in the form of affidavits, but the judge may direct that testimony be taken if he finds that the matter cannot be resolved satisfactorily upon affidavit. If the judge finds that there is a reasonable probability that the informer can give the testimony, and the government elects not to disclose his identity, the judge on motion of the defendant in a criminal case shall dismiss the charges to which the testimony would relate, and the judge may do so on his own motion. In civil cases, he may make any order that justice requires. Evidence submitted to the judge shall be sealed and preserved to be made available to the appellate court in the event of an appeal, and the contents shall not otherwise be revealed without consent of the government. All counsel and parties shall be permitted to be present at every stage of proceedings under this subdivision except a showing *in camera,* at which no counsel or party shall be permitted to be present.

(3) Legality of obtaining evidence. If information from an informer is relied upon to establish the legality of the means by which evidence was obtained and the judge is not satisfied that the information was received from an informer reasonably believed to be reliable or credible, he may require the identity of the informer to be disclosed. The judge shall, on request of the government, direct that the disclosure be made *in camera.* All counsel and parties concerned with the issue of legality shall be permitted to be present at every stage of proceedings under this subdivision except a disclosure *in camera,* at which no counsel or party shall be permitted to be present. If disclosure of the identity of the informer is made *in camera,* the record thereof shall be sealed and preserved to be made available to the appellate court in the event of an appeal, and the contents shall not otherwise be revealed without consent of the government.

Advisory Committee's Note

The rule recognizes the use of informers as an important aspect of law enforcement, whether the informer is a citizen who steps forward with information or a paid undercover agent. In either event, the basic importance of anonymity in the effective use of informers is apparent, Bocchicchio v. Curtis Publishing Co., 203 F.Supp. 403 (E.D.Pa.1962), and the privilege of withholding their identity was well established at common law. Roviaro v. United States, 353 U.S. 53, 59, 77 S.Ct. 623, 1 L.Ed.2d 639 (1957); McCormick § 148; 8 Wigmore § 2374 (McNaughton Rev.1961).

Subdivision (a). The public interest in law enforcement requires that the privilege be that of the government, state, or political subdivision, rather than that of the witness. The rule blankets in as an informer anyone who tells a law enforcement officer about a violation of law without regard to whether the officer is one charged with enforcing the particular law. The rule also applies to disclosures to legislative investigating committees and their staffs, and is sufficiently broad to include continuing investigations.

Although the tradition of protecting the identity of informers has evolved in an essentially criminal setting, noncriminal law enforcement situations involving possibilities of reprisal against informers fall within the purview of the considerations out of which the privilege originated. In Mitchell v. Roma, 265 F.2d 633 (3d Cir.1959), the privilege was given effect with respect to persons informing as to violations of the Fair Labor Standards Act, and in Wirtz v. Continental Finance & Loan Co., 326 F.2d 561 (5th Cir.1964), a similar case, the privilege was recognized, although the basis of decision was lack of relevancy to the issues in the case.

Only identity is privileged; communications are not included except to the extent that disclosure would operate also to disclose the informer's identity. The common law was to the same effect. 8 Wigmore § 2374, at p. 765 (McNaughton Rev.1961). See also Roviaro v. United States, supra, 353 U.S. at p. 60, 77 S.Ct. 623; Bowman Dairy Co. v. United States, 341 U.S. 214, 221, 71 S.Ct. 675, 95 L.Ed. 879 (1951).

The rule does not deal with the question whether presentence reports made under Criminal Procedure Rule 32(c) should be made available to an accused.

Subdivision (b). Normally the "appropriate representative" to make the claim will be counsel. However, it is possible that disclosure of the informer's identity will be sought in proceedings to which the government, state, or subdivision, as the case may be, is not a party. Under these circumstances effective implementation of the privilege requires that other representatives be considered "appropriate." See, for example, Bocchicchio v. Curtis Publishing Co., 203 F.Supp. 403 (E.D.Pa.1962), a civil action for libel, in which a local police officer not represented by counsel successfully claimed the informer privilege.

The privilege may be claimed by a state or subdivision of a state if the information was given to its officer, except that in criminal cases it may not be allowed if the government objects.

Subdivision (c) deals with situations in which the informer privilege either does not apply or is curtailed.

(1) If the identity of the informer is disclosed, nothing further is to be gained from efforts to suppress it. Disclosure may be direct, or the same practical effect may result from action revealing the informer's interest in the subject matter. See, for example, Westinghouse Electric Corp. v. City of Burlington, 122 U.S.App.D.C. 65, 351 F.2d 762 (1965), on remand City of Burlington v. Westinghouse Electric Corp., 246 F.Supp. 839 (D.D.C.1965), which held that the filing of civil antitrust actions destroyed as to plaintiffs the informer privilege claimed by the Attorney General with respect to complaints of criminal antitrust violations. While allowing the privilege in effect to be waived by one not its holder, *i.e.* the informer himself, is something of a novelty in the law of privilege, if the informer chooses to reveal his identity, further efforts to suppress it are scarcely feasible.

The exception is limited to disclosure to "those who would have cause to resent the communication," in the language of Roviaro v. United States, 353 U.S. 53, 60, 77 S.Ct. 623, 1 L.Ed.2d 639 (1957), since disclosure otherwise, *e.g.* to another law enforcing agency, is not calculated to undercut the objects of the privilege.

If the informer becomes a witness for the government, the interests of justice in disclosing his status as a source of bias or possible support are believed to outweigh any remnant of interest in nondisclosure which then remains. See Harris v. United States, 371 F.2d 365 (9th Cir.1967), in which the trial judge permitted detailed inquiry into the relationship between the witness and the government. Cf. Attorney General v. Briant, 15 M. & W. 169, 153 Eng.Rep. 808 (Exch.1846). The purpose of the limitation to witnesses for the government is to avoid the possibility of calling persons as witnesses as a means of discovery whether they are informers.

(2) The informer privilege, it was held by the leading case, may not be used in a criminal prosecution to suppress the identity of a witness when the public interest in protecting the flow of information is outweighed by the individual's right to prepare his defense. Roviaro v. United States, *supra.* The rule extends this balancing to include civil as well as criminal cases and phrases it in terms of "a reasonable probability that the informer may be able to give testimony necessary to a fair determination of the issue of guilt or innocence in a criminal case or of a material issue on the merits in a civil case." Once the privilege is invoked a procedure is provided for determining whether the informer can in fact supply testimony of such nature as to require disclosure of his identity, thus avoiding a "judicial guessing game" on the question. United States v. Day, 384 F.2d 464, 470 (3d Cir.1967). An investigation *in camera* is calculated to accommodate the conflicting interests involved. The rule also spells out specifically the consequences of a successful claim of the privilege in a criminal case; the wider range of possibilities in civil cases demands more flexibility in treatment. See Advisory Committee's Note to Rule 509(e), *supra.*

(3) One of the acute conflicts between the interest of the public in nondisclosure and the avoidance of unfairness to the accused as a result of nondisclosure arises when information from an informer is relied upon to legitimate a search and seizure by furnishing probable cause for an arrest without a warrant or for the issuance of a warrant for arrest or search. McCray v. Illinois, 386 U.S. 300, 87 S.Ct. 1056, 18 L.Ed.2d 62 (1967), rehearing denied 386 U.S. 1042. A hearing *in camera* provides an accommodation of these conflicting interests. United States v. Jackson, 384 F.2d 825 (3d Cir.1967). The limited disclosure to the

judge avoids any significant impairment of secrecy, while affording the accused a substantial measure of protection against arbitrary police action. The procedure is consistent with McCray and the decisions there discussed.

Rule 511. Waiver of Privilege by Voluntary Disclosure [Not enacted.]

A person upon whom these rules confer a privilege against disclosure of the confidential matter or communication waives the privilege if he or his predecessor while holder of the privilege voluntarily discloses or consents to disclosure of any significant part of the matter or communication. This rule does not apply if the disclosure is itself a privileged communication.

Advisory Committee's Note

The central purpose of most privileges is the promotion of some interest or relationship by endowing it with a supporting secrecy or confidentiality. It is evident that the privilege should terminate when the holder by his own act destroys this confidentiality. McCormick §§ 87, 97, 106; 8 Wigmore §§ 2242, 2327–2329, 2374, 2389–2390 (McNaughton Rev.1961).

The rule is designed to be read with a view to what it is that the particular privilege protects. For example, the lawyer-client privilege covers only communications, and the fact that a client has discussed a matter with his lawyer does not insulate the client against disclosure of the subject matter discussed, although he is privileged not to disclose the discussion itself. See McCormick § 93. The waiver here provided for is similarly restricted. Therefore a client, merely by disclosing a subject which he had discussed with his attorney, would not waive the applicable privilege; he would have to make disclosure of the communication itself in order to effect a waiver.

By traditional doctrine, waiver is the intentional relinquishment of a known right. Johnson v. Zerbst, 304 U.S. 458, 464, 58 S.Ct. 1019, 82 L.Ed. 1461 (1938). However, in the confidential privilege situations, once confidentiality is destroyed through voluntary disclosure, no subsequent claim of privilege can restore it, and knowledge or lack of knowledge of the existence of the privilege appears to be irrelevant. California Evidence Code § 912; 8 Wigmore § 2327 (McNaughton Rev.1961).

Rule 512. Privileged Matter Disclosed Under Compulsion or Without Opportunity to Claim Privilege [Not enacted.]

Evidence of a statement or other disclosure of privileged matter is not admissible against the holder of the privilege if the disclosure was (a) compelled erroneously or (b) made without opportunity to claim the privilege.

Advisory Committee's Note

Ordinarily a privilege is invoked in order to forestall disclosure. However, under some circumstances consideration must be given to the status and effect of a disclosure already made. Rule 511, immediately preceding, gives voluntary disclosure the effect of a waiver, while the present rule covers the effect of disclosure made under compulsion or without opportunity to claim the privilege.

Confidentiality, once destroyed, is not susceptible of restoration, yet some measure of repair may be accomplished by preventing use of the evidence against the holder of the privilege. The remedy of exclusion is therefore made available when the earlier disclosure was compelled erroneously or without opportunity to claim the privilege.

With respect to erroneously compelled disclosure, the argument may be made that the holder should be required in the first instance to assert the privilege, stand his ground, refuse to answer, perhaps incur a judgment of contempt, and exhaust all legal recourse, in order to sustain his privilege. See Fraser v. United States, 145 F.2d 139 (6th Cir.1944), cert. denied 324 U.S. 849, 65 S.Ct. 684, 89 L.Ed. 1409; United States v. Johnson, 76 F.Supp. 538 (M.D.Pa. 1947), aff'd 165 F.2d 42 (3d Cir.1947), cert. denied 332 U.S. 852, 68 S.Ct. 355, 92 L.Ed. 422, reh. denied 333 U.S. 834, 68 S.Ct. 457, 92 L.Ed. 1118. However, this exacts of the holder greater fortitude in the face of authority than ordinary individuals are likely to possess, and assumes unrealistically that a judicial remedy is always available. In self-incrimination cases, the writers agree that erroneously compelled disclosures are inadmissible in a subsequent criminal prosecution of the holder, Maguire, Evidence of Guilt 66 (1959); McCormick § 127; 8 Wigmore § 2270 (McNaughton Rev.1961), and the principle is equally sound when applied to other privileges. The modest departure from usual principles of res judicata which occurs when the compulsion is judicial is justified by the advantage of having one simple rule, assuring at least one opportunity for judicial supervision in every case.

The second circumstance stated as a basis for exclusion is disclosure made without opportunity to the holder to assert his privilege. Illustrative possibilities are disclosure by an eavesdropper, by a person used in the transmission of a privileged communication, by a family member participating in psychotherapy, or privileged data improperly made available from a computer bank.

Rule 513. Comment Upon or Inference From Claim of Privilege; Instruction [Not enacted.]

(a) Comment or inference not permitted. The claim of a privilege, whether in the present proceeding or upon a prior occasion, is not a proper subject of comment by judge or counsel. No inference may be drawn therefrom.

(b) Claiming privilege without knowledge of jury. In jury cases, proceedings shall be conducted, to the extent practicable, so as to facilitate the making of claims of privilege without the knowledge of the jury.

(c) Jury instruction. Upon request, any party against whom the jury might draw an adverse inference from a claim of privilege is entitled to an instruction that no inference may be drawn therefrom.

Advisory Committee's Note

Subdivision (a). In Griffin v. California, 380 U.S. 609, 614, 85 S.Ct. 1229, 14 L.Ed.2d 106 (1965), the Court pointed out that allowing comment upon the claim of a privilege "cuts down on the privilege by making its assertion costly." Consequently it was held that comment upon the election of the accused not to take the stand infringed upon his privilege against self-incrimination so substantially as to constitute a constitutional violation. While the privileges governed by these rules are not constitutionally based, they are nevertheless founded upon important policies and are entitled to maximum effect. Hence the present subdivision forbids comment upon the exercise of a privilege, in accord with the weight of authority. Courtney v. United States, 390 F.2d 521 (9th Cir.1968); 8 Wigmore §§ 2243, 2322, 2386; Barnhart, Privilege in the Uniform Rules of Evidence, 24 Ohio St.L.J. 131, 137–138 (1963). Cf. McCormick § 80.

Subdivision (b). The value of a privilege may be greatly depreciated by means other than expressly commenting to a jury upon the fact that it was exercised. Thus, the calling of a witness in the presence of the jury and subsequently excusing him after a sidebar conference may effectively convey to the jury the fact that a privilege has been claimed, even though the actual claim has not been made in their hearing. Whether a privilege will be claimed is usually ascertainable in advance and the handling of the entire matter outside the presence of the jury is feasible. Destruction of the privilege by innuendo can and should be avoided. Tallo v. United States, 344 F.2d 467 (1st Cir.1965); United States v. Tomaiolo, 249 F.2d 683 (2d Cir.1957); San Fratello v. United States, 343 F.2d 711 (5th Cir.1965); Courtney v. United States, 390 F.2d 521 (9th Cir.1968); 6 Wigmore § 1808, pp. 275–276; 6 U.C.L.A.Rev. 455 (1959). This position is in accord with the general agreement of the authorities that an accused cannot be forced to make his election not to testify in the presence of the jury. 8 Wigmore § 2268, p. 407 (McNaughton Rev.1961).

Unanticipated situations are, of course, bound to arise, and much must be left to the discretion of the judge and the professional responsibility of counsel.

Subdivision (c). Opinions will differ as to the effectiveness of a jury instruction not to draw an adverse inference from the making of a claim of privilege. See Bruton v. United States, 389 U.S. 818, 88 S.Ct. 126, 19 L.Ed.2d 70 (1968). Whether an instruction shall be given is left to the sound judgment of counsel for the party against whom the adverse inference may be drawn. The instruction is a matter of right, if requested. This is the result reached in Bruno v. United States, 308 U.S. 287, 60 S.Ct. 198, 84 L.Ed. 257 (1939), holding that an accused is entitled to an instruction under the statute (now 18 U.S.C. § 3481) providing that his failure to testify creates no presumption against him.

The right to the instruction is not impaired by the fact that the claim of privilege is by a witness, rather than by a party, provided an adverse inference against the party may result.

Rule 804. Hearsay Exceptions: Declarant Unavailable [Subdivision (b)(2) not enacted.]

* * *

(b) Hearsay exceptions. The following are not excluded by the hearsay rule if the declarant is unavailable as a witness:

* * *

(2) *Statement of recent perception.* A statement, not in response to the instigation of a person engaged in investigating, litigating, or settling

a claim, which narrates, describes, or explains an event or condition recently perceived by the declarant, made in good faith, not in contemplation of pending or anticipated litigation in which he was interested, and while his recollection was clear.

Note by Federal Judicial Center

Hearsay exception (b)(2) is set forth above as prescribed by the Supreme Court. It was not included in the rules enacted by the Congress but is reproduced here for such value as it may have for purposes of interpretation.

Advisory Committee's Note

Exception (2). The rule finds support in several directions. The well known Massachusetts Act of 1898 allows in evidence the declaration of any deceased person made in good faith before the commencement of the action and upon personal knowledge. Mass.G.L., c. 233, § 65. To the same effect is R.I.G.L. § 9–19–11. Under other statutes, a decedent's statement is admissible on behalf of his estate in actions against it, to offset the presumed inequality resulting from allowing a surviving opponent to testify. California Evidence Code § 1261; Conn.G.S., § 52–172; and statutes collected in 5 Wigmore § 1576. See also Va.Code § 8–286, allowing statements made when capable by a party now incapable of testifying.

In 1938 the Committee on Improvements in the Law of Evidence of the American Bar Association recommended adoption of a statute similar to that of Massachusetts but with the concept of unavailability expanded to include, in addition to death, cases of insanity or inability to produce a witness or take his deposition. 63 A.B.A. Reports 570, 584, 600 (1938). The same year saw enactment of the English Evidence Act of 1938, allowing written statements made on personal knowledge, if declarant is deceased or otherwise unavailable or if the court is satisfied that undue delay or expense would otherwise be caused, unless declarant was an interested person in pending or anticipated relevant proceedings. Evidence Act of 1938, 1 & 2 Geo. 6, c. 28; Cross on Evidence 482 (3rd ed. 1967).

Model Code Rule 503(a) provided broadly for admission of any hearsay declaration of an unavailable declarant. No circumstantial guarantees of trustworthiness were required. Debate upon the floor of the American Law Institute did not seriously question the propriety of the rule but centered upon what should constitute unavailability. 18 A.L.I. Proceedings 90–134 (1941).

The Uniform Rules draftsman took a less advanced position, more in the pattern of the Massachusetts statute, and invoked several assurances of accuracy: recency of perception, clarity of recollection, good faith, and antecedence to the commencement of the action. Uniform Rule 63(4)(c).

Opposition developed to the Uniform Rule because of its countenancing of the use of statements carefully prepared under the tutelage of lawyers, claim adjusters, or investigators with a view to pending or prospective litigation. Tentative Recommendation and a Study Relating to the Uniform Rules of Evidence (Art. VIII. Hearsay Evidence), Cal.Law Rev.Comm'n, 318 (1962); Quick, Excitement, Necessity and the Uniform Rules: A Reappraisal of Rule 63(4), 6 Wayne L.Rev. 204, 219–224 (1960). To meet this objection, the rule excludes statements made at the instigation of a person engaged in investigating, litigating, or setting a claim. It also incorporates as safeguards the good faith and clarity of recollection required by the Uniform Rule and the exclusion of a statement by a person interested in the litigation provided by the English act.

With respect to the question whether the introduction of a statement under this exception against the accused in a criminal case would violate his right of confrontation, reference is made to the last paragraph of the Advisory Committee's Note under Exception (1), *supra*.

Report of House Committee on the Judiciary

Rule 804(b)(2), a hearsay exception submitted by the Court, titled "Statement of recent perception," read as follows:

> A statement, not in response to the instigation of a person engaged in investigating, litigating, or settling a claim, which narrates, describes, or explains an event or condition recently perceived by the declarant, made in good faith, not in contemplation of pending or anticipated litigation in which he was interested, and while his recollection was clear.

The Committee eliminated this Rule as creating a new and unwarranted hearsay exception of great potential breadth. The Committee did not believe that statements of the type referred to bore sufficient guarantees of trustworthiness to justify admissibility.

*

INDEX TO FEDERAL RULES OF EVIDENCE

A

B

INDEX

C

INDEX

INDEX

INDEX

INDEX

INDEX

F

G

INDEX

H

I

J

N

P

Q

R

S

V

W

X

Appendix I

UNIFORM RULES OF EVIDENCE (as amended in 1999)

Table of Contents

APPENDIX I

Rule

504. ~~Husband-Wife Privilege~~ Spousal Privilege
505. Religious Privilege
506. Political Vote
507. Trade Secrets
508. Secrets of State and Other Official Information; Governmental Privileges
509. Identity of Informer
510. Waiver of Privilege ~~by Voluntary Disclosure~~

~~511. Privileged Matter Disclosed Under Compulsion or Without Opportunity to Claim Privilege~~

~~512~~ 511. Comment Upon or Inference From Claim of Privilege; Instruction

ARTICLE VI. WITNESSES

601. General Rule of Competency
602. Lack of Personal Knowledge
603. Oath or Affirmation
604. Interpreters
605. Competency of Judge as Witness
606. Competency of Juror as Witness
607. Who May Impeach
608. Evidence of Character and Conduct of Witness
609. Impeachment by Evidence of Conviction of Crime
610. Religious Beliefs and Opinions
611. Mode and Order of Interrogation and Presentation
612. ~~Writing~~ Record or Object Used to Refresh Memory
613. Prior ~~Statements~~ Statement of Witness
614. Calling and Interrogation of Witnesses by Court
615. Exclusion of Witnesses
616. Bias of Witness

ARTICLE VII. OPINIONS AND EXPERT TESTIMONY

701. Opinion Testimony by Lay Witness
702. Testimony by Experts
703. Basis of Opinion Testimony by ~~Experts~~ Expert
704. Opinion on Ultimate Issue
705. Disclosure of Facts or Data Underlying Expert Opinion
706. Court Appointed ~~Experts~~ Expert Witness

ARTICLE VIII. HEARSAY

801. Definitions; Exclusions
802. Hearsay Rule
803. Hearsay Exceptions~~:~~; Availability of Declarant Immaterial
804. Hearsay Exceptions: Declarant Unavailable
805. Hearsay Within Hearsay
806. Attacking and Supporting Credibility of Declarant
807. ~~Child Victims or Witnesses~~ Statement of Child Victim
808. Residual Exception

ARTICLE IX. AUTHENTICATION AND IDENTIFICATION

901. Requirement of Authentication or Identification
902. Self–Authentication
903. Subscribing Witness' Testimony Unnecessary

ARTICLE X. ~~CONTENTS~~ <u>CONTENT</u> OF ~~WRITINGS, RECORDINGS AND PHOTOGRAPHS~~ <u>RECORD, WRITING, RECORDING, PHOTOGRAPH, AND IMAGE</u>

Rule

~~ARTICLE XI. MISCELLANEOUS RULES~~

UNIFORM RULES OF EVIDENCE (1999)

PREFATORY NOTE

Codification of rules of evidence has proven to be more of a "work in progress" enterprise than was originally anticipated by the various drafting bodies at work in the 1970's. Societal changes, advances in both the hard and soft science and improvements in information technology have exposed many problematic evidentiary situations routinely faced by lawyers and judges. With increasing frequency, the rules fail to fit into a new environment, or alternatively, if they fit, they produce measurable inequity. It is within this context that the Drafting Committee to revise the UNIFORM RULES OF EVIDENCE OF 1974, AS AMENDED, presented its final work product to the National Conference of Commissioners on Uniform State Laws at its 1999 Annual Meeting in December, Colorado.

The assignment from the Conference's Scope and Program and Executive Committees authorized a comprehensive analysis of significant problems, with directions to keep in mind that the law of evidence, being applicable to an almost unlimited range of subject matter, does not reasonably respond to micro-management by the rule maker.

It may be prudent to anticipate one area of inquiry arising from an earlier mandate directed to the Drafting Committee that concluded its work with the 1986 amendments adopted at the Boston Conference. Responding to the expanding interstate and intercourt nature of the practice of law, the Drafting Committee was charged with bringing the language of the UNIFORM RULES OF EVIDENCE into line with comparable provisions in the FEDERAL RULES OF EVIDENCE, where reasonably possible. The underlying theory was, apparently, that a trial practitioner need master only one set of rules to comfortably practice in both federal and state forums located in various States, Districts, and Circuits. However, in practice, this theory does not seem to work as well as expected. In operation, the same words are often construed differently by different courts, even by sister federal circuits and state jurisdictions. Thus, the careful lawyer must continue to research certain rules of evidence on a case-by-case basis.

As a result, the current Drafting Committee has endeavored to draft the amended rules in clear and reasonably understandable terms without slavish regard for other existing work product. In this context, you will note, for the first time, that we have created a definitions rule, as amended RULE 101, containing terms that are used in several different UNIFORM RULES. The Drafting Committee is also proposing a unique approach to accommodate the admissibility of electronic evidence through the use of the term "record" throughout the rules in lieu of the terminology "writings," "recordings," and "photographs" and appropriately defining "record" in RULE 101(3). Numerous stylistic changes have also been made throughout the UNIFORM RULES as recommended by the Committee on Style.

The Drafting Committee also met on October 30–November 1, 1998 and February 26–28, 1999 to consider the comments, criticisms and suggestions of the Committee of the Whole of the Conference at the First Reading in 1988 of proposed amendments to the UNIFORM RULES. Hopefully, the Committee gave due consideration to all of the views expressed by Commissioners at the First Reading even though for various reasons all of them were not recommended or adopted. Among the UNIFORM RULES in which substantive revisions have been made based upon recommendations of the Committee of the Whole are: RULE 404(c) narrowing the scope of the procedural rules to apply in criminal cases when evidence of other crimes, wrongs or acts is offered against an accused; RULE 407 clarifying the meaning of an event in determining the applicability of the rule excluding evidence of subsequent remedial measures; RULES 803(6) and 803(8) to provide that public records inadmissible under RULE 803(8) are inadmissible as business records under RULE 803(6); and RULE 807 which tightens up the criteria for determining the admissibility of statements of children relating to neglect, or physical or sexual abuse.

It should also again be noted that Congress added RULES 413 through 415 of the FEDERAL RULES OF EVIDENCE on September 13, 1994, Pub. L. 103–222, § 320935(a), 108 Stat. 2135, effective July 9, 1995. RULES 413 through 415 permit respectively, (1) the admissibility of evidence of prior offenses of sexual assault when, in a criminal proceeding, a person is accused of such an offense; (2) the admissibility of evidence of prior offenses of child molestation when, in a criminal proceeding, a person is accused of child molestation, and (3) the admissibility of evidence of prior offenses of sexual assault, or of child molestation when, in a civil proceeding, a claim for damages or other relief is sought against a party who is alleged to have committed an act of sexual assault or child molestation.

The overwhelming majority of judges, lawyers, law professors and legal organizations who responded to the Federal Advisory Committee's call for public response opposed the enactment of RULES 413 through 415 without equivocation. The principal objections expressed were twofold. First, the rules would permit the admission of unfairly prejudicial evidence by focusing on convicting a criminal defendant for what the defendant **is** rather than what the defendant **has done**.

Second, the rules contained numerous drafting problems apparently not intended by their authors. For example, mandating the admissibility of the evidence without regard to the other rules of evidence such as the RULE 403 balancing test and the hearsay rule. In turn, it was believed that serious constitutional questions would arise in criminal proceedings in which the rules were invoked. For these and related reasons, the Advisory Committee on the FEDERAL RULES OF EVIDENCE, the Standing Committee on Rules of Practice and Procedure and the Judicial Conference of the United States opposed the enactment of RULES 413 through 415.

Alternatively, the Standing Committee and the Judicial Conference recommended the adoption of an amendment to RULES 404 and 405 of the FEDERAL RULES OF EVIDENCE proposed by the Advisory Committee which would provide for the admission of such evidence under limited conditions. However, Congress elected not to accept the recommendation.

In spite of the expressed concerns for the constitutionality of RULES 413 through 415, they are being given surprising vitality among the federal circuit courts that have considered the issue. These courts have held that the rules do not violate the Due Process Clause subject to the balancing of relevancy against unfair prejudice as provided in RULE 403 of the FEDERAL RULES OF EVIDENCE. *See United States v. Mound*, 149 F.3d 799 (8th Cir. 1998); *United States v. Summer*, 119 F.3d 658 (8th Cir. 1997); *United States v. Castillo*, 140 F.3d 874 (10th Cir. 1998); *United States v. Guardia*, 135 F.3d 1326 (10th Cir. 1998); *United States v. Enjady*, 134 F.3d 1427 (10th Cir. 1998); and *United States v. Larson*, 112 F.3d 600 (2d Cir. 1997).

However, there is still some lingering for the constitutionality of these rules. *See* the dissenting opinion from an order denying a petition for rehearing *en banc* in *United States v. Mound*, 157 F.3d 1153 (8th Cir. 1998), in which it is argued that an *en banc* court ought to consider the constitutionality of Rule 413 because the rule "presents [so] great a risk that the jury will convict a defendant for his past conduct or unsavory character" that it violates due process. *Id.* at 157 F.3d 1153. *See further*, M.A. Sheft, *Federal Rules of Evidence 413: A Dangerous New Frontier*, 33 AM. CRIM. L. REV. 57, 77–82 (1995).

In any event, the propriety of including RULES 413 through 415 in the UNIFORM RULES OF EVIDENCE was considered questionable at best. There is no state which has adopted these rules to date. In Arizona, their adoption was considered by the Supreme Court of Arizona, but was rejected largely for the same reasons they were rejected by the Judicial Conference of the United States. *See* Robert L. Gottsfield, *We Just Don't Get It: Improper Admission of Other Acts Under Evidence Rule 404(B) as Needless Cause of Reversal in Civil and Criminal Cases*, ARIZ. ATT'Y, Apr. 1997 at 24. Connecticut has reprinted FEDERAL RULES 413 through 415 in its Trial Lawyers Guide to Evidence, but they are inapplicable in state court proceedings. Indiana has a rule similar to FEDERAL RULE 414, but it is more carefully drawn with procedural safeguards. *See* Ind. Code Ann. § 35–37–4–15 (West 1997). California also has statutes authorizing the introduction of prior sexual offenses or acts of domestic violence subject to balancing relevancy against unfair prejudice. *See* Cal. Evid. Code §§ 1108, 1109 (West 1997). Section 1108 has been held constitutional by the California Court of Appeal in *People v. Fitch*, (App. 3 Dist. 1997) 63 Cal. Rptr. 753, 55 Cal. App. 4th 172. Missouri also had a blanket statutory rule, since held unconstitutional, admitting evidence of prior acts of child molestation similar to FEDERAL RULE 414. *See* Mo. Ann. Stat. § 566.025 (West 1978).

For the foregoing reasons and apparent lack of support to date among the several states for the enactment of rules similar to RULES 413 through 415, the Drafting Committee, at its meeting in Cleveland, Ohio, on October 4–6, 1996, voted unanimously not to include or recommend the adoption of RULES 413 through 415 by the Conference.

Similarly, the Drafting Committee did not recommend the adoption of the Advisory Committee's earlier carefully drawn proposed amendment to RULE 404 of the FEDERAL RULES OF EVIDENCE to deal with the issue.

These decisions of the Drafting Committee have now been reinforced by the decision of the Supreme Court of Missouri in *State v. Burns*, 978 S.W.2d 759 (Mo. 1998), holding that Section 566.025, *supra*, contravened the Missouri Constitution. In Burns, a prosecution for statutory sodomy, the trial court admitted the testimony of two witnesses relating to prior uncharged acts of sexual abuse committed by the defendant pursuant to Section 566.025, RSMo 1994, providing that evidence of other charged and uncharged crimes "shall be admissible for the purpose of showing the propensity of the defendant to commit the crime or crimes with which he is charged."

The Missouri Supreme Court reasoned that Section 566.025 violated Article I, Section 17 providing "[t]hat no person shall be prosecuted criminally for felony or misdemeanor otherwise than by indictment or information" and Article I, Section 18(a) providing "[t]hat in criminal prosecutions the accused shall have the right . . . to demand the nature and cause of the accusation;. . . ." In doing so it rejected the state's argument that Section 566.062 did not violate Sections 17 and 18(a) of Article I since the defendant was not "on trial" for the uncharged conduct because he could be convicted only for the formally charged crime. This interpretation, the Court reasoned, would enable the jury to "improperly convict the defendant because of his propensity to commit such crimes without regard to whether he is actually guilty of the charged crime. * * * As a result, the defendant is forced to defend against the uncharged conduct in addition to the charged crime."

The Court also rejected the State's argument that in determining the admissibility of propensity evidence under Section 566.025 the trial court can balance the value and effect of evidence of other crimes. This interpretation, the Court also reasoned, would require ignoring the Legislature's use of the mandatory term "shall," an approach which has largely been ignored by the federal circuit courts in dealing with this issue. Finally, the defendant also contended that Section 566.025 violated the Fifth, Sixth, and Fourteenth Amendments to the United States Constitution. However, the Court did not reach these issues by concluding that the challenge under the Missouri Constitution was dispositive.

Within the foregoing approach the proposed amendments of the UNIFORM RULES OF EVIDENCE (1999) were approved and recommended for enactment in all states at the Conference's Annual Meeting, meeting in its One–Hundred-and-Eighth Year in Denver, Colorado, July 23–30, 1999.

ARTICLE I

GENERAL PROVISIONS

Rule 101. ~~Scope~~ Definitions.

~~These rules govern proceedings in the courts of this State to the extent and with the exceptions stated in Rule 1101.~~

In these rules:

(1) "Person" means an individual, corporation, business trust, estate, trust, partnership, limited liability company, association, joint venture, government; governmental subdivision, agency, or instrumentality; public corporation; or any other legal or commercial entity.

(2) "Public record" means a record of a public office or agency in which the record is prepared, filed, or recorded pursuant to law.

(3) "Record" means information that is inscribed on a tangible medium or that is stored in an electronic or other medium and is retrievable in perceivable form.

(4) "State" means a State of the United States, the District of Columbia, Puerto Rico, the United States Virgin Islands, or any territory or insular possession subject to the jurisdiction of the United States.

Rule 102. Scope, Purpose, and Construction.

~~These rules shall be construed to secure fairness in administration, elimination of unjustifiable expense and delay, and promotion of growth and development of the law of evidence, to the end that the truth may be ascertained and proceedings justly determined.~~

(a) Rules applicable. Except as otherwise provided in subdivision (b), these rules apply to all actions and proceedings in the courts of this State.

(b) Rules inapplicable. These rules, other than those applicable to privileges, do not apply in:

(1) ~~Preliminary questions of fact.~~ the determination of questions of fact preliminary to admissibility of evidence if the issue is to be determined by the court under Rule 104(a);

~~Grand jury~~ proceedings before grand juries;

~~(4)~~(3) proceedings for contempt in which the court may act summarily; and

~~(3)~~(4) miscellaneous proceedings, such as proceedings involving extradition or rendition; [preliminary] [probable cause] hearings in criminal cases; [sentencing]; granting or revoking probation; issuance of warrants for arrest, criminal summonses, and search warrants; and release on bail or otherwise.

(c) Purpose and construction. These rules ~~shall~~ must be construed to secure fairness, ~~in administration, elimination of~~ eliminate unjustifiable expense and delay, and ~~promotion of~~ promote the growth and development of the law of evidence, to the end that truth may be ascertained and ~~proceedings~~ issues justly determined.

Rule 103. Rulings on Evidence.

(a) Effect of erroneous ruling. Error may not be predicated upon a ruling ~~which~~ that admits or excludes evidence unless a substantial right of the party is affected, and:

(1) ~~Objection. In case~~ if the ruling is one admitting evidence, a timely objection or motion to strike appears of record, stating the specific ground of objection, if the specific ground was not apparent from the context; or

(2) ~~Offer of proof. In case~~ if the ruling is one excluding evidence, the substance of the evidence was made known to the court by offer or was apparent from the context within which questions were asked.

(b) Record of offer and ruling. The court may add any other or further statement ~~which~~ that shows the character of the evidence, the form in which it was offered, the objection made, and the ruling thereon. It may direct the making of an offer in question and answer form.

(c) Effect of pretrial ruling. If the court makes a definitive pretrial ruling on the record admitting or excluding evidence, a party need not renew an objection or offer of proof at trial to preserve a claim of error for appeal.

~~(c)~~ (d) Hearing of jury. In jury cases, proceedings ~~shall~~ must be conducted, to the extent practicable, so as to prevent inadmissible evidence from being suggested to the jury by any means, such as making statements or offers of proof or asking questions ~~in~~ within the hearing of the jury.

~~(d)~~ (e) Errors affecting substantial rights. ~~Nothing in this~~ This rule ~~precludes~~ does not preclude a court from taking notice of ~~errors~~ an error affecting a substantial ~~rights although they were~~ right even if it was not brought to the attention of the trial court.

Rule 104. Preliminary Questions.

(a) Questions of admissibility generally. Preliminary questions concerning the qualification of ~~a person~~ an individual to be a witness, the existence of a privilege, or the admissibility of evidence ~~shall~~ must be determined by the court, subject to ~~the provisions of~~ subdivision (b). In making its determination, ~~it~~ the court is not bound by the rules of evidence except ~~those~~ the rules with respect to privileges.

(b) Determination of privilege. A person claiming a privilege must prove that the conditions prerequisite to the existence of the privilege are more probably true than not. A person claiming an exception to a privilege must prove that the conditions prerequisite to the applicability of the exception are more probably true than not. If there is a factual basis to support a good faith belief that a review of the allegedly privileged material is necessary, the court, in making its determination, may review the material outside the presence of any other person.

~~(b)~~ (c) Relevancy conditioned on fact. ~~Whenever~~ If the relevancy of evidence depends upon the fulfillment of a condition of fact, the court shall admit it upon~~,~~ or, in the court's discretion, subject to~~,~~ the introduction of evidence sufficient to support a finding of the fulfillment of the condition.

~~(c)~~ (d) Hearing of jury. ~~Hearings~~ A hearing on the admissibility of ~~confessions~~ a confession in a criminal ~~cases shall~~ case must be conducted out of the hearing of the jury. ~~Hearings~~ A hearing on any other preliminary ~~matters in all cases, shall~~ matter must be so conducted ~~whenever~~ if the interests of justice require or, in a criminal ~~cases, whenever~~ case, an accused is a witness~~, if he~~ and so requests.

~~(d)~~ (e) Testimony by accused. ~~The~~ An accused ~~does not~~, by testifying upon a preliminary matter, does not become subject ~~himself~~ to cross-examination as to other issues in the case.

~~(e)~~(f) Weight and credibility. This rule does not limit the right of a party to introduce before the jury evidence relevant to weight or credibility.

Rule 105. Limited Admissibility.

~~Whenever~~ If evidence ~~which~~ that is admissible as to one party or for one purpose but not admissible as to another party or for another purpose is admitted, the court, upon request, shall restrict the evidence to its proper scope and instruct the jury accordingly.

Rule 106. Remainder of, or Related, ~~Writings or Recorded Statements~~ Record.

~~Whenever~~ If a ~~writing or recorded statement~~ record or part thereof is introduced by a party, an adverse party may require ~~him~~ the introduction at that time ~~to introduce~~ of any other part or any other ~~writing or recorded statement which~~ record that in fairness ought to be considered contemporaneously with it.

ARTICLE II

JUDICIAL NOTICE

Rule 201. Judicial Notice of Adjudicative Facts.

(a) Scope of rule. This rule governs only judicial notice of adjudicative facts.

(b) Kinds of facts. A judicially noticed fact must be one that is not subject to reasonable dispute ~~in that~~ because it is: ~~either~~

(1) generally known within the territorial jurisdiction of the trial court; or

(2) capable of accurate and ready determination by resort to sources whose accuracy cannot reasonably be questioned.

(c) When discretionary. A court may take judicial notice, whether requested or not.

(d) When mandatory. A court shall take judicial notice if requested by a party and supplied with the necessary information.

(e) Opportunity to be heard. A party is entitled upon timely request to an opportunity to be heard as to the propriety of taking judicial notice and the tenor of the matter noticed. In the absence of ~~prior~~ earlier notification, the request may be made after judicial notice has been taken.

(f) Time of taking notice. Judicial notice may be taken at any stage of the proceeding.

(g) Instructing jury. The court shall instruct the jury to accept as conclusive ~~any~~ a fact judicially noticed.

ARTICLE III

PRESUMPTIONS

Rule 301. ~~Presumptions in General; in Civil Actions and Proceedings~~ Definitions.

~~(a) Effect. In all actions and proceedings not otherwise provided for by statute or by these rules, a presumption imposes on the party against whom it is directed the burden of proving that the nonexistence of the presumed fact is more probable than its existence.~~

~~(b) Inconsistent Presumptions. If presumptions are inconsistent, the presumption applies that is founded upon weightier considerations of policy. If considerations of policy are of equal weight neither presumption applies.~~

In this article:

(1) "Basic fact" means a fact or group of facts that give rise to a presumption.

(2) "Inconsistent presumption" means that the presumed fact of one presumption is inconsistent with the presumed fact of another presumption.

(3) "Presumed fact" means a fact that is assumed upon the finding of a basic fact.

(4) "Presumption" means that when a basic fact is found to exist, the presumed fact is assumed to exist until the nonexistence of the presumed fact is determined as provided in Rules 302 and 303.

Rule 302. ~~Applicability of Federal Law in Civil Actions and Proceedings~~ Effect of Presumptions in Civil Cases.

~~In civil actions and proceedings, the effect of a presumption respecting a fact which is an element of a claim or defense as to which federal~~

~~law supplies the rule of decision is determined in accordance with federal law.~~

(a) General rule. In a civil action or proceeding, unless otherwise provided by statute, judicial decision, or these rules, a presumption imposes on the party against whom it is directed the burden of proving that the nonexistence of the presumed fact is more probable than its existence.

(b) Inconsistent presumptions. If presumptions are inconsistent, the presumption applies that is founded upon weightier considerations of policy. If considerations of policy are of equal weight, neither presumption applies.

(c) Effect if federal law provides the rule of decision. The effect of presumption respecting a fact that is an element of a claim or defense as to which federal law provides the rule of decision is determined in accordance with federal law.

Rule 303. Scope and Effect of Presumptions in Criminal Cases.

(a) Scope. Except as otherwise provided by statute~~, in criminal cases,~~ or judicial decision, this rule governs presumptions against an accused in criminal cases, recognized at common law or created by statute, including statutory provisions that certain facts are prima facie evidence of other facts or of guilt~~, are governed by this rule~~.

(b) Submission to jury. The court ~~is not authorized to~~ may not direct the jury to find a presumed fact against ~~the~~ an accused. If a presumed fact establishes guilt, ~~or~~ is an element of the offense, or ~~negatives~~ negates a defense, the court may submit the question of guilt or of the existence of the presumed fact to the jury, but only if a reasonable juror on the evidence as a whole, including the evidence of the basic ~~facts~~ fact, could find guilt or the presumed fact beyond a reasonable doubt. If the presumed fact has a lesser effect, the question of its existence may be submitted to the jury ~~provided~~ if the basic ~~facts are~~ fact is supported by substantial evidence or ~~are~~ is otherwise established, unless the court determines that a reasonable juror could not find on the evidence as a whole ~~could not find~~ the existence of the presumed fact.

(c) Instructing the jury. ~~Whenever~~ At the time the existence of a presumed fact against the accused is submitted to the jury, the court shall instruct the jury that it may regard the basic ~~facts~~ fact as sufficient evidence of the presumed fact but is not required to do so. In addition, if ~~the~~ a presumed fact establishes guilt, ~~or~~ is an element of the offense, or ~~negatives~~ negates a defense, the court shall instruct the jury that its existence, on all the evidence, must be proved beyond a reasonable doubt.

ARTICLE IV
RELEVANCY AND ITS LIMITS

Rule 401. Definition of "Relevant Evidence."

In this article, "~~Relevant~~ relevant evidence" means evidence having any tendency to make the existence of any fact that is of consequence to the determination of the action more probable or less probable than it would be without the evidence.

Rule 402. Relevant Evidence Generally Admissible; Irrelevant Evidence Inadmissible.

All relevant evidence is admissible, except as otherwise provided by statute, ~~or by~~ these rules, or ~~by~~ other rules applicable in the courts of this State. Evidence ~~which~~ that is not relevant is not admissible.

Rule 403. Exclusion of Relevant Evidence on Grounds of Prejudice, Confusion, or Waste of Time.

Although relevant, evidence may be excluded if its probative value is substantially outweighed by the danger of unfair prejudice, confusion of the issues, or misleading the jury, or by considerations of undue delay, waste of time, or needless presentation of cumulative evidence.

Rule 404. Character Evidence Not Admissible to Prove Conduct~~.~~, Exceptions: Other Crimes.

(a) Character evidence generally. Evidence of a person's character or a trait of ~~his~~ character is not admissible for the purpose of proving ~~that he acted~~ the person acted in conformity therewith on a particular occasion, except:

(1) ~~Character of accused. Evidence~~ evidence of a pertinent trait of ~~his~~ the accused's character offered by an accused, or by the prosecution to rebut ~~the same~~ that evidence;

(2) ~~Character of victim. Evidence~~ evidence of a pertinent trait of character of the alleged victim of the crime offered by an accused, or by the prosecution to rebut ~~the same~~ that evidence, or evidence of a character trait of peacefulness of the alleged victim offered by the prosecution in a homicide case to rebut evidence that the alleged victim was the first aggressor; and

(3) ~~Character of witness. Evidence~~ evidence of the character of a witness, as provided in Rules 607, 608, and 609.

(b) Other crimes, wrongs, or acts. Evidence of other crimes, wrongs, or acts is not admissible to prove the character of a person in order to show ~~that he acted~~ the person acted in conformity therewith. However, it may ~~It may, however,~~ be admissible for ~~other purposes~~ another purpose, such as proof of motive, opportunity, intent, preparation, plan, knowledge, identity, or absence of mistake or accident.

(c) Determination of admissibility. Evidence is not admissible under subdivision (b) unless:

(1) the proponent gives to all adverse parties reasonable notice in advance of trial, or during trial if the court excuses pretrial notice for good cause shown, of the nature of the evidence the proponent intends to introduce at trial;

(2) if offered against an accused in a criminal case, the court conducts a hearing to determine the admissibility of the evidence and finds:

(A) by clear and convincing evidence, that the other crime, wrong, or act was committed;

(B) that the evidence is relevant to a purpose for which the evidence is admissible under subdivision (b); and

(C) that the probative value of the evidence outweighs the danger of unfair prejudice; and

(3) upon the request of a party, the court gives an instruction on the limited admissibility of the evidence pursuant to Rule 105.

Rule 405. Methods of Proving Character.

(a) Reputation or opinion. ~~In all cases in which~~ If evidence of character or a trait of character of a person is admissible, proof may be ~~made~~ by testimony as to reputation or ~~by testimony~~ in the form of ~~an~~ opinion. On cross-examination, inquiry is allowable into relevant specific instances of conduct.

(b) Specific instances of conduct. ~~In cases in which~~ If character or a trait of character of a person is an essential element of a charge, claim, or defense, proof may also be made of specific instances of ~~his~~ the person's conduct.

Rule 406. Habit~~.~~; Routine Practice.

(a) Admissibility. Evidence of the habit of ~~a person~~ an individual or of the routine practice of ~~an organization~~ a person other than an individual, whether corroborated or not and regardless of the presence of eyewitnesses, is relevant to prove that the conduct of the ~~person~~ individual or ~~organization~~ other person on a particular occasion was in conformity with the habit or routine practice.

(b) Method of proof. Habit or routine practice may be proved by testimony in the form of an opinion or by specific instances of conduct sufficient in number to warrant a finding that the habit existed or that the practice was routine.

Rule 407. Subsequent Remedial Measures.

~~Whenever~~ If, after an event, measures are taken ~~which~~ that, if taken previously, would have made ~~the event~~ injury or harm less likely to occur, evidence of the subsequent measures is not admissible to prove negligence, ~~or~~ culpable conduct, ~~in connection with the event.~~a defect in a product, a defect in a product's design, or a need for a warning or instruction. ~~This rule does not require the exclusion of evidence~~ Evidence of subsequent measures may be admissible if offered for another purpose, such as ~~proving~~ impeachment or, if controverted, proof of ownership, control, or feasibility of precautionary measures~~, if controverted, or impeachment~~. An event includes the sale of a product to a user or consumer.

Rule 408. Compromise and Offers to Compromise.

Evidence of ~~(1)~~ furnishing, offering, ~~or~~ promising to furnish, or ~~(2)~~ accepting, offering, or promising to accept, a valuable consideration in compromising or attempting to compromise a claim ~~which~~ that was disputed as to either validity or amount~~,~~ is not admissible to prove liability for, invalidity of, or amount of the claim, or any other claim. Evidence of conduct or statements made in compromise negotiations is likewise not admissible. This rule does not require the exclusion of ~~any~~ evidence otherwise discoverable merely because it is presented in the course of compromise negotiations. This rule also does not require exclusion if the evidence is offered for another purpose, such as proving bias or prejudice of a witness, ~~negativing~~ negating a contention of undue delay, or proving an effort to obstruct a criminal investigation or prosecution. ~~Compromise negotiations encompass mediation.~~

Rule 409. Payment of Medical and Similar Expenses.

Evidence of furnishing, offering, or promising to pay medical, hospital, or similar expenses occasioned by an injury is not admissible to prove liability for the injury.

Rule 410. ~~Withdrawn Pleas and Offers~~ Inadmissibility of Pleas, Plea Discussions, and Related Statements.

~~Evidence of a plea later withdrawn, of guilty, or admission of the charge, or nolo contendere, or of an offer so to plead to the crime charged or any other crime, or of statements made in connection with any of the foregoing withdrawn pleas or offers, is not admissible in any civil or criminal action, case, or proceeding against the person who made the plea or offer.~~

(a) General. Except as otherwise provided in subdivision (b), evidence of the following is not admissible in a civil or criminal proceeding against the defendant who made the plea or was a participant in the plea discussions:

(1) a plea of guilty that was later withdrawn;

(2) a plea of nolo contendere;

(3) a statement made in the course of any proceedings under Rule 11 of the Federal Rules of Criminal Procedure, [Rules 443 and 444 of the Uniform Rules of Criminal Procedure, or comparable state procedure of this or any other State] regarding either of the foregoing pleas; and

(4) a statement made in the course of plea discussions with an attorney for the prosecuting authority which do not result in a plea of guilty or which result in a plea of guilty later withdrawn.

(b) Exceptions. A statement described in subdivision (a) is admissible:

(1) in a proceeding in which another statement made in the course of the same plea or plea discussions has been introduced and, in fairness, the statement should be considered contemporaneously with the other statement; and

(2) in a criminal proceeding for perjury or false statement if the statement was made by the defendant under oath, on the record, and in the presence of counsel.

Rule 411. Liability Insurance.

Evidence that a person was or was not insured against liability is not admissible upon the issue as to whether ~~he~~ the person acted negligently or otherwise wrongfully. This rule does not require the exclusion of evidence of insurance against liability when offered for another purpose, such as proof of agency, ownership, or control, or bias or prejudice of a witness.

Rule 412. Sexual Behavior.

~~(a) When inadmissible. In a criminal case in which a person is accused of a sexual offense against another person, the following is not admissible:~~

~~(1) Reputation or opinion. Evidence of reputation or opinion regarding other sexual behavior of a victim of the sexual offense alleged.~~

~~(2) Specific instances. Evidence of specific instances of sexual behavior of an alleged victim with persons other than the accused offered on the issue of whether the alleged victim consented to the sexual behavior with respect to the sexual offense alleged.~~

~~(b) Exceptions. This rule does not require the exclusion of evidence of (i) specific instances of sexual behavior if offered for a purpose other than the issue of consent, including proof of the source of semen, pregnancy, disease, injury, mistake, or the intent of the accused; (ii) false allegations of sexual offenses; or (iii) sexual behavior with persons other than the accused which occurs at the time of the event giving rise to the sexual offense alleged.~~

(a) Definition. In this rule, "sexual behavior" means behavior relating to the sexual activities of an individual, including the individual's experience or observation of sexual intercourse or sexual contact, use of contraceptives, history of marriage or divorce, sexual predisposition, expressions of sexual ideas or emotions, and activities of the mind such as fantasies or dreams.

(b) Evidence of sexual behavior generally inadmissible. Except as otherwise provided in subdivisions (c) and (d), in a criminal proceeding involving the alleged sexual misconduct of an accused, evidence may not be admitted to prove that the alleged victim engaged in other sexual behavior.

(c) Exceptions. Evidence of specific instances of an alleged victim's sexual behavior, if otherwise admissible under these rules, is admissible to prove:

(1) that a person other than the accused was the source of the semen, injury, disease, other physical evidence, or pregnancy;

(2) that a person other than the accused was the source of the alleged victim's knowledge of sexual behavior;

(3) consent, if the alleged victim's sexual behavior involved the accused or constituted conduct so distinctive and which so closely resembles the accused's version of the sexual behavior of the alleged victim at the time of the alleged sexual misconduct that it corroborates the accused's claim of reasonable belief that the alleged victim consented to the alleged misconduct; or

(4) a fact of consequence whose exclusion would violate the constitutional rights of the accused.

(d) Procedure to determine admissibility. Evidence is not admissible under subdivision (c) unless:

(1) the proponent gives to all parties and to the alleged victim, or the alleged victim's guardian or representative, reasonable notice in advance of trial, or during trial if the court excuses pretrial notice for good cause shown, of the nature of such evidence the proponent intends to introduce at trial;

(2) the court conducts a hearing in chambers, affords the alleged victim and the parties a right to attend the hearing and be heard, and finds:

(A) that the evidence is relevant to a fact of consequence for which the evidence is admissible under subdivision (c); and

(B) that the probative value of the evidence is not substantially outweighed by the danger of harm to the alleged victim or of unfair prejudice to any party; and

(3) upon request, the court gives an instruction on the limited admissibility of the evidence, pursuant to Rule 105.

ARTICLE V
PRIVILEGES

Rule 501. Privileges Recognized Only As Provided.

Except as otherwise provided by constitution or statute or by these or other rules promulgated by [the Supreme Court of this State], no person has a privilege to:

(1) refuse to be a witness;

(2) refuse to disclose any matter;

(3) refuse to produce any object or ~~writing~~ record; or

(4) prevent another from being a witness or disclosing any matter or producing any object or ~~writing~~ record.

Rule 502. Lawyer–Client Privilege.

(a) Definitions. ~~As used in~~ In this rule:

(1) "Client" means a person~~, including a public officer, corporation, association, or other organization or entity, either public or private, who is rendered~~ for whom a lawyer renders professional legal services ~~by a lawyer,~~ or who consults a lawyer with a view to obtaining professional legal services from the lawyer.

~~(5)~~ (2) A communication is "confidential" if it is not intended to be disclosed to third persons other than those to whom disclosure is made in furtherance of the rendition of professional legal services to the client or those reasonably necessary for the transmission of the communication.

(3) "Lawyer" means a person authorized, or reasonably believed by the client to be authorized, to engage in the practice of law in any ~~state~~ State or ~~nation~~ country.

~~(2)~~ (4) "Representative of the client" means ~~(i)~~ a person having authority to obtain professional legal services, or to act on legal advice ~~thereby~~ rendered, on behalf of the client or ~~(ii) any other~~ a person who, for the purpose of effectuating legal representation for the client, makes or receives a confidential communication while acting in the scope of employment for the client.

~~(4)~~ (5) "Representative of the lawyer" means a person employed, or reasonably believed by the client to be employed, by the lawyer to assist the lawyer in rendering professional legal services.

(b) General rule of privilege. A client has a privilege to refuse to disclose and to prevent any other person from disclosing a confidential communication made for the purpose of facilitating the rendition of professional legal services to the client:

~~(i)~~(1) between the client or a representative of the client and the client's lawyer or a representative of the lawyer~~,~~;

~~(ii)~~(2) between the lawyer and a representative of the lawyer~~,~~;

~~(iii)~~(3) by the client or a representative of the client or the client's lawyer or a representative of the lawyer to a lawyer or a representative of a lawyer representing another party in a pending action and concerning a matter of common interest therein~~,~~;

~~(iv)~~(4) between representatives of the client or between the client and a representative of the client~~,~~; or

~~(v)~~(5) among lawyers and their representatives representing the same client.

(c) Who may claim ~~the~~ privilege. The privilege under this rule may be claimed by the client, the client's guardian or conservator, the personal representative of a deceased client, or the successor, trustee, or similar representative of a corporation, association, or other organization, whether or not in existence. ~~The~~ A person who was the lawyer or the lawyer's representative at the time of the communication is presumed to have authority to claim the privilege, but only on behalf of the client.

(d) Exceptions. There is no privilege under this rule:

(1) ~~Furtherance of crime or fraud. If~~ if the services of the lawyer were sought or obtained to enable or aid anyone to commit or plan to commit what the client knew or reasonably should have known ~~to be~~ was a crime or fraud~~.~~;

(2) ~~Claimants through same deceased client. As~~ as to a communication relevant to an issue between parties who claim through the same deceased client, regardless of whether the claims are by testate or intestate succession or by transaction inter vivos~~.~~;

(3) ~~Breach of duty by a lawyer or client. As~~ as to a communication relevant to an issue of breach of duty by a lawyer to the client or by a client to the lawyer~~.~~;

(4) as to a communication necessary for a lawyer to defend in a legal proceeding an accusation that the lawyer assisted the client in criminal or fraudulent conduct;

~~(4)~~ (5) ~~Documents attested by a lawyer. As~~ as to a communication relevant to an issue concerning an attested document to which the lawyer is an attesting witness~~.~~;

~~(5)~~ (6) ~~Joint Clients. As~~ as to a communication relevant to a matter of common interest between or among two or more clients if the communication was made by any of them to a lawyer retained or consulted in common, when offered in an action between or among any of the clients~~.~~; or

~~(6)~~(7) ~~Public Officer or Agency. As~~ as to a communication between a public officer or agency and its lawyers unless the communication concerns a pending investigation, claim, or action and the court determines that disclosure will seriously impair the ability of the public officer or agency to ~~process~~ act upon the claim or conduct a pending investigation, litigation, or proceeding in the public interest.

Rule 503. ~~Physician and Psychotherapist—Patient Privilege~~ [Psychotherapist] [Physician and Psychotherapist] [Physician and Mental–Health Provider] [Mental–Health Provider]—Patient Privilege.

(a) Definitions. ~~As used in~~ In this rule:

~~(4)~~ (1) A communication is "confidential" if it is not intended to be disclosed to third persons, except those ~~persons~~ present to further the interest of the patient in the consultation, examination, or interview, those ~~persons~~ reasonably necessary for the transmission of the communication, ~~or~~ and persons who are participating in the diagnosis and treatment of the patient under the direction of ~~the [physician or]~~ a [psychotherapist] [physician or psychotherapist] [physician or mental-health provider] [mental-health provider], including members of the patient's family.

[(2) "Mental-health provider" means a person authorized, in any State or country, or reasonably believed by the patient to be authorized, to engage in the diagnosis or treatment of a mental or emotional condition, including addiction to alcohol or drugs.]

~~(1)~~ [(2)] [(3) ~~A "patient" is a person~~ "Patient" means an individual who consults or is examined or interviewed by a ~~[physician, or]~~ [psychotherapist] [physician or psychotherapist] [physician or mental-health provider] [mental-health provider]].

[~~(2)~~[(3)] (4) ~~A "physician" is~~ "Physician" means a person authorized ~~to practice medicine~~ in any ~~state~~ State or ~~nation~~ country, or reasonably believed by the patient ~~so~~ to be authorized to practice medicine.]

~~(3)~~ [(3)] [(5) ~~A "psychotherapist" is (i)~~ "Psychotherapist" means a person authorized ~~to practice medicine~~ in any ~~state~~ State or ~~nation~~ country, or reasonably believed by the patient ~~so~~ to be authorized, to practice medicine, while engaged in the diagnosis or treatment of a mental or emotional condition, including ~~alcohol or drug~~ addiction to alcohol or drugs, or ~~(ii)~~ a person licensed or certified ~~as a psychologist~~ under the laws of any ~~state~~ State or ~~nation~~ country, or reasonably believed by the patient to be licensed or certified, as a psychologist, while similarly engaged.]

(b) General rule of privilege. A patient has a privilege to refuse to disclose and to prevent any other person from disclosing confidential communications made for the purpose of diagnosis or treatment of ~~his~~ the patient's [physical,] mental[,] or emotional condition, including ~~alcohol or drug addiction~~ addiction to alcohol or drugs, among ~~himself~~ the patient, the patient's [physician or] [psychotherapist] [physician or psychotherapist] [physician or mental-health provider] [mental-health provider] and persons, including members of the patient's family, who are participating in the diagnosis or treatment under the direction of the [physician, or] psychotherapist, including members of the patient's family [psychotherapist] [physician or psychotherapist] [physician or mental-health provider] [mental-health provider].

(c) Who may claim the privilege. The privilege under this rule may be claimed by the patient, his the patient's guardian or conservator, or the personal representative of a deceased patient. The person who was the [physician, or] [psychotherapist] [physician or psychotherapist] [physician or mental-health provider] [mental-health provider] at the time of the communication is presumed to have authority to claim the privilege, but only on behalf of the patient.

(d) Exceptions. There is no privilege under this rule for a communication:

(1) Proceedings for hospitalization. There is no privilege under this rule for communications relevant to an issue in proceedings to hospitalize the patient for mental illness, if the [psychotherapist] [physician or psychotherapist] [physician or mental-health provider] [mental-health provider], in the course of diagnosis or treatment, has determined that the patient is in need of hospitalization.;

(2) Examination by order of court. If the court orders an made in the course of a court-ordered investigation or examination of the [physical,] mental[,] or emotional condition of a the patient, whether a party or a witness, communications made in the course thereof are not privileged under this rule with respect to the particular purpose for which the examination is ordered, unless the court orders otherwise.;

(3) Condition an element of claim or defense. There is no privilege under this rule as to a communication relevant to an issue of the [physical,] mental[,] or emotional condition of the patient in any proceeding in which he the patient relies upon the condition as an element of his the patient's claim or defense or, after the patient's death, in any proceeding in which any party relies upon the condition as an element of his the party's claim or defense.;

(4) if the services of the [psychotherapist] [physician or psychotherapist] [physician or mental-health provider] [mental-health provider] were sought or obtained to enable or aid anyone to commit or plan to commit what the patient knew, or reasonably should have known, was a crime or fraud or mental or physical injury to the patient or another individual;

(5) in which the patient has expressed an intent to engage in conduct likely to result in imminent death or serious bodily injury to the patient or another individual;

(6) relevant to an issue in a proceeding challenging the competency of the [psychotherapist] [physician or psychotherapist] [physician or mental-health provider] [mental-health provider];

(7) relevant to a breach of duty by the [psychotherapist] [physician or psychotherapist] [physician or mental-health provider] [mental-health provider]; or

(8) that is subject to a duty to disclose under [statutory law].

Rule 504. ~~Husband-Wife Privilege~~ Spousal Privilege.

(a) Confidential communication. A communication is confidential if it is made privately by an individual to the individual's spouse and is not intended for disclosure to any other person.

~~(a)~~ (b) Marital communications. An individual has a privilege to refuse to testify ~~or to~~ and to prevent ~~his or her~~ the individual's spouse or former spouse from testifying as to any confidential communication made by the individual to the spouse during their marriage. The privilege may be waived only by the individual holding the privilege or by the holder's guardian~~,~~ or conservator, or the individual's personal representative if the individual is deceased.

~~(b)~~ (c) Spousal testimony in criminal ~~proceedings~~ proceeding. The spouse of an accused in a criminal proceeding has a privilege to refuse to testify against the accused spouse.

~~(c)~~ (d) Exceptions. There is no privilege under this rule:

(1) in any civil proceeding in which the spouses are adverse parties~~,~~;

(2) in any criminal proceeding in which ~~a prima facie~~ an unrefuted showing is made that the spouses acted jointly in the commission of the crime charged~~, or~~;

(3) in any proceeding in which one spouse is charged with a crime or tort against the person or property of ~~(i)~~ the other, ~~(ii)~~ a minor child of either, ~~(iii)~~ an individual residing in the household of either, or ~~(iv)~~ a third person if the crime or tort is committed in the course of committing a crime or tort against ~~any of the individuals previously named in this sentence.~~ the other spouse, a minor child of either spouse, or an individual residing in the household of either spouse; or

(4) ~~The court may refuse to allow invocation of the privilege~~ in any other proceeding, in the discretion of the court, if the interests of a minor child of either spouse may be adversely affected by invocation of the privilege.

Rule 505. Religious Privilege.

(a) Definitions. ~~As used in~~ In this rule:

(1) ~~A "clergyman" is~~ "Cleric" means a minister, priest, rabbi, accredited Christian Science Practitioner, or other similar functionary of a religious organization, or an individual reasonably believed so to be by the ~~person~~ individual consulting ~~him~~ the cleric.

(2) A communication is "confidential" if it is made privately and not intended for further disclosure except to other persons present in furtherance of the purpose of the communication.

(b) General rule of privilege. ~~A person~~ An individual has a privilege to refuse to disclose and to prevent another from disclosing a confidential communication by the ~~person~~ individual to a ~~"clergyman"~~ cleric in ~~his~~ the cleric's professional ~~character~~ capacity as spiritual adviser.

(c) Who may claim the privilege. The privilege under this rule may be claimed by ~~the person, by his~~ an individual or the individual's guardian or conservator, or ~~by his~~ the individual's personal representative if ~~he~~ the individual is deceased. The ~~person~~ individual who was the ~~"clergyman"~~ cleric at the time of the communication is presumed to have authority to claim the privilege but only on behalf of the communicant.

Rule 506. Political Vote.

(a) General rule of privilege. ~~Every person~~ An individual has a privilege to refuse to disclose the tenor of ~~his~~ the individual's vote at a political election conducted by secret ballot.

(b) Exceptions. ~~This~~ The privilege under subdivision (a) does not apply if the court finds that the vote was cast illegally or determines that ~~the~~ disclosure should be compelled pursuant to [the election laws of the State].

Rule 507. Trade Secrets.

A person has a privilege, which may be claimed by ~~him~~ the person or ~~his~~ the person's agent or employee, to refuse to disclose and to prevent other persons from disclosing a trade secret owned by ~~him~~ the person, if the allowance of the privilege will not tend to conceal fraud or otherwise work injustice. If disclosure is directed, the court shall take such protective measures as the interest of the holder of the privilege and of the parties and the interests of justice require.

Rule 508. Secrets of State and Other Official Information; Governmental Privileges.

(a) Claim of privilege under law of United States. If the law of the United States creates a governmental privilege that the courts of this State must recognize under the Constitution of the United States, the privilege may be claimed as provided by the law of the United States.

(b) Privileges created by laws of State. No ~~other~~ governmental privilege is recognized except as provided in subdivision (a) or created by the ~~Constitution or~~ constitution, statutes~~,~~, or rules of this State.

(c) Effect of sustaining claim. If a claim of governmental privilege is sustained and it appears that a party is thereby deprived of material evidence, the court shall make any further orders the interests of justice require, including striking the testimony of a witness, declaring a mistrial, finding upon an issue as to which the evidence is relevant, or dismissing the action.

Rule 509. Identity of Informer.

(a) Rule of privilege. The United States or a ~~state or subdivision thereof~~ State has a privilege to refuse to disclose the identity of ~~a person~~ an individual who has furnished information relating to or ~~assisting~~ assisted in an investigation of a possible violation of a law to a law enforcement officer or member of a legislative committee or its staff conducting an investigation.

(b) Who may claim. The privilege under this rule may be claimed by an appropriate representative of the ~~public entity~~ government to which the information was furnished.

(c) Exceptions~~:~~. ~~(1) Voluntary disclosure; informer a witness. No privilege exists under this rule~~ There is no privilege under this rule if the identity of the informer or ~~his~~ the informer's interest in the subject matter of ~~his~~ the informer's communication has been disclosed by a holder of the privilege or by the informer's own action to ~~those~~ persons who would have cause to resent the communication ~~by a holder of the privilege or by the informer's own action,~~ or if the informer appears as a witness for the government.

(d) Procedures. ~~(2) Testimony on relevant issue.~~ If it appears ~~in the case~~ that an informer may be able to give testimony relevant to ~~any~~ an issue in a criminal case, or to a fair determination of a material issue on the merits in a civil case to which ~~a public entity~~ the government is a party, and the informed ~~public entity~~ government invokes the privilege, the court shall give the ~~public entity~~ government an opportunity to show ~~in camera~~ in chambers facts relevant to ~~determining~~ whether the informer can, in fact, supply ~~that~~ the testimony. The showing ~~will~~ ordinarily will be ~~in the form of affidavits~~ by affidavit, but the court may direct that testimony be taken if it finds that the matter cannot be resolved satisfactorily upon affidavit. If the court finds there is a reasonable probability that the informer can give the testimony, and the ~~public entity~~ government elects not to disclose ~~his~~ the informer's identity, in criminal cases the court on motion of the defendant or on its own motion shall grant appropriate relief, which may include one or more of the following: requiring the prosecuting attorney to comply, granting the defendant additional time or a continuance, relieving the defendant from making disclosures otherwise required of ~~him~~ the defendant, prohibiting the prosecuting attorney from introducing specified evidence, and dismissing charges. In civil cases, the court may ~~make~~ issue any order the interests of justice require. Evidence submitted to the court ~~shall~~ must be sealed and preserved to be made available to the appellate court in the event of an appeal, and the contents ~~shall~~ may not otherwise be revealed without consent of the informed ~~public entity~~ government. All counsel and parties ~~are permitted to~~ may be present at every stage of ~~proceedings~~ a proceeding under this subdivision except a showing ~~in camera, at which~~ in chambers, if the court has determined that no counsel or party ~~shall~~ may be ~~permitted to be~~ present.

Rule 510. Waiver of Privilege ~~by Voluntary Disclosure.~~

(a) Voluntary disclosure. A person upon whom these rules confer a privilege against disclosure waives the privilege if ~~he~~ the person or ~~his~~ the person's predecessor, while holder of the privilege, voluntarily discloses or consents to disclosure of any significant part of the privileged matter. This rule does not apply if the disclosure itself is privileged.

(b) Involuntary disclosure. A claim of privilege is not waived by a disclosure that was compelled erroneously or made without an opportunity to claim the privilege.

~~Rule 511. Privileged Matter Disclosed Under Compulsion or Without Opportunity to Claim Privilege.~~

~~A claim of privilege is not defeated by a disclosure which was (a) compelled erroneously or (b) made without opportunity to claim the privilege.~~

Rule ~~512~~ 511. Comment Upon or Inference From Claim of Privilege; Instruction.

(a) Comment or inference not permitted. ~~The~~ A claim of ~~a~~ privilege, whether in the present proceeding or upon a ~~prior~~ previous occasion, is not a proper subject of comment by judge or counsel. No inference may be drawn ~~therefrom~~ from the claim.

(b) Claiming privilege without knowledge of jury. In jury cases, proceedings ~~shall~~ must be conducted, to the extent practicable, so as to facilitate the making of claims of privilege without the knowledge of the jury.

(c) Jury instruction. Upon request, any party against whom the jury might draw an adverse inference from a claim of privilege is entitled to an instruction that no inference may be drawn therefrom.

ARTICLE VI

WITNESSES

Rule 601. General Rule of Competency.

Every ~~person~~ individual is competent to be a witness except as otherwise provided in these rules.

Rule 602. Lack of Personal Knowledge.

A witness may not testify to a matter unless evidence is introduced sufficient to support a finding that ~~he~~ the witness has personal knowledge of the matter. Evidence to prove personal knowledge may, but need not, consist of the witness's own testimony ~~of the witness himself~~. This rule is subject to ~~the provisions of~~ Rule 703, relating to opinion testimony by expert witnesses.

Rule 603. Oath or Affirmation.

Before testifying, ~~every~~ each witness ~~shall be required to~~ must declare under oath or affirmation that ~~he~~ the witness will testify truthfully~~, by~~. The oath or affirmation must be administered in a form calculated to awaken ~~his~~ the witness's conscience and impress ~~his~~ the witness's mind with ~~his~~ the duty to ~~do so~~ testify truthfully.

Rule 604. Interpreters.

An interpreter is subject to the provisions of these rules relating to qualification as an expert and the administration of an oath or affirmation ~~that he will~~ to make a true ~~translation~~ and complete rendition of all communications made during the interpretive process to the best of the interpreter's knowledge and belief.

Rule 605. Competency of Judge as Witness.

The judge presiding at ~~the~~ a trial may not testify in that trial as a witness. ~~No~~ An objection need not be made ~~in order~~ to preserve the point.

Rule 606. Competency of Juror as Witness.

(a) At the trial. A member of ~~the~~ a jury may not testify as a witness before ~~that~~ the jury in the trial of the case in which ~~he~~ the juror is sitting ~~as a juror~~. If ~~he~~ the juror is called so to testify, the ~~opposing party shall~~ parties must be afforded an opportunity to object out of the presence of the jury.

(b) Inquiry into validity of verdict or indictment. Upon an inquiry into the validity of a verdict or indictment the following rules apply:

(1) A juror may not testify ~~as to any~~ to a matter or statement occurring during the course of the jury's deliberations or to the effect of anything upon ~~his~~ that or any other juror's mind or emotions as influencing ~~him~~ the juror to assent to or dissent from the verdict or indictment or concerning ~~his~~ the juror's mental processes in connection therewith~~, nor may his~~.

(2) A juror's affidavit or evidence of any statement by ~~him~~ the juror concerning a matter about which ~~he~~ the juror would be precluded from testifying may not be received~~, but a~~.

(3) A juror may testify ~~on the questions~~ as to whether extraneous prejudicial information was improperly brought to the jury's attention or whether any outside influence was improperly brought to bear upon ~~any~~ a juror.

Rule 607. Who May Impeach.

The credibility of a witness may be attacked by any party, including the party calling ~~him~~ the witness.

Rule 608. Evidence Of Character And Conduct Of Witness.

(a) Opinion and reputation evidence of character. The credibility of a witness may be attacked or supported by evidence in the form of opinion or reputation, ~~but~~ subject to ~~these limitations~~ the following:

(1) ~~the~~ The evidence may refer only to character for truthfulness or untruthfulness, and

(2) ~~evidence~~ Evidence of truthful character is admissible only after the character of the witness for truthfulness has been attacked by opinion or reputation evidence or otherwise.

(b) Specific instances of conduct. Specific instances of the conduct of a witness, for the purpose of attacking or supporting ~~his~~ the witness's credibility, other than conviction of crime as provided in Rule 609, may not be proved by extrinsic evidence. ~~They may, however,~~ However, in the discretion of the court, if probative of truthfulness or untruthfulness, they may be inquired into on cross-examination of the witness ~~(1)~~ (i) concerning ~~his~~ the witness's character for truthfulness or untruthfulness, or ~~(2)~~ (ii) concerning the character for truthfulness or untruthfulness of another witness as to which character the witness being cross-examined has testified.

(c) Privilege against self-incrimination. The giving of testimony, whether by an accused or by any other witness, does not operate as a waiver of ~~his~~ the accused's or the witness's privilege against self-incrimination when examined with respect to matters ~~which~~ that relate only to credibility.

Rule 609. Impeachment by Evidence of Conviction of Crime.

(a) General rule. For the purpose of attacking the credibility of a witness~~, evidence~~:

(1) Evidence that ~~he~~ a witness other than an accused has been convicted of a crime ~~shall be admitted but only~~ is admissible, subject to Rule 403, if the crime ~~(1)~~ was punishable by death or imprisonment in excess of one year under the law under which ~~he~~ the witness was convicted, and evidence that an accused has been convicted of such a crime is admissible if the court determines that the probative value of ~~admitting this~~ the evidence substantially outweighs ~~its prejudicial effect~~ the danger of unfair prejudice to ~~a~~

~~party or a witness, or (2) involved dishonesty or false statement,~~ the accused.

(2) Evidence that a witness has been convicted of a crime of untruthfulness or falsification is admissible, regardless of punishment, if the statutory elements of the crime necessarily involve untruthfulness or falsification.

(b) Time limit. Evidence of a conviction ~~under this rule~~ is not admissible under this rule if a period of more than ~~ten~~ 10 years has elapsed since the date of the conviction or of the release of the witness from the confinement imposed for ~~that~~ the conviction, whichever is the later date, unless the court determines, in the interests of justice, that the probative value of evidence of the conviction supported by specific facts and circumstances substantially outweighs its unfair prejudicial effect.

(c) Effect of pardon, annulment, or certificate of rehabilitation. Evidence of a conviction is not admissible under this rule if ~~(1)~~ the conviction has been:

(1) the subject of a pardon, annulment, certificate of rehabilitation, or other equivalent procedure based on a finding of the rehabilitation of the ~~person~~ individual convicted, and that ~~person~~ individual has not been convicted of a subsequent crime ~~which was~~ punishable by death or imprisonment in excess of one year~~,~~ ;or

(2) ~~the conviction has been~~ the subject of a pardon, annulment, or other equivalent procedure based on a finding of innocence.

(d) Juvenile adjudications. Evidence of a juvenile ~~adjudications~~ adjudication is generally not admissible under this rule. Except as otherwise provided by statute, however, in a criminal case the court may ~~in a criminal case~~ allow evidence of a juvenile adjudication of a witness other than the accused if conviction of the offense would be admissible to attack the credibility of an adult and the court is satisfied that admission ~~in~~ of the evidence is necessary for a fair determination of the issue of guilt or innocence.

(e) Pendency of appeal. The pendency of an appeal ~~therefrom~~ from a conviction does not render evidence of ~~a~~ the conviction inadmissible. Evidence of the pendency of an appeal is admissible.

(f) Notice. Evidence is not admissible under this rule unless the proponent of the evidence gives to all adverse parties reasonable notice in advance of trial, or during trial if the court excuses pretrial notice for good cause shown, of the nature of the conviction.

(g) Record. If objection is made to evidence offered pursuant to subdivision (a)(1) or (2), the court shall state on the record the factors it considered in determining admissibility.

(h) Evidence. If admissible, evidence of a conviction may be by testimony of the witness during direct or cross-examination, by the

<u>introduction of a public record, or by other extrinsic evidence if the public record is not available and good cause is shown.</u>

Rule 610. Religious Beliefs and Opinions.

Evidence of the beliefs or opinions of a witness on matters of religion is not admissible for the purpose of showing that by reason of their nature ~~his~~ <u>the witness's</u> credibility is impaired or enhanced.

Rule 611. Mode and Order of Interrogation and Presentation.

(a) Control by court. The court shall exercise reasonable control over the mode and order of interrogating witnesses and presenting evidence so as to ~~(1)~~ make the interrogation and presentation effective for the ascertainment of the truth, ~~(2)~~ avoid needless consumption of time, <u>and</u> ~~(3)~~ protect witnesses from harassment or undue embarrassment.

(b) Scope of cross-examination. Cross-examination should be limited to the subject matter of the direct examination and matters affecting the credibility of the witness. The court ~~may~~, in the exercise of discretion, <u>may</u> permit inquiry into additional matters as if on direct examination.

(c) Leading questions. Leading questions should not be used on the direct examination of a witness except as ~~may be~~ <u>is</u> necessary to develop ~~his~~ <u>the witness's</u> testimony. Ordinarily leading questions should be permitted on cross-examination. ~~Whenever a~~ <u>A</u> party ~~calls~~ <u>may interrogate</u> a hostile witness, an adverse party, or a witness identified with an adverse party, ~~interrogation may be~~ by leading questions.

Rule 612. ~~Writing~~ <u>Record</u> or Object Used to Refresh Memory.

(a) While testifying. If, while testifying, a witness uses a ~~writing~~ <u>record</u> or object to refresh ~~his~~ <u>the witness's</u> memory, an adverse party is entitled to have the ~~writing~~ <u>record</u> or object produced at the trial, hearing, or deposition in which the witness is testifying.

(b) Before testifying. If, before testifying, a witness uses a ~~writing~~ <u>record</u> or object to refresh ~~his~~ memory for the purpose of testifying and the court in its discretion determines that the interests of justice so require, an adverse party is entitled to have the ~~writing~~ <u>record</u> or object produced, if practicable, at the trial, hearing, or deposition in which the witness is testifying.

(c) Terms and conditions of production and use. A party entitled to have a ~~writing~~ <u>record</u> or object produced under this rule is entitled to inspect it, ~~to~~ cross-examine the witness thereon, and ~~to~~ introduce in evidence ~~those~~ portions <u>of the</u> record which relate to the testimony of the witness. If production of the ~~writing~~ <u>record</u> or object at the trial, hearing, or deposition is impracticable, the court may order it made available for inspection. If it is claimed that the ~~writing~~ <u>record</u> or object contains ~~matters~~ <u>matter</u> not related to the subject matter of the testimony, the court shall examine the ~~writing~~ record or object ~~in camera~~ in chambers, excise any portions not so related, and order delivery of the remainder to the party entitled thereto. Any portion withheld over objections ~~shall~~ must be preserved and made available to the appellate court in the event of an appeal. If a ~~writing~~ record or object is not produced, made available for inspection, or delivered pursuant to order under this rule, the court shall make any order justice requires, but in criminal cases if the prosecution elects not to comply, the order ~~shall~~ must be one striking the testimony or, if the court in its discretion determines that the interests of justice so require, declaring a mistrial.

Rule 613. Prior ~~Statements~~ Statement of Witness.

(a) Examining witness concerning prior statement. In examining a witness concerning a prior statement made by ~~him~~ the witness, whether ~~written~~ in a record or not, the statement need not be shown nor its contents disclosed to ~~him~~ the witness at that time, but on request ~~the same shall~~ it must be shown or disclosed to opposing counsel.

(b) Extrinsic evidence of prior inconsistent statement of witness. Extrinsic evidence of a prior inconsistent statement by a witness is not admissible unless the witness is afforded an opportunity to explain or deny the ~~same~~ statement and the ~~opposite~~ opposing party is afforded an opportunity to interrogate ~~him~~ the witness thereon, or the interests of justice otherwise require. This ~~provision~~ subdivision does not apply to admissions of a party-opponent as defined in Rule 801(d)(2).

Rule 614. Calling and Interrogation of Witnesses by Court.

(a) Calling by court. The court, at the suggestion of a party or on its own motion, may call ~~witnesses~~ a witness, and all parties ~~are entitled to~~ may cross-examine ~~witnesses~~ the witness thus called.

(b) Interrogation by court. The court may interrogate ~~witnesses~~ a witness, whether called by ~~itself~~ the court or ~~by~~ a party.

(c) ~~Objections~~ Objection. ~~Objections~~ An objection to the calling or interrogation of ~~witnesses~~ a witness by the court ~~or to interrogation by it~~ may be made at the time or at the next available opportunity when the jury is not present.

Rule 615. Exclusion oOf Witnesses.

At the request of a party the court shall order witnesses excluded so that they cannot hear the testimony of other witnesses, and it may make the order ~~of~~ on its own motion. This ~~rule~~ Rule does not authorize exclusion of ~~(1)~~ a party who is ~~a natural person~~ an individual, ~~or (2)~~ an officer or employee of a party that is not ~~a natural person~~ an individual designated as its representative by its attorney, or ~~(3) a person~~ an individual whose presence is shown by a party to be essential to the presentation of ~~his~~ the party's cause or is otherwise authorized by statute, judicial decision, or court rule.

Rule 616. Bias of Witness.

For the purpose of attacking the credibility of a witness, evidence of bias, prejudice, or interest of the witness for or against ~~any~~ a party to the case is admissible.

ARTICLE VII

OPINIONS AND EXPERT TESTIMONY

Rule 701. Opinion Testimony by Lay Witnesses.

If ~~the witness is not testifying as an expert, his~~ a witness's testimony is not based on scientific, technical, or other specialized knowledge within the scope of Rule 702, the witness's testimony in the form of opinions or inferences is limited to those opinions or inferences ~~which~~ that are ~~(1)~~ rationally based on the perception of the witness, and ~~(2)~~ helpful to a clear understanding of ~~his~~ the witness's testimony or the determination of a fact in issue.

Rule 702. Testimony by Experts.

~~If scientific, technical, or other specialized knowledge will assist the trier of fact to understand the evidence or to determine a fact in issue, a witness qualified as an expert by knowledge, skill, experience, training, or education, may testify thereto in the form of an opinion or otherwise.~~

(a) General rule. If a witness's testimony is based on scientific, technical, or other specialized knowledge, the witness may testify in the form of opinion or otherwise if the court determines the following are satisfied:

(1) the testimony will assist the trier of fact to understand evidence or determine a fact in issue;

(2) the witness is qualified by knowledge, skill, experience, training, or education as an expert in the scientific, technical, or other specialized field;

(3) the testimony is based upon principles or methods that are reasonably reliable, as established under subdivision (b), (c), (d), or (e);

(4) the testimony is based upon sufficient and reliable facts or data; and

(5) the witness has applied the principles or methods reliably to the facts of the case.

(b) Reliability deemed to exist. A principle or method is reasonably reliable if its reliability has been established by controlling legislation or judicial decision.

(c) Presumption of reliability. A principle or method is presumed to be reasonably reliable if it has substantial acceptance within the relevant scientific, technical, or specialized community. A party may rebut the presumption by proving that it is more probable than not that the principle or method is not reasonably reliable.

(d) Presumption of unreliability. A principle or method is presumed not to be reasonably reliable if it does not have substantial acceptance within the relevant scientific, technical, or specialized community. A party may rebut the presumption by proving that it is more probable than not that the principle or method is reasonably reliable.

(e) Other reliability factors. In determining the reliability of a principle or method, the court shall consider all relevant additional factors, which may include:

(1) the extent to which the principle or method has been tested;

(2) the adequacy of research methods employed in testing the principle or method;

(3) the extent to which the principle or method has been published and subjected to peer review;

(4) the rate of error in the application of the principle or method;

(5) the experience of the witness in the application of the principle or method;

(6) the extent to which the principle or method has gained acceptance within the relevant scientific, technical, or specialized community; and

(7) the extent to which the witness's specialized field of knowledge has gained acceptance within the general scientific, technical, or specialized community.

Rule 703. Basis of Opinion Testimony by ~~Experts~~ Expert.

The facts or data in ~~the~~ a particular case upon which an expert bases an opinion or inference may be those perceived by or made known to ~~him~~ the expert at or before the hearing. If of a type reasonably relied upon by experts in the particular field in forming opinions or inferences upon the subject, the facts or data need not be admissible in evidence for the opinion or inference to be admissible.

Rule 704. Opinion on Ultimate Issue.

Testimony in the form of an opinion or inference otherwise admissible is not objectionable because it embraces an ultimate issue to be decided by the trier of fact.

Rule 705. Disclosure of Facts or Data Underlying Expert Opinion.

~~The~~ An expert may testify in terms of opinion or inference and give ~~his~~ reasons therefore without ~~prior~~ previous disclosure of the underlying facts or data, unless the court requires otherwise. The expert may ~~in any event~~ be required to disclose the underlying facts or data on cross-examination.

Rule 706. Court Appointed ~~Experts~~ Expert Witness.

(a) Appointment. The court, on motion of any party or its own motion, may ~~enter~~ issue an order to show cause why an expert ~~witnesses~~ witness should not be appointed, and may request the parties to submit nominations. The court may appoint ~~any~~ an expert ~~witnesses~~ witness agreed upon by the parties, and may appoint an expert ~~witnesses~~ witness of its own selection. An expert witness ~~shall~~ may not be appointed by the court unless ~~he~~ the witness consents to act. A witness so appointed ~~shall~~ must be informed of ~~his~~ the witness's duties by the court in writing, a copy of which ~~shall~~ must be filed with the clerk, or at a conference in which the parties ~~shall~~ have an opportunity to participate. A witness so appointed shall advise the parties of ~~his~~ the witness's findings, if any~~; his~~. The witness's deposition may be taken by any party~~; and he~~. The witness may be called to testify by the court or any party. ~~He shall be~~ The witness is subject to cross-examination by each party, including a party calling ~~him as a~~ the witness.

(b) Compensation. ~~Expert witnesses so~~ An expert witness appointed ~~are~~ by the court is entitled to reasonable compensation ~~in whatever sum~~ as determined by the court ~~may allow~~. The compensation ~~thus fixed~~ is payable from funds ~~which may be~~ that are provided by law in criminal cases and in civil actions and proceedings involving just compensation for the taking of property. In other civil actions and proceedings the parties shall pay the compensation ~~shall be paid by the parties~~ in such proportion and at such time as the court directs, and ~~thereafter~~ the compensation is to be charged ~~in like manner~~ as ~~other~~ costs.

(c) Disclosure of appointment. ~~In the exercise of its discretion, the~~ The court may authorize disclosure to the jury of the fact that the court appointed the expert witness.

(d) Parties' experts of own selection. ~~Nothing in this rule limits~~ This rule does not limit the parties in calling expert witnesses of their own selection.

ARTICLE VIII

HEARSAY

Rule 801. Definitions; Exclusions.

(a) General. ~~As used in~~ In this ~~Article~~ article:

~~(b)~~ (1) ~~Declarant~~ "Declarant" means ~~an individual~~ a person who makes a statement.

~~(c)~~ (2) ~~Hearsay~~ "Hearsay" means a statement, other than one made by the declarant while testifying at the trial or hearing, offered in evidence to prove the truth of the matter asserted.

~~(a)~~ (3) ~~Statement~~ "Statement" means ~~(i)~~ an oral ~~or written~~ assertion, an assertion in a record, or ~~(ii)~~ nonverbal conduct of ~~an individual~~ a person who intends it as an assertion.

~~(d)~~ (b) ~~Statements that are not hearsay~~. A statement is not hearsay if:

(1) ~~Previous statement by witness~~. ~~The~~ the declarant testifies at the trial or hearing, ~~and~~ is subject to cross-examination concerning the statement, and the statement is:

~~(i)~~ (A) inconsistent with the declarant's testimony and~~, if offered in a criminal proceeding,~~ was given under oath and subject to the penalty of perjury at a trial, hearing, or other proceeding, or in a deposition~~,~~;

~~(ii)~~ (B) consistent with the declarant's testimony, ~~and~~ is offered to rebut an express or implied charge against the declarant of recent fabrication or improper influence or motive~~,~~ and was made before the supposed fabrication, influence, or motive arose; or

~~(iii)~~ (C) one of identification made shortly after perceiving the individual identified.

(2) ~~Admissions by party-opponent~~. ~~The~~ the statement is offered against a party and is:

~~(i)~~ (A) the party's own statement, in either an individual or a representative capacity~~,~~;

~~(ii)~~ (B) a statement of which the party has manifested adoption or belief in its truth~~,~~;

~~(iii)~~ (C) a statement by an individual authorized by the party to make a statement concerning the subject~~,~~;

~~(iv)~~ (D) a statement by the party's agent or servant concerning a matter within the scope of the agency or employment, made during the existence of the relationship~~,~~; or

~~(v)~~ (E) a statement by a ~~co-conspirator~~ coconspirator of a party during the course and in furtherance of the conspiracy.

Rule 802. Hearsay Rule.

Hearsay is not admissible except as provided by law or by these rules.

Rule 803. Hearsay Exceptions~~;~~: Availability of Declarant Immaterial.

The following are not excluded by the hearsay rule, even ~~though~~ if the declarant is available as a witness:

(1) Present sense impression. A statement describing or explaining an event or condition made while the declarant was perceiving the event or condition, or immediately thereafter.

(2) Excited utterance. A statement relating to a startling event or condition made while the declarant was under the stress of excitement caused by the event or condition.

(3) Then existing mental, emotional, or physical condition. A statement of the declarant's then existing state of mind, emotion, sensation, or physical condition, such as intent, plan, motive, design, mental feeling, pain, and bodily health, but not a statement of memory or belief to prove the fact remembered or believed unless it relates to the execution, revocation, identification, or terms of declarant's will.

(4) Statements for purposes of medical diagnosis or treatment. Statements made for purposes of medical diagnosis or treatment and describing medical history, or past or present symptoms, pain, or sensation, or the inception or general character of the cause or external source thereof insofar as reasonably pertinent to diagnosis or treatment.

(5) Recorded recollection. A ~~memorandum or~~ record concerning a matter about which a witness once had knowledge but now has insufficient recollection to testify fully and accurately, shown to have been made or adopted by the witness when the matter was fresh in the ~~witness'~~ witness's memory and to reflect that knowledge correctly~~. If admitted, the memorandum or~~, which record may be read into evidence but may not ~~itself~~ be received as an exhibit unless offered by an adverse party.

(6) ~~Records~~ Record of regularly conducted business activity. A ~~memorandum, report,~~ record~~, or data compilation, in any form,~~ of acts, events, conditions, opinions, or diagnoses, made at or near the time by, or from information transmitted by, a person ~~with~~ having knowledge, if kept in the course of a regularly conducted business activity, and if it was the regular practice of that business activity to make the ~~memorandum, report,~~ record, ~~or data compilation,~~ all as shown by the testimony of the custodian or other qualified witness, or by certification that complies with Rule 902(11) or (12), or with a statute providing for certification, unless the sources of information or the method or circumstances of preparation indicate lack of trustworthiness. ~~As used in~~ In this paragraph, business includes business, institution, association, profession, occupation, and calling of every kind, whether or not conducted for profit. A public record

inadmissible under paragraph (8) is inadmissible under this exception.

(7) Absence of entry in records kept in accordance with paragraph (6). Evidence that a matter is not included in the ~~memoranda, reports,~~ records~~, or data compilations, in any form,~~ kept in accordance with paragraph (6), to prove the nonoccurrence or nonexistence of the matter, if the matter was of a kind of which a ~~memorandum, report,~~ record~~, or data compilation~~ was regularly made and preserved, all as shown by the testimony of the custodian or other qualified witness, or by certification that complies with Rule 902(11) or (12), or with a statute providing for certification, unless the sources of information or other circumstances indicate lack of trustworthiness.

(8) ~~Public records and reports.~~ Record or report of public office. Unless the sources of information or other circumstances indicate lack of trustworthiness, ~~records, reports, statements, or data compilations in any form~~ a record of a public office or agency setting forth its regularly conducted and regularly recorded activities, or matters observed pursuant to duty imposed by law and as to which there was a duty to report, or factual findings resulting from an investigation made pursuant to authority granted by law. The following are not within this exception to the hearsay rule:

~~(i)~~ (A) an investigative ~~reports~~ report by police and other law enforcement personnel, except when offered by an accused in a criminal case;

~~(ii)~~ (B) an investigative ~~reports~~ report prepared by or for a government, ~~a~~ public office, or ~~an~~ agency when offered by it in a case in which it is a party;

~~(iii)~~ (C) factual findings offered by the government in criminal cases; and

~~(iv)~~ (D) factual findings resulting from special investigation of a particular complaint, case, or incident, ~~except when~~ unless offered by an accused in a criminal case.

(9) ~~Records~~ Record of vital statistics. ~~Records or data compilations, in any form,~~ A record of births, fetal deaths, deaths, or marriages, if the report thereof was made to a public office.

(10) Absence of ~~public~~ record or entry. To prove the absence of a record, ~~report, statement, or data compilation, in any form,~~ or the nonoccurrence or nonexistence of a matter of which a record~~, report, statement, or data compilation, in any form,~~ was regularly made and preserved by a public office or agency, evidence in the form of a certification in accordance with Rule 902, or testimony, that diligent search failed to disclose the record, ~~report, statement, or data compilation,~~ or entry.

(11) Records~~s~~ of religious organizations~~s~~. ~~Statements~~ A statement of births~~s~~, marriages~~s~~, divorces~~s~~, death, legitimacy, ancestry, relationship by blood or marriage, or other similar ~~facts~~ fact of personal or family history, contained in a regularly kept record of a religious organization.

(12) Marriage, baptismal, and similar ~~certificates~~ certified record. ~~Statements~~ A statement of fact contained in a ~~certificate~~ certified record that the maker performed a marriage or other ceremony or administered a sacrament, made by a ~~clergyman~~ cleric, public official, or other person authorized by the rules or practices of a religious organization or by law to perform the act certified, and purporting to have been issued at the time of the act or within a reasonable time thereafter.

(13) Family records~~s~~. A statements~~s~~ of fact concerning personal or family history contained in a family Bibles~~s~~, ~~genealogies~~ genealogy, charts~~s~~, engravings~~s~~ on a rings~~s~~, an inscriptions~~s~~ on a family portraits~~s~~, an engravings~~s~~ on an urns, crypts~~s~~, or tombstones~~s~~, or the like.

(14) Records~~s~~ of documents~~s~~ affecting an interest in property. ~~The~~ A public record ~~of a document~~ purporting to establish or affect an interest in property, as proof of the content of the original recorded document and its execution and delivery by each person by whom it purports to have been executed and delivered~~, if the record is a record of a public office and an applicable statute authorizes the recording of documents of that kind in that office~~.

(15) Statements~~s~~ in ~~documents~~ record affecting an interest in property. A statement contained in a ~~document~~ record purporting to establish or affect an interest in property if the matter stated was relevant to the purpose of the ~~document~~ record, unless dealings with the property since the ~~document~~ record was made have been inconsistent with the truth of the statement or the purport of the ~~document~~ record.

(16) Statements~~s~~ in ancient ~~documents~~ record. ~~Statements~~ A statement in a ~~document~~ record in existence ~~twenty~~ 20 years or more, the authenticity of which is established.

(17) Market ~~reports~~ report, commercial ~~publications~~ publication. Market ~~quotations~~ quotation, ~~tabulations~~ tabulation, ~~lists~~ list, ~~directories~~ directory, or other published or publicly recorded compilations, generally used and relied upon by the public or by persons in particular occupations.

(18) Learned treatises~~s~~. To the extent called to the attention of an expert witness upon cross-examination or relied upon by the witness in direct examination, a statements~~s~~ contained in a published treatises~~s~~, periodicals~~s~~, or pamphlets~~s~~ on a subject of history, medicine, or other science or art, established as a reliable authority by testimony or admission of the witness, ~~or~~ by other expert testimony, or by

judicial notice. If admitted, the statements may be read into evidence but may not be received as <u>an</u> exhibits.

(19) Reputation concerning personal or family history. Reputation among members of an individual's family by blood, adoption, or marriage, or among the individual's associates, or in the community, concerning the individual's birth, adoption, marriage, divorce, death, legitimacy, relationship by blood, adoption, or marriage, ancestry, or other similar fact of the individual's personal or family history.

(20) Reputation concerning boundaries or general history. Reputation in a community, arising before the controversy, as to boundaries of or customs affecting ~~lands~~ <u>land</u> in the community, and reputation as to ~~events~~ <u>an event</u> of general history important to the community<u>,</u> ~~or state~~ <u>State,</u> or ~~nation~~ <u>country</u> in which located.

(21) Reputation as to character. Reputation of ~~an individual's~~ <u>a person's</u> character among the ~~individual's~~ <u>person's</u> associates or in the community.

(22) Judgment of previous conviction. Evidence of a final judgment~~, [entered after a trial or upon a plea of guilty,]~~ adjudging a person guilty of a crime punishable by death or imprisonment in excess of one year, to prove any fact essential to sustain the judgment, but not including, when offered by the ~~state~~ <u>State</u> in a criminal prosecution for purposes other than impeachment, ~~judgments~~ <u>a judgment</u> against ~~persons~~ <u>a person</u> other than the accused. The pendency of an appeal may be shown but does not affect admissibility.

(23) Judgment as to personal, family<u>,</u> or general history, or boundaries. ~~Judgments~~ <u>A judgment</u> as proof of ~~matters~~ <u>a matter</u> of personal, family or general history, or boundaries, essential to the judgment, if the matter ~~would be~~ <u>is</u> provable by evidence of reputation.

~~(24) Other exceptions. A statement not specifically covered by any of the foregoing exceptions but having equivalent circumstantial guarantees of trustworthiness, if the court determines that (i) the statement is offered as evidence of a material fact; (ii) the statement is more probative on the point for which it is offered than any other evidence which the proponent can procure through reasonable efforts; and (iii) the general purpose of these rules and the interests of justice will best be served by admission of the statement into evidence. A statement may not be admitted under this exception unless the proponent of it makes known to the adverse party sufficiently in advance to provide the adverse party with a fair opportunity to prepare to meet it, the proponent's intention to offer the statement and the particulars of it, including the name and address of the declarant.~~

<u>~~[As amended 1986.]~~</u>

Rule 804. Hearsay Exceptions: Declarant Unavailable.

(a) Unavailability as a witness. In this rule:

(1) "Unavailability as a witness" includes situations in which the declarant:

~~(1)~~ (A) is exempted by ruling of the court on the ground of privilege from testifying concerning the subject matter of ~~his~~ the declarant's statement;

~~(2)~~ (B) persists in refusing to testify concerning the subject matter of ~~his~~ the declarant's statement despite an order of the court to do so;

~~(3)~~ (C) testifies to a lack of memory of the subject matter of ~~his~~ the declarant's statement;

~~(4)~~ (D) is unable to be present or to testify at the hearing because of death or then existing physical or mental illness or infirmity; or

~~(5)~~ (E) is absent from the hearing and the proponent of ~~his~~ the declarant's statement has been unable to procure ~~his~~ the declarant's attendance, ~~(~~or in the case of a hearsay exception under subdivision (b)(2), (3), or (4), ~~his~~ the declarant's attendance or testimony~~)~~, by process or other reasonable means.

(2) A declarant is not unavailable as a witness if ~~his~~ the declarant's exemption, refusal, claim of lack of memory, inability, or absence is due to the procurement or wrongdoing of the proponent of ~~his~~ the declarant's statement for the purpose of preventing the ~~witness~~ declarant from attending or testifying.

(b) Hearsay exceptions. The following are not excluded by the hearsay rule if the declarant is unavailable as a witness:

(1) Former testimony. Testimony given as a witness at another hearing of the same or a different proceeding, or in a deposition taken in compliance with law in the course of the same or another proceeding, if the party against whom the testimony is now offered, or, in a civil action or proceeding a predecessor in interest, had an opportunity and similar motive to develop the testimony by direct, cross, or redirect examination.

(2) Statement under belief of impending death. A statement made by a declarant while believing that ~~his~~ the declarant's death was imminent, concerning the cause or circumstances of what ~~he~~ the declarant believed to be ~~his~~ the declarant's impending death.

(3) Statement against interest. A statement ~~which was~~ that at the time of its making was so far contrary to the declarant's pecuniary or proprietary interest, or so far tended to subject ~~him [or her]~~ the declarant to civil or criminal liability or to render invalid a claim by ~~him [or her]~~ the declarant against another or to make ~~him~~

the declarant an object of hatred, ridicule, or disgrace, that a reasonable ~~person~~ individual in ~~his [or her]~~ the declarant's position would not have made the statement unless ~~he [or she]~~ the individual believed it to be true. A statement tending to expose the declarant to criminal liability and offered to exculpate ~~the~~ an accused is not admissible unless corroborating circumstances clearly indicate the trustworthiness of the statement. A statement or confession offered against the accused in a criminal case, made by a codefendant or other ~~person~~ individual implicating both ~~himself [or herself]~~ the codefendant or other individual and the accused, is not within this exception.

(4) Statement of personal or family history. ~~(i)~~ A statement concerning ~~the~~:

(A) the declarant's own birth, adoption, marriage, divorce, legitimacy, relationship by blood, adoption, marriage, ancestry, or other similar fact of personal or family history, even though declarant had no means of acquiring personal knowledge of the matter stated~~;~~ or ~~(ii) a statement concerning the foregoing~~

(B) the matters ~~and~~ listed in subparagraph (A) or the death ~~also,~~ of another ~~person,~~ individual if the declarant was related to the other individual by blood, adoption, or marriage or was so intimately associated with the ~~other's~~ other individual's family as to be likely to have accurate information concerning the matter declared.

~~[(5) Statement of recent perception. In a civil action or proceeding, a statement, not in response to the instigation of a person engaged in investigating, litigating, or settling a claim, which narrates, describes, or explains an event or condition recently perceived by the declarant, made in good faith, not in contemplation of pending or anticipated litigation in which the declarant was interested, and while the declarant's recollection was clear.]~~

~~(6) Other exceptions. A statement not specifically covered by any of the foregoing exceptions but having equivalent circumstantial guarantees of trustworthiness, if the court determines that (i) the statement is offered as evidence of a material fact; (ii) the statement is more probative on the point for which it is offered than any other evidence which the proponent can procure through reasonable efforts; and (iii) the general purposes of these rules and the interests of justice will best be served by admission of the statement into evidence. A statement may not be admitted under this exception unless the proponent of it makes known to the adverse party sufficiently in advance to provide the adverse party with a fair opportunity to prepare to meet it, the proponent's intention to offer the statement and the particulars of it, including the name and address of the declarant.~~

~~[As amended 1986.]~~

(5) Forfeiture by wrongdoing. A statement offered against a party that has engaged or acquiesced in wrongdoing that was intended to and did cause the unavailability of the declarant as a witness.

Rule 805. Hearsay Within Hearsay.

Hearsay included within hearsay is not excluded under the hearsay rule if each part of the combined statements conforms with an exception to the hearsay rule provided in these rules.

Rule 806. Attacking and Supporting Credibility of Declarant.

If a hearsay statement, or a statement ~~defined~~ described in Rule ~~801(d)(2)(iii)~~ 801(b)(2)(C), ~~(iv)~~ (D), or ~~(v)~~ (E), has been admitted in evidence, the credibility of the declarant may be attacked, and if attacked may be supported, by any evidence ~~which~~ that would be admissible for those purposes if the declarant had testified as a witness. Evidence of a statement or conduct by the declarant ~~at any time,~~ inconsistent with the declarant's hearsay statement~~,~~ is not subject to ~~any~~ a requirement that the declarant ~~may have~~ has been afforded an opportunity to deny or explain. If the party against whom a hearsay statement has been admitted calls the declarant as a witness, the party ~~is entitled to~~ may examine the declarant on the statement as if under cross-examination.

~~Rule 807. Child Victims or Witnesses.~~

~~(a) A hearsay statement made by a minor who is under the age of [12] years at the time of trial describing an act of sexual conduct or physical violence performed by or with another on or with that minor or any [other individual] [parent, sibling or member of the familial household of the minor] is not excluded by the hearsay rule if, on motion of a party, the minor, or the court and following a hearing [in camera], the court finds that (i) there is a substantial likelihood that the minor will suffer severe emotional or psychological harm if required to testify in open court; (ii) the time, content, and circumstances of the statement provide sufficient circumstantial guarantees of trustworthiness; (iii) the statement was accurately recorded by audio-visual means as may be provided by statute; (iv) the audio-visual record discloses the identity and at all times includes the images and voices of all individuals present during the interview of the minor; (v) the statement was not made in response to questioning calculated to lead the minor to make a particular statement or is clearly shown to be the minor's statement and not the product of improper suggestion; (vi) the individual conducting the interview of the minor is available at trial for examination or cross-examination by any party; and (vii) before the recording is offered into evidence, all parties are afforded an opportunity to view it and are furnished a copy of a written transcript of it.~~

~~(b) Before a statement may be admitted in evidence pursuant to subsection (a) in a criminal case, the court shall, at the request of the defendant, provide for further questioning of the minor in such manner as the court may direct. If the minor refuses to respond to further questioning or is otherwise unavailable, the statement made pursuant to subsection (a) is not admissible under this rule.~~

~~(c) The admission in evidence of a statement of a minor pursuant to subsection (a) does not preclude the court from permitting any party to call the minor as a witness if the interests of justice so require.~~

~~(d) In any proceeding in which a minor under the age of [12] years may be called as a witness to testify concerning an act of sexual conduct or physical violence performed by or with another on or with that minor or any [other individual] [parent, sibling or member of the familial household of the minor], if the court finds that there is a substantial likelihood that the minor will suffer severe emotional or psychological harm if required to testify in open court, the court may, on motion of a party, the minor or the court, order that the testimony of the minor be taken by deposition recorded by audio-visual means or by contemporaneous examination and cross-examination in another place under the supervision of the trial judge and communicated to the courtroom by closed-circuit television. Only the judge, the attorneys for the parties, the parties, individuals necessary to operate the equipment and any individual the court finds would contribute to the welfare and well-being of the minor may be present during the minor's testimony. If the court finds that placing the minor and one or more of the parties in the same room during the testimony of the minor would contribute to the likelihood that the minor will suffer severe emotional or psychological harm, the court shall order that the parties be situated so that they may observe and hear the testimony of the minor and may consult with their attorneys, but the court shall ensure that the minor cannot see or hear them, except, within the discretion of the court, for purposes of identification.~~

~~(e) The requirements for admissibility of a statement under this rule do not preclude admissibility of the statement under any other exception to the hearsay rule.~~

~~[As added 1986.]~~

Rule 807. Statement of Child Victim.

(a) Statement of child not excluded. A statement made by a child under [seven] years of age describing an alleged act of neglect, physical or sexual abuse, or sexual contact performed against, with, or on the child by another individual is not excluded by the hearsay rule if:

(1) subject to subdivision (b), the court conducts a hearing outside the presence of the jury and finds that the statement

concerns an event within the child's personal knowledge and is inherently trustworthy; and

(2) the child testifies at the proceeding [or pursuant to an applicable state procedure for the giving of testimony by a child], or the child is unavailable to testify at the proceeding, as defined in Rule 804(a), and, in the latter case, there is evidence corroborative of the alleged act of neglect, physical or sexual abuse, or sexual contact.

(b) Determining trustworthiness. In determining the trustworthiness of a child's statement, the court shall consider the circumstances surrounding the making of the statement, including:

(1) the child's ability to observe, remember, and relate the details of the event;

(2) the child's age and mental and physical maturity;

(3) whether the child used terminology not reasonably expected of a child of similar age, mental and physical maturity, and socioeconomic circumstances;

(4) the child's relationship to the alleged offender;

(5) the nature and duration of the alleged neglect, physical or sexual abuse, or sexual contact;

(6) whether any other descriptions of the event by the child have been consistent with the statement;

(7) whether the child had a motive to fabricate the statement;

(8) the identity, knowledge and experience of the person taking the statement;

(9) whether there is a video or audio recording of the statement and, if so, the circumstances surrounding the taking of the statement; and

(10) whether the child made the statement spontaneously or in response to suggestive or leading questions.

(c) Making a record. The court shall state on the record the circumstances that support its determination of the admissibility of the statement offered pursuant to subdivision (a).

(d) Notice. Evidence is not admissible under this rule unless the proponent gives to all adverse parties reasonable notice in advance of trial, or during trial if the court excuses pretrial notice for good cause shown, of the nature of any such evidence the proponent intends to introduce at trial.

Rule ~~803(24), 804(b)(5),~~ 808. Residual Exception.

(a) ~~A~~ Exception. In exceptional circumstances a statement not ~~specifically~~ covered by ~~any of the foregoing exceptions~~ Rules 803, 804, or

807 but ~~having~~ possessing equivalent, though not identical, circumstantial guarantees of trustworthiness, is not excluded by the hearsay rule if the court determines that~~:~~

~~(i)~~(1) the statement is offered as evidence of a ~~material fact~~ fact of consequence;

~~(ii)~~(2) the statement is more probative on the point for which it is offered than any other evidence ~~which~~ that the proponent can procure through reasonable efforts; and

~~(iii)~~(3) the general purposes of these rules and the interests of justice will best be served by admission of the statement into evidence.

(b) Making a record. The court shall state on the record the circumstances that support its determination of the admissibility of the statement offered pursuant to subdivision (a)

(c) Notice. A statement ~~may~~ is not ~~be admitted~~ admissible under this exception unless the proponent ~~of it makes known~~ gives to all parties ~~the adverse party sufficiently in advance to provide the adverse party with a fair opportunity to prepare to meet it, the proponent's intention to offer the statement and the particulars of it, including the name and address of the declarant~~ reasonable notice in advance of trial, or during trial if the court excuses pretrial notice for good cause shown, of the substance of the statement and the identity of the declarant.

ARTICLE IX

AUTHENTICATION AND IDENTIFICATION

Rule 901. Requirement of Authentication or Identification.

(a) General provision. The requirement of authentication or identification as a condition precedent to admissibility is satisfied by evidence sufficient to support a finding that the matter in question is what its proponent claims.

(b) Illustrations. By way of illustration only, and not by way of limitation, the following are examples of authentication or identification conforming with the requirements of this rule:

(1) Testimony of witness ~~with~~ having knowledge. Testimony of a witness with knowledge that a matter is what it is claimed to be.

(2) Nonexpert opinion on handwriting. Nonexpert opinion as to the genuineness of handwriting, based upon familiarity not acquired for purposes of the litigation.

(3) Comparison by trier or expert witness. Comparison by the trier of fact or by an expert ~~witnesses~~ witness with ~~specimens which have~~ a specimen that has been authenticated.

(4) Distinctive characteristics and the like. Appearance, contents, substance, internal patterns, or other distinctive characteristics, taken in conjunction with circumstances.

(5) Voice identification. Identification of a voice, whether heard firsthand or through mechanical or electronic transmission or recording, by opinion based upon hearing the voice ~~at any time~~ under circumstances connecting it with the alleged speaker.

(6) Telephone conversations. Telephone conversations, by evidence that a call was made to the number assigned at the time by the telephone company to a particular person ~~or business~~, if:

~~(i)~~ (A) in the case of ~~a person~~ an individual, circumstances, including self-identification, ~~show~~ which show that the ~~person answering to be~~ individual who answered was the one called~~,~~; or

~~(ii)~~ (B) in the case of a ~~business~~ person other than an individual, the call was made to a place of business and the conversation related to business reasonably transacted over the telephone.

(7) Public records or reports. Evidence that a ~~writing authorized by law to be recorded or filed and in fact recorded or filed in a public office,~~ public record or a purported public record~~, report, statement, or data compilation, in any form,~~ is from the public office where items of this nature are kept.

(8) Ancient ~~documents or data compilation~~ records. Evidence that a ~~document or data compilation, in any form, (i)~~ record is in such condition as to create no suspicion concerning its authenticity, ~~(ii)~~ was in a place where it, if authentic, would likely be, and ~~(iii)~~ has been in existence 20 years or more at the time it is offered.

(9) Process or system. Evidence describing a process or system used to produce a result and showing that the process or system produces an accurate result.

(10) ~~Methods~~ Method provided by statute or rule. Any method of authentication or identification provided by [the Supreme Court of this State or by] a statute or as provided in the ~~Constitution~~ constitution of this State.

Rule 902. Self–Authentication.

Extrinsic evidence of authenticity as a condition precedent to admissibility is not required with respect to the following:

(1) Domestic public ~~documents~~ document under seal. A document bearing a seal purporting to be that of the United States, or of any ~~state~~ State, ~~district, commonwealth, territory, or insular possession thereof, or the Panama Canal Zone, or the Trust Territory of the Pacific Islands,~~ or of a political subdivision, department, officer,

or agency ~~thereof~~ of one of them, and a signature purporting to be an attestation or execution.

(2) Domestic public ~~documents~~ document not under seal. A document purporting to bear a signature in the official capacity of an officer or employee of any entity designated in paragraph (1), having no seal, if a public officer having a seal and having official duties in the district or political subdivision of the officer or employee certifies under seal that the signer has the official capacity and that the signature is genuine.

(3) Foreign public ~~documents~~ document. A document purporting to be executed or attested in the official capacity of an individual authorized by the laws of a foreign country to make the execution or attestation, and accompanied by a final certification as to the genuineness of the signature and official position (i) of the executing or attesting individual, or (ii) of any foreign official whose certificate of genuineness of signature and official position relates to the execution or attestation or is in a chain of certificates of genuineness of signature and official position relating to the execution or attestation. A final certification may be made by a secretary of embassy or legation, consul general, consul, vice consul, or consular agent of the United States, or a diplomatic or consular official of the foreign country assigned or accredited to the United States. If all parties have been given a reasonable opportunity ~~has been given to all parties~~ to investigate the authenticity and accuracy of an official ~~documents~~ document, the court may for good cause shown order that ~~they~~ it be treated as presumptively authentic without final certification or permit ~~them~~ it to be evidenced by an attested summary with or without final certification.

(4) Certified ~~copies~~ copy of public ~~records~~ record. A copy of ~~an official~~ a public record or report or entry therein, or of a document authorized by law to be recorded or filed and actually recorded or filed in a public office, ~~including data compilations in any form,~~ certified as correct by the custodian or other authorized person ~~authorized to make the certification,~~ by certificate complying with paragraph (1), (2), or (3) or complying with any law of the United States or of this State.

(5) Official ~~publications~~ publication. ~~Books~~ A book, ~~pamphlets~~ pamphlet, ~~or other publications issued by public authority~~ publication, or other publicly issued record issued by public authority, if in a form indicative of the genuineness of such a record.

(6) ~~Newspapers and periodicals. Printed~~ Newspaper or periodical. Publicly distributed material purporting to be ~~newspapers~~ a newspaper or ~~periodicals~~ periodical.

(7) Trade inscriptions and the like. Inscriptions, signs, tags, or labels purporting to have been affixed in the course of business and indicating ownership, control, or origin.

(8) Acknowledged ~~documents~~ record. ~~Documents~~ A record accompanied by a certificate of acknowledgment executed in the manner provided by law by a notary public or other officer authorized by law to take acknowledgments.

(9) Commercial paper and related ~~documents~~ record. Commercial paper, ~~signatures~~ a signature thereon, and ~~documents~~ a record relating thereto or having the same legal effect as commercial paper, to the extent provided by general commercial law.

(10) ~~Presumptions~~ Presumption created by law. ~~Any~~ A signature, document, or other matter declared by any law of the United States or of this State~~,~~ to be presumptively or prima facie genuine or authentic.

(11) Certified ~~records~~ domestic record of regularly conducted business activity. The original or a duplicate of a domestic record of ~~regularly conducted activity, within the scope of Rule 803(6), which the custodian thereof~~ acts, events, conditions, opinions, or diagnoses if:

(A) the document is accompanied by a written declaration under oath of the custodian of the record or ~~another~~ other qualified individual ~~certifies~~ that the record ~~(i)~~ was made, at or near the time of the occurrence of the matters set forth, by, ~~(~~or from information transmitted by~~)~~, a person ~~with~~ having knowledge of those matters~~,~~; ~~(ii) is~~ was kept in the course of the regularly conducted business activity~~,~~; and ~~(iii)~~ was made ~~by~~ pursuant to the regularly conducted activity; ~~as a regular practice, unless the sources of information or the method or circumstances of preparation indicate lack of trustworthiness; but a record so certified is not self-authenticating under this subsection unless the proponent makes an intention to offer it known to the adverse party and makes it available for inspection sufficiently in advance of its offer in evidence to provide the adverse party with a fair opportunity to challenge it. As used in this subsection, "certifies" means, with respect to a domestic record, a written declaration under oath subject to the penalty of perjury and, with respect to a foreign record, a written declaration signed in a foreign country which, if falsely made, would subject the maker to criminal penalty under the laws of that country. The certificate relating to a foreign record must be accompanied by a final certification as to the genuineness of the signature and official position (i) of the individual executing the certificate or (ii) of any foreign official who certifies the genuineness of signature and official position of the executing indi-~~

~~vidual or is the last in a chain of certificates that collectively certify the genuineness of signature and official position of the executing official. A final certification must be made by a secretary of embassy or legation, consul general, consul, vice consul, or consular agent of the United States, or a diplomatic or consular official of the foreign country who is assigned or accredited to the United States.~~

(B) the party intending to offer the record in evidence gives notice of that intention to all adverse parties and makes the record available for inspection sufficiently in advance of its offer to provide the adverse parties with a fair opportunity to challenge the record; and

(C) notice is not given to the proponent, sufficiently in advance of the offer to provide the proponent with a fair opportunity to meet the objection or obtain the testimony of a foundation witness, raising a genuine question as to the trustworthiness or authenticity of the record.

(12) Certified foreign record of regularly conducted business activity. The original or a duplicate of a record from a foreign country of acts, events, conditions, opinions, or diagnoses if:

(A) the document is accompanied by a written declaration under oath of the custodian of the record or other qualified individual that the record was made, at or near the time of the occurrence of the matters set forth, by or from information transmitted by a person having knowledge of those matters, was kept in the course of a regularly conducted business activity, and was made pursuant to the regularly conducted activity;

(B) the party intending to offer the record in evidence gives notice of that intention to all adverse parties and makes the record available for inspection sufficiently in advance of its offer to provide the adverse parties with a fair opportunity to challenge the record; and

(C) notice is not given to the proponent, sufficiently in advance of the offer to provide the proponent with a fair opportunity to meet the objection or obtain the testimony of a foundation witness, raising a genuine question as to the trustworthiness or authenticity of the record.

Rule 903. Subscribing Witness' Testimony Unnecessary.

The testimony of a subscribing witness is not necessary to authenticate a ~~writing~~ record unless required by the laws of the jurisdiction whose laws govern the validity of the ~~writing~~ record.

ARTICLE X

~~CONTENTS~~ CONTENT OF ~~WRITINGS, RECORDINGS AND PHOTOGRAPHS~~ RECORD, WRITING, RECORDING, PHOTOGRAPH, IMAGE, AND OTHER RECORD

Rule 1001. Definitions.

~~For purposes of this Article the following definitions are applicable~~ In this article:

~~(4)~~ (1) ~~Duplicate. A "duplicate" is~~ "Duplicate" means a counterpart in the form of a record produced by the same impression as the original, ~~or~~ from the same matrix, ~~or~~ by means of photography, including enlargements and miniatures, ~~or~~ by mechanical or electronic re-recording, ~~or~~ by chemical reproduction, or by ~~other~~ another equivalent ~~techniques which~~ technique that accurately reproduces the original.

(2) "Image" means a form of a record which consists of a digitized copy or image of information.

(3) ~~Original.~~ An "original" of a writing, ~~or~~ recording, or other record ~~is~~ means the writing, ~~or~~ recording, or other record itself or any counterpart intended to have the same effect by a person executing or issuing it. ~~An "original" of~~ The term, when applied to a photograph, includes the negative or any print therefrom. The term includes ~~If data are stored in a computer or similar device,~~ a~~ny~~ printout or other perceivable output ~~readable by sight,~~ of a record of data or images stored in a computer or similar device, if shown to reflect the data or images accurately~~, is an "original."~~.

~~(2)~~ (4) ~~Photographs. "Photographs" include~~ "Photograph" means a form of a record which consists of a still ~~photographs~~ photograph, stored image, X-ray ~~films~~ film, video ~~tapes~~ tape, ~~and~~ or motion ~~pictures~~ picture.

~~(1)~~ (5) ~~Writings and recordings. "Writings"~~ "Writing" and ~~"recordings" consist of~~ "recording" mean letters, words, sounds, or numbers, or their equivalent, ~~set down by~~ inscribed on a tangible medium or stored in an electronic or other machine and retrievable in perceivable form by handwriting, typewriting, printing, photostating, photographing, ~~magnetic impulse,~~ mechanical or electronic recording, or other ~~form of data compilation~~ technique.

Rule 1002. Requirement of Original.

To prove the content of a writing, recording, ~~or~~ photograph, or other record, the original record, writing, recording, ~~or~~ photograph, or other record is required, except as otherwise provided in these rules or by [rules adopted by the Supreme Court of this State or by] statute.

Rule 1003. Admissibility of Duplicates.

A duplicate is admissible to the same extent as an original unless ~~(1)~~ a genuine question is raised as to the authenticity or continuing effectiveness of the original or ~~(2)~~ in the circumstances it would be unfair to admit the duplicate in lieu of the original.

Rule 1004. Admissibility of Other Evidence of Contents.

The original is not required, and other evidence of the contents of a ~~writing, recording, or photograph~~ record is admissible if:

(1) ~~Originals lost or destroyed. All~~ all originals are lost or have been destroyed, unless the proponent lost or destroyed them in bad faith;

(2) ~~Original not obtainable. No~~ an original ~~can~~ cannot be obtained by any available judicial process or procedure;

(3) ~~Original in possession of opponent. At~~ at a time when an original was under the control of the party against whom offered, ~~he~~ the party was put on notice, by the pleadings or otherwise, that the contents would be a subject of proof at the hearing~~;~~, and ~~he~~ the party does not produce the original at the hearing; or

(4) ~~Collateral matters. The writing, recording or photograph~~ the record is not closely related to a controlling issue.

Rule 1005. Public Records.

The contents of an official record, or of a ~~document~~ private record authorized to be recorded or filed in the public records and actually recorded or filed, ~~including data compilations in any form,~~ if otherwise admissible, may be proved by a copy in perceivable form, certified as correct in accordance with Rule 902 or testified to be correct by a witness who has compared it with the original. If a copy complying with the foregoing cannot be obtained by the exercise of reasonable diligence, other evidence of the contents may be admitted.

Rule 1006. Summaries.

The contents of voluminous ~~writings, recordings, or photographs~~ records which cannot conveniently be examined in court may be presented in the form of a chart, summary, ~~or~~ calculation, or other perceivable presentation. The ~~originals~~ original, or ~~duplicates~~ a duplicate, ~~shall~~ must be made available for examination or copying, or both, by other parties at a reasonable time and place. The court may order that they be produced in court.

Rule 1007. Testimony, or ~~Written~~ Admission in Record of Party.

~~Contents~~ The contents of a record ~~writings, recordings, or photographs~~ may be proved by the testimony or deposition of the party against whom offered or by ~~his~~ that party's written admission~~,~~ without accounting for the nonproduction of the original.

Rule 1008. Functions of Court and Jury.

~~Whenever~~ If the admissibility under these rules of other evidence of the contents of a record ~~writings, recordings, or photographs under these rules~~ depends upon the fulfillment of a condition of fact, the question whether the condition has been fulfilled is ordinarily for the court to determine in accordance with ~~the provisions of~~ Rule 104. However, ~~when~~ if an issue is raised as to whether ~~(1)~~ the asserted record ~~writing~~ ever existed, ~~or (2)~~ another record ~~writing, recording, or photograph~~ produced at the trial is the original, or ~~(3)~~ other evidence of contents correctly reflects the contents, the issue is for the trier of fact to determine ~~as in the case of other issues of fact~~.

~~ARTICLE XI~~

~~MISCELLANEOUS RULES~~

~~Rule 1101. Rules Applicable.~~

~~(a) Except as otherwise provided in subdivision (b), these rules apply to all actions and proceedings in the [courts of this State].~~

~~(b) Rules inapplicable. The rules other than those with respect to privileges do not apply in the following situations:~~

~~(1) Preliminary questions of fact. The determination of questions of fact preliminary to admissibility of evidence when the issue is to be determined by the court under Rule 104(a).~~

~~(2) Grand jury. Proceedings before grand juries.~~

~~(3) Miscellaneous proceedings. Proceedings for extradition or rendition; [preliminary examination] detention hearing in criminal cases; sentencing, or granting or revoking probation; issuance of warrants for arrest, criminal summonses, and search warrants; and proceedings with respect to release on bail or otherwise.~~

~~(4) **Contempt proceedings** in which the court may act summarily.~~

Appendix II

RESEARCHING EVIDENCE ISSUES ON WESTLAW®

Analysis

Section 1. Introduction

To keep you abreast of current developments, Westlaw provides frequently updated databases. With Westlaw, you have unparalleled legal research resources at your fingertips.

If you have not previously used Westlaw or have questions not covered in this appendix call the West Group Reference Attorneys at 1–800–REF–ATTY (1–800–733–2889). The West Group Reference Attorneys are trained, licensed attorneys, available 24 hours a day to assist you with your Westlaw search questions. To subscribe to Westlaw, call 1–800–344–5008 or visit **www.westlaw.com**.

Section 2. Westlaw Databases

Each database on Westlaw is assigned an abbreviation called an *identifier*, which you use to access the database. You can find identifiers for all databases in the online Westlaw Directory and in the printed *Westlaw Database Directory*. When you need to know more detailed information about a database, use Scope. Scope contains coverage information, lists of related databases and valuable search tips.

The following chart lists Westlaw databases that contain information pertaining to evidence law. For a complete list of databases, see the online Westlaw Directory or the printed *Westlaw Database Directory*. Because new information is continually being added to Westlaw, you should also check Welcome to Westlaw and the Westlaw Directory for new database information.

Selected Westlaw Databases

Database	Identifier	Coverage
Federal Rules, Orders and Statutes		
Federal Rules	US–RULES	Current data
Federal Orders	US–ORDERS	Current data
Federal Rules of Practice & Procedure Advisory Committee Minutes	US–RULESCOMM	Varies by committee
United States Code Annotated®	USCA	Current data
United States Public Laws	US–PL	Current data
Federal and State Case Law Combined		
Federal & State Case Law	ALLCASES	Begins with 1945
Federal & State Case Law–Before 1945	ALLCASES–OLD	1789–1944
Federal Case Law		
Federal Case Law	ALLFEDS	Begins with 1945
Federal Case Law–Before 1945	ALLFEDS–OLD	1789–1944
U.S. Supreme Court Cases	SCT	Begins with 1945
U.S. Supreme Court Cases–Before 1945	SCT–OLD	1790–1944
U.S. Courts of Appeals Cases	CTA	Begins with 1945
U.S. Courts of Appeals Cases–Before 1945	CTA–OLD	1891–1944
U.S. District Courts Cases	DCT	Begins with 1945
U.S. District Courts Cases–Before 1945	DCT–OLD	1789–1944
State Rules, Orders and Statutes		
State Court Rules	RULES–ALL	Varies by state
Individual State Court Rules	XX–RULES (where XX is a state's two-letter postal abbreviation)	Varies by state
State Court Orders	ORDERS–ALL	Varies by state
Individual State Court Orders	XX–ORDERS (where XX is a state's two-letter postal abbreviation)	Varies by state
State Statutes–Annotated	ST–ANN–ALL	Varies by state
Individual State Statutes–Annotated	XX–ST–ANN (where XX is a state's two-letter postal abbreviation)	Varies by state
State Case Law		
State Case Law	ALLSTATES	Begins with 1945

State Case Law Before 1945	ALLSTATES-OLD	1821–1944
Individual State Case Law	XX–CS (where XX is a state's two-letter postal abbreviation)	Varies by state
Texts, Periodicals and Research Tools		
Texts & Periodicals–All Law Reviews, Texts & Bar Journals	TP–ALL	Varies by publication
Bankruptcy Evidence Manual	BKRMANUAL	2002 edition
California Evidence	WITEVID	Fourth edition
Daubert Citator	DAUBERT	Begins with July 1993
Federal Rules Decisions® (Articles from West Reporter)	FEDRDTP	Begins with 1986 (vol. 108)
Handbook of Federal Evidence	FEDEVID	Current data
Reference Manual on Scientific Evidence	RMSCIEVID	Published in 1994
The Rutter Group–California Practice Guide: Civil Trials and Evidence	TRG–CACIVEV	2001 edition
News and Current Events		
All News	ALLNEWS	Varies by source
American Journal of Trial Advocacy	AMJTA	Selected coverage begins with 1982 (vol. 6); full coverage begins with 1993 (vol. 17)
Legal Newspapers	LEGALNP	Varies by publication
National Law Journal, The	NLJ	Begins with October 1989
United States Law Week	BNA–USLW	Begins with January 1986
Westlaw Topical Highlights–Litigation	WTH–LTG	Current data

Section 3. Retrieving a Document with a Citation: Find and Hypertext Links

3.1 Find

Find is a Westlaw service that allows you to retrieve a document by entering its citation. Find allows you to retrieve documents from anywhere in Westlaw without accessing or changing databases. Find is available for many documents, including rules (state and federal), the *United States Code Annotated*®, state statutes, case law (state and federal), administrative materials, texts and periodicals.

To use Find, simply access the Find service and type the citation. The following list provides some examples:

To Find This Document	Access Find and Type
Fed. R. Evid. 612	**fre 612**
Colorado R. Evid. 612	**co st rev 612**
Frye v. United States, 293 F. 1013 (App. D.C. 1923)	**293 f 1013**
State v. Cary, 264 A.2d 209 (N.J. 1970)	**264 a2d 209**

For a complete list of publications that can be retrieved with Find and their abbreviations, consult the Publications list after accessing Find.

3.2 Hypertext Links

Use hypertext links to move from one location to another on Westlaw. For example, use hypertext links to go directly from the statute, case or law review article you are viewing to a cited statute, case or article; from a headnote to the corresponding text in the opinion; or from an entry in a statutes index database to the full text of the statute.

Section 4. Searching with Natural Language: WIN—Westlaw is Natural

Overview: With WIN, you can retrieve documents by simply describing your issue in plain English. If you are a relatively new Westlaw user, Natural Language searching can make it easier for you to retrieve cases that are on point. If you are an experienced Westlaw user, Natural Language gives you a valuable alternative search method.

When you enter a Natural Language description, Westlaw automatically identifies legal phrases, removes common words and generates variations of terms in your description. Westlaw then searches for the concepts in your description. Concepts may include significant terms, phrases, legal citations or topic and key numbers. Westlaw retrieves the 20 documents that most closely match your description, beginning with the document most likely to match.

4.1 Natural Language Search

Access a database, such as Federal Case Law (ALLFEDS). In the text box, type a Natural Language description such as the following:

```
is testimony of a witness after hypnosis admissible
```

4.2 Next Command

Westlaw displays the 20 documents that most closely match your description, beginning with the document most likely to match. If you want to view additional documents, use the Next command or click the right arrow in the left frame.

4.3 Browse Commands

Best Mode: To display the best portion (the portion that most closely matches your description) of each document in your search result, click the **Best Section** or **Best** arrow at the bottom of the window or page.

Standard Browsing Commands: You can also browse your Natural Language search result using standard Westlaw browsing commands, such as citations list, Locate, and term mode.

Section 5. Searching with Terms and Connectors

Overview: With Terms and Connectors searching, you enter a query, which consists of key terms from your issue and connectors specifying the relationship between these terms.

Terms and Connectors searching is useful when you want to retrieve a document for which you know specific details, such as the title or the fact situation. Terms and Connectors searching is also useful when you want to retrieve documents relating to a specific issue.

5.1 Terms

Plurals and Possessives: Plurals are automatically retrieved when you enter the singular form of a term. This is true for both regular and irregular plurals (e.g., **child** retrieves *children*). If you enter the plural form of a term, you will not retrieve the singular form.

If you enter the nonpossessive form of a term, Westlaw automatically retrieves the possessive form as well. However, if you enter the possessive form, only the possessive form is retrieved.

Automatic Equivalencies: Some terms have alternative forms or equivalencies; for example, *5* and *five* are equivalent terms. Westlaw automatically retrieves equivalent terms.

Compound Words, Abbreviations and Acronyms: When a compound word is one of your search terms, use a hyphen to retrieve all forms of the word. For example, the term **cross-claim** retrieves *cross-claim*, *cross claim* and *crossclaim*.

When using an abbreviation or acronym as a search term, place a period after each of the letters to retrieve any of its forms. For example, the term **f.r.e.** retrieves *FRE, F.R.E., F R E* and *F. R. E.* Note: The abbreviation does *not* retrieve *federal rule of evidence* or *Fed.R.Evid.*, so remember to add alternative terms to your query such as **"federal rule of evidence"** or **fed.r.evid**.

The Root Expander and the Universal Character: When you use the Terms and Connectors search method, placing the root expander (!) at the end of a root term generates all other terms with that root. For example, adding the ! to the root *admiss* in the query

```
admiss! /5 evidence
```

instructs Westlaw to retrieve such terms as *admission, admissive, admissible* and *admissibility*.

The universal character (*) stands for one character and can be inserted in the middle or at the end of a term. For example, the term

```
withdr*w
```

will retrieve *withdraw* and *withdrew*. Adding two asterisks to the root *jur*

```
jur**
```

instructs Westlaw to retrieve all forms of the root with up to two additional characters. Terms such as *jury* or *juror* are retrieved by this query. However, terms with more than two letters following the root, such as *jurisdiction*, are not retrieved. Plurals are always retrieved, even if more than two letters follow the root.

Phrase Searching: To search for an exact phrase, place it within quotation marks. For example, to search for references to *judicial notice*, type **"judicial notice"**. When you are using the Terms and Connectors search method, you should use phrase searching only if you are certain that the terms in the phrase will not appear in any other order.

5.2 Alternative Terms

After selecting the terms for your query, consider which alternative terms are necessary. For example, if you are searching for the term *admissible*, you might also want to search for the term *inadmissible*. You should consider both synonyms and antonyms as alternative terms. You can also use the Westlaw thesaurus to add alternative terms to your query.

5.3 Connectors

After selecting terms and alternative terms for your query, use connectors to specify the relationship that should exist between search terms in your retrieved documents. The connectors are described below:

Use:	**To retrieve documents with:**	**Example:**
& (and)	both terms	**expert & opinion**
or (space)	either term or both terms	**relevan! irrelevan!**
/p	search terms in the same paragraph	**hearsay /p exception**
/s	search terms in the same sentence	**character /s witness**
+s	the first search term preceding the second within the same sentence	**burden +s prov*** proof**
/n	search terms within *n* terms of each other (where *n* is a number)	**refresh! /3 memory**
+n	the first search term preceding the second by *n* terms (where *n* is a number)	**excited +3 utterance**
" "	search terms appearing in the same order as in the quotation marks	**"past recollection recorded"**
Use:	**To exclude documents with:**	**Example:**
% (but not)	search terms following the % symbol	**d.n.a. "deoxyribonucleic acid" % criminal**

5.4 Field Restrictions

Overview: Documents in each Westlaw database consist of several segments, or fields. One field may contain the citation, another the title, another the synopsis and so forth. Not all databases contain the same fields. Also depending on the database, fields with the same name may contain different types of information.

To view a list of fields for a specific database and their contents, see Scope for that database. Note that in some databases not every field is available for every document.

To retrieve only those documents containing your search terms in a specific field, restrict your search to that field. To restrict your search to a specific field, type the field name or abbreviation followed by your search terms enclosed in parentheses. For example, to retrieve a case in the Federal & State Case Law database (ALLCASES) entitled *Daubert v. Merrell Dow Pharmaceuticals,* search for your terms in the title field (ti):

ti(daubert & "merrell dow")

The fields discussed below are available in Westlaw databases you might use for researching evidence issues.

Digest and Synopsis Fields: The digest (di) and synopsis (sy) fields, added to case law databases by West's attorney-editors, summarize the main points of a case. The synopsis field contains a brief description of a case. The digest field contains the topic and headnote fields and includes the complete hierarchy of concepts used by West's editors to classify the headnotes to specific West digest topics and key numbers. Restricting your search to the synopsis and digest fields limits your result to cases in which your terms are related to a major issue in the case.

Consider restricting your search to one or both of these fields if

- you are searching for common terms or terms with more than one meaning, and you need to narrow your search; or
- you cannot narrow your search by using a smaller database.

For example, to retrieve state cases that discuss nonverbal conduct as hearsay, access the State Case Law database (ALLSTATES) and type the following query:

sy,di(non-verbal /s conduct /p hearsay)

Headnote Field: The headnote field (he) is part of the digest field, but does not contain topic numbers, hierarchical classification information or key numbers. The headnote field contains a one-sentence summary for each point of law in a case and any supporting citations given by the author of the opinion. A headnote field restriction is useful when you are searching for specific statutory sections or rule numbers. For example, to retrieve headnotes from federal cases that cite Fed. R. Evid. 803(1), access the Federal Case Law database (ALLFEDS) and type the following query:

he(803(1))

Topic Field: The topic field (to) is also part of the digest field. It contains hierarchical classification information, including the West digest topic names and numbers and the key numbers. You should restrict search terms to the topic field in a case law database if

- a digest field search retrieves too many documents; or
- you want to retrieve cases with digest paragraphs classified under more than one topic.

For example, the topic Evidence has the topic number 157. To retrieve U.S. district courts cases that discuss the admissibility of hearsay evidence based on the excited utterance exception, access the U.S. District Courts Cases database (DCT) and type a query like the following:

to(157) /p "excited utterance"

To retrieve cases classified under more than one topic and key number, search for your terms in the topic field. For example, to search for cases discussing hearsay evidence, which may be classified to Criminal Law (110), Evidence (157) or Searches and Seizures (349), among other topics, type a query like the following:

to(hearsay)

For a complete list of West digest topics and their corresponding topic numbers, access the Key Number Service or Custom Digest.

Note Slips opinions and cases from topical services do not contain the digest, headnote and topic fields.

Prelim and Caption Fields: When searching in a database containing statutes, rules or regulations, restrict your search to the prelim (pr) and caption (ca) fields to retrieve documents in which your terms are important enough to appear in a section name or heading. For example, to retrieve federal rules regarding hearsay, access the Federal Rules database (US–RULES) and type the following:

pr,ca(hearsay)

5.5 Date Restrictions

You can use Westlaw to retrieve documents *decided* or *issued* before, after or on a specified date, as well as within a range of dates. The following sample queries contain date restrictions:

da(1999) & "dying declaration"

da(aft 1995) & "dying declaration"

da(10/23/1998) & "dying declaration"

You can also search for documents *added to a database* on or after a specified date, as well as within a range of dates. The following sample queries contain added-date restrictions:

ad(aft 1996) & "dying declaration"

ad(aft 2-1-1998 & bef 2-17-1998) & "dying declaration"

Section 6. Searching with Topic and Key Numbers

To retrieve cases that address a specific point of law, use topic and key numbers as your search terms. If you have an on-point case, run a search using the topic and key number from the relevant headnote in an appropriate database to find other cases containing headnotes classified to that topic and key number. For example, to search for federal cases containing headnotes classified under topic 157 (Evidence) and key number 551 (Hypothetical Questions and Answers), access the Federal Case Law database (ALLFEDS) and enter the following query:

157k551

For a complete list of West digest topic and key numbers, access the Key Number Service or Custom Digest.

Note: Slip opinions and cases from topical services do not contain West topic and key numbers.

Section 7. Verifying Your Research with Citation Research Services

Overview: A citation research service is a tool that helps you ensure that your cases are good law; helps you retrieve cases, legislation or articles that cite a case, rule or statute; and helps you verify that the spelling and format of your citations are correct.

7.1 KeyCite for Cases

KeyCite for cases covers case law on Westlaw, including unpublished opinions. KeyCite for cases provides

- direct appellate history of a case, including related references, which are opinions involving the same parties and facts but resolving different issues
- negative indirect history of a case, which consists of cases outside the direct appellate line that may have a negative impact on its precedential value
- the title, parallel citations, court of decision, docket number and filing date of a case
- citations to cases, administrative decisions and secondary sources on Westlaw that have cited a case
- complete integration with the West Key Number System® so you can track legal issues discussed in a case

7.2 KeyCite for Statutes and Federal Regulations

KeyCite for statutes and federal regulations covers the *United States Code Annotated* (USCA®), the *Code of Federal Regulations* (CFR), and statutes from all 50 states. KeyCite for statutes provides

- links to session laws amending or repealing a statute
- statutory credits and historical notes
- citations to pending legislation affecting a federal statute or a statute from California or New York
- citations to cases, administrative decisions and secondary sources that have cited a statute

7.3 KeyCite for Administrative Materials

KeyCite for administrative materials includes

- National Labor Relations Board decisions beginning with 1935
- Board of Contract Appeals decisions (varies by agency)
- Board of Immigration Appeals decisions beginning with 1940
- Comptroller General decisions beginning with 1921
- Environmental Protection Agency decisions beginning with 1974
- Federal Communications Commission decisions beginning with 1960
- Federal Energy Regulatory Commission (Federal Power Commission) decisions beginning with 1931 (history only)
- Internal Revenue Service revenue rulings beginning with 1954
- Internal Revenue Service revenue procedures beginning with 1954
- Internal Revenue Service private letter rulings beginning with 1954
- Internal Revenue Service technical advice memoranda beginning with 1954
- Public Utilities Reports beginning with 1974 (history only)
- U.S. Merit Systems Protection Board decisions beginning with 1979
- U.S. Patent and Trademark Office decisions beginning with 1987
- U.S. Tax Court (Board of Tax Appeals) decisions beginning with 1924
- U.S. patents beginning with 1976

7.4 KeyCite Alert

KeyCite Alert monitors the status of your cases or statutes and automatically sends you updates at the frequency you specify when their KeyCite information changes.

Section 8. Researching with Westlaw—Examples

8.1 Retrieving Law Review Articles

Recent law review articles are often a good place to begin researching a legal issue because law review articles serve 1) as an excellent introduction to a new topic or review for a stale one, providing terminology to help you formulate a query; 2) as a finding tool for pertinent primary authority, such as rules, statutes and cases; and 3) in some instances, as persuasive secondary authority.

Suppose you need to gain more background information on the factors that courts have considered in determining whether it is appropriate for lay witnesses to give opinion testimony.

Solution

- To retrieve law review articles relevant to your issue, access the Journals & Law Reviews database (JLR). Using the Natural Language search method, enter a description like the following:

  opinion testimony by lay witnesses

- If you have a citation to an article in a specific publication, use Find to retrieve it. For more information on Find, see Section 3.1 of this appendix. For example, to retrieve the article found at 12 Touro L. Rev. 513, access Find and type

  12 touro l rev 513

- If you know the title of an article but not which journal it appeared in, access the Journals & Law Reviews database (JLR) and search for key terms from the title in the title field. For example, to retrieve the article "The Movement from Frye to Daubert: Where Do the States Stand?" type the following Terms and Connectors query:

  ti(movement & frye & daubert & states)

8.2 Retrieving Rules

Suppose you need to retrieve federal rules dealing with relevancy of character evidence.

Solution

- Access the Federal Rules database (US-RULES). Search for your terms in the prelim and caption fields using the Terms and Connectors search method:

  pr,ca(relevan! & character)

- When you know the citation for a specific rule or statute, use Find to retrieve it. For example, to retrieve Fed. R. Evid. 410, access Find and type

```
fre 410
```

- To look at surrounding rules, use the Table of Contents service. Click a hypertext link in the prelim or caption field or click the **TOC** tab in the left frame. You can also use Documents in Sequence to retrieve the rule following Fed. R. Evid. 410, even if that following section was not retrieved with your search or Find request.
- When you retrieve a rule on Westlaw, it will contain a message if a court order amending or repealing it is available online. To display the order, click the hypertext link in the message.

Because slip copy versions of laws are added to Westlaw before they contain full editorial enhancements, they are not retrieved with the update feature. To retrieve slip copy versions of laws, access the United States Public Laws database (US-PL), then type **ci(slip)** and descriptive terms, e.g., **ci(slip) & evidence.** Slip copy documents are replaced by the editorially enhanced versions within a few working days. The update feature also does not retrieve legislation or court orders that enact a new rule. To retrieve these materials, access US-PL or the Federal Orders database (US-ORDERS) and enter a query containing terms that describe the rule.

8.3 Retrieving Case Law

Suppose you need to retrieve New York case law dealing with the priest-penitent privilege.

Solution

- Access the New York Cases database (NY–CS). Type a Natural Language description such as the following:

```
waiver of priest-penitent privilege
```

- When you know the citation for a specific case, use Find to retrieve it. (For more information on Find, see Section 3.1 of this appendix.) For example, to retrieve *Darrow. v. Gunn*, 594 F.2d 767 (9th Cir. 1979), access Find and type

```
594 f2d 767
```

- If you find a topic and key number that is on point, run a search using that topic and key number to retrieve additional cases discussing that point of law. For example, to retrieve cases containing headnotes classified under topic 410 (Witnesses) and key number 215 (Confessions or Other Communications to Clergyman or Minister of Religion), type the following query:

```
410k215
```

- To retrieve cases written by a particular judge, add a judge field (ju) restriction to your query. For example, to retrieve cases written by

Justice White that contain headnotes classified under topic 157 (Evidence), type the following query:

```
ju(white) & to(157)
```

8.4 Using KeyCite

Suppose one of the cases you retrieve in your case law research is *Frye v. United States*, 293 F. 1013 (App. D.C. 1923). You want to determine whether this case is good law and to find other cases that have cited this case.

Solution

- Use KeyCite to retrieve direct history and negative indirect history for *Frye v. United States*.
- Use KeyCite to display citing references for *Frye*.

8.5 Following Recent Developments

As the evidence law specialist in your firm, you are expected to keep up with and summarize recent legal developments in this area of the law. How can you do this efficiently?

Solution

One of the easiest ways to stay abreast of recent developments in the area of evidence and litigation is by accessing the Westlaw Topical Highlights–Litigation database (WTH–LTG). The WTH–LTG database contains summaries of recent legal developments, including court decisions, legislation and changes in the area of litigation. Some summaries also contain suggested queries that combine the proven power of West's topic and key numbers and West's case headnotes to retrieve additional pertinent cases. When you access WTH–LTG you will automatically retrieve a list of documents added to the database in the last two weeks.

Appendix III

CALIFORNIA EVIDENCE CODE*

DIVISION 1. PRELIMINARY PROVISIONS AND CONSTRUCTION

Analysis

DIVISION 2. WORDS AND PHRASES DEFINED

* Current through the 1997-98 legislative sessions.

Sec.
230. "Statute".
235. "Trier of fact".
240. "Unavailable as a witness".
250. "Writing".
255. "Original".
260. "Duplicate".

DIVISION 3. GENERAL PROVISIONS

CHAPTER 1. APPLICABILITY OF CODE

300. Applicability of code.

CHAPTER 2. PROVINCE OF COURT AND JURY

310. Questions of law for court.
311. Foreign law applicable; law undetermined; procedures.
312. Jury as trier of fact.

CHAPTER 3. ORDER OF PROOF

320. Power of court to regulate order of proof.

CHAPTER 4. ADMITTING AND EXCLUDING EVIDENCE

ARTICLE 1. GENERAL PROVISIONS

350. Only relevant evidence admissible.
351. Admissibility of relevant evidence.
351.1. Polygraph examinations; results, opinion of examiner or reference; exclusion.
352. Discretion of court to exclude evidence.
352.1. Criminal sex acts; victim's address and telephone number.
353. Erroneous admission of evidence; effect.
354. Erroneous exclusion of evidence; effect.
355. Limited admissibility.
356. Entire act, declaration, conversation, or writing, to elucidate part offered.

ARTICLE 2. PRELIMINARY DETERMINATIONS ON ADMISSIBILITY OF EVIDENCE

400. "Preliminary Fact".
401. "Proffered evidence".
402. Procedure for determining foundational and other preliminary facts.
403. Determination of foundational and other preliminary facts where relevancy, personal knowledge, or authenticity is disputed.
404. Determination of whether proffered evidence is incriminatory.
405. Determination of foundational and other preliminary facts in other cases.
406. Evidence affecting weight or credibility.

CHAPTER 5. WEIGHT OF EVIDENCE GENERALLY

410. Direct evidence.
411. Direct evidence of one witness sufficient.
412. Party having power to produce better evidence.
413. Party's failure to explain or deny evidence.

CALIFORNIA EVIDENCE CODE

DIVISION 4. JUDICIAL NOTICE

DIVISION 5. BURDEN OF PROOF; BURDEN OF PRODUCING EVIDENCE; PRESUMPTIONS AND INFERENCES

CHAPTER 1. BURDEN OF PROOF

ARTICLE 1. GENERAL

ARTICLE 2. BURDEN OF PROOF ON SPECIFIC ISSUES

CHAPTER 2. BURDEN OF PRODUCING EVIDENCE

CHAPTER 3. PRESUMPTIONS AND INFERENCES

ARTICLE 1. GENERAL

ARTICLE 2. CONCLUSIVE PRESUMPTIONS

APPENDIX III

CHAPTER 4. PARTICULAR PRIVILEGES

CHAPTER 2. MEDIATION

CHAPTER 3. OTHER EVIDENCE AFFECTED OR EXCLUDED BY EXTRINSIC POLICIES

APPENDIX III

CALIFORNIA EVIDENCE CODE

TABLE OF SECTIONS AFFECTED

These tables indicate sections affected by 2002 legislation

Evidence Code

Sec.	Effect	Chap.	Sec.
250	Amended	945	1
300	Amended	784	101
452.5	Amended	784	102
795	Amended	1013	77
912	Amended	72	1
917	Amended	72	2
952	Amended	72	3
1014	Amended	1013	78
prec.1030 (Art. heading)	Amended	806	18
1030	Amended	806	19
1031	Amended	806	20
1032	Amended	806	21
1033	Amended	806	22
1034	Amended	806	23
1037.8	Added	629	1
1043	Amended	391	1
1045	Amended	391	2
1046	Amended	391	3
1047	Amended	391	4
1061	Amended	784	103
1108	Amended	194	1
		828	1
1550	Amended	124	1

APPENDIX III

DIVISION 1. PRELIMINARY PROVISIONS AND CONSTRUCTION

§ 1. Short title

This code shall be known as the Evidence Code.

§ 2. Common law rule construing code abrogated

The rule of the common law, that statutes in derogation thereof are to be strictly construed, has no application to this code. This code establishes the law of this state respecting the subject to which it relates, and its provisions are to be liberally construed with a view to effecting its objects and promoting justice.

§ 3. Severability

If any provision or clause of this code or application thereof to any person or circumstances is held invalid, such invalidity shall not affect other provisions or applications of the code which can be given effect without the invalid provision or application, and to this end the provisions of this code are declared to be severable.

LAW REVISION COMMISSION COMMENT

Section 3 is the same as Section 1108 of the Commercial Code. See also, e.g., Vehicle Code § 5. This general "severability" provision permits the repeal of comparable provisions applicable to specific sections formerly compiled in the Code of Civil Procedure that are now compiled in the Evidence Code and makes it unnecessary to include similar provisions in future amendments to this code. See Code Civ.Proc. § 1928.4 (superseded by the Evidence Code). [7 Cal.L.Rev.Comm. Reports 1 (1965)]

§ 4. Construction of code

Unless the provision or context otherwise requires, these preliminary provisions and rules of construction shall govern the construction of this code.

§ 5. Effect of headings

Division, chapter, article, and section headings do not in any manner affect the scope, meaning, or intent of the provisions of this code.

§ 6. References to statutes

Whenever any reference is made to any portion of this code or of any other statute, such reference shall apply to all amendments and additions heretofore or hereafter made.

§ 7. "Division," "chapter," "article," "section," "subdivision," and "paragraph"

Unless otherwise expressly stated:

(a) "Division" means a division of this code.

(b) "Chapter" means a chapter of the division in which that term occurs.

(c) "Article" means an article of the chapter in which that term occurs.

(d) "Section" means a section of this code.

(e) "Subdivision" means a subdivision of the section in which that term occurs.

(f) "Paragraph" means a paragraph of the subdivision in which that term occurs.

§ 8. Construction of tenses

The present tense includes the past and future tenses; and the future, the present.

§ 9. Construction of genders

The masculine gender includes the feminine and neuter.

§ 10. Construction of singular and plural

The singular number includes the plural; and the plural, the singular.

§ 11. "Shall" and "may"

"Shall" is mandatory and "may" is permissive.

§ 12. Code becomes operative January 1, 1967; effect on pending proceedings

(a) This code shall become operative on January 1, 1967, and shall govern proceedings in actions brought on or after that date and, except as provided in subdivision (b), further proceedings in actions pending on that date.

(b) Subject to subdivision (c), a trial commenced before January 1, 1967, shall not be governed by this code. For the purpose of this subdivision:

(1) A trial is commenced when the first witness is sworn or the first exhibit is admitted into evidence and is terminated when the issue upon which such evidence is received is submitted to the trier of fact. A new trial, or a separate trial of a different issue,

commenced on or after January 1, 1967, shall be governed by this code.

(2) If an appeal is taken from a ruling made at a trial commenced before January 1, 1967, the appellate court shall apply the law applicable at the time of the commencement of the trial.

(c) The provisions of Division 8 (commencing with Section 900) relating to privileges shall govern any claim of privilege made after December 31, 1966.

LEGISLATIVE COMMITTEE COMMENT—ASSEMBLY COMMITTEE ON JUDICIARY

The delayed operative date provides time for California judges and attorneys to become familiar with the code before it goes into effect.

Subdivision (a) makes it clear that the Evidence Code governs all trials commenced after December 31, 1966.

Under subdivision (b), a trial that has actually commenced prior to the operative date of the code will continue to be governed by the rules of evidence (except privileges) applicable at the commencement of the trial. Thus, if the trial court makes a ruling on the admission of evidence in a trial commenced prior to January 1, 1967, such ruling (even when it is made after January 1, 1967) is not affected by the enactment of the Evidence Code; if an appeal is taken from the ruling, Section 12 requires the appellate court to apply the law applicable at the commencement of the trial. On the other hand, any ruling made by the trial court on the admission of evidence in a trial commenced after December 31, 1966, is governed by the Evidence Code, even if a previous trial in the same action was commenced prior to that date.

A hearing on a motion or a similar proceeding is to be treated the same as a trial for the purpose of applying the rules stated in subdivision (b). See subdivision (b)(1).

Under subdivision (c), all claims of privilege made after December 31, 1966, are governed by the Evidence Code in order that there might be no delay in providing protection to the important relationships and interests that are protected by the Privileges Division.

DIVISION 2. WORDS AND PHRASES DEFINED

§ 100. Application of definitions

Unless the provision or context otherwise requires, these definitions govern the construction of this code.

§ 105. "Action"

"Action" includes a civil action and a criminal action.

LAW REVISION COMMISSION COMMENT

Defining the word "action" to include both a civil action or proceeding and a criminal action or proceeding eliminates the necessity of repeating "civil action and criminal action" in numerous code sections. [7 Cal.L.Rev.Comm. Reports 1 (1965)]

§ 110. "Burden of producing evidence"

"Burden of producing evidence" means the obligation of a party to introduce evidence sufficient to avoid a ruling against him on the issue.

COMMENT—ASSEMBLY COMMITTEE ON JUDICIARY

The phrases defined in Sections 110 and 115 provide a convenient means for distinguishing between the burden of proving a fact and the burden of going forward with the evidence. They recognize a distinction that is well established in California. Witkin, California Evidence §§ 53–60 (1958). The practical effect of the distinction is discussed in the Comments to Division 5 (commencing with Section 500), especially in the Comments to Sections 500 and 550.

§ 115. "Burden of proof"

"Burden of proof" means the obligation of a party to establish by evidence a requisite degree of belief concerning a fact in the mind of the trier of fact or the court. The burden of proof may require a party to raise a reasonable doubt concerning the existence or nonexistence of a fact or that he establish the existence or nonexistence of a fact by a preponderance of the evidence, by clear and convincing proof, or by proof beyond a reasonable doubt.

Except as otherwise provided by law, the burden of proof requires proof by a preponderance of the evidence.

COMMENT—ASSEMBLY COMMITTEE ON JUDICIARY

See the Comment to Section 110.

After stating the general definition of "burden of proof," the first paragraph of Section 115 gives examples of specific burdens that may be imposed by statutory or decisional law. The list of examples is not exclusive, and in some cases the law may prescribe some other burden of proof. For example, under Penal Code Section 872, the prosecution's burden of proof at a preliminary hearing is to establish "sufficient cause"—i.e., a "strong suspicion"—of the accused's guilt. Garabedian v. Superior Court, 59 Cal.2d 124, 28 Cal.Rptr. 318, 378 P.2d 590 (1963); Rogers v. Superior Court, 46 Cal.2d 3, 291 P.2d 929 (1955).

The second paragraph of Section 115 makes it clear that "burden of proof" refers to the burden of proving the fact in question by a preponderance of the evidence unless a heavier or lesser burden of proof is specifically required in a particular case by constitutional, statutory, or decisional law. See the definition of "law" in Evidence Code § 160.

§ 120. "Civil action"

"Civil action" includes civil proceedings.

LAW REVISION COMMISSION COMMENT

Defining "civil action" to include civil proceedings eliminates the necessity of repeating "civil action or proceeding" in numerous code sections, and, together with the definition of "criminal action" in Section 130, it assures the applicability of the Evidence Code to all actions and proceedings. See Evidence Code § 300. [7 Cal.L.Rev.Comm. Reports 1 (1965)]

§ 125. "Conduct"

"Conduct" includes all active and passive behavior, both verbal and nonverbal.

§ 130. "Criminal action"

"Criminal action" includes criminal proceedings.

§ 135. "Declarant"

"Declarant" is a person who makes a statement.

LAW REVISION COMMISSION COMMENT

Ordinarily, the word "declarant" is used in the Evidence Code to refer to a person who makes a hearsay statement as distinguished from the witness who testifies to the content of the statement. See Evidence Code § 1200 and the Comment thereto. [7 Cal.L.Rev.Comm. Reports 1 (1965)]

§ 140. "Evidence"

"Evidence" means testimony, writings, material objects, or other things presented to the senses that are offered to prove the existence or nonexistence of a fact.

LAW REVISION COMMISSION COMMENT

"Evidence" is defined broadly to include the testimony of witnesses, tangible objects, sights (such as a jury view or the appearance of a person exhibited to a jury), sounds (such as the sound of a voice demonstrated for a jury), and any other thing that may be presented as a basis of proof. The definition includes anything offered in evidence whether or not it is technically inadmissible and whether or not it is received. For example, Division 10 (commencing with Section 1200) uses "evidence" to refer to hearsay which may be excluded as inadmissible but which may be admitted if no proper objection is made. Thus, when inadmissible hearsay or opinion testimony is admitted without objection, this definition makes it clear that it constitutes evidence that may be considered by the trier of fact.

Section 140 is a better statement of existing law than Code of Civil Procedure Section 1823, which is superseded by Section 140. Although Section 1823 by its terms restricts "judicial evidence" to that "sanctioned by law," the general principle is well established that matter which is technically inadmissible under an exclusionary rule is nonetheless evidence and may be considered in support of a judgment if it is offered and received in evidence without proper objection or motion to strike. E.g., People v. Alexander, 212 Cal.App.2d 84, 98, 27 Cal.Rptr. 720, 727 (1963) ("illustrations of this principle are numerous and cover a wide range of evidentiary topics such as incompetent hearsay, secondary evidence violating the best evidence rule, inadmissible opinions, lack of foundation, incompetent, privileged or unqualified witnesses, and violations of the parol evidence rule"). See Witkin, California Evidence §§ 723–724 (1958).

Under this definition, a presumption is not evidence. See also Evidence Code § 600 and the Comment thereto. [7 Cal.L.Rev.Comm. Reports 1 (1965)]

§ 145. "The hearing"

"The hearing" means the hearing at which a question under this code arises, and not some earlier or later hearing.

LAW REVISION COMMISSION COMMENT

"The hearing" is defined to mean the hearing at which the particular question under the Evidence Code arises, and, unless a particular provision or its context otherwise indicates, not some earlier or later hearing. This definition is much broader than would be a reference to the trial itself; the definition includes, for example, preliminary hearings and post-trial proceedings. [7 Cal.L Rev.Comm. Reports 1 (1965)]

§ 150. "Hearsay evidence"

"Hearsay evidence" is defined in Section 1200.

LAW REVISION COMMISSION COMMENT

Because of its special significance to Division 10, the substantive definition of "hearsay evidence" is contained in Section 1200. See the Comment to Section 1200. [7 Cal.L.Rev.Comm. Reports 1 (1965)]

§ 160. "Law"

"Law" includes constitutional, statutory, and decisional law.

LAW REVISION COMMISSION COMMENT

This definition makes it clear that a reference to "law" includes the law established by judicial decisions as well as by constitutional and statutory provisions. [7 Cal.L.Rev.Comm. Reports 1 (1965)]

§ 165. "Oath"

"Oath" includes affirmation or declaration under penalty of perjury.

§ 170. "Perceive"

"Perceive" means to acquire knowledge through one's senses.

§ 175. "Person"

"Person" includes a natural person, firm, association, organization, partnership, business trust, corporation, limited liability company, or public entity.

§ 180. "Personal property"

"Personal property" includes money, goods, chattels, things in action, and evidences of debt.

§ 185. "Property"

"Property" includes both real and personal property.

§ 190. "Proof"

"Proof" is the establishment by evidence of a requisite degree of belief concerning a fact in the mind of the trier of fact or the court.

LAW REVISION COMMISSION COMMENT

This definition is more accurate than the definition of "proof" in Code of Civil Procedure Section 1824, which is superseded by Section 190. The disjunctive reference to "the trier of fact or the court" is needed because, even when the jury is the trier of fact, the court is required to determine preliminary questions of fact on the basis of proof. [7 Cal.L.Rev.Comm. Reports 1 (1965)]

§ 195. "Public employee"

"Public employee" means an officer, agent, or employee of a public entity.

LAW REVISION COMMISSION COMMENT

This definition specifically includes public officers and agents, thereby eliminating any distinction between employees and officers and making it unnecessary to repeat the phrase "officer, agent, or employee" in numerous code sections. [7 Cal.L.Rev.Comm. Reports 1 (1965)]

§ 200. "Public entity"

"Public entity" includes a nation, state, county, city and county, city, district, public authority, public agency, or any other political subdivision or public corporation, whether foreign or domestic.

LAW REVISION COMMISSION COMMENT

The broad definition of "public entity" includes every form of public authority, both foreign and domestic. Occasionally, "public entity" is used in the Evidence Code with limiting language to refer specifically to entities within this State or the United States. E.g., Evidence Code § 452(b). Cf. Evidence Code § 452(f). [7 Cal.L.Rev.Comm. Reports 1 (1965)]

§ 205. "Real property"

"Real property" includes lands, tenements, and hereditaments.

§ 210. "Relevant evidence"

"Relevant evidence" means evidence, including evidence relevant to the credibility of a witness or hearsay declarant, having any tendency in reason to prove or disprove any disputed fact that is of consequence to the determination of the action.

LAW REVISION COMMISSION COMMENT

This definition restates existing law. E.g., Larson v. Solbakken, 221 Cal.App.2d 410, 419, 34 Cal.Rptr. 450, 455 (1963); People v. Lint, 182 Cal.App.2d 402, 415, 6 Cal.Rptr. 95, 102–103 (1960). Thus, under Section 210, "relevant evidence" includes not only evidence of the ultimate facts actually in dispute but also evidence of other facts from which such ultimate facts may be presumed or inferred. This retains existing law as found in subdivisions 1 and 15 of Code of Civil Procedure Section 1870, which are superseded by the Evidence Code. In addition, Section 210 makes it clear that evidence relating to the credibility of witnesses and hearsay declarants is "relevant evidence." This restates existing law. See Code Civ.Proc. §§ 1868, 1870(16) (credibility of witnesses), which are superseded by the Evidence Code, and Tentative Recommendation and a Study Relating to the Uniform Rules of Evidence (Article VIII. Hearsay Evidence), 6 Cal.Law Revision Comm'n, Rep., Rec. & Studies Appendix at 339–340, 569–575 (1964) (credibility of hearsay declarants). [7 Cal.L.Rev.Comm. Reports 1 (1965)]

§ 220. "State"

"State" means the State of California, unless applied to the different parts of the United States. In the latter case, it includes any state, district, commonwealth, territory, or insular possession of the United States.

§ 225. "Statement"

"Statement" means (a) oral or written verbal expression or (b) nonverbal conduct of a person intended by him as a substitute for oral or written verbal expression.

§ 230. "Statute"

"Statute" includes a treaty and a constitutional provision.

LAW REVISION COMMISSION COMMENT

In the Evidence Code, "statute" includes a constitutional provision. Thus, for example, when a particular section in subject to any exceptions "otherwise provided by statute," exceptions provided by the Constitution also are applicable. [7 Cal.L.Rev.Comm. Reports 1 (1965)]

§ 235. "Trier of fact"

"Trier of fact" includes (a) the jury and (b) the court when the court is trying an issue of fact other than one relating to the admissibility of evidence.

LAW REVISION COMMISSION COMMENT

"Trier of fact" is defined to include not only the jury but also the court when it is trying an issue of fact without a jury. The definition is not exclusive; a referee, court commissioner, or other officer conducting proceedings governed by the Evidence Code may be a trier of fact. See Evidence Code § 300. [7 Cal.L.Rev.Comm. Reports 1 (1965)]

§ 240. "Unavailable as a witness"

(a) Except as otherwise provided in subdivision (b), "unavailable as a witness" means that the declarant is any of the following:

(1) Exempted or precluded on the ground of privilege from testifying concerning the matter to which his or her statement is relevant.

(2) Disqualified from testifying to the matter.

(3) Dead or unable to attend or to testify at the hearing because of then existing physical or mental illness or infirmity.

(4) Absent from the hearing and the court is unable to compel his or her attendance by its process.

(5) Absent from the hearing and the proponent of his or her statement has exercised reasonable diligence but has been unable to procure his or her attendance by the court's process.

(b) A declarant is not unavailable as a witness if the exemption, preclusion, disqualification, death, inability, or absence of the declarant was brought about by the procurement or wrongdoing of the proponent of his or her statement for the purpose of preventing the declarant from attending or testifying.

(c) Expert testimony which establishes that physical or mental trauma resulting from an alleged crime has caused harm to a witness of sufficient severity that the witness is physically unable to testify or is unable to testify without suffering substantial trauma may constitute a sufficient showing of unavailability pursuant to paragraph (3) of subdivision (a). As used in this section, the term "expert" means a physician and surgeon, including a psychiatrist, or any person described by subdivision (b), (c), or (e) of Section 1010.

The introduction of evidence to establish the unavailability of a witness under this subdivision shall not be deemed procurement of unavailability, in absence of proof to the contrary.

COMMENT—ASSEMBLY COMMITTEE ON JUDICIARY

Usually, the phrase "unavailable as a witness" is used in the Evidence Code to state the condition that must be met whenever the admissibility of hearsay evidence is dependent upon the declarant's present unavailability to testify. See, e.g., Evidence Code §§ 1230, 1251, 1291, 1292, 1310, 1311, 1323. See also Code Civ.Proc. § 2016(d)(3) and Penal Code §§ 1345 and 1362, relating to depositions.

"Unavailable as a witness" includes, in addition to cases where the declarant is physically unavailable (i.e., dead, insane, or beyond the reach of the court's process), situations in which the declarant is legally unavailable (i.e., prevented from testifying by a claim of privilege or disqualified from testifying). Of course, if the declaration made out of court is itself privileged, the fact that the declarant is unavailable to testify at the hearing on the ground of privilege does not make the declaration admissible. The exceptions to the hearsay rule that are set forth in Division 10 (commencing with Section 1200) of the Evidence Code do not declare that the evidence described is necessarily admissible. They merely declare that such evidence is not inadmissible under the hearsay rule. If there is some other rule of law—such as privilege—which makes the evidence inadmissible, the court is not authorized to admit the evidence merely because it falls within an exception to the hearsay rule. Accordingly, the hearsay exceptions permit the introduction of evidence where the declarant is unavailable because of privilege only if the declaration itself is not privileged or is not inadmissible for some other reason.

Subdivision (b) is designed to establish safeguards against sharp practices and, in the words of the Commissioners on Uniform State Laws, to assure "that unavailability is honest and not planned in order to gain an advantage." Uniform Rules of Evidence, Rule 62 Comment. Under this subdivision, a party may not arrange a declarant's disappearance in order to use the declarant's out-of-court statement. Moreover, if the out-of- court statement is that of the party himself, he may not create "unavailability" under this section by invoking a privilege not to testify.

Section 240 substitutes a uniform standard for the varying standards of unavailability provided by the superseded Code of Civil Procedure sections providing hearsay exceptions. E.g., Code Civ.Proc. § 1870(4), (8). The conditions constituting unavailability under these superseded sections vary from exception to exception without apparent reason. Under some of these sections, the evidence is admissible if the declarant is dead; under others, the evidence is admissible if the declarant is dead or insane; under still others, the evidence is admissible if the declarant is absent from the jurisdiction. Despite the express language of these superseded sections, Section 24 may, to a considerable extent, restate existing law. Compare People v. Spriggs, 60 Cal.2d 868, 875, 36 Cal.Rptr. 841, 845, 389 P.2d 377, 381 (1964) (generally consistent with Section 240), with the older cases, some but not all of which are inconsistent with the Spriggs case and with Section 240. See the cases cited in Tentative Recommendation and a Study Relating to the Uniform Rules of Evidence (Article VIII. Hearsay Evidence), 6 Cal.Law Revision Comm'n, Rep., Rec. & Studies Appendix at 411 note 7 (1964).

§ 250. "Writing"

"Writing" means handwriting, typewriting, printing, photostating, photographing, photocopying, transmitting by electronic mail or facsimile, and every other means of recording upon any tangible thing any form of communication or representation, including letters, words, pictures, sounds, or symbols, or combinations thereof and any record thereby created, regardless of the manner in which the record has been stored.

LAW REVISION COMMISSION COMMENT

"Writing" is defined very broadly to include all forms of tangible expression, including pictures and sound recordings. [7 Cal.L.Rev. Comm. Reports 1 (1965)]

§ 255. "Original"

"Original" means the writing itself or any counterpart intended to have the same effect by a person executing or issuing it. An "original" of a photograph includes the negative or any print therefrom. If data are stored in a computer or similar device, any printout or other output readable by sight, shown to reflect the data accurately, is an "original."

§ 260. "Duplicate"

A "duplicate" is a counterpart produced by the same impression as the original, or from the same matrix, or by means of photography, including enlargements and miniatures, or by mechanical or electronic rerecording, or by chemical reproduction, or by other equivalent technique which accurately reproduces the original.

DIVISION 3. GENERAL PROVISIONS

CHAPTER 1. APPLICABILITY OF CODE

§ 300. Applicability of code

Except as otherwise provided by statute, this code applies in every action before the Supreme Court or a court of appeal or superior court, including proceedings in such actions conducted by a referee, court commissioner, or similar officer, but does not apply in grand jury proceedings.

LAW REVISION COMMISSION COMMENT

Section 300 makes the Evidence Code applicable to all proceedings conducted by California courts except those court proceedings to which it is made inapplicable by statute. The provisions of the code do not apply in administrative proceedings, legislative hearings, or any other proceedings unless some statute so provides or the agency concerned chooses to apply them.

Various code sections—in the Evidence Code as well as in other codes—make the provisions of the Evidence Code applicable to a certain extent in proceedings other than court proceedings. E.g., Govt.Code § 11513 (a finding in a proceeding conducted under the Administrative Procedure Act may not be based on hearsay evidence unless the evidence would be admissible over objection in a civil action); Penal Code § 939.6 (a grand jury, in investigating a charge, may receive only evidence admissible over objection in a criminal action); Evidence Code § 910 (provisions of the Evidence Code relating to privileges are applicable in all proceedings of every kind in which testimony can be compelled to be given); and Evidence Code § 1566 (Sections 1560–1565 are applicable in nonjudicial proceedings).

Section 300 does not affect any other statute relaxing rules of evidence for specified purposes. See, e.g., Code Civ.Proc. § 117g (judge of small claims court may make informal investigation either in or out of court), § 1768 (hearing of conciliation proceeding to be conducted informally), § 2016(b) (inadmissibility of testimony at trial is not ground for objection to testimony sought from a deponent, provided that such testimony is reasonably calculated to lead to the discovery of admissible evidence); Penal Code § 1203 (judge must consider probation officer's investigative report on question of probation); Welf. & Inst. Code § 706 (juvenile court must consider probation officer's social study in determining disposition to be made of ward or dependent child). [7 Cal. L.Rev.Comm. Reports 1 (1965)]

2002 Amendment

Section 300 is amended to reflect unification of the municipal and superior courts pursuant to Article VI, Section 5(e), of the California Constitution.

1998 Amendment

Section 300 is amended to reflect elimination of the justice court. Cal. Const. art. VI, §§ 1, 51(b).

CHAPTER 2. PROVINCE OF COURT AND JURY

§ 310. Questions of law for court

(a) All questions of law (including but not limited to questions concerning the construction of statutes and other writings, the admissibility of evidence, and other rules of evidence) are to be decided by the court. Determination of issues of fact preliminary to the admission of evidence are to be decided by the court as provided in Article 2 (commencing with Section 400) of Chapter 4.

(b) Determination of the law of an organization of nations or of the law of a foreign nation or a public entity in a foreign nation is a question of law to be determined in the manner provided in Division 4 (commencing with Section 450).

COMMENT—ASSEMBLY COMMITTEE ON JUDICIARY

Subdivision (a) of Section 310 restates the substance of and supersedes the first sentence of Section 2102 of the Code of Civil Procedure. Subdivision (b) restates the existing rule that foreign law is not a question of fact but is a question of law to be decided by the court. See Gallegos v. Union–Tribune Publishing Co., 195 Cal.App.2d 791, 16 Cal.Rptr. 185 (1961).

Section 310 refers specifically to the law of organizations of nations in order to make certain that the law of supranational organizations that have lawmaking authority—such as the European Economic Community—is to be determined as other foreign law is determined. This probably does not change the law of California, for it seems likely that the law of a supranational organization would be regarded as the law in the member nations by virtue of the treaty arrangements among them. Of course, the Evidence Code does not require California courts to give the force of law to anything that does not have the force of law. The Evidence Code merely prescribes the procedure for determining the existing foreign law.

The judicial notice provisions of the Evidence Code have no effect on which party has the burden of establishing the applicable foreign law under Probate Code Section 259 (relating to the right of nonresident aliens to inherit). The applicable foreign law is, however, to be determined in accordance with the judicial notice provisions of the Evidence

Code. Estate of Gogabashvele, 195 Cal.App.2d 503, 16 Cal.Rptr. 77 (1961).

§ 311. Foreign law applicable; law undetermined; procedures

If the law of an organization of nations, a foreign nation or a state other than this state, or a public entity in a foreign nation or a state other than this state, is applicable and such law cannot be determined, the court may, as the ends of justice require, either:

(a) Apply the law of this state if the court can do so consistently with the Constitution of the United States and the Constitution of this state; or

(b) Dismiss the action without prejudice or, in the case of a reviewing court, remand the case to the trial court with directions to dismiss the action without prejudice.

COMMENT—ASSEMBLY COMMITTEE ON JUDICIARY

Insofar as it relates to the law of foreign nations, Section 311 restates the substance of and supersedes the last paragraph of Section 1875 of the Code of Civil Procedure. With respect to sister-state law, the result reached under existing California case law is probably the same as under Section 311. See, e.g., Gagnon Co. v. Nevada Desert Inn, 45 Cal.2d 448, 453–454, 289 P.2d 466, 471 (1955) ("Whether such a judgment is a bar . . . is controlled by Nevada law. . . . We find no Nevada statute or case law covering the case we have here. . . . Under those circumstances we will assume the Nevada law is not out of harmony with ours and thus we look to our law for a solution of the problem.").

The last paragraph of Section 1875, which Section 311 supersedes, applies, "if the court is unable to determine" the applicable foreign law. Instead, Section 311 comes into operation if the applicable out-of-state law "cannot be determined." This revised language emphasizes that every effort should be made by the court to determine the applicable law before the case is otherwise disposed of under Section 311.

The reason why the court cannot determine the applicable foreign or sister-state law may be that the parties have not provided the court with sufficient information to make such determination. In such a case, the court may, of course, grant the parties additional time within which to obtain such information and make it available to the court. If they fail to obtain such information and the court is not satisfied that they made a reasonable effort to do so, the court may dismiss the action without prejudice. On the other hand, where counsel have made a reasonable effort and when all sources of information as to the applicable foreign or sister- state law are exhausted and the court cannot determine it, the court may either apply California law, within constitutional limits, or dismiss the action without prejudice.

§ 312. Jury as trier of fact

Except as otherwise provided by law, where the trial is by jury:

(a) All questions of fact are to be decided by the jury.

(b) Subject to the control of the court, the jury is to determine the effect and value of the evidence addressed to it, including the credibility of witnesses and hearsay declarants.

LAW REVISION COMMISSION COMMENT

Section 312 restates the substance of and supersedes Section 2101 and the first sentence of Section 2061 of the Code of Civil Procedure. The rule stated in Section 312 is subject to such exceptions as are otherwise provided by statutory or decisional law. See, e.g., Evidence Code §§ 310, 311, 457. [7 Cal.L.Rev.Comm. Reports 1 (1965)]

CHAPTER 3. ORDER OF PROOF

§ 320. Power of court to regulate order of proof

Except as otherwise provided by law, the court in its discretion shall regulate the order of proof.

LAW REVISION COMMISSION COMMENT

Section 320 restates the substance of and supersedes the first sentence of Section 2042 of the Code of Civil Procedure. Under Section 320, as under existing law, the trial judge has wide discretion to determine the order of proof. See California Civil Procedure During Trial, Parrish, Order of Proof, 205 (Cal.Cont.Ed.Bar 1960). Of course, the order of proof ordinarily should be as prescribed in Code of Civil Procedure Section 607 or 631.7 (added in this recommendation [Chapter 299, Statutes of 1965])or in Penal Code Sections 1093 and 1094.

Directions of the trial judge which control the order of proof should be distinguished from those which actually exclude evidence. Obviously, it is not permissible, through repeated directions of the order of proof, to prevent a party from presenting relevant evidence on a disputed fact. Foster v. Keating, 120 Cal.App.2d 435, 261 P.2d 529 (1953); California Civil Procedure During Trial, Parrish, Order of Proof, 205, 210 (Cal. Cont.Ed.Bar 1960). See also Murry v. Manley, 170 Cal.App.2d 364, 338 P.2d 976 (1959). [7 Cal.L.Rev.Comm. Reports 1 (1965)]

CHAPTER 4. ADMITTING AND EXCLUDING EVIDENCE

ARTICLE 1. GENERAL PROVISIONS

§ 350. Only relevant evidence admissible

No evidence is admissible except relevant evidence.

LAW REVISION COMMISSION COMMENT

Section 350 restates and supersedes that portion of Code of Civil Procedure Section 1868 requiring the exclusion of irrelevant evidence. [7 Cal.L.Rev.Comm. Reports 1 (1965)]

§ 351. Admissibility of relevant evidence

Except as otherwise provided by statute, all relevant evidence is admissible.

LAW REVISION COMMISSION COMMENT

Section 351 abolishes all limitations on the admissibility of relevant evidence except those that are based on a statute, including a constitutional provision. See Evidence Code § 230. The Evidence Code contains a number of provisions that exclude relevant evidence either for reasons of public policy or because the evidence is too unreliable to be presented to the trier of fact. See, e.g., Evidence Code § 352 (cumulative, unduly prejudicial, etc. evidence), §§ 900–1070 (privileges), §§ 1100–1156 (extrinsic policies), § 1200 (hearsay). Other codes also contain provisions that may in some cases result in the exclusion of relevant evidence. See, e.g., Civil Code §§ 79.06, 79.09, 227; Code Civ.Proc. § 1747; Educ.Code § 14026; Fin.Code § 8754; Fish & Game Code § 7923; Govt.Code §§ 15619, 18573, 18934, 18952, 20134, 31532; Health & Saf.Code §§ 211.5, 410; Ins.Code §§ 735, 855, 10381.5; Labor Code § 6319; Penal Code §§ 290, 938.1, 3046, 3107, 11105; Pub.Res. Code § 3234; Rev. & Tax.Code §§ 16563, 19282–19289; Unempl.Ins.Code §§ 1094, 2111, 2714; Vehicle Code §§ 1808, 16005, 20012–20015, 40803, 40804, 40832, 40833; Water Code § 12516; Welf. & Inst.Code §§ 118, 827. [7 Cal.L.Rev.Comm.Reports 1 (1965)]

§ 351.1. Polygraph examinations; results, opinion of examiner or reference; exclusion

(a) Notwithstanding any other provision of law, the results of a polygraph examination, the opinion of a polygraph examiner, or any reference to an offer to take, failure to take, or taking of a polygraph examination, shall not be admitted into evidence in any criminal proceeding, including pretrial and post conviction motions and hearings, or in any trial or hearing of a juvenile for a criminal offense, whether heard in juvenile or adult court, unless all parties stipulate to the admission of such results.

(b) Nothing in this section is intended to exclude from evidence statements made during a polygraph examination which are otherwise admissible.

§ 352. Discretion of court to exclude evidence

The court in its discretion may exclude evidence if its probative value is substantially outweighed by the probability that its admission will (a) necessitate undue consumption of time or (b) create substantial danger of undue prejudice, of confusing the issues, or of misleading the jury.

LAW REVISION COMMISSION COMMENT

Section 352 expresses a rule recognized by statute and in several California decisions. Code Civ. Proc. §§ 1868, 2044 (superseded by the Evidence Code); Adkins v. Brett, 184 Cal. 252, 258, 193 Pac. 251, 254 (1920) ("the matter [of excluding prejudicial evidence] is largely one of discretion on the part of the trial judge"); Moody v. Peirano, 4 Cal.App. 411, 418, 88 Pac. 380, 382 (1906) ("a wide discretion is left to the trial judge in determining whether [evidence of a collateral nature] is admissible or not"). [7 Cal.L.Rev.Comm.Reports 1 (1965)]

§ 352.1. Criminal sex acts; victim's address and telephone number

In any criminal proceeding under Section 261, 262, or 264.1, subdivision (d) of Section 286, or subdivision (d) of Section 288a of the Penal Code, or in any criminal proceeding under subdivision (c) of Section 286 or subdivision (c) of Section 288a of the Penal Code in which the defendant is alleged to have compelled the participation of the victim by force, violence, duress, menace, or threat of great bodily harm, the district attorney may, upon written motion with notice to the defendant or the defendant's attorney, if he or she is represented by an attorney, within a reasonable time prior to any hearing, move to exclude from evidence the current address and telephone number of any victim at the hearing.

The court may order that evidence of the victim's current address and telephone number be excluded from any hearings conducted pursuant to the criminal proceeding if the court finds that the probative value of the evidence is outweighed by the creation of substantial danger to the victim.

Nothing in this section shall abridge or limit the defendant's right to discover or investigate the information.

§ 353. Erroneous admission of evidence; effect

A verdict or finding shall not be set aside, nor shall the judgment or decision based thereon be reversed, by reason of the erroneous admission of evidence unless:

(a) There appears of record an objection to or a motion to exclude or to strike the evidence that was timely made and so stated as to make clear the specific ground of the objection or motion; and

(b) The court which passes upon the effect of the error or errors is of the opinion that the admitted evidence should have been excluded on the ground stated and that the error or errors complained of resulted in a miscarriage of justice.

COMMENT—ASSEMBLY COMMITTEE ON JUDICIARY

Subdivision (a) of Section 353 codifies the well-settled California rule that a failure to make a timely objection to, or motion to exclude or to strike, inadmissible evidence waives the right to complain of the erroneous admission of evidence. See Witkin, California Evidence §§ 700–702 (1958). Subdivision (a) also codifies the related rule that the objection or motion must specify the ground for objection, a general objection being insufficient. Witkin, California Evidence §§ 703–709 (1958).

Section 353 does not specify the form in which an objection must be made; hence, the use of a continuing objection to a line of questioning would be proper under Section 353 just as it is under existing law. See Witkin, California Evidence § 708 (1958).

Subdivision (b) reiterates the requirement of Section 4½ of Article VI of the California Constitution that a judgment may not be reversed, nor may a new trial be granted, because of an error unless the error is prejudicial.

Section 353 is, of course, subject to the constitutional requirement that a judgment must be reversed if an error has resulted in a denial of due process of law. People v. Matteson, 61 Cal.2d 466, 39 Cal.Rptr. 1, 393 P.2d 161 (1964).

§ 354. Erroneous exclusion of evidence; effect

A verdict or finding shall not be set aside, nor shall the judgment or decision based thereon be reversed, by reason of the erroneous exclusion of evidence unless the court which passes upon the effect of the error or errors is of the opinion that the error or errors complained of resulted in a miscarriage of justice and it appears of record that:

(a) The substance, purpose, and relevance of the excluded evidence was made known to the court by the questions asked, an offer of proof, or by any other means;

(b) The rulings of the court made compliance with subdivision (a) futile; or

(c) The evidence was sought by questions asked during cross-examination or recross-examination.

LAW REVISION COMMISSION COMMENT

Section 354, like Section 353, reiterates the requirement of the California Constitution that a judgment may not be reversed, nor may a new trial be granted, because of an error unless the error is prejudicial. Cal.Const., Art. VI, § 4 1/2.

The provisions of Section 354 that require an offer of proof or other disclosure of the evidence improperly excluded reflect existing law. See Witkin, California Evidence § 713 (1958). The exceptions to this requirement that are stated in Section 354 also reflect existing law. Thus, an offer of proof is unnecessary where the judge has limited the issues so that an offer to prove matters related to excluded issues would be futile. Lawless v. Calaway, 24 Cal.2d 81, 91, 147 P.2d 604, 609 (1944). An offer of proof is also unnecessary when an objection is improperly sustained to a question on cross-examination. Tossman v. Newman, 37 Cal.2d 522, 525–526, 233 P.2d 1, 3 (1951) ("no offer of proof is necessary in order to obtain a review of rulings on cross- examination"); People v. Jones, 160 Cal. 358, 117 Pac. 176 (1911). [7 Cal.L.Rev.Comm. Reports 1 (1965)]

§ 355. Limited admissibility

When evidence is admissible as to one party or for one purpose and is inadmissible as to another party or for another purpose, the court upon request shall restrict the evidence to its proper scope and instruct the jury accordingly.

LAW REVISION COMMISSION COMMENT

Section 355 codifies existing law which requires the court to instruct the jury as to the limited purpose for which evidence may be considered when such evidence is admissible for one purpose and inadmissible for another. See Adkins v. Brett, 184 Cal. 252, 193 Pac. 251 (1920).

Under Section 352, as under existing law, the judge is permitted to exclude such evidence if he deems it so prejudicial that a limiting instruction would not protect a party adequately and the matter in question can be proved sufficiently by other evidence. See discussion in Adkins v. Brett, 184 Cal. 252, 258, 193 Pac. 251, 254 (1920); Tentative Recommendation and a Study Relating to the Uniform Rules of Evidence (Article VI. Extrinsic Policies Affecting Admissibility), 6 Cal.Law Revision Comm'n, Rep., Rec. & Studies 601, 612, 639–640 (1964). [7 Cal.L.Rev.Comm. Reports 1 (1965)]

§ 356. Entire act, declaration, conversation, or writing, to elucidate part offered

Where part of an act, declaration, conversation, or writing is given in evidence by one party, the whole on the same subject may be inquired into by an adverse party; when a letter is read, the answer may be given; and when a detached act, declaration, conversation, or writing is given in evidence, any other act, declaration, conversation, or writing which is necessary to make it understood may also be given in evidence.

COMMENT—ASSEMBLY COMMITTEE ON JUDICIARY

Section 356 restates the substance of and supersedes Section 1854 of the Code of Civil Procedure.

The rule stated in Section 356, like the superseded statement of the rule in the Code of Civil Procedure, only makes admissible such parts of an act, declaration, conversation, or writing as are relevant to the part thereof previously given in evidence. See, e.g., Witt v. Jackson, 57 Cal.2d 57, 67, 17 Cal.Rptr. 369, 374, 366 P.2d 641, 646 (1961) (the rule "is necessarily subject to the qualification that the court may exclude those portions of the conversation not relevant to the items thereof which have been introduced"). See also Evidence Code § 350.

ARTICLE 2. PRELIMINARY DETERMINATIONS ON ADMISSIBILITY OF EVIDENCE

§ 400. "Preliminary Fact"

As used in this article, "preliminary fact" means a fact upon the existence or nonexistence of which depends the admissibility or inadmissibility of evidence. The phrase "the admissibility or inadmissibility of evidence" includes the qualification or disqualification of a person to be a witness and the existence or nonexistence of a privilege.

LAW REVISION COMMISSION COMMENT

"Preliminary fact" is defined to distinguish those facts upon which the admissibility of evidence depends from those facts sought to be proved by that evidence. [7 Cal.L.Rev.Comm. Reports 1 (1965)]

§ 401. "Proffered evidence"

As used in this article, "proffered evidence" means evidence, the admissibility or inadmissibility of which is dependent upon the existence or nonexistence of a preliminary fact.

LAW REVISION COMMISSION COMMENT

"Proffered evidence" is defined to avoid confusion between evidence whose admissibility is in question and evidence offered on the preliminary fact issue. "Proffered evidence" includes such matters as the testimony to be elicited from a witness who is claimed to be disqualified, testimony or tangible evidence claimed to be privileged, and any other evidence to which objection is made. [7 Cal.L.Rev.Comm. Reports 1 (1965)]

§ 402. Procedure for determining foundational and other preliminary facts

(a) When the existence of a preliminary fact is disputed, its existence or nonexistence shall be determined as provided in this article.

(b) The court may hear and determine the question of the admissibility of evidence out of the presence or hearing of the jury; but in a criminal action, the court shall hear and determine the question of the admissibility of a confession or admission of the defendant out of the presence and hearing of the jury if any party so requests.

(c) A ruling on the admissibility of evidence implies whatever finding of fact is prerequisite thereto; a separate or formal finding is unnecessary unless required by statute.

COMMENT—ASSEMBLY COMMITTEE ON JUDICIARY

Under Section 310, the court must decide preliminary questions of fact upon which the admissibility of evidence depends. Section 402 prescribes certain procedures that must be observed by the court when making such preliminary determinations.

Subdivision (a). Subdivision (a) requires the judge to observe the procedures specified in Article 2 (commencing with Section 400) when he is determining disputed factual questions preliminary to the admission or exclusion of evidence. The provisions of Article 2 are designed to distinguish clearly between (1) those situations where the judge must be persuaded of the existence of the preliminary fact upon which admissibility depends and (2) those situations where the judge must admit the proffered evidence merely upon the introduction of evidence sufficient to sustain a finding of the preliminary fact. Under the Evidence Code, as under existing law, the judge determines some preliminary fact questions on the basis of all of the evidence presented to him by both parties, resolving any conflicts in that evidence. Evidence Code § 405. See, e.g., People v. Glab, 13 Cal.App.2d 528, 57 P.2d 588 (1936) (judge considered conflicting evidence and decided that a proposed witness was not married to the defendant and, therefore, was competent to testify). See also Fairbank v. Hughson, 58 Cal. 314 (1881) (error to permit jury to determine whether witness was an expert). On the other hand, the judge does not always resolve conflicts in the evidence submitted on preliminary fact questions; in some cases, the proffered evidence must be admitted if there is evidence sufficient to sustain a finding of the preliminary fact. Evidence Code § 403. See, e.g., Reed v. Clark, 47 Cal. 194, 200 (1873); Verzan v. McGregor, 23 Cal. 339 (1863).

Subdivision (b). Subdivision (b) requires the judge, on request, to determine the admissibility of a confession or admission of a criminal defendant out of the presence and hearing of the jury. Under existing law, whether the preliminary hearing is held out of the presence of the jury is left to the judge's discretion. People v. Gonzales, 24 Cal.2d 870, 151 P.2d 251 (1944); People v. Nelson, 90 Cal.App. 27, 31, 265 Pac. 366, 367 (1928). The existing procedure permits the jury to hear evidence that may be extremely prejudicial. For example, in People v. Black, 73 Cal.App. 13, 238 Pac. 374 (1925), the alleged coercion consisted of threats to send the defendants to New Mexico to be prosecuted for murder. Subdivision (b) prevents this kind of prejudice. Nothing in subdivision (b) precludes a defendant from presenting to the jury evidence attacking the credibility of a confession that is admitted (Evidence

Code § 406), and such evidence may include some of the same matters presented to the judge during the preliminary hearing.

Subdivision (c). Subdivision (c) codifies existing law. Wilcox v. Berry, 32 Cal.2d 189, 195 P.2d 414 (1948) (where evidence is properly received, the ground of the court's ruling is immaterial); City & County of San Francisco v. Western Air Lines, Inc., 204 Cal.App.2d 105, 22 Cal.Rptr. 216 (1962) (where evidence is excluded, the ruling will be upheld if any ground exists for the exclusion).

§ 403. Determination of foundational and other preliminary facts where relevancy, personal knowledge, or authenticity is disputed

(a) The proponent of the proffered evidence has the burden of producing evidence as to the existence of the preliminary fact, and the proffered evidence is inadmissible unless the court finds that there is evidence sufficient to sustain a finding of the existence of the preliminary fact, when:

(1) The relevance of the proffered evidence depends on the existence of the preliminary fact;

(2) The preliminary fact is the personal knowledge of a witness concerning the subject matter of his testimony;

(3) The preliminary fact is the authenticity of a writing; or

(4) The proffered evidence is of a statement or other conduct of a particular person and the preliminary fact is whether that person made the statement or so conducted himself.

(b) Subject to Section 702, the court may admit conditionally the proffered evidence under this section, subject to evidence of the preliminary fact being supplied later in the course of the trial.

(c) If the court admits the proffered evidence under this section, the court:

(1) May, and on request shall, instruct the jury to determine whether the preliminary fact exists and to disregard the proffered evidence unless the jury finds that the preliminary fact does exist.

(2) Shall instruct the jury to disregard the proffered evidence if the court subsequently determines that a jury could not reasonably find that the preliminary fact exists.

COMMENT—ASSEMBLY COMMITTEE ON JUDICIARY

As indicated in the Comment to Section 402, the judge does not determine in all instances whether a preliminary fact exists or does not exist. At times, the judge must admit the proffered evidence if there is evidence sufficient to sustain a finding of the preliminary fact, and the jury must finally decide whether the preliminary fact exists. See, e.g.,

Verzan v. McGregor, 23 Cal. 339 (1863). Section 403 covers those situations in which the judge is required to admit the proffered evidence upon the introduction of evidence sufficient to sustain a finding of the preliminary fact.

Subdivision (a)

Some writers have attempted to distinguish the kinds of questions to be decided under the standard prescribed in Section 403 from the kinds of questions to be decided under the standard described in Section 405 on the ground that the former questions involve the relevancy of the proffered evidence while the latter questions involve the competency of evidence that is relevant. Maguire & Epstein, Preliminary Questions of Fact in Determining the Admissibility of Evidence, 40 Harv.L.Rev. 392 (1927); Morgan, Functions of Judge and Jury in the Determination of Preliminary Questions of Fact, 43 Harv.L.Rev. 165 (1929). It is difficult, however, to distinguish all preliminary fact questions upon this principle. And eminent legal authorities sometimes differ over whether a particular preliminary fact question is one of relevancy or competency. For example, Wigmore classifies admissions with questions of relevancy (4 Wigmore, Evidence 1 (3d ed. 1940))while Morgan classifies admissions with questions of competency to be decided under the standard prescribed in Section 405 (Morgan, Basic Problems of Evidence 244 (1957)).

To eliminate uncertainties of classification, subdivision (a) lists the kinds of preliminary fact questions that are to be determined under the standard prescribed in Section 403. And to eliminate any uncertainties that are not resolved by this listing, various Evidence Code sections state specifically that admissibility depends on "evidence sufficient to sustain a finding" of certain facts. See, e.g., Evidence Code §§ 1222, 1223, 1400.

The preliminary fact questions listed in subdivision (a), or identified elsewhere as matters to be determined under the Section 403 standard, are not finally decided by the judge because they have been traditionally regarded as jury questions. The questions involve the credibility of testimony or the probative value of evidence that is admitted on the ultimate issues. It is the jury's function to determine the effect and value of the evidence addressed to it. Evidence Code § 312. Hence, the judge's function on questions of this sort is merely to determine whether there is evidence sufficient to permit a jury to decide the question. The "question of admissibility ... merges imperceptibly into the weight of the evidence, if admitted." Di Carlo v. United States, 6 F.2d 364, 367 (2d Cir.1925). If the judge finally determined the existence or nonexistence of the preliminary fact, he would deprive a party of a jury decision on a question that the party has a right to have decided by the jury.

For example, if the question of A's title to land is in issue, A may seek to prove his title by a deed from former owner O. Section 1401 requires that the deed be authenticated, and the judge, under Section

403, must rule on the question of authentication. If A introduces evidence sufficient to sustain a finding of the genuineness of the deed, the judge is required to admit it. If the rule were otherwise and the judge, on the basis of the adverse party's evidence, were permitted to decide that the deed was spurious and not admissible, the judge would be resolving the basic factual issue in the case and A would be deprived of a jury finding on the issue, even though he is entitled to a jury decision and even though he has introduced evidence sufficient to warrant a jury finding in his favor.

Illustrative of the preliminary fact questions that should be decided under Section 403 are the following:

Section 350—Relevancy. Under existing law, as under Section 403, if the relevancy of proffered evidence depends on the existence of some preliminary fact, the evidence is admissible if there is evidence sufficient to warrant a jury finding of the preliminary fact. Reed v. Clark, 47 Cal. 194, 200 (1873). Thus, for example, if P sues D upon an alleged agreement, evidence of negotiations with A is inadmissible because irrelevant unless A is shown to be D's agent; but the evidence of the negotiations with A is admissible if there is evidence sufficient to sustain a finding of the agency. Brown v. Spencer, 163 Cal. 589, 126 Pac. 493 (1912). The same rule is applicable when a person is charged with criminal responsibility for the acts of another because they are conspirators. See discussion in People v. Steccone, 36 Cal.2d 234, 238, 223 P.2d 17, 19 (1950).

Section 702—Requirement of personal knowledge. Evidence sufficient to sustain a finding of a witness' personal knowledge seems to be sufficient under the existing California practice. See, e.g., People v. Avery, 35 Cal.2d 487, 492, 218 P.2d 527, 530 (1950) ("Bolton testified that he observed the incident about which he testified. His testimony, therefore, was not incompetent under section 1845 of the Code of Civil Procedure."); People v. McCarthy, 14 Cal.App. 148, 151, 111 Pac. 274, 275 (1910). See also Tentative Recommendation and a Study Relating to the Uniform Rules of Evidence (Article IV. Witnesses), 6 Cal.Law Revision Comm'n, Rep., Rec. & Studies 701, 711–713 (1964).

Section 788—Conviction of a crime when offered to attack credibility. In this situation, the preliminary fact issue to be decided under Section 403 is whether the witness is actually the person who was convicted. This involves the relevancy of the evidence (since, obviously, the conviction of another does not affect the witness' credibility) and should be a question to be resolved by the jury. The judge should not be able to decide finally that it was the witness who was convicted and, thus, to prevent a contest on that issue before the jury. The existing law is uncertain in this regard; however, it seems likely that any evidence sufficient to identify the witness as the person convicted is sufficient to warrant admission of the conviction. See People v. Theodore, 121 Cal.App.2d 17, 28, 262 P.2d 630, 637 (1953) (relying on presumption of identity of person from identity of name).

Section 800—Requirement that lay opinion be based on personal perception. The requirement specified in Section 800 is merely a specific application of the personal knowledge requirement in Section 702. See the discussion of Section 702 in this Comment, supra.

Sections 1200–1341—Identity of hearsay declarant. For most hearsay evidence, admissibility depends upon two preliminary determinations: (1) Did the declarant actually make the statement as claimed by the proponent of the evidence? (2) Does the statement meet certain standards of trustworthiness required by some exception to the hearsay rule?

The first determination involves the relevancy of the evidence. For example, if the issue is the state of mind of X, a person's statement as to his state of mind has no tendency to prove X's state of mind unless the declarant was X. Relevancy depends on the fact that X made the statement. Accordingly, if otherwise competent, a hearsay statement is admitted upon evidence sufficient to sustain a finding that the claimed declarant made the statement.

The second determination involves the competency of the evidence. Unless the evidence meets the requisite standards of an exception to the hearsay rule, it must be kept from the trier of fact despite its relevancy either because it is too unreliable or because public policy requires its suppression. For example, if an admission was in fact made by a defendant to a criminal action, the admission is relevant. But public policy requires that the admission be held inadmissible if it was not given voluntarily.

The admissibility of some hearsay declarations is dependent solely upon the determination that a particular declarant made the statement. Some of these exceptions to the hearsay rule—such as inconsistent statements of trial witnesses and admissions—are mentioned specifically below. Since the only preliminary fact to be determined in regard to these declarations involves the relevancy of the evidence, they should be admitted upon the introduction of evidence sufficient to sustain a finding of the preliminary fact.

When the admissibility of hearsay depends both upon a determination that a particular declarant made the statement and upon a determination that the requisite standards of a hearsay exception have been met, the former determination is to be made upon evidence sufficient to sustain a finding of the preliminary fact. Paragraph (4) is included in subdivision (a) to make this clear.

Section 1220—Admissions of a party. The only preliminary fact that is subject to dispute is the identity of the declarant. Under Section 403(a)(4), an admission is admissible upon the introduction of evidence sufficient to sustain a finding that the party made the statement.

Existing law appears to be in accord. Eastman v. Means, 75 Cal.App. 537, 242 Pac. 1089 (1925).

An admission is not admissible in a criminal case unless it was given voluntarily. The voluntariness of an admission by a criminal defendant is determined under Section 405, not Section 403.

Sections 1221, 1222—Authorized and adoptive admissions. Under existing law, both authorized admissions (by an agent of a party) and adoptive admissions are admitted upon the introduction of evidence sufficient to sustain a finding of the foundational fact. Sample v. Round Mountain Citrus Farm Co., 29 Cal.App. 547, 156 Pac. 983 (1916) (authorized admission); Southers v. Savage, 191 Cal.App.2d 100, 12 Cal.Rptr. 470 (1961) (adoptive admission).

Section 1223—Admission of co-conspirator. The admission of a co-conspirator is another form of an authorized admission. Hence, the proffered evidence is admissible upon the introduction of evidence sufficient to sustain a finding of the conspiracy. Existing law is in accord. People v. Robinson, 43 Cal.2d 132, 137, 271 P.2d 865, 868 (1954).

Sections 1224–1227—Admission of third person whose liability, breach of duty, or right is in issue. The only preliminary fact subject to dispute is the identity of the declarant; and the preliminary showing required in regard to this class of admissions is the same as if the declarant were being sued directly. Any evidence of the making of the statement by the claimed declarant is sufficient to warrant its admission. Existing law is in accord. See Langley v. Zurich General Acc. & Liab. Ins. Co., 219 Cal. 101, 25 P.2d 418 (1933). Although Sections 1226 and 1227 are new to California law, the same principles should be applicable.

Sections 1235, 1236—Previous statements of witnesses. Prior inconsistent statements and prior consistent statements made before bias or other improper motive arose are dealt with in Sections 1235 and 1236. In each case, the evidence is relevant and probative if the witnesses to the statements are credible. The credibility of the witnesses testifying to these statements should be decided finally by the jury. Moreover, the only preliminary fact subject to dispute insofar as alleged inconsistent statements are concerned is the identity of the declarant. Hence, evidence is admitted under these sections upon the introduction of evidence sufficient to sustain a finding of the preliminary fact. The existing practice seems to be consistent with Section 403. See Schneider v. Market Street Ry., 134 Cal. 482, 492, 66 Pac. 734, 738 (1901) ("Whether the [prior inconsistent] statements made to Glassman and Hubbell were made by Meley, or by some other man, was a question for the jury. Both witnesses testified that they were made by him."); People v. Neely, 163 Cal.App.2d 289, 312, 329 P.2d 357, 371 (1958) (two prior consistent statements held admissible because the "jury could properly infer . . . the motive to fabricate did arise after the making of the two statements").

Sections 1400–1402—Authentication of writings. Under existing law, an otherwise competent writing is admissible upon the introduction of evidence sufficient to sustain a finding of the authenticity of the writing. Verzan v. McGregor, 23 Cal. 339 (1863). Section 403(a)(3) retains this existing law.

Sections 1410–1421—Means of authenticating writings. Sections 1410 through 1421 merely state several ways in which the requirements of Sections 1400 through 1402 may be met. Hence, to the extent that Sections 1410 through 1421 specify facts that may be shown to authenticate writings, the same principles apply: In each case, the judge must decide whether the evidence offered is sufficient to sustain a finding of the authenticity of the proffered writing and admit the writing if there is such evidence. Care should be exercised, however, to distinguish those cases where the disputed preliminary fact is the authenticity of an exemplar with which the proffered writing is to be compared (Evidence Code §§ 1417–1419) or the qualification of a witness to give an opinion concerning the authenticity of a writing (Evidence Code §§ 1416, 1418); the judge is required to determine such questions under the provisions of Section 405.

Subdivision (b)

Subdivision (b) restates the apparent meaning of Section 1834 of the Code of Civil Procedure. Under this subdivision, the judge may receive evidence that is conditionally admissible under Section 403, subject to the presentation of evidence of the preliminary fact later in the course of the trial. See Brea v. McGlashan, 3 Cal.App.2d 454, 465, 39 P.2d 877, 882 (1934).

Subdivision (c)

Subdivision (c) relates to the instructions to be given the jury when evidence is admitted whose admissibility depends on the existence of a preliminary fact determined under Section 403. When such evidence is admitted, the jury is required to make the ultimate determination of the existence of the preliminary fact. Unless the jury is persuaded that the preliminary fact exists, it is not permitted to consider the evidence.

For example, if P offers evidence of his negotiations with A in his contract action against D, the judge must admit the evidence if there is other evidence sufficient to sustain a finding that A was D's agent. If the jury is not persuaded that A was in fact D's agent, then it is not permitted to consider the evidence of the negotiations with A in determining D's liability.

Frequently, the jury's duty to disregard conditionally admissible evidence when it is not persuaded of the existence of the preliminary fact on which relevancy is conditioned is so clear that an instruction to this effect is unnecessary. For example, if the disputed preliminary fact is the authenticity of a deed, it hardly seems necessary to instruct the jury to disregard the deed if it should find that the deed is not genuine. No rational jury could find the deed to be spurious and, yet, to be still effective to transfer title from the purported grantor.

At times, however, it is not quite so clear that conditionally admissible evidence should be disregarded unless the preliminary fact is found to exist. In such cases, the jury should be appropriately instructed. For example, the theory upon which agent's and co-conspirator's statements are admissible is that the party is vicariously responsible for the acts and statements of agents and co-conspirators within the scope of the agency or conspiracy. Yet, it is not always clear that statements made by a purported agent or co-conspirator should be disregarded if not made in furtherance of the agency or conspiracy. Hence, the jury should be instructed to disregard such statements unless it is persuaded that the statements were made within the scope of the agency or conspiracy. People v. Geiger, 49 Cal. 643, 649 (1875); People v. Talbott, 65 Cal. App.2d 654, 663, 151 P.2d 317, 322 (1944). Subdivision (c), therefore, permits the judge in any case to instruct the jury to disregard conditionally admissible evidence unless it is persuaded of the existence of the preliminary fact; further, subdivision (c) requires the judge to give such an instruction whenever he is requested by a party to do so.

§ 404. Determination of whether proffered evidence is incriminatory

Whenever the proffered evidence is claimed to be privileged under Section 940, the person claiming the privilege has the burden of showing that the proffered evidence might tend to incriminate him; and the proffered evidence is inadmissible unless it clearly appears to the court that the proffered evidence cannot possibly have a tendency to incriminate the person claiming the privilege.

LAW REVISION COMMISSION COMMENT

Section 404 provides a special procedure to be followed by the judge when an objection is made in reliance upon the privilege against self-incrimination. Under Section 404, the objecting party has the burden of showing that the testimony sought might incriminate him. However, the party is not required to produce evidence as such. In addition to considering evidence, the judge must consider the matters disclosed in argument, the implications of the question, the setting in which it is asked, the applicable statute of limitations, and all other relevant factors. See Cohen v. Superior Court, 173 Cal.App.2d 61, 70, 343 P.2d 286, 291 (1959). Nonetheless, the burden is on the objector to present to the judge information of this sort sufficient to indicate that the proffered evidence might incriminate him. If he presents information of this sort, Section 404 requires the judge to sustain the claim of privilege unless it clearly appears that the proffered evidence cannot possibly have a tendency to incriminate the person claiming the privilege.

Section 404 is consistent with existing law: The party claiming the privilege "has the burden of showing that the testimony which was being required might be used in a prosecution to help establish his guilt"; the court may require testimony to be given only if it clearly appears to the court that the claim of privilege is mistaken and that any answer " 'cannot possibly' " have a tendency to incriminate the witness. Cohen v. Superior Court, 173 Cal.App.2d 61, 68, 70–72, 343 P.2d 286, 290, 291–292 (1959) (italics in original). [7 Cal.L.Rev.Comm. Reports 1 (1965)]

§ 405. Determination of foundational and other preliminary facts in other cases

With respect to preliminary fact determinations not governed by Section 403 or 404:

(a) When the existence of a preliminary fact is disputed, the court shall indicate which party has the burden of producing evidence and the burden of proof on the issue as implied by the rule of law under which the question arises. The court shall determine the existence or nonexistence of the preliminary fact and shall admit or exclude the proffered evidence as required by the rule of law under which the question arises.

(b) If a preliminary fact is also a fact in issue in the action:

(1) The jury shall not be informed of the court's determination as to the existence or nonexistence of the preliminary fact.

(2) If the proffered evidence is admitted, the jury shall not be instructed to disregard the evidence if its determination of the fact differs from the court's determination of the preliminary fact.

COMMENT—ASSEMBLY COMMITTEE ON JUDICIARY

Section 405 requires the judge to determine the existence or nonexistence of disputed preliminary facts except in certain situations covered by Sections 403 and 404. Section 405 deals with evidentiary rules designed to withhold evidence from the jury because it is too unreliable to be evaluated properly or because public policy requires its exclusion.

Under Section 405, the judge first indicates to the parties who has the burden of proof and the burden of producing evidence on the disputed issue as implied by the rule of law under which the question arises. For example, Section 1200 indicates that the burden of proof is usually on the proponent of the evidence to show that the proffered evidence is within a hearsay exception. Thus, if the disputed preliminary fact is whether the proffered statement was spontaneous, as required by Section 1240, the proponent would have the burden of persuading the judge as to the spontaneity of the statement. On the other hand, the privilege rules usually place the burden of proof on the objecting party to show that a privilege is applicable. Thus, if the disputed preliminary fact is whether a person is married to a party and, hence, whether their confidential communications are privileged under Section 980, the burden of proof is on the party asserting the privilege to persuade the judge of the existence of the marriage.

After the judge has indicated to the parties who has the burden of proof and the burden of producing evidence, the parties submit their evidence on the preliminary issue to the judge. If the judge is persuaded by the party with the burden of proof, he finds in favor of that party in regard to the preliminary fact and either admits or excludes the proffered evidence as required by the rule of law under which the question arises. Otherwise, he finds against that party on the preliminary fact and either admits or excludes the proffered evidence as required by such finding.

Section 405 is generally consistent with existing law. Code Civ. Proc. § 2102 ("All questions of law, including the admissibility of testimony, [and] the facts preliminary to such admission, ... are to be decided by the Court") (superseded by Evidence Code § 310).

Examples of preliminary fact issues to be decided under Section 405

Illustrative of the preliminary fact questions that should be decided under Section 405 are the following:

Section 701—Disqualification of a witness for lack of mental capacity. Under existing law, as under this code, the party objecting to a proffered witness has the burden of proving the witness' lack of capacity. People v. Craig, 111 Cal. 460, 469, 44 Pac. 186, 188 (1896); People v. Tyree, 21 Cal.App. 701, 706, 132 Pac. 784, 786 (1913) (disapproved) on other grounds in People v. McCaughan, 49 Cal.2d 409, 420, 317 P.2d 974, 981 (1957).

Section 720—Qualifications of an expert witness. Under Section 720, as under existing law, the proponent must persuade the judge that his expert is qualified, and it is error for the judge to submit the qualifications of the expert to the jury. Fairbank v. Hughson, 58 Cal. 314 (1881); Eble v. Peluso, 80 Cal.App.2d 154, 181 P.2d 680 (1947).

Section 788—Conviction of a crime when offered to attack credibility. If the disputed preliminary fact is whether a pardon or some similar relief has been granted to a witness convicted of a crime, the judge's determination is made under Section 405. Cf. Comment to Section 403.

Section 870—Opinion evidence on sanity. Whether a witness is sufficiently acquainted with a person whose sanity is in question to be qualified to express an opinion on the matter involves, in effect, the expertise of the witness on that limited subject. The witness' qualifications to express such an opinion, therefore, are to be determined by the judge under Section 405 just as the qualifications of other experts are decided by the judge. See the discussion of Section 720 in this Comment, supra. Under existing law, too, determination of whether a witness is an "intimate acquaintance" is a question addressed to the court. Estate of Budan, 156 Cal. 230, 104 Pac. 442 (1909).

Sections 900–1070—Privileges. Under this code, as under existing law, the party claiming a privilege has the burden of proof on the preliminary facts. San Diego Professional Ass'n v. Superior Court, 58 Cal.2d 194, 199, 23 Cal.Rptr. 384, 387, 373 P.2d 448, 451 (1962) ("The burden of establishing that a particular matter is privileged is on the party asserting that privilege."); Chronicle Publishing Co. v. Superior Court, 54 Cal.2d 548, 565, 7 Cal.Rptr. 109, 117, 354 P.2d 637, 645 (1960). The proponent of the proffered evidence, however, has the burden of proof upon any preliminary fact necessary to show that an exception to the privilege is applicable. But see Abbott v. Superior Court, 78 Cal. App.2d 19, 21, 177 P.2d 317, 318 (1947) (suggesting that a prima facie showing by the proponent is sufficient where the issue is whether a communication between attorney and client was made in contemplation of crime).

Sections 1152, 1154—Admissions made during compromise negotiations. With respect to admissions made during compromise negotiations, the disputed preliminary fact to be decided by the judge is whether the admission occurred during compromise negotiations or at some other time. This code places the burden on the objecting party to satisfy the judge that the admission occurred during such negotiations.

Sections 1200–1341—Hearsay evidence. When hearsay evidence is offered, two preliminary fact questions may be raised. The first question relates to the authenticity of the proffered declaration—was the statement actually made by the person alleged to have made it? The second question relates to the existence of those circumstances that make the hearsay sufficiently trustworthy to be received in evidence—e.g., was the declaration spontaneous, the confession voluntary, the business record trustworthy? Under this code, questions relating to the authenticity of the proffered declaration are decided under Section 403. See the Comment to Section 403. But other preliminary fact questions are decided under Section 405.

For example, the court must decide whether a statement offered as a dying declaration was made under a sense of impending death, and the proponent of the evidence has the burden of proof on this issue. People v. Keelin, 136 Cal.App.2d 860, 873, 289 P.2d 520, 528 (1955); People v. Pollock, 31 Cal.App.2d 747, 753–754, 89 P.2d 128, 131 (1939). Under this code, the proponent of a hearsay declaration has the burden of proof on the unavailability of the declarant as a witness under Section 1291 or 1310; but the party objecting to the evidence has the burden of proving that the unavailability of the declarant was procured by the proponent in order to prevent the declarant from testifying. See Evidence Code § 240.

Section 1416—Opinion evidence on handwriting. Whether a witness is sufficiently acquainted with the handwriting of a person to give an opinion on whether a questioned writing is in that person's handwriting involves, in effect, the expertise of the witness on the limited subject of the supposed writer's handwriting. The witness' qualifications to express such an opinion, therefore, are to be determined by the judge under Section 405 just as the qualifications of other experts are decided by the judge. See the discussion of Section 720 in this Comment, supra.

Sections 1417–1419—Comparison of writing with exemplar. Under Sections 1417 through 1419, as under existing law, the judge must be satisfied that a writing is genuine before he may admit it for comparison with other writings whose authenticity is in dispute. People v. Creegan, 121 Cal. 554, 53 Pac. 1082 (1898); Marshall v. Hancock, 80 Cal. 82, 22 Pac. 61 (1889).

Sections 1500–1510—Best evidence rule. Under Section 405, as under existing law, the trial judge is required to determine the preliminary fact necessary to warrant reception of secondary evidence of a writing, and the burden of proof on the issue is on the proponent of the secondary evidence. Cotton v. Hudson, 42 Cal.App.2d 812, 110 P.2d 70 (1941).

Sections 1550, 1551—Photographic copy of writing. Sections 1550 and 1551 are special exceptions to the best evidence rule; hence, Section 405 governs the determination of any disputed preliminary fact under these sections just as it governs the determination of disputed preliminary facts under Sections 1500 through 1510. See the discussion of Sections 1550–1510 in this Comment, supra.

Function of court and jury under Section 405

When preliminary fact question is also an issue involved in merits of case. In some cases, a factual issue to be decided by the judge under Section 405 will coincide with an issue involved in the merits of the case. For example, in People v. MacDonald, 24 Cal.App.2d 702, 76 P.2d 121 (1938), the defendant in an incest prosecution objected to the testimony of the prosecutrix on the ground that she was his wife. The judge, in ruling on the objection, had to determine whether the prosecutrix was also the defendant's daughter and, hence, whether their marriage was incestuous and void. In such a case, it would be prejudicial to the parties for the judge to inform the jury how he had decided the same factual question that it must decide in determining the merits of the case. Subdivision (b), therefore, prohibits a judge from informing the jury how he decided a question under Section 405 that the jury must ultimately resolve on the merits.

The judge is also prohibited from instructing the jury to disregard evidence that has been admitted if the jury's determination of a fact in deciding the merits differs from the judge's determination of the same fact under Section 405. The rules of admissibility being applied by the judge under Section 405 are designed to withhold evidence from the jury because it is too unreliable to be evaluated properly or because public policy requires its exclusion. The policies underlying these rules are served only by the exclusion of the evidence. No valid public or evidentiary purpose is served by submitting the admissibility question again to the jury. For example, the interspousal testimonial privilege involved in People v. MacDonald, 24 Cal.App.2d 702, 76 P.2d 121 (1938), exists to preclude a spouse from being involuntarily compelled to testify against the other spouse. The privilege serves its purpose only if the spouse does not testify. The harm the privilege is designed to prevent has occurred if the spouse testifies. Therefore, subdivision (b) provides for the finality of the judge's rulings on admissibility under Section 405 even in those cases where the factual questions decided by the judge coincide with the factual questions ultimately to be resolved by the jury.

Of course, Section 405 has no effect on the constitutional right of the judge to comment on the evidence and on the testimony and credibility of witnesses. See Cal.Const., Art. I, § 13, and Art. VI, § 19.

Confessions, dying declarations, and spontaneous statements. Although Section 405 is generally consistent with existing law, it will, however, substantially change the law relating to confessions, dying declarations, and spontaneous statements. Under existing law, the judge considers all of the evidence and decides whether evidence of this sort is admissible, as indicated in Section 405. But if he decides the proffered evidence is admissible, he submits the preliminary question to the jury for a final determination whether the confession was voluntary, whether the dying declaration was made in realization of impending doom, or whether the spontaneous statement was in fact spontaneous; and the jury is instructed to disregard the statement if it does not believe that the condition of admissibility has been satisfied. People v. Baldwin, 42 Cal.2d 858, 866–867, 270 P.2d 1028, 1033–1034 (1954) (confession—see the court's instruction, id. at 866, 270 P.2d at 1033); People v. Gonzales, 24 Cal.2d 870, 876–877, 151 P.2d 251, 254 (1944) (confession); People v. Singh, 182 Cal. 457, 476, 188 Pac. 987, 995 (1920) (dying declaration); People v. Keelin, 136 Cal.App.2d 860, 871, 289 P.2d 520, 527 (1955) (spontaneous declaration).

Under Section 405, the judge's rulings on these questions are final; the jury does not have an opportunity to redetermine the issue.

Section 405 will have no effect on the admissibility of confessions where the uncontradicted evidence shows that the confession was not voluntary. Under existing law, as under the Evidence Code, such a confession may not be admitted for consideration by the jury. People v. Trout, 54 Cal.2d 576, 6 Cal.Rptr. 759, 354 P.2d 231 (1960); People v. Jones, 24 Cal.2d 601, 150 P.2d 801 (1944). Section 405 will also have no effect on the admissibility of confessions in those instances where, despite a conflict in the evidence, the court is persuaded that the confession was not voluntary; for, under existing law (as under the

Evidence Code), "if the court concludes that the confession was not free and voluntary it ... is in duty bound to withhold it from the jury's consideration." People v. Gonzales, 24 Cal.2d 870, 876, 151 P.2d 251, 254 (1944).

Hence, Section 405 changes the law relating to confessions only where there is a substantial conflict in the evidence over voluntariness and the court is not persuaded that the confession was involuntary. Under existing law, a court that is in doubt may "pass the buck" concerning such a confession to the jury when there is a difficult factual question to resolve; for "if there is evidence that the confession was free and voluntary, it is within the court's discretion to permit it to be read to the jury, and to submit to the jury for its determination the question whether under all the circumstances the confession was made freely and voluntarily." People v. Gonzales, 24 Cal.2d 870, 876, 151 P.2d 251, 254 (1944). Under the Evidence Code, however, the court is required to withhold a confession from the jury unless the court is persuaded that the confession was made freely and voluntarily. The court has no "discretion" to avoid difficult decisions by shifting the responsibility to the jury. If the court is in doubt, if the prosecution has not persuaded it of the voluntary nature of the confession, Section 405 requires the court to exclude the confession. Thus, Section 405 makes the procedure for determining the admissibility of a confession the same as the procedure for determining the admissibility of physical evidence claimed to have been seized in violation of constitutional guarantees. See People v. Gorg, 45 Cal.2d 776, 291 P.2d 469 (1955); People v. Chavez, 208 Cal.App.2d 248, 24 Cal.Rptr. 895 (1962).

The existing law is based on the belief that a jury, in determining the defendant's guilt or innocence, can and will refuse to consider a confession that it has determined was involuntary even though it believes that the confession is true. Section 405, on the other hand, proceeds upon the belief that it is unrealistic to expect a jury to perform such a feat. Corroborating facts stated in a confession cannot but assist the jury in resolving other conflicts in the evidence. The question of voluntariness will inevitably become merged with the question of guilt and the truth of the confession; and, as a result of this merger, the admitted confession will inevitably be considered on the issue of guilt. The defendant will receive a greater degree of protection if the court is deprived of the power to shift its fact-determining responsibility to the jury and is required to exclude a confession whenever it is not persuaded that the confession was voluntary.

The foregoing discussion has focused on confessions because the case law is well developed there. But the "second crack" doctrine is equally unsatisfactory when applied to dying declarations and spontaneous statements. Hence, Section 405 requires the court to rule finally on the admissibility of these statements as well.

Of course, Section 405 does not prevent the presentation of any evidence to the jury that is relevant to the reliability of the hearsay statement. See Evidence Code § 406. Thus, a party may present evidence of the circumstances under which a confession, dying declaration, or spontaneous statement was made where such evidence is relevant to the credibility of the statement, even though such evidence may duplicate to some degree the evidence presented to the court on the issue of admissibility. But the jury's sole concern is the truth or falsity of the facts stated, not the admissibility of the statement.

§ 406. Evidence affecting weight or credibility

This article does not limit the right of a party to introduce before the trier of fact evidence relevant to weight or credibility.

LAW REVISION COMMISSION COMMENT

Other sections in this article provide that the judge determines whether proffered evidence is admissible, i.e., whether it may be considered by the trier of fact. Section 406 simply makes it clear that the judge's decision on a question of admissibility does not preclude the parties from introducing before the trier of fact evidence relevant to weight and credibility. [7 Cal.L.Rev.Comm. Reports 1 (1965)]

CHAPTER 5. WEIGHT OF EVIDENCE GENERALLY

§ 410. Direct evidence

As used in this chapter, "direct evidence" means evidence that directly proves a fact, without an inference or presumption, and which in itself, if true, conclusively establishes that fact.

§ 411. Direct evidence of one witness sufficient

Except where additional evidence is required by statute, the direct evidence of one witness who is entitled to full credit is sufficient for proof of any fact.

LAW REVISION COMMISSION COMMENT

Section 411 restates the substance of and supersedes Section 1844 of the Code of Civil Procedure. The phrase "except where additional evidence is required by statute" has been substituted for the phrase "except perjury and treason" in Section 1844 because the "perjury and treason" exception to Section 1844 is too limited: Corroboration is required by Section 20 of Article I of the California Constitution (treason) and by Penal Code Sections 653f (solicitation to commit felonies), 1103a (perjury), 1108 (abortion and prostitution cases), 1110 (obtaining property by oral false pretenses), and 1111 (testimony of accomplices); in addition, Civil Code Section 130 provides that divorces cannot be granted on the uncorroborated testimony of the parties. [7 Cal.L.Rev. Comm. Reports 1 (1965)]

§ 412. Party having power to produce better evidence

If weaker and less satisfactory evidence is offered when it was within the power of the party to produce stronger and more satisfactory evidence, the evidence offered should be viewed with distrust.

LAW REVISION COMMISSION COMMENT

Section 412 restates the substance of and supersedes subdivisions 6 and 7 of Section 2061 of the Code of Civil Procedure.

Section 413, taken together with Section 412, restates in substance the meaning that has been given to the presumptions appearing in subdivisions 5 and 6 of Code of Civil Procedure Section 1963.

Evidence Code Section 913 provides that "no presumption shall arise because of the exercise of [a] privilege, and the trier of fact may not draw any inference therefrom," and the trial judge is required to give such an instruction if he is requested to do so. However, there is no inconsistency between Section 913 and Sections 412 and 413. Section 913 deals only with the inferences that may be drawn from the exercise of a privilege; it does not purport to deal with the inferences that may be drawn from the evidence in the case. Sections 412 and 413, on the other hand, deal with the inferences to be drawn from the evidence in the case; and the fact that a privilege has been relied on is irrelevant to the application of these sections. Cf. People v. Adamson, 27 Cal.2d 478, 165 P.2d 3 (1946). [7 Cal.L.Rev.Comm. Reports 1 (1965)]

§ 413. Party's failure to explain or deny evidence

In determining what inferences to draw from the evidence or facts in the case against a party, the trier of fact may consider, among other things, the party's failure to explain or to deny by his testimony such evidence or facts in the case against him, or his willful suppression of evidence relating thereto, if such be the case.

DIVISION 4. JUDICIAL NOTICE

§ 450. Judicial notice may be taken only as authorized by law

Judicial notice may not be taken of any matter unless authorized or required by law.

LAW REVISION COMMISSION COMMENT

Section 450 provides that judicial notice may not be taken of any matter unless authorized or required by law. See Evidence Code § 160, defining "law." Sections 451 and 452 state a number of matters which must or may be judicially noticed. Judicial notice of other matters is authorized or required by other statutes or by decisional law. E.g., Civil Code § 53; Corp.Code § 6602. In this respect, the Evidence Code is consistent with existing law, for the principal judicial notice provision found in existing law—Code of Civil Procedure Section 1875 (superseded by this division of the Evidence Code)—does not limit judicial notice to those matters specified by statute. Judicial notice has been taken of various matters not so specified, principally of those matters of common knowledge which are certain and indisputable. Witkin, California Evidence §§ 50–52 (1958).

Under the Evidence Code, as under existing law, courts may consider whatever materials are appropriate in construing statutes, determining constitutional issues, and formulating rules of law. That a court may consider legislative history, discussions by learned writers in treatises and law reviews, materials that contain controversial economic and social facts or findings or that indicate contemporary opinion, and similar materials is inherent in the requirement that it take judicial notice of the law. In many cases, the meaning and validity of statutes, the precise nature of a common law rule, or the correct interpretation of a constitutional provision can be determined only with the help of such extrinsic aids. Cf. People v. Sterling Refining Co., 86 Cal.App. 558, 564, 261 Pac. 1080, 1083 (1927) (statutory authority to notice "public and private acts" of legislature held to authorize examination of legislative history of certain acts). See also Perez v. Sharp, 32 Cal.2d 711, 198 P.2d 17 (1948) (texts and authorities used by court in opinions determining constitutionality of statute prohibiting interracial marriages). Section 450 will neither broaden nor limit the extent to which a court may resort to extrinsic aids in determining the rules of law that it is required to notice. Nor will Section 450 broaden or limit the extent to which a court may take judicial notice of any other matter not specified in Section 451 or 452. [7 Cal.L.Rev.Comm. Reports 1 (1965)]

§ 451. Matters which must be judicially noticed

Judicial notice shall be taken of the following:

(a) The decisional, constitutional, and public statutory law of this state and of the United States and the provisions of any charter described in Section 3, 4, or 5 of Article XI of the California Constitution.

(b) Any matter made a subject of judicial notice by Section 11343.6, 11344.6, or 18576 of the Government Code or by Section 1507 of Title 44 of the United States Code.[1]

(c) Rules of professional conduct for members of the bar adopted pursuant to Section 6076 of the Business and Professions Code and rules of practice and procedure for the courts of this state adopted by the Judicial Council.

1. 44 U.S.C.A. § 1507.

(d) Rules of pleading, practice, and procedure prescribed by the United States Supreme Court, such as the Rules of the United States Supreme Court, the Federal Rules of Civil Procedure, the Federal Rules of Criminal Procedure, the Admiralty Rules, the Rules of the Court of Claims, the Rules of the Customs Court, and the General Orders and Forms in Bankruptcy.

(e) The true signification of all English words and phrases and of all legal expressions.

(f) Facts and propositions of generalized knowledge that are so universally known that they cannot reasonably be the subject of dispute.

COMMENT—ASSEMBLY COMMITTEE ON JUDICIARY

Judicial notice of the matters specified in Section 451 is mandatory, whether or not the court is requested to notice them. Although the court errs if it fails to take judicial notice of the matters specified in this section, such error is not necessarily reversible error. Depending upon the circumstances, the appellate court may hold that the error was "invited" (and, hence, is not reversible error) or that points not urged in the trial court may not be advanced on appeal. These and similar principles of appellate practice are not abrogated by this section.

Section 451 includes matters both of law and of fact. The matters specified in subdivisions (a), (b), (c), and (d) are all matters that, broadly speaking, can be considered as a part of the "law" applicable to the particular case. The court can reasonably be expected to discover and apply this law even if the parties fail to provide the court with references to the pertinent cases, statutes, regulations and rules. Other matters that also might properly be considered as a part of the law applicable to the case (such as the law of foreign nations and certain regulations and ordinances) are included under Section 452, rather than under Section 451, primarily because of the difficulty of ascertaining such matters. Subdivision (e) of Section 451 requires the court to judicially notice "the true signification of all English words and phrases and of all legal expressions." These are facts that must be judicially noticed in order to conduct meaningful proceedings. Similarly, subdivision (f) of Section 451 covers "universally known" facts.

Listed below are the matters that must be judicially noticed under Section 451.

California and federal law. The decisional, constitutional, and public statutory law of California and of the United States must be judicially noticed under subdivision (a). This requirement states existing law as found in subdivision 3 of Code of Civil Procedure Section 1875 (superseded by the Evidence Code).

Charter provisions of California cities and counties. Judicial notice must be taken under subdivision (a) of the provisions of charters adopted pursuant to Section 7½ or 8 of Article XI of the California Constitution. Notice of these provisions is mandatory under the State Constitution. Cal.Const., Art. XI, § 7½ (county charter), § 8 (charter of city or city and county).

Regulations of California and federal agencies. Judicial notice must be taken under subdivision (b) of the rules, regulations, orders, and standards of general application adopted by California state agencies and filed with the Secretary of State or printed in the California Administrative Code or the California Administrative Register. This is existing law as found in Government Code Sections 11383 and 11384. Under subdivision (b), judicial notice must also be taken of the rules of the State Personnel Board. This, too, is existing law under Government Code Section 18576.

Subdivision (b) also requires California courts to judicially notice documents published in the Federal Register (such as (1) presidential proclamations and executive orders having general applicability and legal effect and (2) orders, regulations, rules, certificates, codes of fair competition, licenses, notices, and similar instruments, having general applicability and legal effect, that are issued, prescribed, or promulgated by federal agencies). There is no clear holding that this is existing California law. Although Section 307 of Title 44 of the United States Code provides that the "contents of the Federal Register shall be judicially noticed," it is not clear that this requires notice by state courts. See Broadway Fed. etc. Loan Ass'n v. Howard, 133 Cal.App.2d 382, 386 note 4, 285 P.2d 61, 64 note 4 (1955) (referring to 44 U.S.C.A. §§ 301–314). Compare Note, 59 Harv.L.Rev. 1137, 1141 (1946) (doubt expressed that notice is required), with Knowlton, Judicial Notice, 10 Rutgers L.Rev. 501, 504 (1956) ("it would seem that this provision is binding upon the state courts"). Livermore v. Beal, 18 Cal.App.2d 535, 542–543, 64 P.2d 987, 992 (1937), suggests that California courts are required to judicially notice pertinent federal official action, and California courts have judicially noticed the contents of various proclamations, orders, and regulations of federal agencies. E.g., Pacific Solvents Co. v. Superior Court, 88 Cal.App.2d 953, 955, 199 P.2d 740, 741 (1948) (orders and regulations); People v. Mason, 72 Cal.App.2d 699, 706–707, 165 P.2d 481, 485 (1946) (presidential and executive proclamations) (disapproved on other grounds in People v. Friend, 50 Cal.2d 570, 578, 327 P.2d 97, 102 (1958)); Downer v. Grizzly Livestock & Land Co., 6 Cal.App.2d 39, 42, 43 P.2d 843, 845 (1935) (rules and regulations). Section 451 makes the California law clear.

Rules of court. Judicial notice of the California Rules of Court is required under subdivision (c). These rules, adopted by the Judicial Council, are as binding on the parties as procedural statutes. Cantillon v. Superior Court, 150 Cal.App.2d 184, 309 P.2d 890 (1957). See Albermont Petroleum, Ltd. v. Cunningham, 186 Cal.App.2d 84, 9 Cal. Rptr. 405 (1960). Likewise, the rules of pleading, practice, and procedure promulgated by the United States Supreme Court are required to be judicially noticed under subdivision (d).

The rules of the California and federal courts which are required to be judicially noticed under subdivisions (c) and (d) are, or should be, familiar to the court or easily discoverable from materials readily available to the court. However, this may not be true of the court rules of sister states or other jurisdictions nor, for example, of the rules of the various United States Courts of Appeals or local rules of a particular superior court. See Albermont Petroleum, Ltd. v. Cunningham, 186 Cal.App.2d 84, 9 Cal.Rptr. 405 (1960). Judicial notice of these rules is permitted under subdivision (e) of Section 452 but is not required unless there is compliance with the provisions of Section 453.

State Bar Rules of Professional Conduct. The Rules of Professional Conduct of the State Bar of California are, in effect, rules of the Supreme Court, for they must be approved by that court. Barton v. State Bar, 209 Cal. 677, 289 Pac. 818 (1930). Subdivision (c), therefore, requires the court to take judicial notice of these rules to the same extent that it takes notice of other rules of court.

Words, phrases, and legal expressions. Subdivision (e) requires the court to take judicial notice of "the true signification of all English words and phrases and of all legal expressions." This restates the same matter covered in subdivision 1 of Code of Civil Procedure Section 1875. Under existing law, however, it is not clear that judicial notice of these matters is mandatory.

"Universally known" facts. Subdivision (f) requires the court to take judicial notice of indisputable facts and propositions universally known. "Universally known" does not mean that every man on the street has knowledge of such facts. A fact known among persons of reasonable and average intelligence and knowledge will satisfy the "universally known" requirement. Cf. People v. Tossetti, 107 Cal.App. 7, 12, 289 Pac. 881, 883 (1930).

Subdivision (f) should be contrasted with subdivisions (g) and (h) of Section 452, which provide for judicial notice of indisputable facts and propositions that are matters of common knowledge or are capable of immediate and accurate determination by resort to sources of reasonably indisputable accuracy. Subdivisions (g) and (h) permit notice of facts and propositions that are indisputable but are not "universally" known.

Judicial notice does not apply to facts merely because they are known to the judge to be indisputable. The facts must fulfill the requirements of subdivision (f) of Section 451 or subdivision (g) or (h) of Section 452. If a judge happens to know a fact that is not widely enough known to be subject to judicial notice under this division, he may not "notice" it.

It is clear under existing law that the court may judicially notice the matters specified in subdivision (f); it is doubtful, however, that the court must notice them. See Varcoe v. Lee, 180 Cal. 338, 347, 181 Pac. 223, 227 (1919) (dictum). Since subdivision (f) covers universally known facts, the parties ordinarily will expect the court to take judicial notice of them; the court should not be permitted to ignore such facts merely because the parties fail to make a formal request for judicial notice.

§ 452. Matters which may be judicially noticed

Judicial notice may be taken of the following matters to the extent that they are not embraced within Section 451:

(a) The decisional, constitutional, and statutory law of any state of the United States and the resolutions and private acts of the Congress of the United States and of the Legislature of this state.

(b) Regulations and legislative enactments issued by or under the authority of the United States or any public entity in the United States.

(c) Official acts of the legislative, executive, and judicial departments of the United States and of any state of the United States.

(d) Records of (1) any court of this state or (2) any court of record of the United States or of any state of the United States.

(e) Rules of court of (1) any court of this state or (2) any court of record of the United States or of any state of the United States.

(f) The law of an organization of nations and of foreign nations and public entities in foreign nations.

(g) Facts and propositions that are of such common knowledge within the territorial jurisdiction of the court that they cannot reasonably be the subject of dispute.

(h) Facts and propositions that are not reasonably subject to dispute and are capable of immediate and accurate determination by resort to sources of reasonably indisputable accuracy.

COMMENT—ASSEMBLY COMMITTEE ON JUDICIARY

Section 452 includes matters both of law and of fact. The court may take judicial notice of these matters, even when not requested to do so; it is required to notice them if a party requests it and satisfies the requirements of Section 453.

The matters of law included under Section 452 may be neither known to the court nor easily discoverable by it because the sources of information are not readily available. However, if a party requests it and furnishes the court with "sufficient information" for it to take judicial notice, the court must do so if proper notice has been given to each adverse party. See Evidence Code § 453. Thus, judicial notice of these matters of law is mandatory only if counsel adequately discharges his responsibility for informing the court as to the law applicable to the case. The simplified process of judicial notice can then be applied to all of the law applicable to the case, including such law as ordinances and the law of foreign nations.

Although Section 452 extends the process of judicial notice to some matters of law which the courts do not judicially notice under existing law, the wider scope of such notice is balanced by the assurance that the matter need not be judicially noticed unless adequate information to support its truth is furnished to the court. Under Section 453, this burden falls upon the party requesting that judicial notice be taken. In addition, the parties are entitled under Section 455 to a reasonable opportunity to present information to the court as to the propriety of taking judicial notice and as to the tenor of the matter to be noticed.

Listed below are the matters that may be judicially noticed under Section 452 (and must be noticed if the conditions specified in Section 453 are met).

Law of sister states. Subdivision (a) provides for judicial notice of the decisional, constitutional, and statutory law in force in sister states. California courts now take judicial notice of the law of sister states under subdivision 3 of Section 1875 of the Code of Civil Procedure. However, Section 1875 seems to preclude notice of sister-state law as interpreted by the intermediate-appellate courts of sister states, whereas Section 452 permits notice of relevant decisions of all sister-state courts. If this be an extension of existing law, it is a desirable one, for the courts of sister states generally can be considered as responsive to the need for properly determining the law as are equivalent courts in California. The existing law also is not clear as to whether a request for judicial notice of sister-state law is required and whether judicial notice is mandatory. On the necessity for a request for judicial notice, see Comment, 24 Cal.L.Rev. 311, 316 (1936). On whether judicial notice is mandatory, see In re Bartges, 44 Cal.2d 241, 282 P.2d 47 (1955), and the opinion of the Supreme Court in denying a hearing in Estate of Moore, 7 Cal.App.2d 722, 726, 48 P.2d 28, 29 (1935).

Law of territories and possessions of the United States. Subdivision (a) also provides for judicial notice of the decisional, constitutional, and statutory law in force in the territories and possessions of the United States. See the broad definition of "state" in Evidence Code § 220. It is not clear under existing California law whether this law is treated as sister-state law or foreign law. See Witkin, California Evidence § 45 (1958).

Resolutions and private acts. Subdivision (a) provides for judicial notice of resolutions and private acts of the Congress of the United States and of the legislature of any state, territory, or possession of the United States. See the broad definition of "state" in Evidence Code § 220.

The California law on this matter is not clear. Our courts are authorized by subdivision 3 of Code of Civil Procedure Section 1875 to take judicial notice of private statutes of this State and the United States, and they probably would take judicial notice of resolutions of this State and the United States under the same subdivision. It is not clear whether such notice is compulsory. It may be that judicial notice of a private act pleaded in a criminal action pursuant to Penal Code Section 963 is mandatory, whereas judicial notice of the same private act may be discretionary when pleaded in a civil action pursuant to Section 459 of the Code of Civil Procedure.

Although no case in point has been found, California courts probably would not take judicial notice of a resolution or private act of a sister state or territory or possession of the United States. Although Section 1875 is not the exclusive list of the matters that will be judicially noticed, the courts did not take judicial notice of a private statute prior to the enactment of Section 1875. Ellis v. Eastman, 32 Cal. 447 (1867).

Regulations, ordinances, and similar legislative enactments. Subdivision (b) provides for judicial notice of regulations and legislative enactments, adopted by or under the authority of the United States or of any state, territory, or possession of the United States, including public entities therein. See the broad definition of "public entity" in Evidence Code § 200. The words "regulations and legislative enactments" include such matters as "ordinances" and other similar legislative enactments. Not all public entities legislate by ordinance.

This subdivision changes existing law. Under existing law, municipal courts take judicial notice of ordinances in force within their jurisdiction. People v. Cowles, 142 Cal.App.2d Supp. 865, 867, 298 P.2d 732, 733–734 (1956); People v. Crittenden, 93 Cal.App.2d Supp. 871, 877, 209 P.2d 161, 165 (1949). In addition, an ordinance pleaded in a criminal action pursuant to Penal Code Section 963 must be judicially noticed. On the other hand, neither the superior court nor a district court of appeal will take judicial notice in a civil action of municipal or county ordinances. Thompson v. Guyer–Hays, 207 Cal.App.2d 366, 24 Cal.Rptr. 461 (1962); County of Los Angeles v. Bartlett, 203 Cal.App.2d 523, 21 Cal.Rptr. 776 (1962); Becerra v. Hochberg, 193 Cal.App.2d 431, 14 Cal.Rptr. 101 (1961). It seems safe to assume that ordinances of sister states and of territories and possessions of the United States would not be judicially noticed under existing law.

Judicial notice of certain regulations of California and federal agencies is mandatory under subdivision (b) of Section 451. Subdivision (b) of Section 452 provides for judicial notice of California and federal regulations that are not included under subdivision (b) of Section 451 and, also, for judicial notice of regulations of other states and territories and possessions of the United States.

Both California and federal regulations have been judicially noticed under subdivision 3 of Code of Civil Procedure Section 1875. 18 Cal. Jur.2d Evidence § 24. Although no case in point has been found, it is unlikely that regulations of other states or of territories or possessions of the United States would be judicially noticed under existing law.

Official acts of the legislative, executive, and judicial departments. Subdivision (c) provides for judicial notice of the official acts of the legislative, executive, and judicial departments of the United States and any state, territory, or possession of the United States. See the broad definition of "state" in Evidence Code § 220. Subdivision (c) states existing law as found in subdivision 3 of Code of Civil Procedure Section 1875. Under this provision, the California courts have taken judicial notice of a wide variety of administrative and executive acts, such as proceedings and reports of the House Committee on Un–American Activities, records of the State Board of Education, and records of a county planning commission. See Witkin, California Evidence § 49 (1958), and 1963 Supplement thereto.

Court records and rules of court. Subdivisions (d) and (e) provide for judicial notice of the court records and rules of court of (1) any court of this State or (2) any court of record of the United States or of any state, territory, or possession of the United States. See the broad definition of "state" in Evidence Code § 220. So far as court records are concerned, subdivision (d) states existing law. Flores v. Arroyo, 56 Cal.2d 492, 15 Cal.Rptr. 87, 364 P.2d 263 (1961). While the provisions of subdivision (c) of Section 452 are broad enough to include court records, specific mention of these records in subdivision (d) is desirable in order to eliminate any uncertainty in the law on this point. See the Flores case, supra.

Subdivision (e) may change existing law so far as judicial notice of rules of court is concerned, but the provision is consistent with the modern philosophy of judicial notice as indicated by the holding in Flores v. Arroyo, supra. To the extent that subdivision (e) overlaps with subdivisions (c) and (d) of Section 451, notice is, of course, mandatory under Section 451.

Foreign law. Subdivision (f) provides for judicial notice of the law of organizations of nations, foreign nations, and public entities in foreign nations. See the broad definition of "public entity" in Evidence Code § 200. Subdivision (f) should be read in connection with Sections 310, 311, 453, and 454. These provisions retain the substance of the existing law which was enacted in 1957 upon recommendation of the California Law Revision Commission. Code Civ.Proc. § 1875. See 1 Cal.Law Revision Comm'n. Rep., Rec. & Studies, Recommendation and Study Relating to Judicial Notice of the Law of Foreign Countries at I–1 (1957).

Subdivision (f) refers to "the law" of organizations of nations, foreign nations, and public entities in foreign nations. This makes all law, in whatever form, subject to judicial notice.

Matters of "common knowledge" and verifiable facts. Subdivision (g) provides for judicial notice of matters of common knowledge within the court's territorial jurisdiction that are not subject to dispute. "Territorial jurisdiction," in this context, refers to the county in which a superior court is located or the judicial district in which a municipal or justice court is located. The fact of which notice is taken need not be something physically located within the court's territorial jurisdiction, but common knowledge of the fact must exist within the court's territorial jurisdiction. Subdivision (g) reflects existing case law. Varcoe v. Lee, 180 Cal. 338, 181 Pac. 223 (1919); 18 Cal.Jur.2d Evidence § 19 at 439–440. The California courts have taken judicial notice of a wide variety of matters of common knowledge. Witkin, California Evidence §§ 50–52 (1958).

Subdivision (h) provides for judicial notice of indisputable facts immediately ascertainable by reference to sources of reasonably indisputable accuracy. In other words, the facts need not be actually known if they are readily ascertainable and indisputable. Sources of "reasonably indisputable accuracy" include not only treatises, encyclopedias, almanacs, and the like, but also persons learned in the subject matter. This would not mean that reference works would be received in evidence or sent to the jury room. Their use would be limited to consultation by the judge and the parties for the purposes of determining whether or not to take judicial notice and determining the tenor of the matter to be noticed.

Subdivisions (g) and (h) include, for example, facts which are accepted as established by experts and specialists in the natural, physical, and social sciences, if those facts are of such wide acceptance that to submit them to the jury would be to risk irrational findings. These subdivisions include such matters listed in Code of Civil Procedure Section 1875 as the "geographical divisions and political history of the world." To the extent that subdivisions (g) and (h) overlap subdivision (f) of Section 451, notice is, of course, mandatory under Section 451.

The matters covered by subdivisions (g) and (h) are included in Section 452, rather than Section 451, because it seems reasonable to put the burden on the parties to bring adequate information before the court if judicial notice of these matters is to be mandatory. See Evidence Code § 453 and the Comment thereto.

Under existing law, courts take judicial notice of the matters that are included under subdivisions (g) and (h), either pursuant to Section 1875 of the Code of Civil Procedure or because such matters are matters of common knowledge which are certain and indisputable. Witkin,

California Evidence §§ 50–52 (1958). Notice of these matters probably is not compulsory under existing law.

§ 452.5. Criminal conviction records; computer-generated records; admissibility

(a) The official acts and records specified in subdivisions (c) and (d) of Section 452 include any computer-generated official court records, as specified by the Judicial Council which relate to criminal convictions, when the record is certified by a clerk of the superior court pursuant to Section 69844.5 of the Government Code at the time of computer entry.

(b) An official record of conviction certified in accordance with subdivision (a) of Section 1530 is admissible pursuant to Section 1280 to prove the commission, attempted commission, or solicitation of a criminal offense, prior conviction, service of a prison term, or other act, condition, or event recorded by the record.

LAW REVISION COMMISSION COMMENTS

2002 Amendment

Subdivision (a) of Section 452.5 is amended to reflect unification of the municipal and superior courts pursuant to Article VI, Section 5(e), of the California Constitution. The reference to former Government Code Section 71280.5 is deleted, because that provision concerned certification and submission of municipal court records relating to criminal convictions. Government Code Section 69844.5 is the comparable superior court provision.

§ 453. Compulsory judicial notice upon request

The trial court shall take judicial notice of any matter specified in Section 452 if a party requests it and:

(a) Gives each adverse party sufficient notice of the request, through the pleadings or otherwise, to enable such adverse party to prepare to meet the request; and

(b) Furnishes the court with sufficient information to enable it to take judicial notice of the matter.

LAW REVISION COMMISSION COMMENT

Section 453 provides that the court must take judicial notice of any matter specified in Section 452 if a party requests that such notice be taken, furnishes the court with sufficient information to enable it to take judicial notice of the matter, and gives each adverse party sufficient notice of the request to prepare to meet it.

Section 453 is intended as a safeguard and not as a rigid limitation on the court's power to take judicial notice. The section does not affect the discretionary power of the court to take judicial notice under Section

452 where the party requesting that judicial notice be taken fails to give the requisite notice to each adverse party or fails to furnish sufficient information as to the propriety of taking judicial notice or as to the tenor of the matter to be noticed. Hence, when he considers it appropriate, the judge may take judicial notice under Section 452 and may consult and use any source of pertinent information, whether or not furnished by the parties. However, where the matter noticed under Section 452 is one that is of substantial consequence to the action—even though the court may take judicial notice under Section 452 when the requirements of Section 453 have not been satisfied—the party adversely affected must be given a reasonable opportunity to present information as to the propriety of taking judicial notice and as to the tenor of the matter to be noticed. See Evidence Code § 455 and the Comment thereto.

The "notice" requirement. The party requesting the court to judicially notice a matter under Section 453 must give each adverse party sufficient notice, through the pleadings or otherwise, to enable him to prepare to meet the request. In cases where the notice given does not satisfy this requirement, the court may decline to take judicial notice. A somewhat similar notice to the adverse parties is required under subdivision 4 of Section 1875 of the Code of Civil Procedure when a request for judicial notice of the law of a foreign country is made. Section 453 broadens this existing requirement to cover all matters specified in Section 452.

The notice requirement is an important one since judicial notice is binding on the jury under Section 457. Accordingly, the adverse parties should be given ample notice so that they will have an opportunity to prepare to oppose the taking of judicial notice and to obtain information relevant to the tenor of the matter to be noticed.

Since Section 452 relates to a wide variety of facts and law, the notice requirement should be administered with flexibility in order to insure that the policy behind the judicial notice rules is properly implemented. In many cases, it will be reasonable to expect the notice to be given at or before the time of the pretrial conference. In other cases, matters of fact or law of which the court should take judicial notice may come up at the trial. Section 453 merely requires reasonable notice, and the reasonableness of the notice given will depend upon the circumstances of the particular case.

The "sufficient information" requirement. Under Section 453, the court is not required to resort to any sources of information not provided by the parties. If the party requesting that judicial notice be taken under Section 453 fails to provide the court with "sufficient information," the judge may decline to take judicial notice. For example, if the party requests the court to take judicial notice of the specific gravity of gold, the party requesting that notice be taken must furnish the judge with definitive information as to the specific gravity of gold. The judge is not required to undertake the necessary research to determine the fact, though, of course, he is not precluded from doing such research if he so desires.

Section 453 does not define "sufficient information"; this will necessarily vary from case to case. While the parties will understandably use the best evidence they can produce under the circumstances, mechanical requirements that are ill-suited to the individual case should be avoided. The court justifiably might require that the party requesting that judicial notice be taken provide expert testimony to clarify especially difficult problems.

Burden on party requesting that judicial notice be taken. Where a request is made to take judicial notice under Section 453, the court may decline to take judicial notice unless the party requesting that notice be taken persuades the judge that the matter is one that properly may be noticed under Section 452 and also persuades the judge as to tenor of the matter to be noticed. The degree of the judge's persuasion regarding a particular matter is determined by the subdivision of Section 452 which authorizes judicial notice of the matter. For example, if the matter is claimed to be a fact of common knowledge under paragraph (g) of Section 452, the party must persuade the judge that the fact is of such common knowledge within the territorial jurisdiction of the court that it cannot reasonably be subject to dispute, i.e., that no reasonable person having the same information as is available to the judge could rationally disbelieve the fact. On the other hand, if the matter to be noticed is a city ordinance under paragraph (b) of Section 452, the party must persuade the judge that a valid ordinance exists and also as to its tenor; but the judge need not believe that not reasonable person could conclude otherwise.

Without regard to the evidence supplied by the party requesting that judicial notice be taken, the judge's determination to take judicial notice of a matter specified in Section 452 will be upheld on appeal if the matter was properly noticed. The reviewing court may resort to any information, whether or not available at the trial, in order to sustain the proper taking of judicial notice. See Evidence Code § 459. On the other hand, even though a party requested that judicial notice be taken under Section 453 and gave notice to each adverse party in compliance with subdivision (a) of Section 453, the decision of the judge not to take judicial notice will be upheld on appeal unless the reviewing court determines that the party furnished information to the judge that was so persuasive that no reasonable judge would have refused to take judicial notice of the matter. [7 Cal.L.Rev.Comm. Reports 1 (1965)]

§ 454. Information that may be used in taking judicial notice

(a) In determining the propriety of taking judicial notice of a matter, or the tenor thereof:

(1) Any source of pertinent information, including the advice of persons learned in the subject matter, may be consulted or used, whether or not furnished by a party.

(2) Exclusionary rules of evidence do not apply except for Section 352 and the rules of privilege.

(b) Where the subject of judicial notice is the law of an organization of nations, a foreign nation, or a public entity in a foreign nation and the court resorts to the advice of persons learned in the subject matter, such advice, if not received in open court, shall be in writing.

COMMENT—ASSEMBLY COMMITTEE ON JUDICIARY

Since one of the purposes of judicial notice is to simplify the process of proofmaking, the judge should be given considerable latitude in deciding what sources are trustworthy. This section permits the court to use any source of pertinent information, including the advice of persons learned in the subject matter. It probably restates existing law as found in Section 1875 of the Code of Civil Procedure. See Estate of McNamara, 181 Cal. 82, 89–91, 183 Pac. 552, 555 (1919); Rogers v. Cady, 104 Cal. 288, 290, 38 Pac. 81 (1894) (dictum); Tentative Recommendation and a Study Relating to the Uniform Rules of Evidence (Article II. Judicial Notice), 6 Cal.Law Revision Comm'n, Rep., Rec. & Studies 801, 850–851 (1964).

Subdivision (b) preserves a limitation, now appearing in the next to the last paragraph of Code of Civil Procedure Section 1875, on the form in which expert advice on foreign law may be received.

§ 455. Opportunity to present information to court

With respect to any matter specified in Section 452 or in subdivision (f) of Section 451 that is of substantial consequence to the determination of the action:

(a) If the trial court has been requested to take or has taken or proposes to take judicial notice of such matter, the court shall afford each party reasonable opportunity, before the jury is instructed or before the cause is submitted for decision by the court, to present to the court information relevant to (1) the propriety of taking judicial notice of the matter and (2) the tenor of the matter to be noticed.

(b) If the trial court resorts to any source of information not received in open court, including the advice of persons learned in the subject matter, such information and its source shall be made a part of the record in the action and the court shall afford each party reasonable opportunity to meet such information before judicial notice of the matter may be taken.

LAW REVISION COMMISSION COMMENT

Section 455 provides procedural safeguards designed to afford the parties reasonable opportunity to be heard both as to the propriety of taking judicial notice of a matter and as to the tenor of the matter to be noticed.

Subdivision (a). This subdivision guarantees to the parties a reasonable opportunity to present information to the court as to the propriety of taking judicial notice and as to the tenor of the matter to be noticed. In a jury case, the subdivision provides the parties with an opportunity to present their information to the judge before a jury instruction based on a matter judicially noticed is given. Where the matter subject to judicial notice relates to a cause tried by the court, the subdivision guarantees the parties an opportunity to dispute the taking of judicial notice of the matter before the cause is submitted for decision. If the judge does not discover that a matter should be judicially noticed until after the cause is submitted for decision, he may, of course, order the cause to be reopened for the purpose of permitting the parties to provide him with information concerning the matter.

Subdivision (a) is limited in its application to those matters specified in subdivision (f) of Section 451 or in Section 452 that are of substantial consequence to the determination of the action, for it would not be practicable to make the subdivision applicable to the other matters listed in Section 451 or to matters that are of inconsequential significance.

What constitutes a "reasonable opportunity" to "present ... information" will depend upon the complexity of the matter and its importance to the case. For example, in a case where there is no dispute as to the existence and validity of a city ordinance, no formal hearing would be necessary to determine the propriety of taking judicial notice of the ordinance and of its tenor. But, where there is a complex question as to the tenor of foreign law applicable to the case, the granting of a hearing under subdivision (a) would be mandatory. The New York courts have so construed their judicial notice statute, saying that an opportunity for a litigant to know what the deciding tribunal is considering and to be heard with respect to both law and fact is guaranteed by due process of law. Arams v. Arams, 182 Misc. 328, 182 Misc. 336, 45 N.Y.S.2d 251 (Sup.Ct.1943).

Subdivision (b). If the court resorts to sources of information not previously known to the parties, this subdivision requires that such information and its source be made a part of the record when it relates to taking judicial notice of a matter specified in subdivision (f) of Section 451 or in Section 452 that is of substantial consequence to the determination of the action. This requirement is based on a somewhat similar requirement found in Code of Civil Procedure Section 1875 regarding the law of a foreign nation. Making the information and its source a part of the record assures its availability for examination by the parties and by a reviewing court. In addition, subdivision (b) requires the court to give the parties a reasonable opportunity to meet such additional information before judicial notice of the matter may be taken. [7 Cal.L.Rev.Comm. Report 1 (1965)]

§ 456. Noting denial of request to take judicial notice

If the trial court denies a request to take judicial notice of any matter, the court shall at the earliest practicable time so advise the parties and indicate for the record that it has denied the request.

LAW REVISION COMMISSION COMMENT

Section 456 requires the judge to advise the parties and indicate for the record at the earliest practicable time any denial of a request to take judicial notice of a matter. The requirement is imposed in order to provide the parties with an adequate opportunity to submit evidence on any matter as to which judicial notice was anticipated but not taken. No comparable requirement is found in existing law. Compare Evidence Code § 455 and the Comment thereto. [7 Cal.L.Rev.Comm. Reports 1 (1965)]

§ 457. Instructing jury on matter judicially noticed

If a matter judicially noticed is a matter which would otherwise have been for determination by the jury, the trial court may, and upon request shall, instruct the jury to accept as a fact the matter so noticed.

LAW REVISION COMMISSION COMMENT

Section 457 makes matters judicially noticed binding on the jury and thereby eliminates any possibility of presenting to the jury evidence disputing the fact as noticed by the court. The section is limited to instruction on a matter that would otherwise have been for determination by the jury; instruction of juries on matters of law is not a matter of evidence and is covered by the general provisions of law governing instruction of juries. The section states the substance of the existing law as found in Code of Civil Procedure Section 2102. See People v. Mayes, 113 Cal. 618, 625–626, 45 Pac. 860, 862 (1896); Gallegos v. Union–Tribune Publishing Co., 195 Cal.App.2d 791, 797–798, 16 Cal. Rptr. 185, 189–190 (1961). [7 Cal.L.Rev.Comm. Reports 1 (1965)]

§ 458. Judicial notice by trial court in subsequent proceedings

The failure or refusal of the trial court to take judicial notice of a matter, or to instruct the jury with respect to the matter, does not preclude the trial court in subsequent proceedings in the action from taking judicial notice of the matter in accordance with the procedure specified in this division.

LAW REVISION COMMISSION COMMENT

This section provides that the failure or even the refusal of the court to take judicial notice of a matter at the trial does not bar the trial judge, or another trial judge, from taking judicial notice of that matter in a subsequent proceeding, such as a hearing on a motion for new trial or the like. Although no California case in point has been found, it seems safe to assume that the trial judge has the power to take judicial notice of a matter in subsequent proceedings, since the appellate court can properly take judicial notice of any matter that the trial court could properly notice. See People v. Tossetti, 107 Cal.App. 7, 12, 289 Pac. 881, 883 (1930). [7 Cal.L.Rev.Comm. Reports 1 (1965)]

§ 459. Judicial notice by reviewing court

(a) The reviewing court shall take judicial notice of (1) each matter properly noticed by the trial court and (2) each matter that the trial court was required to notice under Section 451 or 453. The reviewing court may take judicial notice of any matter specified in Section 452. The reviewing court may take judicial notice of a matter in a tenor different from that noticed by the trial court.

(b) In determining the propriety of taking judicial notice of a matter, or the tenor thereof, the reviewing court has the same power as the trial court under Section 454.

(c) When taking judicial notice under this section of a matter specified in Section 452 or in subdivision (f) of Section 451 that is of substantial consequence to the determination of the action, the reviewing court shall comply with the provisions of subdivision (a) of Section 455 if the matter was not theretofore judicially noticed in the action.

(d) In determining the propriety of taking judicial notice of a matter specified in Section 452 or in subdivision (f) of Section 451 that is of substantial consequence to the determination of the action, or the tenor thereof, if the reviewing court resorts to any source of information not received in open court or not included in the record of the action, including the advice of persons learned in the subject matter, the reviewing court shall afford each party reasonable opportunity to meet such information before judicial notice of the matter may be taken.

LAW REVISION COMMISSION COMMENT

Section 459 sets forth a separate set of rules for the taking of judicial notice by a reviewing court.

Subdivision (a). Subdivision (a) requires that a reviewing court take judicial notice of any matter that the trial court properly noticed or was obliged to notice. This means that the matters specified in Section 451 must be judicially noticed by the reviewing court even though the trial court failed to take judicial notice of such matters. A matter specified in Section 452 also must be judicially noticed by the reviewing court if such matter was properly noticed by the trial court in the exercise of its discretion or an appropriate request was made at the trial level and the party making the request satisfied the conditions specified in Section 453. However, if the trial court erred, the reviewing court is not bound by the tenor of the notice taken by the trial court.

Having taken judicial notice of such a matter, the reviewing court may or may not apply it in the particular case on appeal. The effect to be given to matters judicially noticed on appeal, where the question has not been raised below, depends on factors that are not evidentiary in character and are not mentioned in this code. For example, the appellate court is required to notice the matters of law mentioned in Section 451, but it may hold that an error which the appellant has "invited" is not reversible error or that points not urged in the trial court may not be advanced on appeal, and refuse, therefore, to apply the law to the pending case. These principles do not mean that the appellate court does not take judicial notice of the applicable law; they merely mean that, for reasons of policy governing appellate review, the appellate court may refuse to apply the law to the case before it.

In addition to requiring the reviewing court to judicially notice those matters which the trial court properly noticed or was required to notice, the subdivision also provides authority for the reviewing court to exercise the same discretionary power to take judicial notice as is possessed by the trial court.

Subdivision (b). The reviewing court may consult any source of pertinent information for the purpose of determining the propriety of taking judicial notice or the tenor of the matter to be noticed. This includes, of course, the power to consult such sources for the purpose of sustaining or reversing the taking of judicial notice by the trial court. As to the rights of the parties when the reviewing court consults such materials, see subdivision (d) and the Comment thereto.

Subdivision (c). This subdivision provides the parties with the same procedural protection when judicial notice is taken by the reviewing court as is provided by Section 455(a).

Subdivision (d). This subdivision assures the parties the same procedural safeguard at the appellate level that they have in the trial court: If the appellate court resorts to sources of information not included in the record in the action or proceeding, or not received in open court at the appellate level, either to sustain the tenor of the notice taken by the trial court or to notice a matter in a tenor different from that noticed by the trial court, the parties must be given a reasonable opportunity to meet such additional information before judicial notice of the matter may be taken. See Evidence Code § 455(b) and the Comment thereto. [7 Cal.L.Rev.Comm. Reports 1 (1965)]

§ 460. Appointment of expert by court

Where the advice of persons learned in the subject matter is required in order to enable the court to take judicial notice of a matter, the court on its own motion or on motion of any party may appoint one or more such persons to provide such advice. If the court determines to appoint such a person, he shall be appointed and compensated in the manner provided in Article 2 (commencing with Section 730) of Chapter 3 of Division 6.

COMMENT—ASSEMBLY COMMITTEE ON JUDICIARY

Section 460 makes it clear that a court may appoint experts on matters that are subject to judicial notice when the advice of such persons is required in order to enable the court to take such notice. Such persons are to be appointed and compensated in the same manner as expert witnesses are appointed and compensated under the provisions of Evidence Code Sections 730–733. In the normal case, the parties may be expected to produce the advice of experts if it is needed. Section 460, however, enables the court to appoint experts in those cases where the advice of an expert not identified with a party seems desirable.

DIVISION 5. BURDEN OF PROOF; BURDEN OF PRODUCING EVIDENCE; PRESUMPTIONS AND INFERENCES

CHAPTER 1. BURDEN OF PROOF

ARTICLE 1. GENERAL

§ 500. Party who has the burden of proof

Except as otherwise provided by law, a party has the burden of proof as to each fact the existence or nonexistence of which is essential to the claim for relief or defense that he is asserting.

LAW REVISION COMMISSION COMMENT

As used in Section 500, the burden of proof means the obligation of a party to produce a particular state of conviction in the mind of the trier of fact as to the existence or nonexistence of a fact. See Evidence Code §§ 115, 190. If this requisite degree of conviction is not achieved as to the existence of a particular fact, the trier of fact must assume that the fact does not exist. Morgan, Basic Problems of Evidence 19 (1957); 9 Wigmore, Evidence § 2485 (3d ed. 1940). Usually, the burden of proof requires a party to convince the trier of fact that the existence of a particular fact is more probable than its nonexistence—a degree of proof usually described as proof by a preponderance of the evidence. Evidence Code § 115; Witkin, California Evidence § 59 (1958). However, in some instances, the burden of proof requires a party to produce a substantially greater degree of belief in the mind of the trier of fact concerning the existence of the fact—a burden usually described by stating that the party must introduce clear and convincing proof (Witkin, California Evidence § 60 (1958)) or, with respect to the prosecution in a criminal case, proof beyond a reasonable doubt (Penal Code § 1096).

The defendant in a criminal case sometimes has the burden of proof in regard to a fact essential to negate his guilt. However, in such cases, he usually is not required to persuade that trier of fact as to the existence of such fact; he is merely required to raise a reasonable doubt in the mind of the trier of fact as to his guilty. Evidence Code § 501; People v. Bushton, 80 Cal. 160, 22 Pac. 127 (1889). If the defendant produces no evidence concerning the fact, there is no issue on the matter to be decided by the jury; hence, the jury may be instructed that the nonexistence of the fact must be assumed. See, e.g., People v. Harmon, 89 Cal.App.2d 55, 58, 200 P.2d 32, 34 (1948) (prosecution for narcotics possession; jury instructed "that the burden of proof is upon the defendant that he possessed a written prescription and that in the absence of such evidence it must be assumed that he had no such prescription"). See also People v. Boo Doo Hong, 122 Cal. 606, 607, 55 Pac. 402, 403 (1898).

Section 1981 of the Code of Civil Procedure (superseded by Evidence Code Section 500) provides that the party holding the affirmative of the issue must produce the evidence to prove it and that the burden of proof lies on the party who would be defeated if no evidence were given on either side. This section has been criticized as establishing a meaningless standard:

The "affirmative of the issue" lacks any substantial objective meaning, and the allocation of the burden actually requires the application of several rules of practice and policy, not entirely consistent and not wholly reliable. [Witkin, California Evidence § 56 at 72–73 (1958).]

That the burden is on the party having the affirmative [or] that a party is not required to prove a negative . . . is no more than a play on words, since practically any proposition may be stated in either affirmative or negative form. Thus a plaintiff's exercise of ordinary care equals absence of contributory negligence, in the minority of jurisdictions which place this element in plaintiff's case. In any event, the proposition seems simply not to be so. [Cleary, Presuming and Pleading: An Essay on Juristic Immaturity, 12 Stan.L.Rev. 5, 11 (1959).]

"The basic rule, which covers most situations, is that whatever facts a party must affirmatively plead he also has the burden of proving." Witkin, California Evidence § 56 at 73 (1958). Section 500 follows this basic rule. However, Section 500 is broader, applying to issues not necessarily raised in the pleadings.

Under Section 500, the burden of proof as to a particular fact is normally on the party to whose case the fact is essential. "[W]hen a party seeks relief the burden is upon him to prove his case, and he cannot depend wholly upon the failure of the defendant to prove his defenses." Cal. Employment Comm'n v. Malm, 59 Cal.App.2d 322, 323, 138 P.2d 744, 745 (1943). And, "as a general rule, the burden is on the defendant to prove new matter alleged as a defense . . ., even though it requires the proof of a negative." Wilson v. California Cent. R.R., 94 Cal. 166, 172, 29 Pac. 861, 864 (1892).

Section 500 does not attempt to indicate what facts may be essential to a particular party's claim for relief or defense. The facts that must be shown to establish a cause of action or a defense are determined by the substantive law, not the law of evidence.

The general rule allocating the burden of proof applies "except as otherwise provided by law." The exception is included in recognition of the fact that the burden of proof is sometimes allocated in a manner that is at variance with the general rule. In determining whether the normal allocation of the burden of proof should be altered, the courts consider a number of factors: the knowledge of the parties concerning the particular fact, the availability of the evidence to the parties, the most desirable result in terms of public policy in the absence of proof of the particular fact, and the probability of the existence or nonexistence of the fact. In determining the incidence of the burden of proof, "the truth is that there is not and cannot be any one general solvent for all cases. It is merely a question of policy and fairness based on experience in the different situations." 9 Wigmore, Evidence § 2486 at 275 (3d ed. 1940).

Under existing California law, certain matters have been called "presumptions" even though they do not fall within the definition contained in Code of Civil Procedure Section 1959 (superseded by Evidence Code Section 600). Both Section 1959 and Evidence Code Section 600 define a presumption to be an assumption or conclusion of fact that the law requires to be drawn from the proof or establishment of some other fact. Despite the statutory definition, subdivisions 1 and 4 of Code of Civil Procedure Section 1963 (superseded by Sections 520 and 521 of the Evidence Code) provide presumptions that a person is innocent of crime or wrong and that a person exercises ordinary care for his own concerns. Similarly, some cases refer to a presumption of sanity. It is apparent that these so-called presumptions do not arise from the establishment or proof of a fact in the action. In fact, they are not presumptions at all but are preliminary allocations of the burden of proof in regard to the particular issue. This preliminary allocation of the burden of proof may be satisfied in particular cases by proof of a fact giving rise to a presumption that does affect the burden of proof. For example, the initial burden of proving negligence may be satisfied in a particular case by proof that undamaged goods were delivered to a bailee and that such goods were lost or damaged while in the bailee's possession. Upon such proof, the bailee would have the burden of proof as to his lack of negligence. George v. Bekins Van & Storage Co., 33 Cal.2d 834, 205 P.2d 1037 (1949). Cf. Com. Code § 7403.

Because the assumptions referred to above do not meet the definition of a presumption contained in Section 600, they are not continued in this code as presumptions. Instead, they appear in the next article in several sections allocating the burden of proof on specific issues. See Article 2 (Sections 520–522). [7 Cal.L.Rev.Comm. Reports 1 (1965)]

§ 501. Criminal actions; statutory assignment of burden of proof; controlling section

Insofar as any statute, except Section 522, assigns the burden of proof in a criminal action, such statute is subject to Penal Code Section 1096.

LAW REVISION COMMISSION COMMENT

A statute assigning the burden of proof may require the party to whom the burden is assigned to raise a reasonable doubt in the mind of the trier of fact or to persuade the trier of fact by a preponderance of evidence, by clear and convincing proof, or by proof beyond a reasonable doubt. See Evidence Code § 115.

Sections 520–522 (Which assign the burden of proof on specific issues) may, at times, assign the burden of proof to the defendant in a criminal action. Elsewhere in the codes are other sections that either specifically allocate the burden of proof to the defendant in a criminal action or have been construed to allocate the burden of proof to the defense. For example, Health and Safety Code Section 11721 provides specifically that, in a prosecution for the use of narcotics, it is the burden of the defense to show that the narcotics were administered by or under the direction of a person licensed to prescribe and administer narcotics. Health and Safety Code Section 11500, on the other hand, prohibits the possession of narcotics but provides an exception for narcotics possessed pursuant to a prescription. The courts have construed this section to place the burden of proof on the defense to show that the exception applies and that the narcotics were possessed pursuant to a prescription. People v. Marschalk, 206 Cal.App.2d 346, 23 Cal.Rptr. 743 (1962); People v. Bill, 140 Cal.App. 389, 392–394, 35 P.2d 645, 647–648 (1934).

Section 501 is intended to make it clear that the statutory allocations of the burden of proof appearing in this chapter and elsewhere in the codes are subject to Penal Code Section 1096, which requires that a criminal defendant be proved guilty beyond a reasonable doubt, i.e., that the statutory allocations do not (except on the issue of insanity) require the defendant to persuade the trier of fact of his innocence. Under Evidence Code Section 522, as under existing law, the defendant must prove his insanity by a preponderance of the evidence. People v. Daugherty, 40 Cal.2d 876, 256 P.2d 911 (1953). However, where a statute allocates the burden of proof to the defendant on any other issue relating to the defendant's guilt, the defendant's burden, as under existing law, is merely to raise a reasonable doubt as to his guilt. People

v. Bushton, 80 Cal. 160, 22 Pac. 127 (1889). Section 501 also makes it clear that, when a statute assigns the burden of proof to the prosecution in a criminal action, the prosecution must discharge that burden by proof beyond a reasonable doubt. [7 Cal L.Rev.Comm. Reports 1 (1965)]

§ 502. Instructions on burden of proof

The court on all proper occasions shall instruct the jury as to which party bears the burden of proof on each issue and as to whether that burden requires that a party raise a reasonable doubt concerning the existence or nonexistence of a fact or that he establish the existence or nonexistence of a fact by a preponderance of the evidence, by clear and convincing proof, or by proof beyond a reasonable doubt.

LAW REVISION COMMISSION COMMENT

Section 502 supersedes subdivision 5 of Code of Civil Procedure Section 2061. [7 Cal.L.Rev.Comm. Reports 1 (1965)]

ARTICLE 2. BURDEN OF PROOF ON SPECIFIC ISSUES

§ 520. Claim that person guilty of crime or wrongdoing

The party claiming that a person is guilty of crime or wrongdoing has the burden of proof on that issue.

§ 521. Claim that person did not exercise care

The party claiming that a person did not exercise a requisite degree of care has the burden of proof on that issue.

LAW REVISION COMMISSION COMMENT

Section 521 supersedes the presumption in subdivision 4 of Code of Civil Procedure Section 1963. Under existing law, the presumption is considered "evidence"; while under the Evidence Code, it is not. See Evidence Code § 600 and the Comment thereto. [7 Cal.L.Rev.Comm. Reports 1 (1965)]

§ 522. Claim that person is or was insane

The party claiming that any person, including himself, is or was insane has the burden of proof on that issue.

LAW REVISION COMMISSION COMMENT

Section 522 codifies an allocation of the burden of proof that is frequently referred to in the cases as a presumption. See, e.g., People v. Daugherty, 40 Cal.2d 876, 899, 256 P.2d 911, 925–926 (1953). [7 Cal. L.Rev.Comm. Reports 1 (1965)]

§ 523. Historic locations of water; claims involving state land patents or grants

In any action where the state is a party, regardless of who is the moving party, where (a) the boundary of land patented or otherwise granted by the state is in dispute, or (b) the validity of any state patent or grant dated prior to 1950 is in dispute, the state shall have the burden of proof on all issues relating to the historic locations of rivers, streams, and other water bodies and the authority of the state in issuing the patent or grant.

This section is not intended to nor shall it be construed to supersede existing statutes governing disputes where the state is a party and regarding title to real property.

CHAPTER 2. BURDEN OF PRODUCING EVIDENCE

§ 550. Party who has the burden of producing evidence

(a) The burden of producing evidence as to a particular fact is on the party against whom a finding on that fact would be required in the absence of further evidence.

(b) The burden of producing evidence as to a particular fact is initially on the party with the burden of proof as to that fact.

LAW REVISION COMMISSION COMMENT

Section 550 deals with the allocation of the burden of producing evidence. At the outset of the case, this burden will coincide with the burden of proof. 9 Wigmore, Evidence § 2487 at 279 (3d ed. 1940). However, during the course of the trial, the burden may shift from one party to another, irrespective of the incidence of the burden of proof. For example, if the party with the initial burden of producing evidence establishes a fact giving rise to a presumption, the burden of producing evidence will shift to the other party, whether or not the presumption is one that affects the burden of proof. In addition, a party may introduce evidence of such overwhelming probative force that no person could reasonably disbelieve it in the absence of countervailing evidence, in which case the burden of producing evidence would shift to the opposing party to produce some evidence. These principles are in accord with well- settled California law. See Discussion in Witkin, California Evidence §§ 53–56 (1958). See also 9 Wigmore, Evidence § 2487 (3d ed. 1940). [7 Cal.L.Rev.Comm. Reports 1 (1965)]

CHAPTER 3. PRESUMPTIONS AND INFERENCES

ARTICLE 1. GENERAL

§ 600. Presumption and inference defined

(a) A presumption is an assumption of fact that the law requires to be made from another fact or group of facts found or otherwise established in the action. A presumption is not evidence.

(b) An inference is a deduction of fact that may logically and reasonably be drawn from another fact or group of facts found or otherwise established in the action.

COMMENT—ASSEMBLY COMMITTEE ON JUDICIARY

The definition of a presumption in Section 600 is substantially the same as that contained in Code of Civil Procedure Section 1959: "A presumption is a deduction which the law expressly directs to be made from particular facts." Section 600 was derived from Rule 13 of the Uniform Rules of Evidence and supersedes Code of Civil Procedure Section 1959.

The second sentence of subdivision (a) may be unnecessary in light of the definition of "evidence" in Section 140—"testimony, writings, material objects, or other things presented to the senses that are offered to prove the existence or nonexistence of a fact." Presumptions, then, are not "evidence" but are conclusions that the law requires to be drawn (in the absence of a sufficient contrary showing) when some other fact is proved or otherwise established in the action.

Nonetheless, the second sentence has been added here to repudiate specifically the rule of Smellie v. Southern Pac. Co., 212 Cal. 540, 299 Pac. 529 (1931). That case held that a presumption is evidence that must be weighed against conflicting evidence; and in Scott v. Burke, 39 Cal.2d 388, 247 P.2d 313 (1952), the Supreme Court held that conflicting presumptions must be weighed against each other. These decisions require the jury to perform an intellectually impossible task. The jury is required to weigh the testimony of witnesses and other evidence as to the circumstances of a particular event against the fact that the law requires an opposing conclusion in the absence of contrary evidence and to determine which "evidence" is of greater probative force. Or else, the jury is required to accept the fact that the law requires two opposing conclusions and to determine which required conclusion is of greater probative force.

Moreover, the doctrine that a presumption is evidence imposes upon the party with the burden of proof a much higher burden of proof than is warranted. For example, if a party with the burden of proof has a presumption invoked against him and if the presumption remains in the case as evidence even though the jury believes that he has produced a preponderance of the evidence, the effect is that he must produce some additional but unascertainable quantum of proof in order to dispel the effect of the presumption. See Scott v. Burke, 39 Cal.2d 388, 405–406, 247 P.2d 313, 323–324 (1952) (dissenting opinion). The doctrine that a presumption is evidence gives no guidance to the jury or to the parties as to the amount of this additional proof. The most that should be expected of a party in a civil case is that he prove his case by a preponderance of the evidence (unless some specific presumption or rule of law requires proof of a particular issue by clear and convincing evidence). The most that should be expected of the prosecution in a criminal case is that it establish the defendant's guilt beyond a reasonable doubt. To require some additional quantum of proof, unspecified and uncertain in amount, to dispel a presumption which persists as evidence in the case unfairly weights the scales of justice against the party with the burden of proof.

To avoid the confusion engendered by the doctrine that a presumption is evidence, this code describes "evidence" as the matters presented in judicial proceedings and uses presumptions solely as devices to aid in determining the facts from the evidence presented.

The definition of "inference" in subdivision (b) restates in substance the definition contained in Code of Civil Procedure Sections 1958 and 1960. Under the Evidence Code, an inference is not itself evidence; it is the result of reasoning from evidence.

In the sections that follow, the Evidence Code classifies presumptions and lists a number of specific presumptions. Some presumptions that have been listed in the Code of Civil Procedure have not been listed as presumptions in the Evidence Code. But the fact that a statutory presumption has been repealed will not preclude the drawing of any appropriate inferences from the facts that would have given rise to the presumption. And, in appropriate cases, the court may instruct the jury on the propriety of drawing particular inferences.

§ 601. Classification of presumptions

A presumption is either conclusive or rebuttable. Every rebuttable presumption is either (a) a presumption affecting the burden of producing evidence or (b) a presumption affecting the burden of proof.

LAW REVISION COMMISSION COMMENT

Under existing law, some presumptions are conclusive. The court or jury is required to find the existence of the presumed fact regardless of the strength of the opposing evidence. The conclusive presumptions are specified in Section 1962 of the Code of Civil Procedure (superseded by Article 2 (Sections 620–624) of this chapter).

Under existing law, too, all presumptions that are not conclusive are rebuttable presumptions. Code Civ.Proc. § 1961 (superseded by Evidence Code § 601). However, the existing statutes make no attempt to classify the rebuttable presumptions.

For several decades, courts and legal scholars have wrangled over the purpose and function of presumptions. The view espoused by Professors Thayer (Thayer, Preliminary Treatise on Evidence 313–352 (1898)) and Wigmore (9 Wigmore, Evidence §§ 2485–2491 (3d ed. 1940)), accepted by most courts (see Morgan, Presumptions, 10 Rutgers L.Rev. 512, 516 (1956)), and adopted by the American Law Institute's Model Code of Evidence, is that a presumption is a preliminary assumption of fact that disappears from the case upon the introduction of evidence sufficient to sustain a finding of the nonexistence of the presumed fact. In Professor Thayer's view, a presumption merely reflects the judicial determination that the same conclusionary fact exists so frequently when the preliminary fact exists that, once the preliminary fact is established, proof of the conclusionary fact may be dispensed with unless there is actually some contrary evidence:

Many facts and groups of facts often recur, and when a body of men with a continuous tradition has carried on for some length of time this process of reasoning upon facts that often repeat themselves, they cut short the process and lay down a rule. To such facts they affix, by a general declaration, the character and operation which common experience has assigned to them. [Thayer, Preliminary Treatise on Evidence 326 (1898).]

Professors Morgan and McCormick argue that a presumption should shift the burden of proof to the adverse party. Morgan, Some Problems of Proof 81 (1956); McCormick, Evidence § 317 at 671–672 (1954). They believe that presumptions are created for reasons of policy and argue that, if the policy underlying a presumption is of sufficient weight to require a finding of the presumed fact when there is no contrary evidence, it should be of sufficient weight to require a finding when the mind of the trier of fact is in equilibrium, and, a fortiori, it should be of sufficient weight to require a finding if the trier of fact does not believe the contrary evidence.

The classification of presumptions in the Evidence Code is based on a third view suggested by Professor Bohlen in 1920. Bohlen, The Effect of Rebuttable Presumptions of Law Upon the Burden of Proof, 68 U.Pa.L.Rev. 307 (1920). Underlying the presumptions provisions of the Evidence Code is the conclusion that the Thayer view is correct as to some presumptions, but that the Morgan view is right as to others. The fact is that presumptions are created for a variety of reasons, and no single theory or rationale of presumptions can deal adequately with all of them. Hence, the Evidence Code classifies all rebuttable presumptions as either (1) presumptions affecting the burden of producing evidence (essentially Thayer presumptions), or (2) presumptions affecting the burden of proof (essentially Morgan presumptions).

Sections 603 and 605 set forth the criteria by which the two classes of rebuttable presumptions may be distinguished, and Sections 604, 606, and 607 prescribe their effect. Articles 3 and 4 (Sections 630–668) classify many presumptions found in California law; but many other presumptions, both statutory and common law, must await classification by the courts in accordance with the criteria contained in Sections 603 and 605.

The classification scheme contained in the Evidence Code follows a distinction that appears in the California cases. Thus, for example, the courts have at times held that presumptions do not affect the burden of proof. Estate of Eakle, 33 Cal.App.2d 379, 91 P.2d 954 (1939) (presumption of undue influence); Valentine v. Provident Mut. Life Ins. Co., 12 Cal.App.2d 616, 55 P.2d 1243 (1936) (presumption of death from seven years' absence). And at other times the courts have held that certain presumptions do affect the burden of proof. Estate of Nickson, 187 Cal. 603, 203 Pac. 106 (1921) ("clear and convincing proof" required to overcome presumption of community property); Estate of Walker, 180 Cal. 478, 181 Pac. 792 (1919) ("clear and satisfactory proof" required to overcome presumption of legitimacy). The cases have not, however, explicitly recognized the distinction, nor have they applied it consistently. Compare Estate of Eakle, supra (presumption of undue influence does not affect burden of proof), with Estate of Witt, 198 Cal. 407, 245 Pac. 197 (1926) (presumption of undue influence must be overcome with "the clearest and most satisfactory evidence"). The Evidence Code clarifies the law relating to presumptions by identifying the distinguishing factors, and it provides a measure of certainty by classifying a number of specific presumptions. [7 Cal.L.Rev.Comm. Reports 1 (1965)]

§ 602. Statute making one fact prima facie evidence of another fact

A statute providing that a fact or group of facts is prima facie evidence of another fact establishes a rebuttable presumption.

LAW REVISION COMMISSION COMMENT

Section 602 indicates the construction to be given to the large number of statutes scattered through the codes that state that one fact or group of facts is prima facie evidence of another fact. See, e.g., Agric.Code § 18, Com.Code § 1202, Rev. & Tax.Code § 6714. In some instances, these statutes have been enacted for reasons of public policy that require them to be treated as presumptions affecting the burden of proof. See People v. Schwartz, 31 Cal.2d 59, 63, 187 P.2d 12, 14 (1947); People v. Mahoney, 13 Cal.2d 729, 732–733, 91 P.2d 1029, 1030–1031 (1939). It seems likely, however, that in many instances such statutes are not intended to affect the burden of proof but only the burden of producing evidence. Section 602 provides that these statutes are to be regarded as rebuttable presumptions. Hence, unless some specific language applicable to the particular statute in question indicates whether it affects the burden of proof or only the burden of producing evidence, the courts will be required to classify these statutes as presumptions affecting the burden of proof or the burden of producing evidence in accordance with the criteria set forth in Sections 603 and 605. [7 Cal.L.Rev.Comm. Reports 1 (1965)]

§ 603. Presumption affecting the burden of producing evidence defined

A presumption affecting the burden of producing evidence is a presumption established to implement no public policy other than to facilitate the determination of the particular action in which the presumption is applied.

LAW REVISION COMMISSION COMMENT

Sections 603 and 605 set forth the criteria for determining whether a particular presumption is a presumption affecting the burden of producing evidence or a presumption affecting the burden of proof. Many presumptions are classified in Articles 3 and 4 (Sections 630–668) of this chapter. In the absence of specific statutory classification, the courts may determine whether a presumption is a presumption affecting the burden of producing evidence or a presumption affecting the burden of proof by applying the standards contained in Sections 603 and 605.

Section 603 describes those presumptions that are not based on any public policy extrinsic to the action in which they are invoked. These presumptions are designed to dispense with unnecessary proof of facts that are likely to be true if not disputed. Typically, such presumptions are based on an underlying logical inference. In some cases, the presumed fact is so likely to be true and so little likely to be disputed that the law requires it to be assumed in the absence of contrary evidence. In other cases, evidence of the nonexistence of the presumed fact, if there is any, is so much more readily available to the party against whom the presumption operates that he is not permitted to argue that the presumed fact does not exist unless he is willing to produce such evidence. In still other cases, there may be no direct evidence of the existence or nonexistence of the presumed fact; but, because the case must be decided, the law requires a determination that the presumed fact exists in light of common experience indicating that it usually exists in such cases. Cf. Bohlen, Studies in the Law of Torts 644 (1926). Typical of such presumptions are the presumption that a mailed letter was received (Section 641) and presumptions relating to the authenticity of documents (Sections 643–645).

The presumptions described in Section 603 are not expressions of policy; they are expressions of experience. They are intended solely to eliminate the need for the trier of fact to reason from the proven or established fact to the presumed fact and to forestall argument over the existence of the presumed fact when there is no evidence tending to prove the nonexistence of the presumed fact. [7 Cal.L.Rev.Comm. Reports 1 (1965)]

§ 604. Effect of presumption affecting burden of producing evidence

The effect of a presumption affecting the burden of producing evidence is to require the trier of fact to assume the existence of the presumed fact unless and until evidence is introduced which would support a finding of its nonexistence, in which case the trier of fact shall determine the existence or nonexistence of the presumed fact from the evidence and without regard to the presumption. Nothing in this section shall be construed to prevent the drawing of any inference that may be appropriate.

COMMENT—ASSEMBLY COMMITTEE ON JUDICIARY

Section 604 describes the manner in which a presumption affecting the burden of producing evidence operates. Such a presumption is merely a preliminary assumption in the absence of contrary evidence, i.e., evidence sufficient to sustain a finding of the nonexistence of the presumed fact. If contrary evidence is introduced, the trier of fact must weigh the inferences arising from the facts that gave rise to the presumption against the contrary evidence and resolve the conflict. For example, if a party proves that a letter was mailed, the trier of fact is required to find that the letter was received in the absence of any believable contrary evidence. However, if the adverse party denies receipt, the presumption is gone from the case. The trier of fact must then weigh the denial of receipt against the inference of receipt arising from proof of mailing and decide whether or not the letter was received.

If a presumption affecting the burden of producing evidence is relied on, the judge must determine whether there is evidence sufficient to sustain a finding of the nonexistence of the presumed fact. If there is such evidence, the presumption disappears and the judge need say nothing about it in his instructions. If there is not evidence sufficient to sustain a finding of the nonexistence of the presumed fact, the judge should instruct the jury concerning the presumption. If the basic fact from which the presumption arises is established (by the pleadings, by stipulation, by judicial notice, etc.) so that the existence of the basic fact is not a question of fact for the jury, the jury should be instructed that the presumed fact is also established. If the basic fact is a question of fact for the jury, the judge should charge the jury that, if it finds the basic fact, the jury must also find the presumed fact. Morgan, Basic Problems of Evidence 36–38 (1957).

Of course, in a criminal case, the jury has the power to disregard the judge's instructions and find a defendant guilty of a lesser crime than that shown by the evidence or acquit a defendant despite the facts established by the undisputed evidence. Cf. People v. Powell, 34 Cal.2d 196, 208 P.2d 974 (1949); Pike, What Is Second Degree Murder in California?, 9 So.Cal.L.Rev. 112, 128–132 (1936). Nonetheless, the jury should be instructed on the rules of law applicable, including those rules of law called presumptions. The fact that the jury may choose to disregard the applicable rules of law should not affect the nature of the instructions given. See People v. Lem You, 97 Cal. 224, 32 Pac. 11 (1893); People v. Macken, 32 Cal.App.2d 31, 89 P.2d 173 (1939).

§ 605. Presumption affecting the burden of proof defined

A presumption affecting the burden of proof is a presumption established to implement some public policy other than to facilitate the determination of the particular action in which the presumption is applied, such as the policy in favor of establishment of a parent and child relationship, the validity of marriage, the stability of titles to property, or the security of those who entrust themselves or their property to the administration of others.

LAW REVISION COMMISSION COMMENT

Section 605 describes a presumption affecting the burden of proof. Such presumptions are established in order to carry out or to effectuate some public policy other than or in addition to the policy of facilitating the trial of actions.

Frequently, presumptions affecting the burden of proof are designed to facilitate determination of the action in which they are applied. Superficially, therefore, such presumptions may appear merely to be presumptions affecting the burden of producing evidence. What makes a presumption one affecting the burden of proof is the fact that there is always some further reason of policy for the establishment of the presumption. It is the existence of this further basis in policy that distinguishes a presumption affecting the burden of proof from a presumption affecting the burden of producing evidence. For example, the presumption of death from seven years' absence (Section 667) exists in part to facilitate the disposition of actions by supplying a rule of thumb to govern certain cases in which there is likely to be no direct evidence of the presumed fact. But the policy in favor of distributing estates, of settling titles, and of permitting life to proceed normally at some time prior to the expiration of the absentee's normal life expectancy (perhaps 30 or 40 years) that underlies the presumption indicates that it should be a presumption affecting the burden of proof.

Frequently, too, a presumption affecting the burden of proof will have an underlying basis in probability and logical inference. For example, the presumption of the validity of a ceremonial marriage may be based in part on the probability that most marriages are valid. However, an underlying logical inference is not essential. In fact, the lack of an underlying inference is a strong indication that the presumption affects the burden of proof. Only the needs of public policy can justify the direction of a particular assumption that is not warranted by the application of probability and common experience to the known facts. Thus, the total lack of any inference underlying the presumption of the negligence of an employer that arises from his failure to secure the payment of workmen's compensation (Labor Code § 3708) is a clear indication that the presumption is based on public policy and affects the burden of proof. Similarly, the fact that the presumption of death from seven years' absence may conflict directly with the logical inference that life continues for its normal expectancy is an indication that the presumption is based on public policy and, hence, affects the burden of proof. [7 Cal.L.Rev.Comm. Reports 1 (1965)]

§ 606. Effect of presumption affecting burden of proof

The effect of a presumption affecting the burden of proof is to impose upon the party against whom it operates the burden of proof as to the nonexistence of the presumed fact.

COMMENT—ASSEMBLY COMMITTEE ON JUDICIARY

Section 606 describes the manner in which a presumption affecting the burden of proof operates. In the ordinary case, the party against whom it is invoked will have the burden of proving the nonexistence of the presumed fact by a preponderance of the evidence. Certain presumptions affecting the burden of proof may be overcome only by clear and convincing proof. When such a presumption is relied on, the party against whom the presumption operates will have a heavier burden of proof and will be required to persuade the trier of fact of the nonexistence of the presumed fact by proof " 'sufficiently strong to command the unhesitating assent of every reasonable mind.' " Sheehan v. Sullivan, 126 Cal. 189, 193, 58 Pac. 543, 544 (1899).

If the party against whom the presumption operates already has the same burden of proof as to the nonexistence of the presumed fact that is assigned by the presumption, the presumption can have no effect on the case and no instruction in regard to the presumption should be given. See Speck v. Sarver, 20 Cal.2d 585, 590, 128 P.2d 16, 19 (1942) (dissenting opinion by Traynor, J.); Morgan, Instructing the Jury Upon Presumptions and Burden of Proof, 47 Harv.L.Rev. 59, 69 (1933). If the evidence is not sufficient to sustain a finding of the nonexistence of the presumed fact, the judge's instructions will be the same as if the presumption were merely a presumption affecting the burden of producing evidence. See the Comment to Section 604. If there is evidence of the nonexistence of the presumed fact, the judge should instruct the jury on the manner in which the presumption affects the factfinding process. If the basic fact from which the presumption arises is so established that the existence of the basic fact is not a question of fact for the jury (as, for example, by the pleadings, by judicial notice, or by stipulation of the parties), the judge should instruct the jury that the existence of the presumed fact is to be assumed until the jury is persuaded to the contrary by the requisite degree of proof (proof by a preponderance of the evidence, clear and convincing proof, etc.). See McCormick, Evidence § 317 at 672 (1954). If the basic fact is a question of fact for the jury, the judge should instruct the jury that, if it finds the basic fact, it must also find the presumed fact unless persuaded of the nonexistence of the presumed fact by the requisite degree of proof. Morgan, Basic Problems of Evidence 38 (1957).

In a criminal case, a presumption affecting the burden of proof may be relied upon by the prosecution to establish an element of the crime with which the defendant is charged. The effect of the presumption on the factfinding process and the nature of the instructions in such a case are described in Section 607 and the Comment thereto. On other issues, a presumption affecting the burden of proof will have the same effect in a criminal case as it does in a civil case, and the instructions will be the same.

§ 607. Effect of certain presumptions in a criminal action

When a presumption affecting the burden of proof operates in a criminal action to establish presumptively any fact that is essential to the defendant's guilt, the presumption operates only if the facts that give rise to the presumption have been found or otherwise established beyond a reasonable doubt and, in such case, the defendant need only raise a reasonable doubt as to the existence of the presumed fact.

COMMENT—ASSEMBLY COMMITTEE ON JUDICIARY

If a presumption affecting the burden of proof is relied upon by the prosecution in a criminal case to establish a fact essential to the defendant's guilt, the defendant will not be required to overcome the presumption by clear and convincing evidence or even by a preponderance of the evidence; the defendant will be required merely to raise a reasonable doubt as to the existence of the presumed fact. This is the effect of a presumption in a criminal case under existing law. People v. Hardy, 33 Cal.2d 52, 198 P.2d 865 (1948); People v. Scott, 24 Cal.2d 774, 151 P.2d 517 (1944); People v. Agnew, 16 Cal.2d 655, 107 P.2d 601 (1940).

Instructions in criminal cases on presumptions affecting the burden of proof will be similar to the instructions given on presumptions and on issues where the defendant has the burden of proof under existing law. Where no evidence has been introduced to show the nonexistence of the presumed fact, the court should instruct the jury that, if it finds beyond a reasonable doubt the facts giving rise to the presumption, it should also find the presumed fact. Where some evidence of the nonexistence of the presumed fact has been introduced, the court should instruct the jury that, if it finds beyond a reasonable doubt the facts giving rise to the presumption, it should also find the presumed fact unless the contrary evidence has raised a reasonable doubt as to the existence of the presumed fact. Cf. People v. Hardy, 33 Cal.2d 52, 63–64, 198 P.2d 865, 871–872 (1948); People v. Agnew, 16 Cal.2d 655, 661–667, 107 P.2d 601, 603–607 (1940); People v. Martina, 140 Cal.App.2d 17, 25, 294 P.2d 1015, 1019 (1956). The judge must be careful to specify that a presumption is rebutted by any evidence that raises a reasonable doubt as to the presumed fact. In the absence of this qualification, the jury may be led to believe that the defendant has the burden of disproof of the presumed fact by a preponderance of the evidence and the instruction will be erroneous. People v. Agnew, 16 Cal.2d 655, 107 P.2d 601 (1940). Cf. People v. Hardy, 33 Cal.2d 52, 198 P.2d 865 (1948).

Of course, in a criminal case, the jury may choose to disregard the instructions relating to presumptions. But this should not affect the duty of the court to instruct the jury on the rules of law, including presumptions, applicable to the case. See the Comment to Section 604.

Section 607 does not apply to the "presumption" of sanity. Under the Evidence Code, the burden of proof on the issue of sanity is allocated by Section 522, and there is no "presumption" of sanity. See Evidence Code § 522 and the Comment thereto. Hence, notwithstanding the provisions of Section 607, a defendant who pleads insanity has the burden of proving by a preponderance of the evidence that he was insane. See the Comment to Section 501.

ARTICLE 2. CONCLUSIVE PRESUMPTIONS

§ 620. Conclusive presumptions

The presumptions established by this article, and all other presumptions declared by law to be conclusive, are conclusive presumptions.

LAW REVISION COMMISSION COMMENT

This article supersedes and continues in effect without substantive change the provisions of subdivisions 2, 3, 4, and 5 of Section 1962 of the Code of Civil Procedure. Other statutes not listed in this article also provide conclusive presumptions. See, e.g., Civil Code § 3440. There may also be a few nonstatutory conclusive presumptions. See Witkin, California Evidence § 63 (1958).

Conclusive presumptions are not evidentiary rules so much as they are rules of substantive law. Hence, the Commission has not recommended any substantive revision of the conclusive presumptions contained in this article. [7 Cal.L.Rev.Comm. Reports 1 (1965)]

§ 621. Repealed by Stats.1992, c. 162 (A.B.2650), § 8, operative Jan. 1, 1994

§ 621.1. Repealed by Stats.1993, c. 219 (A.B.1500), § 76

Repeal

Former Section 621.1 was without substantive change continued in Family Code Sections 20100–20104 (paternity pilot projects). See 1993 Cal. Stat. ch. 219, § 211. Family Code Sections 20100–20104 have been superseded by Family Code Sections 7570–7577. See 1993 Cal. Stat. ch. 1240. [23 Cal.L.Rev.Comm. Reports 1 (1993)]

LAW REVISION COMMISSION COMMENT

Repeal

Former Section 621.1 was without substantive change continued in Family Code Sections 20100–20104 (paternity pilot projects). See 1993

Cal. Stat. ch. 219, § 211. Family Code Sections 20100–20104 have been superseded by Family Code Sections 7570–7577. See 1993 Cal. Stat. ch. 1240. [23 Cal.L.Rev.Comm. Reports 1 (1993)]

§ 622. Facts recited in written instrument

The facts recited in a written instrument are conclusively presumed to be true as between the parties thereto, or their successors in interest; but this rule does not apply to the recital of a consideration.

§ 623. Estoppel by own statement or conduct

Whenever a party has, by his own statement or conduct, intentionally and deliberately led another to believe a particular thing true and to act upon such belief, he is not, in any litigation arising out of such statement or conduct, permitted to contradict it.

§ 624. Estoppel of tenant to deny title of landlord

A tenant is not permitted to deny the title of his landlord at the time of the commencement of the relation.

ARTICLE 3. PRESUMPTIONS AFFECTING THE BURDEN OF PRODUCING EVIDENCE

§ 630. Presumptions affecting the burden of producing evidence

The presumptions established by this article, and all other rebuttable presumptions established by law that fall within the criteria of Section 603, are presumptions affecting the burden of producing evidence.

LAW REVISION COMMISSION COMMENT

Article 3 sets forth a list of presumptions, recognized in existing law, that are classified here as presumptions affecting the burden of producing evidence. The list is not exhaustive. Other presumptions affecting the burden of producing evidence may be found in other codes. Others will be found in the common law. Specific statutes will classify some of these, but some must await classification by the courts. The list here, however, will eliminate any uncertainty as to the proper classification for the presumptions in this article. [7 Cal.L.Rev.Comm. Reports 1 (1965)]

§ 631. Money delivered by one to another

Money delivered by one to another is presumed to have been due to the latter.

§ 632. Thing delivered by one to another

A thing delivered by one to another is presumed to have belonged to the latter.

§ 633. Obligation delivered up to the debtor

An obligation delivered up to the debtor is presumed to have been paid.

§ 634. Person in possession of order on self

A person in possession of an order on himself for the payment of money, or delivery of a thing, is presumed to have paid the money or delivered the thing accordingly.

§ 635. Obligation possessed by creditor

An obligation possessed by the creditor is presumed not to have been paid.

§ 636. Payment of earlier rent or installments

The payment of earlier rent or installments is presumed from a receipt for later rent or installments.

§ 637. Ownership of things possessed

The things which a person possesses are presumed to be owned by him.

§ 638. Property ownership acts

A person who exercises acts of ownership over property is presumed to be the owner of it.

LAW REVISION COMMISSION COMMENT

Section 638 restates and supersedes the presumption found in subdivision 12 of Code of Civil Procedure Section 1963. Subdivision 12 of Code of Civil Procedure Section 1963 provides that a presumption of ownership arises from common reputation of ownership. This is inaccurate, however, for common reputation is not admissible to prove private title to property. Berniaud v. Beecher, 76 Cal. 394, 18 Pac. 598 (1888); Simons v. Inyo Cerro Gordo Co., 48 Cal.App. 524, 192 Pac. 144 (1920). [7 Cal.L.Rev.Comm. Reports 1 (1965)]

§ 639. Judgment correctly determines rights of parties

A judgment, when not conclusive, is presumed to correctly determine or set forth the rights of the parties, but there is no presumption that the facts essential to the judgment have been correctly determined.

LAW REVISION COMMISSION COMMENT

Section 639 restates and supersedes the presumption found in subdivision 17 of Code of Civil Procedure Section 1963. The presumption involved here is that the judgment correctly determines that one party owes another money, or that the parties are divorced, or their marriage has been annulled, or any similar rights of the parties. The presumption does not apply to the facts underlying the judgment. For example, a judgment of annulment is presumed to determine correctly that the marriage is void. Clark v. City of Los Angeles, 187 Cal.App.2d 792, 9 Cal.Rptr. 913 (1960). However, the judgment may not be used to establish presumptively that one of the parties was guilty of fraud as against some third party who is not bound by the judgment.

In a few cases, a judgment may be used as evidence of the facts necessarily determined by the judgment. See, e.g., Evidence Code §§ 1300–1302. But, even in those cases, the judgments do not presumptively establish the facts determined; they are merely evidence. [7 Cal.L.Rev.Comm. Reports 1 (1965)]

§ 640. Writing truly dated

A writing is presumed to have been truly dated.

§ 641. Letter received in ordinary course of mail

A letter correctly addressed and properly mailed is presumed to have been received in the ordinary course of mail.

§ 642. Conveyance by person having duty to convey real property

A trustee or other person, whose duty it was to convey real property to a particular person, is presumed to have actually conveyed to him when such presumption is necessary to perfect title of such person or his successor in interest.

§ 643. Authenticity of ancient document

A deed or will or other writing purporting to create, terminate, or affect an interest in real or personal property is presumed to be authentic if it:

(a) Is at least 30 years old;

(b) Is in such condition as to create no suspicion concerning its authenticity;

(c) Was kept, or if found was found, in a place where such writing, if authentic, would be likely to be kept or found; and

(d) Has been generally acted upon as authentic by persons having an interest in the matter.

LAW REVISION COMMISSION COMMENT

Section 643 restates and supersedes the presumption found in subdivision 34 of Code of Civil Procedure Section 1963. Although the statement of the ancient documents rule in Section 1963 requires the document to have been acted upon as if genuine before the presumption applies, some recent cases have not insisted upon this requirement. Estate of Nidever, 181 Cal.App.2d 367, 5 Cal.Rptr. 343 (1960); Kirkpatrick v. Tapo Oil Co., 144 Cal.App.2d 404, 301 P.2d 274 (1956). The requirement that the document be acted upon as genuine is, in substance, a requirement of the possession of property by those persons who would be entitled to such possession under the document if it were genuine. See 7 Wigmore, Evidence §§ 2141, 2146 (3d ed. 1940); Tentative Recommendation and a Study Relating to the Uniform Rules of Evidence (Article IX. Authentication and Content of Writings), 6 Cal. Law Revision Comm'n, Rep., Rec. & Studies 101, 135–137 (1964). Giving the ancient documents rule a presumptive effect—i.e., requiring a finding of the authenticity of an ancient document—seems justified when it is a dispositive instrument and the persons interested in the matter have acted upon the instrument for a period of at least 30 years as if it were genuine. Evidence which is not of this strength may be sufficient in particular cases to warrant an inference of genuineness and thus justify the admission of the document into evidence, but the presumption should be confined to those cases where the evidence of genuineness is not likely to be disputed. See 7 Wigmore, Evidence § 2146 (3d ed. 1940). Accordingly, Section 643 limits the presumptive application of the ancient documents rule to dispositive instruments. [7 Cal.L.Rev.Comm. Reports 1 (1965)]

§ 644. Book purporting to be published by public authority

A book, purporting to be printed or published by public authority, is presumed to have been so printed or published.

§ 645. Book purporting to contain reports of cases

A book, purporting to contain reports of cases adjudged in the tribunals of the state or nation where the book is published, is presumed to contain correct reports of such cases.

§ 645.1. Printed materials purporting to be particular newspaper or periodical

Printed materials, purporting to be a particular newspaper or periodical, are presumed to be that newspaper or periodical if regularly issued at average intervals not exceeding three months.

§ 646. Res ipsa loquitur; instruction

(a) As used in this section, "defendant" includes any party against whom the res ipsa loquitur presumption operates.

(b) The judicial doctrine of res ipsa loquitur is a presumption affecting the burden of producing evidence.

(c) If the evidence, or facts otherwise established, would support a res ipsa loquitur presumption and the defendant has introduced evidence which would support a finding that he was not negligent or that any negligence on his part was not a proximate cause of the occurrence, the court may, and upon request shall, instruct the jury to the effect that:

> (1) If the facts which would give rise to a res ipsa loquitur presumption are found or otherwise established, the jury may draw the inference from such facts that a proximate cause of the occurrence was some negligent conduct on the part of the defendant; and
>
> (2) The jury shall not find that a proximate cause of the occurrence was some negligent conduct on the part of the defendant unless the jury believes, after weighing all the evidence in the case and drawing such inferences therefrom as the jury believes are warranted, that it is more probable than not that the occurrence was caused by some negligent conduct on the part of the defendant.

LAW REVISION COMMISSION COMMENT

1970 Addition

Section 646 is designed to clarify the manner in which the doctrine of res ipsa loquitur functions under the provisions of the Evidence Code relating to presumptions.

The doctrine of res ipsa loquitur, as developed by the California courts, is applicable in an action to recover damages for negligence when the plaintiff establishes three conditions:

First, that it is the kind of [accident] [injury] which ordinarily does not occur in the absence of someone's negligence;

Second, that it was caused by an agency or instrumentality in the exclusive control of the defendant [originally, and which was not mishandled or otherwise changed after defendant relinquished control]; and

Third, that the [accident] [injury] was not due to any voluntary action or contribution on the part of the plaintiff which was the responsible cause of his injury [BAJI (5th ed.1969) No. 4.00 (brackets in original).]

This section provides that the doctrine of res ipsa loquitur is a presumption affecting the burden of producing evidence. Therefore, when the plaintiff has established the three conditions that give rise to the doctrine, the jury is required to find that the accident resulted from the defendant's negligence unless the defendant comes forward with evidence that would support a contrary finding. EVIDENCE CODE 604. If evidence is produced that would support a finding that the defendant was not negligent or that any negligence on his part was not a proximate cause of the accident, the presumptive effect of the doctrine vanishes.

However, the jury may still be able to draw an inference that the accident was caused by the defendant's lack of due care from the facts that gave rise to the presumption. See EVIDENCE CODE § 604 and the Comment thereto. In rare cases, the defendant may produce such conclusive evidence that the inference of negligence is dispelled as a matter of law. See, e.g., Leonard v. Watsonville Community Hosp., 47 Cal.2d 509, 305 P.2d 36 (1956). But, except in such a case, the facts giving rise to the doctrine will support an inference of negligence even after its presumptive effect has disappeared.

To assist the jury in the performance of its factfinding function, the court may instruct that the facts that give rise to res ipsa loquitur are themselves circumstantial evidence from which the jury can infer that the accident resulted from the defendant's failure to exercise due care. This section requires the court to give such an instruction when a party so requests. Whether the jury should so find will depend on whether the jury believes that the probative force of the circumstantial and other evidence of the defendant's negligence exceeds the probative force of the contrary evidence and, therefore, that it is more probable than not that the accident resulted from the defendant's negligence.

At times the doctrine of res ipsa loquitur will coincide in a particular case with another presumption or with another rule of law that requires the defendant to discharge the burden of proof on the issue. See Prosser, Res Ipsa Loquitur in California, 37 Cal.L.Rev. 183 (1949). In such cases the defendant will have the burden of proof on issues where res ipsa loquitur appears to apply. But because of the allocation of the burden of proof to the defendant, the doctrine of res ipsa loquitur will serve no function in the disposition of the case. However, the facts that would give rise to the doctrine may nevertheless be used as circumstantial evidence tending to rebut the evidence produced by the party with the burden of proof.

For example, a bailee who has received undamaged goods and returns damaged goods has the burden of proving that the damage was not caused by his negligence unless the damage resulted from a fire. See discussion in Redfoot v. J. T. Jenkins Co., 138 Cal.App.2d 108, 112, 291 P.2d 134, 135 (1955). See Com. Code § 7403(1) (b). When the defendant has produced evidence of his exercise of care in regard to the bailed goods, the facts that would give rise to the doctrine of res ipsa loquitur may be weighed against the evidence produced by the defendant in determining whether it is more likely than not that the goods were damaged without fault on the part of the bailee. But because the bailee has both the burden of producing evidence and the burden of proving that the damage was not caused by his negligence, the presumption of negligence arising from res ipsa loquitur cannot have any effect on the proceeding. Effect of the Failure of the Plaintiff to Establish All the Preliminary Facts That Give Rise to the Presumption.

The fact that the plaintiff fails to establish all of the facts giving rise to the res ipsa presumption does not necessarily mean that he has not produced sufficient evidence of negligence to sustain a jury finding in his favor. The requirements of res ipsa loquitur are merely those that must be met to give rise to a compelled conclusion (or presumption) of negligence in the absence of contrary evidence. An inference of negligence may well be warranted from all of the evidence in the case even though the plaintiff fails to establish all the elements of res ipsa loquitur. See Prosser, Res Ipsa Loquitur: A Reply to Professor Carpenter, 10 So.Cal.L.Rev. 459 (1937). In appropriate cases, therefore, the jury may be instructed that, even though it does not find that the facts giving rise to the presumption have been proved by a preponderance of the evidence, it may nevertheless find the defendant negligent if it concludes from a consideration of all the evidence that it is more probable than not that the defendant was negligent. Such an instruction would be appropriate, for example, in a case where there was evidence of the defendant's negligence apart from the evidence going to the elements of the res ipsa loquitur doctrine. Examples of Operation of Res Ipsa Loquitur Presumption.

The doctrine of res ipsa loquitur may be applicable to a case under four varying sets of circumstances:

(1) Where the facts giving rise to the doctrine are established as a matter of law (by the pleadings by stipulation, by pretrial order, or by some other means) and there is no evidence sufficient to sustain a finding either that the accident resulted from some cause other than the defendant's negligence or that he exercised due care in all possible respects wherein he might have been negligent.

(2) Where the facts giving rise to the doctrine are established as a matter of law, but the defendant has introduced evidence sufficient to sustain a finding either of his due care or of some cause for the accident other than his negligence.

(3) Where the defendant introduces evidence tending to show the nonexistence of the essential conditions of the doctrine but does not introduce evidence to rebut the presumption.

(4) Where the defendant introduces evidence to contest both the conditions of the doctrine and the conclusion that his negligence caused the accident.

Set forth below is an explanation of the manner in which this section functions in each of these situations.

Basic facts established as a matter of law; no rebuttal evidence. If the basic facts that give rise to the presumption are established as a matter of law (by the pleadings, by stipulation, by pretrial order, etc.), the presumption requires that the jury find that the defendant's negligence was the proximate cause of the accident unless evidence is introduced sufficient to sustain a finding either that the accident resulted from some cause other than the defendant's negligence or that he exercised due care in all possible respects wherein he might have been negligent. When the defendant fails to introduce such evidence, the court must simply instruct the jury that it is required to find that the accident was caused by the defendant's negligence.

For example, if a plaintiff automobile passenger sues the driver for injuries sustained in an accident, the defendant may determine not to contest the fact that the accident was of a type that ordinarily does not occur unless the driver was negligent. Moreover, the defendant may introduce no evidence that he exercised due care in the driving of the automobile. Instead, the defendant may rest his defense solely on the ground that the plaintiff was a guest and not a paying passenger. In this case, the court should instruct the jury that it must assume that the defendant was negligent. Cf. Phillips v. Noble, 50 Cal.2d 163, 323 P.2d 385 (1958); Fiske v. Wilkie, 67 Cal.App.2d 440, 154 P.2d 725 (1945).

Basic facts established as matter of law; evidence introduced to rebut presumption. Where the facts giving rise to the doctrine are established as a matter of law but the defendant has introduced evidence sufficient to sustain a finding either of his due care or of a cause for the accident other than his negligence, the presumptive effect of the doctrine vanishes. Except in those rare cases where the inference is dispelled as a matter of law, the court may instruct the jury that it may infer from the established facts that negligence on the part of the defendant was a proximate cause of the accident. The court is required to give such an instruction when requested. The instruction should make it clear, however, that the jury should not find that a proximate cause of the occurrence was some negligent conduct on the part of the defendant unless the jury believes, after weighing all the evidence in the case, that it is more probable than not that the accident was caused by the defendant's negligence.

Basic facts contested; no rebuttal evidence. The defendant may attack only the elements of the doctrine. His purpose in doing so would be to prevent the application of the doctrine. In this situation, the court cannot determine whether the doctrine is applicable or not because the basic facts that give rise to the doctrine must be determined by the jury. Therefore, the court must give an instruction on what has become known as conditional res ipsa loquitur.

Where the basic facts contested by evidence, but there is no rebuttal evidence, the court should instruct the jury that, if it finds that the basic facts have been established by a preponderance of the evidence, then it must also find that the accident was caused by some negligent conduct on the part of the defendant.

Basic facts contested; evidence introduced to rebut presumption. The defendant may introduce evidence that both attacks the basic facts that underlie the doctrine of res ipsa loquitur and tends to show that the accident was not caused by his failure to exercise due care. Because of the evidence contesting the presumed conclusion of negligence, the presumptive effect of the doctrine vanishes, and the greatest effect the doctrine can have in the case is to support an inference that the accident resulted from the defendant's negligence.

In this situation, the court should instruct the jury that, if it finds that the basic facts have been established by a preponderance of the evidence, then it may infer from those facts that the accident was caused because the defendant was negligent. But the court shall also instruct the jury that it should not find that a proximate cause of the accident was some negligent conduct on the part of the defendant unless it believes, after weighing all of the evidence, that it is more probable than not that the defendant was negligent and that the accident resulted from his negligence. Other Appropriate Instructions.

The jury instructions referred to in Section 646 do not preclude the judge from giving the jury any additional instructions on res ipsa loquitur that are appropriate to the particular case. [9 Cal.L.Rev.Comm. Reports 137 (1970)]

§ 647. Return of process served by registered process server

The return of a process server registered pursuant to Chapter 16 (commencing with Section 22350) of Division 8 of the Business and Professions Code upon process or notice establishes a presumption, affecting the burden of producing evidence, of the facts stated in the return.

ARTICLE 4. PRESUMPTIONS AFFECTING THE BURDEN OF PROOF

§ 660. Presumptions affecting the burden of proof

The presumptions established by this article, and all other rebuttable presumptions established by law that fall within the criteria of Section 605, are presumptions affecting the burden of proof.

LAW REVISION COMMISSION COMMENT

In some cases it may be difficult to determine whether a particular presumption is a presumption affecting the burden of proof or a presumption affecting the burden of producing evidence. To avoid uncertainty, it is desirable to classify as many presumptions as possible. Article 4 (§§ 660–668), therefore, lists several presumptions that are to be regarded as presumptions affecting the burden of proof. The list is not exclusive. Other statutory and common law presumptions that affect the burden of proof must await classification by the courts. [7 Cal. L.Rev.Comm. Reports 1 (1965)]

§ 661. Repealed by Stats.1975, c. 1244, p. 3202, § 14

§ 662. Owner of legal title to property is owner of beneficial title

The owner of the legal title to property is presumed to be the owner of the full beneficial title. This presumption may be rebutted only by clear and convincing proof.

LAW REVISION COMMISSION COMMENT

Section 662 codifies a common law presumption recognized in the California cases. The presumption may be overcome only by clear and convincing proof. Olson v. Olson, 4 Cal.2d 434, 437, 49 P.2d 827, 828 (1935); Rench v. McMullen, 82 Cal.App.2d 872, 187 P.2d 111 (1947). [7 Cal.L.Rev.Comm. Reports 1 (1965)]

§ 663. Ceremonial marriage

A ceremonial marriage is presumed to be valid.

LAW REVISION COMMISSION COMMENT

Section 663 codifies a common law presumption recognized in the California cases. Estate of Hughson, 173 Cal. 448, 160 Pac. 548 (1916); Wilcox v. Wilcox, 171 Cal. 770, 155 Pac. 95 (1916); Freeman S.S. Co. v. Pillsbury, 172 F.2d 321 (9th Cir.1949). [7 Cal.L.Rev.Comm. Reports 1 (1965)]

§ 664. Official duty regularly performed

It is presumed that official duty has been regularly performed. This presumption does not apply on an issue as to the lawfulness of an arrest if it is found or otherwise established that the arrest was made without a warrant.

COMMENT—ASSEMBLY COMMITTEE ON JUDICIARY

The first sentence of Section 664 restates and supersedes subdivision 15 of Code of Civil Procedure Section 1963.

Under existing law, there is a common law presumption that an arrest made without a warrant is unlawful. People v. Agnew, 16 Cal.2d 655, 107 P.2d 601 (1940). Under this common law presumption, if a person arrests another without the color of legality provided by a warrant, the person making the arrest must prove the circumstances that justified the arrest without a warrant. Badillo v. Superior Court, 46 Cal.2d 269, 294 P.2d 23 (1956); Dragna v. White, 45 Cal.2d 469, 471, 289 P.2d 428, 430 (1955) ("Upon proof of [arrest without process] the burden is on the defendants to prove justification for the arrest."). The second sentence of Section 664 makes it clear that the presumption of regular performance of official duty is inapplicable whenever facts have been established that give rise to the common law presumption regarding the illegality of an arrest made without a warrant.

§ 665. Ordinary consequences of voluntary act

A person is presumed to intend the ordinary consequences of his voluntary act. This presumption is inapplicable in a criminal action to establish the specific intent of the defendant where specific intent is an element of the crime charged.

COMMENT—ASSEMBLY COMMITTEE ON JUDICIARY

Section 665 restates and supersedes the presumption in subdivision 3 of Code of Civil Procedure Section 1963. The second sentence in this section also appears in Section 668 (restating the presumption in subdivision 2 of Code of Civil Procedure Section 1963). These sentences reflect the fact that it is error to rely on these presumptions when specific intent is in issue in a criminal case. See People v. Snyder, 15 Cal.2d 706, 104 P.2d 639 (1940); People v. Maciel, 71 Cal.App. 213, 234 Pac. 877 (1925).

§ 666. Judicial action lawful exercise of jurisdiction

Any court of this state or the United States, or any court of general jurisdiction in any other state or nation, or any judge of such a court, acting as such, is presumed to have acted in the lawful exercise of its jurisdiction. This presumption applies only when the act of the court or judge is under collateral attack.

COMMENT—ASSEMBLY COMMITTEE ON JUDICIARY

Section 666 restates and supersedes the presumption in subdivision 16 of Code of Civil Procedure Section 1963. Under existing law, the presumption applies only to courts of general jurisdiction; the presumption has been held inapplicable to a superior court in California when acting in a special or limited jurisdiction. Estate of Sharon, 179 Cal. 447, 177 Pac. 283 (1918). The presumption also has been held inapplicable to courts of inferior jurisdiction. Santos v. Dondero, 11 Cal.App.2d 720, 54 P.2d 764 (1936). There is no reason to perpetuate this distinction insofar as the courts of California and of the United States are concerned. California's municipal and justice courts are served by able and conscientious judges and are no more likely to act beyond their jurisdiction than are the superior courts. Moreover, there is no reason to suppose that a superior court or a federal court is less respectful of its jurisdiction when acting in a limited capacity (for example, as a juvenile court) than it is when acting in any other capacity. Section 666, therefore, applies to any court or judge of any court of California or of the United States. So far as other states are concerned, the distinction is still applicable, and the presumption applies only to courts of general jurisdiction.

Under Section 666, as under existing law, the presumption applies only when the act of the court or judge is under collateral attack. See City of Los Angeles v. Glassell, 203 Cal. 44, 262 Pac. 1084 (1928).

§ 667. Death of person not heard from in five years

A person not heard from in five years is presumed to be dead.

LAW REVISION COMMISSION COMMENT

1965 Enactment

Section 667 restates and supersedes the presumption in subdivision 26 of Code of Civil Procedure Section 1963. [7 Cal.L.Rev.Comm. Reports 1 (1965)]

1983 Amendment

Section 667 is amended to adopt a five-year missing period. This period is consistent with Probate Code Section 1301 (administration of estates of persons missing five years) and Civil Code Sections 4401(2), 4425(b) (five-year absence in bigamy situations). Except for the change in the duration of the missing period from seven to five years, the amendment of Section 667 has no effect on the case law interpreting this section. [16 Cal.L.Rev.Comm. Reports 105 (1982)].

§ 668. Unlawful intent

An unlawful intent is presumed from the doing of an unlawful act. This presumption is inapplicable in a criminal action to establish the specific intent of the defendant where specific intent is an element of the crime charged.

COMMENT—ASSEMBLY COMMITTEE ON JUDICIARY

Section 668 restates and supersedes the presumption in subdivision 2 of Code of Civil Procedure Section 1963. See the Comment to Section 665.

§ 669. Due care; failure to exercise

(a) The failure of a person to exercise due care is presumed if:

(1) He violated a statute, ordinance, or regulation of a public entity;

(2) The violation proximately caused death or injury to person or property;

(3) The death or injury resulted from an occurrence of the nature which the statute, ordinance, or regulation was designed to prevent; and

(4) The person suffering the death or the injury to his person or property was one of the class of persons for whose protection the statute, ordinance, or regulation was adopted.

(b) This presumption may be rebutted by proof that:

(1) The person violating the statute, ordinance, or regulation did what might reasonably be expected of a person of ordinary prudence, acting under similar circumstances, who desired to comply with the law; or

(2) The person violating the statute, ordinance, or regulation was a child and exercised the degree of care ordinarily exercised by persons of his maturity, intelligence, and capacity under similar circumstances, but the presumption may not be rebutted by such proof if the violation occurred in the course of an activity normally engaged in only by adults and requiring adult qualifications.

LAW REVISION COMMISSION COMMENT

1967 Addition

Section 669 codifies a common law presumption that is frequently applied in the California cases. See Alarid v. Vanier, 50 Cal.2d 617, 327 P.2d 897 (1958). The presumption may be used to establish a plaintiff's contributory negligence as well as a defendant's negligence. Nevis v. Pacific Gas & Elec. Co., 43 Cal.2d 626, 275 P.2d 761 (1954).

Effect of Presumption

If the conditions listed in subdivision (a) are established, a presumption of negligence arises which may be rebutted by proof of the facts specified in subdivision (b). The presumption is one of simple negligence only, not gross negligence. Taylor v. Cockrell, 116 Cal.App. 596, 3 P.2d 16 (1931).

Section 669 appears in Article 4 (beginning with Section 660), Chapter 3, of Division 5 of the Evidence Code and, therefore, is a presumption affecting the burden of proof. Evidence Code § 660. Thus, if it is established that a person violated a statute under the conditions specified in subdivision (a), the opponent of the presumption is required to prove to the trier of fact that it is more probable than not that the violation of the statute was reasonable and justifiable under the circumstances. See Evidence Code § 606 and the Comment thereto. Since the ultimate question is whether the opponent of the presumption was negligent rather than whether he violated the statute, proof of justification or excuse under subdivision (b) negates the existence of negligence instead of merely establishing an excuse for negligent conduct. Therefore, if the presumption is rebutted by proof of justification or excuse under subdivision (b), the trier of fact is required to find that the violation of the statute was not negligent.

Violations by children. Section 669 applies to the violation of a statute, ordinance, or regulation by a child as well as by an adult. But in the case of a violation by a child, the presumption may be rebutted by a showing that the child, in spite of the violation, exercised the care that children of his maturity, intelligence, and capacity ordinarily exercise under similar circumstances. Daun v. Truax, 56 Cal.2d 647, 16 Cal. Rptr. 351, 365 P.2d 407 (1961). However, if a child engages in an activity normally engaged in only by adults and requiring adult qualifications, the "reasonable" behavior he must show to establish justification or excuse under subdivision (b) must meet the standard of conduct established primarily for adults. Cf. Prichard v. Veterans Cab Co., 63 Cal.2d 727, 47 Cal.Rptr. 904, 408 P.2d 360 (1965) (minor operating a motorcycle).

Failure to establish conditions of presumption. Even though a party fails to establish that a violation occurred or that a proven violation meets all the requirements of subdivision (a), it is still possible for the party to recover by proving negligence apart from any statutory violation. Nunneley v. Edgar Hotel, 36 Cal.2d 493, 225 P.2d 497 (1950) (plaintiff permitted to recover even though her injury was not of the type to be prevented by statute).

Functions of Judge and Jury

If a case is tried without a jury, the judge is responsible for deciding both questions of law and questions of fact arising under Section 669. However, in a case tried by a jury, there is an allocation between the judge and jury of the responsibility for determining the existence or nonexistence of the elements underlying the presumption and the existence of excuse or justification.

Subdivision (a), paragraph (3) and (4). Whether the death or injury involved in an action resulted from an occurrence of the nature which the statute, ordinance, or regulation was designed to prevent (paragraph (3) of subdivision (a))and whether the plaintiff was one of the class of persons for whose protection the statute, ordinance, or regulation was adopted (paragraph (4) of subdivision (a))are questions of law. Nunneley v. Edgar Hotel, 36 Cal.2d 493, 225 P.2d 497 (1950) (statute requiring parapet of particular height at roofline of vent shaft designed to protect against walking into shaft, not against falling into shaft while sitting on parapet). If a party were relying solely on the violation of a statute to establish the other party's negligence or contributory negligence, his opponent would be entitled to a directed verdict on the issue if the judge failed to find either of the above elements of the presumption. See Nunneley v. Edgar Hotel, 36 Cal.2d 493, 225 P.2d 497 (1950) (by implication).

Subdivision (a), paragraphs (1) and (2). Whether or not a party to an action has violated a statute, ordinance, or regulation (paragraph (1) of subdivision (a))is generally a question of fact. However, if a party admits the violation or if the evidence of the violation is undisputed, it is appropriate for the judge to instruct the jury that a violation of the statute, ordinance, or regulation has been established as a matter of law. Alarid v. Vanier, 50 Cal.2d 617, 327 P.2d 897 (1958) (undisputed evidence of driving with faulty brakes).

The question of whether the violation has proximately caused or contributed to the plaintiff's death or injury (paragraph (2) of subdivision (a))is normally a question for the jury. Satterlee v. Orange Glenn School Dist., 29 Cal.2d 581, 177 P.2d 279 (1947). However, the existence or nonexistence of proximate cause becomes a question of law to be decided by the judge if reasonable men can draw but one inference from the facts. Satterlee v. Orange Glenn School Dist., 29 Cal.2d 581, 177 P.2d 279 (1947). See also Alarid v. Vanier, 50 Cal.2d 617, 327 P.2d 897 (1958) (defendant's admission establishes proximate cause); Moon v. Payne, 97 Cal.App.2d 717, 218 P.2d 550 (1950) (failure to obtain permit to burn weeds not proximate cause of child's burns).

Subdivision (b). Normally, the question of justification or excuse is a jury question. Fuentes v. Panella, 120 Cal.App.2d 175, 260 P.2d 853 (1953). The jury should be instructed on the issue of justification or excuse whether the excuse or justification appears from the circumstances surrounding the violation itself or appears from evidence offered specifically to show justification. Fuentes v. Panella, 120 Cal.App.2d 175, 260 P.2d 853 (1953) (instruction on justification proper in light of conflicting testimony concerning violation itself and surrounding circumstances). However, an instruction on the issue of excuse or justification should not be given if there is no evidence that would sustain a finding by the jury that the violation was excused. McCaughan v. Hansen Pac. Lumber Co., 176 Cal.App.2d 827, 833–834, 1 Cal.Rptr. 796, 800 (1959) (evidence went to contributory negligence, not to excuse); Fuentes v. Panella, 120 Cal.App.2d 175, 260 P.2d 853 (1953) (dictum). [8 Cal.L.Rev. Comm. Reports 101 (1967)]

§ 669.1. Standards of conduct for public employees; presumption of failure to exercise due care

A rule, policy, manual, or guideline of state or local government setting forth standards of conduct or guidelines for its employees in the conduct of their public employment shall not be considered a statute, ordinance, or regulation of that public entity within the meaning of Section 669, unless the rule, manual, policy, or guideline has been formally adopted as a statute, as an ordinance of a local governmental entity in this state empowered to adopt ordinances, or as a regulation by an agency of the state pursuant to the Administrative Procedure Act (Chapter 3.5 (commencing with Section 11340) of Division 3 of Title 2 of the Government Code), or by an agency of the United States government pursuant to the federal Administrative Procedure Act (Chapter 5 (commencing with Section 5001) of Title 5 of the United States Code). This section affects only the presumption set forth in Section 669, and is not otherwise intended to affect the admissibility or inadmissibility of the rule, policy, manual, or guideline under other provisions of law.

§ 669.5. Ordinances limiting building permits or development of buildable lots for residential purposes; impact on supply of residential units; actions challenging validity

(a) Any ordinance enacted by the governing body of a city, county, or city and county which (1) directly limits, by number, the building permits that may be issued for residential construction or the buildable lots which may be developed for residential purposes, or (2) changes the standards of residential development on vacant land so that the governing body's zoning is rendered in violation of Section 65913.1 of the Government Code is presumed to have an impact on the supply of residential units available in an area which includes territory outside the jurisdiction of the city, county, or city and county.

(b) With respect to any action which challenges the validity of an ordinance specified in subdivision (a) the city, county, or city and county enacting the ordinance shall bear the burden of proof that the ordinance is necessary for the protection of the public health, safety, or welfare of the population of the city, county, or city and county.

(c) This section does not apply to state and federal building code requirements or local ordinances which (1) impose a moratorium, to protect the public health and safety, on residential construction for a specified period of time, if, under the terms of the ordinance, the moratorium will cease when the public health or safety is no longer jeopardized by the construction, (2) create agricultural preserves under Chapter 7 (commencing with Section 51200) of Part 1 of Division 1 of Title 5 of the Government Code, or (3) restrict the number of buildable parcels or designate lands within a zone for nonresidential uses in order to protect agricultural uses as defined in subdivision (b) of Section 51201 of the Government Code or open-space land as defined in subdivision (b) of Section 65560 of the Government Code.

(d) This section shall not apply to a voter approved ordinance adopted by referendum or initiative prior to the effective date of this section which (1) requires the city, county, or city and county to establish a population growth limit which represents its fair share of each year's statewide population growth, or (2) which sets a growth rate of no more than the average population growth rate experienced by the state as a whole. Paragraph (2) of subdivision (a) does not apply to a voter-approved ordinance adopted by referendum or initiative which exempts housing affordable to persons and families of low or moderate income, as defined in Section 50093 of the Health and Safety Code, or which otherwise provides low- and moderate-income housing sites equivalent to such an exemption.

§ 670. Payments by check

(a) In any dispute concerning payment by means of a check, a copy of the check produced in accordance with Section 1550 of the Evidence Code, together with the original bank statement that reflects payment of the check by the bank on which it was drawn or a copy thereof produced in the same manner, creates a presumption that the check has been paid.

(b) As used in this section:

(1) "Bank" means any person engaged in the business of banking and includes, in addition to a commercial bank, a savings and loan association, savings bank, or credit union.

(2) "Check" means a draft, other than a documentary draft, payable on demand and drawn on a bank, even though it is described by another term, such as "share draft" or "negotiable order of withdrawal."

DIVISION 6. WITNESSES

CHAPTER 1. COMPETENCY

§ 700. General rule as to competency

Except as otherwise provided by statute, every person, irrespective of age, is qualified to be a witness and no person is disqualified to testify to any matter.

LAW REVISION COMMISSION COMMENT

Section 700 makes it clear that all grounds for disqualification of witnesses must be based on statute. There can be no nonstatutory grounds for disqualification. The section is similar to and supersedes Section 1879 of the Code of Civil Procedure, which provides that "all persons ... who, having organs of sense, can perceive, and perceiving, can make known their perceptions to others, may be witnesses."

Just as Code of Civil Procedure Section 1879 is limited by various statutory restrictions on the competency of witnesses, the broad rule stated in Section 700 is also substantially qualified by statutory restrictions appearing in the Evidence Code and in other California codes. See, e.g., Evidence Code § 701 (mental or physical capacity to be a witness), § 702 (requirement of personal knowledge), § 703 (judge as a witness), § 704 (juror as a witness), §§ 900–1070 (privileges), § 1150 (continuing existing law limiting use of juror's evidence concerning jury misconduct); Vehicle Code § 40804 (speed trap evidence). [7 Cal.L.Rev.Comm. Reports 1 (1965)]

§ 701. Disqualification of witness

(a) A person is disqualified to be a witness if he or she is:

(1) Incapable of expressing himself or herself concerning the matter so as to be understood, either directly or through interpretation by one who can understand him; or

(2) Incapable of understanding the duty of a witness to tell the truth.

(b) In any proceeding held outside the presence of a jury, the court may reserve challenges to the competency of a witness until the conclusion of the direct examination of that witness.

LAW REVISION COMMISSION COMMENT

Under existing law, the competency of a person to be a witness is a question to be determined by the court and depends upon his capacity to understand the oath and to perceive, recollect, and communicate that which he is offered to relate. "Whether he did perceive accurately, does recollect, and is communicating accurately and truthfully are questions of credibility to be resolved by the trier of fact." People v. McCaughan, 49 Cal.2d 409, 420, 317 P.2d 974, 981 (1957).

Under the Evidence Code, too, the competency of a person to be a witness is a question to be determined by the court. See Evidence Code § 405 and the Comment thereto. However, Section 701 requires the court to determine only the prospective witness' capacity to communicate and his understanding of the duty to tell the truth. The missing qualifications—the capacity to perceive and to recollect—are determined in a different manner. Because a witness, qualified under Section 701, must have personal knowledge of the facts to which he testifies (Section 702), he must, of course, have the capacity to perceive and to recollect those facts. But the court may exclude the testimony of a witness for lack of personal knowledge only if no jury could reasonably find that he has such knowledge. See Evidence Code § 403 and the Comment thereto. Thus, the Evidence Code has made a person's capacity to perceive and to recollect a condition for the admission of his testimony concerning a particular matter instead of a condition for his competency to be a witness. And, under the Evidence Code, if there is evidence that the witness has those capacities, the determination whether he in fact perceived and does recollect is left to the trier of fact. See Evidence Code §§ 403 and 702 and the Comments thereto.

Although Section 701 modifies the existing law with respect to determining the competency of witnesses, it seems unlikely that the change will have much practical significance. Theoretically, Section 701 may permit children and persons suffering from mental impairment to testify in some instances where they are now disqualified from testifying; in practice, however, the California courts have permitted children of very tender years and persons with mental impairment to testify. See Witkin, California Evidence §§ 389, 390 (1958). See also Bradburn v. Peacock, 135 Cal.App.2d 161, 164–165, 286 P.2d 972, 974 (1955) (reversible error to preclude a child from testifying without conducting a voir dire examination to determine his competency: "We cannot say that no child of 3 years and 3 months is capable of receiving just impressions of the facts that a man whom he knows in a truck which he knows ran over his little sister. Nor can we say that no child of 3 years and 3 months would remember such facts and be able to relate them truly at the age of 5." (Emphasis in original.)); People v. McCaughan, 49 Cal.2d 409, 317 P.2d 974 (1957) (indicating that committed mental patients may be competent witnesses). For further discussion, see Tentative Recommendation and a Study Relating to the Uniform Rules of Evidence (Article IV. Witnesses), 6 Cal. Law Revision Comm'n, Rep., Rec. & Studies 701, 709–710 (1964). [7 Cal.L.Rev.Comm. Reports 1 (1965)]

§ 702. Personal knowledge of witness

(a) Subject to Section 801, the testimony of a witness concerning a particular matter is inadmissible unless he has personal knowledge of the matter. Against the objection of a party, such personal knowledge must be shown before the witness may testify concerning the matter.

(b) A witness' personal knowledge of a matter may be shown by any otherwise admissible evidence, including his own testimony.

LAW REVISION COMMISSION COMMENT

Section 702 states the general requirement that a witness must have personal knowledge of the facts to which he testifies. "Personal knowledge" means a present recollection of an impression derived from the exercise of the witness' own senses. 2 Wigmore, Evidence § 657 at 762 (3d ed. 1940). Cf. Evidence Code § 170, defining "perceive." Section 702 restates the substance of and supersedes Code of Civil Procedure Section 1845.

Except to the extent that experts may give opinion testimony not based on personal knowledge (see Evidence Code § 801), the requirement of Section 702 is applicable to all witnesses, whether expert or not. Certain additional qualifications that an expert witness must possess are set forth in Article 1 (commencing with Section 720) of Chapter 3.

Under existing law, as under Section 702, an objection must be made to the testimony of a witness who does not have personal knowledge; but, if there is no reasonable opportunity to object before the testimony is given, a motion to strike is appropriate after lack of knowledge has been shown. Fildew v. Shattuck & Nimmo Warehouse Co., 39 Cal.App. 42, 46, 177 Pac. 866, 867 (1918) (objection to question properly sustained when foundational showing of personal knowledge was not made); Sneed v. Marysville Gas & Elec. Co., 149 Cal. 704, 709, 87 Pac. 376, 378 (1906) (error to overrule motion to strike testimony after lack of knowledge shown on cross-examination); Parker v. Smith, 4

Cal. 105 (1854) (testimony properly stricken by court when lack of knowledge shown on cross-examination).

If a timely objection is made that a witness lacks personal knowledge, the court may not receive his testimony subject to the condition that evidence of personal knowledge be supplied later in the trial. Section 702 thus limits the ordinary power of the court with respect to the order of proof. See Evidence Code § 403(b). See also Evidence Code § 320. [7 Cal.L.Rev.Comm. Reports 1 (1965)]

§ 703. Judge as witness

(a) Before the judge presiding at the trial of an action may be called to testify in that trial as a witness, he shall, in proceedings held out of the presence and hearing of the jury, inform the parties of the information he has concerning any fact or matter about which he will be called to testify.

(b) Against the objection of a party, the judge presiding at the trial of an action may not testify in that trial as a witness. Upon such objection, the judge shall declare a mistrial and order the action assigned for trial before another judge.

(c) The calling of the judge presiding at a trial to testify in that trial as a witness shall be deemed a consent to the granting of a motion for mistrial, and an objection to such calling of a judge shall be deemed a motion for mistrial.

(d) In the absence of objection by a party, the judge presiding at the trial of an action may testify in that trial as a witness.

COMMENT—ASSEMBLY COMMITTEE ON JUDICIARY

Under existing law, a judge may be called as a witness even if a party objects, but the judge in his discretion may order the trial to be postponed or suspended and to take place before another judge. Code Civ.Proc. § 1883 (superseded by Evidence Code §§ 703 and 704). But see People v. Connors, 77 Cal.App. 438, 450–457, 246 Pac. 1072, 1076–1079 (1926) (dictum) (abuse of discretion for the presiding judge to testify to important and necessary facts).

Section 703, however, precludes the judge from testifying if a party objects. Before the judge may be called to testify in a civil or criminal action, he must disclose to the parties out of the presence and hearing of the jury the information he has concerning the case. After such disclosure, if no party objects, the judge is permitted—but not required—to testify.

Section 703 is based on the fact that examination and cross-examination of a judge-witness may be embarrassing and prejudicial to a party. By testifying as a witness for one party a judge appears in a partisan attitude before the jury. Objections to questions and to his testimony must be ruled on by the witness himself. The extent of cross-examination and the introduction of impeaching and rebuttal evidence may be limited by the fear of appearing to attack the judge personally. For these and other reasons, Section 703 is preferable to Code of Civil Procedure Section 1883.

Subdivision (c) is designed to prevent a plea of double jeopardy by a defendant who either calls or objects to the calling of the judge to testify. Under subdivision (c), the defendant will, in effect, have consented to the mistrial and thus waived any objection to a retrial. See Witkin, California Crimes § 193 (1963).

§ 703.5. Judges, arbitrators or mediators as witnesses; subsequent civil proceeding

No person presiding at any judicial or quasi-judicial proceeding, and no arbitrator or mediator, shall be competent to testify, in any subsequent civil proceeding, as to any statement, conduct, decision, or ruling, occurring at or in conjunction with the prior proceeding, except as to a statement or conduct that could (a) give rise to civil or criminal contempt, (b) constitute a crime, (c) be the subject of investigation by the State Bar or Commission on Judicial Performance, or (d) give rise to disqualification proceedings under paragraph (1) or (6) of subdivision (a) of Section 170.1 of the Code of Civil Procedure. However, this section does not apply to a mediator with regard to any mediation under Chapter 11 (commencing with Section 3160) of Part 2 of Division 8 of the Family Code.

LAW REVISION COMMISSION COMMENT

1994 Amendment

Section 703.5 is amended to correct the cross-reference to former Family Code Section 3155 to reflect the reorganization of those sections in 1993 Cal. Stat. ch. 219. This is a technical, nonsubstantive change. [24 Cal.L.Rev.Comm.Reports ___ (1994), Annual Report for 1994, App. 5]

§ 704. Juror as witness

(a) Before a juror sworn and impaneled in the trial of an action may be called to testify before the jury in that trial as a witness, he shall, in proceedings conducted by the court out of the presence and hearing of the remaining jurors, inform the parties of the information he has concerning any fact or matter about which he will be called to testify.

(b) Against the objection of a party, a juror sworn and impaneled in the trial of an action may not testify before the jury in that trial as a witness. Upon such objection, the court shall declare a mistrial and order the action assigned for trial before another jury.

(c) The calling of a juror to testify before the jury as a witness shall be deemed a consent to the granting of a motion for mistrial, and an objection to such calling of a juror shall be deemed a motion for mistrial.

(d) In the absence of objection by a party, a juror sworn and impaneled in the trial of an action may be compelled to testify in that trial as a witness.

COMMENT—ASSEMBLY COMMITTEE ON JUDICIARY

Under existing law, a juror may be called as a witness even if a party objects, but the judge in his discretion may order the trial to be postponed or suspended and to take place before another jury. Code Civ.Proc. § 1883 (superseded by Evidence Code §§ 703 and 704). Section 704, on the other hand, prevents a juror from testifying before the jury if any party objects.

A juror-witness is in an anomalous position. He manifestly cannot weigh his own testimony impartially. A party affected adversely by the juror's testimony is placed in an embarrassing position. He cannot freely cross- examine or impeach the juror for fear of antagonizing the juror—and perhaps his fellow jurors as well. And, if he does not attack the juror's testimony, the other jurors may give his testimony undue weight. For these and other reasons, Section 704 forbids jurors to testify over the objection of any party.

Before a juror may be called to testify before the jury in a civil or criminal action, he is required to disclose to the parties out of the presence and hearing of the remaining jurors the information he has concerning the case. After such disclosure, if no party objects, the juror is required to testify. If a party objects, the objection is deemed a motion for mistrial and the judge is required to declare a mistrial and order the action assigned for trial before another jury.

Section 704 is concerned only with the problem of a juror who is called to testify before the jury. Section 704 does not deal with voir dire examinations of jurors, with testimony of jurors in post-verdict proceedings (such as on motions for new trial), or with the testimony of jurors on any other matter that is to be decided by the court. Cf. Evidence Code § 1150 and the Comment thereto.

Subdivision (c) is designed to prevent a plea of double jeopardy by a defendant who either calls or objects to the calling of the juror to testify. Under subdivision (c), the defendant will, in effect, have consented to the mistrial and thus waived any objection to a retrial. See Witkin, California Crimes § 193 (1963).

CHAPTER 2. OATH AND CONFRONTATION

§ 710. Oath required

Every witness before testifying shall take an oath or make an affirmation or declaration in the form provided by law, except that a child under the age of 10, in the court's discretion, may be required only to promise to tell the truth.

§ 711. Confrontation

At the trial of an action, a witness can be heard only in the presence and subject to the examination of all the parties to the action, if they choose to attend and examine.

§ 712. Blood samples; technique in taking; affidavits in criminal actions; service; objections

Notwithstanding Sections 711 and 1200, at the trial of a criminal action, evidence of the technique used in taking blood samples may be given by a registered nurse, licensed vocational nurse, or licensed clinical laboratory technologist or clinical laboratory bioanalyst, by means of an affidavit. The affidavit shall be admissible, provided the party offering the affidavit as evidence has served all other parties to the action, or their counsel, with a copy of the affidavit no less than 10 days prior to trial. Nothing in this section shall preclude any party or his counsel from objecting to the introduction of the affidavit at any time, and requiring the attendance of the affiant, or compelling attendance by subpoena.

CHAPTER 3. EXPERT WITNESSES

ARTICLE 1. EXPERT WITNESSES GENERALLY

§ 720. Qualification as an expert witness

(a) A person is qualified to testify as an expert if he has special knowledge, skill, experience, training, or education sufficient to qualify him as an expert on the subject to which his testimony relates. Against the objection of a party, such special knowledge, skill, experience, training, or education must be shown before the witness may testify as an expert.

(b) A witness' special knowledge, skill, experience, training, or education may be shown by any otherwise admissible evidence, including his own testimony.

LAW REVISION COMMISSION COMMENT

This section states existing law as declared in subdivision 9 (last clause) of Code of Civil Procedure Section 1870, which is superseded by Sections 720 and 801.

The judge must be satisfied that the proposed witness is an expert. People v. Haeussler, 41 Cal.2d 252, 260 P.2d 8 (1953); Pfingsten v. Westenhaver, 39 Cal.2d 12, 244 P.2d 395 (1952); Bossert v. Southern Pac. Co., 172 Cal. 504, 157 Pac. 597 (1916); People v. Pacific Gas & Elec. Co., 27 Cal.App.2d 725, 81 P.2d 584 (1938).

Against the objection of a party, the special qualifications of the proposed witness must be shown as a prerequisite to his testimony as an expert. With the consent of the parties, the judge may receive a witness' testimony conditionally, subject to the necessary foundation being supplied later in the trial. See Evidence Code § 320. Unless the foundation is subsequently supplied, however, the judge should grant a motion to strike or should order the testimony stricken from the record on his own motion.

The judge's determination that a witness qualifies as an expert witness is binding on the trier of fact, but the trier of fact may consider the witness' qualifications as an expert in determining the weight to be given his testimony. Pfingsten v. Westenhaver, 39 Cal.2d 12, 244 P.2d 395 (1952); Howland v. Oakland Consol. St. Ry., 110 Cal. 513, 42 Pac. 983 (1895); Estate of Johnson, 100 Cal.App.2d 73, 223 P.2d 105 (1950). See Evidence Code §§ 405 and 406 and the Comments thereto. [7 Cal.L.Rev.Comm. Reports 1 (1965)]

§ 721. Cross-examination of expert witness

(a) Subject to subdivision (b), a witness testifying as an expert may be cross-examined to the same extent as any other witness and, in addition, may be fully cross-examined as to (1) his or her qualifications, (2) the subject to which his or her expert testimony relates, and (3) the matter upon which his or her opinion is based and the reasons for his or her opinion.

(b) If a witness testifying as an expert testifies in the form of an opinion, he or she may not be cross-examined in regard to the content or tenor of any scientific, technical, or professional text, treatise, journal, or similar publication unless any of the following occurs:

(1) The witness referred to, considered, or relied upon such publication in arriving at or forming his or her opinion * * *.

(2) The publication has been admitted in evidence.

(3) The publication has been established as a reliable authority by the testimony or admission of the witness or by other expert testimony or by judicial notice.

If admitted, relevant portions of the publication may be read into evidence but may not be received as exhibits.

LAW REVISION COMMISSION COMMENT

Under Section 721, a witness who testifies as an expert may, of course, be cross-examined to the same extent as any other witness. See Chapter 5 (commencing with Section 760). But, under subdivision (a) of Section 721, as under existing law, the expert witness is also subject to a somewhat broader cross-examination: "Once an expert offers his opinion, however, he exposes himself to the kind of inquiry which ordinarily would have no place in the cross-examination of a factual witness. The expert invites investigation into the extent of his knowledge, the reasons for his opinion including facts and other matters upon which it is based (Code Civ.Proc., § 1872), and which he took into consideration; and he may be 'subjected to the most rigid cross examination' concerning his qualifications, and his opinion and its sources [citation omitted]." Hope v. Arrowhead & Puritas Waters, Inc., 174 Cal.App.2d 222, 230, 344 P.2d 428, 433 (1959). The cross-examination rule stated in subdivision (a) is based in part on the last clause of Code of Civil Procedure Section 1872.

Subdivision (b) clarifies a matter concerning which there is considerable confusion in the California decisions. It is at least clear under existing law that an expert witness may be cross-examined in regard to those books on which he relied in forming or arriving at his opinion. Lewis v. Johnson, 12 Cal.2d 558, 86 P.2d 99 (1939); People v. Hooper, 10 Cal.App.2d 332, 51 P.2d 1131 (1935). Dicta in some decisions indicate that the cross-examiner is strictly limited to the books relied on by the expert witness. See, e.g., Baily v. Kreutzmann, 141 Cal. 519, 75 Pac. 104 (1904). Other cases, however, suggest that an expert witness may be cross- examined in regard to any book of the same character as the books on which he relied in forming his opinion. Griffith v. Los Angeles Pac. Co., 14 Cal.App. 145, 111 Pac. 107 (1910). See Salgo v. Leland Stanford etc. Bd. Trustees, 154 Cal.App.2d 560, 317 P.2d 170 (1957); Gluckstein v. Lipsett, 93 Cal.App.2d 391, 209 P.2d 98 (1949) (reviewing California authorities). (Possibly, the cross-examiner is restricted under this view to the use of such books as "are not in harmony with the testimony of the witness." Griffith v. Los Angeles Pac. Co., supra.) Language in several earlier cases indicated that the cross-examiner could use books to test the competency of an expert witness, whether or not the expert relied on books in forming his opinion. Fisher v. Southern Pac. R.R., 89 Cal. 399, 26 Pac. 894 (1891); People v. Hooper, 10 Cal.App.2d 332, 51 P.2d 1131 (1935). More recent decisions indicate, however, that the opinion of an expert witness must be based either generally or specifically on books before the expert can be cross-examined concerning them. Lewis v. Johnson, 12 Cal.2d 558, 86 P.2d 99 (1939); Salgo v. Leland Stanford etc. Bd. Trustees, 154 Cal.App.2d 560, 317 P.2d 170 (1957); Gluckstein v. Lipsett, 93 Cal.App.2d 391, 209 P.2d 98 (1949). The conflicting California cases are gathered in Annot., 60 A.L.R.2d 77 (1958).

If an expert witness has relied on a particular publication in forming his opinion, it is necessary to permit cross-examination in regard to that publication in order to show whether the expert correctly read, interpreted, and applied the portions he relied on. Similarly, it is important to permit an expert witness to be cross-examined concerning those publications referred to or considered by him even though not specifically relied on by him in forming his opinion. An expert's reasons for not relying on particular publications that were referred to or considered by him while forming his opinion may reveal important information bearing upon the credibility of his testimony. However, a rule permitting cross-examination on technical treatises not considered by the expert witness would permit the cross-examiner to utilize this opportunity not for its ostensible purpose—to test the expert's opinion—but to bring before the trier of fact the opinions of absentee authors without the safeguard of cross-examination. Although the court would be required upon request to caution the jury that the statements read are not to be considered evidence of the truth of the propositions stated, there is a danger that at least some jurors might rely on the author's statements for this purpose. Yet, the statements in the text might be based on inadequate background research, might be subject to unexpressed qualifications that would be applicable to the case before the court, or might be unreliable for some other reason that could be revealed if the author were subject to cross-examination. Therefore, subdivision (b) does not permit cross-examination of an expert witness on scientific, technical, or professional works not referred to, considered, or relied on by him.

If a particular publication has already been admitted in evidence, however, the reason for subdivision (b)—to prevent inadmissible evidence from being brought before the jury—is inapplicable. Hence, the subdivision permits an expert witness to be examined concerning such a publication without regard to whether he referred to, considered, or relied on it in forming his opinion. Cf. Laird v. T. W. Mather, Inc., 51 Cal.2d 210, 331 P.2d 617 (1958).

The rule state in subdivision (b) thus provides a fair and workable solution to this conflict of competing interests with respect to the permissible use of scientific, technical, or professional publications by the cross-examiner. [7 Cal.L.Rev.Comm. Reports 1 (1965)]

§ 722. Credibility of expert witness

(a) The fact of the appointment of an expert witness by the court may be revealed to the trier of fact.

(b) The compensation and expenses paid or to be paid to an expert witness by the party calling him is a proper subject of inquiry by any adverse party as relevant to the credibility of the witness and the weight of his testimony.

LAW REVISION COMMISSION COMMENT

Subdivision (a) of Section 722 codifies a rule recognized in the California decisions. People v. Cornell, 203 Cal. 144, 263 Pac. 216 (1928); People v. Strong, 114 Cal.App. 522, 300 Pac. 84 (1931).

Subdivision (b) of Section 722 restates the substance of Section 1256.2 of the Code of Civil Procedure. Section 1256.2, however, applies only in condemnation cases, while Section 722 is not so limited. It is uncertain whether the California law in other fields of litigation is as stated in Section 722. At least one California case has held that an expert could be asked whether he was being compensated but that he could not be asked the amount of the compensation. People v. Tomalty, 14 Cal.App. 224, 111 Pac. 513 (1910). However, the decision may have been based on the discretionary right of the trial judge to curtail collateral inquiry.

In any event, the rule enunciated in Section 722 is a desirable rule. The tendency of some experts to become advocates for the party employing them has been recognized. 2 Wigmore, Evidence § 563 (3d ed. 1940); Friedenthal, Discovery and Use of an Adverse Party's Expert Information, 14 Stan.L.Rev. 455, 485–486 (1962). The jury can better appraise the extent to which bias may have influenced an expert's opinion if it is informed of the amount of his fee—and, hence, the extent of his possible feeling of obligation to the party calling him. [7 Cal. L.Rev.Comm. Reports 1 (1965)]

§ 723. Limit on number of expert witnesses

The court may, at any time before or during the trial of an action, limit the number of expert witnesses to be called by any party.

ARTICLE 2. APPOINTMENT OF EXPERT WITNESS BY COURT

§ 730. Appointment of expert by court

When it appears to the court, at any time before or during the trial of an action, that expert evidence is or may be required by the court or by any party to the action, the court on its own motion or on motion of any party may appoint one or more experts to investigate, to render a report as may be ordered by the court, and to testify as an expert at the trial of the action relative to the fact or matter as to which the expert evidence is or may be required. The court may fix the compensation for these services, if any, rendered by any person appointed under this section, in addition to any service as a witness, at the amount as seems reasonable to the court.

Nothing in this section shall be construed to permit a person to perform any act for which a license is required unless the person holds the appropriate license to lawfully perform that act.

§ 731. Payment of court-appointed expert

(a) In all criminal actions and juvenile court proceedings, the compensation fixed under Section 730 shall be a charge against the county in which such action or proceeding is pending and shall be paid out of the treasury of such county on order of the court.

(b) In any county in which the board of supervisors so provides, the compensation fixed under Section 730 for medical experts in civil actions in such county shall be a charge against and paid out of the treasury of such county on order of the court.

(c) Except as otherwise provided in this section, in all civil actions, the compensation fixed under Section 730 shall, in the first instance, be apportioned and charged to the several parties in such proportion as the court may determine and may thereafter be taxed and allowed in like manner as other costs.

§ 732. Calling and examining court-appointed expert

Any expert appointed by the court under Section 730 may be called and examined by the court or by any party to the action. When such witness is called and examined by the court, the parties have the same right as is expressed in Section 775 to cross-examine the witness and to object to the questions asked and the evidence adduced.

LAW REVISION COMMISSION COMMENT

Section 732 restates the substance of and supersedes the fourth paragraph of Section 1871 of the Code of Civil Procedure. Section 732 refers to Section 775, which is based on language originally contained in Section 1871. Section 775 permits each party to the action to object to questions asked and evidence adduced and, also, to cross-examine any person called by the court as a witness to the same extent as if such person were called as a witness by an adverse party. [7 Cal.L.Rev. Comm. Reports 1 (1965)]

§ 733. Right to produce other expert evidence

Nothing contained in this article shall be deemed or construed to prevent any party to any action from producing other expert evidence on the same fact or matter mentioned in Section 730; but, where other expert witnesses are called by a party to the action, their fees shall be paid by the party calling them and only ordinary witness fees shall be taxed as costs in the action.

CHAPTER 4. INTERPRETERS AND TRANSLATORS

§ 750. Rules relating to witnesses apply to interpreters and translators

A person who serves as an interpreter or translator in any action is subject to all the rules of law relating to witnesses.

LAW REVISION COMMISSION COMMENT

Section 750 codifies existing law. E.g., People v. Lem Deo, 132 Cal. 199, 201, 64 Pac. 265, 266 (1901) (interpreter); People v. Bardin, 148 Cal.App.2d 776, 307 P.2d 384 (1957) (translator). [7 Cal.L.Rev.Comm. Reports 1 (1965)]

§ 751. Oath required of interpreters and translators

(a) An interpreter shall take an oath that he or she will make a true interpretation to the witness in a language that the witness understands and that he or she will make a true interpretation of the witness' answers to questions to counsel, court, or jury, in the English language, with his or her best skill and judgment.

(b) In any proceeding in which a deaf or hard-of-hearing person is testifying under oath, the interpreter certified pursuant to subdivision (f) of Section 754 shall advise the court whenever he or she is unable to comply with his or her oath taken pursuant to subdivision (a).

(c) A translator shall take an oath that he or she will make a true translation in the English language of any writing he or she is to decipher or translate.

(d) An interpreter or translator regularly employed by the court and certified or registered in accordance with Article 4 (commencing with Section 68560) of Chapter 2 of Title 8 of the Government Code, or a translator regularly employed by the court, may file an oath as prescribed by this section with the clerk of the court. The filed oath shall serve for all subsequent court proceedings until the appointment is revoked by the court.

LAW REVISION COMMISSION COMMENT

1995 Main Volume

Section 751 is based on language presently contained in subdivision (c) of Section 1885 of the Code of Civil Procedure. [7 Cal.L.Rev.Comm. Reports 1 (1965)]

§ 752. Interpreters for witnesses

(a) When a witness is incapable of understanding the English language or is incapable of expressing himself or herself in the English language so as to be understood directly by counsel, court, and jury, an interpreter whom he or she can understand and who can understand him or her shall be sworn to interpret for him or her.

(b) The record shall identify the interpreter who may be appointed and compensated as provided in Article 2 (commencing with Section 730) of Chapter 3.

LAW REVISION COMMISSION COMMENT

Section 752 restates the substance of and supersedes Section 1884 of the Code of Civil Procedure. It is drawn broadly enough to authorize the use of an interpreter for a person whose inability to be understood directly stems from physical disability as well as from lack of understanding of the English language. See discussion in People v. Walker, 69 Cal.App. 475, 231 Pac. 572 (1924). Under Section 752, as under existing law, whether an interpreter should be appointed is largely within the discretion of the trial judge. People v. Holtzclaw, 76 Cal.App. 168, 243 Pac. 894 (1926).

Subdivision (b) of Section 752 substitutes for the detailed language in Code of Civil Procedure Section 1884 a reference to the general authority of a court to appoint expert witnesses, since interpreters are treated as expert witnesses and subject to the same rules of competency and examination as are experts generally. The existing procedure provided by Code of Civil Procedure Section 1884 does not insure that an interpreter who is required to testify will be paid reasonable compensation for his services. Section 752 corrects this deficiency in the existing law. [7 Cal.L.Rev.Comm. Reports 1 (1965)]

§ 753. Translators of writings

(a) When the written characters in a writing offered in evidence are incapable of being deciphered or understood directly, a translator who can decipher the characters or understand the language shall be sworn to decipher or translate the writing.

(b) The record shall identify the translator who may be appointed and compensated as provided in Article 2 (commencing with Section 730) of Chapter 3.

LAW REVISION COMMISSION COMMENT

Section 753 restates the substance of and supersedes Section 1863 of the Code of Civil Procedure, but the language of Section 753 is new. The same principles that require the appointment of an interpreter for a witness who is incapable of expressing himself so as to be understood directly apply with equal force to documentary evidence. See Evidence Code § 752 and the Comment thereto. [7 Cal.L.Rev.Comm. Reports 1 (1965)]

§ 754. Deaf or hearing impaired persons; interpreters; qualifications; guidelines; compensation; questioning; use of statements

(a) As used in this section, "individual who is deaf or hearing impaired" means an individual with a hearing loss so great as to prevent his or her understanding language spoken in a normal tone, but does not include an individual who is hearing impaired provided with, and able to fully participate in the proceedings through the use of, an assistive listening system or computer-aided transcription equipment provided pursuant to Section 54.8 of the Civil Code.

(b) In any civil or criminal action, including, but not limited to, any action involving a traffic or other infraction , any small claims court proceeding, any juvenile court proceeding, any family court proceeding or service, or any proceeding to determine the mental competency of a person, in any court-ordered or court-provided alternative dispute resolution, including mediation and arbitration, or any administrative hearing, where a party or witness is an individual who is deaf or hearing impaired and the individual who is deaf or hearing impaired is present and participating, the proceedings shall be interpreted in a language that the individual who is deaf or hearing impaired understands by a qualified interpreter appointed by the court or other appointing authority, or as agreed upon.

(c) For purposes of this section, "appointing authority" means a court, department, board, commission, agency, licensing or legislative body, or other body for proceedings requiring a qualified interpreter.

(d) For the purposes of this section, "interpreter" includes, but is not limited to, an oral interpreter, a sign language interpreter, or a deaf-blind interpreter, depending upon the needs of the individual who is deaf or hearing impaired.

(e) For purposes of this section, "intermediary interpreter" means an individual who is deaf or hearing impaired, or a hearing individual who is able to assist in providing an accurate interpretation between spoken English and sign language or between variants of sign language or between American Sign Language and other foreign languages by acting as an intermediary between the individual who is deaf or hearing impaired and the qualified interpreter.

(f) For purposes of this section, "qualified interpreter" means an interpreter who has been certified as competent to interpret court proceedings by a testing organization, agency, or educational institution approved by the Judicial Council as qualified to administer tests to court interpreters for individuals who are deaf or hearing impaired.

(g) In the event that the appointed interpreter is not familiar with the use of particular signs by the individual who is deaf or hearing impaired or his or her particular variant of sign language, the court or other appointing authority shall, in consultation with the individual who is deaf or hearing impaired or his or her representative, appoint an intermediary interpreter.

(h) Prior to July 1, 1992, the Judicial Council shall conduct a study to establish the guidelines pursuant to which it shall determine which testing organizations, agencies, or educational institutions will be approved to administer tests for certification of court interpreters for individuals who are deaf or hearing impaired. It is the intent of the Legislature that the study obtain the widest possible input from the public, including, but not limited to, educational institutions, the judiciary, linguists, members of the State Bar, court interpreters, members of professional interpreting organizations, and members of the deaf and hearing-impaired communities. After obtaining public comment and completing its study, the Judicial Council shall publish these guidelines. By January 1, 1997, the Judicial Council shall approve one or more entities to administer testing for court interpreters for individuals who are deaf or hearing impaired. Testing entities may include educational institutions, testing organizations, joint powers agencies or public agencies.

Commencing July 1, 1997, court interpreters for individuals who are deaf or hearing impaired shall meet the qualifications specified in subdivision (f).

(i) Persons appointed to serve as interpreters under this section shall be paid, in addition to actual travel costs, the prevailing rate paid to persons employed by the court to provide other interpreter services unless such service is considered to be a part of the person's regular duties as an employee of the state, county, or other political subdivision of the state. Payment of the interpreter's fee shall be a charge against the county, or other political subdivision of the state, in which that action is pending. Payment of the interpreter's fee in administrative proceedings shall be a charge against the appointing board or authority.

(j) Whenever a peace officer or any other person having a law enforcement or prosecutorial function in any criminal or quasi-criminal investigation or proceeding questions or otherwise interviews an alleged victim or witness who demonstrates or alleges deafness or hearing impairment, a good faith effort to secure the services of an interpreter shall be made, without any unnecessary delay unless either the individual who is deaf or hearing impaired affirmatively indicates that he or she does not need or cannot use an interpreter, or an interpreter is not otherwise required by Title II of the Americans with Disabilities Act of 1990 (Public Law 101–336)[1] and federal regulations adopted thereunder.

(k) No statement, written or oral, made by an individual who the court finds is deaf or hearing impaired in reply to a question of a peace officer, or any other person having a law enforcement or prosecutorial function in any criminal or quasi-criminal investigation or proceeding, may be used against that individual who is deaf or hearing impaired unless the question was accurately interpreted and the statement was made knowingly, voluntarily, and intelligently and was accurately interpreted, or the court makes special findings that either the individual could not have used an interpreter or an interpreter was not otherwise required by Title II of the Americans with Disabilities Act of 1990 (Public Law 101–336)[1] and federal regulations adopted thereunder and that the statement was made knowingly, voluntarily, and intelligently.

(*l*) In obtaining services of an interpreter for purposes of subdivision (j) or (k), priority shall be given to first obtaining a qualified interpreter.

(m) Nothing in subdivision (j) or (k) shall be deemed to supersede the requirement of subdivision (b) for use of a qualified interpreter for

1. 42 U.S.C.A. § 12101 et seq.

individuals who are deaf or hearing impaired participating as parties or witnesses in a trial or hearing.

(n) In any action or proceeding in which an individual who is deaf or hearing impaired is a participant, the appointing authority shall not commence proceedings until the appointed interpreter is in full view of and spatially situated to assure proper communication with the participating individual who is deaf or hearing impaired.

(*o*) Each superior court shall maintain a current roster of qualified interpreters certified pursuant to subdivision (f).

LAW REVISION COMMISSION COMMENT

Section 754 restates the substance of and supersedes Section 1885 of the Code of Civil Procedure. Subdivision (c) of Section 1885 is not continued in Section 754 but is restated in substance in Section 751.

The phrase "with or without a hearing aid" has been deleted from the definition of "deaf person" as unnecessary. The court's inquiry should be directed towards the ability of the person to hear; the court should not be concerned with the means by which he might be enabled to hear. [7 Cal.L.Rev.Comm. Reports 1 (1965)]

§ 754.5. Privileged statements; deaf or hearing impaired persons; use of interpreter

Whenever an otherwise valid privilege exists between an individual who is deaf or hearing impaired and another person, that privilege is not waived merely because an interpreter was used to facilitate their communication.

§ 755. Hearings or proceedings related to domestic violence; party not proficient in English; interpreters; fees

(a) In any action or proceeding under Division 10 (commencing with Section 6200) of the Family Code, and in any action or proceeding under the Uniform Parentage Act (Part 3 (commencing with Section 7600) of Division 12 of the Family Code) or for dissolution or nullity of marriage or legal separation of the parties in which a protective order has been granted or is being sought pursuant to Section 6221 of the Family Code, in which a party does not proficiently speak or understand the English language, and that party is present, an interpreter, as provided in this section, shall be present to interpret the proceedings in a language that the party understands, and to assist communication between the party and his or her attorney. Notwithstanding this requirement, a court may issue an ex parte order pursuant to Sections 2045 and 7710 of, and Article 1 (commencing with Section 6320) of Chapter 2 of Part 4 of Division 10 of the Family Code, without the presence of an interpreter. The interpreter selected shall be certified pursuant to Article 4 (commencing with Section 68560) of Chapter 2 of Title 8 of the Government

Code, unless the court in its discretion appoints an interpreter who is not certified.

(b) The fees of interpreters utilized under this section shall be paid as provided in subdivision (b) of Section 68092 of the Government Code. However, the fees of an interpreter shall be waived for a party who needs an interpreter and appears in forma pauperis pursuant to Section 68511.3 of the Government Code. The Judicial Council shall amend subdivision (i) of California Rule of Court 985 and revise its forms accordingly by July 1, 1996.

(c) In any civil action in which an interpreter is required under this section, the court shall not commence proceedings until the appointed interpreter is present and situated near the party and his or her attorney. However, this section shall not prohibit the court from doing any of the following:

(1) Issuing an order when the necessity for the order outweighs the necessity for an interpreter.

(2) Extending the duration of a previously issued temporary order if an interpreter is not readily available.

(3) Issuing a permanent order where a party who requires an interpreter fails to make appropriate arrangements for an interpreter after receiving proper notice of the hearing with information about obtaining an interpreter.

(d) This section does not prohibit the presence of any other person to assist a party.

(e) A local public entity may, and the Judicial Council shall, apply to the appropriate state agency that receives federal funds authorized pursuant to the federal Violence Against Women Act (P.L. 103–322) for these federal funds or for funds from sources other than the state to implement this section. A local public entity and the Judicial Council shall comply with the requirements of this section only to the extent that any of these funds are made available.

(f) The Judicial Council shall draft rules and modify forms necessary to implement this section, including those for the petition for a temporary restraining order and related forms, to inform both parties of their right to an interpreter pursuant to this section.

§ 755.5. Medical examinations; parties not proficient in English language; interpreters; fees; admissibility of record

(a) During any medical examination, requested by an insurer or by the defendant, of a person who is a party to a civil action and who does not proficiently speak or understand the English language, conducted for the purpose of determining damages in a civil action, an interpreter shall be present to interpret the examination in a language that the person understands. * * * The interpreter shall be certified pursuant to Article 8 (commencing with Section * * * 11435.05) of Chapter 4.5 of Part 1 of Division 3 of Title 2 of the Government Code.

(b) The fees of interpreters used under subdivision (a) shall be paid by the insurer or defendant requesting the medical examination.

(c) The record of, or testimony concerning, any medical examination conducted in violation of subdivision (a) shall be inadmissible in the civil action for which it was conducted or any other civil action.

(d) This section does not prohibit the presence of any other person to assist a party.

(e) In the event that interpreters certified pursuant to Article 8 (commencing with Section * * * 11435.05) of Chapter 4.5 of Part 1 of Division 3 of Title 2 of the Government Code cannot be present at the medical examination, upon stipulation of the parties the requester specified in subdivision (a) shall have the discretionary authority to provisionally qualify and use other interpreters.

CHAPTER 5. METHOD AND SCOPE OF EXAMINATION

ARTICLE 1. DEFINITIONS

§ 760. Direct examination

"Direct examination" is the first examination of a witness upon a matter that is not within the scope of a previous examination of the witness.

LAW REVISION COMMISSION COMMENT

Section 760 restates the substance of and supersedes the first clause of Code of Civil Procedure Section 2045 and the last clause of Code of Civil Procedure Section 2048. Under Section 760, an examination of a witness called by another party is direct examination if the examination relates to a matter that is not within the scope of the previous examination of the witness. [7 Cal.L.Rev.Comm. Reports 1 (1965)]

§ 761. Cross-examination

"Cross-examination" is the examination of a witness by a party other than the direct examiner upon a matter that is within the scope of the direct examination of the witness.

LAW REVISION COMMISSION COMMENT

Section 761 restates the substance of and supersedes the definition of "cross-examination" found in Section 2045 of the Code of Civil Procedure. In accordance with existing law, it limits cross-examination of a witness to the scope of the witness' direct examination. See generally Witkin, California Evidence §§ 622–638 (1958).

Section 761, together with Section 773, retains the cross-examination rule now applicable to a defendant in a criminal action who testifies as a witness in that action. See People v. McCarthy, 88 Cal.App.2d 883, 200 P.2d 69 (1948). See also People v. Arrighini, 122 Cal. 121, 54 Pac. 591 (1898); People v. O'Brien, 66 Cal. 602, 6 Pac. 695 (1885); Witkin, California Evidence § 629 (1958). See also Evidence Code § 772(d). [7 Cal.L.Rev.Comm. Reports 1 (1965)]

§ 762. Redirect examination

"Redirect examination" is an examination of a witness by the direct examiner subsequent to the cross-examination of the witness.

LAW REVISION COMMISSION COMMENT

"Redirect examination" and "recross-examination" are not defined in existing statutes, but the terms are recognized in practice. See Witkin, California Evidence §§ 697, 698 (1958). The scope of redirect and recross-examination is limited by Section 774.

The definition of "redirect examination" embraces not only the examination immediately following cross-examination of the witness but also any subsequent re-examination of the witness by the direct examiner. [7 Cal.L.Rev.Comm. Reports 1 (1965)]

§ 763. Recross-examination

"Recross-examination" is an examination of a witness by a cross-examiner subsequent to a redirect examination of the witness.

LAW REVISION COMMISSION COMMENT

See the Comment to Section 762. The definition of "recross-examination" embraces not only the examination immediately following the first redirect examination of the witness but also any subsequent re-examination of the witness by a cross-examiner. [7 Cal.L.Rev.Comm. Reports 1 (1965)]

§ 764. Leading question

A "leading question" is a question that suggests to the witness the answer that the examining party desires.

LAW REVISION COMMISSION COMMENT

Section 764 restates the substance of and supersedes the first sentence of Section 2046 of the Code of Civil Procedure. For restrictions on the use of leading questions in the examination of a witness, see Evidence Code § 767 and the Comment thereto. [7 Cal.L.Rev.Comm. Reports 1 (1965)]

ARTICLE 2. EXAMINATION OF WITNESSES

§ 765. Court to control mode of interrogation

(a) The court shall exercise reasonable control over the mode of interrogation of a witness so as to make such interrogation as rapid, as distinct, and as effective for the ascertainment of the truth, as may be, and to protect the witness from undue harassment or embarrassment.

(b) With a witness under the age of 14, the court shall take special care to protect him or her from undue harassment or embarrassment, and to restrict the unnecessary repetition of questions. The court shall also take special care to insure that questions are stated in a form which is appropriate to the age of the witness. The court may in the interests of justice, on objection by a party, forbid the asking of a question which is in a form that is not reasonably likely to be understood by a person of the age of the witness.

LAW REVISION COMMISSION COMMENT

Section 765 restates the substance of and supersedes Section 2044 of the Code of Civil Procedure. As to the latitude permitted the judge in controlling the examination of witnesses under existing law, which is continued in effect by Section 765, see Commercial Union Assur. Co. v. Pacific Gas & Elec. Co., 220 Cal. 515, 31 P.2d 793 (1934). See also People v. Davis, 6 Cal.App. 229, 91 Pac. 810 (1907). [7 Cal.L.Rev.Comm. Reports 1 (1965)]

§ 766. Responsive answers

A witness must give responsive answers to questions, and answers that are not responsive shall be stricken on motion of any party.

§ 767. Leading questions

(a) Except under special circumstances where the interests of justice otherwise require:

(1) A leading question may not be asked of a witness on direct or redirect examination.

(2) A leading question may be asked of a witness on cross-examination or recross-examination.

(b) The court may in the interests of justice permit a leading question to be asked of a child under 10 years of age in a case involving a prosecution under Section 273a, 273d, 288, or 288.5 of the Penal Code.

COMMENT—ASSEMBLY COMMITTEE ON JUDICIARY

Subdivision (a) restates the substance of and supersedes the last sentence of Section 2046 of the Code of Civil Procedure. Subdivision (b) is based on and supersedes a phrase that appears in Code of Civil Procedure Section 2048.

The exception stated at the beginning of the section continues the present law that permits leading questions on direct examination where there is little danger of improper suggestion or where such questions are necessary to obtain relevant evidence. This would permit leading questions on direct examination for preliminary matters, refreshing recollection, and examining handicapped witnesses, expert witnesses, and hostile witnesses. See Witkin, California Evidence §§ 591, 592 (1958); 3 Wigmore, Evidence § 769 et seq. (3d ed. 1940). The court may also forbid the asking of leading questions on cross-examination where the witness is biased in favor of the cross-examiner and would be unduly susceptible to the influence of questions that suggested the desired answer. See 3 Wigmore, Evidence § 773 (3d ed. 1940).

§ 768. Writings

(a) In examining a witness concerning a writing, it is not necessary to show, read, or disclose to him any part of the writing.

(b) If a writing is shown to a witness, all parties to the action must be given an opportunity to inspect it before any question concerning it may be asked of the witness.

COMMENT—ASSEMBLY COMMITTEE ON JUDICIARY

Existing law apparently does not require that a writing (other than one containing prior inconsistent statements used for impeachment purposes) be shown to a witness before he can be examined concerning it. Section 2054 of the Code of Civil Procedure, which seems to so require, actually requires only that the adverse party be given an opportunity to inspect any writing that is actually shown to a witness before the witness can be examined concerning the writing. See People v. Briggs, 58 Cal.2d 385, 413, 24 Cal.Rptr. 417, 435, 374 P.2d 257, 275 (1962); People v. Keyes, 103 Cal.App. 624, 284 Pac. 1096 (1930) (hearing denied); People v. De Angelli, 34 Cal.App. 716, 168 Pac. 699 (1917). Section 768 clarifies whatever doubt may exist in this regard by declaring that such a writing need not be shown to the witness before he can be examined concerning it. Of course, the best evidence rule may in some cases preclude eliciting testimony concerning the content of a writing. See Evidence Code § 1500 and the Comment thereto.

Insofar as Section 768 relates to prior inconsistent statements that are in writing, see the Comment to Section 769.

Subdivision (b) of Section 768 preserves the right of the adverse party to inspect a writing that is actually shown to a witness before the witness can be examined concerning it. As indicated above, this preserves the existing requirement declared in Code of Civil Procedure

Section 2054. However, the right of inspection has been extended to all parties to the action.

§ 769. Inconsistent statement or conduct

In examining a witness concerning a statement or other conduct by him that is inconsistent with any part of his testimony at the hearing, it is not necessary to disclose to him any information concerning the statement or other conduct.

COMMENT—ASSEMBLY COMMITTEE ON JUDICIARY

Section 769 is consistent with the existing California law regarding the examination of a witness concerning prior inconsistent oral statements. Under existing law, a party need not disclose to a witness any information concerning a prior inconsistent oral statement of the witness before asking him questions about the statement. People v. Kidd, 56 Cal.2d 759, 765, 16 Cal.Rptr. 793, 796–797, 366 P.2d 49, 52–53 (1961); People v. Campos, 10 Cal.App.2d 310, 317, 52 P.2d 251, 254 (1935). However, if a witness' prior inconsistent statements are in writing or, as in the case of former oral testimony, have been reduced to writing, "they must be shown to the witness before any question is put to him concerning them." Code Civ.Proc. § 2052 (superseded by Evidence Code § 768); Umemoto v. McDonald, 6 Cal.2d 587, 592, 58 P.2d 1274, 1276 (1936).

Section 769 eliminates the distinction made in existing law between oral and written statements and permits a witness to be asked questions concerning a prior inconsistent statement, whether written or oral, even though no disclosure is made to him concerning the prior statement. (Whether a foundational showing is required before other evidence of the prior statement may be admitted is not covered in Section 769; the prerequisites for the admission of such evidence are set forth in Section 770.) The disclosure of inconsistent written statements that is required under existing law limits the effectiveness of cross-examination by removing the element of surprise. The forewarning gives the dishonest witness the opportunity to reshape his testimony in conformity with the prior statement. The existing rule is based on an English common law rule that has been abandoned in England for 100 years. See McCormick, Evidence § 28 at 53 (1954).

§ 770. Evidence of inconsistent statement of witness; exclusion; exceptions

Unless the interests of justice otherwise require, extrinsic evidence of a statement made by a witness that is inconsistent with any part of his testimony at the hearing shall be excluded unless:

(a) The witness was so examined while testifying as to give him an opportunity to explain or to deny the statement; or

(b) The witness has not been excused from giving further testimony in the action.

LAW REVISION COMMISSION COMMENT

Under Section 2052 of the Code of Civil Procedure, extrinsic evidence of a witness' inconsistent statement may be admitted only if the witness was given the opportunity, while testifying, to explain or deny the contradictory statement. Permitting a witness to explain or deny an alleged inconsistent statement is desirable, but there is no compelling reason to provide the opportunity for explanation before the inconsistent statement is introduced in evidence. Accordingly, unless the interests of justice otherwise require, Section 770 permits the judge to exclude evidence of an inconsistent statement only if the witness during his examination was not given an opportunity to explain or deny the statement and he has been unconditionally excused and is not subject to being recalled as a witness. Among other things, Section 770 will permit more effective cross-examination and impeachment of several collusive witnesses, since there need be no disclosure of prior inconsistency before all such witnesses have been examined.

Where the interests of justice require it, the court may permit extrinsic evidence of an inconsistent statement to be admitted even though the witness has been excused and has had no opportunity to explain or deny the statement. An absolute rule forbidding introduction of such evidence where the specified conditions are not met may cause hardship in some cases. For example, the party seeking to introduce the statement may not have learned of its existence until after the witness has left the court and is no longer available to testify. For the foundational requirements for the admission of a hearsay declarant's inconsistent statement, see Evidence Code § 1202 and the Comment thereto. [7 Cal.L.Rev.Comm.Reports 1 (1965)]

§ 771. Production of writing used to refresh memory

(a) Subject to subdivision (c), if a witness, either while testifying or prior thereto, uses a writing to refresh his memory with respect to any matter about which he testifies, such writing must be produced at the hearing at the request of an adverse party and, unless the writing is so produced, the testimony of the witness concerning such matter shall be stricken.

(b) If the writing is produced at the hearing, the adverse party may, if he chooses, inspect the writing, cross-examine the witness concerning it, and introduce in evidence such portion of it as may be pertinent to the testimony of the witness.

(c) Production of the writing is excused, and the testimony of the witness shall not be stricken, if the writing:

(1) Is not in the possession or control of the witness or the party who produced his testimony concerning the matter; and

(2) Was not reasonably procurable by such party through the use of the court's process or other available means.

COMMENT—ASSEMBLY COMMITTEE ON JUDICIARY

Section 771 grants to an adverse party the right to inspect any writing used to refresh a witness' recollection, whether the writing is used by the witness while testifying or prior thereto. The right of inspection granted by Section 771 may be broader than the similar right of inspection granted by Section 2047 of the Code of Civil Procedure, for Section 2047 has been interpreted by the courts to grant a right of inspection of only those writings used by the witness while he is testifying. People v. Gallardo, 41 Cal.2d 57, 257 P.2d 29 (1953); People v. Grayson, 172 Cal.App.2d 372, 341 P.2d 820 (1959); Smith v. Smith, 135 Cal.App.2d 100, 286 P.2d 1009 (1955). In a criminal case, however, the defendant can compel the prosecution to produce any written statement of a prosecution witness relating to matters covered in the witness' testimony. People v. Estrada, 54 Cal.2d 713, 7 Cal.Rptr. 897, 355 P.2d 641 (1960). The extent to which the public policy reflected in criminal discovery practice overrides the restrictive interpretation of Code of Civil Procedure Section 2047 is not clear. See Witkin, California Evidence § 602 (Supp. 1963). In any event, Section 771 follows the lead of the criminal cases, such as People v. Silberstein, 159 Cal.App.2d Supp. 848, 323 P.2d 591 (1958) (defendant entitled to inspect police report used by police officer to refresh his recollection before testifying), and grants a right of inspection without regard to when the writing is used to refresh recollection. If a witness' testimony depends upon the use of a writing to refresh his recollection, the adverse party's right to inspect the writing should not be made to depend upon the happenstance of when the writing is used.

Subdivision (b) gives an adverse party the right to introduce the refreshing memorandum into evidence. An adverse party has a similar right under Code of Civil Procedure Section 2047, which is superseded by this section. This right is not unlimited, however. Only those parts of the refreshing memorandum that are pertinent to the testimony given by the witness are admissible under this rule. Cf. People v. Silberstein, 159 Cal.App.2d Supp. 848, 851–852, 323 P.2d 591, 593 (1958) ("the right to inspect [a refreshing writing] cannot be denied although its admission in evidence may be refused if . . . its contents are immaterial"); Dragash v. Western Pac. R.R., 161 Cal.App.2d 233, 326 P.2d 649 (1958). See also Evidence Code § 356 and the Comment thereto.

Subdivision (c) excuses the nonproduction of the memory-refreshing writing where the writing cannot be produced through no fault of the witness or the party eliciting his testimony concerning the matter. The rule is analogous to the rule announced in People v. Parham, 60 Cal.2d

378, 33 Cal.Rptr. 497, 384 P.2d 1001 (1963), which affirmed an order denying defendant's motion to strike certain witnesses' testimony where the witnesses' prior statements were withheld by the Federal Bureau of Investigation.

It should be noted that there is no restriction in the Evidence Code on the means that may be used to refresh recollection. Thus, the limitations on the types of writings that may be used as recorded memory under Section 1237 do not limit the types of writings that may be used to refresh recollection under Section 771.

§ 772. Order of examination

(a) The examination of a witness shall proceed in the following phases: direct examination, cross-examination, redirect examination, recross- examination, and continuing thereafter by redirect and recross-examination.

(b) Unless for good cause the court otherwise directs, each phase of the examination of a witness must be concluded before the succeeding phase begins.

(c) Subject to subdivision (d), a party may, in the discretion of the court, interrupt his cross-examination, redirect examination, or recross-examination of a witness, in order to examine the witness upon a matter not within the scope of a previous examination of the witness.

(d) If the witness is the defendant in a criminal action, the witness may not, without his consent, be examined under direct examination by another party.

COMMENT—ASSEMBLY COMMITTEE ON JUDICIARY

Subdivision (a) codifies existing but nonstatutory California law. See Witkin, California Evidence § 576 at 631 (1958).

Subdivision (b) is based on and supersedes the second sentence of Section 2045 of the Code of Civil Procedure. The language of the existing section has been expanded, however, to require completion of each phase of examination of the witness, not merely the direct examination.

Under subdivision (c), as under existing law, a party examining a witness under cross-examination, redirect examination, or recross-examination may go beyond the scope of the initial direct examination if the court permits. See Code Civ.Proc. §§ 2048 (last clause), 2050; Witkin, California Evidence §§ 627, 697 (1958). Under the definition in Section 760, such an extended examination is direct examination. Cf. Code Civ.Proc. § 2048 ("such examination is to be subject to the same rules as a direct examination"). Such direct examination may, however, be subject to the rules applicable to a cross-examination by virtue of the provisions of Section 776, 804, or 1203.

Subdivision (d) states an exception for the defendant-witness in a criminal action that reflects existing law. See Witkin, California Evidence § 629 at 676 (1958).

§ 773. Cross-examination

(a) A witness examined by one party may be cross-examined upon any matter within the scope of the direct examination by each other party to the action in such order as the court directs.

(b) The cross-examination of a witness by any party whose interest is not adverse to the party calling him is subject to the same rules that are applicable to the direct examination.

LAW REVISION COMMISSION COMMENT

Subdivision (a) restates the substance of Sections 2045 (part) and 2048 of the Code of Civil Procedure and Section 1323 of the Penal Code.

Subdivision (b) is based on the holding in Atchison, T. & S.F. Ry. v. Southern Pac. Co., 13 Cal.App.2d 505, 57 P.2d 575 (1936). That case held that a party not adverse to the direct examiner of a witness did not have the right to cross-examine the witness. Under subdivision (a), such a party would have the right to cross-examine the witness upon any matter within the scope of the direct examination, but he would be prohibited by Section 767 from asking leading questions during such examination. If the witness testifies on direct examination to matters that are, in fact, antagonistic to a party's position, he may be permitted to cross-examine with leading questions even though from a technical point of view the interest of the cross-examiner is not adverse to that of the direct examiner. Cf. McCarthy v. Mobile Cranes, Inc., 199 Cal. App.2d 500, 18 Cal.Rptr. 750 (1962). [7 Cal.L.Rev.Comm. Reports 1 (1965)]

§ 774. Re-examination

A witness once examined cannot be reexamined as to the same matter without leave of the court, but he may be reexamined as to any new matter upon which he has been examined by another party to the action. Leave may be granted or withheld in the court's discretion.

LAW REVISION COMMISSION COMMENT

Section 774 is based on and supersedes the first and third sentences of Section 2050 of the Code of Civil Procedure. The nature of a reexamination is to be determined in accordance with the definitions in Sections 760–763. [7 Cal.L.Rev.Comm. Reports 1 (1965)]

§ 775. Court may call witnesses

The court, on its own motion or on the motion of any party, may call witnesses and interrogate them the same as if they had been produced by a party to the action, and the parties may object to the questions asked and the evidence adduced the same as if such witnesses were called and examined by an adverse party. Such witnesses may be cross-examined by all parties to the action in such order as the court directs.

COMMENT—ASSEMBLY COMMITTEE ON JUDICIARY

The power of the judge to call expert witnesses is well recognized by statutory and case law in California. Code Civ.Proc. § 1871 (recodified as Section 723 and Article 2 (commencing with Section 730) of Chapter 3); Penal Code § 1027; Citizens State Bank v. Castro, 105 Cal.App. 284, 287 Pac. 559 (1930). See also Code Civ.Proc. §§ 1884 and 1885 (interpreters), continued in substance by Chapter 4 (commencing with Section 750).

The power of the judge to call other witnesses is also recognized by case law. Travis v. Southern Pac. Co., 210 Cal.App.2d 410, 425, 26 Cal.Rptr. 700, 707–708 (1962) ("[W]e have been cited to no case, nor has our independent research disclosed any case, dealing with a civil action in which a witness has been called to the stand by the court, over objection of a party. However, we can see no difference in this respect between a civil and a criminal case. In both, the endeavor of the court and the parties should be to get at the truth of the matter in contest. Fundamentally, there is no reason why the court in the interests of justice should not call to the stand anyone who appears to have relevant, competent and material information.").

Of course, the judge would be guilty of misconduct were he to show partiality or bias in calling and interrogating witnesses. See 2 Witkin, California Procedure, Trial §§ 14–17 (1954).

§ 776. Examination of adverse party or person identified with adverse party

(a) A party to the record of any civil action, or a person identified with such a party, may be called and examined as if under cross-examination by any adverse party at any time during the presentation of evidence by the party calling the witness.

(b) A witness examined by a party under this section may be cross-examined by all other parties to the action in such order as the court directs; but, subject to subdivision (e), the witness may be examined only as if under redirect examination by:

(1) In the case of a witness who is a party, his own counsel and counsel for a party who is not adverse to the witness.

(2) In the case of a witness who is not a party, counsel for the party with whom the witness is identified and counsel for a party who is not adverse to the party with whom the witness is identified.

(c) For the purpose of this section, parties represented by the same counsel are deemed to be a single party.

(d) For the purpose of this section, a person is identified with a party if he is:

(1) A person for whose immediate benefit the action is prosecuted or defended by the party.

(2) A director, officer, superintendent, member, agent, employee, or managing agent of the party or of a person specified in paragraph (1), or any public employee of a public entity when such public entity is the party.

(3) A person who was in any of the relationships specified in paragraph (2) at the time of the act or omission giving rise to the cause of action.

(4) A person who was in any of the relationships specified in paragraph (2) at the time he obtained knowledge of the matter concerning which he is sought to be examined under this section.

(e) Paragraph (2) of subdivision (b) does not require counsel for the party with whom the witness is identified and counsel for a party who is not adverse to the party with whom the witness is identified to examine the witness as if under redirect examination if the party who called the witness for examination under this section:

(1) Is also a person identified with the same party with whom the witness is identified.

(2) Is the personal representative, heir, successor, or assignee of a person identified with the same party with whom the witness is identified.

LAW REVISION COMMISSION COMMENT

1965 Enactment

Section 776 restates the substance of Code of Civil Procedure Section 2055 as it has been interpreted by the courts. See Witkin, California Evidence §§ 607–613 (1958), and pertinent cases cited and discussed therein.

Subdivision (a). Subdivision (a) restates the provisions of Section 2055 that permit a party to call and examine as if under cross-examination an adverse party and certain adverse witnesses. However, Section 776 substitutes the phrase "or a person identified with such a party" for the confusing enumeration of persons listed in the first sentence of Section 2055. This phrase is defined in subdivision (d) of Section 776 to include all of the persons presently named in Section 2055. See the Comment to subdivision (d), infra.

Subdivision (b). Subdivision (b) is based in part on similar provisions contained in Code of Civil Procedure Section 2055. Unlike Section

2055, however, this subdivision is drafted in recognition of the problems involved in multiple party litigation. Thus, the introductory portion of subdivision (b) states the general rule that a witness examined under this section may be cross-examined by all other parties to the action in such order as the court directs. For example, a party whose interest in the action is identical with that of the party who called the witness for examination under this section has a right to cross-examine the witness fully because he, too, has the right to call the witness for examination under this section. Similarly, a party whose interest in the action is adverse to the party who calls the witness for examination under this section has the right to cross-examine the witness fully unless he is identified with the witness as described in paragraphs (1) and (2) of this subdivision. Paragraphs (1) and (2) restrict the nature of the cross-examination permitted of a witness by a party with whom the witness is identified and by parties whose interest in the action is not adverse to the party with whom the witness is identified. These parties are limited to examination of the witness as if under redirect examination. In essence, this means that leading questions cannot be asked of the witness by these parties. See Evidence Code § 767. Although the examination must proceed as if it were a redirect examination, under Section 761 it is in fact a cross-examination and limited to the scope of the direct. See also Evidence Code §§ 760, 773.

Subdivision (c). Subdivision (c) codifies a principle that has been recognized in the California cases even though not explicitly stated in Code of Civil Procedure Section 2055. See Gates v. Pendleton, 71 Cal.App. 752, 236 Pac. 365 (1925); Goehring v. Rogers, 67 Cal.App. 260, 227 Pac. 689 (1924).

Subdivision (d). Subdivision (d) lists the classes of persons who are "identified with a party" as that phrase and variations of it are used in subdivisions (a) and (b) of Section 776. The persons named in paragraphs (1) and (2) are those described in the first sentence of Code of Civil Procedure Section 2055 as being subject to examination pursuant to the section because of a particular relationship to a party. See the definitions of "person," "public employee," and "public entity" in Evidence Code §§ 175, 195, and 200, respectively. In addition, paragraph (3) of this subdivision describes persons who were in any of the requisite relationships at the time of the act or omission giving rise to the cause of action. This states existing case law. Scott v. Del Monte Properties, Inc., 140 Cal.App.2d 756, 295 P.2d 947 (1956); Wells v. Lloyd, 35 Cal.App.2d 6, 94 P.2d 373 (1939). Similarly, paragraph (4) extends this principle to include any person who obtained relevant knowledge as a result of such a relationship but who does not fit the precise descriptions contained in paragraphs (1) through (3). For example, a person whose employment by a party began after the cause of action arose and terminated prior to the time of his examination at the trial would be included in the description contained in paragraph (4) if he obtained relevant knowledge of the incident as a result of his employment. It is not clear whether this states existing law, for no California decision has been found that decides this question. The paragraph is necessary, however, to preclude a party from preventing examination of his employee pursuant to this section by the simple expedient of discharging the employee prior to trial and reinstating him afterwards. Cf. Wells v. Lloyd, 35 Cal.App.2d 6, 12, 94 P.2d 373, 376–377 (1939). [7 Cal.L.Rev. Comm. Reports 1 (1965)]

1967 Amendment

Section 776 permits a party calling as a witness an employee of (or someone similarly identified in interest with) an adverse party to examine the witness as if under cross-examination, i.e., to use leading questions in his examination. Section 776 requires the party whose employee was thus called and examined to examine the witness as if under redirect examination, i.e., to refrain from the use of leading questions. If a party is able to persuade the court that the usual rule prescribed by Section 776 is not in the interest of justice in a particular case, the court may enlarge or restrict the right to use leading questions as provided in Section 767.

These rules are based on the premise that ordinarily such a witness will have a feeling of identification in the lawsuit with his employer rather than with the other party to the action.

Subdivision (b) has been amended, and subdivision (e) has been added, because the premise upon which Section 776 is based does not necessarily apply when the party calling the witness is also closely identified with the adverse party; hence, the adverse party should be entitled to the usual rights of a cross-examiner when he examines the witness. For example, when an employee sues his employer and calls a co-employee as a witness, there is no reason to assume that the witness will be adverse to the employee-party and in sympathy with the employer-party. The reverse may be the case. The amendment to Section 776 will permit an employer, as a general rule to use leading questions in his cross-examination of an employee-witness who has been called to testify under Section 776 by a co-employee. However, if the party calling the witness can satisfy the court that the witness is in fact identified in interest with the employer or for some other reason is amenable to suggestive questioning by the employer, the court may limit the employer's use of leading questions during his examination of the witness pursuant to Section 767. See J. & B. Motors, Inc. v. Margolis, 75 Ariz. 392, 257 P.2d 588 (1953). [8 Cal.L.Rev.Comm. Reports 101 (1967)]

§ 777. Exclusion of witness

(a) Subject to subdivisions (b) and (c), the court may exclude from the courtroom any witness not at the time under examination so that such witness cannot hear the testimony of other witnesses.

(b) A party to the action cannot be excluded under this section.

(c) If a person other than a natural person is a party to the action, an officer or employee designated by its attorney is entitled to be present.

LAW REVISION COMMISSION COMMENT

Section 777 is based on and supersedes Section 2043 of the Code of Civil Procedure. Under the existing law, the judge exercises broad discretion in regard to the exclusion of witnesses. People v. Lariscy, 14 Cal.2d 30, 92 P.2d 638 (1939); People v. Garbutt, 197 Cal. 200, 239 Pac. 1080 (1925). Cf. Penal Code § 867 (power of magistrate to exclude witnesses during preliminary examination). See also Code Civ.Proc. § 125 (general discretionary power of the court to exclude witnesses).

Under the existing law, the judge may not exclude a party to an action. If the party is a corporation, an officer designated by its attorney is entitled to be present. Section 777 permits the right of presence to be exercised by an employee as well as an officer. Also, because there is little practical distinction between corporations and other artificial entities and organizations, Section 777 extends the right of presence to all artificial parties. [7 Cal.L.Rev.Comm. Reports 1 (1965)]

§ 778. Recall of witness

After a witness has been excused from giving further testimony in the action, he cannot be recalled without leave of the court. Leave may be granted or withheld in the court's discretion.

LAW REVISION COMMISSION COMMENT

Section 778 restates the substance of and supersedes the second and third sentences of Section 2050 of the Code of Civil Procedure. [7 Cal.L.Rev.Comm. Reports 1 (1965)]

CHAPTER 6. CREDIBILITY OF WITNESSES

ARTICLE 1. CREDIBILITY GENERALLY

§ 780. Testimony; proof of truthfulness; considerations

Except as otherwise provided by statute, the court or jury may consider in determining the credibility of a witness any matter that has any tendency in reason to prove or disprove the truthfulness of his testimony at the hearing, including but not limited to any of the following:

(a) His demeanor while testifying and the manner in which he testifies.

(b) The character of his testimony.

(c) The extent of his capacity to perceive, to recollect, or to communicate any matter about which he testifies.

(d) The extent of his opportunity to perceive any matter about which he testifies.

(e) His character for honesty or veracity or their opposites.

(f) The existence or nonexistence of a bias, interest, or other motive.

(g) A statement previously made by him that is consistent with his testimony at the hearing.

(h) A statement made by him that is inconsistent with any part of his testimony at the hearing.

(i) The existence or nonexistence of any fact testified to by him.

(j) His attitude toward the action in which he testifies or toward the giving of testimony.

(k) His admission of untruthfulness.

LAW REVISION COMMISSION COMMENT

Section 780 is a restatement of the existing California law as declared in several sections of the Code of Civil Procedure, all of which are superseded by this section and other sections in Article 2 (commencing with Section 785) of this chapter. See, e.g., Code Civ.Proc. §§ 1847, 2049, 2051, 2052, 2053.

Section 780 is a general catalog of those matters that have any tendency in reason to affect the credibility of a witness. So far as the admissibility of evidence relating to credibility is concerned, Section 780 is technically unnecessary because Section 351 declares that "all relevant evidence is admissible." However, this section makes it clear that matters that may not be "evidence" in a technical sense can affect the credibility of a witness, and it provides a convenient list of the most common factors that bear on the question of credibility. See Davis v. Judson, 159 Cal. 121, 128, 113 Pac. 147, 150 (1910); La Jolla Casa de Manana v. Hopkins, 98 Cal.App.2d 339, 346, 219 P.2d 871, 876 (1950). See generally Witkin, California Evidence §§ 480–485 (1958). Limitations on the admissibility of evidence offered to attack or support the credibility of a witness are stated in Article 2 (commencing with Section 785).

There is no specific limitation in the Evidence Code on the use of impeaching evidence on the ground that it is "collateral". The so-called "collateral matter" limitation on attacking the credibility of a witness excludes evidence relevant to credibility unless such evidence is independently relevant to the issue being tried. It is based on the sensible notion that trials should be confined to settling those disputes between the parties upon which their rights in the litigation depend. Under existing law, this "collateral matter" doctrine has been treated as an inflexible rule excluding evidence relevant to the credibility of the witness. See, e.g., People v. Wells, 33 Cal.2d 330, 340, 202 P.2d 53, 59 (1949), and cases cited therein.

The effect of Section 780 (together with Section 351) is to eliminate this inflexible rule of exclusion. This is not to say that all evidence of a collateral nature offered to attack the credibility of a witness would be admissible. Under Section 352, the court has substantial discretion to exclude collateral evidence. The effect of Section 780, therefore, is to change the present somewhat inflexible rule of exclusion to a rule of discretion to be exercised by the trial judge.

There is no limitation in the Evidence Code on the use of opinion evidence to prove the character of a witness for honesty, veracity, or the lack thereof. Hence, under Sections 780 and 1100, such evidence is admissible. This represents a change in the present law. See People v. Methvin, 53 Cal. 68 (1878). However, the opinion evidence that may be offered by those persons intimately familiar with the witness is likely to be of more probative value than the generally admissible evidence of reputation. See 7 Wigmore, Evidence § 1986 (3d ed. 1940). [7 Cal. L.Rev.Comm. Reports 1 (1965)]

§ 782. Sexual offenses; evidence of sexual conduct of complaining witness; procedure for admissibility

(a) In any prosecution under Section 261, 262, 264.1, 286, 288, 288a, 288.5, or 289 of the Penal Code, or for assault with intent to commit, attempt to commit, or conspiracy to commit any crime defined in any of those sections, except where the crime is alleged to have occurred in a local detention facility, as defined in Section 6031.4, or in a state prison, as defined in Section 4504, if evidence of sexual conduct of the complaining witness is offered to attack the credibility of the complaining witness under Section 780, the following procedure shall be followed:

(1) A written motion shall be made by the defendant to the court and prosecutor stating that the defense has an offer of proof of the relevancy of evidence of the sexual conduct of the complaining witness proposed to be presented and its relevancy in attacking the credibility of the complaining witness.

(2) The written motion shall be accompanied by an affidavit in which the offer of proof shall be stated.

(3) If the court finds that the offer of proof is sufficient, the court shall order a hearing out of the presence of the jury, if any, and at the hearing allow the questioning of the complaining witness regarding the offer of proof made by the defendant.

(4) At the conclusion of the hearing, if the court finds that evidence proposed to be offered by the defendant regarding the sexual conduct of the complaining witness is relevant pursuant to

Section 780, and is not inadmissible pursuant to Section 352 of this code, the court may make an order stating what evidence may be introduced by the defendant, and the nature of the questions to be permitted. The defendant may then offer evidence pursuant to the order of the court.

(b) As used in this section, "complaining witness" means the alleged victim of the crime charged, the prosecution of which is subject to this section.

§ 783. Sexual harassment, sexual assault, or sexual battery cases; admissibility of evidence of plaintiff's sexual conduct; procedure

In any civil action alleging conduct which constitutes sexual harassment, sexual assault, or sexual battery, if evidence of sexual conduct of the plaintiff is offered to attack credibility of the plaintiff under Section 780, the following procedures shall be followed:

(a) A written motion shall be made by the defendant to the court and the plaintiff's attorney stating that the defense has an offer of proof of the relevancy of evidence of the sexual conduct of the plaintiff proposed to be presented.

(b) The written motion shall be accompanied by an affidavit in which the offer of proof shall be stated.

(c) If the court finds that the offer of proof is sufficient, the court shall order a hearing out of the presence of the jury, if any, and at the hearing allow the questioning of the plaintiff regarding the offer of proof made by the defendant.

(d) At the conclusion of the hearing, if the court finds that evidence proposed to be offered by the defendant regarding the sexual conduct of the plaintiff is relevant pursuant to Section 780, and is not inadmissible pursuant to Section 352, the court may make an order stating what evidence may be introduced by the defendant, and the nature of the questions to be permitted. The defendant may then offer evidence pursuant to the order of the court.

ARTICLE 2. ATTACKING OR SUPPORTING CREDIBILITY

§ 785. Parties may attack or support credibility

The credibility of a witness may be attacked or supported by any party, including the party calling him.

LAW REVISION COMMISSION COMMENT

Section 785 eliminates the present restriction on attacking the credibility of one's own witness. Under the existing law, a party is precluded from attacking the credibility of his own witness unless he has been surprised and damaged by the witness' testimony. Code Civ.Proc.

§§ 2049, 2052 (superseded by Evidence Code §§ 768, 769, 770, 785); People v. LeBeau, 39 Cal.2d 146, 148, 245 P.2d 302, 303 (1952). In large part, the present law rests upon the theory that a party producing a witness is bound by his testimony. See discussion in Smellie v. Southern Pac. Co., 212 Cal. 540, 555–556, 299 Pac. 529, 535 (1931). This theory has long been abandoned in several jurisdictions where the practical exigencies of litigation have been recognized. See McCormick, Evidence § 38 (1954). A party has no actual control over a person who witnesses an event and is required to testify to aid the trier of fact in its function of determining the truth. Hence, a party should not be "bound" by the testimony of a witness produced by him and should be permitted to attack the credibility of the witness without anachronistic limitations. Denial of the right to attack credibility may often work a hardship on a party where by necessity he must call a hostile witness. Expanded opportunity for testing credibility is in keeping with the interest of providing a forum for full and free disclosure. In regard to attacking the credibility of a "necessary" witness, see generally People v. McFarlane, 134 Cal. 618, 66 Pac. 865 (1901); Anthony v. Hobbie, 85 Cal.App.2d 798, 803–804, 193 P.2d 748, 751 (1948); First Nat'l Bank v. De Moulin, 56 Cal.App. 313, 321, 205 Pac. 92, 96 (1922). [7 Cal.L.Rev. Comm. Reports 1 (1965)]

§ 786. Character evidence generally

Evidence of traits of his character other than honesty or veracity, or their opposites, is inadmissible to attack or support the credibility of a witness.

LAW REVISION COMMISSION COMMENT

Section 786 limits evidence relating to the character of a witness to the character traits necessarily involved in a proper determination of credibility. Other character traits are not sufficiently probative of a witness' honesty or veracity to warrant their consideration on the issue of credibility.

Section 786 is substantially in accord with the present California law. Code Civ.Proc. § 2051 (superseded by Evidence Code §§ 780, 785–788); People v. Yslas, 27 Cal. 630, 633 (1865). [7 Cal.L.Rev.Comm. Reports 1 (1965)]

§ 787. Specific instances of conduct

Subject to Section 788, evidence of specific instances of his conduct relevant only as tending to prove a trait of his character is inadmissible to attack or support the credibility of a witness.

LAW REVISION COMMISSION COMMENT

Under Section 787, as under existing law, evidence of specific instances of a witness' conduct is inadmissible to prove a trait of his character for the purpose of attacking or supporting his credibility. See Sharon v. Sharon, 79 Cal. 633, 673–674, 22 Pac. 26, 38 (1889); Code Civ.Proc. § 2051 (superseded by Section 787 and several other sections in Chapter 6). Section 787 is subject, however, to Section 788, which permits certain kinds of criminal convictions to be used for the purpose of attacking a witness' credibility. [7 Cal.L.Rev.Comm. Reports 1 (1965)]

§ 788. Prior felony conviction

For the purpose of attacking the credibility of a witness, it may be shown by the examination of the witness or by the record of the judgment that he has been convicted of a felony unless:

(a) A pardon based on his innocence has been granted to the witness by the jurisdiction in which he was convicted.

(b) A certificate of rehabilitation and pardon has been granted to the witness under the provisions of Chapter 3.5 (commencing with Section 4852.01) of Title 6 of Part 3 of the Penal Code.

(c) The accusatory pleading against the witness has been dismissed under the provisions of Penal Code Section 1203.4, but this exception does not apply to any criminal trial where the witness is being prosecuted for a subsequent offense.

(d) The conviction was under the laws of another jurisdiction and the witness has been relieved of the penalties and disabilities arising from the conviction pursuant to a procedure substantially equivalent to that referred to in subdivision (b) or (c).

COMMENT—SENATE COMMITTEE ON JUDICIARY

Under Section 787, evidence of specific instances of a witness' conduct is inadmissible for the purpose of attacking or supporting his credibility. Section 788 states an exception to this general rule where the evidence of the witness' misconduct consists of his conviction of a felony. A judgment of conviction that is offered to prove that the person adjudged guilty committed the crime is hearsay. See Evidence Code §§ 1200 and 1300 and the Comments thereto. But the hearsay objection to the evidence specified in Section 788 is overcome by the declaration in the section that such evidence "may be shown" for the purpose of attacking a witness' credibility.

Section 788 is based on Section 2051 of the Code of Civil Procedure. Under Section 788, as under Section 2051, only the testimony of the witness himself or the record of the judgment of conviction may be used to prove the fact of conviction. As Section 788 is, in substance, a recodification of the existing law, it will have no effect on the case-developed rules limiting the circumstances under which a witness may be asked whether he was convicted of a felony. See People v. Perez, 58

Cal.2d 229, 23 Cal.Rptr. 569, 373 P.2d 617 (1962); People v. Darnold, 219 Cal.App.2d 561, 33 Cal.Rptr. 369 (1963).

Subdivision (a) prohibits the use of a conviction to attack the credibility of a witness if a pardon has been granted to the witness on the ground that he was innocent and was erroneously convicted. Subdivision (a) changes the existing California law. Under the existing law, the conviction is admissible to attack credibility, and the pardon—even though based on innocence—is admissible merely to mitigate the effect of the conviction. People v. Hardwick, 204 Cal. 582, 269 Pac. 427 (1928).

Subdivision (b) recodifies the provision of Section 2051 that prohibits the use of a conviction to attack credibility if a pardon has been granted upon the basis of a certificate of rehabilitation. See also Code Civ.Proc. § 2065.

Subdivision (c) recodifies the existing law that prohibits the use of a conviction to attack the credibility of a witness if the conviction has been set aside under Penal Code Section 1203.4. See People v. Mackey, 58 Cal.App. 123, 208 Pac. 135 (1922). The exception that permits the use of such a conviction to attack the credibility of a criminal defendant who testifies as a witness also reflects existing law. See People v. James, 40 Cal.App.2d 740, 105 P.2d 947 (1940).

Subdivision (d) merely provides that a witness who has been relieved of the penalties and disabilities of a prior conviction under the laws of another jurisdiction will be subject to attacks on his credibility under the same conditions that would be applicable if such relief had been granted him under the laws of California.

§ 789. Religious belief

Evidence of his religious belief or lack thereof is inadmissible to attack or support the credibility of a witness.

LAW REVISION COMMISSION COMMENT

Section 789 codifies existing law as expressed in People v. Copsey, 71 Cal. 548, 12 Pac. 721 (1887), where the Supreme Court held that evidence relating to a witness' religious belief or lack thereof is incompetent on the issue of his credibility as a witness. See Cal.Const., Art. I, § 4. [7 Cal.L.Rev.Comm. Reports 1 (1965)]

§ 790. Good character of witness

Evidence of the good character of a witness is inadmissible to support his credibility unless evidence of his bad character has been admitted for the purpose of attacking his credibility.

LAW REVISION COMMISSION COMMENT

Section 790 restates without substantive change a rule that is well recognized by statutory and case law in California. Code Civ.Proc. § 2053 (superseded by Evidence Code §§ 790, 1101); People v. Bush, 65 Cal. 129, 131, 3 Pac. 590, 591 (1884). Unless the credibility of a witness is put in issue by an attack impugning his character for honesty or veracity (see Section 786), evidence of the witness' good character admitted merely to support his credibility introduces collateral material that is unnecessary to a proper determination of any legitimate issue in the action. See People v. Sweeney, 55 Cal.2d 27, 38–39, 9 Cal.Rptr. 793, 799, 357 P.2d 1049, 1055 (1960). [7 Cal.L.Rev.Comm. Reports 1 (1965)]

§ 791. Prior consistent statement of witness

Evidence of a statement previously made by a witness that is consistent with his testimony at the hearing is inadmissible to support his credibility unless it is offered after:

(a) Evidence of a statement made by him that is inconsistent with any part of his testimony at the hearing has been admitted for the purpose of attacking his credibility, and the statement was made before the alleged inconsistent statement; or

(b) An express or implied charge has been made that his testimony at the hearing is recently fabricated or is influenced by bias or other improper motive, and the statement was made before the bias, motive for fabrication, or other improper motive is alleged to have arisen.

LAW REVISION COMMISSION COMMENT

Section 791 sets forth the conditions for admitting a witness' prior consistent statements for the purpose of supporting his credibility as a witness. For a discussion of the effect to be given to the evidence admitted under this section, see Evidence Code § 1236 and the Comment thereto.

Subdivision (a). Subdivision (a) permits the introduction of a witness' prior consistent statement if evidence of an inconsistent statement of the witness has been admitted for the purpose of attacking his credibility and if the consistent statement was made before the alleged inconsistent statement.

Under existing California law, evidence of a prior consistent statement is admissible to rebut a charge of bias, interest, recent fabrication, or other improper motive. See the Comment to subdivision (b), infra. Existing law may preclude admission of a prior consistent statement to rehabilitate a witness where only a prior inconsistent statement has been admitted for the purpose of attacking his credibility. See People v. Doyell, 48 Cal. 85, 90–91 (1874). However, recent cases indicate that the offering of a prior inconsistent statement necessarily is an implied charge that the witness has fabricated his testimony since the time the inconsistent statement was made and justifies the admission of a consistent statement made prior to the alleged inconsistent statement. People v. Bias, 170 Cal.App.2d 502, 511–512, 339 P.2d 204, 210–211 (1959). Subdivision (a) makes it clear that evidence of a previous consistent statement is admissible under these circumstances to show that no such fabrication took place. Subdivision (a), thus, is no more than a logical extension of the general rule that evidence of a prior consistent statement is admissible to rehabilitate a witness following an express or implied charge of recent fabrication.

Subdivision (b). This subdivision codifies existing law. See People v. Kynette, 15 Cal.2d 731, 104 P.2d 794 (1940) (overruled on other grounds in People v. Snyder, 50 Cal.2d 190, 197, 324 P.2d 1, 6 (1958)). Of course, if the consistent statement was made after the time the improper motive is alleged to have arisen, the logical thrust of the evidence is lost and the statement is inadmissible. See People v. Doetschman, 69 Cal.App.2d 486, 159 P.2d 418 (1945). [7 Cal.L.Rev.Comm. Reports 1 (1965)]

CHAPTER 7. HYPNOSIS OF WITNESSES

§ 795. Testimony of hypnosis subject; admissibility; conditions

(a) The testimony of a witness is not inadmissible in a criminal proceeding by reason of the fact that the witness has previously undergone hypnosis for the purpose of recalling events which are the subject of the witness' testimony, if all of the following conditions are met:

(1) The testimony is limited to those matters which the witness recalled and related prior to the hypnosis.

(2) The substance of the prehypnotic memory was preserved in written, audiotape, or videotape form prior to the hypnosis.

(3) The hypnosis was conducted in accordance with all of the following procedures:

(A) A written record was made prior to hypnosis documenting the subject's description of the event, and information which was provided to the hypnotist concerning the subject matter of the hypnosis.

(B) The subject gave informed consent to the hypnosis.

(C) The hypnosis session, including the pre- and post-hypnosis interviews, was videotape recorded for subsequent review.

(D) The hypnosis was performed by a licensed medical doctor, psychologist, licensed clinical social worker, or a licensed marriage and family therapist experienced in the use of hypnosis and independent of and not in the presence of law enforcement, the prosecution, or the defense.

(4) Prior to admission of the testimony, the court holds a hearing pursuant to Section 402 of the Evidence Code at which the proponent of the evidence proves by clear and convincing evidence that the hypnosis did not so affect the witness as to render the witness' prehypnosis recollection unreliable or to substantially impair the ability to cross-examine the witness concerning the witness' prehypnosis recollection. At the hearing, each side shall have the right to present expert testimony and to cross-examine witnesses.

(b) Nothing in this section shall be construed to limit the ability of a party to attack the credibility of a witness who has undergone hypnosis, or to limit other legal grounds to admit or exclude the testimony of that witness.

DIVISION 7. OPINION TESTIMONY AND SCIENTIFIC EVIDENCE

CHAPTER 1. EXPERT AND OTHER OPINION TESTIMONY

ARTICLE 1. EXPERT AND OTHER OPINION TESTIMONY GENERALLY

§ 800. Lay witnesses; opinion testimony

If a witness is not testifying as an expert, his testimony in the form of an opinion is limited to such an opinion as is permitted by law, including but not limited to an opinion that is:

(a) Rationally based on the perception of the witness; and

(b) Helpful to a clear understanding of his testimony.

LAW REVISION COMMISSION COMMENT

This section codifies existing law. A witness who is not testifying as an expert may testify in the form of an opinion only if the opinion is based on his own perception. Stuart v. Dotts, 89 Cal.App.2d 683, 201 P.2d 820 (1949). See discussion in Manney v. Housing Authority, 79 Cal.App.2d 453, 459–460, 180 P.2d 69, 73 (1947). And, in addition, the opinion must be "helpful to a clear understanding of his testimony." See Tentative Recommendation and a Study Relating to the Uniform Rules of Evidence (Article VII. Expert and Other Opinion Testimony), 6 Cal.Law Revision Comm'n, Rep., Rec. & Studies 901, 931–935 (1964).

Section 800 does not make inadmissible an opinion that is admissible under existing law, even though the requirements of subdivisions (a) and (b) are not satisfied. Thus, the section does not affect the existing rule that a nonexpert witness may give his opinion as to the value of his property or the value of his own services. See Witkin, California Evidence § 179 (1958). The words "such an opinion as is permitted by law" in Section 800 make this clear. [7 Cal.L.Rev.Comm. Reports 1 (1965)]

§ 801. Expert witness; opinion testimony

If a witness is testifying as an expert, his testimony in the form of an opinion is limited to such an opinion as is:

(a) Related to a subject that is sufficiently beyond common experience that the opinion of an expert would assist the trier of fact; and

(b) Based on matter (including his special knowledge, skill, experience, training, and education) perceived by or personally known to the witness or made known to him at or before the hearing, whether or not admissible, that is of a type that reasonably may be relied upon by an expert in forming an opinion upon the subject to which his testimony relates, unless an expert is precluded by law from using such matter as a basis for his opinion.

LAW REVISION COMMISSION COMMENT

Section 801 deals with opinion testimony of a witness testifying as an expert; it sets the standard for admissibility of such testimony.

Subdivision (a), which states when an expert may give his opinion upon a subject that is within the scope of his expertise, codifies the existing rule that expert opinion is limited to those subjects that are beyond the competence of persons of common experience, training, and education. People v. Cole, 47 Cal.2d 99, 103, 301 P.2d 854, 856 (1956). For examples of the variety of subjects upon which expert testimony is admitted, see Witkin, California Evidence §§ 190–195 (1958).

Subdivision (b) states a general rule in regard to the permissible bases upon which the opinion of an expert may be founded. The California courts have made it clear that the nature of the matter upon which an expert may base his opinion varies from case to case. In some fields of expert knowledge, an expert may rely on statements made by and information received from other persons; in some other fields of expert knowledge, an expert may not do so. For example, a physician may rely on statements made to him by the patient concerning the history of his condition. People v. Wilson, 25 Cal.2d 341, 153 P.2d 720 (1944). A physician may also rely on reports and opinions of other physicians. Kelley v. Bailey, 189 Cal.App.2d 728, 11 Cal.Rptr. 448 (1961); Hope v. Arrowhead & Puritas Waters, Inc., 174 Cal.App.2d 222, 344 P.2d 428 (1959). An expert on the valuation of real or personal property, too, may rely on inquiries made of others, commercial reports, market quotations, and relevant sales known to the witness. Betts v. Southern Cal. Fruit Exchange, 144 Cal. 402, 77 Pac. 993 (1904); Hammond Lumber Co. v. County of Los Angeles, 104 Cal.App. 235, 285 Pac. 896 (1930); Glantz v. Freedman, 100 Cal.App. 611, 280 Pac. 704 (1929).

On the other hand, an expert on automobile accidents may not rely on extrajudicial statements of others as a partial basis for an opinion as to the point of impact, whether or not the statements would be admissible evidence. Hodges v. Severns, 201 Cal.App.2d 99, 20 Cal.Rptr. 129 (1962); Ribble v. Cook, 111 Cal.App.2d 903, 245 P.2d 593 (1952). See also Behr v. County of Santa Cruz, 172 Cal.App.2d 697, 342 P.2d 987 (1959) (report of fire ranger as to cause of fire held inadmissible because it was based primarily upon statements made to him by other persons).

Likewise, under existing law, irrelevant or speculative matters are not a proper basis for an expert's opinion. See Roscoe Moss Co. v. Jenkins, 55 Cal.App.2d 369, 130 P.2d 477 (1942) (expert may not base opinion upon a comparison if the matters compared are not reasonably comparable); People v. Luis, 158 Cal. 185, 110 Pac. 580 (1910) (physician may not base opinion as to person's feeblemindedness merely upon the person's exterior appearance); Long v. Cal.-Western States Life Ins. Co., 43 Cal.2d 871, 279 P.2d 43 (1955) (speculative or conjectural data); Eisenmayer v. Leonardt, 148 Cal. 596, 84 Pac. 43 (1906) (speculative or conjectural data). Compare People v. Wochnick, 98 Cal.App.2d 124, 219 P.2d 70 (1950) (expert may not give opinion as to the truth or falsity of certain statements on basis of lie detector test), with People v. Jones, 42 Cal.2d 219, 266 P.2d 38 (1954) (psychiatrist may consider an examination given under the influence of sodium pentothal—the so-called "truth serum"—in forming an opinion as to the mental state of the person examined).

The variation in the permissible bases of expert opinion is unavoidable in light of the wide variety of subjects upon which such opinion can be offered. In regard to some matters of expert opinion, an expert must, if he is going to give an opinion that will be helpful to the jury, rely on reports, statements, and other information that might not be admissible evidence. A physician in many instances cannot make a diagnosis without relying on the case history recited by the patient or on reports from various technicians or other physicians. Similarly, an appraiser must rely on reports of sales and other market data if he is to give an opinion that will be of value to the jury. In the usual case where a physician's or an appraiser's opinion is required, the adverse party also will have its expert who will be able to check the data relied upon by the adverse expert. On the other hand, a police officer can analyze skid marks, debris, and the condition of vehicles that have been involved in an accident without relying on the statements of bystanders; and it seems likely that the jury would be as able to evaluate the statements of others in the light of the physical facts, as interpreted by the officer, as would the officer himself. It is apparent that the extent to which an expert may base his opinion upon the statements of others is far from clear. It is at least clear, however, that it is permitted in a number of instances. See Young v. Bates Valve Bag Corp., 52 Cal.App.2d 86, 96–

97, 125 P.2d 840, 846 (1942), and cases therein cited. Cf. People v. Alexander, 212 Cal.App.2d 84, 27 Cal.Rptr. 720 (1963).

It is not practical to formulate a detailed statutory rule that lists all of the matters upon which an expert may properly base his opinion, for it would be necessary to prescribe specific rules applicable to each field of expertise. This is clearly impossible; the subjects upon which expert opinion may be received are too numerous to make statutory prescription of applicable rules a feasible venture. It is possible, however, to formulate a general rule that specifies the minimum requisites that must be met in every case, leaving to the courts the task of determining particular detail within this general framework. This standard is expressed in subdivision (b) which states a general rule that is applicable whenever expert opinion is offered on a given subject.

Under subdivision (b), the matter upon which an expert's opinion is based must meet each of three separate but related tests. First, the matter must be perceived by or personally known to the witness or must be made known to him at or before the hearing at which the opinion is expressed. This requirement assures the expert's acquaintance with the facts of a particular case either by his personal perception or observation or by means of assuming facts not personally known to the witness. Second, and without regard to the means by which an expert familiarizes himself with the matter upon which his opinion is based, the matter relied upon by the expert in forming his opinion must be of a type that reasonably may be relied upon by experts in forming an opinion upon the subject to which his testimony relates. In large measure, this assures the reliability and trustworthiness of the information used by experts in forming their opinions. Third, an expert may not base his opinion upon any matter that is declared by the constitutional, statutory, or decisional law of this State to be an improper basis for an opinion. For example, the statements of bystanders as to the cause of a fire may be considered reliable for some purposes by an investigator of the fire, particularly when coupled with physical evidence found at the scene, but the courts have determined this to be an improper basis for an opinion since the trier of fact is as capable as the expert of evaluating such statements in light of the physical facts as interpreted by the expert. Behr v. County of Santa Cruz, 172 Cal.App.2d 697, 342 P.2d 987 (1959).

The rule stated in subdivision (b) thus permits an expert to base his opinion upon reliable matter, whether or not admissible, of a type that may reasonably be used in forming an opinion upon the subject to which his expert testimony relates. In addition, it provides assurance that the courts and the Legislature are free to continue to develop specific rules regarding the proper bases for particular kinds of expert opinion in specific fields. See, e.g., 3 Cal.Law Revision Comm'n, Rep., Rec. & Studies, Recommendation and Study Relating to Evidence in Eminent Domain Proceedings at A–1 (1961), Subdivision (b) thus provides a sensible standard of admissibility while, at the same time, it continues in effect the discretionary power of the courts to regulate abuses, thereby retaining in large measure the existing California law. [7 Cal.L.Rev. Comm. Reports 1 (1965)]

§ 802. Statement of basis of opinion

A witness testifying in the form of an opinion may state on direct examination the reasons for his opinion and the matter (including, in the case of an expert, his special knowledge, skill, experience, training, and education) upon which it is based, unless he is precluded by law from using such reasons or matter as a basis for his opinion. The court in its discretion may require that a witness before testifying in the form of an opinion be first examined concerning the matter upon which his opinion is based.

LAW REVISION COMMISSION COMMENT

Section 802 restates the substance of and supersedes a portion of Section 1872 of the Code of Civil Procedure. Section 802, however, relates to all witnesses who testify in the form of opinion, while Section 1872 relates only to experts.

Although Section 802 (like its predecessor, Code of Civil Procedure Section 1872) provides that a witness may state the basis for his opinion on direct examination, it is clear that in some cases, a witness is required to do so in order to show that his opinion is applicable to the action before the court. Under existing law, where a witness testifies in the form of opinion not based upon his personal observation, the assumed facts upon which his opinion is based must be stated in order to show that the witness has some basis for forming an intelligent opinion and to permit the trier of fact to determine the applicability of the opinion in light of the existence or nonexistence of such facts. Eisenmayer v. Leonardt, 148 Cal. 596, 84 Pac. 43 (1906); Lemley v. Doak Gas Engine Co., 40 Cal.App. 146, 180 Pac 671 (1919) (hearing denied). Evidence Code Section 802 will not affect the rule set forth in these cases, for it is based essentially on the requirement that all evidence must be shown to be applicable—or relevant—to the action. Evidence Code §§ 350, 403. But under Section 802, as under existing law, a witness testifying from his personal observation of the facts upon which his opinion is based need not be examined concerning such facts before testifying in the form of opinion; his personal observation is a sufficient basis upon which to found his opinion. Lumbermen's Mut. Cas. Co. v. Industrial Acc. Comm'n, 29 Cal.2d 492, 175 P.2d 823 (1946); Hart v. Olson, 68 Cal.App.2d 657, 157 P.2d 385 (1945); Lemley v. Doak Gas Engine Co., supra. However, the court may require a witness to state the facts observed before stating his opinion. In this respect Section 802 codifies the existing rule concerning lay witnesses and, although the existing law is unclear, probably states the existing rule as to expert witnesses. See Tentative Recommendation and a Study Relating to the

Uniform Rules of Evidence (Article VII. Expert and Other Opinion Testimony), 6 Cal.Law Revision Comm'n, Rep., Rec. & Studies 901, 934 (lay witness), 939 (expert witness) (1964). [7 Cal.L.Rev.Comm. Reports 1 (1965)]

§ 803. Opinion based on improper matter

The court may, and upon objection shall, exclude testimony in the form of an opinion that is based in whole or in significant part on matter that is not a proper basis for such an opinion. In such case, the witness may, if there remains a proper basis for his opinion, then state his opinion after excluding from consideration the matter determined to be improper.

LAW REVISION COMMISSION COMMENT

Under Section 803, as under existing law, an opinion may be held inadmissible or may be stricken if it is based wholly or in substantial part upon improper considerations. Whether or not the opinion should be held inadmissible or stricken will depend in a particular case on the extent to which the improper considerations have influenced the opinion. "The question is addressed to the discretion of the trial court." People v. Lipari, 213 Cal.App.2d 485, 493, 28 Cal.Rptr. 808, 813–814 (1963). See discussion in City of Gilroy v. Filice, 221 Cal.App.2d 259, 271–272, 34 Cal.Rptr. 368, 375–376 (1963), and cases cited therein. If a witness' opinion is stricken because of reliance upon improper considerations, the second sentence of Section 803 assures the witness the opportunity to express his opinion after excluding from his consideration the matter determined to be improper. [7 Cal.L.Rev.Comm. Reports 1 (1965)]

§ 804. Opinion based on opinion or statement of another

(a) If a witness testifying as an expert testifies that his opinion is based in whole or in part upon the opinion or statement of another person, such other person may be called and examined by any adverse party as if under cross-examination concerning the opinion or statement.

(b) This section is not applicable if the person upon whose opinion or statement the expert witness has relied is (1) a party, (2) a person identified with a party within the meaning of subdivision (d) of Section 776, or (3) a witness who has testified in the action concerning the subject matter of the opinion or statement upon which the expert witness has relied.

(c) Nothing in this section makes admissible an expert opinion that is inadmissible because it is based in whole or in part on the opinion or statement of another person.

(d) An expert opinion otherwise admissible is not made inadmissible by this section because it is based on the opinion or statement of a person who is unavailable for examination pursuant to this section.

LAW REVISION COMMISSION COMMENT

Section 804 is designed to provide protection to a party who is confronted with an expert witness who relies on the opinion or statement of some other person. (See the Comment to Section 801 for examples of opinions that may be based on the statements and opinions of others.) In such a situation, a party may find that cross-examination of the witness will not reveal the weakness in his opinion, for the crucial parts are based on the observations or opinions of someone else. Under existing law, if that other person is called as a witness, he is the witness of the party calling him and, therefore, that party may not subject him to cross-examination.

The existing law operates unfairly, for it unnecessarily restricts meaningful cross-examination. Hence, Section 804 permits a party to extend his cross-examination into the underlying bases of the opinion testimony introduced against him by calling the authors of opinions and statements relied on by adverse witnesses and examining them as if under cross- examination concerning the subject matter of their opinions and statements. See the Comment to Evidence Code § 1203. [7 Cal. L.Rev.Comm. Reports 1 (1965)]

§ 805. Opinion on ultimate issue

Testimony in the form of an opinion that is otherwise admissible is not objectionable because it embraces the ultimate issue to be decided by the trier of fact.

LAW REVISION COMMISSION COMMENT

Although several older cases indicated that an opinion could not be received on an ultimate issue, more recent cases have repudiated this rule. Hence, this section is declarative of existing law. People v. Wilson, 25 Cal.2d 341, 349–350, 153 P.2d 720, 725 (1944); Wells Truckways, Ltd. v. Cebrian, 122 Cal.App.2d 666, 265 P.2d 557 (1954); People v. King, 104 Cal.App.2d 298, 231 P.2d 156 (1951). [7 Cal.L.Rev.Comm. Reports 1 (1965)]

ARTICLE 2. EVIDENCE OF MARKET VALUE OF PROPERTY

§ 810. Application of article

(a) Except where another rule is provided by statute, this article provides special rules of evidence applicable to any action in which the value of property is to be ascertained.

(b) This article does not govern ad valorem property tax assessment or equalization proceedings.

LEGISLATIVE COMMITTEE COMMENT— SENATE 1978 AMENDMENT

1995 Interim Update Section 810 defines the scope of this article. This article expressly applies only to the determination of the value of property in eminent domain and inverse condemnation proceedings. However, nothing in this article precludes a court from using the rules prescribed in this article in valuation proceedings to which the article is not made applicable, where the court determines that the rules prescribed are appropriate. See In re Marriage of Folb, 53 Cal.App.3d 862, 868–71, 126 Cal.Rptr. 306, 310–12 (1975).

1980 Amendment

Section 810 is amended to remove the limitation on application of this article to eminent domain and inverse condemnation proceedings. This article does not attempt to define market value and does not apply the eminent domain definition of market value to other cases; it it limited to procedural rules for determining market value, however defined.

This article applies to any action or proceeding in which the value of real property, or real and personal property taken as a unit, is to be determined. See Section 811 and Comment thereto ("value of property" defined). See also Sections 105 and 120 ("action" includes action or proceeding). These cases include, but are not limited to, the following:

(1) Eminent domain proceedings. See, e.g., Code Civ.Proc. § 1263.310 (measure of compensation is fair market value of property taken).

(2) Inheritance taxation. See, e.g., Rev. & Tax. Code §§ 13311, 13951 (property taxed on basis of market value).

(3) Breach of contract of sale. See, e.g., Civil Code §§ 3306, 3307 (damages for breach of real property contract based on value of property).

(4) Mortgage deficiency judgments. See, e.g., Code Civ.Proc. §§ 580a, 726 (judgments calculated on fair market value or fair value of property).

(5) Gift taxation. See, e.g., Rev. & Tax. Code § 15203 (gift tax computed on market value of property).

(6) Fraud in the purchase, sale, or exchange of property. See, e.g., Civil Code § 3343 (measure of damages includes damages based on actual value of property).

(7) Other cases in which no statutory standard of market value or its equivalent is prescribed but in which the court is required to make a determination of market value, such as marriage dissolution. See, e.g., In re Marriage of Folb, 53 Cal.App.3d 862, 126 Cal.Rptr. 306 (1975).

This article applies only where market value is to be determined, whether for computing damages and benefits or for any other purpose. In cases involving some other standard of value, the rules provided in this article are not made applicable by statute.

The introductory proviso of subdivision (a) ensures that, where a particular provision requires a special rule relating to value, the special rule prevails over this article. By virtue of subdivision (b), property tax assessment and equalization proceedings, whether judicial or administrative, are not subject to this article. They are governed by a well-developed and adequate set of rules that are comparable to the Evidence Code rules. See, e.g., Rev. & Tax. Code §§ 402.1, 402.5 (valuation and assessment rules); Rev. & Tax. Code §§ 1606, 1609, 1609.4, 1636–1641 (equalization proceedings); Cal.Admin. Code, Tit. 18 (public revenues regulations).

Nothing in this section is intended to require a hearing to ascertain the value of property where a hearing is not required by statute. See, e.g., Rev. & Tax. Code §§ 14501–14505 (Inheritance Tax Referee permitted but not required to conduct hearing to ascertain value of property).

§ 811. Value of property

As used in this article, "value of property" means market value of any of the following:

(a) Real property or any interest therein.

(b) Real property or any interest therein and tangible personal property valued as a unit.

LEGISLATIVE COMMITTEE COMMENT— SENATE 1978 AMENDMENT

1995 Interim Update Section 811 is amended to make clear the limited application of this article. This article applies only where market value of real property, an interest in real property (e.g., a leasehold), or tangible personal property is to be determined, whether for computing damages and benefits or otherwise. This article does not apply to the valuation of intangible personal property that is not an interest in real property, such as goodwill of a business; valuation of such property is governed by the rules of evidence otherwise applicable. However, nothing in this article precludes a court from using the rules prescribed in this article in valuation proceedings to which the article is not made applicable, where the court determines that the rules prescribed are appropriate. See Comment to Section 810.

1980 Amendment

Subdivision (b) of Section 811 is amended to include personal property only when valued together with real property. The effect of this amendment is to limit the scope of the evidence of market value provisions to actions involving real property or real and personal property combined. See Section 810 (article provides rules applicable to action in which "value of property" to be ascertained). Actions involving personal property alone are governed by general law, including the general rules of evidence prescribed in this code, although where appropriate the court may look to the special rules prescribed in this article.

LAW REVISION COMMISSION COMMENT 1975 AMENDMENT

Section 811 is amended to conform to the numbering of the Eminent Domain Law.

Section 811 makes clear that this article as applied to eminent domain proceedings governs only evidence relating to the determination of property value and damages and benefits to the remainder. This article does not govern evidence relating to the determination of loss of goodwill (Code Civ.Proc. § 1263.510).

The evidence admissible to prove loss of goodwill is governed by the general provisions of the Evidence Code. Hence, nothing in this article should be deemed a limitation on the admissibility of evidence to prove loss of goodwill if such evidence is otherwise admissible. [12 Cal.L.Rev. Comm. Reports 1601 (1975)]

LEGISLATIVE COMMITTEE COMMENT— SENATE 1978 AMENDMENT

Section 811 is amended to make clear the limited application of this article. This article applies only where market value of real property, an interest in real property (e.g., a leasehold), or tangible personal property is to be determined, whether for computing damages and benefits or otherwise. This article does not apply to the valuation of intangible personal property that is not an interest in real property, such as goodwill of a business; valuation of such property is governed by the rules of evidence otherwise applicable. However, nothing in this article precludes a court from using the rules prescribed in this article in valuation proceedings to which the article is not made applicable, where the court determines that the rules prescribed are appropriate. See Comment to Section 810.

1980 Amendment

Subdivision (b) of Section 811 is amended to include personal property only when valued together with real property. The effect of this amendment is to limit the scope of the evidence of market value provisions to actions involving real property or real and personal property combined. See Section 810 (article provides rules applicable to action in which "value of property" to be ascertained). Actions involving personal property alone are governed by general law, including the general rules of evidence prescribed in this code, although where appropriate the court may look to the special rules prescribed in this article.

§ 812. Market value; interpretation of meaning

This article is not intended to alter or change the existing substantive law, whether statutory or decisional, interpreting the meaning of "market value," whether denominated "fair market value" or otherwise.

LAW REVISION COMMISSION COMMENT 1975 AMENDMENT

Section 812 is amended to conform to the numbering and terminology of the Eminent Domain Law. [12 Cal.L.Rev.Comm. Reports 1601 (1975)].

LEGISLATIVE COMMITTEE COMMENT—
SENATE 1978 AMENDMENT

Section 812 is amended to take into account the limited application of this article. See Section 811 and Comment thereto.

§ 813. Value of property; authorized opinions; view of property; admissible evidence

(a) The value of property may be shown only by the opinions of any of the following:

(1) Witnesses qualified to express such opinions.

(2) The owner or the spouse of the owner of the property or property interest being valued.

(3) An officer, regular employee, or partner designated by a corporation, partnership, or unincorporated association that is the owner of the property or property interest being valued, if the designee is knowledgeable as to the value of the property or property interest.

(b) Nothing in this section prohibits a view of the property being valued or the admission of any other admissible evidence (including but not limited to evidence as to the nature and condition of the property and, in an eminent domain proceeding, the character of the improvement proposed to be constructed by the plaintiff) for the limited purpose of enabling the court, jury, or referee to understand and weigh the testimony given under subdivision (a); and such evidence, except evidence of the character of the improvement proposed to be constructed by the plaintiff in an eminent domain proceeding, is subject to impeachment and rebuttal.

(c) For the purposes of subdivision (a), "owner of the property or property interest being valued" includes, but is not limited to, the following persons:

(1) A person entitled to possession of the property.

(2) Either party in an action or proceeding to determine the ownership of the property between the parties if the court determines that it would not be in the interest of efficient administration

of justice to determine the issue of ownership prior to the admission of the opinion of the party.

LEGISLATIVE COMMITTEE COMMENT—
SENATE 1980 AMENDMENT

1995 Interim Update Paragraph (2) of Section 813(a) is amended by make clear that either spouse may testify as to the value of community property since both spouses are the owners. In addition, paragraph (2) authorizes either spouse to testify as to the value of the separate property of the other spouse as well as to his or her own separate property. This authority may be useful in cases under the Family Law Act where the character of the property is in dispute as well as in other cases requiring valuation where the nonowning spouse may be a more competent valuation witness than the owning spouse.

Subdivision (c) of Section 813 is amended to make clear that a person claiming to be an owner may testify as an owner in litigation over title. Such litigation may arise, for example, between a buyer and seller concerning title to and value of real property under a contract of sale, or between a landlord and tenant concerning characterization and value of property as trade fixtures.

LAW REVISION COMMISSION COMMENT 1978 AMENDMENT

Paragraph (3) is added to Section 813(a) to make clear that, where a corporation, partnership, or unincorporated association owns property being valued, a designated officer, regular employee, or partner who is knowledgeable as to the value of the property may testify to an opinion of its value as an owner, notwithstanding any contrary implications in City of Pleasant Hill v. First Baptist Church, 1 Cal.App.3d 384, 82 Cal.Rptr. 1 (1969). The designee may be knowledgeable as to the value of the property as a result of being instrumental in its acquisition or management or as a result of being knowledgeable as to its character and use; the designee need not qualify as a general valuation expert. Compare Section 720 (qualification as an expert witness). Nothing in Section 813 affects the authority of the court to limit the number of expert witnesses to be called by any party (see Section 723) or to limit cumulative evidence (see Section 352).

The phrase "value of property," as used in this section, is defined in Section 811. [14 Cal.L.Rev.Comm. Reports 105 (1978)]

LEGISLATIVE COMMITTEE COMMENT—
SENATE 1980 AMENDMENT

Paragraph (2) of Section 813(a) is amended by make clear that either spouse may testify as to the value of community property since both spouses are the owners. In addition, paragraph (2) authorizes either spouse to testify as to the value of the separate property of the other spouse as well as to his or her own separate property. This authority may be useful in cases under the Family Law Act where the character of the property is in dispute as well as in other cases requiring valuation where the nonowning spouse may be a more competent valuation witness than the owning spouse.

Subdivision (c) of Section 813 is amended to make clear that a person claiming to be an owner may testify as an owner in litigation over title. Such litigation may arise, for example, between a buyer and seller concerning title to and value of real property under a contract of sale, or between a landlord and tenant concerning characterization and value of property as trade fixtures.

§ 814. Matter upon which opinion must be based

The opinion of a witness as to the value of property is limited to such an opinion as is based on matter perceived by or personally known to the witness or made known to the witness at or before the hearing, whether or not admissible, that is of a type that reasonably may be relied upon by an expert in forming an opinion as to the value of property, including but not limited to the matters listed in Sections 815 to 821, inclusive, unless a witness is precluded by law from using such matter as a basis for an opinion.

§ 814.5. Repealed by Stats.1971, c. 1574, p. 3154, § 1.4, operative July 1, 1972

§ 815. Sales of subject property

When relevant to the determination of the value of property, a witness may take into account as a basis for an opinion the price and other terms and circumstances of any sale or contract to sell and purchase which included the property or property interest being valued or any part thereof if the sale or contract was freely made in good faith within a reasonable time before or after the date of valuation, except that in an eminent domain proceeding where the sale or contract to sell and purchase includes only the property or property interest being taken or a part thereof, such sale or contract to sell and purchase may not be taken into account if it occurs after the filing of the lis pendens.

§ 816. Comparable sales

When relevant to the determination of the value of property, a witness may take into account as a basis for his opinion the price and other terms and circumstances of any sale or contract to sell and purchase comparable property if the sale or contract was freely made in good faith within a reasonable time before or after the date of valuation. In order to be considered comparable, the sale or contract must have been made sufficiently near in time to the date of valuation, and the property sold must be located sufficiently near the property being valued, and must be sufficiently alike in respect to character, size, situation, usability, and improvements, to make it clear that the property sold and the property being valued are comparable in value and that the price realized for the property sold may fairly be considered as shedding light on the value of the property being valued.

§ 817. Leases of subject property

(a) Subject to subdivision (b), when relevant to the determination of the value of property, a witness may take into account as a basis for an opinion the rent reserved and other terms and circumstances of any lease which included the property or property interest being valued or any part thereof which was in effect within a reasonable time before or after the date of valuation, except that in an eminent domain proceeding where the lease includes only the property or property interest being taken or a part thereof, such lease may not be taken into account in the determination of the value of property if it is entered into after the filing of the lis pendens.

(b) A witness may take into account a lease providing for a rental fixed by a percentage or other measurable portion of gross sales or gross income from a business conducted on the leased property only for the purpose of arriving at an opinion as to the reasonable net rental value attributable to the property or property interest being valued as provided in Section 819 or determining the value of a leasehold interest.

LAW REVISION COMMISSION COMMENT 1978 AMENDMENT

Subdivision (a) of Section 817 is amended to add the limitation that a lease of the subject property is not a proper basis for an opinion of value of the property after the filing of the lis pendens in an eminent domain proceeding. This is comparable to a provision of Section 815 (sale of subject property). Nothing in subdivision (a) should be construed to limit the use of leases created after filing of the lis pendens to show damages to the property, such as those authorized by Klopping v. City of Whittier, 8 Cal.3d 39, 500 P.2d 1345, 104 Cal.Rptr. 1 (1972).

Subdivision (b) limits the extent to which a witness may take into account a lease based on gross sales or gross income of a business conducted on the property. This limitation applies only to valuation of the real property or an interest therein, or of tangible personal property, and does not apply to the determination of loss of goodwill. See Section 811 and Comment thereto; Code Civ.Proc. § 1263.510 and Comment thereto.

The phrase "value of property," as used in this section, is defined in Section 811. [14 Cal.L.Rev.Comm. Reports 105 (1978)]

§ 818. Comparable leases

For the purpose of determining the capitalized value of the reasonable net rental value attributable to the property or property interest being valued as provided in Section 819 or determining the value of a leasehold interest, a witness may take into account as a basis for his opinion the rent reserved and other terms and circumstances of any lease of comparable property if the lease was freely made in good faith within a reasonable time before or after the date of valuation.

§ 819. Capitalization of income

When relevant to the determination of the value of property, a witness may take into account as a basis for his opinion the capitalized value of the reasonable net rental value attributable to the land and existing improvements thereon (as distinguished from the capitalized value of the income or profits attributable to the business conducted thereon).

§ 820. Reproduction cost

When relevant to the determination of the value of property, a witness may take into account as a basis for his opinion the value of the property or property interest being valued as indicated by the value of the land together with the cost of replacing or reproducing the existing improvements thereon, if the improvements enhance the value of the property or property interest for its highest and best use, less whatever depreciation or obsolescence the improvements have suffered.

§ 821. Conditions in general vicinity of subject property

When relevant to the determination of the value of property, a witness may take into account as a basis for his opinion the nature of the improvements on properties in the general vicinity of the property or property interest being valued and the character of the existing uses being made of such properties.

§ 822. Matter upon which opinion may not be based

(a) In an eminent domain or inverse condemnation proceeding, notwithstanding the provisions of Sections 814 to 821, inclusive, the following matter is inadmissible as evidence and shall not be taken into account as a basis for an opinion as to the value of property:

(1) The price or other terms and circumstances of an acquisition of property or a property interest if the acquisition was for a public use for which the property could have been taken by eminent domain.

The price or other terms and circumstances shall not be excluded pursuant to this paragraph if the proceeding relates to the valuation of all or part of a water system as defined in section 240 of the Public Utilities Code.

(2) The price at which an offer or option to purchase or lease the property or property interest being valued or any other property was made, or the price at which such property or interest was optioned, offered, or listed for sale or lease, except that an option,

offer, or listing may be introduced by a party as an admission of another party to the proceeding; but nothing in this subdivision permits an admission to be used as direct evidence upon any matter that may be shown only by opinion evidence under Section 813.

(3) The value of any property or property interest as assessed for taxation purposes or the amount of taxes which may be due on the property, but nothing in this subdivision prohibits the consideration of actual or estimated taxes for the purpose of determining the reasonable net rental value attributable to the property or property interest being valued.

(4) An opinion as to the value of any property or property interest other than that being valued.

(5) The influence upon the value of the property or property interest being valued of any noncompensable items of value, damage, or injury.

(6) The capitalized value of the income or rental from any property or property interest other than that being valued.

(b) In an action other than an eminent domain or inverse condemnation proceeding, the matters listed in subdivision (a) are not admissible as evidence, and may not be taken into account as a basis for an opinion as to the value of property, except to the extent permitted under the rules of law otherwise applicable.

LAW REVISION COMMISSION COMMENT

2000 Amendment

Subdivision (a)(1) of Section 822 is amended to delete the special exception relating to property appropriated to public use, in reliance on general evidentiary principles. See, e.g., Section 823 ("Notwithstanding any other provision of this article, the value of property for which there is no relevant, comparable market may be determined by any method of valuation that is just and equitable."); see also Code Civ. Proc. § 1263.320(b) (fair market value). Thus, evidence of an acquisition that is otherwise inadmissible under subdivision (a)(1) may, in an appropriate case, be admissible under Section 823 if a private market is lacking, e.g., the acquisition involves a special purpose property such as a school, church, cemetery, park, utility corridor, or similar property.

The new exception added to subdivision (a)(1) is intended to apply in an eminent domain or inverse condemnation proceeding that relates to a public agency's acquisition or taking of all or any part of a water system owned by a water company.

Subdivision (c) is deleted as obsolete.

LEGISLATIVE COMMITTEE COMMENT— SENATE 1980 AMENDMENT

1995 Interim Update Section 822 is amended to limit the application of subdivision (a) to eminent domain and inverse condemnation cases despite the general expansion of this article to cover real property valuation cases generally. See Sections 810 and 811 and Comments thereto. The introductory portion of subdivision (a) is also amended to make clear that subdivision (a) regulates only the bases for an opinion of value admissible in evidence; it does not purport to prescribe rules or regulations governing the practice of the appraisal profession outside of expert testimony in a case.

Subdivision (b) is added to make clear that the exclusion of the matters listed in subdivision (a) in eminent domain and inverse condemnation cases does not imply that those matters are admissible in other cases. The rules governing admissibility in other cases of matters listed in subdivision (a) are found in Section 814 and in the general Evidence Code rules relating to relevance, prejudice, and the like.

LAW REVISION COMMISSION COMMENT 1978 AMENDMENT

Subdivision (c) of Section 822 is amended to incorporate a provision formerly found in Revenue and Taxation Code Section 4986(b). Unlike the former provision, subdivision (c) does not provide for a mistrial for mention of the amount of taxes which may be due. Whether such mention is grounds for a mistrial is governed by the general principles of court discretion to declare a mistrial when evidence has been presented which is inadmissible, highly prejudicial, and cannot be corrected by an admonition to the jury.

Subdivision (d) does not prohibit a witness from testifying to adjustments made in sales of comparable property used as a basis for an opinion. Merced Irrigation Dist. v. Woolstenhulme, 4 Cal.3d 478, 501–03, 483 P.2d 1, 16–17, 93 Cal.Rptr. 833, 848–49 (1971).

Section 822 does not prohibit cross-examination of a witness on any matter precluded from admission as evidence if such cross-examination is for the limited purpose of determining whether a witness based an opinion in whole or in part on matter that is not a proper basis for an opinion; such cross-examination may not, however, serve as a means of placing improper matters before the trier of fact. See Evid. Code §§ 721, 802, 803.

The phrase "value of property," as used in this section, is defined in Section 811. [14 Cal.L.Rev.Comm. Reports 105 (1978)]

LEGISLATIVE COMMITTEE COMMENT— SENATE 1980 AMENDMENT

Section 822 is amended to limit the application of subdivision (a) to eminent domain and inverse condemnation cases despite the general expansion of this article to cover real property valuation cases generally. See Sections 810 and 811 and Comments thereto. The introductory portion of subdivision (a) is also amended to make clear that subdivision

(a) regulates only the bases for an opinion of value admissible in evidence; it does not purport to prescribe rules or regulations governing the practice of the appraisal profession outside of expert testimony in a case.

Subdivision (b) is added to make clear that the exclusion of the matters listed in subdivision (a) in eminent domain and inverse condemnation cases does not imply that those matters are admissible in other cases. The rules governing admissibility in other cases of matters listed in subdivision (a) are found in Section 814 and in the general Evidence Code rules relating to relevance, prejudice, and the like.

§ 823. Property with no relevant, comparable market

Notwithstanding any other provision of this article, the value of property for which there is no relevant, comparable market may be determined by any method of valuation that is just and equitable.

LEGISLATIVE COMMITTEE COMMENT—SENATE 1980 ADDITION

1995 Interim Update Section 823 is drawn from Code of Civil Procedure Section 1263.320(b) (fair market value in eminent domain proceeding of property for which there is no relevant market). Section 823 is included because there may be no relevant market for some types of special purpose properties such as schools, churches, cemeteries, parks, utilities, and similar properties. See Code Civ.Proc. § 1263.320(b) and Comment thereto.

§ 824. Nonprofit, special use property

(a) Notwithstanding any other provision of this article, a just and equitable method of determining the value of nonprofit, special use property, as defined by Section 1235.155 of the Code of Civil Procedure, for which there is no relevant, comparable market, is the cost of purchasing land and the reasonable cost of making it suitable for the conduct of the same nonprofit, special use, together with the cost of constructing similar improvements. The method for determining compensation for improvements shall be as set forth in subdivision (b).

(b) Notwithstanding any other provision of this article, a witness providing opinion testimony on the value of nonprofit, special use property, as defined by Section 1235.155 of the Code of Civil Procedure, for which there is no relevant, comparable market, shall base his or her opinion on the value of reproducing the improvements without taking into consideration any depreciation or obsolescence of the improvements.

(c) This section does not apply to actions or proceedings commenced by a public entity or public utility to acquire real property or any interest in real property for the use of water, sewer, electricity, telephone, natural gas, or flood control facilities or rights-of-way where those acquisitions neither require removal or destruction of existing improvements, nor render the property unfit for the owner's present or proposed use.

ARTICLE 3. OPINION TESTIMONY ON PARTICULAR SUBJECTS

§ 870. Opinion as to sanity

A witness may state his opinion as to the sanity of a person when:

(a) The witness is an intimate acquaintance of the person whose sanity is in question;

(b) The witness was a subscribing witness to a writing, the validity of which is in dispute, signed by the person whose sanity is in question and the opinion relates to the sanity of such person at the time the writing was signed; or

(c) The witness is qualified under Section 800 or 801 to testify in the form of an opinion.

LAW REVISION COMMISSION COMMENT

Subdivisions (a) and (b) restate the substance of and supersede subdivision 10 of Section 1870 of the Code of Civil Procedure. Subdivision (c) merely makes it clear that a witness who meets the requirements of Section 800 or Section 801 is qualified to testify in the form of an opinion as to the sanity of a person. Section 870 does not disturb the present rule that permits a witness to testify to a person's rational or irrational appearance or conduct, even though the witness is not qualified under Section 870 to express an opinion on the person's sanity. See Pfingst v. Goetting, 96 Cal.App.2d 293, 215 P.2d 93 (1950). [7 Cal. L.Rev.Comm. Reports 1 (1965)]

CHAPTER 2. BLOOD TESTS TO DETERMINE PATERNITY [REPEALED]

§ 890 to 895. Repealed by Stats.1992, c. 162 (A.B.2650), § 9, operative Jan. 1, 1994

§ 895.5. Repealed by Stats.1993, c. 219 (A.B.1500), § 77

§ 896, 897. Repealed by Stats.1992, c. 162 (A.B.2650), § 9, operative Jan. 1, 1994

DIVISION 8. PRIVILEGES

CHAPTER 1. DEFINITIONS

§ 900. Application of definitions

Unless the provision or context otherwise requires, the definitions in this chapter govern the construction of this division. They do not govern the construction of any other division.

LAW REVISION COMMISSION COMMENT

Section 900 makes it clear that the definitions in Sections 901 through 905 apply only to Division 8 (Privileges) and that these definitions are not applicable where the context or language of a particular section in Division 8 requires that a word or phrase used in that section be given a different meaning. The definitions contained in Division 2 (commencing with Section 100) apply to the entire code, including Division 8. Definitions applicable only to a particular article are found in that article. [7 Cal.L.Rev.Comm. Reports 1 (1965)]

§ 901. Proceeding

"Proceeding" means any action, hearing, investigation, inquest, or inquiry (whether conducted by a court, administrative agency, hearing officer, arbitrator, legislative body, or any other person authorized by law) in which, pursuant to law, testimony can be compelled to be given.

LAW REVISION COMMISSION COMMENT

"Proceeding" is defined to mean all proceedings of whatever kind in which testimony can be compelled by law be to given. It includes civil and criminal actions and proceedings, administrative proceedings, legislative hearings, grand jury proceedings, coroners' inquests, arbitration proceedings, and any other kind of proceeding in which a person can be compelled by law to appear and give evidence. This broad definition is necessary in order that Division is may be made applicable to all situations where a person can be compelled to testify. The reasons for giving this broad scope to Division 8 are stated in the Comment to Section 910. [7 Cal.L.Rev.Comm. Reports 1 (1965)]

§ 902. Civil proceeding

"Civil proceeding" means any proceeding except a criminal proceeding.

LAW REVISION COMMISSION COMMENT

"Civil proceeding" includes not only a civil action or proceeding, but also any nonjudicial proceeding in which, pursuant to law, testimony can be compelled to be given. See Evidence Code §§ 901 and 903. [7 Cal.L.Rev.Comm. Reports 1 (1965)]

§ 903. Criminal proceeding

"Criminal proceeding" means:

(a) A criminal action; and

(b) A proceeding pursuant to Article 3 (commencing with Section 3060) of Chapter 7 of Division 4 of Title 1 of the Government Code to determine whether a public officer should be removed from office for willful or corrupt misconduct in office.

LAW REVISION COMMISSION COMMENT

This division treats a proceeding by accusation for the removal of a public officer under Government Code Sections 3060–3073 the same as a criminal action. Proceedings by accusation and criminal actions are so nearly alike in their basic nature that, so far as privileges are concerned, this similar treatment is justified. [7 Cal.L.Rev.Comm. Reports 1 (1965)]

§ 904. Blank

§ 905. Presiding officer

"Presiding officer" means the person authorized to rule on a claim of privilege in the proceeding in which the claim is made.

LAW REVISION COMMISSION COMMENT

"Presiding officer" is defined so that reference may be made in Division 8 to the person who makes rulings on questions of privilege in nonjudicial proceedings. The term includes arbitrators, hearing officers, referees, and any other person who is authorized to make rulings on claims of privilege. It, of course, includes the judge or other person presiding in a judicial proceeding. [7 Cal.L.Rev.Comm. Reports 1 (1965)]

CHAPTER 2. APPLICABILITY OF DIVISION

§ 910. Applicability of division

Except as otherwise provided by statute, the provisions of this division apply in all proceedings. The provisions of any statute making rules of evidence inapplicable in particular proceedings, or limiting the applicability of rules of evidence in particular proceedings, do not make this division inapplicable to such proceedings.

LAW REVISION COMMISSION COMMENT

Most rules of evidence are designed for use in courts. Generally, their purpose is to keep unreliable or prejudicial evidence from being presented to the trier of fact. Privileges are granted, however, for reasons of policy unrelated to the reliability of the information involved. A privilege is granted because it is considered more important to keep certain information confidential than it is to require disclosure of all the information relevant to the issues in a pending proceeding. Thus, for example, to protect the attorney-client relationship, it is necessary to prevent disclosure of confidential communications made in the course of that relationship.

If confidentiality is to be protected effectively by a privilege, the privilege must be recognized in proceedings other than judicial proceedings. The protection afforded by a privilege would be insufficient if a court were the only place where the privilege could be invoked. Every officer with power to issue subpoenas for investigative purposes, every administrative agency, every local governing board, and many more persons could pry into the protected information if the privilege rules were applicable only in judicial proceedings.

Therefore, the policy underlying the privilege rules requires their recognition in all proceedings of any nature in which testimony can be compelled by law to be given. Section 910 makes the privilege rules applicable to all such proceedings. In this respect, it follows the precedent set in New Jersey when privilege rules, based in part on the Uniform Rules of Evidence, were enacted. See N.J.Laws 1960, Ch. 52, p. 452 (N.J.Rev.Stat. §§ 2A:84A–1 to 2A:84A–49).

Statutes that relax the rules of evidence in particular proceedings do not have the effect of making privileges inapplicable in such proceedings. For example, Labor Code Section 5708, which provides that the officer conducting an Industrial Accident Commission proceeding "shall not be bound by the common law or statutory rules of evidence," does not make privileges inapplicable in such proceedings. Thus, the lawyer-client privilege must be recognized in an Industrial Accident Commission proceeding. On the other hand, Division 8 and other statutes provide exceptions to particular privileges for particular types of proceedings. E. g., Evidence Code § 998 (physician-patient privilege inapplicable in criminal proceeding); Labor Code §§ 4055, 6407, 6408 (testimony by physician and certain reports of physicians admissible as evidence in Industrial Accident Commission proceedings).

Whether Section 910 is declarative of existing law is uncertain. No California case has squarely decided whether the privileges which are recognized in judicial proceedings are also applicable in nonjudicial proceedings. By statute, however, they have been made applicable in all adjudicatory proceedings conducted under the terms of the Administrative Procedure Act. Govt. Code § 11513. The reported decisions indicate that, as a general rule, privileges are assumed to be applicable in nonjudicial proceedings. See, e. g., McKnew v. Superior Court, 23 Cal.2d 58, 142 P.2d 1 (1943); Ex parte McDonough, 170 Cal. 230, 149 P. 566 (1915); Board of Educ. v. Wilkinson, 125 Cal.App.2d 100, 270 P.2d 82 (1954); In re Bruns, 15 Cal.App.2d 1, 58 P.2d 1318 (1936). Thus, Section 910 appears to be declarative of existing practice, but there is no authority as to whether it is declarative of existing law. Its enactment will remove the existing uncertainty concerning the right to claim a privilege in a nonjudicial proceeding. See generally Tentative Recommendation and a Study Relating to the Uniform Rules of Evidence (Article V. Privileges), 6 Cal.Law Revision Comm'n, Rep., Rec. & Studies 201, 309–327 (1964). [7 Cal.L.Rev.Comm. Reports 1 (1965)]

CHAPTER 3. GENERAL PROVISIONS RELATING TO PRIVILEGES

§ 911. Refusal to be or have another as witness, or disclose or produce any matter

Except as otherwise provided by statute:

(a) No person has a privilege to refuse to be a witness.

(b) No person has a privilege to refuse to disclose any matter or to refuse to produce any writing, object, or other thing.

(c) No person has a privilege that another shall not be a witness or shall not disclose any matter or shall not produce any writing, object, or other thing.

LAW REVISION COMMISSION COMMENT

This section codifies the existing law that privileges are not recognized in the absence of statute. See Chronicle Pub. Co. v. Superior Court, 54 Cal.2d 548, 565, 7 Cal.Rptr. 109, 117, 354 P.2d 637, 645 (1960); Tatkin v. Superior Court, 160 Cal.App.2d 745, 753, 326 P.2d 201, 205–206 (1958); Whitlow v. Superior Court, 87 Cal.App.2d 175, 196 P.2d 590 (1948). See also 8 Wigmore, Evidence § 2286 (McNaughton rev. 1961); Witkin, California Evidence § 396 at 446 (1958). This is one of the few instances where the Evidence Code precludes the courts from elaborating upon the statutory scheme. Even with respect to privileges, however, the courts to a limited extent are permitted to develop the details of declared principles. See, e. g., Section 1060 (trade secret). [7 Cal.L.Rev.Comm. Reports 1 (1965)]

§ 912. Waiver of privilege

(a) Except as otherwise provided in this section, the right of any person to claim a privilege provided by Section 954 (lawyer-client privilege), 980 (privilege for confidential marital communications), 994 (physician-patient privilege), 1014 (psychotherapist-patient privilege), 1033 (privilege of penitent), 1034 (privilege of clergyman), 1035.8 (sexual assault victim- counselor privilege), or 1037.5 (domestic violence victim-counselor privilege) is waived with respect to a communication protected by such privilege if any holder of the privilege, without coercion, has disclosed a significant part of the communication or has consented to such disclosure made by anyone. Consent to disclosure is manifested by any statement or other conduct of the holder of the privilege indicating consent to the disclosure, including failure to claim the privilege in any proceeding in which the holder has the legal standing and opportunity to claim the privilege.

(b) Where two or more persons are joint holders of a privilege provided by Section 954 (lawyer-client privilege), 994 (physician-patient privilege), 1014 (psychotherapist-patient privilege), 1035.8 (sexual assault victim-counselor privilege), or 1037.5 (domestic violence victim-counselor privilege) a waiver of the right of a particular joint holder of the privilege to claim the privilege does not affect the right of another joint holder to claim the privilege. In the case of the privilege provided by Section 980 (privilege for confidential marital communications), a waiver of the right of one spouse to claim the privilege does not affect the right of the other spouse to claim the privilege.

(c) A disclosure that is itself privileged is not a waiver of any privilege.

(d) A disclosure in confidence of a communication that is protected by a privilege provided by Section 954 (lawyer-client privilege), 994 (physician- patient privilege), 1014 (psychotherapist-patient privilege), 1035.8 (sexual assault victim-counselor privilege), or 1037.5 (domestic violence victim-counselor privilege), when disclosure is reasonably necessary for the accomplishment of the purpose for which the lawyer, physician, psychotherapist, sexual assault counselor, or domestic violence counselor was consulted, is not a waiver of the privilege.

LAW REVISION COMMISSION COMMENTS

2002 Amendment

Section 912 is amended to make clear that it applies to the privilege for confidential communications between a domestic violence victim and counselor, which did not exist when the statute was originally enacted in 1965. See Sections 1037–1037.7 (domestic violence victim).

COMMENT—SENATE COMMITTEE ON JUDICIARY

This section covers in some detail the matter of waiver of those privileges that protect confidential communications.

Subdivision (a). Subdivision (a) states the general rule with respect to the manner in which a privilege is waived. Failure to claim the privilege where the holder of the privilege has the legal standing and the opportunity to claim the privilege constitutes a waiver. This seems to be the existing law. See City & County of San Francisco v. Superior Court, 37 Cal.2d 227, 233, 231 P.2d 26, 29 (1951); Lissak v. Crocker Estate Co., 119 Cal. 442, 51 P. 688 (1897). There is, however, at least one case that is out of harmony with this rule. People v. Kor, 129 Cal.App.2d 436, 277 P.2d 94 (1954) (defendant's failure to claim privilege to prevent a witness from testifying to a communication between the defendant and his attorney held not to waive the privilege to prevent the attorney from similarly testifying).

Subdivision (b). A waiver of the privilege by a joint holder of the privilege does not operate to waive the privilege for any of the other joint holders of the privilege. This codifies existing law. See People v. Kor, 129 Cal.App.2d 436, 277 P.2d 94 (1954); People v. Abair, 102 Cal.App.2d 765, 228 P.2d 336 (1951).

Subdivision (c). A privilege is not waived when a revelation of the privileged matter takes place in another privileged communication. Thus, for example, a person does not waive his lawyer-client privilege by telling his wife in confidence what it was that he told his attorney. Nor does a person waive the marital communication privilege by telling his attorney in confidence in the course of the attorney-client relationship what it was that he told his wife. And a person does not waive the lawyer-client privilege as to a communication by relating it to another attorney in the course of a separate relationship. A privileged communication should not cease to be privileged merely because it has been related in the course of another privileged communication. The theory underlying the concept of waiver is that the holder of the privilege has abandoned the secrecy to which he is entitled under the privilege. Where the revelation of the privileged matter takes place in another privileged communication, there has not been such an abandonment. Of course, this rule does not apply unless the revelation was within the scope of the relationship in which it was made; a client consulting his lawyer on a contract matter who blurts out that he told his doctor that he had a venereal disease has waived the privilege, even though he intended the revelation to be confidential, because the revelation was not necessary to the contract business at hand.

Subdivision (d). Subdivision (d) is designed to maintain the confidentiality of communications in certain situations where the communications are disclosed to others in the course of accomplishing the purpose for which the lawyer, physician, or psychotherapist was consulted. For example, where a confidential communication from a client is related by his attorney to a physician, appraiser, or other expert in order to obtain that person's assistance so that the attorney will better be able to advise his client, the disclosure is not a waiver of the privilege, even though the disclosure is made with the client's knowledge and consent. Nor would a physician's or psychotherapist's keeping of confidential records necessary to diagnose or treat a patient, such a confidential hospital records, be a waiver of the privilege, even though other authorized persons have access to the records. Similarly, the patient's presentation of a physician's prescription to a registered pharmacist would not constitute a waiver of the physician-patient privilege because such disclosure is reasonably necessary for the accomplishment of the purpose for which the physician is consulted. See also Evidence Code § 992. Communications such as these, when made in confidence, should not operate to destroy the privilege even when they are made with the consent of the client or patient. Here, again, the privilege holder has not evidenced any abandonment of secrecy. Hence, he should be entitled to maintain the confidential nature of his communications to his attorney or physician despite the necessary further disclosure.

Subdivision (d) may change California law. Green v. Superior Court, 220 Cal.App.2d 121, 33 Cal.Rptr. 604 (1963) (hearing denied), held that the physician-patient privilege did not provide protection against disclosure by a pharmacist of information concerning the nature of drugs dispensed upon prescription. See also Himmelfarb v. United States, 175 F.2d 924 (9th Cir.1949) (applying the California law of privileges and holding that a lawyer's revelation to an accountant of a client's communication to the lawyer waived the client's privilege if such revelation was authorized by the client).

§ 913. Comment on, and inferences from, exercise of privilege

(a) If in the instant proceeding or on a prior occasion a privilege is or was exercised not to testify with respect to any matter, or to refuse to disclose or to prevent another from disclosing any matter, neither the presiding officer nor counsel may comment thereon, no presumption shall arise because of the exercise of the privilege, and the trier of fact may not draw any inference therefrom as to the credibility of the witness or as to any matter at issue in the proceeding.

(b) The court, at the request of a party who may be adversely affected because an unfavorable inference may be drawn by the jury because a privilege has been exercised, shall instruct the jury that no presumption arises because of the exercise of the privilege and that the jury may not draw any inference therefrom as to the credibility of the witness or as to any matter at issue in the proceeding.

COMMENT—ASSEMBLY COMMITTEE ON JUDICIARY

Section 913 prohibits any comment on the exercise of a privilege and provides that the trier of fact may not draw any inference therefrom. Except as noted below, this probably states existing law. See People v. Wilkes, 44 Cal.2d 679, 284 P.2d 481 (1955). In addition, the court is required, upon request of a party who may be adversely affected, to instruct the jury that no presumption arises and that no inference is to be drawn from the exercise of a privilege. If comment could be made on the exercise of a privilege and adverse inferences drawn therefrom, a litigant would be under great pressure to forgo his claim of privilege and the protection sought to be afforded by the privilege would be largely negated. Moreover, the inferences which might be drawn would, in many instances, be quite unwarranted.

It should be noted that Section 913 deals only with comment upon, and the drawing of adverse inferences from, the exercise of a privilege. Section 913 does not purport to deal with the inferences that may be drawn from, or the comment that may be made upon, the evidence in the case.

Section 13 of Article I of the California Constitution provides that, in a criminal case, the failure of the defendant to explain or to deny by his testimony the evidence in the case against him may be commented upon. The courts, in reliance on this provision, have held that the failure of a party in either a civil or criminal case to explain or to deny the evidence against him may be considered in determining what inferences should be drawn from that evidence. People v. Adamson, 27 Cal.2d 478, 165 P.2d 3 (1946); Fross v. Wotton, 3 Cal.2d 384, 44 P.2d 350 (1935). However, the cases have emphasized that this right of comment and consideration does not extend in criminal cases to the drawing of inferences from the claim of privilege itself. Inferences may be drawn only from the evidence in the case and the defendant's failure to explain or deny such evidence. People v. Ashley, 42 Cal.2d 246, 267 P.2d 271 (1954); People v. Adamson, supra, 27 Cal.2d 478, 165 P.2d 3 (1946). Section 413 of the Evidence Code expresses the principle underlying this constitutional provision; nothing in Section 913 affects the application of Section 413 in either criminal or civil cases. See the Comment to Evidence Code § 413. Thus, for example, it is perfectly proper under the Evidence Code for counsel to point out that the evidence against the other party is uncontradicted.

Section 913 may modify existing California law as it applies in civil cases. In Nelson v. Southern Pacific Co., 8 Cal.2d 648, 67 P.2d 682 (1937), the Supreme Court held that evidence of a person's exercise of the privilege against self-incrimination in a prior proceeding may be shown for impeachment purposes if he testifies in a self-exculpatory manner in a subsequent proceeding. The Supreme Court within recent years has overruled statements in certain criminal cases declaring a similar rule. People v. Snyder, 50 Cal.2d 190, 197, 324 P.2d 1, 6 (1958) (overruling or disapproving several cases there cited). See also People v. Sharer, 61 Cal.2d 869, 40 Cal.Rptr. 851, 395 P.2d 899 (1964). Section 913 Will, in effect, overrule the holding in the Nelson case, for it declares that no inference may be drawn from an exercise of a privilege either on the issue of credibility or on any other issue, whether the privilege was exercised in the instant proceeding or on a prior occasion. The status of the rule in the Nelson case has been in doubt because of the recent holdings in criminal cases; Section 913 eliminates any remaining basis for applying a different rule in civil cases.

There is some language in Fross v. Wotton, 3 Cal.2d 384, 44 P.2d 350 (1935), that indicates that unfavorable inferences may be drawn in a civil case from a party's claim of the privilege against self-incrimination during the case itself. Such language was unnecessary to that decision; but, if it does indicate California law, that law is changed by Evidence Code Sections 413 and 913. Under these sections, it is clear that, in civil cases as well as criminal cases, inferences may be drawn only from the evidence in the case, not from the claim of privilege.

§ 914. Determination of claim of privilege; limitation on punishment for contempt

(a) The presiding officer shall determine a claim of privilege in any proceeding in the same manner as a court determines such a claim under Article 2 (commencing with Section 400) of Chapter 4 of Division 3.

(b) No person may be held in contempt for failure to disclose information claimed to be privileged unless he has failed to comply with an order of a court that he disclose such information. This subdivision does not apply to any governmental agency that has constitutional contempt power, nor does it apply to hearings and investigations of the Industrial Accident Commission, nor does it impliedly repeal Chapter 4 (commencing with Section 9400) of Part 1 of Division 2 of Title 2 of the Government Code. If no other statutory procedure is applicable, the procedure prescribed by Section 1991 of the Code of Civil Procedure shall be followed in seeking an order of a court that the person disclose the information claimed to be privileged.

COMMENT—ASSEMBLY COMMITTEE ON JUDICIARY

Subdivision (a) makes the general provisions concerning preliminary determinations on admissibility of evidence (Sections 400–406) applicable when a presiding officer who is not a judge is called upon to determine whether or not a privilege exists. Subdivision (a) is necessary because Sections 400–406, by their terms, apply only to determinations by a court.

Subdivision (b) is needed to protect persons claiming privileges in nonjudicial proceedings. Because such proceedings are often conducted by persons untrained in law, it is desirable to have a judicial determination of whether a person is required to disclose information claimed to be privileged before he can be held in contempt for failing to disclose such information. What is contemplated is that, if a claim of privilege is made in a nonjudicial proceeding and is overruled, application must be made to a court for an order compelling the witness to answer. Only if such order is made and is disobeyed may a witness be held in contempt. That the determination of privilege in a judicial proceeding is a question for the judge is well-established California law. See, e.g., Holm v. Superior Court, 42 Cal.2d 500, 507, 267 P.2d 1025, 1029 (1954).

Subdivision (b), of course, does not apply to any body—such as the Public Utilities Commission—that has constitutional power to impose punishment for contempt. See, e.g., Cal.Const., Art. XII, § 22. Nor does this subdivision apply to witnesses before the State Legislature or its committees. See Govt.Code §§ 9400–9414. Likewise, subdivision (b) does not apply to hearings and investigations of the State Industrial Accident Commission.

§ 915. Disclosure of privileged information in ruling on claim of privilege

(a) Subject to subdivision (b), the presiding officer may not require disclosure of information claimed to be privileged under this division or attorney work product under subdivision (c) of Section 2018 of the Code of Civil Procedure in order to rule on the claim of privilege; provided, however, that in any hearing conducted pursuant to subdivision (c) of Section 1524 of the Penal Code in which a claim of privilege is made and the court determines that there is no other feasible means to rule on the validity of the claim other than to require disclosure, the court shall proceed in accordance with subdivision (b).

(b) When a court is ruling on a claim of privilege under Article 9 (commencing with Section 1040) of Chapter 4 (official information and identity of informer) or under Section 1060 (trade secret) or under subdivision (b) of Section 2018 of the Code of Civil Procedure (attorney work product) and is unable to do so without requiring disclosure of the information claimed to be privileged, the court may require the person from whom disclosure is sought or the person authorized to claim the privilege, or both, to disclose the information in chambers out of the presence and hearing of all persons except the person authorized to claim the privilege and any other persons as the person authorized to claim the privilege is willing to have present. If the judge determines that the information is privileged, neither the judge nor any other person may ever disclose, without the consent of a person authorized to permit disclosure, what was disclosed in the course of the proceedings in chambers.

LAW REVISION COMMISSION COMMENT

Subdivision (a) state the general rule that revelation of the information asserted to be privileged may not be compelled in order to determine whether or not it is privileged. This codifies existing law. See Collette v. Sarrasin, 184 Cal. 283, 288–289, 193 Pac. 571, 573 (1920); People v. Glen Arms Estate, Inc., 230 Cal.App.2d 841, 846 note 1, 41 Cal.Rptr. 303, 305 note 1 (1964).

Subdivision (b) provides an exception to this general rule for information claimed to be privileged under Section 1040 (official information), Section 1041 (identity of an informer), or Section 1060 (trade secret). These privileges exist only if the interest in maintaining the secrecy of the information outweighs the interest in seeing that justice is done in the particular case. In at least some cases, it will be necessary for the judge to examine the information claimed to be privileged in order to balance these competing considerations intelligently. See People v. Glen Arms Estate, Inc., 230 Cal.App.2d 841, 846 note 1, 41 Cal.Rptr. 303, 305 note 1 (1964), and the cases cited in 8 Wigmore, Evidence § 2379 at 812 note 6 (McNaughton rev. 1961). And see United States v. Reynolds, 345 U.S. 1, 7–11 (1953), and pertinent discussion thereof in 8 Wigmore, Evidence § 2379 (McNaughton rev. 1961). Even in these cases, Section 915 undertakes to give adequate protection to the person claiming the privilege by providing that the information be disclosed in confidence to the judge and requiring that it be kept in confidence if it is found to be privileged.

The exception in subdivision (b) applies only when a court is ruling on the claim of privilege. Thus, in view of subdivision (a), disclosure of the information cannot be required, for example, in an administrative proceeding. [7 Cal.L.Rev.Comm. Reports 1 (1965)]

§ 916. Exclusion of privileged information where persons authorized to claim privilege are not present

(a) The presiding officer, on his own motion or on the motion of any party, shall exclude information that is subject to a claim of privilege under this division if:

(1) The person from whom the information is sought is not a person authorized to claim the privilege; and

(2) There is no party to the proceeding who is a person authorized to claim the privilege.

(b) The presiding officer may not exclude information under this section if:

(1) He is otherwise instructed by a person authorized to permit disclosure; or

(2) The proponent of the evidence establishes that there is no person authorized to claim the privilege in existence.

COMMENT—ASSEMBLY COMMITTEE ON JUDICIARY

Section 916 is needed to protect the holder of a privilege when he is not available to protect his own interest. For example, a third party—perhaps the lawyer's secretary—may have been present when a confidential communication to a lawyer was made. In the absence of both the holder himself and the lawyer, the secretary could be compelled to testify concerning the communication if there were no provision such as Section 916 which requires the presiding officer to recognize the privilege.

Section 916 is designed to protect only privileged information that the holder of the privilege could protect by claiming the privilege at the hearing. It is not designed to protect unprivileged information. For example, if the statement offered in evidence is a declaration against the penal interest of the declarant, Section 916 does not authorize the presiding officer to exclude the evidence on the ground of the declarant's privilege against self-incrimination. If the declarant were present, his self-incrimination privilege would merely preclude his giving self- incriminating testimony at the hearing; it could not be asserted to prevent the disclosure of previously made self-incriminating statements.

The erroneous exclusion of information pursuant to Section 916 on the ground that it is privileged might amount to prejudicial error. On the other hand, the erroneous failure to exclude information pursuant to Section 916 could not amount to prejudicial error. See Evidence Code § 918.

Section 916 may be declarative of the existing law. No case in point has been found, but see the language in People v. Atkinson, 40 Cal. 284, 285 (1870) (attorney-client privilege).

§ 917. Presumption that certain communications are confidential

(a) Whenever a privilege is claimed on the ground that the matter sought to be disclosed is a communication made in confidence in the course of the lawyer-client, physician-patient, psychotherapist-patient, cleryman-penitent,[1] husband-wife, sexual assault victim-counselor, or domestic violence victim-counselor relationship, the communication is presumed to have been made in confidence and the opponent of the claim of privilege has the burden of proof to establish that the communication was not confidential.

(b) A communication between persons in a relationship listed in subdivision (a) does not lose its privileged character for the sole reason that it is communicated by electronic means or because persons involved in the delivery, facilitation, or storage of electronic communication may have access to the content of the communication.

(c) For purposes of this section, "electronic" has the same meaning provided in Section 1633.2 of the Civil Code.

COMMENT—ASSEMBLY COMMITTEE ON JUDICIARY

A number of sections provide privileges for communications made "in confidence" in the course of certain relationships. Although there appear to have been no cases involving the question in California, the general rule elsewhere is that a communication made in the course of such a relationship is presumed to be confidential and the party objecting to the claim of privilege has the burden of showing that it was not. See generally, with respect to the marital communication privilege, 8 Wigmore, Evidence § 2336 (McNaughton rev. 1961). See also Blau v. United States, 340 U.S. 332, 333–335 (1951) (holding that marital communications are presumed to be confidential). In adopting by statute a revised version of the privileges article of the Uniform Rules of Evidence, New Jersey included such a provision in its statement of the lawyer-client privilege. N.J.Rev.Stat. § 2A:84A–20(3), added by N.J.Laws 1960, Ch. 52, p. 452.

If the privilege claimant were required to show that the communication was made in confidence, he would be compelled, in many cases, to reveal the subject matter of the communication in order to establish his right to the privilege. Hence, Section 917 is included to establish a presumption of confidentiality, if this is not already the existing law in California. See Sharon v. Sharon, 79 Cal. 633, 678, 22 Pac. 26, 40 (1889) (attorney- client privilege); Hager v. Shindler, 29 Cal. 47, 63 (1865) ("Prima facie, all communications made by a client to his attorney or counsel [in the course of that relationship] must be regarded as confidential.").

1. So in enrolled bill.

To overcome the presumption, the proponent of the evidence must persuade the presiding officer that the communication was not made in confidence. Of course, if the facts show that the communication was not intended to be kept in confidence, the communication is not privileged. See Solon v. Lichtenstein, 39 Cal.2d 75, 244 P.2d 907 (1952). And the fact that the communication was made under circumstances where others could easily overhear is a strong indication that the communication was not intended to be confidential and is, therefore, unprivileged. See Sharon v. Sharon, 79 Cal. 633, 677, 22 Pac. 26, 39 (1889); People v. Castiel, 153 Cal.App.2d 653, 315 P.2d 79 (1957).

LAW REVISION COMMISSION COMMENTS

2002 Amendment

Subdivision (a) of Section 917 is amended to make clear that it also applies to confidential communication privileges created after its original enactment in 1965. See Sections 1035–1036.2 (sexual assault victim), 1037–1037.7 (domestic violence victim). The presumption set forth in subdivision (a) applies regardless of how a communication is transmitted. In each instance, the opponent of the claim of privilege has the burden of proof to establish that the communication was not confidential.

Subdivision (b) is drawn from New York law (N.Y. C.P.L.R. 4548 (McKinney 2001)) and from language formerly found in Section 952 relating to confidentiality of an electronic communication between a client and a lawyer. For waiver of privileges, see Section 912 & Comment.

Under subdivision (c), the definition of "electronic" is broad, including any "intangible media which are technologically capable of storing, transmitting and reproducing information in human perceivable form." Unif. Electronic Transactions Act, § 2 comment (1999) (enacted as Civ. Code § 1633.2).

For discussion of ethical considerations where a lawyer communicates with a client by electronic means, see Bus. & Prof. Code § 6068(e) (attorney has duty to "maintain inviolate the confidence, and at every peril to himself or herself to preserve the secrets, of his or her client"); ABA Standing Committee on Ethics & Professional Responsibility, Formal Op. 99–413 ("Protecting the Confidentiality of Unencrypted E–Mail"); ABA Standing Committee on Ethics & Professional Responsibility, Formal Op. 92–368 ("Inadvertent Disclosure of Confidential Materials").

For examples of provisions on the admissibility of electronic communications, see Evid. Code §§ 1521 & Comment (Secondary Evidence Rule), 1552 (printed representation of computer information or computer program), 1553 (printed representation of images stored on video or digital medium); Civ. Code § 1633.13 ("In a proceeding, evidence of a record or signature may not be excluded solely because it is in electronic form."). See also People v. Martinez, 22 Cal. 4th 106, 990 P.2d 563, 91 Cal. Rptr. 2d 687 (2000); People v. Hernandez, 55 Cal. App. 4th 225, 63 Cal. Rptr. 2d 769 (1997); *Aguimatang* v. California State Lottery, 234 Cal. App. 3d 769, 286 Cal. Rptr. 57 (1991); People v. Lugashi, 205 Cal. App. 3d 632, 252 Cal. Rptr. 434 (1988).

§ 918. Error in overruling claim of privilege

A party may predicate error on a ruling disallowing a claim of privilege only if he is the holder of the privilege, except that a party may predicate error on a ruling disallowing a claim of privilege by his spouse under Section 970 or 971.

LAW REVISION COMMISSION COMMENT

This section is consistent with existing law. See People v. Gonzales, 56 Cal.App. 330, 204 Pac. 1088 (1922), and discussion of similar cases cited in Tentative Recommendation and a Study Relating to the Uniform Rules of Evidence (Article V. Privileges) 6 Cal.Law Revision Comm'n, Rep., Rec. & Studies 201, 525 note 5 (1964). [7 Cal.L.Rev.Comm. Reports 1 (1965)]

§ 919. Admissibility where disclosure erroneously compelled; claim of privilege; coercion

(a) Evidence of a statement or other disclosure of privileged information is inadmissible against a holder of the privilege if:

(1) A person authorized to claim the privilege claimed it but nevertheless disclosure erroneously was required to be made; or

(2) The presiding officer did not exclude the privileged information as required by Section 916.

(b) If a person authorized to claim the privilege claimed it, whether in the same or a prior proceeding, but nevertheless disclosure erroneously was required by the presiding officer to be made, neither the failure to refuse to disclose nor the failure to seek review of the order of the presiding officer requiring disclosure indicates consent to the disclosure or constitutes a waiver and, under these circumstances, the disclosure is one made under coercion.

LAW REVISION COMMISSION COMMENT 1965 ENACTMENT

Section 919 protects a holder of a privilege from the detriment he would otherwise suffer in a later proceeding when, in a prior proceeding, the presiding officer erroneously overruled a claim of privilege and compelled revelation of the privileged information. Although Section 912 provides that such a coerced disclosure does not waive a privilege, it does not provide specifically that evidence of the prior disclosure is inadmissible; Section 919 assures the inadmissibility of such evidence in the subsequent proceeding.

Section 919 probably states existing law. See People v. Abair, 102 Cal.App.2d 765, 228 P.2d 336 (1951) (prior disclosure by an attorney held inadmissible in a later proceeding where the holder of the privilege had first opportunity to object to attorney's testifying). See also People v. Kor, 129 Cal.App.2d 436, 277 P.2d 94 (1954). However, there is little case authority upon the proposition. [7 Cal.L.Rev.Comm. Reports 1 (1965)]

1974 Amendment

Subdivision (b) has been added to Section 919 to make clear that, after disclosure of privileged information has been erroneously required to be made by order of a trial court or other presiding officer, neither the failure to refuse to disclose nor the failure to challenge the order (by, for example, a petition for a writ of habeas corpus or other special writ or by an appeal from a contempt order) amounts to a waiver and the disclosure is one made under coercion for the purposes of Sections 912(a) and 919(a) (1). See Section 905 (defining "presiding officer"). The addition of subdivision (b) will preclude any possibility of a contrary interpretation of Sections 912 and 919 based on the language found in Markwell v. Sykes, 173 Cal.App.2d 642, 649–650, 343 P.2d 769, 773–774 (1959). See Recommendation Relating to Erroneously Ordered Disclosure of Privileged Information, 11 Cal.L. Revision Comm'n Reports 1163 (1973).

The phrase "whether in the same or a prior proceeding" has been included in subdivision (b) to avoid any implication that might be drawn from the original Law Revision Commission Comment to Section 919 that subdivision (a) (1) applies only where the privilege was claimed in a prior proceeding. The protection afforded by Section 919, of course, also applies where a claim of privilege is made at an earlier stage in the same proceeding and the presiding officer erroneously overruled the claim and ordered disclosure of the privileged information to be made. [11 Cal. L.Rev.Comm. Reports 1163 (1974)]

§ 920. Implied repeal of other statutes related to privileges

Nothing in this division shall be construed to repeal by implication any other statute relating to privileges.

LAW REVISION COMMISSION COMMENT

Some of the statutes relating to privileges are found in other codes and are continued in force. See, e.g., Penal Code §§ 266h and 266i (making the marital communications privilege inapplicable in prosecutions for pimping and pandering respectively). Section 920 assures that nothing in this division makes privileged any information declared by statute to be unprivileged or makes unprivileged any information declared by statute to be privileged. [7 Cal.L.Rev. Reports 1 (1965)]

CHAPTER 4. PARTICULAR PRIVILEGES

ARTICLE 1. PRIVILEGE OF DEFENDANT IN CRIMINAL CASE

§ 930. Privilege not to be called as a witness and not to testify

To the extent that such privilege exists under the Constitution of the United States or the State of California, a defendant in a criminal case has a privilege not to be called as a witness and not to testify.

LAW REVISION COMMISSION COMMENT

Section 930 recognizes that the defendant in a criminal case has a constitutional privilege not to be called as a witness and not to testify. Cal.Const., Art. I, § 13. See Killpatrick v. Superior Court, 153 Cal. App.2d 146, 314 P.2d 164 (1957); People v. Talle, 111 Cal.App.2d 650, 245 P.2d 633 (1952). Section 930 also recognizes that the defendant may have a similar privilege under the United States Constitution. See Malloy v. Hogan, 378 U.S. 1 (1964). [7 Cal.L.Rev.Comm. Reports 1 (1965)]

ARTICLE 2. PRIVILEGE AGAINST SELF-INCRIMINATION

§ 940. Privilege against self-incrimination

To the extent that such privilege exists under the Constitution of the United States or the State of California, a person has a privilege to refuse to disclose any matter that may tend to incriminate him.

LAW REVISION COMMISSION COMMENT

Section 940 recognizes the privilege (derived from the California and United States Constitutions) of a person to refuse, when testifying, to give information that might tend to incriminate him. See Fross v. Wotton, 3 Cal.2d 384, 44 P.2d 350 (1935); In re Leavitt, 174 Cal.App.2d 535, 345 P.2d 75 (1959). This privilege should be distinguished from the privilege stated in Section 930 (privilege of defendant in a criminal case to refuse to testify at all).

Section 940 does not determine the scope of the privilege against self-incrimination; the scope of the privilege is determined by the pertinent provisions of the California and United States Constitutions as interpreted by the courts. See Cal.Const., Art. I, § 13. See also Malloy v. Hogan, 378 U.S. 1 (1964). Nor does Section 940 prescribe the exceptions to the privilege or indicate when it has been waived. This, too, is determined by the cases interpreting the pertinent provisions of the California and United States Constitutions. For a statement of the scope of the constitutional privilege and some of its exceptions, see Tentative Recommendation and a Study Relating to the Uniform Rules of Evidence (Article V. Privileges), 6 Cal.Law Revision Comm'n, Rep., Rec. & Studies 201, 215–218, 343–377 (1964). [7 Cal.L.Rev.Comm. Reports 1 (1965)]

ARTICLE 3. LAWYER–CLIENT PRIVILEGE

§ 950. Lawyer

As used in this article, "lawyer" means a person authorized, or reasonably believed by the client to be authorized, to practice law in any state or nation.

LAW REVISION COMMISSION COMMENT

"Lawyer" is defined to include a person "reasonably believed by the client to be authorized" to practice law. Since the privilege is intended to encourage full disclosure, the client's reasonable belief that the person he is consulting is an attorney is sufficient to justify application of the privilege. See 8 Wigmore, Evidence § 2302 (McNaughton rev. 1961), and cases there cited in note 1. See also McCormick, Evidence § 92 (1954).

There is no requirement that the lawyer be licensed to practice in a jurisdiction that recognizes the lawyer-client privilege. Legal transactions frequently cross state and national boundaries and require consultation with attorneys from many different jurisdictions. When a California resident travels outside the State and has occasion to consult a lawyer during such travel, or when a lawyer from another state or nation participates in a transaction involving a California client, the client should be entitled to assume that his communications will be given as much protection as they would be if he consulted a California lawyer in California. A client should not be forced to inquire about the jurisdictions where the lawyer is authorized to practice and whether such jurisdictions recognize the lawyer-client privilege before he may safely communicate with the lawyer. [7 Cal.L.Rev.Comm. Reports 1 (1965)]

§ 951. Client

As used in this article, "client" means a person who, directly or through an authorized representative, consults a lawyer for the purpose of retaining the lawyer or securing legal service or advice from him in his professional capacity, and includes an incompetent (a) who himself so consults the lawyer or (b) whose guardian or conservator so consults the lawyer in behalf of the incompetent.

LAW REVISION COMMISSION COMMENT

Under Section 951, public entities have a privilege insofar as communications made in the course of the lawyer-client relationship are concerned. This codifies existing law. See Holm v. Superior Court, 42 Cal.2d 500, 267 P.2d 1025 (1954). Likewise, such unincorporated organizations as labor unions, social clubs, and fraternal societies have a lawyer-client privilege when the organization (rather than its individual members) is the client. See Evidence Code § 175 (defining "person") and § 200 (defining "public entity"). [7 Cal.L.Rev.Comm. Reports 1 (1965)]

§ 952. Confidential communication between client and lawyer

As used in this article, "confidential communication between client and lawyer" means information transmitted between a client and his or her lawyer in the course of that relationship and in confidence by a means which, so far as the client is aware, discloses the information to no third persons other than those who are present to further the interest of the client in the consultation or those to whom disclosure is reasonably necessary for the transmission of the information or the accomplishment of the purpose for which the lawyer is consulted, and includes a legal opinion formed and the advice given by the lawyer in the course of that relationship.

LAW REVISION COMMISSION COMMENTS

2002 Amendment

Section 952 is amended to delete the last sentence concerning confidentiality of electronic communications, because this rule is generalized in Section 917(b)-(c) applicable to all confidential communication privileges.

1965 Amendment

The requirement that the communication be made in the course of the lawyer-client relationship and be confidential is in accord with existing law. See City & County of San Francisco v. Superior Court, 37 Cal.2d 227, 234–235, 231 P.2d 26, 29–30 (1951).

Confidential communications also include those made to third parties—such as the lawyer's secretary, a physician, or similar expert—for the purpose of transmitting such information to the lawyer because they are "reasonably necessary for the transmission of the information." This codifies existing law. See, e.g., City & County of San Francisco v. Superior Court, supra (communication to a physician); Loftin v. Glaser, Civil No. 789604 (L.A.Super.Ct., July 23, 1964) (communication to an accountant), as reported in Los Angeles Daily Journal Report Section, August 25, 1964 (memorandum opinion of Judge Philbrick McCoy).

A lawyer at times may desire to have a client reveal information to an expert consultant in order that the lawyer may adequately advise his client. The inclusion of the words "or the accomplishment of the purpose for which the lawyer is consulted" assures that these communications, too, are within the scope of the privilege. This part of the definition may change existing law. Himmelfarb v. United States, 175 F.2d 924, 938–939 (9th Cir.1949), applying California law, held that the presence of an accountant during a lawyer-client consultation destroyed the privilege, but no California case directly in point has been found. Of course, if the expert consultant is acting merely as a conduit for communications from the client to the attorney, the doctrine of City & County of San Francisco v. Superior Court, supra, applies and the communication would be privileged under existing law as well as under this section. See also Evidence Code § 912(d) and the Comment thereto.

The words "other than those who are present to further the interest of the client in the consultation" indicate that a communication to a lawyer is nonetheless confidential even though it is made in the presence of another person—such as a spouse, parent, business associate, or joint client—who is present to further the interest of the client in the consultation. These words refer, too, to another person and his attorney who may meet with the client and his attorney in regard to a matter of joint concern. This may change existing law, for the presence of a third person sometimes has been held to destroy the confidential character of the consultation, even where the third person was present because of his concern for the welfare of the client. See Attorney–Client Privilege in California, 10 Stan.L.Rev. 297, 308 (1958), and authorities there cited in notes 67–71. See also Himmelfarb v. United States, supra. [7 Cal.L.Rev. Comm. Reports 1 (1965)]

1967 Amendment

The express inclusion of "a legal opinion" in the last clause will preclude a possible construction of this section that would leave the attorney's uncommunicated legal opinion—which includes his impressions and conclusions—unprotected by the privilege. Such a construction would virtually destroy the privilege. [8 Cal.L.Rev.Comm. Reports 101 (1967)]

§ 953. Holder of the privilege

As used in this article, "holder of the privilege" means:

(a) The client when he has no guardian or conservator.

(b) A guardian or conservator of the client when the client has a guardian or conservator.

(c) The personal representative of the client if the client is dead.

(d) A successor, assign, trustee in dissolution, or any similar representative of a firm, association, organization, partnership, business trust, corporation, or public entity that is no longer in existence.

LAW REVISION COMMISSION COMMENT

Under subdivisions (a) and (b), the guardian of a client is the holder of the privilege if the client has a guardian, and the client becomes the holder of the privilege when he no longer has a guardian. For example, if an underage client or his guardian consults a lawyer, the guardian is the holder of the privilege under subdivision (b) until the guardianship is terminated; thereafter, the client himself is the holder of the privilege. The present California law is uncertain. The statutes do not deal with the problem, and no appellate decision has discussed it.

Under subdivision (c), the personal representative of a client is the holder of the privilege when the client is dead. He may either claim or waive the privilege on behalf of the deceased client. This may be a change in California law. Under existing law, it seems probable that the privilege survives the death of the client and that no one can waive it after the client's death. See Collette v. Sarrasin, 184 Cal. 283, 289, 193 Pac. 571, 573 (1920). Hence, the privilege apparently is recognized even when it would be clearly to the interest of the estate of the deceased client to waive it. Under Section 953, however, the personal representative of a deceased client may waive the privilege. The purpose underlying the privilege—to provide a client with the assurance of confidentiality—does not require the recognition of the privilege when to do so is detrimental to his interest or to the interests of his estate. [7 Cal.L.Rev. Comm. Reports 1 (1965)]

§ 954. Lawyer-client privilege

Subject to Section 912 and except as otherwise provided in this article, the client, whether or not a party, has a privilege to refuse to disclose, and to prevent another from disclosing, a confidential communication between client and lawyer if the privilege is claimed by:

(a) The holder of the privilege;

(b) A person who is authorized to claim the privilege by the holder of the privilege; or

(c) The person who was the lawyer at the time of the confidential communication, but such person may not claim the privilege if there is no holder of the privilege in existence or if he is otherwise instructed by a person authorized to permit disclosure.

The relationship of attorney and client shall exist between a law corporation as defined in Article 10 (commencing with Section 6160) of Chapter 4 of Division 3 of the Business and Professions Code and the persons to whom it renders professional services, as well as between such persons and members of the State Bar employed by such corporation to render services to such persons. The word "persons" as used in this subdivision includes partnerships, corporations, limited liability companies, associations and other groups and entities.

LAW REVISION COMMISSION COMMENT

Section 954 is the basic statement of the lawyer-client privilege. Exceptions to this privilege are stated in Sections 956–962.

Persons entitled to claim the privilege. The persons entitled to claim the privilege are specified in subdivisions (a), (b), and (c). See Evidence Code § 953 for the definition of "holder of the privilege."

Eavesdroppers. Under Section 954, the lawyer-client privilege can be asserted to prevent anyone from testifying to a confidential communication. Thus, clients are protected against the risk of disclosure by eavesdroppers and other wrongful interceptors of confidential communications between lawyer and client. Probably no such protection was provided prior to the enactment of Penal Code Sections 653i and 653j. See People v. Castiel, 153 Cal.App.2d 653, 315 P.2d 79 (1957). See also Attorney–Client Privilege in California, 10 Stan.L.Rev. 297, 310–312 (1958), and cases there cited in note 84.

Penal Code Section 653j makes evidence obtained by electronic eavesdropping or recording in violation of the section inadmissible in "any judicial, administrative, legislative, or other proceeding." The section also provides a criminal penalty and contains definitions and exceptions. Penal Code Section 653i makes it a felony to eavesdrop by an electronic or other device upon a conversation between a person in custody of a public officer or on public property and that person's lawyer, religious advisor, or physician.

Section 954 is consistent with Penal Code Sections 653i and 653j but provides broader protection, for it protects against disclosure of confidential communications by anyone who obtained knowledge of the communication without the client's consent. See also Evidence Code § 912 (when disclosure with client's consent constitutes a waiver of the privilege). The use of the privilege to prevent testimony by eavesdroppers and those to whom the communication was wrongfully disclosed does not, however, affect the rule that the making of the communication under circumstances where others could easily overhear it is evidence that the client did not intend the communication to be confidential. See Sharon v. Sharon, 79 Cal. 633, 677, 22 Pac. 26, 39 (1889).

Termination of privilege. The privilege may be claimed by a person listed in Section 954, or the privileged information excluded by the presiding officer under Section 916, only if there is a holder of the privilege in existence. Hence, the privilege ceases to exist when the client's estate is finally distributed and his personal representative is discharged. This is apparently a change in California law. Under the existing law, it seems likely that the privilege continues to exist indefinitely after the client's death and that no one has authority to waive the privilege. See Collette v. Sarrasin, 184 Cal. 283, 193 Pac. 571 (1920). See generally Paley v. Superior Court, 137 Cal.App.2d 450, 290 P.2d 617 (1955), and discussion of the analogous situation in connection with the physician- patient privilege in Tentative Recommendation and a Study Relating to the Uniform Rules of Evidence (Article V. Privileges), 6 Cal.Law Revision Comm'n, Rep., Rec. & Studies 201, 408–410 (1964). Although there is good reason for maintaining the privilege while the estate is being administered—particularly if the estate is involved in litigation—there is little reason to preserve secrecy at the expense of excluding relevant evidence after the estate is wound up and the representative is discharged. [7 Cal.L.Rev.Comm. Reports 1 (1965)]

§ 955. When lawyer required to claim privilege

The lawyer who received or made a communication subject to the privilege under this article shall claim the privilege whenever he is present when the communication is sought to be disclosed and is authorized to claim the privilege under subdivision (c) of Section 954.

LAW REVISION COMMISSION COMMENT

The obligation of the lawyer to claim the privilege on behalf of the client, unless otherwise instructed by a person authorized to permit disclosure, is consistent with Section 6068(e) of the Business and Professions Code. [7 Cal.L.Rev.Comm. Reports 1 (1965)]

§ 956. Exception: Crime or fraud

There is no privilege under this article if the services of the lawyer were sought or obtained to enable or aid anyone to commit or plan to commit a crime or a fraud.

LAW REVISION COMMISSION COMMENT

California now recognizes this exception. Abbott v. Superior Court, 78 Cal.App.2d 19, 177 P.2d 317 (1947). Cf. Nowell v. Superior Court, 223 Cal.App.2d 652, 36 Cal.Rptr. 21 (1963). [7 Cal.L.Rev.Comm. Reports 1 (1965)]

§ 956.5. Reasonable belief that disclosure of confidential communication is necessary to prevent criminal act resulting in death or bodily harm; exception to privilege

There is no privilege under this article if the lawyer reasonably believes that disclosure of any confidential communication relating to representation of a client is necessary to prevent the client from committing a criminal act that the lawyer believes is likely to result in death or substantial bodily harm.

§ 957. Exception: Parties claiming through deceased client

There is no privilege under this article as to a communication relevant to an issue between parties all of whom claim through a deceased client, regardless of whether the claims are by testate or intestate succession or by inter vivos transaction.

LAW REVISION COMMISSION COMMENT

The lawyer-client privilege does not apply to a communication relevant to an issue between parties all of whom claim through a deceased client. Under existing law, all must claim through the client by testate or intestate succession in order for this exception to be applicable; a claim by inter vivos transaction apparently is not within the exception. Paley v. Superior Court, 137 Cal.App.2d 450, 457–460, 290 P.2d 617, 621–623 (1955). Section 957 extends this exception to include inter vivos transactions.

The traditional exception for litigation between claimants by testate or intestate succession is based on the theory that claimants in privity with the estate claim through the client, not adversely, and the deceased client presumably would want his communications disclosed in litigation between such claimants so that his desires in regard to the disposition of his estate might be correctly ascertained and carried out. This rationale is equally applicable where one or more of the parties is claiming by inter vivos transaction as, for example, in an action between a party who claims under a deed (executed by a client in full possession of his faculties) and a party who claims under a will executed while the client's mental stability was dubious. See the discussion in Tentative Recommendation and a Study Relating to the Uniform Rules of Evidence (Article V. Privileges), 6 Cal.Law Revision Comm'n, Rep., Rec. & Studies 201, 392–396 (1964). [7 Cal.L.Rev.Comm. Reports 1 (1965)]

§ 958. Exception: Breach of duty arising out of lawyer-client relationship

There is no privilege under this article as to a communication relevant to an issue of breach, by the lawyer or by the client, of a duty arising out of the lawyer-client relationship.

LAW REVISION COMMISSION COMMENT

This exception has not been recognized by a holding in any California case, although dicta in several opinions indicate that it would be recognized if the question were presented in a proper case. People v. Tucker, 61 Cal.2d 828, 40 Cal.Rptr. 609, 395 P.2d 449 (1964); Henshall v. Coburn, 177 Cal. 50, 169 Pac. 1014 (1917); Pacific Tel. & Tel. Co. v. Fink, 141 Cal.App.2d 332, 335, 296 P.2d 843, 845 (1956); Fleschler v. Strauss, 15 Cal.App.2d 735, 60 P.2d 193 (1936). See generally Witkin, California Evidence § 419 (1958).

It would be unjust to permit a client either to accuse his attorney of a breach of duty and to invoke the privilege to prevent the attorney from bringing forth evidence in defense of the charge or to refuse to pay his attorney's fee and invoke the privilege to defeat the attorney's claim. Thus, for example, if the defendant in a criminal action claims that his lawyer did not provide him with an adequate defense, communications between the lawyer and client relevant to that issue are not privileged. See People v. Tucker, 61 Cal.2d 828, 40 Cal.Rptr. 609, 395 P.2d 449 (1964). The duty involved must, of course, be one arising out of the lawyer-client relationship, e.g., the duty of the lawyer to exercise reasonable diligence on behalf of his client, the duty of the lawyer to care faithfully and account for his client's property, or the client's duty to pay for the lawyer's services. [7 Cal.L.Rev.Comm. Reports 1 (1965)]

§ 959. Exception: Lawyer as attesting witness

There is no privilege under this article as to a communication relevant to an issue concerning the intention or competence of a client executing an attested document of which the lawyer is an attesting witness, or concerning the execution or attestation of such a document.

LAW REVISION COMMISSION COMMENT

This exception relates to the type of communication about which an attesting witness would testify. The mere fact that an attorney acts as an attesting witness should not destroy the lawyer-client privilege as to all statements made concerning the document attested; but the privilege should not prohibit the lawyer from performing the duties expected of an attesting witness. Under existing law, the attesting witness exception is broader, having been used as a device to obtain information which the lawyer who is an attesting witness received in his capacity as a lawyer rather than as an attesting witness. See In re Mullin, 110 Cal. 252, 42 Pac. 645 (1895). [7 Cal.L.Rev.Comm. Reports 1 (1965)]

§ 960. Exception: Intention of deceased client concerning writing affecting property interest

There is no privilege under this article as to a communication relevant to an issue concerning the intention of a client, now deceased, with respect to a deed of conveyance, will, or other writing, executed by the client, purporting to affect an interest in property.

LAW REVISION COMMISSION COMMENT

Although the attesting witness exception stated in Section 959 is limited to information of the kind to which one would expect an attesting witness to testify, there is merit to having an exception that applies to all dispositive instruments. A client ordinarily would desire his lawyer to communicate his true intention with regard to a dispositive instrument if the instrument itself leaves the matter in doubt and the client is deceased. Likewise, the client ordinarily would desire his attorney to testify to communications relevant to the validity of such instruments after the client dies. Accordingly, two additional exceptions—Sections 960 and 961—are provided for this purpose. These exceptions have been recognized by the California decisions only in cases where the lawyer is an attesting witness. See the Comment to Evidence Code § 959. [7 Cal.L.Rev.Comm. Reports 1 (1965)]

§ 961. Exception: Validity of writing affecting property interest

There is no privilege under this article as to a communication relevant to an issue concerning the validity of a deed of conveyance, will, or other writing, executed by a client, now deceased, purporting to affect an interest in property.

LAW REVISION COMMISSION COMMENT

See the Comment to Section 960. [7 Cal.L.Rev.Comm. Reports 1 (1965)]

§ 962. Exception:Joint clients

Where two or more clients have retained or consulted a lawyer upon a matter of common interest, none of them, nor the successor in interest of any of them, may claim a privilege under this article as to a communication made in the course of that relationship when such communication is offered in a civil proceeding between one of such clients (or his successor in interest) and another of such clients (or his successor in interest).

LAW REVISION COMMISSION COMMENT

This section states existing law. Clyne v. Brock, 82 Cal.App.2d 958, 965, 188 P.2d 263, 267 (1947); Croce v. Superior Court, 21 Cal.App.2d 18, 68 P.2d 369 (1937). See also Harris v. Harris, 136 Cal. 379, 69 Pac. 23 (1902). [7 Cal.L.Rev.Comm. Reports 1 (1965)]

ARTICLE 4. PRIVILEGE NOT TO TESTIFY AGAINST SPOUSE

§ 970. Spouse's privilege not to testify against spouse; exception

Except as otherwise provided by statute, a married person has a privilege not to testify against his spouse in any proceeding.

LAW REVISION COMMISSION COMMENT

Under this article, a married person has two privileges: (1) a privilege not to testify against his spouse in any proceeding (Section 970) and (2) a privilege not to be called as a witness in any proceeding to which his spouse is a party (Section 971).

The privileges under this article are not as broad as the privilege provided by existing law. Under existing law, a married person has a privilege to prevent his spouse from testifying against him, but only the witness spouse has a privilege under this article. Under the existing law, a married person may refuse to testify for the other spouse, such privilege exists under this article. For a discussion of the reasons for these changes in existing law, see the Law Revision Commission's Comment to Code of Civil Procedure Section 1881 (superseded by the Evidence Code).

The rationale of the privilege provided by Section 970 not to testify against one's spouse is that such testimony would seriously disturb or disrupt the marital relationship. Society stands to lose more from such disruption than it stands to gain from the testimony which would be available if the privilege did not exist. The privilege is based in part on a previous recommendation and study of the California Law Revision Commission. See 1 Cal.Law Revision Comm'n, Rep., Rec. & Studies, Recommendation and Study Relating to the Marital "For and Against" Testimonial Privilege at F-1 (1957). [7 Cal.L.Rev.Comm. Reports 1 (1965)]

§ 971. Privilege not to be called as a witness against spouse

Except as otherwise provided by statute, a married person whose spouse is a party to a proceeding has a privilege not to be called as a witness by an adverse party to that proceeding without the prior express consent of the spouse having the privilege under this section unless the party calling the spouse does so in good faith without knowledge of the marital relationship.

LAW REVISION COMMISSION COMMENT

The privilege of a married person not to be called as a witness against his spouse is somewhat similar to the privilege given the defendant in a criminal case not to be called as a witness (Section 930). This privilege is necessary to avoid the prejudicial effect. For example, of the prosecution's calling the defendant's wife as a witness, thus forcing her to object before the jury. The privilege not to be called as a witness does not apply, however, in a proceeding where the other spouse is not a party. Thus, a married person may be called as a witness in a grand jury proceeding because his spouse is not a party to that proceeding, but the witness in the grand jury proceeding may claim the privilege under Section 970 to refuse to answer a question that would compel him to testify against his spouse. [7 Cal.L.Rev.Comm. Reports 1 (1965)]

§ 972. Exceptions to privilege

A married person does not have a privilege under this article in:

(a) A proceeding brought by or on behalf of one spouse against the other spouse.

(b) A proceeding to commit or otherwise place his or her spouse or his or her spouse's property, or both, under the control of another because of the spouse's alleged mental or physical condition.

(c) A proceeding brought by or on behalf of a spouse to establish his or her competence.

(d) A proceeding under the Juvenile Court Law, Chapter 2 (commencing with Section 200) of Part 1 of Division 2 of the Welfare and Institutions Code.

(e) A criminal proceeding in which one spouse is charged with:

(1) A crime against the person or property of the other spouse or of a child, parent, relative, or cohabitant of either, whether committed before or during marriage.

(2) A crime against the person or property of a third person committed in the course of committing a crime against the person or property of the other spouse, whether committed before or during marriage.

(3) Bigamy.

(4) A crime defined by Section 270 or 270a of the Penal Code.

(f) A proceeding resulting from a criminal act which occurred prior to legal marriage of the spouses to each other regarding knowledge acquired prior to that marriage if prior to the legal marriage the witness spouse was aware that his or her spouse had been arrested for or had been formally charged with the crime or crimes about which the spouse is called to testify.

(g) A proceeding brought against the spouse by a former spouse so long as the property and debts of the marriage have not been adjudicated, or in order to establish, modify, or enforce a child, family or spousal support obligation arising from the marriage to the former spouse; in a proceeding brought against a spouse by the other parent in order to establish, modify, or enforce a child support obligation for a child of a nonmarital relationship of the spouse; or in a proceeding brought against a spouse by the guardian of a child of that spouse in order to establish, modify, or enforce a child support obligation of the spouse. The married person does not have a privilege under this subdivision to refuse to provide information relating to the issues of income, expenses, assets, debts, and employment of either spouse, but may assert the privilege as otherwise provided in this article if other information is requested by the former spouse, guardian, or other parent of the child.

Any person demanding the otherwise privileged information made available by this subdivision, who also has an obligation to support the child for whom an order to establish, modify, or enforce child support is sought, waives his or her marital privilege to the same extent as the spouse as provided in this subdivision.

LAW REVISION COMMISSION COMMENT

The exceptions to the privileges under this article are similar to those contained in Code of Civil Procedure Section 1881(1) and Penal Code Section 1322, both of which are superseded by the Evidence Code. However, the exceptions in this section have been drafted so that they are consistent with those provided in Article 5 (commencing with Section 980) of this chapter (the privilege for confidential marital communications).

A discussion of comparable exceptions may be found in the Comments to the sections in Article 5 of this chapter. [7 Cal.L.Rev.Comm. Reports 1 (1965)]

§ 973. Waiver of privilege

(a) Unless erroneously compelled to do so, a married person who testifies in a proceeding to which his spouse is a party, or who testifies against his spouse in any proceeding, does not have a privilege under this article in the proceeding in which such testimony is given.

(b) There is no privilege under this article in a civil proceeding brought or defended by a married person for the immediate benefit of his spouse or of himself and his spouse.

COMMENT—ASSEMBLY COMMITTEE ON JUDICIARY

Section 973 contains special waiver provisions for the privileges provided by this article.

Subdivision (a). Under subdivision (a), a married person who testifies in a proceeding to which his spouse is a party waives both privileges provided for in this article. Thus, for example, a married person cannot call his spouse as a witness to give favorable testimony and have that spouse invoke the privilege provided in Section 970 to keep from testifying on cross-examination to unfavorable matters; nor can a married person testify for an adverse party as to particular matters and then invoke the privilege not to testify against his spouse as to other matters.

In any proceeding where a married person's spouse is not a party, the privilege not to be called as a witness is not available, and a married person may testify like any other witness without waiving the privilege provided under Section 970 so long as he does not testify against his spouse. However, under subdivision (a), the privilege not to testify against his spouse in that proceeding is waived as to all matters if he testifies against his spouse as to any matter.

The word "proceeding" is defined in Section 901 to include any action, civil or criminal. Hence, the privilege is waived for all purposes in an action if the spouse entitled to claim the privilege testifies at any time during the action. For example, if a civil action involves issues being separately tried, a wife whose husband is a party to the litigation may not testify for her husband at one trial and invoke and privilege in order to avoid testifying against him at a separate trial of a different issue. Nor may a wife testify against her husband at a preliminary hearing of a criminal action and refuse to testify against him at the trial.

Subdivision (b). This subdivision precludes married persons from taking unfair advantage of their marital status to escape their duty to give testimony under Section 776, which supersedes Code of Civil Procedure Section 2055. It recognizes a doctrine of waiver that has been developed in the California cases. Thus, for example, when suit is brought to set aside a conveyance from husband to wife allegedly in fraud of the husband's creditors, both spouses being named as defendants, it has been held that setting up the conveyance in the answer as a defense waives the privilege. Tobias v. Adams, 201 Cal. 689, 258 Pac. 588 (1927); Schwartz v. Brandon, 97 Cal.App. 30, 275 Pac. 448 (1929). But cf. Marple v. Jackson, 184 Cal. 411, 193 Pac. 940 (1920). Also, when husband and wife are joined as defendants in a quiet title action and assert a claim to the property, they have been held to have waived the privilege. Hagen v. Silva, 139 Cal.App.2d 199, 293 P.2d 143 (1956). And when both spouses joined as plaintiffs in an action to recover damages to one of them, each was held to have waived the privilege as to the testimony of the other. In re Strand, 123 Cal.App. 170, 11 P.2d 89 (1932). (It should be noted that, with respect to damages for personal injuries, Civil Code Section 163.5 (added by Cal.Stats.1957, Ch. 2334, § 1, p. 4066) provides that all damages awarded to a married person in a civil action for personal injuries are the separate property of such married person.) This principle of waiver has seemingly been developed by the case law to prevent a spouse from refusing to testify as to matters which affect his own interest on the ground that such testimony would also be "against" his spouse. It has been held, however, that a spouse does not waive the privilege by making the other spouse his agent, even as to transactions involving the agency. Ayres v. Wright, 103 Cal.App. 610, 284 Pac. 1077 (1930).

ARTICLE 5. PRIVILEGE FOR CONFIDENTIAL MARITAL COMMUNICATIONS

§ 980. Confidential marital communication privilege

Subject to Section 912 and except as otherwise provided in this article, a spouse (or his guardian or conservator when he has a guardian or conservator), whether or not a party, has a privilege during the marital relationship and afterwards to refuse to disclose, and to prevent another from disclosing, a communication if he claims the privilege and the communication was made in confidence between him and the other spouse while they were husband and wife.

LAW REVISION COMMISSION COMMENT

Section 980 is the basic statement of the privilege for confidential marital communications. Exceptions to this privilege are stated in Sections 981–987.

Who can claim the privilege. Under Section 980, both spouses are the holders of the privilege and either spouse may claim it. Under existing law, the privilege may belong only to the nontestifying spouse inasmuch as Code of Civil Procedure Section 1881(1), superseded by the Evidence Code, provides: "[N]or can either . . . be, without the consent of the other, examined as to any communication made by one to the other during the marriage." (Emphasis added.) It is likely, however, that Section 1881(1) would be construed to grant the privilege to both spouses. See In re De Neef, 42 Cal.App.2d 691, 109 P.2d 741 (1941). But see People v. Keller, 165 Cal.App.2d 419, 423–424, 332 P.2d 174, 176 (1958) (dictum).

A guardian of an incompetent spouse may claim the privilege on behalf of that spouse. However, when a spouse is dead, no one can claim the privilege for him; the privilege, if it is to be claimed at all, can be claimed only by or on behalf of the surviving spouse.

Termination of marriage. The privilege may be claimed as to confidential communications made during a marriage even though the marriage has been terminated at the time the privilege is claimed. This states existing law. Code Civ.Proc. § 1881(1) (superseded by the Evidence Code; People v. Mullings, 83 Cal. 138, 23 Pac. 229 (1890)). Free and open communication between spouses would be unduly inhibited if one of the spouses could be compelled to testify as to the nature of such communications after the termination of the marriage.

Eavesdroppers. The privilege may be asserted to prevent testimony by anyone, including eavesdroppers. To a limited extent, this constitutes a change in California law. See the Comment to Evidence Code § 954. See generally People v. Peak, 66 Cal.App.2d 894, 153 P.2d 464 (1944); People v. Morhar, 78 Cal.App. 380, 248 Pac. 975 (1926); People v. Mitchell, 61 Cal.App. 569, 215 Pac. 117 (1923). Section 980 also changes the existing law which permits a third party, to whom one of the spouses had revealed a confidential communication, to testify concerning it. People v. Swaile, 12 Cal.App. 192, 195–196, 107 Pac. 134, 137 (1909); People v. Chadwick, 4 Cal.App. 63, 72, 87 Pac. 384, 387, 388 (1906). See also Wolfle v. United States, 291 U.S. 7 (1934). Under Section 912, such conduct would constitute a waiver of the privilege only as to the spouse who makes the disclosure. [7 Cal.L.Rev.Comm. Reports 1 (1965)]

§ 981. Exception: Crime or fraud

There is no privilege under this article if the communication was made, in whole or in part, to enable or aid anyone to commit or plan to commit a crime or a fraud.

LAW REVISION COMMISSION COMMENT

California recognizes this as an exception to the lawyer-client privilege, but it does not appear to have been recognized in the California cases dealing with the confidential marital communications privilege. Nonetheless, the exception does not seem so broad that it would impair the values that the privilege is intended to preserve; in many cases, the evidence which would be admissible under this exception will be vital in order to do justice between the parties to a lawsuit. This exception would not, of course, infringe on the privileges accorded to a married person under Sections 970 and 971.

It is important to note that the exception provided by Section 981 is quite limited. It does not permit disclosure of communications that merely reveal a plan to commit a crime or fraud; it permits disclosure only of communications made to enable or aid anyone to commit or plan to commit a crime or fraud. Thus, unless the communication is for the purpose of obtaining assistance in the commission of the crime or fraud or in furtherance thereof, it is not made admissible by the exception provided in this section. Cf. People v. Pierce, 61 Cal.2d 879, 40 Cal.Rptr. 845, 395 P.2d 893 (1964) (husband and wife who conspire only between themselves against others cannot claim immunity from prosecution for conspiracy on the basis of their marital status). [7 Cal.L.Rev.Comm. Reports 1 (1965)]

§ 982. Commitment or similar proceeding

There is no privilege under this article in a proceeding to commit either spouse or otherwise place him or his property, or both, under the control of another because of his alleged mental or physical condition.

LAW REVISION COMMISSION COMMENT

Sections 982 and 983 express existing law. Code Civ.Proc. § 1881(1) (superseded by the Evidence Code). Commitment and competency proceedings are undertaken for the benefit of the subject person. Frequently, much or all of the evidence bearing on a spouse's competency or lack of competency will consist of communications to the other spouse. It would be undesirable to permit either spouse to invoke a privilege to prevent the presentation of this vital information inasmuch as these proceedings are of such vital importance both to society and to the spouse who is the subject of the proceedings. [7 Cal.L.Rev.Comm. Reports 1 (1965)]

§ 983. Competency proceedings

There is no privilege under this article in a proceeding brought by or on behalf of either spouse to establish his competence.

LAW REVISION COMMISSION COMMENT

See the Comment to Section 982. [7 Cal.L.Rev.Comm. Reports 1 (1965)]

§ 984. Proceeding between spouses

There is no privilege under this article in:

(a) A proceeding brought by or on behalf of one spouse against the other spouse.

(b) A proceeding between a surviving spouse and a person who claims through the deceased spouse, regardless of whether such claim is by testate or intestate succession or by inter vivos transaction.

LAW REVISION COMMISSION COMMENT

The exception to the marital communications privilege for litigation between the spouses states existing law. Code Civ.Proc. § 1881(1) (superseded by the Evidence Code). Section 984 extends the principle to cases where one of the spouses is dead and the litigation is between his successor and the surviving spouse. See generally Estate of Gillett, 73 Cal.App.2d 588, 166 P.2d 870 (1946). [7 Cal.L.Rev.Comm. Reports 1 (1965)]

§ 985. Criminal proceedings

There is no privilege under this article in a criminal proceeding in which one spouse is charged with:

(a) A crime committed at any time against the person or property of the other spouse or of a child of either.

(b) A crime committed at any time against the person or property of a third person committed in the course of committing a crime against the person or property of the other spouse.

(c) Bigamy.

(d) A crime defined by Section 270 or 270a of the Penal Code.

LAW REVISION COMMISSION COMMENT

This exception restates with minor variations an exception that is recognized under existing law. Code Civ.Proc. § 1881(1) (superseded by the Evidence Code). Sections 985 and 986 together create an exception for all the proceedings mentioned in Section 1322 of the Penal Code (superseded by the Evidence Code). [7 Cal.L.Rev.Comm. Reports 1 (1965)]

§ 986. Juvenile court proceedings

There is no privilege under this article in a proceeding under the Juvenile Court Law, Chapter 2 (commencing with Section 200) of Part 1 of Division 2 of the Welfare and Institutions Code.

LAW REVISION COMMISSION COMMENT

See the Comment to Section 985. [7 Cal.L.Rev.Comm. Reports 1 (1965)]

§ 987. Exception—Communication offered by spouse who is criminal defendant

There is no privilege under this article in a criminal proceeding in which the communication is offered in evidence by a defendant who is one of the spouses between whom the communication was made.

LAW REVISION COMMISSION COMMENT

This exception does not appear to have been recognized in any California case. Nonetheless, it is a desirable exception. When a married person is the defendant in a criminal proceeding and seeks to introduce evidence which is material to his defense, his spouse (or his former spouse) should not be privileged to withhold the information. [7 Cal.L.Rev.Comm. Reports 1 (1965)]

ARTICLE 6. PHYSICIAN–PATIENT PRIVILEGE

§ 990. Physician

As used in this article, "physician" means a person authorized, or reasonably believed by the patient to be authorized, to practice medicine in any state or nation.

LAW REVISION COMMISSION COMMENT

Defining "physician" to include a person "reasonably believed by the patient to be authorized" to practice medicine changes the existing law which requires that the physician be licensed. See Code Civ.Proc. § 1881(4) (superseded by the Evidence Code). But, if this privilege is to be recognized, it should protect the patient from reasonable mistakes as to unlicensed practitioners. The privilege also should be applicable to communications made to a physician authorized to practice in any state or nation. When a California resident travels outside the State and has occasion to visit a physician during such travel, or when a physician from another state or nation participates in the treatment of a person in California, the patient should be entitled to assume that his communications will be given as much protection as they would be if he consulted a California physician in California. A patient should not be forced to inquire about the jurisdictions where the physician is authorized to practice medicine and whether such jurisdictions recognize the physician-patient privilege before he may safely communicate with the physician. [7 Cal.L.Rev.Comm. Reports 1 (1965)]

§ 991. Patient

As used in this article, "patient" means a person who consults a physician or submits to an examination by a physician for the purpose of securing a diagnosis or preventive, palliative, or curative treatment of his physical or mental or emotional condition.

COMMENT—SENATE COMMITTEE ON JUDICIARY

"Patient" means a person who consults a physician for the purpose of diagnosis or treatment. This definition modifies existing California law; under existing law, a person who consults a physician for diagnosis only has no physician-patient privilege. City & County of San Francisco v. Superior Court, 37 Cal.2d 227, 231, 231 P.2d 26, 28 (1951) (physician-patient privilege "cannot be invoked when no treatment is contemplated or given").

There seems to be little reason to perpetuate the distinction made between consultations for the purpose of diagnosis and consultations for the purpose of treatment. Persons do not ordinarily consult physicians from idle curiosity. They may be sent by their attorney to obtain a diagnosis in contemplation of some legal proceeding—in which case the attorney- client privilege will afford protection. See, e.g., City & County of San Francisco v. Superior Court, 37 Cal.2d 227, 231 P.2d 26 (1951). They may submit to an examination for insurance purposes—in which case the insurance contract will contain appropriate waiver provisions. They may seek diagnosis from one physician to check the diagnosis made by another. They may seek diagnosis from one physician in contemplation of seeking treatment from another. Communications made under such circumstances are as deserving of protection as are communications made to a treating physician.

§ 992. Confidential communication between patient and physician

As used in this article, "confidential communication between patient and physician" means information, including information obtained by an examination of the patient, transmitted between a patient and his physician in the course of that relationship and in confidence by a means which, so far as the patient is aware, discloses the information to no third persons other than those who are present to further the interest of the patient in the consultation or those to whom disclosure is reasonably necessary for the transmission of the information or the accomplishment of the purpose for which the physician is consulted, and includes a diagnosis made and the advice given by the physician in the course of that relationship.

COMMENT—ASSEMBLY COMMITTEE ON JUDICIARY

This section generally restates existing law, except that it is uncertain whether a doctor's statement to a patient giving his diagnosis is presently covered by the privilege. See Code Civ.Proc. § 1881(4) (superseded by the Evidence Code). See also the Comment to Evidence Code § 952.

The definition here is sufficiently broad to include matters that are not ordinarily thought of as "communications." It is the communications that are defined here, however, to which reference is made throughout the remainder of the article. Under Section 994, the privilege applies to the communications defined here. And the exceptions in Sections 996–1007 that relate to particular communications also apply to the communications defined here. Thus, there is no information protected by the privilege in Section 994 to which the exceptions cannot be applied in an appropriate case.

LAW REVISION COMMISSION COMMENT 1967 AMENDMENT

The express inclusion of "a diagnosis" in the last clause will preclude a possible construction of this section that would leave an uncommunicated diagnosis unprotected by the privilege. Such a construction would virtually destroy the privilege. [8 Cal.L.Rev.Comm. Reports 101 (1967)]

§ 993. Holder of the privilege

As used in this article, "holder of the privilege" means:

(a) The patient when he has no guardian or conservator.

(b) A guardian or conservator of the patient when the patient has a guardian or conservator.

(c) The personal representative of the patient if the patient is dead.

LAW REVISION COMMISSION COMMENT

A guardian of the patient is the holder of the privilege if the patient has a guardian. If the patient has separate guardians of his estate and of his person, either guardian may claim the privilege. The provision making the personal representative of the patient the holder of the privilege when the patient is dead may change California law. The existing law may be that the privilege survives the death of the patient in some cases and that no one can waive it on behalf of the patient. See the discussion in Tentative Recommendation and a Study Relating to the Uniform Rules of Evidence (Article V. Privileges), 6 Cal.Law Revision Comm'n, Rep., Rec. & Studies 201, 408–410 (1964). Sections 993 and 994 enable the personal representative to protect the interest of the patient's estate in the confidentiality of these statements and to waive the privilege when the estate would benefit by waiver. When the patient's estate has no interest in preserving confidentiality, or when the estate has been distributed and the representative discharged, the importance of providing complete access to information relevant to a particular proceeding should prevail over whatever remaining interest the decedent may have had in secrecy. [7 Cal.L.Rev.Comm. Reports 1 (1965)]

§ 994. Physician-patient privilege

Subject to Section 912 and except as otherwise provided in this article, the patient, whether or not a party, has a privilege to refuse to disclose, and to prevent another from disclosing, a confidential communication between patient and physician if the privilege is claimed by:

(a) The holder of the privilege;

(b) A person who is authorized to claim the privilege by the holder of the privilege; or

(c) The person who was the physician at the time of the confidential communication, but such person may not claim the privilege if there is no holder of the privilege in existence or if he or she is otherwise instructed by a person authorized to permit disclosure.

The relationship of a physician and patient shall exist between a medical or podiatry corporation as defined in the Medical Practice Act and the patient to whom it renders professional services, as well as between such patients and licensed physicians and surgeons employed by such corporation to render services to such patients. The word "persons" as used in this subdivision includes partnerships, corporations, limited liability companies, associations, and other groups and entities.

LAW REVISION COMMISSION COMMENT

This section, like Section 954 (lawyer-client privilege), is based on the premise that the privilege must be claimed by a person who is authorized to claim the privilege. If there is no claim of privilege by a person with authority to make the claim, the evidence is admissible. See the Comments to Evidence Code §§ 993 and 954.

For the reasons indicated in the Comment to Section 954, an eavesdropper or other interceptor of a communication privileged under this section is not permitted to testify to the communication. [7 Cal. L.Rev.Comm. Reports 1 (1965)]

§ 995. When physician required to claim privilege

The physician who received or made a communication subject to the privilege under this article shall claim the privilege whenever he is present when the communication is sought to be disclosed and is authorized to claim the privilege under subdivision (c) of Section 994.

LAW REVISION COMMISSION COMMENT

The obligation of the physician to claim the privilege on behalf of the patient, unless otherwise instructed by a person authorized to permit disclosure, is consistent with Section 2379 of the Business and Professions Code. [7 Cal.L.Rev.Comm. Reports 1 (1965)]

§ 996. Patient-litigant exception

There is no privilege under this article as to a communication relevant to an issue concerning the condition of the patient if such issue has been tendered by:

(a) The patient;

(b) Any party claiming through or under the patient;

(c) Any party claiming as a beneficiary of the patient through a contract to which the patient is or was a party; or

(d) The plaintiff in an action brought under Section 376 or 377 of the Code of Civil Procedure for damages for the injury or death of the patient.

LAW REVISION COMMISSION COMMENT

Section 996 provides that the physician-patient privilege does not exist in any proceeding in which an issue concerning the condition of the patient has been tendered by the patient. If the patient himself tenders the issue of his condition, he should not be able to withhold relevant evidence from the opposing party by the exercise of the physician-patient privilege.

A limited form of this exception is recognized by Code of Civil Procedure Section 1881(4) (superseded by the Evidence Code) which makes the privilege inapplicable in personal injury actions. This exception is also recognized in various types of administrative proceedings where the patient tenders the issue of his condition. E.g., Labor Code §§ 4055, 5701, 5703, 6407, 6408 (proceedings before the Industrial Accident Commission). The exception provided by Section 996 applies not only to proceedings before the Industrial Accident Commission but also to any other proceeding where the patient tenders the issue of his condition. The exception in Section 996 also states existing law in applying the exception to other situations where the patient himself has raised the issue of his condition. In re Cathey, 55 Cal.2d 679, 690–692, 12 Cal.Rptr. 762, 768, 361 P.2d 426, 432 (1961) (prisoner in state medical facility waived physician-patient privilege by putting his mental condition in issue by application for habeas corpus); see also City & County of San Francisco v. Superior Court, 37 Cal.2d 227, 232, 231 P.2d 26, 28 (1951) (personal injury case).

Section 996 also provides that there is no privilege in an action brought under Section 377 of the Code of Civil Procedure (wrongful death). Under Code of Civil Procedure Section 1881(4) (superseded by the Evidence Code), a person authorized to bring the wrongful death action may consent to the testimony by the physician. As far as testimony by the physician is concerned, there is no reason why the rules of evidence should be different in a case where the patient brings the action and a case where someone else sues for the patient's wrongful death.

Section 996 also provides that there is no privilege in an action brought under Section 376 of the Code of Civil Procedure (parent's action for injury to child). In this case, as in a case under the wrongful death statute, the same rule of evidence should apply when the parent brings the action as applies when the child is the plaintiff. [7 Cal.L.Rev. Comm. Reports 1 (1965)]

§ 997. Exception: Crime or tort

There is no privilege under this article if the services of the physician were sought or obtained to enable or aid anyone to commit or plan to commit a crime or a tort or to escape detection or apprehension after the commission of a crime or a tort.

LAW REVISION COMMISSION COMMENT

This section is considerably broader in scope than Section 956 which provides that the lawyer-client privilege does not apply when the communication was made to enable anyone to commit or plan to commit a crime or a fraud. Section 997 creates an exception to the physician-patient privilege where the services of the physician were sought or obtained to enable or aid anyone to commit or plan to commit a crime or a tort, or to escape detection or apprehension after commission of a crime or a tort. People seldom, if ever, consult their physicians in regard to matters which might subsequently be determined to be a tort, and there is no desirable end to be served by encouraging such communications. On the other hand, people often consult lawyers about matters which may later turn out to be torts and it is desirable to encourage discussion of such matters with lawyers. Whether the exception provided by Section 997 now exists in California has not been determined in any decided case, but it probably would be recognized in an appropriate case in view of the similar court- created exception to the lawyer-client privilege. See the Comment to Evidence Code § 956. [7 Cal.L.Rev. Comm. Reports 1 (1965)]

§ 998. Exception: Criminal proceeding

There is no privilege under this article in a criminal proceeding.

COMMENT—ASSEMBLY COMMITTEE ON JUDICIARY

The physician-patient privilege is not now applicable in a criminal proceeding. Code Civ.Proc. § 1881(4) (superseded by the Evidence Code). See also People v. Griffith, 146 Cal. 339, 80 Pac. 68 (1905).

§ 999. Communication relating to patient condition in proceeding to recover damages; good cause

There is no privilege under this article as to a communication relevant to an issue concerning the condition of the patient in a proceeding to recover damages on account of the conduct of the patient if good cause for disclosure of the communication is shown.

COMMENT

Section 999 makes the physician-patient privilege inapplicable in civil actions to recover damages for any criminal conduct, whether or not felonious, on the part of the patient. Under Sections 1290–1292 (hearsay), the evidence admitted in the criminal trial would be admissible in a subsequent civil trial as former testimony. Thus, if the exception provided by Section 999 did not exist, the evidence subject to the privilege would be available in a civil trial only if a criminal trial were conducted first; it would not be available if the civil trial were conducted first. The admissibility of evidence should not depend on the order in which civil and criminal matters are tried. This exception is provided, therefore, so that the same evidence is available in the civil case without regard to when the criminal case is tried.

§ 1000. Parties claiming through deceased patient

There is no privilege under this article as to a communication relevant to an issue between parties all of whom claim through a deceased patient, regardless of whether the claims are by testate or intestate succession or by inter vivos transaction.

LAW REVISION COMMISSION COMMENT

See the Comment to Section 957. [7 Cal.L.Rev.Comm. Reports 1 (1965)]

§ 1001. Breach of duty arising out of physician-patient relationship

There is no privilege under this article as to a communication relevant to an issue of breach, by the physician or by the patient, of a duty arising out of the physician-patient relationship.

LAW REVISION COMMISSION COMMENT

See the Comment to Section 658. [7 Cal.L.Rev.Comm. Reports 1 (1965)]

§ 1002. Intention of deceased patient concerning writing affecting property interest

There is no privilege under this article as to a communication relevant to an issue concerning the intention of a patient, now deceased, with respect to a deed of conveyance, will, or other writing, executed by the patient, purporting to affect an interest in property.

LAW REVISION COMMISSION COMMENT

Existing law provides exceptions virtually coextensive with those provided in Sections 1002 and 1003. Code Civ.Proc. § 1881(4) (superseded by the Evidence Code). See the Comment to Section 960. [7 Cal.L.Rev.Comm. Reports 1 (1965)]

§ 1003. Validity of writing affecting property interest

There is no privilege under this article as to a communication relevant to an issue concerning the validity of a deed of conveyance, will, or other writing, executed by a patient, now deceased, purporting to affect an interest in property.

LAW REVISION COMMISSION COMMENT

See the Comment to Section 1002. [7 Cal.L.Rev.Comm. Reports 1 (1965)]

§ 1004. Commitment or similar proceeding

There is no privilege under this article in a proceeding to commit the patient or otherwise place him or his property, or both, under the control of another because of his alleged mental or physical condition.

LAW REVISION COMMISSION COMMENT

This exception covers not only commitments of mentally ill persons but also such cases as the appointment of a conservator under Probate Code Section 1751. In these cases, the proceedings are being conducted for the benefit of the patient and he should not have a privilege to withhold evidence that the court needs in order to act properly for his welfare. There is no similar exception in existing law. McClenahan v. Keyes, 188 Cal. 574, 584, 206 Pac. 454, 458 (1922) (dictum). But see 35 Ops.Cal.Atty.Gen. 226 (1960), regarding the unavailability of the present physician-patient privilege where the physician acts pursuant to court appointment for the explicit purpose of giving testimony. [7 Cal.L.Rev. Comm. Reports 1 (1965)]

§ 1005. Proceeding to establish competence

There is no privilege under this article in a proceeding brought by or on behalf of the patient to establish his competence.

LAW REVISION COMMISSION COMMENT

This exception is new to California law. When a patient has placed his mental condition in issue by instituting a proceeding to establish his competence, he should not be permitted to withhold the most vital evidence relating thereto. [7 Cal.L.Rev.Comm. Reports 1 (1965)]

§ 1006. Required report

There is no privilege under this article as to information that the physician or the patient is required to report to a public employee, or as to information required to be recorded in a public office, if such report or record is open to public inspection.

LAW REVISION COMMISSION COMMENT

This exception is not recognized by existing law. However, no valid purpose is served by preventing the use of relevant information when the law requiring the information to be reported to a public office does not restrict disclosure. [7 Cal.L.Rev.Comm. Reports 1 (1965)]

§ 1007. Exception—Proceeding to terminate right, license or privilege

There is no privilege under this article in a proceeding brought by a public entity to determine whether a right, authority, license, or privilege (including the right or privilege to be employed by the public entity or to hold a public office) should be revoked, suspended, terminated, limited, or conditioned.

ARTICLE 7. PSYCHOTHERAPIST–PATIENT PRIVILEGE

§ 1010. Psychotherapist

As used in this article, "psychotherapist" means a person who is, or is reasonably believed by the patient to be:

(a) A person authorized to practice medicine in any state or nation who devotes, or is reasonably believed by the patient to devote, a substantial portion of his or her time to the practice of psychiatry.

(b) A person licensed as a psychologist under Chapter 6.6 (commencing with Section 2900) of Division 2 of the Business and Professions Code.

(c) A person licensed as a clinical social worker under Article 4 (commencing with Section 4996) of Chapter 14 of Division 2 of the Business and Professions Code, when he or she is engaged in applied psychotherapy of a nonmedical nature.

(d) A person who is serving as a school psychologist and holds a credential authorizing that service issued by the state.

(e) A person licensed as a marriage and family therapist under Chapter 13 (commencing with Section 4980) of Division 2 of the Business and Professions Code.

(f) A person registered as a psychological assistant who is under the supervision of a licensed psychologist or board certified psychiatrist as required by Section 2913 of the Business and Professions Code, or a person registered as a marriage and family therapist intern who is under the supervision of a licensed marriage and family therapist, a licensed clinical social worker, a licensed psychologist, or a licensed physician certified in psychiatry, as specified in Section 4980.44 of the Business and Professions Code.

(g) A person registered as an associate clinical social worker who is under the supervision of a licensed clinical social worker, a licensed psychologist, or a board certified psychiatrist as required by Section 4996.20 or 4996.21 of the Business and Professions Code.

(h) A person exempt from the Psychology Licensing Law pursuant to subdivision (d) of Section 2909 of the Business and Professions Code who is under the supervision of a licensed psychologist or board certified psychiatrist.

(i) A psychological intern as defined in Section 2911 of the Business and Professions Code who is under the supervision of a licensed psychologist or board certified psychiatrist.

(j) A trainee, as defined in subdivision (c) of Section 4980.03 of the Business and Professions Code, who is fulfilling his or her supervised practicum required by subdivision (b) of Section 4980.40 of the Business and Professions Code and is supervised by a licensed psychologist, board certified psychiatrist, a licensed clinical social worker, or a licensed marriage and family therapist.

(k) A person licensed as a registered nurse pursuant to Chapter 6 (commencing with Section 2700) of Division 2 of the Business and Professions Code, who possesses a master's degree in psychiatric mental health nursing.

(*l*) A person rendering mental health treatment or counseling services as authorized pursuant to Section 6924 of the Family Code.

LAW REVISION COMMISSION COMMENT

A "psychotherapist" is defined to include only a person who is or who is reasonably believed to be a psychiatrist or who is a California certified psychologist (see Bus. & Prof.Code § 2900 et seq.). See the Comment to Section 990. [7 Cal.L.Rev.Comm. Reports 1 (1965)]

§ 1010.5. Privileged communication between patient and educational psychologist

A communication between a patient and an educational psychologist, licensed under Article 5 (commencing with Section 4986) of Chapter 13 of Division 2 of the Business and Professions Code, shall be privileged to the same extent, and subject to the same limitations, as a communication between a patient and a psychotherapist described in subdivisions (c), (d), and (e) of Section 1010.

§ 1011. Patient

As used in this article, "patient" means a person who consults a psychotherapist or submits to an examination by a psychotherapist for the purpose of securing a diagnosis or preventive, palliative, or curative treatment of his mental or emotional condition or who submits to an examination of his mental or emotional condition for the purpose of scientific research on mental or emotional problems.

COMMENT—ASSEMBLY COMMITTEE ON JUDICIARY

See the Comment to Section 991. Section 1011 is comparable to Section 991 (physician-patient privilege) except that the definition of "patient" in Section 1011 includes not only persons seeking diagnosis or treatment of a mental or emotional condition but also persons who submit to examination for purposes of psychiatric or psychological research. See the Comment to Section 1014.

§ 1012. Confidential communication between patient and psychotherapist

As used in this article, "confidential communication between patient and psychotherapist" means information, including information obtained by an examination of the patient, transmitted between a patient and his psychotherapist in the course of that relationship and in confidence by a means which, so far as the patient is aware, discloses the information to no third persons other than those who are present to further the interest of the patient in the consultation, or those to whom disclosure is reasonably necessary for the transmission of the information or the accomplishment of the purpose for which the psychotherapist is consulted, and includes a diagnosis made and the advice given by the psychotherapist in the course of that relationship.

LAW REVISION COMMISSION COMMENT

1965 Enactment

See the Comment to Section 992. [7 Cal.L.Rev.Comm. Reports 1 (1965)]

1967 Amendment

The express inclusion of "a diagnosis" in the last clause will preclude a possible construction of this section that would leave an uncommunicated diagnosis unprotected by the privilege. Such a construction would virtually destroy the privilege. [8 Cal.L.Rev.Comm. Reports 101 (1967)]

1970 Amendment

Section 1012 is amended to add "including other patients present at joint therapy" in order to foreclose the possibility that the section would be construed not to embrace marriage counseling, family counseling, and other forms of group therapy. However, it should be noted that communications made in the course of joint therapy are within the privilege only if they are made "in confidence" and "by a means which ... discloses the information to no third persons other than those ... to whom disclosure is reasonably necessary for ... the accomplishment of the purpose for which the psychotherapist is consulted." The making of a communication that meets these two requirements in the course of joint therapy would not amount to a waiver of the privilege. See Evidence Code Section 912(c) and (d).

The other amendments are technical and conform the language of Section 1012 to that of Section 992, the comparable section relating to the physician-patient privilege. Deletion of the words "or examination" makes no substantive change since "consultation" is broad enough to cover an examination. See Section 992. Substitution of "for which the psychotherapist is consulted" for "of the consultation or examination" adopts the broader language used in subdivision (d) of Section 912 and in Section 992. [9 Cal.L.Rev.Comm. Reports 153 (1969)]

§ 1013. Holder of the privilege

As used in this article, "holder of the privilege" means:

(a) The patient when he has no guardian or conservator.

(b) A guardian or conservator of the patient when the patient has a guardian or conservator.

(c) The personal representative of the patient if the patient is dead.

LAW REVISION COMMISSION COMMENT

See the Comment to Section 993. [7 Cal.L.Rev.Comm. Reports 1 (1965)]

§ 1014. Psychotherapist-patient privilege; application to individuals and entities

Subject to Section 912 and except as otherwise provided in this article, the patient, whether or not a party, has a privilege to refuse to disclose, and to prevent another from disclosing, a confidential communication between patient and psychotherapist if the privilege is claimed by:

(a) The holder of the privilege.

(b) A person who is authorized to claim the privilege by the holder of the privilege.

(c) The person who was the psychotherapist at the time of the confidential communication, but such person may not claim the privilege if there is no holder of the privilege in existence or if he or she is otherwise instructed by a person authorized to permit disclosure.

The relationship of a psychotherapist and patient shall exist between a psychological corporation as defined in Article 9 (commencing with Section 2995) of Chapter 6.6 of Division 2 of the Business and Professions Code, a marriage and family therapy corporation as defined in Article 6 (commencing with Section 4987.5) of Chapter 13 of Division 2 of the Business and Professions Code, or a licensed clinical social workers corporation as defined in Article 5 (commencing with Section 4998) of Chapter 14 of Division 2 of the Business and Professions Code, and the patient to whom it renders professional services, as well as between those patients and psychotherapists employed by those corporations to render services to those patients. The word "persons" as used in this subdivision includes partnerships, corporations, limited liability companies, associations and other groups and entities.

COMMENT—SENATE COMMITTEE ON JUDICIARY

This article creates a psychotherapist-patient privilege that provides much broader protection than the physician-patient privilege.

Psychiatrists now have only the physician-patient privilege which is enjoyed by physicians generally. On the other hand, persons who consult certified psychologists have a much broader privilege under Business and Professions Code Section 2904 (superseded by the Evidence Code). There is no rational basis for this distinction.

A broad privilege should apply to both psychiatrists and certified psychologists. Psychoanalysis and psychotherapy are dependent upon the fullest revelation of the most intimate and embarrassing details of the patient's life. Research on mental or emotional problems requires similar disclosure. Unless a patient or research subject is assured that such information can and will be held in utmost confidence, he will be reluctant to make the full disclosure upon which diagnosis and treatment or complete and accurate research depends.

The Law Revision Commission has received several reliable reports that persons in need of treatment sometimes refuse such treatment from psychiatrists because the confidentiality of their communications cannot be assured under existing law. Many of these persons are seriously disturbed and constitute threats to other persons in the community. Accordingly, this article establishes a new privilege that grants to patients of psychiatrists a privilege much broader in scope than the ordinary physician-patient privilege. Although it is recognized that the granting of the privilege may operate in particular cases to withhold relevant information, the interests of society will be better served if psychiatrists are able to assure patients that their confidences will be protected.

The Commission has also been informed that adequate research cannot be carried on in this field unless persons examined in connection therewith can be guaranteed that their disclosures will be kept confidential.

The privilege also applies to psychologists and supersedes the psychologist-patient privilege provided in Section 2904 of the Business and Professions Code. The new privilege is one for psychotherapists generally.

Generally, the privilege provided by this article follows the physician- patient privilege, and the Comments to Sections 990 through 1007 are pertinent. The following differences, however, should be noted:

(1) The psychotherapist-patient privilege applies in all proceedings. The physician-patient privilege does not apply in criminal proceedings. This difference in the scope of the two privileges is based on the fact that the Law Revision Commission has been advised that proper psychotherapy often is denied a patient solely because he will not walk freely to a psychotherapist for fear that the latter may be compelled in a criminal proceeding to reveal what he has been told. The Commission has also been advised that research in this field will be unduly hampered unless the privilege is available in criminal proceedings.

Although the psychotherapist-patient privilege applies in a criminal proceeding, the privilege is not available to a defendant who puts his mental or emotional condition in issue, as, for example, by a plea of insanity or a claim of diminished responsibility. See Evidence Code §§ 1016 and 1023. In such a proceeding, the trier of fact should have available to it all information that can be obtained in regard to the defendant's mental or emotional condition. That evidence can often be furnished by the psychotherapist who examined or treated the patient-defendant.

(2) There is an exception in the physician-patient privilege for commitment or guardianship proceedings for the patient. Evidence Code § 1004. Section 1024 provides a considerably narrower exception in the psychotherapist-patient privilege.

(3) The physician-patient privilege does not apply in civil actions for damages arising out of the patient's criminal conduct. Evidence Code § 999. Nor does it apply in certain administrative proceedings. Evidence Code § 1007. No similar exceptions are provided in the psychotherapist- patient privilege. These exceptions appear in the physician-patient privilege because that privilege does not apply in criminal proceedings. See Evidence Code § 998. Therefore, an exception is also created for comparable civil and administrative cases. The psychotherapist-patient privilege, however, does

apply in criminal cases; hence, there is no similar exception in administrative proceedings or civil actions involving the patient's criminal conduct.

§ 1014.5. Repealed by Stats.1994, c. 1270 (A.B.2659), § 2

§ 1015. When psychotherapist required to claim privilege

The psychotherapist who received or made a communication subject to the privilege under this article shall claim the privilege whenever he is present when the communication is sought to be disclosed and is authorized to claim the privilege under subdivision (c) of Section 1014.

LAW REVISION COMMISSION COMMENT

See the Comment to Section 995. [7 Cal.L.Rev.Comm. Reports 1 (1965)]

§ 1016. Exception: Patient-litigant exception

There is no privilege under this article as to a communication relevant to an issue concerning the mental or emotional condition of the patient if such issue has been tendered by:

(a) The patient;

(b) Any party claiming through or under the patient;

(c) Any party claiming as a beneficiary of the patient through a contract to which the patient is or was a party; or

(d) The plaintiff in an action brought under Section 376 or 377 of the Code of Civil Procedure for damages for the injury or death of the patient.

LAW REVISION COMMISSION COMMENT

See the Comment to Section 996. [7 Cal.L.Rev.Comm. Reports 1 (1965)]

§ 1017. Exception: Psychotherapist appointed by court or board of prison terms

(a) There is no privilege under this article if the psychotherapist is appointed by order of a court to examine the patient, but this exception does not apply where the psychotherapist is appointed by order of the court upon the request of the lawyer for the defendant in a criminal proceeding in order to provide the lawyer with information needed so that he or she may advise the defendant whether to enter or withdraw a plea based on insanity or to present a defense based on his or her mental or emotional condition.

(b) There is no privilege under this article if the psychotherapist is appointed by the Board of Prison Terms to examine a patient pursuant to the provisions of Article 4 (commencing with Section 2960) of Chapter 7 of Title 1 of Part 3 of the Penal Code.

LAW REVISION COMMISSION COMMENT

1965 Enactment

Section 1017 provides an exception to the psychotherapist-patient privilege if the psychotherapist is appointed by order of a court to examine the patient. Generally, where the relationship of psychotherapist and patient is created by court order, there is not a sufficiently confidential relationship to warrant extending the privilege to communications made in the course of that relationship. Moreover, when the psychotherapist is appointed by the court, it is most often for the purpose of having the psychotherapist testify concerning his conclusions as to the patient's condition. It would be inappropriate to have the privilege apply in this situation. See generally 35 Ops.Cal.Atty.Gen. 226 (1960), regarding the unavailability of the present physician-patient privilege under these circumstances.

On the other hand, it is essential that the privilege apply where the psychotherapist is appointed by order of the court to provide the defendant's lawyer with information needed so that he may advise the defendant whether to enter a plea based on insanity or to present a defense based on his mental or emotional condition. If the defendant determines not to tender the issue of his mental or emotional condition, the privilege will protect the confidentiality of the communication between him and his court-appointed psychotherapist. If, however, the defendant determines to tender this issue—by a plea of not guilty by reason of insanity, by presenting a defense based on his mental or emotional condition, or by raising the question of his sanity at the time of the trial—the exceptions provided in Sections 1016 and 1023 make the privilege unavailable to prevent disclosure of the communications between the defendant and the psychotherapist. [7 Cal.L.Rev.Comm. Reports 1 (1965)]

1967 Amendment

The words "or withdraw" are added to Section 1017 to make it clear that the psychotherapist-patient privilege applies in a case where the defendant in a criminal proceeding enters a plea based on insanity, submits to an examination by a court-appointed psychotherapist, and later withdraws the plea based on insanity prior to the trial on that issue. In such case, since the defendant does not tender an issue based on his mental or emotional condition at the trial, the privilege should remain applicable. Of course, if the defendant determines to go to trial on the plea based on insanity, the psychotherapist-patient privilege will not be applicable. See Section 1016.

It should be noted that violation of the constitutional right to counsel may require the exclusion of evidence that is not privileged under this article; and, even in cases where this constitutional right is not violated, the protection that this right affords may require certain procedural safeguards in the examination procedure and a limiting instruction if the psychotherapist's testimony is admitted. See In re Spencer, 63 Cal.2d 400, 46 Cal.Rptr. 753, 406 P.2d 33 (1965).

It is important to recognize that the attorney-client privilege may provide protection in some cases where an exception to the psychotherapist- patient privilege is applicable. See Section 952 and the Comment thereto. See also Sections 912(d) and 954 and the Comments thereto. [8 Cal.L.Rev.Comm. Reports 101 (1967)]

§ 1018. Exception: Crime or tort

There is no privilege under this article if the services of the psychotherapist were sought or obtained to enable or aid anyone to commit or plan to commit a crime or a tort or to escape detection or apprehension after the commission of a crime or a tort.

LAW REVISION COMMISSION COMMENT

See the Comment to Section 997. [7 Cal.L.Rev.Comm. Reports 1 (1965)]

§ 1019. Exception: Parties claiming through deceased patient

There is no privilege under this article as to a communication relevant to an issue between parties all of whom claim through a deceased patient, regardless of whether the claims are by testate or intestate succession or by inter vivos transaction.

LAW REVISION COMMISSION COMMENT

See the Comment to Section 957. [7 Cal.L.Rev.Comm. Reports 1 (1965)]

§ 1020. Exception: Breach of duty arising out of psychotherapist-patient relationship

There is no privilege under this article as to a communication relevant to an issue of breach, by the psychotherapist or by the patient, of a duty arising out of the psychotherapist-patient relationship.

LAW REVISION COMMISSION COMMENT

See the Comment to Section 958. [7 Cal.L.Rev.Comm. Reports 1 (1965)]

§ 1021. Exception: Intention of deceased patient concerning writing affecting property interest

There is no privilege under this article as to a communication relevant to an issue concerning the intention of a patient, now deceased, with respect to a deed of conveyance, will, or other writing, executed by the patient, purporting to affect an interest in property.

LAW REVISION COMMISSION COMMENT

See the Comment to Section 1002. [7 Cal.L.Rev.Comm. Reports 1 (1965)]

§ 1022. Exception: Validity of writing affecting property interest

There is no privilege under this article as to a communication relevant to an issue concerning the validity of a deed of conveyance, will, or other writing, executed by a patient, now deceased, purporting to affect an interest in property.

LAW REVISION COMMISSION COMMENT

See the Comment to Section 1002. [7 Cal.L.Rev.Comm. Reports 1 (1965)]

§ 1023. Exception: Proceeding to determine sanity of criminal defendant

There is no privilege under this article in a proceeding under Chapter 6 (commencing with Section 1367) of Title 10 of Part 2 of the Penal Code initiated at the request of the defendant in a criminal action to determine his sanity.

LAW REVISION COMMISSION COMMENT

Section 1023 is included to make it clear that the psychotherapist-patient privilege does not apply when the defendant raises the issue of his sanity at the time of trial. The section probably is unnecessary because the exception provided by Section 1016 is broad enough to cover this situation. [7 Cal.L.Rev.Comm. Reports 1 (1965)]

§ 1024. Exception: Patient dangerous to himself or others

There is no privilege under this article if the psychotherapist has reasonable cause to believe that the patient is in such mental or emotional condition as to be dangerous to himself or to the person or property of another and that disclosure of the communication is necessary to prevent the threatened danger.

LAW REVISION COMMISSION COMMENT

This section provides a narrower exception to the psychotherapist-patient privilege than the comparable exceptions provided by Section 982 (privilege for confidential marital communications) and Section 1004 (physician- patient privilege). Although this exception might inhibit the relationship between the patient and his psychotherapist to a limited extent, it is essential that appropriate action be taken if the psychotherapist becomes convinced during the course of treatment that the patient is a menace to himself or others and the patient refuses to permit the psychotherapist to make the disclosure necessary to prevent the threatened danger. [7 Cal.L.Rev.Comm. Reports 1 (1965)]

§ 1025. Exception: Proceeding to establish competence

There is no privilege under this article in a proceeding brought by or on behalf of the patient to establish his competence.

LAW REVISION COMMISSION COMMENT

See the Comment to Section 1005. [7 Cal.L.Rev.Comm. Reports 1 (1965)]

§ 1026. Exception: Required report

There is no privilege under this article as to information that the psychotherapist or the patient is required to report to a public employee or as to information required to be recorded in a public office, if such report or record is open to public inspection.

LAW REVISION COMMISSION COMMENT

See the Comment to Section 1006. [7 Cal.L.Rev.Comm. Reports 1 (1965)]

§ 1027. Exception: Child under 16 victim of crime

There is no privilege under this article if all of the following circumstances exist:

(a) The patient is a child under the age of 16.

(b) The psychotherapist has reasonable cause to believe that the patient has been the victim of a crime and that disclosure of the communication is in the best interest of the child.

LAW REVISION COMMISSION COMMENT 1970 ADDITION

Section 1027 provides an exception to the psychotherapist-patient privilege that is analogous to the exception provided by Section 1024 (patient dangerous to himself or others). The exception provided by Section 1027 is necessary to permit court disclosure of communications to a psychotherapist by a child who has been the victim of a crime (such as child abuse) in a proceeding in which the commission of such crime is a subject of inquiry. Although the exception provided by Section 1027 might inhibit the relationship between the patient and his psychotherapist to a limited extent, it is essential that appropriate action be taken if the psychotherapist becomes convinced during the course of treatment that the patient is the victim of a crime and that disclosure of the communication would be in the best interest of the child.

The text of both 1970 additions was identical. [9 Cal.L.Rev.Comm. Reports 137 (1970)]

§ 1028. Repealed by Stats.1985, c. 1077, §§ 1, 2

ARTICLE 8. CLERGYMAN–PENITENT PRIVILEGES

§ 1030. Member of the Clergy

As used in this article, a "member of the clergy" means a priest, minister, religious practitioner, or similar functionary of a church or of a religious denomination or religious organization.

LAW REVISION COMMISSION COMMENT

"Clergyman" is broadly defined in this section. [7 Cal.L.Rev.Comm. Reports 1 (1965)]

§ 1031. Penitent

As used in this article, "penitent" means a person who has made a penitential communication to a member of the clergy.

LAW REVISION COMMISSION COMMENT

This section defines "penitent" by incorporating the definitions in Sections 1030 and 1032. [7 Cal.L.Rev.Comm. Reports 1 (1965)]

§ 1032. Penitential communication

As used in this article, "penitential communication" means a communication made in confidence, in the presence of no third person so far as the penitent is aware, to a member of the clergy who, in the course of the discipline or practice of the clergy member's church, denomination, or organization, is authorized or accustomed to hear those communications and, under the discipline or tenets of his or her church, denomination, or organization, has a duty to keep those communications secret.

LAW REVISION COMMISSION COMMENT

Under existing law, the communication must be a "confession." Code Civ.Proc. § 1881(3) (superseded by the Evidence Code). Section 1032 extends the protection that traditionally has been provided only to those persons whose religious practice involves "confessions." [7 Cal. L.Rev.Comm. Reports 1 (1965)]

§ 1033. Privilege of penitent

Subject to Section 912, a penitent, whether or not a party, has a privilege to refuse to disclose, and to prevent another from disclosing, a penitential communication if he or she claims the privilege.

LAW REVISION COMMISSION COMMENT

This section provides the penitent with a privilege to refuse to disclose, and to prevent another from disclosing, a penitential communication. Because of the definition of "penitential communication," Section 1033 provides a broader privilege than the existing law.

Section 1033 differs from Code of Civil Procedure Section 1881(3) (superseded by the Evidence Code) in that Section 1881(3) gives a penitent a privilege only to prevent a clergyman from disclosing the communication. Literally, Section 1881(3) does not give the penitent himself the right to refuse disclosure. However, similar privilege statutes have been held to grant a privilege both to refuse to disclose and to prevent the other communicant from disclosing the privileged statement. See City & County of San Francisco v. Superior Court, 37 Cal.2d 227, 236, 231 P.2d 26, 31 (1951) (attorney-client privilege); Verdelli v. Gray's Harbor Commercial Co., 115 Cal. 517, 525–526, 47 Pac. 364, 366 (1897) ("a client cannot be compelled to disclose communications which his attorney cannot be permitted to disclose"). Hence, it is likely that Section 1881 (3) would be similarly construed.

Section 1033 also protects against disclosure by eavesdroppers. In this respect, the section provides the same scope of protection that is provided by the other confidential communication privileges. See the Comment to Section 954. [7 Cal.L.Rev.Comm. Reports 1 (1965)]

§ 1034. Privilege of clergy

Subject to Section 912, a member of the clergy, whether or not a party, has a privilege to refuse to disclose a penitential communication if he or she claims the privilege.

LAW REVISION COMMISSION COMMENT

This section provides the clergyman with a privilege in his own right. Moreover, he may claim this privilege even if the penitent has waived the privilege granted him by Section 1033.

There may be several reasons for granting clergyman the traditional priest-penitent privilege. At least one underlying reason seems to be that the law will not compel a clergyman to violate—nor punish him for refusing to violate—the tenets of his church which require him to maintain secrecy as to confidential statements made to him in the course of his religious duties. See generally 8 Wigmore, Evidence §§ 2394–2396 (McNaughton rev. 1961).

The clergyman is under no legal compulsion to claim the privilege. Hence, a penitential communication will be admitted if the clergyman fails to claim the privilege and the penitent is deceased, incompetent, absent, or fails to claim the privilege. This probably changes existing law; but, if so, the change is desirable. For example, if a murderer had confessed the crime to a clergyman, the clergyman might under some circumstances (e.g., if the murderer has died) decline to claim the privilege and instead, give the evidence on behalf of an innocent third party who had been indicted for the crime. The extent to which a clergyman should keep secret or reveal penitential communications is not an appropriate subject for legislation; the matter is better left to the discretion of the individual clergyman involved and the discipline of the religious body of which he is a member. [7 Cal.L.Rev.Comm. Reports 1 (1965)]

ARTICLE 8.5. SEXUAL ASSAULT VICTIM–COUNSELOR PRIVILEGE

§ 1035. Victim

As used in this article, "victim" means a person who consults a sexual assault victim counselor for the purpose of securing advice or assistance concerning a mental, physical, or emotional condition caused by a sexual assault.

§ 1035.2. Sexual assault victim counselor

As used in this article, "sexual assault victim counselor" means any of the following:

(a) A person who is engaged in any office, hospital, institution, or center commonly known as a rape crisis center, whose primary purpose is the rendering of advice or assistance to victims of sexual assault and who has received a certificate evidencing completion of a training program in the counseling of sexual assault victims issued by a counseling center that meets the criteria for the award of a grant established pursuant to Section 13837 of the Penal Code and who meets one of the following requirements:

(1) Is a psychotherapist as defined in Section 1010; has a master's degree in counseling or a related field; or has one year of counseling experience, at least six months of which is in rape crisis counseling.

(2) Has 40 hours of training as described below and is supervised by an individual who qualifies as a counselor under paragraph (1). The training, supervised by a person qualified under paragraph (1), shall include, but not be limited to, the following areas: law, medicine, societal attitudes, crisis intervention and counseling techniques, role playing, referral services, and sexuality.

(b) A person who is employed by any organization providing the programs specified in Section 13835.2 of the Penal Code, whether financially compensated or not, for the purpose of counseling and assisting sexual assault victims, and who meets one of the following requirements:

(1) Is a psychotherapist as defined in Section 1010; has a master's degree in counseling or a related field; or has one year of counseling experience, at least six months of which is in rape assault counseling.

(2) Has the minimum training for sexual assault counseling required by guidelines established by the employing agency pursuant to subdivision (c) of Section 13835.10 of the Penal Code, and is supervised by an individual who qualifies as a counselor under paragraph (1). The training, supervised by a person qualified under paragraph (1), shall include, but not be limited to, the following areas: law, victimology, counseling techniques, client and system advocacy, and referral services.

§ 1035.4. Confidential communication between the sexual assault counselor and the victim; disclosure

As used in this article, "confidential communication between the sexual assault counselor and the victim" means information transmitted between the victim and the sexual assault counselor in the course of their relationship and in confidence by a means which, so far as the victim is aware, discloses the information to no third persons other than those who are present to further the interests of the victim in the consultation or those to whom disclosures are reasonably necessary for the transmission of the information or an accomplishment of the purposes for which the sexual assault counselor is consulted. The term includes all information regarding the facts and circumstances involving the alleged sexual assault and also includes all information regarding the victim's prior or subsequent sexual conduct, and opinions regarding the victim's sexual conduct or reputation in sexual matters.

The court may compel disclosure of information received by the sexual assault counselor which constitutes relevant evidence of the facts and circumstances involving an alleged sexual assault about which the victim is complaining and which is the subject of a criminal proceeding if the court determines that the probative value outweighs the effect on the victim, the treatment relationship, and the treatment services if disclosure is compelled. The court may also compel disclosure in proceedings related to child abuse if the court determines the probative value outweighs the effect on the victim, the treatment relationship, and the treatment services if disclosure is compelled.

When a court is ruling on a claim of privilege under this article, the court may require the person from whom disclosure is sought or the person authorized to claim the privilege, or both, to disclose the information in chambers out of the presence and hearing of all persons except the person authorized to claim the privilege and such other persons as the person authorized to claim the privilege is willing to have present. If the judge determines that the information is privileged and must not be disclosed, neither he or she nor any other person may ever disclose, without the consent of a person authorized to permit disclosure, what was disclosed in the course of the proceedings in chambers.

If the court determines certain information shall be disclosed, the court shall so order and inform the defendant. If the court finds there is a reasonable likelihood that particular information is subject to disclosure pursuant to the balancing test provided in this section, the following procedure shall be followed:

(1) The court shall inform the defendant of the nature of the information which may be subject to disclosure.

(2) The court shall order a hearing out of the presence of the jury, if any, and at the hearing allow the questioning of the sexual assault counselor regarding the information which the court has determined may be subject to disclosure.

(3) At the conclusion of the hearing, the court shall rule which items of information, if any, shall be disclosed. The court may make an order stating what evidence may be introduced by the defendant and the nature of questions to be permitted. The defendant may then offer evidence pursuant to the order of the court. Admission of evidence concerning the sexual conduct of the complaining witness is subject to Sections 352, 782, and 1103.

§ 1035.6. Holder of the privilege

As used in this article, "holder of the privilege" means:

(a) The victim when such person has no guardian or conservator.

(b) A guardian or conservator of the victim when the victim has a guardian or conservator.

(c) The personal representative of the victim if the victim is dead.

§ 1035.8. Sexual assault victim-counselor privilege

A victim of a sexual assault, whether or not a party, has a privilege to refuse to disclose, and to prevent another from disclosing, a confidential communication between the victim and a sexual assault victim counselor if the privilege is claimed by:

(a) The holder of the privilege;

(b) A person who is authorized to claim the privilege by the holder of the privilege; or

(c) The person who was the sexual assault victim counselor at the time of the confidential communication, but such person may not claim the privilege if there is no holder of the privilege in existence or if he is otherwise instructed by a person authorized to permit disclosure.

§ 1036. Claim of privilege by sexual assault victim counselor

The sexual assault victim counselor who received or made a communication subject to the privilege under this article shall claim the privilege whenever he is present when the communication is sought to be disclosed and is authorized to claim the privilege under subdivision (c) of Section 1035.8.

§ 1036.2. Sexual assault

As used in this article, "sexual assault" includes all of the following:

(a) Rape, as defined in Section 261 of the Penal Code.

(b) Unlawful sexual intercourse, as defined in Section 261.5 of the Penal Code.

(c) Rape in concert with force and violence, as defined in Section 264.1 of the Penal Code.

(d) Rape of a spouse, as defined in Section 262 of the Penal Code.

(e) Sodomy, as defined in Section 286 of the Penal Code, except a violation of subdivision (e) of that section.

(f) A violation of Section 288 of the Penal Code.

(g) Oral copulation, as defined in Section 288a of the Penal Code, except a violation of subdivision (e) of that section.

(h) Sexual penetration, as defined in Section 289 of the Penal Code.

(i) Annoying or molesting a child under 18, as defined in Section 647a of the Penal Code.

(j) Any attempt to commit any of the above acts.

ARTICLE 8.7. DOMESTIC VIOLENCE VICTIM–COUNSELOR PRIVILEGE

§ 1037. Victim

As used in this article, "victim" means any person who suffers domestic violence, as defined in Section 1037.7.

§ 1037.1. Domestic violence counselor; qualifications

As used in this article "domestic violence counselor" means any of the following:

(a) A person who is employed by any organization providing the programs specified in Section 18294 of the Welfare and Institutions Code, whether financially compensated or not, for the purpose of rendering advice or assistance to victims of domestic violence, who has received specialized training in the counseling of domestic violence victims, and who meets one of the following requirements:

(1) Has a master's degree in counseling or a related field; or has one year of counseling experience, at least six months of which is in the counseling of domestic violence victims.

(2) Has at least 40 hours of training as specified in this paragraph and is supervised by an individual who qualifies as a counselor under paragraph (1); or is a psychotherapist, as defined in Section 1010. The training, supervised by a person qualified under paragraph (1), shall include, but need not be limited to, the following areas: history of domestic violence, civil and criminal law as it relates to domestic violence, societal attitudes towards domestic violence, peer counseling techniques, housing, public assistance and other financial resources available to meet the financial needs of domestic violence victims, and referral services available to domestic violence victims.

(b) A person who is employed by any organization providing the programs specified in Section 13835.2 of the Penal Code, whether financially compensated or not, for the purpose of counseling and assisting victims of domestic violence, and who meets one of the following requirements:

(1) Is a psychotherapist as defined in Section 1010; has a master's degree in counseling or a related field; or has one year of counseling experience, at least six months of which is in counseling victims of domestic violence.

(2) Has the minimum training for counseling victims of domestic violence required by guidelines established by the employing agency pursuant to subdivision (c) of Section 13835.10 of the Penal Code, and is supervised by an individual who qualifies as a counselor under paragraph (1). The training, supervised by a person qualified under paragraph (1), shall include, but not be limited to, the following areas: law, victimology, counseling techniques, client and system advocacy, and referral services.

§ 1037.2. Confidential communication; compulsion of disclosure by court; claim of privilege

As used in this article, "confidential communication" means information transmitted between the victim and the counselor in the course of their relationship and in confidence by a means which, so far as the victim is aware, discloses the information to no third persons other than those who are present to further the interests of the victim in the consultation or those to whom disclosures are reasonably necessary for the transmission of the information or an accomplishment of the purposes for which the domestic violence counselor is consulted. It includes all information regarding the facts and circumstances involving all incidences of domestic violence, as well as all information about the children of the victim or abuser and the relationship of the victim with the abuser.

The court may compel disclosure of information received by a domestic violence counselor which constitutes relevant evidence of the facts and circumstances involving a crime allegedly perpetrated against the victim or another household member and which is the subject of a criminal proceeding, if the court determines that the probative value of the information outweighs the effect of disclosure of the information on the victim, the counseling relationship, and the counseling services. The court may compel disclosure if the victim is either dead or not the complaining witness in a criminal action against the perpetrator. The court may also compel disclosure in proceedings related to child abuse if the court determines that the probative value of the evidence outweighs the effect of the disclosure on the victim, the counseling relationship, and the counseling services.

When a court rules on a claim of privilege under this article, it may require the person from whom disclosure is sought or the person authorized to claim the privilege, or both, to disclose the information in chambers out of the presence and hearing of all persons except the person authorized to claim the privilege and such other persons as the person authorized to claim the privilege consents to have present. If the judge determines that the information is privileged and shall not be disclosed, neither he nor she nor any other person may disclose, without the consent of a person authorized to permit disclosure, any information disclosed in the course of the proceedings in chambers.

If the court determines that information shall be disclosed, the court shall so order and inform the defendant in the criminal action. If the court finds there is a reasonable likelihood that any information is subject to disclosure pursuant to the balancing test provided in this section, the procedure specified in subdivisions (1), (2), and (3) of Section 1035.4 shall be followed.

§ 1037.3. Child abuse; reporting

Nothing in this article shall be construed to limit any obligation to report instances of child abuse as required by Section 11166 of the Penal Code.

§ 1037.4. Holder of the privilege

As used in this article, "holder of the privilege" means:

(a) The victim when he or she has no guardian or conservator.

(b) A guardian or conservator of the victim when the victim has a guardian or conservator.

§ 1037.5. Privilege of refusal to disclose communication; claimants

A victim of domestic violence, whether or not a party to the action, has a privilege to refuse to disclose, and to prevent another from disclosing, a confidential communication between the victim and a domestic violence counselor if the privilege is claimed by any of the following persons:

(a) The holder of the privilege.

(b) A person who is authorized to claim the privilege by the holder of the privilege.

(c) The person who was the domestic violence counselor at the time of the confidential communication. However, that person may not claim the privilege if there is no holder of the privilege in existence or if he or she is otherwise instructed by a person authorized to permit disclosure.

§ 1037.6. Claim of privilege by counselor

The domestic violence counselor who received or made a communication subject to the privilege granted by this article shall claim the privilege whenever he or she is present when the communication is sought to be disclosed and he or she is authorized to claim the privilege under subdivision (c) of Section 1037.5.

§ 1037.7. Domestic violence

As used in this article, "domestic violence" means "domestic violence" as defined in Section 6211 of the Family Code.

LAW REVISION COMMISSION COMMENT

1993 Addition

Section 1037.7 substitutes a reference to the Family Code provision defining "domestic violence" for the definitions of "abuse," "domestic violence," and "family or household member" in the former section. This is not a substantive change, since the Family Code definition of "domestic violence" continues the substance of the omitted definitions. See Fam. Code § 6211 ("domestic violence" defined) & Comment. See also Fam. Code §§ 6203 ("abuse" defined), 6209 ("cohabitant" and "former cohabitant" defined). [23 Cal.L.Rev.Comm. Reports 1 (1993)]

LAW REVISION COMMISSION COMMENT

1993 Addition

Section 1037.7 substitutes a reference to the Family Code provision defining "domestic violence" for the definitions of "abuse," "domestic violence," and "family or household member" in the former section. This is not a substantive change, since the Family Code definition of "domestic violence" continues the substance of the omitted definitions. See Fam. Code § 6211 ("domestic violence" defined) & Comment. See also Fam. Code §§ 6203 ("abuse" defined), 6209 ("cohabitant" and "former cohabitant" defined). [23 Cal.L.Rev.Comm. Reports 1 (1993)]

§ 1037.8. Notice; limitations on confidential communications

A domestic violence counselor shall inform a domestic violence victim of any applicable limitations on confidentiality of communications between the victim and the domestic violence counselor. This information may be given orally.

ARTICLE 9. OFFICIAL INFORMATION AND IDENTITY OF INFORMER

§ 1040. Privilege for official information

(a) As used in this section, "official information" means information acquired in confidence by a public employee in the course of his or her duty and not open, or officially disclosed, to the public prior to the time the claim of privilege is made.

(b) A public entity has a privilege to refuse to disclose official information, and to prevent another from disclosing official information, if the privilege is claimed by a person authorized by the public entity to do so and:

(1) Disclosure is forbidden by an act of the Congress of the United States or a statute of this state; or

(2) Disclosure of the information is against the public interest because there is a necessity for preserving the confidentiality of the information that outweighs the necessity for disclosure in the interest of justice; but no privilege may be claimed under this paragraph if any person authorized to do so has consented that the information be disclosed in the proceeding. In determining whether disclosure of the information is against the public interest, the interest of the public entity as a party in the outcome of the proceeding may not be considered.

(c) Notwithstanding any other provision of law, the Employment Development Department shall disclose to law enforcement agencies, in accordance with the provisions of subdivision (k) of Section 1095 and subdivision (b) of Section 2714 of the Unemployment Insurance Code, information in its possession relating to any person if an arrest warrant has been issued for the person for commission of a felony.

COMMENT—ASSEMBLY COMMITTEE ON JUDICIARY

Under existing law, official information is protected either by subdivision 5 of Code of Civil Procedure Section 1881 (which, like Section 1040, prohibits disclosure when the interest of the public would suffer thereby) or by specific statutes such as the provisions of the Revenue and Taxation Code prohibiting disclosure of information reported in tax returns. See, e.g., Rev. & Tax.Code §§ 19281–19289. Section 1881 is superseded by the Evidence Code, but the specific statutes protecting official information remain in effect. Evidence Code § 1040(b)(1).

Section 1040 permits the official information privilege to be invoked by the public entity or its authorized representative. Since the privilege is granted to enable the government to protect its secrets, no reason exists for permitting the privilege to be exercised by persons who are not concerned with the public interest. It should be noted, however, that another statute may provide a person with a privilege not to disclose a report he made to the government; the Evidence Code has no effect on that privilege. See the Comment to Evidence Code § 920. Where the government has received a report from an informant, the official information privilege may apply to that report. It does not apply, however, to the knowledge of the informant. The government does not acquire a privilege to prevent an informant from revealing his knowledge merely because that knowledge has been communicated to the government.

The official information privilege provided in Section 1040 does not extend to the identity of an informer. Section 1041 provides special rules for determining when the government has a privilege to keep secret the identity of an informer.

The privilege may be asserted to prevent testimony by anyone who has official information. This provides the public entity with more protection than existing law. See the Comment to Evidence Code § 954 (attorney-client privilege).

Official information is absolutely privileged if its disclosure is forbidden by either a federal or state statute. Other official information is subject to a conditional privilege: The judge must determine in each instance the consequences to the public of disclosure and the consequences to the litigant of nondisclosure and then decide which outweighs the other. He should, of course, be aware that the public has an interest in seeing that justice is done in the particular cause as well as an interest in the secrecy of the information.

§ 1041. Privilege for identity of informer

(a) Except as provided in this section, a public entity has a privilege to refuse to disclose the identity of a person who has furnished information as provided in subdivision (b) purporting to disclose a violation of a law of the United States or of this state or of a public entity in this state, and to prevent another from disclosing such identity, if the privilege is claimed by a person authorized by the public entity to do so and:

(1) Disclosure is forbidden by an act of the Congress of the United States or a statute of this state; or

(2) Disclosure of the identity of the informer is against the public interest because there is a necessity for preserving the confidentiality of his identity that outweighs the necessity for disclosure in the interest of justice; but no privilege may be claimed under this paragraph if any person authorized to do so has consented that the identity of the informer be disclosed in the proceeding. In determining whether disclosure of the identity of the informer is against the public interest, the interest of the public entity as a party in the outcome of the proceeding may not be considered.

(b) This section applies only if the information is furnished in confidence by the informer to:

(1) A law enforcement officer;

(2) A representative of an administrative agency charged with the administration or enforcement of the law alleged to be violated; or

(3) Any person for the purpose of transmittal to a person listed in paragraph (1) or (2).

(c) There is no privilege under this section to prevent the informer from disclosing his identity.

LAW REVISION COMMISSION COMMENT

Under existing law, the identity of an informer is protected by subdivision 5 of Code of Civil Procedure Section 1881 (which, like Section 1041, prohibits disclosure when the interest of the public would suffer thereby). Section 1881 is superseded by the Evidence Code.

This privilege may be claimed under the same conditions as the official information privilege may be claimed, except that it does not apply if a person is called as a witness and asked if he is the informer. [7 Cal.L.Rev.Comm. Reports 1 (1965)]

§ 1042. Adverse order or finding in certain cases

(a) Except where disclosure is forbidden by an act of the Congress of the United States, if a claim of privilege under this article by the state or a public entity in this state is sustained in a criminal proceeding, the presiding officer shall make such order or finding of fact adverse to the public entity bringing the proceeding as is required by law upon any issue in the proceeding to which the privileged information is material.

(b) Notwithstanding subdivision (a), where a search is made pursuant to a warrant valid on its face, the public entity bringing a criminal proceeding is not required to reveal to the defendant official information or the identity of an informer in order to establish the legality of the search or the admissibility of any evidence obtained as a result of it.

(c) Notwithstanding subdivision (a), in any preliminary hearing, criminal trial, or other criminal proceeding, any otherwise admissible evidence of information communicated to a peace officer by a confidential informant, who is not a material witness to the guilt or innocence of the accused of the offense charged, is admissible on the issue of reasonable cause to make an arrest or search without requiring that the name or identity of the informant be disclosed if the judge or magistrate is satisfied, based upon evidence produced in open court, out of the presence of the jury, that such information was received from a reliable informant and in his discretion does not require such disclosure.

(d) When, in any such criminal proceeding, a party demands disclosure of the identity of the informant on the ground the informant is a material witness on the issue of guilt, the court shall conduct a hearing at which all parties may present evidence on the issue of disclosure. Such hearing shall be conducted outside the presence of the jury, if any. During the hearing, if the privilege provided for in Section 1041 is claimed by a person authorized to do so or if a person who is authorized to claim such privilege refuses to answer any question on the ground that the answer would tend to disclose the identity of the informant, the prosecuting attorney may request that the court hold an in camera hearing. If such a request is made, the court shall hold such a hearing outside the presence of the defendant and his counsel. At the in camera hearing, the prosecution may offer evidence which would tend to disclose or which discloses the identity of the informant to aid the court in its determination whether there is a reasonable possibility that nondisclosure might deprive the defendant of a fair trial. A reporter shall be present at the in camera hearing. Any transcription of the proceedings at the in camera hearing, as well as any physical evidence presented at the hearing, shall be ordered sealed by the court, and only a court may have access to its contents. The court shall not order disclosure, nor strike the testimony of the witness who invokes the privilege, nor dismiss the criminal proceeding, if the party offering the witness refuses to disclose the identity of the informant, unless, based upon the evidence presented at the hearing held in the presence of the defendant and his counsel and the evidence presented at the in camera hearing, the court concludes that there is a reasonable possibility that nondisclosure might deprive the defendant of a fair trial.

COMMENT—ASSEMBLY COMMITTEE ON JUDICIARY

Section 1042 provides special rules regarding the consequences of invocation of the privileges provided in this article by the prosecution in a criminal proceeding.

Subdivision (a). This subdivision recognizes the existing California rule in a criminal case. As was stated by the United States Supreme Court in United States v. Reynolds, 345 U.S. 1, 12 (1953), "since the Government which prosecutes an accused also has the duty to see that justice is done, it is unconscionable to allow it to undertake prosecution and then invoke its governmental privileges to deprive the accused of anything which might be material to his defense." This policy applies if either the official information privilege (Section 1040) or the informer privilege (Section 1041) is exercised in a criminal proceeding.

In some cases, the privileged information will be material to the issue of the defendant's guilt or innocence; in such cases, the law requires that the court dismiss the case if the public entity does not reveal the information. People v. McShann, 50 Cal.2d 802, 330 P.2d 33 (1958). In other cases, the privileged information will relate to narrower issues, such as the legality of a search without a warrant; in those cases, the law requires that the court strike the testimony of a particular witness or make some other order appropriate under the circumstances if the public entity insists upon its privilege. Priestly v. Superior Court, 50 Cal.2d 812, 330 P.2d 39 (1958).

In cases where the legality of an arrest is in issue, Section 1042 does not require disclosure of the privileged information if there was reasonable cause for the arrest aside from the privileged information, for in such a case the identity of the informer is immaterial. Cf. People v. Hunt, 216 Cal.App.2d 753, 756–757, 31 Cal.Rptr. 221, 223 (1963) ("The rule requiring disclosure of an informer's identity has no application in situations where reasonable cause for arrest and search exists aside from the informer's communication.")

Subdivision (a) applies only if the privilege is asserted by the State of California or a public entity in the State of California. Subdivision (a) does not require the imposition of its sanction if the privilege is invoked in an action prosecuted by the State and the information is withheld by the federal government or another state. Nor may the sanction be imposed where disclosure is forbidden by federal statute. In these respects, subdivision (a) states existing California law. People v. Parham, 60 Cal.2d 378, 33 Cal.Rptr. 497, 384 P.2d 1001 (1963) (prior statements of prosecution witnesses withheld by the Federal Bureau of Investigation); denial of motion to strike witnesses' testimony affirmed.

Subdivision (b). This subdivision codifies the rule declared in People v. Keener, 55 Cal.2d 714, 723, 12 Cal.Rptr. 859, 864, 361 P.2d 587, 592 (1961), in which the court held that "where a search is made pursuant to a warrant valid on its face, the prosecution is not required to reveal the identity of the informer in order to establish the legality of the search and the admissibility of the evidence obtained as a result of it." Subdivision (b), however, applies to all official information, not merely to the identity of an informer.

Subdivision (b) does not affect the rule that a defendant is entitled to know the identity of an informer in a case where the informer is a material witness with respect to facts directly relating to the defendant's guilt.

§ 1043. Peace officer personnel records; discovery or disclosure; procedure

(a) In any case in which discovery or disclosure is sought of peace or custodial officer personnel records or records maintained pursuant to Section 832.5 of the Penal Code or information from those records, the party seeking the discovery or disclosure shall file a written motion with the appropriate court or administrative body upon written notice to the governmental agency which has custody and control of the records. The written notice shall be given at the times prescribed by subdivision (b) of Section 1005 of the Code of Civil Procedure. Upon receipt of the notice the governmental agency served shall immediately notify the individual whose records are sought.

(b) The motion shall include all of the following:

(1) Identification of the proceeding in which discovery or disclosure is sought, the party seeking discovery or disclosure, the peace or custodial officer whose records are sought, the governmental agency which has custody and control of the records, and the time and place at which the motion for discovery or disclosure shall be heard.

(2) A description of the type of records or information sought.

(3) Affidavits showing good cause for the discovery or disclosure sought, setting forth the materiality thereof to the subject matter involved in the pending litigation and stating upon reasonable belief that the governmental agency identified has the records or information from the records.

(c) No hearing upon a motion for discovery or disclosure shall be held without full compliance with the notice provisions of this section except upon a showing by the moving party of good cause for noncompliance, or upon a waiver of the hearing by the governmental agency identified as having the records.

§ 1044. Medical or psychological history records; right of access

Nothing in this article shall be construed to affect the right of access to records of medical or psychological history where such access would otherwise be available under Section 996 or 1016.

§ 1045. Peace officers; access to records of complaints or discipline imposed; relevancy; protective orders

(a) Nothing in this article shall be construed to affect the right of access to records of complaints, or investigations of complaints, or discipline imposed as a result of those investigations, concerning an event or transaction in which the peace officer or custodial officer, as defined in Section 831.5 of the Penal Code, participated, or which he or she perceived, and pertaining to the manner in which he or she performed his or her duties, provided that information is relevant to the subject matter involved in the pending litigation.

(b) In determining relevance the court shall examine the information in chambers in conformity with Section 915, and shall exclude from disclosure:

(1) Information consisting of complaints concerning conduct occurring more than five years before the event or transaction that is the subject of the litigation in aid of which discovery or disclosure is sought.

(2) In any criminal proceeding the conclusions of any officer investigating a complaint filed pursuant to Section 832.5 of the Penal Code.

(3) Facts sought to be disclosed that are so remote as to make disclosure of little or no practical benefit.

(c) In determining relevance where the issue in litigation concerns the policies or pattern of conduct of the employing agency, the court shall consider whether the information sought may be obtained from order records maintained by the employing agency in the regular course of agency business which would not necessitate the disclosure of individual personnel records.

(d) Upon motion seasonably made by the governmental agency which has custody or control of the records to be examined or by the officer whose records are sought, and upon good cause showing the necessity thereof, the court may make any order which justice requires to protect the officer or agency from unnecessary annoyance, embarrassment or oppression.

(e) The court shall, in any case or proceeding permitting the disclosure or discovery of any peace or custodial officer records requested pursuant to Section 1043, order that the records disclosed or discovered may not be used for any purpose other than a court proceeding pursuant to applicable law.

§ 1046. Allegation of excessive force by peace officer during arrest; police arrest report

In any case, otherwise authorized by law, in which the party seeking disclosure is alleging excessive force by a peace officer or custodial officer, as defined in Section 831.5 of the Penal Code, in connection with the arrest of that party, or for conduct alleged to have occurred within a jail facility, the motion shall include a copy of the police report setting forth the circumstances under which the party was stopped and arrested, or a copy of the crime report setting forth the circumstances under which the conduct is alleged to have occurred within a jail facility.

§ 1047. Arrests; records of peace officers; exemption from disclosure

Records of peace officers or custodial officers, as defined in Section 831.5 of the Penal Code, including supervisorial peace officers, who either were not present during the arrest or had no contact with the party seeking disclosure from the time of the arrest until the time of booking, or who were not present at the time the conduct is alleged to have occurred within a jail facility, shall not be subject to disclosure.

ARTICLE 10. POLITICAL VOTE

§ 1050. Privilege to protect secrecy of vote

If he claims the privilege, a person has a privilege to refuse to disclose the tenor of his vote at a public election where the voting is by secret ballot unless he voted illegally or he previously made an unprivileged disclosure of the tenor of his vote.

LAW REVISION COMMISSION COMMENT

Section 1050 declares existing law. The California cases declaring such a privilege have relied upon the provision of the Constitution that "secrecy in voting be preserved." Cal.Const., Art. II, § 5. See Bush v. Head, 154 Cal. 277, 97 Pac. 512 (1908); Smith v. Thomas, 121 Cal. 533, 54 Pac. 71 (1898). Since the policy of ballot secrecy extends only to legally cast ballots, the California cases—as well as Section 1050—recognize that there is no privilege as to the tenor of an illegal vote. Patterson v. Hanley, 136 Cal. 265, 68 Pac. 821 (1902). [7 Cal.L.Rev. Comm. Reports 1 (1965)]

ARTICLE 11. TRADE SECRET

§ 1060. Privilege to protect trade secret

If he or his agent or employee claims the privilege, the owner of a trade secret has a privilege to refuse to disclose the secret, and to prevent another from disclosing it, if the allowance of the privilege will not tend to conceal fraud or otherwise work injustice.

LAW REVISION COMMISSION COMMENT

This privilege is granted so that secret information essential to the continued operation of a business or industry may be afforded some measure of protection against unnecessary disclosure. Thus, the privilege prevents the use of the witness' duty to testify as the means for injuring an otherwise profitable business where more important interests will not be jeopardized. See generally 8 Wigmore, Evidence § 2212(3) (McNaughton rev. 1961). Nevertheless, there are dangers in the recognition of such a privilege. Copyright and patent laws provide adequate protection for many of the matters that might otherwise be classified as trade secrets. Recognizing the privilege as to such information would serve only to hinder the courts in determining the truth without providing the owner of the secret any needed protection. Again, disclosure of the matters protected by the privilege may be essential to disclose unfair competition or fraud or to reveal the improper use of dangerous materials by the party asserting the privilege. Recognizing the privilege in such cases would amount to a legally sanctioned license to commit the wrongs complained of, for the wrongdoer would be privileged to withhold his wrongful conduct from legal scrutiny.

Therefore, the privilege exists under this section only if its application will not tend to conceal fraud or otherwise work injustice. The limits of the privilege are necessarily uncertain and will have to be worked out through judicial decisions.

Although no California case has been found holding evidence of a trade secret to be privileged, at least one California case has recognized that such a privilege may exist unless its holder has injured another and the disclosure of the secret is indispensable to the ascertainment of the truth and the ultimate determination of the rights of the parties. Willson v. Superior Court, 66 Cal.App. 275, 225 Pac. 881 (1924) (trade secret held not subject to privilege because of plaintiff's need for information to establish case against the person asserting the privilege). Indirect recognition of such a privilege has also been given in Code of Civil Procedure Section 2019, which provides that in discovery proceedings the court may make protective orders prohibiting inquiry into "secret processes, developments or research." [7 Cal.L.Rev.Comm. Reports 1 (1965)]

§ 1061. Procedure for assertion of trade secret privilege

(a) For purposes of this section, and Sections 1062 and 1063:

(1) "Trade secret" means "trade secret," as defined in subdivision (d) of Section 3426.1 of the Civil Code, or paragraph (9) of subdivision (a) of Section 499c of the Penal Code.

(2) "Article" means "article," as defined in paragraph (2) of subdivision (a) of Section 499c of the Penal Code.

(b) In addition to Section 1062, the following procedure shall apply whenever the owner of a trade secret wishes to assert his or her trade secret privilege, as provided in Section 1060, during a criminal proceeding:

(1) The owner of the trade secret shall file a motion for a protective order, or the people may file the motion on the owner's behalf and with the owner's permission. The motion shall include an affidavit based upon personal knowledge listing the affiant's qualifications to give an opinion concerning the trade secret at issue, identifying, without revealing, the alleged trade secret and articles which disclose the secret, and presenting evidence that the secret

qualifies as a trade secret under either subdivision (d) of Section 3426.1 of the Civil Code or paragraph (9) of subdivision (a) of Section 499c of the Penal Code. The motion and affidavit shall be served on all parties in the proceeding.

(2) Any party in the proceeding may oppose the request for the protective order by submitting affidavits based upon the affiant's personal knowledge. The affidavits shall be filed under seal, but shall be provided to the owner of the trade secret and to all parties in the proceeding. Neither the owner of the trade secret nor any party in the proceeding may disclose the affidavit to persons other than to counsel of record without prior court approval.

(3) The movant shall, by a preponderance of the evidence, show that the issuance of a protective order is proper. The court may rule on the request without holding an evidentiary hearing. However, in its discretion, the court may choose to hold an in camera evidentiary hearing concerning disputed articles with only the owner of the trade secret, the people's representative, the defendant, and defendant's counsel present. If the court holds such a hearing, the parties' right to examine witnesses shall not be used to obtain discovery, but shall be directed solely toward the question of whether the alleged trade secret qualifies for protection.

(4) If the court finds that a trade secret may be disclosed during any criminal proceeding unless a protective order is issued and that the issuance of a protective order would not conceal a fraud or work an injustice, the court shall issue a protective order limiting the use and dissemination of the trade secret, including, but not limited to, articles disclosing that secret. The protective order may, in the court's discretion, include the following provisions:

(A) That the trade secret may be disseminated only to counsel for the parties, including their associate attorneys, paralegals, and investigators, and to law enforcement officials or clerical officials.

(B) That the defendant may view the secret only in the presence of his or her counsel, or if not in the presence of his or her counsel, at counsel's offices.

(C) That any party seeking to show the trade secret, or articles containing the trade secret, to any person not designated by the protective order shall first obtain court approval to do so:

(i) The court may require that the person receiving the trade secret do so only in the presence of counsel for the party requesting approval.

(ii) The court may require the person receiving the trade secret to sign a copy of the protective order and to agree to be bound by its terms. The order may include a provision recognizing the owner of the trade secret to be a third-party beneficiary of that agreement.

(iii) The court may require a party seeking disclosure to an expert to provide that expert's name, employment history, and any other relevant information to the court for examination. The court shall accept that information under seal, and the information shall not be disclosed by any court except upon termination of the action and upon a showing of good cause to believe the secret has been disseminated by a court-approved expert. The court shall evaluate the expert and determine whether the expert poses a discernible risk of disclosure. The court shall withhold approval if the expert's economic interests place the expert in a competitive position with the victim, unless no other experts are available. The court may interview the expert in camera in aid of its ruling. If the court rejects the expert, it shall state its reasons for doing so on the record and a transcript of those reasons shall be prepared and sealed.

(D) That no articles disclosing the trade secret shall be filed or otherwise made a part of the court record available to the public without approval of the court and prior notice to the owner of the secret. The owner of the secret may give either party permission to accept the notice on the owner's behalf.

(E) Other orders as the court deems necessary to protect the integrity of the trade secret.

(c) A ruling granting or denying a motion for a protective order filed pursuant to subdivision (b) shall not be construed as a determination that the alleged trade secret is or is not a trade secret as defined by subdivision (d) of Section 3426.1 of the Civil Code or paragraph (9) of subdivision (a) of Section 499c of the Penal Code. Such a ruling shall not have any effect on any civil litigation.

(d) This section shall have prospective effect only and shall not operate to invalidate previously entered protective orders.

LAW REVISION COMMISSION COMMENTS

2002 Amendment

Former subdivision (d) of Section 1061 is deleted to reflect unification of the municipal and superior courts pursuant to Article VI, Section 5(e), of the California Constitution. On unification of the municipal and superior courts in a county, preexisting records of the municipal court automatically become records of the superior court. Cal. Const. art. VI, § 23(c)(3); Gov't Code § 70212(c).

§ 1062. Exclusion of public from criminal proceeding; motion; contents; hearing; determination

(a) Notwithstanding any other provision of law, in a criminal case, the court, upon motion of the owner of a trade secret, or upon motion by the People with the consent of the owner, may exclude the public from any portion of a criminal proceeding where the proponent of closure has demonstrated a substantial probability that the trade secret would otherwise be disclosed to the public during that proceeding and a substantial probability that the disclosure would cause serious harm to the owner of the secret, and where the court finds that there is no overriding public interest in an open proceeding. No evidence, however, shall be excluded during a criminal proceeding pursuant to this section if it would conceal a fraud, work an injustice, or deprive the People or the defendant of a fair trial.

(b) The motion made pursuant to subdivision (a) shall identify, without revealing, the trade secrets which would otherwise be disclosed to the public. A showing made pursuant to subdivision (a) shall be made during an in camera hearing with only the owner of the trade secret, the People's representative, the defendant, and defendant's counsel present. A court reporter shall be present during the hearing. Any transcription of the proceedings at the in camera hearing, as well as any articles presented at that hearing, shall be ordered sealed by the court and only a court may allow access to its contents upon a showing of good cause. The court, in ruling upon the motion made pursuant to subdivision (a), may consider testimony presented or affidavits filed in any proceeding held in that action.

(c) If, after the in camera hearing described in subdivision (b), the court determines that exclusion of trade secret information from the public is appropriate, the court shall close only that portion of the criminal proceeding necessary to prevent disclosure of the trade secret. Before granting the motion, however, the court shall find and state for the record that the moving party has met its burden pursuant to subdivision (b), and that the closure of that portion of the proceeding will not deprive the People or the defendant of a fair trial.

(d) The owner of the trade secret, the People, or the defendant may seek relief from a ruling denying or granting closure by petitioning a higher court for extraordinary relief.

(e) Whenever the court closes a portion of a criminal proceeding pursuant to this section, a transcript of that closed proceeding shall be made available to the public as soon as practicable. The court shall redact any information qualifying as a trade secret before making that transcript available.

(f) The court, subject to Section 867 of the Penal Code, may allow witnesses who are bound by a protective order entered in the criminal proceeding protecting trade secrets, pursuant to Section 1061, to remain within the courtroom during the closed portion of the proceeding.

§ 1063. Sealing of articles protected by protective order; procedures

The following provisions shall govern requests to seal articles which are protected by a protective order entered pursuant to Evidence Code Section 1060 or 1061:

(a) The People shall request sealing of articles reasonably expected to be filed or admitted into evidence as follows:

(1) No less than 10 court days before trial, and no less than five court days before any other criminal proceeding, the People shall file with the court a list of all articles which the People reasonably expect to file with the court, or admit into evidence, under seal at that proceeding. That list shall be available to the public. The People may be relieved from providing timely notice upon showing that exigent circumstances prevent that notice.

(2) The court shall not allow the listed articles to be filed, admitted into evidence, or in any way made a part of the court record otherwise open to the public before holding a hearing to consider any objections to the People's request to seal the articles. The court at that hearing shall allow those objecting to the sealing to state their objections.

(3) After hearing any objections to sealing, the court shall conduct an in camera hearing with only the owner of the trade secret contained within those articles, the People's representative, defendant, and defendant's counsel present. The court shall review the articles sought to be sealed, evaluate objections to sealing, and determine whether the People have satisfied the constitutional standards governing public access to articles which are part of the judicial record. The court may consider testimony presented or affidavits filed in any proceeding held in that action. The People, defendant, and the owner of the trade secret may file affidavits based on the affiant's personal knowledge to be considered at that hearing. Those affidavits are to be sealed and not released to the public, but shall be made available to the parties. The court may rule on the request to seal without taking testimony. If the court takes testimony, examination of witnesses shall not be used to obtain discovery, but shall be directed solely toward whether sealing is appropriate.

(4) If the court finds that the movant has satisfied appropriate constitutional standards with respect to sealing particular articles, the court shall seal those articles if and when they are

filed, admitted into evidence, or in any way made a part of the court record otherwise open to the public. The articles shall not be unsealed absent an order of a court upon a showing of good cause. Failure to examine the court file for notice of a request to seal shall not constitute good cause to consider objections to sealing.

(b) The following procedure shall apply to other articles made a part of the court record:

(1) Where any articles protected by a protective order entered pursuant to Section 1060 or 1061 are filed, admitted into evidence, or in any way made a part of the court record in such a way as to be otherwise open to the public, the People, a defendant, or the owner of a trade secret contained within those articles may request the court to seal those articles.

(2) The request to seal shall be made by noticed motion filed with the court. It may also be made orally in court at the time the articles are made a part of the court record. Where the request is made orally, the movant must file within 24 hours a written description of that request, including a list of the articles which are the subject of that request. These motions and lists shall be available to the public.

(3) The court shall promptly conduct hearings as provided in paragraphs (2), (3), and (4) of subdivision (a). The court shall, pending the hearings, seal those articles which are the subject of the request. Where a request to seal is made orally, the court may conduct hearings at the time the articles are made a part of the court record, but shall reconsider its ruling in light of additional objections made by objectors within two court days after the written record of the request to seal is made available to the public.

(4) Any articles sealed pursuant to these hearings shall not be unsealed absent an order of a court upon a showing of good cause. Failure to examine the court file for notice of a request to seal shall not constitute good cause to consider objections to sealing.

CHAPTER 5. IMMUNITY OF NEWSMAN FROM CITATION FOR CONTEMPT

§ 1070. Refusal to disclose news source

(a) A publisher, editor, reporter, or other person connected with or employed upon a newspaper, magazine, or other periodical publication, or by a press association or wire service, or any person who has been so connected or employed, cannot be adjudged in contempt by a judicial, legislative, administrative body, or any other body having the power to issue subpoenas, for refusing to disclose, in any proceeding as defined in Section 901, the source of any information procured while so connected or employed for publication in a newspaper, magazine or other periodical publication, or for refusing to disclose any unpublished information obtained or prepared in gathering, receiving or processing of information for communication to the public.

(b) Nor can a radio or television news reporter or other person connected with or employed by a radio or television station, or any person who has been so connected or employed, be so adjudged in contempt for refusing to disclose the source of any information procured while so connected or employed for news or news commentary purposes on radio or television, or for refusing to disclose any unpublished information obtained or prepared in gathering, receiving or processing of information for communication to the public.

(c) As used in this section, "unpublished information" includes information not disseminated to the public by the person from whom disclosure is sought, whether or not related information has been disseminated and includes, but is not limited to, all notes, outtakes, photographs, tapes or other data of whatever sort not itself disseminated to the public through a medium of communication, whether or not published information based upon or related to such material has been disseminated.

DIVISION 9. EVIDENCE AFFECTED OR EXCLUDED BY EXTRINSIC POLICIES

CHAPTER 1. EVIDENCE OF CHARACTER, HABIT, OR CUSTOM

§ 1100. Manner of proof of character

Except as otherwise provided by statute, any otherwise admissible evidence (including evidence in the form of an opinion, evidence of reputation, and evidence of specific instances of such person's conduct) is admissible to prove a person's character or a trait of his character.

LAW REVISION COMMISSION COMMENT

Section 1100 states the kinds of evidence that may be used to prove a person's character or a trait of his character. The section makes it clear that reputation evidence, opinion evidence, and evidence of specific instances of conduct are admissible for this purpose.

Section 1100 is technically unnecessary because Section 351 declares that all relevant evidence is admissible. Hence, all of the evidence declared to be admissible by Section 1100 would be admissible anyway under the general provisions of Section 351. Section 1100 is included in the Evidence Code, however, to forestall the argument that Section 351 does not remove all judicially created restrictions on the kinds of evidence that may be used to prove character or a trait of character.

Subject to certain statutory restrictions, the character evidence described in Section 1100 is admissible under Section 351 whenever it is relevant. Evidence of a person's character or a trait of his character is relevant in three situations: (1) when offered on the issue of his credibility as a witness, (2) when offered as circumstantial evidence of his conduct in conformity with such character or trait of character, and (3) when his character or a trait of his character is an ultimate fact in dispute in the action.

Sections 786–790 establish restrictions that are applicable when character evidence is offered to attack or to support the credibility of a witness. See the Comments to Sections 787 and 788 for a discussion of the restrictions on the kinds of evidence admissible for this purpose.

Sections 1101–1104 substantially restrict the extent to which character evidence may be used as circumstantial evidence of conduct. See the Comments to those sections for a discussion of the restrictions on the kinds of evidence admissible for this purpose.

Section 1100 applies without restriction only when character or a trait of character is an ultimate fact in dispute in the action. As applied to this situation, Section 1100 is generally consistent with existing law, although the existing law is uncertain in some respects. Cases involving character as an ultimate issue have admitted opinion evidence (People v. Wade, 118 Cal. 672, 50 Pac. 841 (1897); People v. Samonset, 97 Cal. 448, 450, 32 Pac. 520, 521 (1893)), reputation evidence (Estate of Akers, 184 Cal. 514, 519–520, 194 Pac. 706, 708–709 (1920); People v. Samonset, supra), and evidence of specific acts (Guardianship of Wisdom, 146 Cal.App.2d 635, 304 P.2d 221 (1956); Currin v. Currin, 125 Cal.App.2d 644, 271 P.2d 61 (1954); Guardianship of Casad, 106 Cal.App.2d 134, 234 P.2d 647 (1951)). However, there are cases which exclude some kinds of evidence where particular traits are involved. For example, in cases involving the unfitness or incompetency of an employee, evidence of specific acts is admissible to prove such unfitness or incompetency, while evidence of reputation is not. E.g., Gier v. Los Angeles Consol. Elec. Ry., 108 Cal. 129, 41 Pac. 22 (1895). Section 1100 eliminates the uncertainties in existing law and makes admissible any evidence that is relevant to prove the character in issue. [7 Cal.L.Rev.Comm. Reports 1 (1965)]

§ 1101. Evidence of character to prove conduct

(a) Except as provided in this section and in Sections 1102, 1103, 1108, and 1109, evidence of a person's character or a trait of his or her character (whether in the form of an opinion, evidence of reputation, or evidence of specific instances of his or her conduct) is inadmissible when offered to prove his or her conduct on a specified occasion.

(b) Nothing in this section prohibits the admission of evidence that a person committed a crime, civil wrong, or other act when relevant to prove some fact (such as motive, opportunity, intent, preparation, plan, knowledge, identity, absence of mistake or accident, or whether a defendant in a prosecution for an unlawful sexual act or attempted unlawful sexual act did not reasonably and in good faith believe that the victim consented) other than his or her disposition to commit such an act.

(c) Nothing in this section affects the admissibility of evidence offered to support or attack the credibility of a witness.

LAW REVISION COMMISSION COMMENT

Section 1101 is concerned with evidence of a person's character (i.e., his propensity or disposition to engage in a certain type of conduct) that is offered as a basis for an inference that he behaved in conformity with that character on a particular occasion. Section 1101 is not concerned with evidence offered to prove a person's character when that character is itself in issue; the admissibility of character evidence offered for this purpose is determined under Sections 351 and 1100. Nor is Section 1101 concerned with evidence of character offered on the issue of the credibility of a witness; the admissibility of such evidence is determined under Section 786–790. See Evidence Code § 1101(c).

Civil cases. Section 1101 excludes evidence of character to prove conduct in a civil case for the following reasons. First, character evidence is of slight probative value and may be very prejudicial. Second, character evidence tends to distract the trier of fact from the main question of what actually happened on the particular occasion and permits the trier of fact to reward the good man and to punish the bad man because of their respective characters. Third, introduction of character evidence may result in confusion of issues and require extended collateral inquiry.

Section 1101 states the general rule recognized under existing law. Code Civ.Proc. § 2053 ("Evidence of the good character of a party is not admissible in a civil action...." (Section 2053 is superseded by various Evidence Code sections.)); Deevy v. Tassi, 21 Cal.2d 109, 130 P.2d 389 (1942) (assault; evidence of defendant's bad character for peace and quiet held inadmissible); Vance.v Richardson, 110 Cal. 414, 42 Pac. 909 (1895) (assault; evidence of defendant's good character for peace and quiet held inadmissible); Van Horn v. Van Horn, 5 Cal.App. 719, 91 Pac. 260 (1907) (divorce for adultery; evidence of defendant's and the non-party-corespondent's good character held inadmissible). Under existing law, however, there may be an exception to this general rule. Existing law may permit evidence to be introduced of the unchaste character of a plaintiff to show the likelihood of her consent to an alleged rape. Valencia v. Milliken, 31 Cal.App. 533, 160 Pac. 1086 (1916) (civil action for rape; error, but nonprejudicial, to limit evidence of unchaste character of plaintiff to issue of damages). The Evidence Code has no such exception for civil cases. But see Evidence Code § 1103 (criminal cases).

Criminal cases. Section 1101 states the general rule that evidence of character to prove conduct is inadmissible in a criminal case. Sections 1102 and 1103 state exceptions to this general principle. See the Comment to Section 1102.

Evidence of misconduct to show fact other than character. Section 1101 does not prohibit the admission of evidence of misconduct when it is offered as evidence of some other fact in issue, such as motive, common scheme or plan, preparation, intent, knowledge, identity, or absence of mistake or accident. Subdivision (b) of Section 1101 makes this clear. This codifies existing law. People v. Lisenba, 14 Cal.2d 403, 94 P.2d 569 (1939) (prior crime admissible to show general criminal plan and absence of accident); People v. David, 12 Cal.2d 639, 86 P.2d 811 (1939) (prior robbery admissible to show defendant's sanity and ability to devise and execute deliberate plan); People v. Morani, 196 Cal. 154, 236 Pac. 135 (1925) (prior abortion admissible to show that operation was not performed in ignorance of effect and, hence, to show necessary intent). See discussion in California Criminal Law Practice 491–498 (Cal.Cont.Ed.Bar 1964). [7 Cal.L.Rev.Comm. Reports 1 (1965)]

§ 1102. Opinion and reputation evidence of character of criminal defendant to prove conduct

In a criminal action, evidence of the defendant's character or a trait of his character in the form of an opinion or evidence of his reputation is not made inadmissible by Section 1101 if such evidence is:

(a) Offered by the defendant to prove his conduct in conformity with such character or trait of character.

(b) Offered by the prosecution to rebut evidence adduced by the defendant under subdivision (a).

LAW REVISION COMMISSION COMMENT

Section 1102 and 1103 state exceptions (applicable only in criminal cases) to the general rule of Section 1101 that character evidence is not admissible to prove conduct in conformity with that character.

Sections 1102 and 1103 generally

Under Section 1102, the accused in a criminal case may introduce evidence of his good character to show his innocence of the alleged crime—provided that the character or trait of character to be shown is relevant to the charge made against him. This codifies existing law. People v. Chrisman, 135 Cal. 282, 67 Pac. 136 (1901). Sections 1101 and 1102 make it clear that the prosecution may not, on its own initiative, use character evidence to prove that the defendant had the disposition to commit the crime charged; but, if the defendant first introduces evidence of his good character to show the likelihood of innocence, the prosecution may meet his evidence by introducing evidence of the defendant's bad character to show the likelihood of guilt. This also codifies existing law. People v. Jones, 42 Cal.2d 219, 266 P.2d 38 (1954) (prosecution for sexual molestation of child; error to exclude expert psychiatric opinion that defendant was not a sexual psychopath); People v. Stewart, 28 Cal. 395 (1865) (murder prosecution; error to exclude evidence of defendant's good character for peace and quiet); People v. Hughes, 123 Cal.App.2d 767, 267 P.2d 376 (1954) (assault prosecution; evidence of defendant's violent nature held admissible after introduction of evidence showing his good character for peace and quiet). See California Criminal Law Practice 489–490 (Cal.Cont.Ed.Bar 1964).

Likewise, under Section 1103, the defendant may introduce evidence of the character of the victim of the crime where the conduct of the victim in conformity with his character would tend to exculpate the defendant; and, if the defendant introduces evidence of the bad character of the victim, the prosecution may introduce evidence of the victim's good character. This codifies existing law. People v. Hoffman, 195 Cal. 295, 311–312, 232 Pac. 974, 980 (1925) (murder prosecution; evidence of victim's good reputation for peace and quiet held inadmissible when defendant had not attacked reputation of victim); People v. Lamar, 148 Cal. 564, 83 Pac. 993 (1906) (murder prosecution; error to exclude evidence of victim's bad character for violence offered to prove victim was aggressor and defendant acted in self-defense); People v. Shea, 125 Cal. 151, 57 Pac. 885 (1899) (rape prosecution; error to exclude evidence of the prosecutrix's unchaste character offered to prove the likelihood of consent); People v. Fitch, 28 Cal.App.2d 31, 81 P.2d 1019 (1938) (murder prosecution; evidence of victim's good character for peace and quiet held admissible after defendant introduced evidence of victim's violent nature). See also Comment, 25 Cal.L.Rev. 459 (1937).

Thus, under Sections 1102 and 1103, the defendant in a criminal case is given the right to introduce character evidence that would be inadmissible in a civil case. However, evidence of the character of the defendant or the victim—though weak—may be enough to raise a reasonable doubt in the mind of the trier of fact concerning the defendant's guilt. And, since his life or liberty is at stake, the defendant should not be deprived of the right to introduce evidence even of such slight probative value.

Kinds of character evidence admissible to prove conduct under Sections 1102 and 1103.

The three kinds of evidence that might be offered to prove character as circumstantial evidence of conduct are: (1) evidence as to reputation, (2) opinion evidence as to character, and (3) evidence of specific acts indicating character. The admissibility of each of these kinds of evidence when character is sought to be proved as circumstantial evidence of conduct under Sections 1102 and 1103 is discussed below.

Reputation evidence. Reputation evidence is the ordinary means sanctioned by the cases for proving character as circumstantial evidence of conduct. Witkin, California Evidence § 125 (1958). See People v. Fair, 43 Cal. 137 (1872). Both Sections 1102 and 1103 codify the existing law permitting character to be proved by reputation.

Opinion evidence. There is recent authority for the admission of opinion evidence to prove character as circumstantial evidence of conduct. People v. Jones, 42 Cal.2d 219, 266 P.2d 38 (1954) (error to exclude expert psychiatric opinion that the defendant was not a sexual psychopath and, hence, unlikely to have violated Penal Code Section 288). However, opinion evidence generally has been held inadmissible. See People v. Spigno, 156 Cal.App.2d 279, 319 P.2d 458 (1957) (full discussion of the Jones case); California Criminal Law Practice 489–490 (Cal.Cont.Ed.Bar 1964).

The general rule under existing law excludes the most reliable form of character evidence and admits the least reliable. The opinions of those whose personal intimacy with a person gives them firsthand knowledge of that person's character are a far more reliable indication of that character than is reputation, which is little more than accumulated hearsay. See 7 Wigmore, Evidence § 1986 (3d ed. 1940). The danger of collateral issues seems no greater than that inherent in reputation evidence. Accordingly, both Section 1102 and Section 1103 permit character to be proved by opinion evidence.

Evidence of specific acts. Under existing law, the admissibility of evidence of specific acts to prove character as circumstantial evidence of conduct depends upon the nature of the conduct sought to be proved. Evidence of specific acts of the accused is excluded as a general rule in order to avoid the possibility of prejudice, undue confusion of the issues with collateral matters, unfair surprise, and the like. Thus, it is usually held that evidence of specific acts by the defendant is inadmissible to prove his guilt even though the defendant has opened the question by introducing evidence of his good character. See discussion in People v. Gin Shue, 58 Cal.App.2d 625, 634, 137 P.2d 742, 747–748 (1943). On the other hand, it is well settled that in a rape case the defendant may show the unchaste character of the prosecutrix by evidence of prior voluntary intercourse in order to indicate the unlikelihood of resistance on the occasion in question. People v. Shea, 125 Cal. 151, 57 Pac. 885 (1899); People v. Benson, 6 Cal. 221 (1856); People v. Battilana, 52 Cal.App.2d 685, 126 P.2d 923 (1942). However, in a homicide or assault case where the defense is self-defense, evidence of specific acts of violence by the victim is inadmissible to prove his violent nature (and, hence, that the victim was the aggressor) unless the prior acts were directed against the defendant himself. People v. Yokum, 145 Cal. App.2d 245, 302 P.2d 406 (1956); People v. Soules, 41 Cal.App.2d 298, 106 P.2d 639 (1940). But see People v. Carmichael, 198 Cal. 534, 548, 246 Pac. 62, 68 (1926) (if defendant had knowledge of victim's statement evidencing violent nature, the "statement was material and might have had an important bearing upon his plea of self-defense"); People v. Swigart, 80 Cal.App. 31, 251 Pac. 343 (1926). See also Comment, 25 Cal.L.Rev. 459, 466–469 (1937).

Section 1102 codifies the general rule under existing law which precludes evidence of specific acts of the defendant to prove character as circumstantial evidence of his innocence or of his disposition to commit the crime with which he is charged.

Section 1103 permits both the defendant and the prosecution to use evidence of specific acts of the victim of the crime to prove the victim's character as circumstantial evidence of his conduct. In this respect, the section harmonizes conflicting rules found in existing law. [7 Cal.L.Rev. Comm. Reports 1 (1965)]

§ 1103. Character evidence of crime victim to prove conduct; evidence of defendant's character or trait for violence; evidence of manner of dress of victim; evidence of complaining witness' sexual conduct

(a) In a criminal action, evidence of the character or a trait of character (in the form of an opinion, evidence of reputation, or evidence of specific instances of conduct) of the victim of the crime for which the defendant is being prosecuted is not made inadmissible by Section 1101 if the evidence is:

(1) Offered by the defendant to prove conduct of the victim in conformity with the character or trait of character.

(2) Offered by the prosecution to rebut evidence adduced by the defendant under paragraph (1).

(b) In a criminal action, evidence of the defendant's character for violence or trait of character for violence (in the form of an opinion, evidence of reputation, or evidence of specific instances of conduct) is not made inadmissible by Section 1101 if the evidence is offered by the prosecution to prove conduct of the defendant in conformity with the character or trait of character and is offered after evidence that the victim had a character for violence or a trait of character tending to show violence has been adduced by the defendant under paragraph (1) of subdivision (a).

(c) (1) Notwithstanding any other provision of this code to the contrary, and except as provided in this subdivision, in any prosecution under Section 261, 262, or 264.1 of the Penal Code, or under Section 286, 288a, or 289 of the Penal Code, or for assault with intent to commit, attempt to commit, or conspiracy to commit a crime defined in any of those sections, except where the crime is alleged to have occurred in a local detention facility, as defined in Section 6031.4, or in a state prison, as defined in Section 4504, opinion evidence, reputation evidence, and evidence of specific instances of the complaining witness' sexual conduct, or any of that evidence, is not admissible by the defendant in order to prove consent by the complaining witness.

(2) Notwithstanding paragraph (3), evidence of the manner in which the victim was dressed at the time of the commission of the offense shall not be admissible when offered by either party on the issue of consent in any prosecution for an offense specified in paragraph (1), unless the evidence is determined by the court to be relevant and admissible in the interests of justice. The proponent of the evidence shall make an offer of proof outside the hearing of the jury. The court shall then make its determination and at that time, state the reasons for its ruling on the record. For the purposes of this paragraph, "manner of dress" does not include the condition of the victim's clothing before, during, or after the commission of the offense.

(3) Paragraph (1) shall not be applicable to evidence of the complaining witness' sexual conduct with the defendant.

(4) If the prosecutor introduces evidence, including testimony of a witness, or the complaining witness as a witness gives testimony, and that evidence or testimony relates to the complaining witness' sexual conduct, the defendant may cross-examine the witness who gives the testimony and offer relevant evidence limited specifically to the rebuttal of the evidence introduced by the prosecutor or given by the complaining witness.

(5) Nothing in this subdivision shall be construed to make inadmissible any evidence offered to attack the credibility of the complaining witness as provided in Section 782.

(6) As used in this section, "complaining witness" means the alleged victim of the crime charged, the prosecution of which is subject to this subdivision.

LAW REVISION COMMISSION COMMENT

See the Comment to Section 1102. [7 Cal.L.Rev.Comm. Reports 1 (1965)]

§ 1104. Character trait for care or skill

Except as provided in Sections 1102 and 1103, evidence of a trait of a person's character with respect to care or skill is inadmissible to prove the quality of his conduct on a specified occasion.

LAW REVISION COMMISSION COMMENT

Section 1104 places a further limitation on the use of character evidence. Under Section 1104, character evidence with respect to care or skill is inadmissible to prove that conduct on a specific occasion was either careless or careful, skilled or unskilled, except to the extent permitted by Sections 1102 and 1103.

Section 1104 codifies well-settled California law. Towle v. Pacific Improvement Co., 98 Cal. 342, 33 Pac. 207 (1893). The purpose of the rule is to prevent collateral issues from consuming too much time and distracting the attention of the trier of fact from what was actually done on the particular occasion. Here, the slight probative value of the evidence balanced against the danger of confusion of issues, collateral inquiry, prejudice, and the like, warrants a fixed exclusionary rule. [7 Cal.L.Rev.Comm. Reports 1 (1965)]

§ 1105. Habit or custom to prove specific behavior

Any otherwise admissible evidence of habit or custom is admissible to prove conduct on a specified occasion in conformity with the habit or custom.

LAW REVISION COMMISSION COMMENT

Section 1105, like Section 1100, declares that certain evidence is admissible. Hence, Section 1105 is technically unnecessary because Section 351 declares that all relevant evidence is admissible. Nonetheless, Section 1105 is desirable to assure that evidence of custom or habit (a regular response to a repeated specific situation) is admissible even where evidence of a person's character (his general disposition or propensity to engage in a certain type of conduct) is inadmissible.

The admissibility of habit evidence to prove conduct in conformity with the habit has long been established in California. Wallis v. Southern Pac. Co., 184 Cal. 662, 195 Pac. 408 (1921) (distinguishing cases holding character evidence as to care or skill inadmissible); Craven v. Central Pac. R.R., 72 Cal. 345, 13 Pac. 878 (1887). The admissibility of evidence of the custom of a business or occupation is also well established. Hughes v. Pacific Wharf & Storage Co., 188 Cal. 210, 205 Pac. 105 (1922) (mailing letter). However, under existing law, evidence of habit is admissible only if there are no eyewitnesses. Boone v. Bank of America, 220 Cal. 93, 29 P.2d 409 (1934). In earlier cases, the Supreme Court criticized the "no eyewitness" limitation:

> This limitation upon the introduction of such testimony seems rather illogical. If the fact of the existence of habits of caution in a given particular has any legitimate evidentiary weight, the party benefited ought to have the advantage of it for whatever it is worth, even against adverse eye-witnesses; and if the testimony of the eye-witnesses is in his favor, it would be at least a harmless cumulation of evidence to permit testimony of his custom or habit. [Wallis v. Southern Pac. Co., 184 Cal. 662, 665, 195 Pac. 408, 409 (1921).]

The "no eyewitness" limitation is undesirable. Eyewitnesses frequently are mistaken, and some are dishonest. The trier of fact should be entitled to weigh the habit evidence against the eyewitness testimony as well as all of the other evidence in the case. Hence, Section 1105 does not contain the "no eyewitness" limitation. [7 Cal.L.Rev.Comm. Reports 1 (1965)]

§ 1106. Sexual harassment, sexual assault, or sexual battery cases; opinion or reputation evidence of plaintiff's sexual conduct; inadmissibility; exception; cross-examination

(a) In any civil action alleging conduct which constitutes sexual harassment, sexual assault, or sexual battery, opinion evidence, reputation evidence, and evidence of specific instances of plaintiff's sexual conduct, or any of such evidence, is not admissible by the defendant in order to prove consent by the plaintiff or the absence of injury to the plaintiff, unless the injury alleged by the plaintiff is in the nature of loss of consortium.

(b) Subdivision (a) shall not be applicable to evidence of the plaintiff's sexual conduct with the alleged perpetrator.

(c) If the plaintiff introduces evidence, including testimony of a witness, or the plaintiff as a witness gives testimony, and the evidence or testimony relates to the plaintiff's sexual conduct, the defendant may cross-examine the witness who gives the testimony and offer relevant evidence limited specifically to the rebuttal of the evidence introduced by the plaintiff or given by the plaintiff.

(d) Nothing in this section shall be construed to make inadmissible any evidence offered to attack the credibility of the plaintiff as provided in Section 783.

§ 1107. Battered women's syndrome; expert testimony in criminal actions; exception; sufficiency of foundation; abuse and domestic violence; applicability to Penal Code

(a) In a criminal action, expert testimony is admissible by either the prosecution or the defense regarding battered women's syndrome, including the nature and effect of physical, emotional, or mental abuse on the beliefs, perceptions, or behavior of victims of domestic violence, except when offered against a criminal defendant to prove the occurrence of the act or acts of abuse which form the basis of the criminal charge.

(b) The foundation shall be sufficient for admission of this expert testimony if the proponent of the evidence establishes its relevancy and the proper qualifications of the expert witness. Expert opinion testimony on battered women's syndrome shall not be considered a new scientific technique whose reliability is unproven.

(c) For purposes of this section, "abuse" is defined in Section 6203 of the Family Code and "domestic violence" is defined in Section 6211 of the Family Code or acts defined in Section 242, subdivision (e) of Section 243, or Section 262, 273.5, 273.6, 422 or 653m of the Penal Code.

(d) This section is intended as a rule of evidence only and no substantive change affecting the Penal Code is intended.

(e) This section shall be known, and may be cited as, the Expect Witness Testimony on Battered Women's Experiences Section of the Evidence Code.

LAW REVISION COMMISSION COMMENT

1992 Amendment (Revised Comment)

Subdivision (c) of Section 1107 is amended to substitute references to the provisions of the Family Code that replaced the relevant provisions of former Code of Civil Procedure Section 542. [23 Cal.L.Rev. Comm. Reports 1 (1993)]

LAW REVISION COMMISSION COMMENT

1992 Amendment (Revised Comment)

Subdivision (c) of Section 1107 is amended to substitute references to the provisions of the Family Code that replaced the relevant provisions of former Code of Civil Procedure Section 542. [23 Cal.L.Rev. Comm. Reports 1 (1993)]

§ 1108. Evidence of another sexual offense by defendant; disclosure; construction of section

(a) In a criminal action in which the defendant is accused of a sexual offense, evidence of the defendant's commission of another sexual offense or offenses is not made inadmissible by Section 1101, if the evidence is not inadmissible pursuant to Section 352.

(b) In an action in which evidence is to be offered under this section, the people shall disclose the evidence to the defendant, including statements of witnesses or a summary of the substance of any testimony that is expected to be offered in compliance with the provisions of Section 1054.7 of the Penal Code.

(c) This section shall not be construed to limit the admission or consideration of evidence under any other section of this code.

(d) As used in this section, the following definitions shall apply:

(1) "Sexual offense" means a crime under the law of a state or of the United States that involves any of the following:

(A) Any conduct proscribed by Section 243.4, 261, 261.5, 262, 264.1, 266c, 269, 286, 288, 288a, 288.2, 288.5, or 289, or subdivision (b), (c), or (d) of Section 311.2 or Section 311.3, 311.4, 311.10, 311.11, 314, or 647.6, of the Penal Code.

(B) Any conduct proscribed by Section 220 of the Penal Code, except assault with intent to commit mayhem.

(C) Contact, without consent, between any part of the defendant's body or an object and the genitals or anus of another person.

(D) Contact, without consent, between the genitals or anus of the defendant and any part of another person's body.

(E) Deriving sexual pleasure or gratification from the infliction of death, bodily injury, or physical pain on another person.

(F) An attempt or conspiracy to engage in conduct described in this paragraph.

(2) "Consent" shall have the same meaning as provided in Section 261.6 of the Penal Code, except that it does not include consent which is legally ineffective because of the age, mental disorder, or developmental or physical disability of the victim.

§ 1109. Evidence of defendant's other acts of domestic violence

(a)(1) Except as provided in subdivision (e) or (f), in a criminal action in which the defendant is accused of an offense involving domestic violence, evidence of the defendant's commission of other domestic violence is not made inadmissible by Section 1101, if the evidence is not inadmissible pursuant to Section 352.

(2) Except as provided in subdivision (e) or (f), in a criminal action in which the defendant is accused of an offense involving abuse of an elder or dependent adult, evidence of the defendant's commission of other abuse of an elder or dependent adult is not made inadmissible by Section 1101 if the evidence is not inadmissible pursuant to Section 352.

(b) In an action in which evidence is to be offered under this section, the people shall disclose the evidence to the defendant, including statements of witnesses or a summary of the substance of any testimony that is expected to be offered, in compliance with the provisions of Section 1054.7 of the Penal Code.

(c) This section shall not be construed to limit or preclude the admission or consideration of evidence under any other statute or case law.

(d) As used in this section, "domestic violence" has the meaning set forth in Section 13700 of the Penal Code. "Abuse of an elder or a dependent adult" has the meaning set forth in Section 15610.07 of the Welfare and Institutions Code.

(e) Evidence of acts occurring more than 10 years before the charged offense is inadmissible under this section, unless the court determines that the admission of this evidence is in the interest of justice.

(f) Evidence of the findings and determinations of administrative agencies regulating the conduct of health facilities licensed under Section 1250 of the Health and Safety Code is inadmissible under this section.

CHAPTER 2. MEDIATION

§ 1115. Definitions

For purposes of this chapter:

(a) "Mediation" means a process in which a neutral person or persons facilitate communication between the disputants to assist them in reaching a mutually acceptable agreement.

(b) "Mediator" means a neutral person who conducts a mediation. "Mediator" includes any person designated by a mediator either to assist in the mediation or to communicate with the participants in preparation for a mediation.

(c) "Mediation consultation" means a communication between a person and a mediator for the purpose of initiating, considering, or reconvening a mediation or retaining the mediator.

LAW REVISION COMMISSION COMMENTS

1997 Addition

Subdivision (a) of Section 1115 is drawn from Code of Civil Procedure Section 1775.1. To accommodate a wide range of mediation styles, the definition is broad, without specific limitations on format. For example, it would include a mediation conducted as a number of sessions, only some of which involve the mediator. The definition focuses on the nature of a proceeding, not its label. A proceeding may be a "mediation" for purposes of this chapter, even though it is denominated differently.

Under subdivision (b), a mediator must be neutral. The neutrality requirement is drawn from Code of Civil Procedure Section 1775.1. An attorney or other representative of a party is not neutral and so does not qualify as a "mediator" for purposes of this chapter.

A "mediator" may be an individual, group of individuals, or entity. See Section 175 ("person" defined). See also Section 10 (singular includes the plural). This definition of mediator encompasses not only the neutral person who takes the lead in conducting a mediation, but also any neutral who assists in the mediation, such as a case-developer, interpreter, or secretary. The definition focuses on a person's role, not the person's title. A person may be a "mediator" under this chapter even though the person has a different title, such as "ombudsperson." Any person who meets the definition of "mediator" must comply with Section 1121 (mediator reports and communications), which generally prohibits a mediator from reporting to a court or other tribunal concerning the mediated dispute.

Subdivision (c) is drawn from former Section 1152.5, which was amended in 1996 to explicitly protect mediation intake communications. See 1996 Cal. Stat. ch. 174, § 1. Subdivision (c) is not limited to communications to retain a mediator. It also encompasses contacts concerning whether to mediate, such as where a mediator contacts a disputant because another disputant desires to mediate, and contacts concerning initiation or recommencement of mediation, such as where a case-developer meets with a disputant before mediation.

For the scope of this chapter, see Section 1117. [1997–98 Annual Report, 27 Cal.L.Rev.Comm. Reports App. 5 (1997)]

§ 1116. Effect of chapter

(a) Nothing in this chapter expands or limits a court's authority to order participation in a dispute resolution proceeding. Nothing in this chapter authorizes or affects the enforceability of a contract clause in which parties agree to the use of mediation.

(b) Nothing in this chapter makes admissible evidence that is inadmissible under Section 1152 or any other statute.

LAW REVISION COMMISSION COMMENTS

1997 Addition

Subdivision (a) of Section 1116 establishes guiding principles for applying this chapter.

Subdivision (b) continues the first sentence of former Section 1152.5(c) without substantive change. [1997–98 Annual Report, 27 Cal. L.Rev.Comm. Reports App. 5 (1997)]

§ 1117. Application of chapter

(a) Except as provided in subdivision (b), this chapter applies to a mediation as defined in Section 1115.

(b) This chapter does not apply to either of the following:

(1) A proceeding under Part 1 (commencing with Section 1800) of Division 5 of the Family Code or Chapter 11 (commencing with Section 3160) of Part 2 of Division 8 of the Family Code.

(2) A settlement conference pursuant to Rule 222 of the California Rules of Court.

(Added by Stats.1997, c. 772 (A.B.939), § 3.)

LAW REVISION COMMISSION COMMENTS

1997 Addition

Under subdivision (a) of Section 1117, mediation confidentiality and the other safeguards of this chapter apply to a broad range of mediations. See Section 1115 Comment.

Subdivision (b) sets forth two exceptions. Section 1117(b)(1) continues without substantive change former Section 1152.5(b). Special confidentiality rules apply to a proceeding in family conciliation court or a mediation of child custody or visitation issues. See Section 1040; Fam. Code §§ 1818, 3177.

Section 1117(b)(2) establishes that a court settlement conference is not a mediation within the scope of this chapter. A settlement conference is conducted under the aura of the court and is subject to special rules. [1997–98 Annual Report, 27 Cal.L.Rev.Comm. Reports App. 5 (1997)]

§ 1118. Oral agreements

An oral agreement "in accordance with Section 1118" means an oral agreement that satisfies all of the following conditions:

(a) The oral agreement is recorded by a court reporter, tape recorder, or other reliable means of sound recording.

(b) The terms of the oral agreement are recited on the record in the presence of the parties and the mediator, and the parties express on the record that they agree to the terms recited.

(c) The parties to the oral agreement expressly state on the record that the agreement is enforceable or binding or words to that effect.

(d) The recording is reduced to writing and the writing is signed by the parties within 72 hours after it is recorded.

(Added by Stats.1997, c. 772 (A.B.939), § 3.)

LAW REVISION COMMISSION COMMENTS

1997 Addition

Section 1118 establishes a procedure for orally memorializing an agreement, in the interest of efficiency. Provisions permitting use of that procedure for certain purposes include Sections 1121 (mediator reports and communications), 1122 (disclosure by agreement), 1123 (written settlement agreements reached through mediation), and 1124 (oral agreements reached through mediation). See also Section 1125 (when mediation ends). For guidance on authority to bind a litigant, see Williams v. Saunders, 55 Cal. App. 4th 1158, 64 Cal. Rptr. 2d 571 (1997) ("The litigants' direct participation tends to ensure that the settlement is the result of their mature reflection and deliberate assent.") [1997–98 Annual Report, 27 Cal.L.Rev.Comm. Reports App. 5 (1997)]

§ 1119. Written or oral communications during mediation process; admissibility

Except as otherwise provided in this chapter:

(a) No evidence of anything said or any admission made for the purpose of, in the course of, or pursuant to, a mediation or a mediation consultation is admissible or subject to discovery, and disclosure of the evidence shall not be compelled, in any arbitration, administrative adjudication, civil action, or other noncriminal proceeding in which, pursuant to law, testimony can be compelled to be given.

(b) No writing, as defined in Section 250, that is prepared for the purpose of, in the course of, or pursuant to, a mediation or a mediation consultation, is admissible or subject to discovery, and disclosure of the writing shall not be compelled, in any arbitration, administrative adjudication, civil action, or other noncriminal proceeding in which, pursuant to law, testimony can be compelled to be given.

(c) All communications, negotiations, or settlement discussions by and between participants in the course of a mediation or a mediation consultation shall remain confidential.

(Added by Stats.1997, c. 772 (A.B.939), § 3.)

LAW REVISION COMMISSION COMMENTS

1997 Addition

Subdivision (a) of Section 1119 continues without substantive change former Section 1152.5(a)(1), except that its protection explicitly applies in a subsequent arbitration or administrative adjudication, as well as in any civil action or proceeding. See Section 120 ("civil action" includes civil proceedings). In addition, the protection of Section 1119(a) extends to oral communications made for the purpose of or pursuant to a mediation, not just oral communications made in the course of the mediation.

Subdivision (b) continues without substantive change former Section 1152.5(a)(2), except that its protection explicitly applies in a subsequent arbitration or administrative adjudication, as well as in any civil action or proceeding. See Section 120 ("civil action" includes civil proceedings). In addition, subdivision (b) expressly encompasses any type of "writing" as defined in Section 250, regardless of whether the representations are on paper or on some other medium.

Subdivision (c) continues former Section 1152.5(a)(3) without substantive change. A mediation is confidential notwithstanding the presence of an observer, such as a person evaluating or training the mediator or studying the mediation process.

See Sections 1115(a) ("mediation" defined), 1115(c) ("mediation consultation" defined). See also Section 703.5 (testimony by a judge, arbitrator, or mediator).

For examples of specialized mediation confidentiality provisions, see Bus. & Prof. Code §§ 467.4–467.5 (community dispute resolution programs), 6200 (attorney-client fee disputes); Code Civ. Proc. §§ 1297.371 (international commercial disputes), 1775.10 (civil action mediation in participating courts); Fam. Code §§ 1818 (family conciliation court), 3177 (child custody); Food & Agric. Code § 54453 (agricultural cooperative bargaining associations); Gov't Code §§ 11420.20–11420.30 (administrative adjudication), 12984–12985 (housing discrimination), 66032–66033 (land use); Ins. Code § 10089.80 (earthquake insurance); Lab. Code § 65 (labor disputes); Welf. & Inst. Code § 350 (dependency mediation). See also Cal. Const. art. I, § 1 (right to privacy); Garstang v. Superior Court, 39 Cal. App. 4th 526, 46 Cal. Rptr. 2d 84, 88 (1995) (constitutional right of privacy protected communications made during mediation sessions before an ombudsperson). [1997–98 Annual Report, 27 Cal.L.Rev.Comm. Reports App. 5 (1997)]

§ 1120. Evidence otherwise admissible

(a) Evidence otherwise admissible or subject to discovery outside of a mediation or a mediation consultation shall not be or become inadmissible or protected from disclosure solely by reason of its introduction or use in a mediation or a mediation consultation.

(b) This chapter does not limit any of the following:

(1) The admissibility of an agreement to mediate a dispute.

(2) The effect of an agreement not to take a default or an agreement to extend the time within which to act or refrain from acting in a pending civil action.

(3) Disclosure of the mere fact that a mediator has served, is serving, will serve, or was contacted about serving as a mediator in a dispute.

LAW REVISION COMMISSION COMMENTS

1997 Addition

Subdivision (a) of Section 1120 continues former Section 1152.5(a)(6) without change. It limits the scope of Section 1119 (mediation confidentiality), preventing parties from using a mediation as a pretext to shield materials from disclosure.

Subdivision (b)(1) makes explicit that Section 1119 does not restrict admissibility of an agreement to mediate. Subdivision (b)(2) continues former Section 1152.5(e) without substantive change, but also includes an express exception for extensions of litigation deadlines. Subdivision (b)(3) makes clear that Section 1119 does not preclude a disputant from obtaining basic information about a mediator's track record, which may be significant in selecting an impartial mediator. Similarly, mediation participants may express their views on a mediator's performance, so long as they do not disclose anything said or done at the mediation.

See Sections 1115(a) ("mediation" defined), 1115(b) ("mediator" defined), 1115(c) ("mediation consultation" defined). [1997–98 Annual Report, 27 Cal.L.Rev.Comm. Reports App. 5 (1997)]

§ 1121. Mediator's reports and findings

Neither a mediator nor anyone else may submit to a court or other adjudicative body, and a court or other adjudicative body may not consider, any report, assessment, evaluation, recommendation, or finding of any kind by the mediator concerning a mediation conducted by the mediator, other than a report that is mandated by court rule or other law and that states only whether an agreement was reached, unless all parties to the mediation expressly agree otherwise in writing, or orally in accordance with Section 1118.

LAW REVISION COMMISSION COMMENTS

1997 Addition

Section 1121 continues the first sentence of former Section 1152.6 without substantive change, except to make clear that (1) the section applies to all submissions, not just filings, (2) the section is not limited to court proceedings but rather applies to all types of adjudications, including arbitrations and administrative adjudications, (3) the section applies to any report or statement of opinion, however denominated, and (4) neither a mediator nor anyone else may submit the prohibited information. The section does not prohibit a mediator from providing a mediation participant with feedback on the dispute in the course of the mediation.

Rather, the focus is on preventing coercion. As Section 1121 recognizes, a mediator should not be able to influence the result of a mediation or adjudication by reporting or threatening to report to the decisionmaker on the merits of the dispute or reasons why mediation failed to resolve it. Similarly, a mediator should not have authority to resolve or decide the mediated dispute, and should not have any function for the adjudicating tribunal with regard to the dispute, except as a non-decisionmaking neutral. See Section 1117 (scope of chapter), which excludes settlement conferences from this chapter.

The exception to Section 1121 (permitting submission and consideration of a mediator's report where "all parties to the mediation expressly agree" in writing) is modified to allow use of the oral procedure in Section 1118 (recorded oral agreement) and to permit making of the agreement at any time, not just before the mediation. A mediator's report to a court may disclose mediation communications only if all parties to the mediation agree to the reporting and all persons who participate in the mediation agree to the disclosure. See Section 1122 (disclosure by agreement).

The second sentence of former Section 1152.6 is continued without substantive change in Section 1117 (scope of chapter), except that Section 1117 excludes proceedings under Part 1 (commencing with Section 1800) of Division 5 of the Family Code, as well as proceedings under Chapter 11 (commencing with Section 3160) of Part 2 of Division 8 of the Family Code.

See Sections 1115(a) ("mediation" defined), 1115(b) ("mediator" defined). See also Sections 703.5 (testimony by a judge, arbitrator, or mediator), 1127 (attorney's fees), 1128 (irregularity in proceedings). [1997–98 Annual Report, 27 Cal.L.Rev.Comm. Reports App. 5 (1997)]

§ 1122. Communications or writings; conditions to admissibility

(a) A communication or a writing, as defined in Section 250, that is made or prepared for the purpose of, or in the course of, or pursuant to, a mediation or a mediation consultation, is not made inadmissible, or protected from disclosure, by provisions of this chapter if either of the following conditions is satisfied:

(1) All persons who conduct or otherwise participate in the mediation expressly agree in writing, or orally in accordance with Section 1118, to disclosure of the communication, document, or writing.

(2) The communication, document, or writing was prepared by or on behalf of fewer than all the mediation participants, those participants expressly agree in writing, or orally in accordance with Section 1118, to its disclosure, and the communication, document, or writing does not disclose anything said or done or any admission made in the course of the mediation.

(b) For purposes of subdivision (a), if the neutral person who conducts a mediation expressly agrees to disclosure, that agreement also binds any other person described in subdivision (b) of Section 1115.

LAW REVISION COMMISSION COMMENTS

1997 Addition

Section 1122 supersedes former Section 1152.5(a)(4) and part of former Section 1152.5(a)(2), which were unclear regarding precisely whose agreement was required for admissibility or disclosure of mediation communications and documents.

Subdivision (a)(1) states the general rule that mediation documents and communications may be admitted or disclosed only upon agreement of all participants, including not only parties but also the mediator and other nonparties attending the mediation (e.g., a disputant not involved in litigation, a spouse, an accountant, an insurance representative, or an employee of a corporate affiliate). Agreement must be express, not implied. For example, parties cannot be deemed to have agreed in advance to disclosure merely because they agreed to participate in a particular dispute resolution program.

Subdivision (a)(2) facilitates admissibility and disclosure of unilaterally prepared materials, but it only applies so long as those materials may be produced in a manner revealing nothing about the mediation discussion. Materials that necessarily disclose mediation communications may be admitted or disclosed only upon satisfying the general rule of subdivision (a)(1).

Mediation materials that satisfy the requirements of subdivisions (a)(1) or (a)(2) are not necessarily admissible or subject to disclosure. Although the provisions on mediation confidentiality do not bar admissibility or disclosure, there may be other bases for exclusion.

Subdivision (b) makes clear that if the person who takes the lead in conducting a mediation agrees to disclosure, it is unnecessary to seek out and obtain assent from each assistant to that person, such as a case developer, interpreter, or secretary.

For exceptions to Section 1122, see Sections 1123 (written settlement agreements reached through mediation) and 1124 (oral agreements reached through mediation) & Comments.

See Section 1115(a) ("mediation" defined), 1115(c) ("mediation consultation" defined). See also Sections 703.5 (testimony by a judge, arbitrator, or mediator), 1119 (mediation confidentiality), 1121 (mediator reports and communications). [1997–98 Annual Report, 27 Cal.L.Rev. Comm. Reports App. 5 (1997)]

§ 1123. Written settlement agreements; conditions to admissibility

A written settlement agreement prepared in the course of, or pursuant to, a mediation, is not made inadmissible, or protected from disclosure, by provisions of this chapter if the agreement is signed by the settling parties and any of the following conditions are satisfied:

(a) The agreement provides that it is admissible or subject to disclosure, or words to that effect.

(b) The agreement provides that it is enforceable or binding or words to that effect.

(c) All parties to the agreement expressly agree in writing, or orally in accordance with Section 1118, to its disclosure.

(d) The agreement is used to show fraud, duress, or illegality that is relevant to an issue in dispute.

LAW REVISION COMMISSION COMMENTS

1997 Addition

Section 1123 consolidates and clarifies provisions governing written settlements reached through mediation. For guidance on binding a disputant to a written settlement agreement, see Williams v. Saunders, 55 Cal. App. 4th 1158, 64 Cal. Rptr. 2d 571 (1997) ("The litigants' direct participation tends to ensure that the settlement is the result of their mature reflection and deliberate assent.").

As to an executed written settlement agreement, subdivision (a) continues part of former Section 1152.5(a)(2). See also Ryan v. Garcia, 27 Cal. App. 4th 1006, 1012, 33 Cal. Rptr. 2d 158, 162 (1994) (Section 1152.5 "provides a simple means by which settlement agreements executed during mediation can be made admissible in later proceedings," i.e., the "parties may consent, as part of a writing, to subsequent admissibility of the agreement").

Subdivision (b) is new. It is added due to the likelihood that parties intending to be bound will use words to that effect, rather than saying their agreement is intended to be admissible or subject to disclosure.

As to fully executed written settlement agreements, subdivision (c) supersedes former Section 1152.5(a)(4). To facilitate enforceability of such agreements, disclosure pursuant to subdivision (c) requires only agreement of the parties. Agreement of the mediator and other mediation participants is not necessary. Subdivision (c) is thus an exception to the general rule governing disclosure of mediation communications by agreement. See Section 1122.

Subdivision (d) continues former Section 1152.5(a)(5) without substantive change.

A written settlement agreement that satisfies the requirements of subdivision (a), (b), (c), or (d) is not necessarily admissible or subject to disclosure. Although the provisions on mediation confidentiality do not bar admissibility or disclosure, there may be other bases for exclusion.

See Section 1115(a) ("mediation" defined). [1997–98 Annual Report, 27 Cal.L.Rev.Comm. Reports App. 5 (1997)]

§ 1124. Oral agreements; conditions to admissibility

An oral agreement made in the course of, or pursuant to, a mediation is not made inadmissible, or protected from disclosure, by the provisions of this chapter if any of the following conditions are satisfied:

(a) The agreement is in accordance with Section 1118.

(b) The agreement is in accordance with subdivisions (a), (b), and (d) of Section 1118, and all parties to the agreement expressly agree, in writing or orally in accordance with Section 1118, to disclosure of the agreement.

(c) The agreement is in accordance with subdivisions (a), (b), and (d) of Section 1118, and the agreement is used to show fraud, duress, or illegality that is relevant to an issue in dispute.

LAW REVISION COMMISSION COMMENTS

1997 Addition

Section 1124 sets forth specific circumstances under which mediation confidentiality is inapplicable to an oral agreement reached through mediation. Except in those circumstances, Sections 1119 (mediation confidentiality) and 1124 codify the rule of Ryan v. Garcia, 27 Cal. App. 4th 1006, 33 Cal. Rptr. 2d 158 (1994) (mediation confidentiality applies to oral statement of settlement terms), and reject the contrary approach of Regents of University of California v. Sumner, 42 Cal. App. 4th 1209, 50 Cal. Rptr. 2d 200 (1996) (mediation confidentiality does not protect oral statement of settlement terms).

Subdivision (a) of Section 1124 facilitates enforcement of an oral agreement that is recorded and memorialized in writing in accordance with Section 1118. For guidance in applying subdivision (a), see Section 1125 (when mediation ends) & Comment.

Subdivision (b) parallels Section 1123(c).

Subdivision (c) parallels Section 1123(d).

An oral agreement that satisfies the requirements of subdivision (a), (b), or (c) is not necessarily admissible or subject to disclosure. Although the provisions on mediation confidentiality do not bar admissibility or disclosure, there may be other bases for exclusion. For guidance on binding a disputant to a settlement agreement, see Williams v. Saunders, 55 Cal. App. 4th 1158, 64 Cal. Rptr. 2d 571 (1997) ("The litigants' direct participation tends to ensure that the settlement is the result of their mature reflection and deliberate assent.").

See Section 1115(a) ("mediation" defined). [1997–98 Annual Report, 27 Cal.L.Rev.Comm. Reports App. 5 (1997)]

§ 1125. End of mediation; satisfaction of conditions

(a) For purposes of confidentiality under this chapter, a mediation ends when any one of the following conditions is satisfied:

(1) The parties execute a written settlement agreement that fully resolves the dispute.

(2) An oral agreement that fully resolves the dispute is reached in accordance with Section 1118.

(3) The mediator provides the mediation participants with a writing signed by the mediator that states that the mediation is terminated, or words to that effect, which shall be consistent with Section 1121.

(4) A party provides the mediator and the other mediation participants with a writing stating that the mediation is terminated, or words to that effect, which shall be consistent with Section 1121. In a mediation involving more than two parties, the mediation may

continue as to the remaining parties or be terminated in accordance with this section.

(5) For 10 calendar days, there is no communication between the mediator and any of the parties to the mediation relating to the dispute. The mediator and the parties may shorten or extend this time by agreement.

(b) For purposes of confidentiality under this chapter, if a mediation partially resolves a dispute, mediation ends when either of the following conditions is satisfied:

(1) The parties execute a written settlement agreement that partially resolves the dispute.

(2) An oral agreement that partially resolves the dispute is reached in accordance with Section 1118.

(c) This section does not preclude a party from ending a mediation without reaching an agreement. This section does not otherwise affect the extent to which a party may terminate a mediation.

LAW REVISION COMMISSION COMMENTS

1997 Addition

By specifying when a mediation ends, Section 1125 provides guidance on which communications are protected by Section 1119 (mediation confidentiality).

Under subdivision (a)(1), if mediation participants reach an oral compromise and reduce it to a written settlement fully resolving their dispute, confidentiality extends until the agreement is signed by all the parties. For guidance on binding a disputant to a settlement agreement, see Williams v. Saunders, 55 Cal. App. 4th 1158, 64 Cal. Rptr. 2d 571 (1997) ("The litigants' direct participation tends to ensure that the settlement is the result of their mature reflection and deliberate assent.").

Subdivision (a)(2) applies where mediation participants fully resolve their dispute by an oral agreement that is recorded and memorialized in writing in accordance with Section 1118. The mediation is over upon completion of that procedure, and the confidentiality protections of this chapter do not apply to any later proceedings, such as attempts to further refine the content of the agreement. See Section 1124 (oral agreements reached through mediation). Subdivisions (a)(3) and (a)(4) are drawn from Rule 14 of the American Arbitration Association's Commercial Mediation Rules (as amended, Jan. 1, 1992). Subdivision (a)(5) applies where an affirmative act terminating a mediation for purposes of this chapter does not occur.

Subdivision (b) applies where mediation partially resolves a dispute, such as when the disputants resolve only some of the issues (e.g., contract, but not tort, liability) or when only some of the disputants settle.

Subdivision (c) limits the effect of Section 1125.

See Sections 1115(a) ("mediation" defined), 1115(b) ("mediator" defined). [1997–98 Annual Report, 27 Cal.L.Rev.Comm. Reports App. 5 (1997)]

§ 1126. Protections before and after mediation ends

Anything said, any admission made, or any writing that is inadmissible, protected from disclosure, and confidential under this chapter before a mediation ends, shall remain inadmissible, protected from disclosure, and confidential to the same extent after the mediation ends.

LAW REVISION COMMISSION COMMENTS

1997 Addition

Section 1126 clarifies that mediation materials are confidential not only during a mediation, but also after the mediation ends pursuant to Section 1125 (when mediation ends).

See Section 1115(a) ("mediation" defined). [1997–98 Annual Report, 27 Cal.L.Rev.Comm. Reports App. 5 (1997)]

§ 1127. Attorney's fees and costs

If a person subpoenas or otherwise seeks to compel a mediator to testify or produce a writing, as defined in Section 250, and the court or other adjudicative body determines that the testimony or writing is inadmissible under this chapter, or protected from disclosure under this chapter, the court or adjudicative body making the determination shall award reasonable attorney's fees and costs to the mediator against the person seeking the testimony or writing.

LAW REVISION COMMISSION COMMENTS

1997 Addition

Section 1127 continues former Section 1152.5(d) without substantive change, except to clarify that either a court or another adjudicative body (e.g., an arbitrator or an administrative tribunal) may award the fees and costs. Because Section 1115 (definitions) defines "mediator" to include not only the neutral person who takes the lead in conducting a mediation, but also any neutral who assists in the mediation, fees are available regardless of the role played by the person subjected to discovery.

See Section 1115(b) ("mediator" defined). [1997–98 Annual Report, 27 Cal.L.Rev.Comm. Reports App. 5 (1997)]

§ 1128. Subsequent trials; references to mediation

Any reference to a mediation during any subsequent trial is an irregularity in the proceedings of the trial for the purposes of Section 657 of the Code of Civil Procedure. Any reference to a mediation during any other subsequent noncriminal proceeding is grounds for vacating or modifying the decision in that proceeding, in whole or in part, and granting a new or further hearing on all or part of the issues, if the reference materially affected the substantial rights of the party requesting relief.

LAW REVISION COMMISSION COMMENTS

1997 Addition

Section 1128 is drawn from Code of Civil Procedure Section 1775.12. The first sentence makes it an irregularity to refer to a mediation in a subsequent civil trial; the second sentence extends that rule to other noncriminal proceedings, such as an administrative adjudication. An appropriate situation for invoking this section is where a party urges the trier of fact to draw an adverse inference from an adversary's refusal to disclose mediation communications.

See Section 1115 (“mediation” defined). [1997–98 Annual Report, 27 Cal.L.Rev.Comm. Reports App. 5 (1997)]

CHAPTER 3. OTHER EVIDENCE AFFECTED OR EXCLUDED BY EXTRINSIC POLICIES

§ 1150. Evidence to test a verdict

(a) Upon an inquiry as to the validity of a verdict, any otherwise admissible evidence may be received as to statements made, or conduct, conditions, or events occurring, either within or without the jury room, of such a character as is likely to have influenced the verdict improperly. No evidence is admissible to show the effect of such statement, conduct, condition, or event upon a juror either in influencing him to assent to or dissent from the verdict or concerning the mental processes by which it was determined.

(b) Nothing in this code affects the law relating to the competence of a juror to give evidence to impeach or support a verdict.

§ 1151. Subsequent remedial conduct

When, after the occurrence of an event, remedial or precautionary measures are taken, which, if taken previously, would have tended to make the event less likely to occur, evidence of such subsequent measures is inadmissible to prove negligence or culpable conduct in connection with the event.

LAW REVISION COMMISSION COMMENT

Section 1151 codifies well-settled law. Helling v. Schindler, 145 Cal. 303, 78 Pac. 710 (1904); Sappenfield v. Main Street etc. R.R., 91 Cal. 48,

27 Pac. 590 (1891). The admission of evidence of subsequent repairs to prove negligence would substantially discourage persons from making repairs after the occurrence of an accident.

Section 1151 does not prevent the use of evidence of subsequent remedial conduct for the purpose of impeachment in appropriate cases. This is in accord with Pierce v. J. C. Penney Co., 167 Cal.App.2d 3, 334 P.2d 117 (1959). [7 Cal.L.Rev.Comm. Reports 1 (1965)]

§ 1152. Offer to compromise

(a) Evidence that a person has, in compromise or from humanitarian motives, furnished or offered or promised to furnish money or any other thing, act, or service to another who has sustained or will sustain or claims that he or she has sustained or will sustain loss or damage, as well as any conduct or statements made in negotiation thereof, is inadmissible to prove his or her liability for the loss or damage or any part of it.

(b) In the event that evidence of an offer to compromise is admitted in an action for breach of the covenant of good faith and fair dealing or violation of subdivision (h) of Section 790.03 of the Insurance Code, then at the request of the party against whom the evidence is admitted, or at the request of the party who made the offer to compromise that was admitted, evidence relating to any other offer or counteroffer to compromise the same or substantially the same claimed loss or damage shall also be admissible for the same purpose as the initial evidence regarding settlement. Other than as may be admitted in an action for breach of the covenant of good faith and fair dealing or violation of subdivision (h) of Section 790.03 of the Insurance Code, evidence of settlement offers shall not be admitted in a motion for a new trial, in any proceeding involving an additur or remittitur, or on appeal.

(c) This section does not affect the admissibility of evidence of any of the following:

(1) Partial satisfaction of an asserted claim or demand without questioning its validity when such evidence is offered to prove the validity of the claim.

(2) A debtor's payment or promise to pay all or a part of his or her preexisting debt when such evidence is offered to prove the creation of a new duty on his or her part or a revival of his or her preexisting duty.

LAW REVISION COMMISSION COMMENT

1965 Enactment

Section 1152, like Section 2078 of the Code of Civil Procedure which it supersedes, declares that compromise offers are inadmissible to prove liability. Because of the particular wording of Section 2078, an offer of compromise probably may not be considered as an admission even though admitted without objection. See Tentative Recommendation and a Study Relating to the Uniform Rules of Evidence (Article VI. Extrinsic Policies Affecting Admissibility), 6 Cal.Law Revision Comm'n, Rep., Rec. & Studies 601, 675–676 (1964). See also Scott v. Wood, 81 Cal. 398, 405–406, 22 Pac. 871, 873 (1889). Under Section 1152, however, nothing prohibits the consideration of an offer of settlement on the issue of liability if the evidence is received without objection. This modest change in the law is desirable. An offer of compromise, like other incompetent evidence, should be considered to the extent that it is relevant when it is presented to the trier of fact without objection.

The words "as well as any conduct or statements made in negotiation thereof" make it clear that statements made by parties during negotiations for the settlement of a claim may not be used as admissions in later litigation. This language will change the existing law under which certain statements made during settlement negotiations may be used as admissions. People v. Forster, 58 Cal.2d 257, 23 Cal.Rptr. 582, 373 P.2d 630 (1962). The rule excluding offers is based upon the public policy in favor of the settlement of disputes without litigation. The same public policy requires that admissions made during settlement negotiations also be excluded. The rule of the Forster case that permits such statements to be admitted places a premium on the form of the statement. The statement "Assuming, for the purposes of these negotiations, that I was negligent . . ." is inadmissible; but the statement "All right, I was negligent! Let's talk about damages . . ." may be admissible. See the discussion in People v. Glen Arms Estate, Inc., 230 Cal.App.2d 841, 863, 864, 41 Cal.Rptr. 303, 316 (1964). The rule of the Forster case is changed by Section 1152 because that rule prevents the complete candor between the parties that is most conducive to settlement. [7 Cal.L.Rev.Comm. Reports 1 (1965)]

1967 Amendment

The amendment to Section 1152 is intended to clarify the meaning of the section without changing its substantive effect. The words "or will sustain" have been added to make it clear that the section applies to statements made in the course of negotiations concerning future loss or damage as well as past loss or damage. Such negotiations might occur as a result of an alleged anticipatory breach of contract or as an incident of an eminent domain proceeding. [8 Cal.L.Rev.Comm. Reports 101 (1967)]

§ 1152.5. Repealed by Stats.1997, c. 772 (A.B.939), § 5

§ 1152.6. Repealed by Stats.1997, c. 772 (A.B.939), § 6

§ 1153. Offer to plead guilty or withdrawn plea of guilty by criminal defendant

Evidence of a plea of guilty, later withdrawn, or of an offer to plead guilty to the crime charged or to any other crime, made by the defendant in a criminal action is inadmissible in any action or in any proceeding of any nature, including proceedings before agencies, commissions, boards, and tribunals.

LAW REVISION COMMISSION COMMENT

Section 1153 is consistent with existing law. Under existing law, evidence of a rejected offer to plead guilty to the crime charged or to a lesser crime is inadmissible. Penal Code § 1192.4; People v. Wilson, 60 Cal.2d 139, 155–156, 32 Cal.Rptr. 44, 54–55, 383 P.2d 452, 462–463 (1963); People v. Hamilton, 60 Cal.2d 105, 113–114, 32 Cal.Rptr. 4, 8–9, 383 P.2d 412, 146–417 (1963). Likewise, a plea of guilty, later withdrawn, is inadmissible. People v. Quinn, 61 Cal.2d 551, 39 Cal.Rptr. 393, 393 P.2d 705 (1964). [7 Cal.L.Rev.Comm. Reports 1 (1965)]

§ 1153.5. Offer for civil resolution of crimes against property

Evidence of an offer for civil resolution of a criminal matter pursuant to the provisions of Section 33 of the Code of Civil Procedure, or admissions made in the course of or negotiations for the offer shall not be admissible in any action.

§ 1154. Offer to discount a claim

Evidence that a person has accepted or offered or promised to accept a sum of money or any other thing, act, or service in satisfaction of a claim, as well as any conduct or statements made in negotiation thereof, is inadmissible to prove the invalidity of the claim or any part of it.

LAW REVISION COMMISSION COMMENT

Section 1154 stems from the same policy of encouraging settlement and compromise that is reflected in Section 1152. Except for the language "as well as any conduct or statements made in negotiation thereof," this section codifies existing law. Dennis v. Belt, 30 Cal. 247 (1866); Anderson v. Yousem, 177 Cal.App.2d 135, 1 Cal.Rptr. 889 (1960); Cramer v. Lee Wa Corp., 109 Cal.App.2d 591, 241 P.2d 550 (1952). The significance of the quoted language is indicated in the Comment to Section 1152. [7 Cal.L.Rev.Comm. Reports 1 (1965)]

§ 1155. Liability insurance

Evidence that a person was, at the time a harm was suffered by another, insured wholly or partially against loss arising from liability for that harm is inadmissible to prove negligence or other wrongdoing.

LAW REVISION COMMISSION COMMENT

Section 1155 codifies existing law. Roche v. Llewellyn Iron Works Co., 140 Cal. 563, 74 Pac. 147 (1903). Evidence of liability insurance might be inadmissible in the absence of Section 1155 because it is not relevant; Section 1155 assures its inadmissibility. [7 Cal.L.Rev.Comm. Reports 1 (1965)]

§ 1156. Records of medical study of in-hospital staff committee

(a) In-hospital medical or medical-dental staff committees of a licensed hospital may engage in research and medical or dental study for the purpose of reducing morbidity or mortality, and may make findings and recommendations relating to such purpose. Except as provided in subdivision (b), the written records of interviews, reports, statements, or memoranda of such in-hospital medical or medical-dental staff committees relating to such medical or dental studies are subject to Sections 2016 to 2036, inclusive, of the Code of Civil Procedure (relating to discovery proceedings) but, subject to subdivisions (c) and (d), shall not be admitted as evidence in any action or before any administrative body, agency, or person.

(b) The disclosure, with or without the consent of the patient, of information concerning him to such in-hospital medical or medical-dental staff committee does not make unprivileged any information that would otherwise be privileged under Section 994 or 1014; but, notwithstanding Sections 994 and 1014, such information is subject to discovery under subdivision (a) except that the identity of any patient may not be discovered under subdivision (a) unless the patient consents to such disclosure.

(c) This section does not affect the admissibility in evidence of the original medical or dental records of any patient.

(d) This section does not exclude evidence which is relevant evidence in a criminal action.

§ 1156.1. Records of medical or psychiatric studies of quality assurance committees

(a) A committee established in compliance with Sections 4070 and 5624 of the Welfare and Institutions Code may engage in research and medical or psychiatric study for the purpose of reducing morbidity or mortality, and may make findings and recommendations to the county and state relating to such purpose. Except as provided in subdivision (b), the written records of interviews, reports, statements, or memoranda of such committees relating to such medical or psychiatric studies are subject to Sections 2016 to 2036, inclusive, of the Code of Civil Procedure but, subject to subdivisions (c) and (d), shall not be admitted as evidence in any action or before any administrative body, agency, or person.

(b) The disclosure, with or without the consent of the patient, of information concerning him or her to such committee does not make unprivileged any information that would otherwise be privileged under Section 994 or 1014. However, notwithstanding Sections 994 and 1014, such information is subject to discovery under subdivision (a) except that the identity of any patient may not be discovered under subdivision (a) unless the patient consents to such disclosure.

(c) This section does not affect the admissibility in evidence of the original medical or psychiatric records of any patient.

(d) This section does not exclude evidence which is relevant evidence in a criminal action.

§ 1157. Proceedings and records of organized committees having responsibility of evaluation and improvement of quality of care; exceptions

(a) Neither the proceedings nor the records of organized committees of medical, medical-dental, podiatric, registered dietitian, psychological, marriage and family therapist, licensed clinical social worker, or veterinary staffs in hospitals, or of a peer review body, as defined in Section 805 of the Business and Professions Code, having the responsibility of evaluation and improvement of the quality of care rendered in the hospital, or for that peer review body, or medical or dental review or dental hygienist review or chiropractic review or podiatric review or registered dietitian review or veterinary review or acupuncturist review committees of local medical, dental, dental hygienist, podiatric, dietetic, veterinary, acupuncture, or chiropractic societies, marriage and family therapist, licensed clinical social worker, or psychological review committees of state or local marriage and family therapist, state or local psychological associations or societies having the responsibility of evaluation and improvement of the quality of care, shall be subject to discovery.

(b) Except as hereinafter provided, no person in attendance at a meeting of any of those committees shall be required to testify as to what transpired at that meeting.

(c) The prohibition relating to discovery or testimony does not apply to the statements made by any person in attendance at a meeting of any of those committees who is a party to an action or proceeding the subject matter of which was reviewed at that meeting, or to any person requesting hospital staff privileges, or in any action against an insurance carrier alleging bad faith by the carrier in refusing to accept a settlement offer within the policy limits.

(d) The prohibitions in this section do not apply to medical, dental, dental hygienist, podiatric, dietetic, psychological, marriage and family therapist, licensed clinical social worker, veterinary, acupuncture, or chiropractic society committees that exceed 10 percent of the membership of the society, nor to any of those committees if any person serves upon the committee when his or her own conduct or practice is being reviewed.

(e) The amendments made to this section by Chapter 1081 of the Statutes of 1983, or at the 1985 portion of the 1985–86 Regular Session of the Legislature, or at the 1990 portion of the 1989–90 Regular Session of the Legislature, or at the 2000 portion of the 1999-2000 Regular Session of the Legislature, do not exclude the discovery or use of relevant evidence in a criminal action.

§ 1157.5. Organized committee of nonprofit medical care foundation or professional standards review organization; proceedings and records

Except in actions involving a claim of a provider of health care services for payment for such services, the prohibition relating to discovery or testimony provided by Section 1157 shall be applicable to the proceedings or records of an organized committee of any nonprofit medical care foundation or professional standards review organization which is organized in a manner which makes available professional competence to review health care services with respect to medical necessity, quality of care, or economic justification of charges or level of care.

§ 1157.6. Proceedings and records of quality assurance committees for county health facilities

Neither the proceedings nor the records of a committee established in compliance with Sections 4070 and 5624 of the Welfare and Institutions Code having the responsibility of evaluation and improvement of the quality of mental health care rendered in county operated and contracted mental health facilities shall be subject to discovery. Except as provided in this section, no person in attendance at a meeting of any such committee shall be required to testify as to what transpired thereat. The prohibition relating to discovery or testimony shall not apply to the statements made by any person in attendance at such a meeting who is a party to an action or proceeding the subject matter of which was reviewed at such meeting, or to any person requesting facility staff privileges.

§ 1157.7. Application of Section 1157 discovery or testimony prohibitions; application of public records and meetings provisions

The prohibition relating to discovery or testimony provided in Section 1157 shall be applicable to proceedings and records of any committee established by a local governmental agency to monitor, evaluate, and report on the necessity, quality, and level of specialty health services, including, but not limited to, trauma care services, provided by a general acute care hospital which has been designated or recognized by that governmental agency as qualified to render specialty health care services. The provisions of Chapter 3.5 (commencing with Section 6250) of Division 7 of Title 1 of the Government Code and Chapter 9 (commencing with Section 54950) of Division 2 of Title 5 of the Government Code shall not be applicable to the committee records and proceedings.

§ 1158. Inspection and copying of patient's records; authorization; failure to comply; costs

Whenever, prior to the filing of any action or the appearance of a defendant in an action, an attorney at law or his or her representative presents a written authorization therefor signed by an adult patient, by the guardian or conservator of his or her person or estate, or, in the case of a minor, by a parent or guardian of the minor, or by the personal representative or an heir of a deceased patient, or a copy thereof, a physician and surgeon, dentist, registered nurse, dispensing optician, registered physical therapist, podiatrist, licensed psychologist, osteopathic physician and surgeon, chiropractor, clinical laboratory bioanalyst, clinical laboratory technologist, or pharmacist or pharmacy, duly licensed as such under the laws of the state, or a licensed hospital, shall make all of the patient's records under his, hers or its custody or control available for inspection and copying by the attorney at law or his, or her, representative, promptly upon the presentation of the written authorization.

No copying may be performed by any medical provider or employer enumerated above, or by an agent thereof, when the requesting attorney has employed a professional photocopier or anyone identified in Section 22451 of the Business and Professions Code as his or her representative to obtain or review the records on his or her behalf. The presentation of the authorization by the agent on behalf of the attorney shall be sufficient proof that the agent is the attorney's representative.

Failure to make the records available, during business hours, within five days after the presentation of the written authorization, may subject the person or entity having custody or control of the records to liability for all reasonable expenses, including attorney's fees, incurred in any proceeding to enforce this section.

All reasonable costs incurred by any person or entity enumerated above in making patient records available pursuant to this section may be charged against the person whose written authorization required the availability of the records.

"Reasonable cost," as used in this section, shall include, but not be limited to, the following specific costs: ten cents ($0.10) per page for standard reproduction of documents of a size 8 ½ by 14 inches or less; twenty cents ($0.20) per page for copying of documents from microfilm; actual costs for the reproduction of oversize documents or the reproduction of documents requiring special processing which are made in response to an authorization; reasonable clerical costs incurred in locating and making the records available to be billed at the maximum rate of sixteen dollars ($16) per hour per person, computed on the basis of four dollars ($4) per quarter hour or fraction thereof; actual postage charges; and actual costs, if any, charged to the witness by a third person for the retrieval and return of records held by that third person.

Where the records are delivered to the attorney or the attorney's representative for inspection or photocopying at the record custodian's place of business, the only fee for complying with the authorization shall not exceed fifteen dollars ($15), plus actual costs, if any, charged to the record custodian by a third person for retrieval and return of records held offsite by the third person.

§ 1159. Animal experimentation in product liability actions

(a) No evidence pertaining to live animal experimentation, including, but not limited to, injury, impact, or crash experimentation, shall be admissible in any product liability action involving a motor vehicle or vehicles.

(b) This section shall apply to cases for which a trial has not actually commenced, as described in paragraph (6) of subdivision (a) of Section 581 of the Code of Civil Procedure, on January 1, 1993.

§ 1160. Admissibility of expressions of sympathy or benevolence; definitions

(a) The portion of statements, writings, or benevolent gestures expressing sympathy or a general sense of benevolence relating to the pain, suffering, or death of a person involved in an accident and made to that person or to the family of that person shall be inadmissible as evidence of an admission of liability in a civil action. A statement of fault, however, which is part of, or in addition to, any of the above shall not be inadmissible pursuant to this section.

(b) For purposes of this section:

(1) "Accident" means an occurrence resulting in injury or death to one or more persons which is not the result of willful action by a party.

(2) "Benevolent gestures" means actions which convey a sense of compassion or commiseration emanating from humane impulses.

(3) "Family" means the spouse, parent, grandparent, stepmother, stepfather, child, grandchild, brother, sister, half brother, half sister, adopted children of parent, or spouse's parents of an injured party.

DIVISION 10. HEARSAY EVIDENCE

CHAPTER 1. GENERAL PROVISIONS

§ 1200. The hearsay rule

(a) "Hearsay evidence" is evidence of a statement that was made other than by a witness while testifying at the hearing and that is offered to prove the truth of the matter stated.

(b) Except as provided by law, hearsay evidence is inadmissible.

(c) This section shall be known and may be cited as the hearsay rule.

§ 1201. Multiple hearsay

A statement within the scope of an exception to the hearsay rule is not inadmissible on the ground that the evidence of such statement is hearsay evidence if such hearsay evidence consists of one or more statements each of which meets the requirements of an exception to the hearsay rule.

LAW REVISION COMMISSION COMMENT

1965 Enactment

Section 1201 makes it possible to use admissible hearsay to prove another statement that is also admissible hearsay. For example, under Section 1201, an official reporter's transcript of the testimony at a previous trial may be used to prove the testimony previously given (Evidence Code § 1280); the former testimony may be used as evidence (Evidence Code § 1291) to prove that a party made a statement; and the party's statement is admissible against him as an admission (Evidence Code § 1220). Thus, under Section 1201, the evidence of the admission contained in the transcript is admissible because each of the hearsay statements involved is within an exception to the hearsay rule.

Although no California case has been found where the admissibility of "multiple hearsay" has been analyzed and discussed, the practice is apparently in accord with the rule stated in Section 1201. See, e.g., People v. Collup, 27 Cal.2d 829, 167 P.2d 714 (1946) (transcript of former testimony used to prove admission). [7 Cal.L.Rev.Comm. Reports 1 (1965)]

1967 Amendment

This amendment is designed to clarify the meaning of Section 1201 without changing its substantive effect. [8 Cal.L.Rev.Comm. Reports 101 (1967)]

§ 1202. Credibility of hearsay declarant

Evidence of a statement or other conduct by a declarant that is inconsistent with a statement by such declarant received in evidence as hearsay evidence is not inadmissible for the purpose of attacking the credibility of the declarant though he is not given and has not had an opportunity to explain or to deny such inconsistent statement or other conduct. Any other evidence offered to attack or support the credibility of the declarant is admissible if it would have been admissible had the declarant been a witness at the hearing. For the purposes of this section, the deponent of a deposition taken in the action in which it is offered shall be deemed to be a hearsay declarant.

LAW REVISION COMMISSION COMMENT

Section 1202 deals with the impeachment of a declarant whose hearsay statement is in evidence as distinguished from the impeachment of a witness who has testified. It clarifies two points. First, evidence to impeach a hearsay declarant is not to be excluded on the ground that it is collateral. Second, the rule applying to the impeachment of a witness—that a witness may be impeached by an inconsistent statement only if he is provided with an opportunity to explain or deny it—does not apply to a hearsay declarant.

When hearsay evidence in the form of former testimony has been admitted, the California courts have permitted a party to impeach the hearsay declarant with evidence of an inconsistent statement made by the hearsay declarant after the former testimony was given, even though the declarant was never given an opportunity to explain or deny the inconsistency. People v. Collup, 27 Cal.2d 829, 167 P.2d 714 (1946). Apparently, however, former testimony may not be impeached by evidence of an inconsistent statement made prior to the former testimony unless the would- be impeacher either did not know of the inconsistent statement at the time the former testimony was given or unless he had provided the declarant with an opportunity to explain or deny the inconsistent statement. People v. Greenwell, 20 Cal.App.2d 266, 66 P.2d 674 (1937), as limited by People v. Collup, 27 Cal.2d 829, 167 P.2d 714 (1946). The courts permit dying declarations to be impeached by evidence of contradictory statements by the deceased despite the lack of any foundation, for only in very rare cases would it be possible to provide the declarant with an opportunity to explain or deny the inconsistency. People v. Lawrence, 21 Cal. 368 (1863).

Section 1202 substitutes for this case law a uniform rule permitting a hearsay declarant to be impeached by inconsistent statements in all cases, whether or not the declarant has been given an opportunity to explain or deny the inconsistency. If the hearsay declarant is unavailable as a witness, the party against whom the evidence is admitted should not be deprived of both his right to cross-examine and his right to impeach. Cf. People v. Lawrence, 21 Cal. 368, 372 (1863). If the hearsay declarant is available, the party electing to use the hearsay of such a declarant should have the burden of calling him to explain or deny any alleged inconsistencies.

Of course, the trial judge may curb efforts to impeach hearsay declarants if he determines that the inquiry is becoming too remote from the issues that are actually at stake in the litigation. Evidence Code § 352.

Section 1235 provides that evidence of inconsistent statements made by a trial witness may be admitted to prove the truth of the matter stated. No similar exception to the hearsay rule is applicable to a hearsay declarant's inconsistent statements that are admitted under Section 1202. Hence, the hearsay rule prohibits any such statement from being used to prove the truth of the matter stated. If the declarant is not a witness and is not subject to cross-examination upon the subject matter of his statements, there is no sufficient guarantee of the trustworthiness of the statements he has made out of court to warrant their reception as substantive evidence unless they fall within some recognized exception to the hearsay rule. [7 Cal.L.Rev.Comm. Reports 1 (1965)]

§ 1203. Cross-examination of hearsay declarant

(a) The declarant of a statement that is admitted as hearsay evidence may be called and examined by any adverse party as if under cross-examination concerning the statement.

(b) This section is not applicable if the declarant is (1) a party, (2) a person identified with a party within the meaning of subdivision (d) of Section 776, or (3) a witness who has testified in the action concerning the subject matter of the statement.

(c) This section is not applicable if the statement is one described in Article 1 (commencing with Section 1220), Article 3 (commencing with Section 1235), or Article 10 (commencing with Section 1300) of Chapter 2 of this division.

(d) A statement that is otherwise admissible as hearsay evidence is not made inadmissible by this section because the declarant who made the statement is unavailable for examination pursuant to this section.

§ 1203.1. Hearsay offered at preliminary examination; inapplication of § 1203

Section 1203 is not applicable if the hearsay statement is offered at a preliminary examination, as provided in Section 872 of the Penal Code.

§ 1204. Hearsay statement offered against criminal defendant

A statement that is otherwise admissible as hearsay evidence is inadmissible against the defendant in a criminal action if the statement was made, either by the defendant or by another, under such circumstances that it is inadmissible against the defendant under the Constitution of the United States or the State of California.

§ 1205. No implied repeal

Nothing in this division shall be construed to repeal by implication any other statute relating to hearsay evidence.

LAW REVISION COMMISSION COMMENT

Although some of the statutes providing for the admission of hearsay evidence will be repealed when the Evidence Code is enacted, a number of statutes will remain in the various codes. For the most part, these statutes are narrowly drawn to make a particular type of hearsay evidence admissible under specifically limited circumstances. To assure the continued validity of these provisions, Section 1205 states that they will not be impliedly repealed by the enactment of the Evidence Code. [7 Cal.L.Rev.Comm. Reports 1 (1965)]

CHAPTER 2. EXCEPTIONS TO THE HEARSAY RULE

ARTICLE 1. CONFESSIONS AND ADMISSIONS

§ 1220. Admission of party

Evidence of a statement is not made inadmissible by the hearsay rule when offered against the declarant in an action to which he is a party in either his individual or representative capacity, regardless of whether the statement was made in his individual or representative capacity.

LAW REVISION COMMISSION COMMENT

Section 1220 states existing law as found in subdivision 2 of Section 1870 of the Code of Civil Procedure. The rationale underlying this exception is that the party cannot object to the lack of the right to cross-examine the declarant since the party himself made the statement. Moreover, the party can cross-examine the witness who testifies to the party's statement and can explain or deny the purported admission. The statement need not be one which would be admissible if made at the hearing. See Shields v. Oxnard Harbor Dist., 46 Cal.App.2d 477, 116 P.2d 121 (1941).

In a criminal action, a defendant's statement is not admissible under this section unless it was made voluntarily. Evidence Code § 1204. [7 Cal.L.Rev.Comm. Reports 1 (1965)]

§ 1221. Adoptive admission

Evidence of a statement offered against a party is not made inadmissible by the hearsay rule if the statement is one of which the party, with knowledge of the content thereof, has by words or other conduct manifested his adoption or his belief in its truth.

LAW REVISION COMMISSION COMMENT

Section 1221 restates an exception found in subdivision 3 of Section 1870 of the Code of Civil Procedure. [7 Cal.L.Rev.Comm. Reports 1 (1965)]

§ 1222. Authorized admission

Evidence of a statement offered against a party is not made inadmissible by the hearsay rule if:

(a) The statement was made by a person authorized by the party to make a statement or statements for him concerning the subject matter of the statement; and

(b) The evidence is offered either after admission of evidence sufficient to sustain a finding of such authority or, in the court's discretion as to the order of proof, subject to the admission of such evidence.

LAW REVISION COMMISSION COMMENT

Section 1222 provides a hearsay exception for authorized admissions. Under this exception, if a party authorized an agent to make statements on his behalf, such statements may be introduced against the party under the same conditions as if they had been made by the party himself. The authority of the declarant to make the statement need not be express; it may be implied. It is to be determined in each case under the substantive law of agency. Section 1222 restates an exception found in the first portion of subdivision 5 of Section 1870 of the Code of Civil Procedure. See Tentative Recommendation and a Study Relating to the Uniform Rules of Evidence (Article VIII. Hearsay Evidence), 6 Cal.Law Revision Comm'n, Rep., Rec. & Studies Appendix at 484–490 (1964). [7 Cal.L.Rev.Comm. Reports 1 (1965)]

§ 1223. Admission of co-conspirator

Evidence of a statement offered against a party is not made inadmissible by the hearsay rule if:

(a) The statement was made by the declarant while participating in a conspiracy to commit a crime or civil wrong and in furtherance of the objective of that conspiracy;

(b) The statement was made prior to or during the time that the party was participating in that conspiracy; and

(c) The evidence is offered either after admission of evidence sufficient to sustain a finding of the facts specified in subdivisions (a) and (b) or, in the court's discretion as to the order of proof, subject to the admission of such evidence.

LAW REVISION COMMISSION COMMENT

Section 1223 is a specific example of a kind of authorized admission that is admissible under Section 1222 The statement is admitted because it is an act of the conspiracy for which the party, as a co-conspirator, is legally responsible. People v. Lorraine, 90 Cal.App. 317, 327, 265 Pac. 893, 897 (1928). See California Criminal Law Practice

471–472 (Cal.Cont.Ed.Bar 1964). Section 1223 restates an exception found in subdivision 6 of Section 1870 of the Code of Civil Procedure. [7 Cal.L.Rev.Comm. Reports 1 (1965)]

§ 1224. Statement of declarant whose liability or breach of duty is in issue

When the liability, obligation, or duty of a party to a civil action is based in whole or in part upon the liability, obligation, or duty of the declarant, or when the claim or right asserted by a party to a civil action is barred or diminished by a breach of duty by the declarant, evidence of a statement made by the declarant is as admissible against the party as it would be if offered against the declarant in an action involving that liability, obligation, duty, or breach of duty.

LAW REVISION COMMISSION COMMENT

Section 1224 restates in substance a hearsay exception found in Code of Civil Procedure Section 1851 (superseded by Evidence Code Sections 1224 and 1302). See Butte County v. Morgan, 76 Cal. 1, 18 Pac. 115 (1888); Ingram v. Bob Jaffe Co., 139 Cal.App.2d 193, 293 P.2d 132 (1956); Standard Oil Co. v. Houser, 101 Cal.App.2d 480, 225 P.2d 539 (1950). Section 1224, however, limits this hearsay exception to civil actions. Much of the evidence within this exception is also covered by Section 1230, which makes declarations against interest admissible. However, to be admissible under Section 1230, the statement must have been against the declarant's interest when made; this requirement is not stated in Section 1224.

Code of Civil Procedure Section 1851 provides for the admission of a declarant's statements in an action where the liability of the party against whom the statements are offered is based on the declarant's breach of duty. Butte County v. Morgan, 76 Cal. 1, 18 Pac. 115 (1888); Nye & Nissen v. Central etc. Ins. Corp., 71 Cal.App.2d 570, 163 P.2d 100 (1945). Section 1224 of the Evidence Code refers specifically to "breach of duty" in order to admit statements of a declarant whose breach of duty is in issue without regard to whether that breach gives rise to a liability of the party against whom the statements are offered or merely defeats a right being asserted by that party. For example, in Ingram v. Bob Jaffe Co., 139 Cal.App.2d 193, 293 P.2d 132 (1956), a statement of a person permitted to operate a vehicle was admitted against the owner of the vehicle in an action seeking to hold the owner liable on the derivative liability of vehicle owners established by Vehicle Code Section 17150. Under Section 1224, the statement of the declarant would also be admissible against the owner in an action brought by the owner to recover for damage to his vehicle where the defense is based on the contributory negligence of the declarant.

Section 1302 supplements the rule stated in Section 1224. Section 1302 creates an exception for judgments against a third person when one of the issues between the parties is the liability, obligation, or duty of the third person and the judgment determines that liability, obligation, or duty. Together, Sections 1224 and 1302 codify the holdings of the cases applying Code of Civil Procedure Section 1851. See Tentative Recommendation and a Study Relating to the Uniform Rules of Evidence (Article VIII. Hearsay Evidence), 6 Cal.Law Revision Comm'n, Rep., Rec. & Studies Appendix at 491–496 (1964). [7 Cal.L.Rev.Comm. Reports 1 (1965)]

§ 1225. Statement of declarant whose right or title is in issue

When a right, title, or interest in any property or claim asserted by a party to a civil action requires a determination that a right, title, or interest exists or existed in the declarant, evidence of a statement made by the declarant during the time the party now claims the declarant was the holder of the right, title, or interest is as admissible against the party as it would be if offered against the declarant in an action involving that right, title, or interest.

LAW REVISION COMMISSION COMMENT

Section 1225 expresses a common law exception to the hearsay rule that is recognized in part in Section 1849 of the Code of Civil Procedure. Section 1849 (which is superseded by Section 1225) permits the statements of predecessors in interest of real property to be admitted against the successors; however, the California cases follow the general rule of permitting predecessors' statements to be admitted against successors of either real or personal property. Smith v. Goethe, 159 Cal. 628, 115 Pac. 223 (1911); 4 Wigmore, Evidence § 1082 et seq. (3d ed. 1940).

It should be noted that "statements made before title accrued in the declarant will not be receivable. On the other hand, the time of divestiture, after which no statements could be treated as admissions, is the time when the party against whom they are offered has by his own hypothesis acquired the title; thus, in a suit, for example, between A's heir and A's grantee, A's statements at any time before his death are receivable against the heir; but only his statements before the grant are receivable against the grantee." 4 Wigmore, Evidence § 1082 at 153 (3d ed. 1940).

Despite the limitations of Section 1225, some statements of a grantor made after divestiture of title will be admissible; but another theory of admissibility must be found. For example, later statement of his state of mind may be admissible on the issue of his intent. Evidence Code §§ 1950 and 1251. Where it is claimed that a conveyance was in fraud of creditors, the later statements of the grantor may be admissible not as hearsay but as evidence of the fraud itself (cf. Bush & Mallett Co. v. Helbing, 134 Cal. 676, 66 Pac. 967 (1901))or as declarations of a co-conspirator in the fraud (cf. McGee v. Allen, 7 Cal.2d 468, 60 P.2d 1026 (1936)). See generally 4 Wigmore, Evidence § 1086 (3d ed. 1940).

Section 1225 supplements the rule provided in Section 1224. Under Section 1224, for example, a party suing an executor on an obligation incurred by the decedent prior to his death may introduce admissions of the decedent. Similarly, under Section 1225, a party sued by an executor on an obligation claimed to have been owed to the decedent may introduce admissions of the decedent. [7 Cal.L.Rev.Comm. Reports 1 (1965)]

§ 1226. Statement of minor child in parent's action for child's injury

Evidence of a statement by a minor child is not made inadmissible by the hearsay rule if offered against the plaintiff in an action brought under Section 376 of the Code of Civil Procedure for injury to such minor child.

LAW REVISION COMMISSION COMMENT

See the Comment to Section 1227. [7 Cal.L.Rev.Comm. Reports 1 (1965)]

§ 1227. Statement of declarant in action for his wrongful death

Evidence of a statement by the deceased is not made inadmissible by the hearsay rule if offered against the plaintiff in an action for wrongful death brought under Section 377 of the Code of Civil Procedure.

LAW REVISION COMMISSION COMMENT

Under existing law, an admission by a decedent is not admissible against his heirs or representatives in a wrongful death action brought by them. Marks v. Reissinger, 35 Cal.App. 44, 169 Pac. 243 (1917). Cf. Hedge v. Williams, 131 Cal. 455, 63 Pac. 721 (1901). The reason is that the action is a new action, but merely a survival of the decedent's action. This rule has been severely criticized and is contrary to the rule adopted by most American courts. Carr v. Duncan, 90 Cal.App.2d 282, 285, 202 P.2d 855, 856 (1949).

Under Section 1224, the admissions of a decedent are admissible to establish the liability of his executor. Similarly, when the executor brings an action for the decedent's death under Code of Civil Procedure Section 377, the defendant should be permitted to introduce the admissions of the decedent. Without Section 1227, in an action between two executors arising out of an accident which was fatal to both participants, the plaintiff executor would be able to introduce admissions of the defendant's decedent, but the defending executor would be unable to introduce admissions of the plaintiff's decedent.

Section 1227 changes the rule announced in the California cases and makes the admissions of the decedent admissible in wrongful death actions. Section 1226 provides a similar rule for the analogous cases arising under Code of Civil Procedure Section 376 (action by parent of injured child).

Section 1227 recognizes that, in an action brought under Code of Civil Procedure Section 377, the only reason for treating the admissions of a plaintiff's decedent differently from those of a defendant's decedent is a technical procedural rule. The plaintiff in a wrongful death action—and the parent of an injured child in an action under Code of Civil Procedure Section 376—stands in reality so completely on the right of the deceased or injured person that such person's admissions should be admitted against the plaintiff, even though (as a technical matter) the plaintiff is asserting an independent right. [7 Cal.L.Rev.Comm. Reports 1 (1965)]

§ 1228. Admissibility of certain out-of-court statements of minors under the age of 12; establishing elements of certain sexually oriented crimes; notice to defendant

Notwithstanding any other provision of law, for the purpose of establishing the elements of the crime in order to admit as evidence the confession of a person accused of violating Section 261, 264.1, 285, 286, 288, 288a, 289, or 647a of the Penal Code, a court, in its discretion, may determine that a statement of the complaining witness is not made inadmissible by the hearsay rule if it finds all of the following:

(a) The statement was made by a minor child under the age of 12, and the contents of the statement were included in a written report of a law enforcement official or an employee of a county welfare department.

(b) The statement describes the minor child as a victim of sexual abuse.

(c) The statement was made prior to the defendant's confession. The court shall view with caution the testimony of a person recounting hearsay where there is evidence of personal bias or prejudice.

(d) There are no circumstances, such as significant inconsistencies between the confession and the statement concerning material facts establishing any element of the crime or the identification of the defendant, that would render the statement unreliable.

(e) The minor child is found to be unavailable pursuant to paragraph (2) or (3) of subdivision (a) of Section 240 or refuses to testify.

(f) The confession was memorialized in a trustworthy fashion by a law enforcement official.

If the prosecution intends to offer a statement of the complaining witness pursuant to this section, the prosecution shall serve a written notice upon the defendant at least 10 days prior to the hearing or trial at which the prosecution intends to offer the statement.

If the statement is offered during trial, the court's determination shall be made out of the presence of the jury. If the statement is found to be admissible pursuant to this section, it shall be admitted out of the presence of the jury and solely for the purpose of determining the admissibility of the confession of the defendant.

§ 1228.1. Signature of parent or guardian on child welfare services case plan; acceptance of services; use in court of law; failure to cooperate

(a) Except as provided in subdivision (b), neither the signature of any parent or legal guardian on a child welfare services case plan nor the acceptance of any services prescribed in the child welfare services case plan by any parent or legal guardian shall constitute an admission of guilt or be used as evidence against the parent or legal guardian in a court of law.

(b) A parent's or guardian's failure to cooperate, except for good cause, in the provision of services specified in the child welfare services case plan may be used as evidence, if relevant, in any hearing held pursuant to Section * * * 366.21, 366.22, or 388 of the Welfare and Institutions Code * * * and at any jurisdictional or dispositional hearing held on a petition filed pursuant to Section 300, 342, or 387 of the Welfare and Institutions Code.

(Added by Stats.1995, c. 540 (A.B.1523), § 1. Amended by Stats.1997, c. 793 (A.B.1544), § 1.)

ARTICLE 2. DECLARATIONS AGAINST INTEREST

§ 1230. Declarations against interest

Evidence of a statement by a declarant having sufficient knowledge of the subject is not made inadmissible by the hearsay rule if the declarant is unavailable as a witness and the statement, when made, was so far contrary to the declarant's pecuniary or proprietary interest, or so far subjected him to the risk of civil or criminal liability, or so far tended to render invalid a claim by him against another, or created such a risk of making him an object of hatred, ridicule, or social disgrace in the community, that a reasonable man in his position would not have made the statement unless he believed it to be true.

ARTICLE 2.5. SWORN STATEMENTS REGARDING GANG–RELATED CRIMES

§ 1231. Prior statements of deceased declarant; hearsay exception

Evidence of a prior statement made by a declarant is not made inadmissible by the hearsay rule if the declarant is deceased and the proponent of introducing the statement establishes each of the following:

(a) The statement relates to acts or events relevant to a criminal prosecution under provisions of the California Street Terrorism Enforcement and Prevention Act (Chapter 11 (commencing with Section 186.20) of Title 7 of Part 1 of the Penal Code).

(b) A verbatim transcript, copy, or record of the statement exists. A record may include a statement preserved by means of an audio or video recording or equivalent technology.

(c) The statement relates to acts or events within the personal knowledge of the declarant.

(d) The statement was made under oath or affirmation in an affidavit; or was made at a deposition, preliminary hearing, grand jury hearing, or other proceeding in compliance with law, and was made under penalty of perjury.

(e) The declarant died from other than natural causes.

(f) The statement was made under circumstances that would indicate its trustworthiness and render the declarant's statement particularly worthy of belief. For purposes of this subdivision, circumstances relevant to the issue of trustworthiness include, but are not limited to, all of the following:

(1) Whether the statement was made in contemplation of a pending or anticipated criminal or civil matter, in which the declarant had an interest, other than as a witness.

(2) Whether the declarant had a bias or motive for fabricating the statement, and the extent of any bias or motive.

(3) Whether the statement is corroborated by evidence other than statements that are admissible only pursuant to this section.

Whether the statement was a statement against the declarant's interest.

(Added by Stats.1997, c. 499 (S.B.941), § 1.)

§ 1231.1. Statements made by deceased declarant; admissibility; notice of statement to adverse party

A statement is admissible pursuant to Section 1231 only if the proponent of the statement makes known to the adverse party the intention to offer the statement and the particulars of the statement sufficiently in advance of the proceedings to provide the adverse party with a fair opportunity to prepare to meet the statement.

(Added by Stats.1997, c. 499 (S.B.941), § 1.)

§ 1231.2. Administer and certify oaths

A peace officer may administer and certify oaths for purposes of this article.

(Added by Stats.1997, c. 499 (S.B.941), § 1.)

§ 1231.3. Testimony of law enforcement officer; hearsay

Any law enforcement officer testifying as to any hearsay statement pursuant to this article shall either have five years of law enforcement experience or have completed a training course certified by the Commission on Peace Officer Standards and Training which includes training in the investigation and reporting of cases and testifying at preliminary hearings and trials.

(Added by Stats.1997, c. 499 (S.B.941), § 1.)

§ 1231.4. Cause of death; deceased declarant

If evidence of a prior statement is introduced pursuant to this article, the jury may not be told that the declarant died from other than natural causes, but shall merely be told that the declarant is unavailable.

(Added by Stats.1997, c. 499 (S.B.941), § 1.)

ARTICLE 3. PRIOR STATEMENTS OF WITNESSES

§ 1235. Inconsistent statement

Evidence of a statement made by a witness is not made inadmissible by the hearsay rule if the statement is inconsistent with his testimony at the hearing and is offered in compliance with Section 770.

LAW REVISION COMMISSION COMMENT

Under existing law, when a prior statement of a witness that is inconsistent with his testimony at the trial is admitted in evidence, it may not be used as evidence of the truth of the matters stated. Because of the hearsay rule, a witness' prior inconsistent statement may be used only to discredit his testimony given at the trial. Albert v. McKay & Co., 174 Cal. 451, 456, 163 Pac. 666, 668 (1917).

Because a witness' inconsistent statement is not substantive evidence, the courts do not permit a party—even when surprised by the testimony—to impeach his own witness with inconsistent statements if the witness' testimony at the trial has not damaged the party's case in any way. Evidence tending only to discredit the witness is irrelevant and immaterial when the witness has not given damaging testimony. People v. Crespi, 115 Cal. 50, 46 Pac. 863 (1896); People v. Mitchell, 94 Cal. 550, 29 Pac. 1106 (1892); People v. Brown, 81 Cal.App. 226, 253 Pac. 735 (1927).

Section 1235 permits an inconsistent statement of a witness to be used as substantive evidence if the statement is otherwise admissible under the conditions specified in Section 770—which do not include surprise on the part of the party calling the witness if he is the party offering the inconsistent statement. Because Section 1235 permits a witness' inconsistent statements to be considered as evidence of the matters stated and not merely as evidence casting discredit on the witness, it follows that a party may introduce evidence of inconsistent statements of his own witness whether or not the witness gave damaging testimony and whether or not the party was surprised by the testimony, for such evidence is no longer irrelevant (and, hence, inadmissible).

Section 1235 admits inconsistent statements of witnesses because the dangers against which the hearsay rule is designed to protect are largely nonexistent. The declarant is in court and may be examined and cross- examined in regard to his statements and their subject matter. In many cases, the inconsistent statement is more likely to be true than the testimony of the witness at the trial because it was made nearer in time to the matter to which it relates and is less likely to be influenced by the controversy that gave rise to the litigation. The trier of fact has the declarant before it and can observe his demeanor and the nature of his testimony as he denies or tries to explain away the inconsistency. Hence, it is in as good a position to determine the truth or falsity of the prior statement as it is to determine the truth or falsity of the inconsistent testimony given in court. Moreover, Section 1235 will provide a party with desirable protection against the "turn-coat" witness who changes his story on the stand and deprives the party calling him of evidence essential to his case. [7 Cal.L.Rev.Comm. Reports 1 (1965)]

§ 1236. Prior consistent statement

Evidence of a statement previously made by a witness is not made inadmissible by the hearsay rule if the statement is consistent with his testimony at the hearing and is offered in compliance with Section 791.

LAW REVISION COMMISSION COMMENT

Under existing law, a prior statement of a witness that is consistent with his testimony at the trial is admissible under certain conditions when the credibility of the witness has been attacked. The statement is admitted, however, only to rehabilitate the witness—to support his credibility—and not as evidence of the truth of the matter stated. People v. Kynette, 15 Cal.2d 731, 753–754, 104 P.2d 794, 805–806 (1940) (overruled on other grounds in People v. Snyder, 50 Cal.2d 190, 197, 324 P.2d 1, 6 (1958)).

Section 1236, however, permits a prior consistent statement of a witness to be used as substantive evidence if the statement is otherwise admissible under the rules relating to the rehabilitation of impeached witnesses. See Evidence Code § 791.

There is no reason to perpetuate the subtle distinction made in the cases. It is not realistic to expect a jury to understand that it cannot believe that a witness was telling the truth on a former occasion even though it believes that the same story given at the hearing is true. [7 Cal.L.Rev.Comm. Reports 1 (1965)]

§ 1237. Past recollection recorded

(a) Evidence of a statement previously made by a witness is not made inadmissible by the hearsay rule if the statement would have been admissible if made by him while testifying, the statement concerns a matter as to which the witness has insufficient present recollection to enable him to testify fully and accurately, and the statement is contained in a writing which:

(1) Was made at a time when the fact recorded in the writing actually occurred or was fresh in the witness' memory;

(2) Was made (i) by the witness himself or under his direction or (ii) by some other person for the purpose of recording the witness' statement at the time it was made;

(3) Is offered after the witness testifies that the statement he made was a true statement of such fact; and

(4) Is offered after the writing is authenticated as an accurate record of the statement.

(b) The writing may be read into evidence, but the writing itself may not be received in evidence unless offered by an adverse party.

§ 1238. Prior identification

Evidence of a statement previously made by a witness is not made inadmissible by the hearsay rule if the statement would have been admissible if made by him while testifying and:

(a) The statement is an identification of a party or another as a person who participated in a crime or other occurrence;

(b) The statement was made at a time when the crime or other occurrence was fresh in the witness' memory; and

(c) The evidence of the statement is offered after the witness testifies that he made the identification and that it was a true reflection of his opinion at that time.

LAW REVISION COMMISSION COMMENT

Under Section 1235, evidence of a prior identification is admissible if the witness denies having made the prior identification or in any other way testifies inconsistently with the prior statement. Under Section 1238, evidence of a prior identification is admissible if the witness admits the prior identification and vouches for its accuracy.

Sections 1235 and 1238 codify exceptions to the hearsay rule similar to that which was recognized in People v. Gould, 54 Cal.2d 621, 7 Cal.Rptr. 273, 354 P.2d 865 (1960). In the Gould case, evidence of a prior identification made by a witness who could not repeat the identification at the trial was held admissible "because the earlier identification has greater probative value than an identification made in the courtroom after the suggestions of others and the circumstances of the trial may have intervened to create a fancied recognition in the witness' mind. [Citations omitted.] The failure of the witness to repeat the extrajudicial identification in court does not destroy its probative value, for such failure may be explained by loss of memory or other circumstances. [Moreover,] the principal danger of admitting hearsay evidence is not present since the witness is available at the trial for cross-examination." 54 Cal.2d at 626, 7 Cal.Rptr. at 275, 354 P.2d at 867.

As there was no discussion in the Gould opinion of the preliminary showing necessary to warrant admission of evidence of a prior identification, it cannot be determined whether Sections 1235 and 1238 modify the law as declared in that case.

Sections 1235 and 1238 deal only with the admissibility of evidence; they do not determine what constitutes evidence sufficient to sustain a verdict or finding. Hence, these sections have no effect on the holding of the Gould case that evidence of an extrajudicial identification that cannot be confirmed by an identification at the trial is insufficient to sustain a criminal conviction in the absence of other evidence tending to connect the defendant with the crime. [7 Cal.L.Rev.Comm. Reports 1 (1965)]

ARTICLE 4. SPONTANEOUS, CONTEMPORANEOUS, AND DYING DECLARATIONS

§ 1240. Spontaneous statement

Evidence of a statement is not made inadmissible by the hearsay rule if the statement:

(a) Purports to narrate, describe, or explain an act, condition, or event perceived by the declarant; and

(b) Was made spontaneously while the declarant was under the stress of excitement caused by such perception.

LAW REVISION COMMISSION COMMENT

Section 1240 is a codification of the existing exception to the hearsay rule for statements made spontaneously under the stress of excitement engendered by the event to which they relate. Showalter v. Western Pacific R.R., 16 Cal.2d 460, 106 P.2d 895 (1940). See Tentative Recommendation and a study relating to the Uniform Rules of Evidence, (Article, VIII. Hearsay Evidence), 6 Cal.Law Revision Comm'n, Rep., Rec. & Studies Appendix at 465–466 (1964). The rationale of this exception is that the spontaneity of such statements and the consequent lack of opportunity for reflection and deliberate fabrication provide an adequate guarantee of their trustworthiness. [7 Cal.L.Rev.Comm. Reports 1 (1965)]

§ 1241. Contemporaneous statement

Evidence of a statement is not made inadmissible by the hearsay rule if the statement:

(a) Is offered to explain, qualify, or make understandable conduct of the declarant; and

(b) Was made while the declarant was engaged in such conduct.

§ 1242. Dying declaration

Evidence of a statement made by a dying person respecting the cause and circumstances of his death is not made inadmissible by the hearsay rule if the statement was made upon his personal knowledge and under a sense of immediately impending death.

LAW REVISION COMMISSION COMMENT

Section 1242 is a broadened form of the well-established exception to the hearsay rule for dying declarations relating to the cause and circumstances of the declarant's death. The existing law—Code of Civil Procedure Section 1870(4) as interpreted by the courts—makes such declarations admissible only in criminal homicide actions. People v. Hall, 94 Cal. 595, 30 Pac. 7 (1892); Thrasher v. Board of Medical Examiners, 44 Cal.App. 26, 185 Pac. 1006 (1919). For the purpose of the admissibility of dying declarations, there is no rational basis for differentiating between civil and criminal actions or among various types of criminal actions. Hence, Section 1242 makes the exception applicable in all actions.

Under Section 1242, as under existing law, the dying declaration is admissible only if the declarant made the statement on personal knowledge. People v. Wasson, 65 Cal. 538, 4 Pac. 555 (1884); People v. Taylor, 59 Cal. 640 (1881). [7 Cal.L.Rev.Comm. Reports 1 (1965)]

ARTICLE 5. STATEMENTS OF MENTAL OR PHYSICAL STATE

§ 1250. Statement of declarant's then existing mental or physical state

(a) Subject to Section 1252, evidence of a statement of the declarant's then existing state of mind, emotion, or physical sensation (including a statement of intent, plan, motive, design, mental feeling, pain, or bodily health) is not made inadmissible by the hearsay rule when:

(1) The evidence is offered to prove the declarant's state of mind, emotion, or physical sensation at that time or at any other time when it is itself an issue in the action; or

(2) The evidence is offered to prove or explain acts or conduct of the declarant.

(b) This section does not make admissible evidence of a statement of memory or belief to prove the fact remembered or believed.

§ 1251. Statement of declarant's previously existing mental or physical state

Subject to Section 1252, evidence of a statement of the declarant's state of mind, emotion, or physical sensation (including a statement of intent, plan, motive, design, mental feeling, pain, or bodily health) at a time prior to the statement is not made inadmissible by the hearsay rule if:

(a) The declarant is unavailable as a witness; and

(b) The evidence is offered to prove such prior state of mind, emotion, or physical sensation when it is itself an issue in the action and the evidence is not offered to prove any fact other than such state of mind, emotion, or physical sensation.

LAW REVISION COMMISSION COMMENT

Section 1250 forbids the use of a statement of memory or belief to prove the fact remembered or believed. Section 1251, however, permits a statement of memory or belief of a past mental or physical state to be used to prove the previous mental or physical state when the previous mental or physical state is itself an issue in the case. If the past mental or physical state is to be used merely as circumstantial evidence of some other fact, the limitation in Section 1250 still applies and the statement of the past mental state is inadmissible hearsay.

The rule stated in Section 1251 is consistent with the California case law to the extent that it permits a statement of a prior mental state to be used as evidence of that mental state. See, e.g. People v. One 1948 Chevrolet Conv. Coupe, 45 Cal.2d 613, 290 P.2d 538 (1955) (statement of prior knowledge admitted to prove such knowledge); Kelly v. Bank of America, 112 Cal.App.2d 388, 246 P.2d 92 (1952) (statement of previous intent to retain title admitted to prove such intent). However, the California cases have held that statements of previous bodily conditions and symptoms are inadmissible to prove the existence of such conditions or symptoms, although they may be admitted as a basis for an expert's opinion. People v. Brown, 49 Cal.2d 577, 320 P.2d 5 (1958); Willoughby v. Zylstra, 5 Cal.App.2d 297, 42 P.2d 685 (1935). Section 1251 eliminates the distinction between statements of previous mental conditions and statements of previous physical sensations; it permits both to be admitted as evidence of the matters stated. Both kinds of statements are equally subjective, and there is no reason to believe that one kind is more unreliable than the other.

Section 1251 requires that the declarant be unavailable as a witness. Some California cases seem to indicate that the unavailability of the declarant is a necessary condition for the admission of his statements to prove a previous state of mind. See, e.g., Whitlow v. Durst, 20 Cal.2d 523, 524, 127 P.2d 530, 531 (1942) ("declarations of a decedent" admissible to show previous mental state); Kelly v. Bank of America, 112 Cal.App.2d 388, 246 P.2d 92 (1952). But other cases have admitted such statements without insisting on the declarant's unavailability. People v. One 1948 Chevrolet Conv. Coupe, 45 Cal.2d 613, 290 P.2d 538 (1955). Section 1251 requires a showing of the declarant's unavailability because the statements involved are narrations of past conditions. There is, therefore, a greater opportunity for the declarant to remember inaccurately or even to fabricate. Hence, Section 1251 permits such statements to be admitted only when the declarant's unavailability necessitates reliance upon his out-of-court statements.

A statement is not admissible under Section 1251 if the statement was made under circumstances indicating that the statement is not trustworthy. See Evidence Code 1252 and the Comment thereto. [7 Cal.L.Rev.Comm. Reports 1 (1965)]

§ 1252. Restriction on admissibility of statement of mental or physical state

Evidence of a statement is inadmissible under this article if the statement was made under circumstances such as to indicate its lack of trustworthiness.

LAW REVISION COMMISSION COMMENT

Section 1252 limits the admissibility of hearsay statements that would otherwise be admissible under Sections 1250 and 1251. If a statement of mental or physical state was made with a motive to misrepresent or to manufacture evidence, the statement is not sufficiently reliable to warrant its reception in evidence. The limitation expressed in Section 1252 has been held to be a condition of admissibility in some of the California cases. See, e.g., People v. Hamilton, 55 Cal.2d 881, 893, 895, 13 Cal.Rptr. 649, 656, 657, 362 P.2d 473, 480, 481 (1961); People v. Alcalde, 24 Cal.2d 177, 187, 148 P.2d 627, 632 (1944).

The Hamilton case mentions some additional limitations on the admissibility of statements offered in a criminal action to prove the declarant's mental statement. These additional limitations do not appear in the Evidence Code. In the Hamilton case, the court was concerned with a murder victim's statements that she was afraid of the accused, that the accused had threatened to kill her, and that the accused had beaten her. The statements were ostensibly offered to prove that the victim feared the accused and, therefore, to cast doubt on the accused's testimony that the victim had invited him to her house on the night of the murder. As the case was tried, however, the victim's declarations were used repeatedly in argument as a basis for the prosecution's claim that the beatings actually occurred, that the threats were actually made, and that the threats were carried out in the murder.

The court said that "testimony as to the 'state of mind' of the declarant ... is admissible, but only when such testimony refers to threats as to future conduct on the part of the accused ... and when [such declarations] show primarily the then state of mind of the declarant and not the state of mind of the accused. But ... such testimony is not admissible if it refers solely to alleged past conduct on the part of the accused." 55 Cal.2d at 893–894, 13 Cal.Rptr. at 656, 362 P.2d at 480.

These additional limitations on the admissibility of state of mind evidence are not mentioned in the Evidence Code for two reasons. First, they are confusing and contradictory: The declarations are inadmissible if they refer to past conduct of the accused; nevertheless, they are admissible "only" when they refer to his past conduct, i.e., his threats. The declarations, to be admissible, must show primarily the state of mind of the declarant and not the state of mind of the accused; nevertheless, such declarations are admissible "only" if they refer to the accused's statements of his state of mind, i.e., his intent to do future harm to the victim.

Second, these additional limitations are unnecessary. Section 1200 makes it clear that statements of past events cannot be used to prove those events unless they fall within an exception to the hearsay rule; and Sections 1250 and 1251 make it clear that statements of a declarant's past state of mind may be used to prove only that state of mind and no other fact. The real problem in the Hamilton case was the fact that much of the evidence was offered ostensibly not as hearsay but as circumstantial evidence of the victim's fear (see Section 1200 and the Comment thereto); but the prosecution endeavored nevertheless to have the jury consider the evidence as hearsay evidence, i.e., as evidence that the events related actually occurred. Evidence Code Section 352 provides the judge with ample power to exclude evidence of this sort where its prejudicial effect outweighs its probative value. But, under Section 352, the judge must weigh the need for the evidence against the danger of its misuse in each case. The Evidence Code does not freeze the courts to the arbitrary and contradictory standards mentioned in the Hamilton case for determining when prejudicial effect outweighs probative value. [7 Cal.L.Rev.Comm. Reports 1 (1965)]

§ 1253. Statements for purposes of medical diagnosis or treatment; contents of statement; child abuse or neglect; age limitations

Subject to Section 1252, evidence of a statement is not made inadmissible by the hearsay rule if the statement was made for purposes of medical diagnosis or treatment and describes medical history, or past or present symptoms, pain, or sensations, or the inception or general character of the cause or external source thereof insofar as reasonably pertinent to diagnosis or treatment. This section applies only to a statement made by a victim who is a minor at the time of the proceedings, provided the statement was made when the victim was under the age of 12 describing any act, or attempted act, of child abuse or neglect. "Child abuse" and "child neglect," for purposes of this section, have the meanings provided in subdivision (c) of Section 1360. In addition, "child abuse" means any act proscribed by Chapter 5 (commencing with Section 281) of Title 9 of Part 1 of the Penal Code committed against a minor.

ARTICLE 6. STATEMENTS RELATING TO WILLS AND TO CLAIMS AGAINST ESTATES

§ 1260. Statement concerning declarant's will

(a) Evidence of a statement made by a declarant who is unavailable as a witness that he has or has not made a will, or has or has not revoked his will, or that identifies his will, is not made inadmissible by the hearsay rule.

(b) Evidence of a statement is inadmissible under this section if the statement was made under circumstances such as to indicate its lack of trustworthiness.

LAW REVISION COMMISSION COMMENT

Section 1260 codifies an exception recognized in California case law. Estate of Morrison, 198 Cal. 1, 242 Pac. 939 (1926); Estate of Thompson, 44 Cal.App.2d 774, 112 P.2d 937 (1941). The section is, of course, subject to the provisions of Probate Code Sections 350 and 351 which relate to the establishment of a lost or destroyed will.

The limitation in subdivision (b) is not mentioned in the few court decisions involving this exception. The limitation is desirable, however, to assure the reliability of the hearsay that is admissible under this section. [7 Cal.L.Rev.Comm. Reports 1 (1965)]

§ 1261. Statement of decedent offered in action against his estate

(a) Evidence of a statement is not made inadmissible by the hearsay rule when offered in an action upon a claim or demand against the estate of the declarant if the statement was made upon the personal knowledge of the declarant at a time when the matter had been recently perceived by him and while his recollection was clear.

(b) Evidence of a statement is inadmissible under this section if the statement was made under circumstances such as to indicate its lack of trustworthiness.

LAW REVISION COMMISSION COMMENT

The dead man statute (subdivision 3 of Section 1880 of the Code of Civil Procedure) prohibits a party who sues on a claim against a decedent's estate from testifying to any fact occurring prior to the decedent's death. The theory apparently underlying the statute is that it would be unfair to permit the surviving claimant to testify to such facts when the decedent is precluded by his death from doing so. To balance the positions of the parties, the living may not speak because the dead cannot.

The dead man statute operates unsatisfactorily. It prohibits testimony concerning matters of which the decedent had no knowledge and, hence, to which he could not have testified even if he had survived. It operates unevenly since it does not prohibit testimony relating to claims under, as distinguished from claims against, the decedent's estate even though the effect of such a claim may be to frustrate the decedent's plan for the disposition of his property. See the Law Revision Commission's Comment to Code of Civil Procedure Section 1880 and 1 Cal.Law Revision Comm'n, Rep., Rec. & Studies, Recommendation and Study Relating to the Dead Man Statute at D–1 (1957). The dead man statute excludes otherwise relevant and competent evidence—even if it is the only available evidence—and frequently this forces the courts to decide cases with a minimum of information concerning the actual facts. See the Supreme Court's complaint in Light v. Stevens, 159 Cal. 288, 292, 113 Pac. 659, 660 (1911) ("Owing to the fact that the lips of one of the parties to the transaction are closed by death and those of the other party by the law, the evidence on this question is somewhat unsatisfactory."). Hence, the dead man statute is not continued in the Evidence Code.

Under the Evidence Code, the positions of the parties are balanced by throwing more light, not less, on the actual facts. Repeal of the dead man statute permits the claimant to testify without restriction. To balance this advantage, Section 1261 permits hearsay evidence of the decedent's statements to be admitted. Certain safeguards—i.e., personal knowledge, recent perception, and circumstantial evidence of trustworthiness—are included in the section to provide some protection for the party against whom the statements are offered, for he has no opportunity to test the hearsay by cross-examination. [7 Cal.L.Rev.Comm. Reports 1 (1965)]

ARTICLE 7. BUSINESS RECORDS

§ 1270. A business

As used in this article, "a business" includes every kind of business, governmental activity, profession, occupation, calling, or operation of institutions, whether carried on for profit or not.

LAW REVISION COMMISSION COMMENT

This article restates and supersedes the Uniform Business Records as Evidence Act appearing in Sections 1953e through 1953h of the Code of Civil Procedure. The definition of "a business" in Section 1270 is substantially the same as that appearing in Code of Civil Procedure Section 1953e. A reference to "governmental activity" has been added to the Evidence Code definition to codify the decisions in cases holding the Uniform Act applicable to governmental records. See, e.g., Nichols v. McCoy, 38 Cal.2d 447, 240 P.2d 569 (1952); Fox v. San Francisco Unified School Dist., 111 Cal.App.2d 885, 245 P.2d 603 (1952).

The definition is sufficiently broad to encompass institutions not customarily thought of as businesses. For example, the baptismal and wedding records of a church would be admissible under the section to prove the events recorded. 5 Wigmore, Evidence § 1523 (3d ed. 1940). Cf. Evidence Code § 1315. [7 Cal.L.Rev.Comm. Reports 1 (1965)].

§ 1271. Admissible writings

Evidence of a writing made as a record of an act, condition, or event is not made inadmissible by the hearsay rule when offered to prove the act, condition, or event if:

(a) The writing was made in the regular course of a business;

(b) The writing was made at or near the time of the act, condition, or event;

(c) The custodian or other qualified witness testifies to its identity and the mode of its preparation; and

(d) The sources of information and method and time of preparation were such as to indicate its trustworthiness.

LAW REVISION COMMISSION COMMENT

Section 1271 is the business records exception to the hearsay rule. It is stated in language taken from the Uniform Business Records as Evidence Act (Sections 1953e–1953h of the Code of Civil Procedure) and from Rule 63(13) of the Uniform Rules of Evidence.

Section 1271 requires the judge to find that the sources of information and the method and time of preparation of the record "were such as to indicate its trustworthiness." Under the language of Code of Civil Procedure Section 1953f, the judge must determine that the sources of information and method and time of preparation "were such as to justify its admission." The language of Section 1271 is more accurate, for the cases hold that admission of a business record is not justified when there is no preliminary showing that the record is reliable or trustworthy. E.g., People v. Grayson, 172 Cal.App.2d 372, 341 P.2d 820 (1959) (hotel register rejected because "not shown to be true and complete").

"The chief foundation of the special reliability of business records is the requirement that they must be based upon the first-hand observation of someone whose job it is to know the facts recorded.... But if the evidence in the particular case discloses that the record was not based upon the report of an informant having the business duty to observe and report, then the record is not admissible under this exception, to show the truth of the matter reported to the recorder." McCormick, Evidence § 286 at 602 (1954), as quoted in MacLean v. City & County of San Francisco, 151 Cal.App.2d 133, 143, 311 P.2d 158, 164 (1957).

Applying this standard, the cases have rejected a variety of business records on the ground that they were not based on the personal knowledge of the recorder or of someone with a business duty to report to the recorder. Police accident and arrest reports are usually held inadmissible because they are based on the narrations of persons who have no business duty to report to the police. MacLean v. City & County of San Francisco, 151 Cal.App.2d 133, 311 P.2d 158 (1957); Hoel v. City of Los Angeles, 136 Cal.App.2d 295, 288 P.2d 989 (1955). They are admissible, however, to prove the fact of the arrest. Harris v. Alcoholic Bev. Con. Appeals Bd., 212 Cal.App.2d 106, 23 Cal.Rptr. 74 (1963). Similar investigative reports on the origin of fires have been held inadmissible because they were not based on personal knowledge. Behr v. County of Santa Cruz, 172 Cal.App.2d 697, 342 P.2d 987 (1959); Harrigan v. Chaperon, 118 Cal.App.2d 167, 257 P.2d 716 (1953).

Section 1271 will continue the law developed in these cases that a business report is admissible only if the sources of information and the time and method of preparation are such as to indicate its trustworthiness. [7 Cal.L.Rev.Comm. Reports 1 (1965)]

§ 1272. Absence of entry in business records

Evidence of the absence from the records of a business of a record of an asserted act, condition, or event is not made inadmissible by the hearsay rule when offered to prove the nonoccurrence of the act or event, or the nonexistence of the condition, if:

(a) It was the regular course of that business to make records of all such acts, conditions, or events at or near the time of the act, condition, or event and to preserve them; and

(b) The sources of information and method and time of preparation of the records of that business were such that the absence of a record of an act, condition, or event is a trustworthy indication that the act or event did not occur or the condition did not exist.

LAW REVISION COMMISSION COMMENT

Technically, evidence of the absence of a record may not be hearsay. Section 1272 removes any doubt that might otherwise exist concerning the admissibility of such evidence under the hearsay rule. It codifies existing case law. People v. Torres, 201 Cal.App.2d 290, 20 Cal.Rptr. 315 (1962). [7 Cal.L.Rev.Comm. Reports 1 (1965)]

ARTICLE 8. OFFICIAL RECORDS AND OTHER OFFICIAL WRITINGS

§ 1280. Record by public employee

Evidence of a writing made as a record of an act, condition, or event is not made inadmissible by the hearsay rule when offered in any civil or criminal proceeding to prove the act, condition, or event if all of the following applies:

(a) The writing was made by and within the scope of duty of a public employee.

(b) The writing was made at or near the time of the act, condition, or event.

(c) The sources of information and method and time of preparation were such as to indicate its trustworthiness.

LAW REVISION COMMISSION COMMENT

Section 1280 restates the substance of and supersedes Sections 1920 and 1926 of the Code of Civil Procedure. Although Sections 1920 and 1926 declare unequivocally that entries in public records are prima facie evidence of the facts stated, "it has been held repeatedly that those sections cannot have universal literal application." Chandler v. Hibberd, 165 Cal.App.2d 39, 65, 332 P.2d 133, 149 (1958). In fact, the cases require the same showing of trustworthiness in regard to an official record as is required under the business records exception. Behr v. County of Santa Cruz, 172 Cal.App.2d 697, 342 P.2d 987 (1959); Hoel v. City of Los Angeles, 136 Cal.App.2d 295, 288 P.2d 989 (1955). Section 1280 continues the law declared in these cases by explicitly requiring the same showing of trustworthiness that is required in Section 1271. See the Comment to Section 1271.

The evidence that is admissible under this section is also admissible under Section 1271, the business records exception. However, Section 1271 requires a witness to testify as to the identity of the record and its mode of preparation in every instance. In contrast, Section 1280, as does existing law, permits the court to admit an official record or report without necessarily requiring a witness to testify as to its identity and mode of preparation if the court takes judicial notice or if sufficient independent evidence shows that the record or report was prepared in such a manner as to assure its trustworthiness. See, e.g., People v. Williams, 64 Cal. 87, 27 Pac. 939 (1883) (census report admitted, the court judicially noticing the statutes prescribing the method of preparing the report); Vallejo etc. R.R. v. Reed Orchard Co., 169 Cal. 545, 571, 147

Pac. 238, 250 (1915) (statistical report of state agency admitted, the court judicially noticing the statutory duty to prepare the report). [7 Cal.L.Rev.Comm. Reports 1 (1965)]

§ 1281. Vital statistics record

Evidence of a writing made as a record of a birth, fetal death, or marriage is not made inadmissible by the hearsay rule if the maker was required by law to file the writing in a designated public office and the writing was made and filed as required by law.

LAW REVISION COMMISSION COMMENT

Section 1281 provides a hearsay exception for official reports concerning birth, death, and marriage. Official reports of such events occurring within California are now admissible under the provisions of Section 10577 of the Health and Safety Code. Section 1281 provides a broader exception which includes similar reports from other jurisdictions. [7 Cal.L.Rev.Comm. Reports 1 (1965)]

§ 1282. Finding of presumed death by authorized federal employee

A written finding of presumed death made by an employee of the United States authorized to make such finding pursuant to the Federal Missing Persons Act (56 Stats. 143, 1092, and P.L. 408, Ch. 371, 2d Sess. 78th Cong.; 59 U.S.C. App. 1001–1016), as enacted or as heretofore or hereafter amended, shall be received in any court, office, or other place in this state as evidence of the death of the person therein found to be dead and of the date, circumstances, and place of his disappearance.

LAW REVISION COMMISSION COMMENT

Section 1282 restates and supersedes the provisions of Code of Civil Procedure Section 1928.1. The evidence made admissible under Section 1282 is limited to evidence of the fact of death and of the date, circumstances, and place of disappearance.

The determination by the federal employee of the date of the presumed death is a determination ordinarily made for the purpose of determining whether the pay of a missing person should be stopped and his name stricken from the payroll. The date so determined should not be given any consideration in the California courts since the issues involved in the California proceedings require determination of the date of death for a different purpose. Hence, Section 1282 does not make admissible the finding of the date of presumed death. On the other hand, the determination of the date, circumstances, and place of disappearance is reliable information that will assist the trier of fact in determining the date when the person died and is admissible under this section. Often the date of death may be inferred from the circumstances of the disappearance. See In re Thornburg's Estate, 186 Ore. 570, 208

P.2d 349 (1949); Lukens v. Camden Trust Co., 2 N.J.Super. 214, 62 A.2d 886 (Super.Ct.1948).

Section 1282 provides a convenient and reliable method of proof of death of persons covered by the Federal Missing Persons Act. See, e.g., In re Jacobsen's Estate, 208 Misc. 443, 143 N.Y.S.2d 432 (1955) (proof of death of 2–year-old dependent of serviceman where child was passenger on plane lost at sea). [7 Cal.L.Rev.Comm. Reports 1 (1965)]

§ 1283. Record by federal employee that person is missing, captured, beleaguered, beseiged, detained, or dead

An official written report or record that a person is missing, missing in action, interned in a foreign country, captured by a hostile force, beleaguered by a hostile force, besieged by a hostile force, or detained in a foreign country against his will, or is dead or is alive, made by an employee of the United States authorized by any law of the United States to make such report or record shall be received in any court, office, or other place in this state as evidence that such person is missing, missing in action, interned in a foreign country, captured by a hostile force, beleaguered by a hostile force, besieged by a hostile force, or detained in a foreign country against his will, or is dead or is alive.

LAW REVISION COMMISSION COMMENT

Section 1283 restates and supersedes the provisions of Code of Civil Procedure Section 1928.2. The language of Section 1928.2 has been revised to reflect the 1953 and 1964 amendments to the Federal Missing Persons Act. [7 Cal.L.Rev.Comm. Reports 1 (1965)]

§ 1284. Statement of absence of public record

Evidence of a writing made by the public employee who is the official custodian of the records in a public office, reciting diligent search and failure to find a record, is not made inadmissible by the hearsay rule when offered to prove the absence of a record in that office.

ARTICLE 9. FORMER TESTIMONY

§ 1290. Former testimony

As used in this article, "former testimony" means testimony given under oath in:

(a) Another action or in a former hearing or trial of the same action;

(b) A proceeding to determine a controversy conducted by or under the supervision of an agency that has the power to determine such a controversy and is an agency of the United States or a public entity in the United States;

(c) A deposition taken in compliance with law in another action; or

(d) An arbitration proceeding if the evidence of such former testimony is a verbatim transcript thereof.

LAW REVISION COMMISSION COMMENT

The purpose of Section 1290 is to provide a convenient term for use in the substantive provisions in the remainder of this article. It should be noted that depositions taken in another action are considered former testimony under Section 1290, and their admissibility is determined by Sections 1291 and 1292. The use of a deposition taken in the same action, however, is not covered by this article. Code of Civil Procedure Sections 2016–2036 deal comprehensively with the conditions and circumstances under which a deposition taken in a civil action may be used at the trial of the action in which the deposition was taken, and Penal Code Sections 1345 and 1362 prescribe the conditions for admitting the deposition of a witness that has been taken in the same criminal action. These sections will continue to govern the use of depositions in the action in which they are taken. [7 Cal.L.Rev.Comm. Reports 1 (1965)]

§ 1291. Former testimony offered against party to former proceeding

(a) Evidence of former testimony is not made inadmissible by the hearsay rule if the declarant is unavailable as a witness and:

(1) The former testimony is offered against a person who offered it in evidence in his own behalf on the former occasion or against the successor in interest of such person; or

(2) The party against whom the former testimony is offered was a party to the action or proceeding in which the testimony was given and had the right and opportunity to cross-examine the declarant with an interest and motive similar to that which he has at the hearing.

(b) The admissibility of former testimony under this section is subject to the same limitations and objections as though the declarant were testifying at the hearing, except that former testimony offered under this section is not subject to:

(1) Objections to the form of the question which were not made at the time the former testimony was given.

(2) Objections based on competency or privilege which did not exist at the time the former testimony was given.

§ 1292. Former testimony offered against person not a party to former proceeding

(a) Evidence of former testimony is not made inadmissible by the hearsay rule if:

(1) The declarant is unavailable as a witness;

(2) The former testimony is offered in a civil action; and

(3) The issue is such that the party to the action or proceeding in which the former testimony was given had the right and opportunity to cross-examine the declarant with an interest and motive similar to that which the party against whom the testimony is offered has at the hearing.

(b) The admissibility of former testimony under this section is subject to the same limitations and objections as though the declarant were testifying at the hearing, except that former testimony offered under this section is not subject to objections based on competency or privilege which did not exist at the time the former testimony was given.

§ 1293. Former testimony by minor child complaining witness at preliminary examination

(a) Evidence of former testimony made at a preliminary examination by a minor child who was the complaining witness is not made inadmissible by the hearsay rule if:

(1) The former testimony is offered in a proceeding to declare the minor a dependent child of the court pursuant to Section 300 of the Welfare and Institutions Code.

(2) The issues are such that a defendant in the preliminary examination in which the former testimony was given had the right and opportunity to cross- examine the minor child with an interest and motive similar to that which the parent or guardian against whom the testimony is offered has at the proceeding to declare the minor a dependent child of the court.

(b) The admissibility of former testimony under this section is subject to the same limitations and objections as though the minor child were testifying at the proceeding to declare him or her a dependent child of the court.

(c) The attorney for the parent or guardian against whom the former testimony is offered or, if none, the parent or guardian may make a motion to challenge the admissibility of the former testimony upon a showing that new substantially different issues are present in the proceeding to declare the minor a dependent child than were present in the preliminary examination.

(d) As used in this section, "complaining witness" means the alleged victim of the crime for which a preliminary examination was held.

(e) This section shall apply only to testimony made at a preliminary examination on and after January 1, 1990.

§ 1294. Unavailable witnesses; prior inconsistent statements; preliminary hearing or prior proceeding

(a) The following evidence of prior inconsistent statements of a witness properly admitted in a preliminary hearing or trial of the same criminal matter pursuant to Section 1235 is not made inadmissible by the hearsay rule if the witness is unavailable and former testimony of the witness is admitted pursuant to Section 1291:

(1) A videotaped statement introduced at a preliminary hearing or prior proceeding concerning the same criminal matter.

(2) A transcript, containing the statements, of the preliminary hearing or prior proceeding concerning the same criminal matter.

(b) The party against whom the prior inconsistent statements are offered, at his or her option, may examine or cross-examine any person who testified at the preliminary hearing or prior proceeding as to the prior inconsistent statements of the witness.

ARTICLE 10. JUDGMENTS

§ 1300. Judgment of conviction of crime punishable as felony

Evidence of a final judgment adjudging a person guilty of a crime punishable as a felony is not made inadmissible by the hearsay rule when offered in a civil action to prove any fact essential to the judgment whether or not the judgment was based on a plea of nolo contendere.

LAW REVISION COMMISSION COMMENT

Analytically, a judgment that is offered to prove the matters determined by the judgment is hearsay evidence. Uniform Rules of Evidence, Rule 63(20) Comment (1953); Tentative Recommendation and a Study Relating to the Uniform Rules of Evidence (Article VIII. Hearsay Evidence), 6 Cal.Law Revision Comm'n, Rep., Rec. & Studies Appendix at 539–541 (1964). It is in substance a statement of the court that determined the previous action ("a statement that was made other than by a witness while testifying at the hearing") that is offered "to prove the truth of the matter stated." Evidence Code § 1200. Therefore, unless an exception to the hearsay rule is provided, a judgment would be inadmissible if offered in a subsequent action to prove the matters determined.

Of course, a judgment may, as a matter of substantive law, conclusively establish certain facts insofar as a party is concerned. Teitlebaum Furs, Inc. v. Dominion Ins. Co., 58 Cal.2d 601, 25 Cal.Rptr. 559, 375 P.2d 439 (1962); Bernhard v. Bank of America, 19 Cal.2d 807, 122 P.2d 892 (1942). The sections of this article do not purport to deal with the doctrines of res judicata and estoppel by judgment. These sections deal only with the evidentiary use of judgments in those cases where the substantive law does not require that the judgments be given conclusive effect.

Section 1300 provides an exception to the hearsay rule for a final judgment adjudging a person guilty of a crime punishable as a felony. Hence, if a plaintiff sues to recover a reward offered by the defendant for the arrest and conviction of a person who committed a particular crime, Section 1300 permits the plaintiff to use a judgment of conviction as evidence that the person convicted committed the crime. The exception does not, however, apply in criminal actions. Thus, Section 1300 does not permit the judgment to be used in a criminal action as evidence of the identity of the person who committed the crime or as evidence that the crime was committed.

Section 1300 will change the California law. Under existing law, a conviction of a crime is inadmissible as evidence in a subsequent action. Marceau v. Travelers' Ins. Co., 101 Cal. 338, 35 Pac. 856 (1894) (evidence of a murder conviction held inadmissible to prove the insured was intentionally killed); Burke v. Wells, Fargo & Co., 34 Cal. 60 (1867) (evidence of a robbery conviction held inadmissible to prove the identity of robber in an action to recover reward). The change, however, is desirable, for the evidence involved is peculiarly reliable. The seriousness of the charge assures that the facts will be thoroughly litigated, and the fact that the judgment must be based upon a determination that there was no reasonable doubt concerning the defendant's guilt assures that the question of guilt will be thoroughly considered.

Section 1300 applies to any crime punishable as a felony. The fact that a misdemeanor sentence is imposed does not affect the admissibility of the judgment of a conviction under this section. Cf. Penal Code § 17. The exclusion of judgments based on a plea of nolo contendere from the exception in Section 1300 is a reflection of the policy expressed in Penal Code Section 1016. [7 Cal.L.Rev.Comm. Reports 1 (1965)]

§ 1301. Judgment against person entitled to indemnity

Evidence of a final judgment is not made inadmissible by the hearsay rule when offered by the judgment debtor to prove any fact which was essential to the judgment in an action in which he seeks to:

(a) Recover partial or total indemnity or exoneration for money paid or liability incurred because of the judgment;

(b) Enforce a warranty to protect the judgment debtor against the liability determined by the judgment; or

(c) Recover damages for breach of warranty substantially the same as the warranty determined by the judgment to have been breached.

LAW REVISION COMMISSION COMMENT

If a person entitled to indemnity, or if the obligee under a warranty contract, complies with certain conditions relating to notice and defense, the indemnitor or warrantor is conclusively bound by any judgment recovered. Civil Code § 2778 (5); Code Civ.Proc. § 1912; McCormick v. Marcy, 165 Cal. 386, 132 Pac. 449 (1913).

Where a judgment against an indemnitee or person protected by a warranty is not made conclusive on the indemnitor or warrantor, Section 1301 permits the judgment to be used as hearsay evidence in an action to recover on the indemnity or warranty. Section 1301 reflects the existing law relating to indemnity agreements. Civil Code § 2778(6). Section 1301 probably restates the law relating to warranties, too, but the law in that regard is not altogether clear. Eric City Iron Works v. Tatum, 1 Cal.App. 286, 82 Pac. 92 (1905). But see Peabody v. Phelps, 9 Cal. 213 (1858). [7 Cal.L.Rev.Comm. Reports 1 (1965)]

§ 1302. Judgment determining liability of third person

When the liability, obligation, or duty of a third person is in issue in a civil action, evidence of a final judgment against that person is not made inadmissible by the hearsay rule when offered to prove such liability, obligation, or duty.

LAW REVISION COMMISSION COMMENT

Section 1302 expresses an exception contained in Code of Civil Procedure Section 1851. Ellsworth v. Bradford, 186 Cal. 316, 199 Pac. 335 (1921); Nordin v. Bank of America, 11 Cal.App.2d 98, 52 P.2d 1018 (1936). Evidence Code Sections 1302 and 1224 together restate and supersede the provisions of Code of Civil Procedure Section 1851. [7 Cal.L.Rev.Comm. Reports 1 (1965)]

ARTICLE 11. FAMILY HISTORY

§ 1310. Statement concerning declarant's own family history

(a) Subject to subdivision (b), evidence of a statement by a declarant who is unavailable as a witness concerning his own birth, marriage, divorce, a parent and child relationship, relationship by blood or marriage, race, ancestry, or other similar fact of his family history is not made inadmissible by the hearsay rule, even though the declarant had no means of acquiring personal knowledge of the matter declared.

(b) Evidence of a statement is inadmissible under this section if the statement was made under circumstances such as to indicate its lack of trustworthiness.

LAW REVISION COMMISSION COMMENT

Section 1310 provides a hearsay exception for a statement concerning the declarant's own family history. It restates in substance and supersedes Section 1870(4) of the Code of Civil Procedure. Section 1870(4), however, requires that the declarant be dead whereas unavailability of the declarant for any of the reasons specified in Section 240 makes the statement admissible under Section 1310.

The statement is not admissible if it was made under circumstances such as to indicate its lack of trustworthiness. The requirement is similar to the requirement of existing case law that the statement be made at a time when no controversy existed as to the matters stated. See, e.g., Estate of Walden, 166 Cal. 446, 137 Pac. 35 (1913); Estate of Nidever, 181 Cal.App.2d 367, 5 Cal.Rptr. 343 (1960). However, the language of Section 1310 permits the judge to consider the declarant's motives to tell the truth as well as his reasons to deviate therefrom in determining whether the statement is sufficiently trustworthy to be admitted as evidence. [7 Cal.L.Rev.Comm. Reports 1 (1965)]

§ 1311. Statement concerning family history of another

(a) Subject to subdivision (b), evidence of a statement concerning the birth, marriage, divorce, death, parent and child relationship, race, ancestry, relationship by blood or marriage, or other similar fact of the family history of a person other than the declarant is not made inadmissible by the hearsay rule if the declarant is unavailable as a witness and:

(1) The declarant was related to the other by blood or marriage; or

(2) The declarant was otherwise so intimately associated with the other's family as to be likely to have had accurate information concerning the matter declared and made the statement (i) upon information received from the other or from a person related by blood or marriage to the other or (ii) upon repute in the other's family.

(b) Evidence of a statement is inadmissible under this section if the statement was made under circumstances such as to indicate its lack of trustworthiness.

LAW REVISION COMMISSION COMMENT

Section 1311 provides a hearsay exception for a statement concerning the family history of another. Paragraph (1) of subdivision (a) restates in substance existing law as found in Section 1870(4) of the Code of Civil Procedure which it supersedes. Paragraph (2) is new to California law, but it is a sound extension of the present law to cover a situation where the declarant was a family housekeeper or doctor or so close a friend as to be included by the family in discussions of its family history.

There are two limitations on admissibility of a statement under Section 1311. First, a statement is admissible only if the declarant is unavailable as a witness within the meaning of Section 240. (Section 1870(4) requires that the declarant be deceased in order for his statement to be admissible.) Second, a statement is not admissible if it was made under circumstances such as to indicate its lack of trustworthiness. For a discussion of this requirement, see the Comment to Evidence Code § 1310. [7 Cal.L.Rev.Comm. Reports 1 (1965)]

§ 1312. Entries in family records and the like

Evidence of entries in family Bibles or other family books or charts, engravings on rings, family portraits, engravings on urns, crypts, or tombstones, and the like, is not made inadmissible by the hearsay rule when offered to prove the birth, marriage, divorce, death, parent and child relationship, race, ancestry, relationship by blood or marriage, or other similar fact of the family history of a member of the family by blood or marriage.

LAW REVISION COMMISSION COMMENT

Section 1312 restates the substance of and supersedes the provisions of Code of Civil Procedure Section 1870(13). [7 Cal.L.Rev.Comm. Reports 1 (1965)]

§ 1313. Reputation in family concerning family history

Evidence of reputation among members of a family is not made inadmissible by the hearsay rule if the reputation concerns the birth, marriage, divorce, death, parent and child relationship, race, ancestry, relationship by blood or marriage, or other similar fact of the family history of a member of the family by blood or marriage.

LAW REVISION COMMISSION COMMENT

Section 1313 restates the substance of and supersedes the provisions of Code of Civil Procedure Sections 1852 and 1870(11). See Estate of Connors, 53 Cal.App.2d 484, 128 P.2d 200 (1942); Estate of Newman, 34 Cal.App.2d 706, 94 P.2d 356 (1939). However, Section 1870(11) requires the family reputation in question to have existed "previous to the controversy." This qualification is not included in Section 1313 because it is unlikely that a family reputation on a matter of pedigree would be influenced by the existence of a controversy even though the declaration of an individual member of the family covered in Sections 1310 and 1311, might be.

The family reputation admitted under Section 1313 is necessarily multiple hearsay. If, however, such reputation were inadmissible because of the hearsay rule, and if direct statements of pedigree were inadmissible because they are based on such reputation (as most of them are), the courts would be virtually helpless in determining matters of pedigree. See Tentative Recommendation and a Study Relating to the Uniform Rules of Evidence (Article VIII. Hearsay Evidence), 6 Cal.Law Revision Comm'n, Rep., Rec. & Studies Appendix at 548 (1964). [7 Cal.L.Rev.Comm. Reports 1 (1965)]

§ 1314. Reputation in community concerning family history

Evidence of reputation in a community concerning the date or fact of birth, marriage, divorce, or death of a person resident in the community at the time of the reputation is not made inadmissible by the hearsay rule.

LAW REVISION COMMISSION COMMENT

Section 1314 restates what has been held to be existing law under Code of Civil Procedure Section 1963(30) with respect to proof of the fact of marriage. See People v. Vogel, 46 Cal.2d 798, 299 P.2d 850 (1956); Estate of Baldwin, 162 Cal. 471, 123 Pac. 267 (1912). However, Section 1314 has no counterpart in California law insofar as proof of the date or fact of birth, divorce, or death is concerned, since proof of such facts by reputation is presently limited to reputation in the family. See Estate of Heaton, 135 Cal. 385, 67 Pac. 321 (1902). [7 Cal.L.Rev.Comm. Reports 1 (1965)]

§ 1315. Church records concerning family history

Evidence of a statement concerning a person's birth, marriage, divorce, death, parent and child relationship, race, ancestry, relationship by blood or marriage, or other similar fact of family history which is contained in a writing made as a record of a church, religious denomination, or religious society is not made inadmissible by the hearsay rule if:

(a) The statement is contained in a writing made as a record of an act, condition, or event that would be admissible as evidence of such act, condition, or event under Section 1271; and

(b) The statement is of a kind customarily recorded in connection with the act, condition, or event recorded in the writing.

LAW REVISION COMMISSION COMMENT

Church records generally are admissible as business records under the provisions of Section 1271. Under Section 1271, such records would be admissible to prove the occurrence of the church activity—the baptism, confirmation, or marriage—recorded in the writing. However, it is unlikely that Section 1271 would permit such records to be used as evidence of the age or relationship of the participants, for the business records act has been held to authorize business records to be used to prove only facts known personally to the recorder of the information or to other employees of the business. Patek & Co. v. Vineberg, 210 Cal.App.2d 20, 23, 26 Cal.Rptr. 293, 294 (1962) (hearing denied); People v. Williams, 187 Cal.App.2d 355, 9 Cal.Rptr. 722 (1960); Gough v. Security Trust & Sav. Bank, 162 Cal.App.2d 90, 327 P.2d 555 (1958).

Section 1315 permits church records to be used to prove certain additional information. Facts of family history, such as birth dates, relationships, marital histories, etc., that are ordinarily reported to church authorities and recorded in connection with the church's baptismal, confirmation, marriage, and funeral records may be proved by such records under Section 1315.

Section 1315 continues in effect and supersedes the provisions of Code of Civil Procedure Section 1919a without, however, the special and cumbersome authentication procedure specified in Code of Civil Procedure Section 1919b. Under Section 1315, church records may be authenticated in the same manner that other business records are authenticated. [7 Cal.L.Rev.Comm. Reports 1 (1965)]

§ 1316. Marriage, baptismal and similar certificates

Evidence of a statement concerning a person's birth, marriage, divorce, death, parent and child relationship, race, ancestry, relationship by blood or marriage, or other similar fact of family history is not made inadmissible by the hearsay rule if the statement is contained in a certificate that the maker thereof performed a marriage or other ceremony or administered a sacrament and:

(a) The maker was a clergyman, civil officer, or other person authorized to perform the acts reported in the certificate by law or by the rules, regulations, or requirements of a church, religious denomination, or religious society; and

(b) The certificate was issued by the maker at the time and place of the ceremony or sacrament or within a reasonable time thereafter.

LAW REVISION COMMISSION COMMENT

Section 1316 provides a hearsay exception for marriage, baptismal, and similar certificates. This exception is somewhat broader than that found in Sections 1919a and 1919b of the Code of Civil Procedure (superseded by Evidence Code Sections 1315 and 1316). Sections 1919a and 1919b are limited to church records and, hence, with respect to marriages, to those performed by clergymen. Moreover, they establish an elaborate and detailed authentication procedure, whereas certificates made admissible by Section 1316 need meet only the general authentication requirement of Section 1401. [7 Cal.L.Rev.Comm. Reports 1 (1965)]

ARTICLE 12. REPUTATION AND STATEMENTS CONCERNING COMMUNITY HISTORY, PROPERTY INTERESTS, AND CHARACTER

§ 1320. Reputation concerning community history

Evidence of reputation in a community is not made inadmissible by the hearsay rule if the reputation concerns an event of general history of the community or of the state or nation of which the community is a part and the event was of importance to the community.

LAW REVISION COMMISSION COMMENT

Section 1320 provides a wider rule of admissibility than does Code of Civil Procedure Section 1870(11) which it supersedes in part. Section 1870 provides in relevant part that proof may be made of "common reputation existing previous to the controversy, respecting facts of a public or general interest more than thirty years old." The 30–year limitation is essentially arbitrary. The important question would seem to be whether a community reputation on the matter involved exists; its age would appear to go more to its venerability than to its truth. Nor is it necessary to include in Section 1320 the requirement that the reputation existed previous to controversy. It is unlikely that a community reputation respecting an event of general history would be influenced by the existence of a controversy. [7 Cal.L.Rev.Comm. Reports 1 (1965)]

§ 1321. Reputation concerning public interest in property

Evidence of reputation in a community is not made inadmissible by the hearsay rule if the reputation concerns the interest of the public in property in the community and the reputation arose before controversy.

LAW REVISION COMMISSION COMMENT

Section 1321 preserves the rule in Simons v. Inyo Cerro Gordo Co., 48 Cal.App. 524, 192 Pac. 144 (1920). It does not require, however, that the reputation be more than 30 years old; it requires merely that the reputation arose before there was a controversy concerning the matter. See the Comment to Section 1320. [7 Cal.L.Rev.Comm. Reports 1 (1965)]

§ 1322. Reputation concerning boundary or custom affecting land

Evidence of reputation in a community is not made inadmissible by the hearsay rule if the reputation concerns boundaries of, or customs affecting, land in the community and the reputation arose before controversy.

LAW REVISION COMMISSION COMMENT

Section 1322 restates the substance of existing law as found in Code of Civil Procedure Section 1870(11) which it supersedes in part. See Muller v. So. Pac. Branch Ry., 83 Cal. 240, 23 Pac. 265 (1890); Ferris v. Emmons, 214 Cal. 501, 6 P.2d 950 (1931). [7 Cal.L.Rev.Comm. Reports 1 (1965)]

§ 1323. Statement concerning boundary

Evidence of a statement concerning the boundary of land is not made inadmissible by the hearsay rule if the declarant is unavailable as a witness and had sufficient knowledge of the subject, but evidence of a statement is not admissible under this section if the statement was made under circumstances such as to indicate its lack of trustworthiness.

LAW REVISION COMMISSION COMMENT

Section 1323 codifies existing law found in such cases as Morton v. Folger, 15 Cal. 275 (1860), and Morcom v. Baiersky, 16 Cal.App. 480, 117 Pac. 560 (1911). [7 Cal.L.Rev.Comm. Reports 1 (1965)]

§ 1324. Reputation concerning character

Evidence of a person's general reputation with reference to his character or a trait of his character at a relevant time in the community in which he then resided or in a group with which he then habitually associated is not made inadmissible by the hearsay rule.

LAW REVISION COMMISSION COMMENT

Section 1324 codifies a well-settled exception to the hearsay rule. See, e.g., People v. Cobb, 45 Cal.2d 158, 287 P.2d 752 (1955). Of course, character evidence is admissible only when the question of character is material to the matter being litigated. The only purpose of Section 1324 is to declare that reputation evidence as to character or a trait of character is not inadmissible under the hearsay rule. [7 Cal.L.Rev. Comm. Reports 1 (1965)]

ARTICLE 13. DISPOSITIVE INSTRUMENTS AND ANCIENT WRITINGS

§ 1330. Recitals in writings affecting property

Evidence of a statement contained in a deed of conveyance or a will or other writing purporting to affect an interest in real or personal property is not made inadmissible by the hearsay rule if:

(a) The matter stated was relevant to the purpose of the writing;

(b) The matter stated would be relevant to an issue as to an interest in the property; and

(c) The dealings with the property since the statement was made have not been inconsistent with the truth of the statement.

LAW REVISION COMMISSION COMMENT

Section 1330 restates the substance of existing California law relating to recitals in dispositive instruments. Although language in some cases appears to require that the dispositive instrument be ancient, cases may be found in which recitals in dispositive instruments have been admitted without regard to the age of the instrument. See Russell v. Langford, 135 Cal. 356, 67 Pac. 331 (1902) (recital in will); Pearson v. Pearson, 46 Cal. 609 (1873) (recital in will); Culver v. Newhart, 18 Cal.App. 614, 123 Pac. 975 (1912) (bill of sale). There is a sufficient likelihood that the statements made in a dispositive document, when related to the purpose of the document, will be true to warrant the admissibility of such documents without regard to their age. [7 Cal. L.Rev.Comm. Reports 1 (1965)]

§ 1331. Recitals in ancient writings

Evidence of a statement is not made inadmissible by the hearsay rule if the statement is contained in a writing more than 30 years old and the statement has been since generally acted upon as true by persons having an interest in the matter.

LAW REVISION COMMISSION COMMENT

Section 1331 clarifies the existing law relating to the admissibility of recitals in ancient documents by providing that such recitals are admissible under an exception to the hearsay rule. Code of Civil Procedure Section 1963(34) (superseded by the Evidence Code) provides that a document more than 30 years old is presumed genuine if it has been generally acted upon as genuine by persons having an interest in the matter. The Supreme Court has held that a document meeting this section's requirements is presumed to be genuine—presumed to be what it purports to be—but that the genuineness of the document imports no verity to the recitals contained therein. Gwin v. Calegaris, 139 Cal. 384, 389, 73 Pac. 851, 853 (1903). Recent cases decided by district courts of appeal, however, have held that the recitals in such a document are admissible to prove the truth of the facts recited. Estate of Nidever, 181 Cal.App.2d 367, 5 Cal.Rptr. 343 (1960); Kirkpatrick v. Tapo Oil Co., 144 Cal.App.2d 404, 301 P.2d 274 (1956). In these latter cases, the courts have not insisted that the hearsay statement itself be acted upon as true by persons with an interest in the matter; the evidence has been admitted merely upon a showing that the document containing the statement is genuine. The age of a document alone is not a sufficient guarantee of the trustworthiness of a statement contained therein to warrant the admission of the statement into evidence. Accordingly, Section 1331 makes it clear that the statement itself must have been generally acted upon as true for at least 30 years by persons having an interest in the matter. [7 Cal.L.Rev.Comm. Reports 1 (1965)]

ARTICLE 14. COMMERCIAL, SCIENTIFIC, AND SIMILAR PUBLICATIONS

§ 1340. Publications relied upon as accurate in the course of business

Evidence of a statement, other than an opinion, contained in a tabulation, list, directory, register, or other published compilation is not made inadmissible by the hearsay rule if the compilation is generally used and relied upon as accurate in the course of a business as defined in Section 1270.

LAW REVISION COMMISSION COMMENT

Section 1340 codifies an exception that has been recognized by statute and by the courts in specific situations. See, e.g., Com.Code § 2724; Emery v. So. Cal. Gas Co., 72 Cal.App.2d 821, 165 P.2d 695 (1946); Christiansen v. Hollings, 44 Cal.App.2d 332, 112 P.2d 723 (1941). [7 Cal.L.Rev.Comm. Reports 1 (1965)]

§ 1341. Publications concerning facts of general notoriety and interests

Historical works, books of science or art, and published maps or charts, made by persons indifferent between the parties, are not made inadmissible by the hearsay rule when offered to prove facts of general notoriety and interest.

LAW REVISION COMMISSION COMMENT

Section 1341 recodifies without substantive change Section 1936 of the Code of Civil Procedure. [7 Cal.L.Rev.Comm. Reports 1 (1965)]

ARTICLE 15. DECLARANT UNAVAILABLE AS WITNESS

§ 1350. Unavailable declarant; hearsay rule

(a) In a criminal proceeding charging a serious felony, evidence of a statement made by a declarant is not made inadmissible by the hearsay rule if the declarant is unavailable as a witness, and all of the following are true:

(1) There is clear and convincing evidence that the declarant's unavailability was knowingly caused by, aided by, or solicited by the party against whom the statement is offered for the purpose of preventing the arrest or prosecution of the party and is the result of the death by homicide or the kidnapping of the declarant.

(2) There is no evidence that the unavailability of the declarant was caused by, aided by, solicited by, or procured on behalf of, the party who is offering the statement.

(3) The statement has been memorialized in a tape recording made by a law enforcement official, or in a written statement prepared by a law enforcement official and signed by the declarant and notorized in the presence of the law enforcement official, prior to the death or kidnapping of the declarant.

(4) The statement was made under circumstances which indicate its trustworthiness and was not the result of promise, inducement, threat, or coercion.

(5) The statement is relevant to the issues to be tried.

(6) The statement is corroborated by other evidence which tends to connect the party against whom the statement is offered with the commission of the serious felony with which the party is charged. The corroboration is not sufficient if it merely shows the commission of the offense or the circumstances thereof.

(b) If the prosecution intends to offer a statement pursuant to this section, the prosecution shall serve a written notice upon the defendant at least 10 days prior to the hearing or trial at which the prosecution intends to offer the statement, unless the prosecution shows good cause for the failure to provide that notice. In the event that good cause is shown, the defendant shall be entitled to a reasonable continuance of the hearing or trial.

(c) If the statement is offered during trial, the court's determination shall be made out of the presence of the jury. If the defendant elects to testify at the hearing on a motion brought pursuant to this section, the court shall exclude from the examination every person except the clerk, the court reporter, the bailiff, the prosecutor, the investigating officer, the defendant and his or her counsel, an investigator for the defendant, and the officer having custody of the defendant. Notwithstanding any other provision of law, the defendant's testimony at the hearing shall not be admissible in any other proceeding except the hearing brought on the motion pursuant to this section. If a transcript is made of the defendant's testimony, it shall be sealed and transmitted to the clerk of the court in which the action is pending.

(d) As used in this section, "serious felony" means any of the felonies listed in subdivision (c) of Section 1192.7 of the Penal Code or any violation of Section 11351, 11352, 11378, or 11379 of the Health and Safety Code.

(e) If a statement to be admitted pursuant to this section includes hearsay statements made by anyone other than the declarant who is unavailable pursuant to subdivision (a), those hearsay statements are inadmissible unless they meet the requirements of an exception to the hearsay rule.

ARTICLE 16. STATEMENTS BY CHILDREN UNDER THE AGE OF 12 IN CHILD NEGLECT AND ABUSE PROCEEDINGS

§ 1360. Statements describing an act or attempted act of child abuse or neglect; criminal prosecutions; requirements

(a) In a criminal prosecution where the victim is a minor, a statement made by the victim when under the age of 12 describing any act of child abuse or neglect performed with or on the child by another, or describing any attempted act of child abuse or neglect with or on the child by another, is not made inadmissible by the hearsay rule if all of the following apply:

(1) The statement is not otherwise admissible by statute or court rule.

(2) The court finds, in a hearing conducted outside the presence of the jury, that the time, content, and circumstances of the statement provide sufficient indicia of reliability.

(3) The child either:

(A) Testifies at the proceedings.

(B) Is unavailable as a witness, in which case the statement may be admitted only if there is evidence of the child abuse or neglect that corroborates the statement made by the child.

(b) A statement may not be admitted under this section unless the proponent of the statement makes known to the adverse party the intention to offer the statement and the particulars of the statement sufficiently in advance of the proceedings in order to provide the adverse party with a fair opportunity to prepare to meet the statement.

(c) For purposes of this section, "child abuse" means an act proscribed by Section 273a, 273d, or 288.5 of the Penal Code, or any of the acts described in Section 11165.1 of the Penal Code, and "child neglect" means any of the acts described in Section 11165.2 of the Penal Code.

ARTICLE 17. PHYSICAL ABUSE

§ 1370. Threat of infliction of injury

(a) Evidence of a statement by a declarant is not made inadmissible by the hearsay rule if all of the following conditions are met:

(1) The statement purports to narrate, describe, or explain the infliction or threat of physical injury upon the declarant.

(2) The declarant is unavailable as a witness pursuant to Section 240.

(3) The statement was made at or near the time of the infliction or threat of physical injury. Evidence of statements made more than five years before the filing of the current action or proceeding shall be inadmissible under this section.

(4) The statement was made under circumstances that would indicate its trustworthiness.

(5) The statement was made in writing, was electronically recorded, or made to a physician, nurse, paramedic or to a law enforcement official.

(b) For purposes of paragraph (4) of subdivision (a), circumstances relevant to the issue of trustworthiness include, but are not limited to, the following:

(1) Whether the statement was made in contemplation of pending or anticipated litigation in which the declarant was interested.

(2) Whether the declarant has a bias or motive for fabricating the statement, and the extent of any bias or motive.

(3) Whether the statement is corroborated by evidence other than statements that are admissible only pursuant to this section.

(c) A statement is admissible pursuant to this section only if the proponent of the statement makes known to the adverse party the intention to offer the statement and the particulars of the statement sufficiently in advance of the proceedings in order to provide the adverse party with a fair opportunity to prepare to meet the statement.

§ 1380. Elder and dependent adults; statements by victims of abuse

(a) In a criminal proceeding charging a violation, or attempted violation, of *Section 368 of the Penal Code*, evidence of a statement made by a declarant is not made inadmissible by the hearsay rule if the declarant is unavailable as a witness, as defined in subdivisions (a) and (b) of Section 240, and all of the following are true:

(1) The party offering the statement has made a showing of particularized guarantees of trustworthiness regarding the statement, the statement was made under circumstances which indicate its trustworthiness, and the statement was not the result of promise, inducement, threat, or coercion. In making its determination, the court may consider only the circumstances that surround the making of the statement and that render the declarant particularly worthy of belief.

(2) There is no evidence that the unavailability of the declarant was caused by, aided by, solicited by, or procured on behalf of, the party who is offering the statement.

(3) The entire statement has been memorialized in a videotape recording made by a law enforcement official, prior to the death or disabling of the declarant.

(4) The statement was made by the victim of the alleged violation.

(5) The statement is supported by corroborative evidence.

(6) The victim of the alleged violation is an individual who meets both of the following requirements:

(A) Was 65 years of age or older or was a dependent adult when the alleged violation or attempted violation occurred.

(B) At the time of any criminal proceeding, including, but not limited to, a preliminary hearing or trial, regarding the alleged violation or attempted violation, is either deceased or suffers from the infirmities of aging as manifested by advanced age or organic brain damage, or other physical, mental, or emotional dysfunction, to the extent that the ability of the person to provide adequately for the person's own care or protection is impaired.

(b) If the prosecution intends to offer a statement pursuant to this section, the prosecution shall serve a written notice upon the defendant at least 10 days prior to the hearing or trial at which the prosecution intends to offer the statement, unless the prosecution shows good cause for the failure to provide that notice. In the event that good cause is shown, the defendant shall be entitled to a reasonable continuance of the hearing or trial.

(c) If the statement is offered during trial, the court's determination as to the availability of the victim as a witness shall be made out of the presence of the jury. If the defendant elects to testify at the hearing on a motion brought pursuant to this section, the court shall exclude from the examination every person except the clerk, the court reporter, the bailiff, the prosecutor, the investigating officer, the defendant and his or her counsel, an investigator for the defendant, and the officer having custody of the defendant. Notwithstanding any other provision of law, the defendant's testimony at the hearing shall not be admissible in any other proceeding except the hearing brought on the motion pursuant to this section. If a transcript is made of the defendant's testimony, it shall be sealed and transmitted to the clerk of the court in which the action is pending.

(Added by Stats. 1999, c. 383 (A.B.526 § 1.))

DIVISION 11. WRITINGS

CHAPTER 1. AUTHENTICATION AND PROOF OF WRITINGS

ARTICLE 1. REQUIREMENT OF AUTHENTICATION

§ 1400. Authentication

Authentication of a writing means (a) the introduction of evidence sufficient to sustain a finding that it is the writing that the proponent of the evidence claims it is or (b) the establishment of such facts by any other means provided by law.

LAW REVISION COMMISSION COMMENT

Before any tangible object may be admitted into evidence, the party seeking to introduce the object must make a preliminary showing that the object is in some way relevant to the issues to be decided in the action. When the object sought to be introduced is a writing, this preliminary showing of relevancy usually entails some proof that the writing is authentic—i.e., that the writing was made or signed by its purported maker. Hence, this showing is normally referred to as "authentication" of the writing. But authentication, correctly understood, may involve a preliminary showing that the writing is a forgery or is a writing found in particular files regardless of its authorship. Cf. People v. Adamson, 118 Cal.App.2d 714, 258 P.2d 1020 (1953). When the requisite preliminary showing has been made, the judge admits the writing into evidence for consideration by the trier of fact. However, the fact that the judge permits the writing to be admitted in evidence does not necessarily establish the authenticity of the writing; all that the judge has determined is that there has been a sufficient showing of the authenticity of the writing to permit the trier of fact to find that it is authentic. The trier of fact independently determines the question of authenticity, and, if the trier of fact does not believe the evidence of authenticity, it may find that the writing is not authentic despite the fact that the judge has determined that it was "authenticated." See 7 Wigmore, Evidence §§ 2129–2135 (3d ed. 1940).

This chapter sets forth the rules governing this process of authentication. Sections 1400–1402 (Article 1) define and state the general requirement of authentication—either by evidence sufficient to sustain a finding of authenticity or by other means sanctioned by law. Sections 1410–1454 (Articles 2 and 3) set forth some of the means that may be used to authenticate certain kinds of writings. The operation and effect of these sections is explained in separate Comments relating to them.

Under Section 1400, as under existing law, a writing may be authenticated by the presentation of evidence sufficient to sustain a finding of its authenticity. See Verzan v. McGregor, 23 Cal. 339, 342–343 (1863). Under Section 1400, as under existing law, the authenticity of a particular writing also may be established by some means other than the introduction of evidence of authenticity. Thus, the authenticity of a writing may be established by stipulation or by the pleadings. See e.g., Code Civ.Proc. §§ 447 and 448. The requisite preliminary showing may also be supplied by a presumption. See, e.g., Evidence Code §§ 1450–1454, 1530. In some instances, a presumption of authenticity may also attach to a writing authenticated in a particular manner. See, e.g., Evidence Code § 643 (the ancient documents rule). Where a presumption applies, the trier of fact is required to find that the writing is authentic unless the requisite contrary showing is made. Evidence Code §§ 600, 604, 606. [7 Cal.L.Rev.Comm. Reports 1 (1965)]

§ 1401. Authentication required

(a) Authentication of a writing is required before it may be received in evidence.

(b) Authentication of a writing is required before secondary evidence of its content may be received in evidence.

§ 1402. Authentication of altered writing

The party producing a writing as genuine which has been altered, or appears to have been altered, after its execution, in a part material to the question in dispute, must account for the alteration or appearance thereof. He may show that the alteration was made by another, without his concurrence, or was made with the consent of the parties affected by it, or otherwise properly or innocently made, or that the alteration did not change the meaning or language of the instrument. If he does that, he may give the writing in evidence, but not otherwise.

LAW REVISION COMMISSION COMMENT

Section 1402 restates and supersedes Code of Civil Procedure Section 1982. See Miller v. Luco, 80 Cal. 257, 265, 22 Pac. 195, 197 (1889); King v. Tarabino, 53 Cal.App. 157, 199 Pac. 890 (1921). [7 Cal.L.Rev. Comm. Reports 1 (1965)]

ARTICLE 2. MEANS OF AUTHENTICATING AND PROVING WRITINGS

§ 1410. Article not exclusive

Nothing in this article shall be construed to limit the means by which a writing may be authenticated or proved.

LAW REVISION COMMISSION COMMENT

This article (Sections 1410–1421) lists many of the evidentiary means for authenticating writings and supersedes the existing statutory expressions of such means.

Section 1410 is included in this article in recognition of the fact that it would be impossible to specify all of the varieties of circumstantial evidence that may be sufficient in particular cases to sustain a finding of the authenticity of a writing. Hence, Section 1410 ensures that the means of authentication listed in this article or stated elsewhere in the codes will not be considered the exclusive means of authenticating writings. Although Section 1410 has no counterpart in previous legislation, the California courts have never considered the listing of certain means of authentication in the various California statutes as precluding reliance upon other means of authentication. See, e.g., People v. Ramsey, 83 Cal.App.2d 707, 189 P.2d 802 (1948) (authentication by evidence of possession); Geary St. etc. R.R. v. Campbell, 39 Cal.App. 496, 179 Pac. 453 (1919) (corporate stock record book authenticated by age, appropriate custody, and unsuspicious appearance). See also the Comments to Sections 1420 and 1421. [7 Cal.L.Rev.Comm. Reports 1 (1965)]

§ 1410.5. Graffiti constitutes a writing; admissibility

(a) For purposes of this chapter, a writing shall include any graffiti consisting of written words, insignia, symbols, or any other markings which convey a particular meaning.

(b) Any writing described in subdivision (a), or any photograph thereof, may be admitted into evidence in an action for vandalism, for the purpose of proving that the writing was made by the defendant.

(c) The admissibility of any fact offered to prove that the writing was made by the defendant shall, upon motion of the defendant, be ruled upon outside the presence of the jury, and is subject to the requirements of Sections 1416, 1417, and 1418.

§ 1411. Subscribing witness' testimony unnecessary

Except as provided by statute, the testimony of a subscribing witness is not required to authenticate a writing.

LAW REVISION COMMISSION COMMENT

When Section 1940 of the Code of Civil Procedure was enacted in 1872, it stated the common law rule that a subscribing witness to a witnessed writing must be produced to authenticate the writing or his absence must be satisfactorily accounted for. See Stevens v. Irwin, 12 Cal. 306 (1859). Section 1940 was amended by the Code Amendments of 1873–74 to remove the requirement that the subscribing witness be produced. Cal.Stats.1873–74, Ch. 383, § 231 (Code Amdts., p. 386). Instead, three alternative methods of authenticating a writing were listed.

Section 1411 states directly what the 1873–74 amendment to Code of Civil Procedure Section 1940 stated indirectly—that the common law rule requiring the production of a subscribing witness to a witnessed writing is not the law in California unless a statute specifically so requires. [7 Cal.L.Rev.Comm. Reports 1 (1965)]

§ 1412. Use of other evidence when subscribing witness' testimony required

If the testimony of a subscribing witness is required by statute to authenticate a writing and the subscribing witness denies or does not recollect the execution of the writing, the writing may be authenticated by other evidence.

LAW REVISION COMMISSION COMMENT

When enacted in 1872, Code of Civil Procedure Section 1941 stated a limitation on the common law rule requiring proof of witnessed writings by a subscribing witness. Section 1941 provided, in effect, that this rule did not prohibit the authentication of a witnessed writing by other evidence if the subscribing witness denied or did not remember the execution of the writing. Evidence Code Section 1412, which supersedes Code of Civil Procedure Section 1941, retains this limitation on the subscribing witness rule in those few cases, such as those involving wills, where a statute requires the testimony of a subscribing witness to authenticate a writing. [7 Cal.L.Rev.Comm Reports 1 (1965)]

§ 1413. Witness to the execution of a writing

A writing may be authenticated by anyone who saw the writing made or executed, including a subscribing witness.

§ 1414. Admission of authenticity; acting upon writing as authentic

A writing may be authenticated by evidence that:

(a) The party against whom it is offered has at any time admitted its authenticity; or

(b) The writing has been acted upon as authentic by the party against whom it is offered.

LAW REVISION COMMISSION COMMENT

Section 1414 restates and supersedes the provisions of Code of Civil Procedure Section 1942. Section 1942 is difficult to understand. It was amended in 1901 to make it more intelligible. Cal.Stats.1901, Ch. 102, § 480, p. 247. However, the code revision of which the 1901 amendment was a part was held unconstitutional because of technical defects in the title of the act and because the act embraced more than one subject. Lewis v. Dunne, 134 Cal. 291, 66 Pac 478 (1901). Evidence Code Section 1414 is based on the 1901 amendment of Section 1942. [7 Cal.L.Rev.Comm. Reports 1 (1965)]

§ 1415. Authentication by handwriting evidence

A writing may be authenticated by evidence of the genuineness of the handwriting of the maker.

§ 1416. Proof of handwriting by person familiar therewith

A witness who is not otherwise qualified to testify as an expert may state his opinion whether a writing is in the handwriting of a supposed writer if the court finds that he has personal knowledge of the handwriting of the supposed writer. Such personal knowledge may be acquired from:

(a) Having seen the supposed writer write;

(b) Having seen a writing purporting to be in the handwriting of the supposed writer and upon which the supposed writer has acted or been charged;

(c) Having received letters in the due course of mail purporting to be from the supposed writer in response to letters duly addressed and mailed by him to the supposed writer; or

(d) Any other means of obtaining personal knowledge of the handwriting of the supposed writer.

§ 1417. Comparison of handwriting by trier of fact

The genuineness of handwriting, or the lack thereof, may be proved by a comparison made by the trier of fact with handwriting (a) which the court finds was admitted or treated as genuine by the party against whom the evidence is offered or (b) otherwise proved to be genuine to the satisfaction of the court.

LAW REVISION COMMISSION COMMENT

Section 1417 is based on that portion of Code of Civil Procedure Section 1944 that permits the trier of fact to compare questioned handwriting with handwriting the court has found to be genuine. [7 Cal.L.Rev.Comm. Reports 1 (1965)]

§ 1418. Comparison of writing by expert witness

The genuineness of writing, or the lack thereof, may be proved by a comparison made by an expert witness with writing (a) which the court finds was admitted or treated as genuine by the party against whom the evidence is offered or (b) otherwise proved to be genuine to the satisfaction of the court.

LAW REVISION COMMISSION COMMENT

Section 1418 is based on that portion of Code of Civil Procedure Section 1944 that permits a witness to compare questioned handwriting with handwriting the court has found to be genuine. However, Section 1418 applies to any form of writing, not just handwriting. This is in recognition of the fact that experts can now compare typewriting specimens and other forms of writing as accurately as they could compare handwriting specimens in 1872.

Although Code of Civil Procedure Section 1944 does not expressly require that the witness making the comparison be an expert witness (as Evidence Code Section 1418 does), the cases have nonetheless imposed this requirement. E.g., Spottiswood v. Weir, 80 Cal. 448, 22 Pac. 289 (1889). The witness' expertise may, of course, be derived from practical experience instead of from technical training. In re Newell's Estate, 75 Cal.App. 554, 243 Pac. 33 (1926) (experienced banker). [7 Cal.L.Rev. Comm. Reports 1 (1965)]

§ 1419. Exemplars when writing is 30 years old

Where a writing whose genuineness is sought to be proved is more than 30 years old, the comparison under Section 1417 or 1418 may be made with writing purporting to be genuine, and generally respected and acted upon as such, by persons having an interest in knowing whether it is genuine.

LAW REVISION COMMISSION COMMENT

Section 1419 restates and supersedes the provisions of Code of Civil Procedure Section 1945. The apparent purpose of Section 1945, continued without substantive change in Evidence Code Section 1419, is to permit the judge to be satisfied with a lesser degree of proof of the authenticity of an exemplar when the writing offered in evidence is more than 30 years old. [7 Cal.L.Rev.Comm. Reports 1 (1965)]

§ 1420. Authentication by evidence of reply

A writing may be authenticated by evidence that the writing was received in response to a communication sent to the person who is claimed by the proponent of the evidence to be the author of the writing.

LAW REVISION COMMISSION COMMENT

Section 1420 provides a method of authentication recognized in California case law but not previously reflected in California statutes. House Grain Co. v. Finerman & Sons, 116 Cal.App.2d 485, 253 P.2d 1034 (1953). [7 Cal.L.Rev.Comm. Reports 1 (1965)]

§ 1421. Authentication by content

A writing may be authenticated by evidence that the writing refers to or states matters that are unlikely to be known to anyone other than the person who is claimed by the proponent of the evidence to be the author of the writing.

LAW REVISION COMMISSION COMMENT

Section 1421 provides a method of authentication recognized in California case law but not previously reflected in California statutes. Chaplin v. Sullivan, 67 Cal.App.2d 728, 734, 155 P.2d 368, 372 (1945). [7 Cal.L.Rev.Comm. Reports 1 (1965)]

ARTICLE 3. PRESUMPTIONS AFFECTING ACKNOWLEDGED WRITINGS AND OFFICIAL

§ 1450. Classification of presumptions in article

The presumptions established by this article are presumptions affecting the burden of producing evidence.

LAW REVISION COMMISSION COMMENT

This article (Sections 1450–1454) lists several presumptions that may be used to authenticate particular kinds of writings. Section 1450 prescribes the effect of these presumptions. They require a finding of authenticity unless the adverse party produces evidence sufficient to sustain a finding that the writing in question is not authentic. See Evidence Code § 604 and the Comment thereto. [7 Cal.L.Rev.Comm. Reports 1 (1965)]

§ 1451. Acknowledged writings

A certificate of the acknowledgment of a writing other than a will, or a certificate of the proof of such a writing, is prima facie evidence of the facts recited in the certificate and the genuineness of the signature of each person by whom the writing purports to have been signed if the certificate meets the requirements of Article 3 (commencing with Section 1180) of Chapter 4, Title 4, Part 4, Division 2 of the Civil Code.

LAW REVISION COMMISSION COMMENT

Section 1451 continues in effect and restates a method of authenticating private writings that is contained in Code of Civil Procedure Section 1948. [7 Cal.L.Rev.Comm. Reports 1 (1965)]

§ 1452. Official seals

A seal is presumed to be genuine and its use authorized if it purports to be the seal of:

(a) The United States or a department, agency, or public employee of the United States.

(b) A public entity in the United States or a department, agency, or public employee of such public entity.

(c) A nation recognized by the executive power of the United States or a department, agency, or officer of such nation.

(d) A public entity in a nation recognized by the executive power of the United States or a department, agency, or officer of such public entity.

(e) A court of admiralty or maritime jurisdiction.

(f) A notary public within any state of the United States.

LAW REVISION COMMISSION COMMENT

Sections 1452 and 1453 eliminate the need for formal proof of the genuineness of certain official seals and signatures when such proof would otherwise be required by the general requirement of authentication.

Under existing law, formal proof of many of the signatures and seals mentioned in Sections 1452 and 1453 is not required because such signatures and seals are the subject of judicial notice. Code Civ.Proc. § 1875 (5), (6), (7), (8). (Section 1875 is superseded by Division 4 (Sections 450–460) of the Evidence Code.) The parties may not dispute a matter that has been judicially noticed. Code Civ.Proc. § 2102 (superseded by Evidence Code § 457). Hence, judicial notice of facts should be confined to matters concerning which there can be no reasonable dispute. The authenticity of writings purporting to be official writings should not be determined conclusively by the judge when there is serious dispute as to such authenticity. Therefore, Sections 1452 and 1453 provide that the official seals and signatures mentioned shall be presumed genuine and authorized until evidence is introduced sufficient to sustain a finding that they are not genuine or authorized. When there is such evidence disputing the authenticity of an official seal or signature, the trier of fact is required to determine the question of authenticity without regard to any presumption created by this section. See Evidence Code § 604 and the Comment thereto.

This procedure will dispense with the necessity for proof of authenticity when there is no real dispute as to such authenticity, but it will assure the parties the right to contest the authenticity of official writings when there is a real dispute as to such authenticity. [7 Cal.L.Rev. Comm. Reports 1 (1965)]

§ 1453. Domestic official signatures

A signature is presumed to be genuine and authorized if it purports to be the signature, affixed in his official capacity, of:

(a) A public employee of the United States.

(b) A public employee of any public entity in the United States.

(c) A notary public within any state of the United States.

LAW REVISION COMMISSION COMMENT

See the Comment to Section 1452. [7 Cal.L.Rev.Comm. Reports 1 (1965)]

§ 1454. Foreign official signatures

A signature is presumed to be genuine and authorized if it purports to be the signature, affixed in his official capacity, of an officer, or deputy of an officer, of a nation or public entity in a nation recognized by the executive power of the United States and the writing to which the signature is affixed is accompanied by a final statement certifying the genuineness of the signature and the official position of (a) the person who executed the writing or (b) any foreign official who has certified either the genuineness of the signature and official position of the person executing the writing or the genuineness of the signature and official position of another foreign official who has executed a similar certificate in a chain of such certificates beginning with a certificate of the genuineness of the signature and official position of the person executing the writing. The final statement may be made only by a secretary of an embassy or legation, consul general, consul, vice consul, consular agent, or other officer in the foreign service of the United States stationed in the nation, authenticated by the seal of his office.

LAW REVISION COMMISSION COMMENT

Section 1454 supersedes the somewhat complex procedure for authenticating foreign official writings that is contained in subdivision 8 of Code of Civil Procedure Section 1918. Section 1454 is based on a proposed amendment to Rule 44 of the Federal Rules of Civil Procedure that has been prepared by the Advisory Committee on Civil Rules, the Commission and Advisory Committee on International Rules of Judicial Procedure, and the Columbia Law School Project on International Procedure. Proposed Amendments to Rules of Civil Procedure for the United States District Courts with Advisory Committee's Notes (mimeo., Feb. 25, 1964). Rule 44 and the proposed amendment, however, deal only with the question of authenticating copies of foreign official writings. Section 1454 relates to the authentication of any foreign official writing, whether it be an original or a copy.

The procedure set forth in Section 1454 is necessary for the reason that a United States foreign service officer may not be able to certify to the official position and signature of a particular foreign official. Accordingly, this section permits the original signature to be certified by a higher foreign official, whose signature can in turn be certified by a still higher official, and such certifications can be continued in a chain until a foreign official is reached as to whom the United States foreign service officer has adequate information upon which to base his final certification. See, e.g., New York Life Ins. Co. v. Aronson, 38 F.Supp. 687 (W.D.Pa.1941).

See also the Comment to Section 1452. [7 Cal.L.Rev.Comm. Reports 1 (1965)]

CHAPTER 2. SECONDARY EVIDENCE OF WRITINGS

§§ 1500 to 1511. Repealed by Stats.1998, c. 100 (S.B.177), § 1, operative Jan. 1, 1999

§ 1520. Content of writing; proof

The content of a writing may be proved by an otherwise admissible original.

LAW REVISION COMMISSION COMMENT

1998 Addition

Section 1520 continues former Section 1500 insofar as it permitted proof of the content of a writing by an original of the writing. See also Sections 1521 (Secondary Evidence Rule), 1522 (exclusion of secondary evidence in criminal action), 1523 (oral testimony of content of writing). [26 Cal.L.Rev.Comm. Reports 369 (1996)].

§ 1521. Secondary evidence rule

(a) The content of a writing may be proved by otherwise admissible secondary evidence. The court shall exclude secondary evidence of the content of writing if the court determines either of the following:

(1) A genuine dispute exists concerning material terms of the writing and justice requires the exclusion.

(2) Admission of the secondary evidence would be unfair.

(b) Nothing in this section makes admissible oral testimony to prove the content of a writing if the testimony is inadmissible under Section 1523 (oral testimony of the content of a writing).

(c) Nothing in this section excuses compliance with Section 1401 (authentication).

(d) This section shall be known as the "Secondary Evidence Rule."

LAW REVISION COMMISSION COMMENT

1998 Addition

Sections 1520 (proof of content of writing by original), 1521 (Secondary Evidence Rule), 1522 (exclusion of secondary evidence in criminal action), and 1523 (oral testimony of content of writing) replace the Best Evidence Rule and its exceptions. For background, see Best Evidence Rule, 26 Cal. L. Revision Comm'n Reports 369 (1996). Because of the breadth of the exceptions to the Best Evidence Rule, this reform is not a major departure from former law, but primarily a matter of clarification and simplification. Discovery principles remain unchanged.

Subdivision (a) makes secondary evidence generally admissible to prove the content of a writing. The nature of the evidence offered affects its weight, not its admissibility. The normal motivation of parties to support their cases with convincing evidence is a deterrent to introduction of unreliable secondary evidence. See also Section 412 (if party offers weaker and less satisfactory evidence despite ability to produce stronger and more satisfactory evidence, the evidence offered should be viewed with distrust).

The mandatory exceptions set forth in subdivisions (a)(1) and (a)(2) provide further protection against unreliable secondary evidence. Those exceptions are modeled on the exceptions to former Section 1511 and to *Rule 1003 of the Federal Rules of Evidence*. Cases interpreting those statutes provide guidance in applying subdivisions (a)(1) and (a)(2). *See, e.g., United States v. Sinclair*, 74 F.3d 753, 760–61 (7th Cir. 1996) (admitting copies of expense account reports was not unfair); *Ruberto v. Commissioner of Internal Revenue*, 774 F.2d 61, 64 (2d Cir. 1985) (tax court did not err in excluding photocopies of canceled checks, "since problems in matching the copies of the backs of the checks with copies of the fronts made them somewhat suspect''); *Amoco Production Co. v. United States*, 619 F.2d 1383, 1391 (10th Cir. 1980) (upholding trial court's determination that ''admission of the file copy would be unfair because the most critical part of the original conformed copy.... is not completely reproduced in the 'duplicate' ''); *People v. Garcia*, 201 Cal. App. 3d 324, 330, 247 Cal. Rptr. 94 (1988) (claim of unfairness ''must be based on substance, not mere speculation that the original might contain some relevant difference''). Courts may consider a broad range of factors, for example: (1) whether the proponent attempts to use the writing in a manner that could not reasonably have been anticipated, (2) whether the original was suppressed in discovery, (3) whether discovery conducted in a reasonably diligent (as opposed to exhaustive) manner failed to result in production of the original, (4) whether there are dramatic differences between the original and the secondary evidence (e.g., the original but not the secondary evidence is in color and the colors provide significant clues to interpretation), (5) whether the original is unavailable and, if so, why, and (6) whether the writing is central to the case or collateral. A classic circumstance for exclusion pursuant to subdivision (a)(2) is if the proponent destroyed the original with fraudulent intent or the doctrine of spoliation of evidence otherwise applies.

Subdivision (b) explicitly establishes that Section 1523 (oral testimony of the content of writing), not Section 1521, governs the admissibility of oral testimony to prove the content of a writing.

Subdivision (c) makes clear that like other evidence, secondary evidence is admissible only if it is properly authenticated. Under Section 1401, the proponent must not only authenticate the original writing, but must also establish that the proffered evidence is secondary evidence of the original. See B. Jefferson, Jefferson's Synopsis of California Evidence Law, 30.1, at 470–71 (1985). [26 Cal.L.Rev.Comm. Reports 369 (1996)].

§ 1522. Additional grounds for exclusion of secondary evidence

(a) In addition to the grounds for exclusion authorized by Section 1521, in a criminal action the court shall exclude secondary evidence of the content of a writing if the court determines that the original is in the proponent's possession, custody, or control, and the proponent has not made the original reasonably available for inspection at or before trial. This section does not apply to any of the following:

(1) A duplicate as defined in Section 260.

(2) A writing that is not closely related to the controlling issues in the action.

(3) A copy of a writing in the custody of a public entity.

(4) A copy of a writing that is recorded in the public records, if the record or a certified copy of it is made evidence of the writing by statute.

(b) In a criminal action, a request to exclude secondary evidence of the content of a writing, under this section or any other law, shall not be made in the presence of the jury.

LAW REVISION COMMISSION COMMENT

1998 Addition

Subdivision (a) of Section 1522 sets forth a mandatory exception applicable only in criminal cases, which are governed by narrower discovery rules than civil cases. See Section 130 ("criminal action" includes criminal proceedings). See also *Penal Code §§ 1054-1054.7* (discovery in criminal cases). Section 1522 does not expand discovery obligations, it simply conditions use of secondary evidence on making the original reasonably available for inspection if the proponent has it. In determining whether the proponent of secondary evidence has made the original "reasonably available," the court should examine specific circumstances, such as the time, place, and manner of allowing inspection. The concept is fluid, not rigid. For example, making the original available moments before using secondary evidence may in general suffice if a defendant is rebutting a surprise contention, but not if the prosecution is presenting its case in chief. Similarly, what constitutes reasonable access to computer evidence may vary from system to system.

The exceptions in subdivisions (a)(1)-(a)(4) are drawn from exceptions to the former Best Evidence Rule (former Section 1500). Subdivision (a)(1) is drawn from former Section 1511. Subdivision (a)(2) is drawn from former Section 1504. Subdivision (a)(3) is drawn from former Section 1506. Subdivision (a)(4) is drawn from former Section 1507.

Subdivision (b) continues the requirement of the second sentence of former Section 1503(a), but applies it to all requests for exclusion of secondary evidence in a criminal trial.

See also Sections 1520 (proof of content of writing by original), 1521 (Secondary Evidence Rule), and 1523 (oral testimony of content of writing). [26 Cal.L.Rev.Comm. Reports 369 (1996)].

§ 1523. Oral testimony of the content of a writing; admissibility

(a) Except as otherwise provided by statute, oral testimony is not admissible to prove the content of a writing.

(b) Oral testimony of the content of a writing is not made inadmissible by subdivision (a) if the proponent does not have possession or control of a copy of the writing and the original is lost or has been destroyed without fraudulent intent on the part of the proponent of the evidence.

(c) Oral testimony of the content of a writing is not made inadmissible by subdivision (a) if the proponent does not have possession or control of the original or a copy of the writing and either of the following conditions is satisfied:

(1) Neither the writing nor a copy of the writing was reasonably procurable by the proponent by use of the court's process or by other available means.

(2) The writing is not closely related to the controlling issues and it would be inexpedient to require its production.

(d) Oral testimony of the content of a writing is not made inadmissible by subdivision (a) if the writing consists of numerous accounts or other writings that cannot be examined in court without great loss of time, and the evidence sought from them is only the general result of the whole.

LAW REVISION COMMISSION COMMENT

1998 Addition

Section 1523 preserves former law governing the admissibility of oral testimony to prove the content of a writing. See former Sections 1500, 1501–1509.

Subdivision (a) is based on an assumption that oral testimony as to the content of a writing is typically less reliable than other proof of the content of a writing. For background, see Best Evidence Rule, 26 Cal. L. Revision Comm'n Reports 369 (1996).

Subdivision (b) continues former Sections 1501 and 1505 without substantive change as to oral testimony of the content of a writing that is lost or has been destroyed.

Subdivision (c)(1) continues former Sections 1502 and 1505 without substantive change as to oral testimony of the content of a writing that was not reasonably procurable. In effect, subdivision (c)(1) also continues former Sections 1503 and 1505 without substantive change as to oral testimony of the content of a writing that the opponent has, but failed to produce at the hearing despite being expressly or impliedly notified that it would be needed. Under such circumstances, the writing was not reasonably procurable. Finally, subdivision (c)(1) continues former Sections 1506–1508 without substantive change as to oral testimony of the content of a writing where (1) the writing is in the custody of a public entity and the proponent could not have obtained it or a copy of it in the exercise of reasonable diligence, or (2) the writing has been recorded in the public records, the record or a certified copy of the writing is made evidence of the writing by statute, and the proponent could not have obtained it or a copy of it in the exercise of reasonable diligence. Subdivision (c)(2) continues former Sections 1504 and 1505 without substantive change as to oral testimony of the content of a collateral writing.

Subdivision (d) continues former Section 1509 without substantive change as to oral testimony of a voluminous writing.

See Sections 1520 (proof of content of writing by original), 1521 (Secondary Evidence Rule), and 1522 (exclusion of secondary evidence in criminal action). [26 Cal.L.Rev.Comm. Reports 369 (1996)].

ARTICLE 2. OFFICIAL WRITINGS AND RECORDED WRITINGS

§ 1530. Copy of writing in official custody

(a) A purported copy of a writing in the custody of a public entity, or of an entry in such a writing, is prima facie evidence of the existence and content of such writing or entry if:

(1) The copy purports to be published by the authority of the nation or state, or public entity therein in which the writing is kept;

(2) The office in which the writing is kept is within the United States or within the Panama Canal Zone, the Trust Territory of the Pacific Islands, or the Ryukyu Islands, and the copy is attested or certified as a correct copy of the writing or entry by a public employee, or a deputy of a public employee, having the legal custody of the writing; or

(3) The office in which the writing is kept is not within the United States or any other place described in paragraph (2) and the copy is attested as a correct copy of the writing or entry by a person having authority to make attestation. The attestation must be accompanied by a final statement certifying the genuineness of the signature and the official position of (i) the person who attested the copy as a correct copy or (ii) any foreign official who has certified either the genuineness of the signature and official position of the person attesting the copy or the genuineness of the signature and official position of another foreign official who has executed a similar certificate in a chain of such certificates beginning with a certificate of the genuineness of the signature and official position of the person attesting the copy. Except as provided in the next sentence, the final statement may be made only by a secretary of an embassy or legation, consul general, consul, vice consul, or consular agent of the United States, or a diplomatic or consular official of the foreign country assigned or accredited to the United States. Prior to January 1, 1971, the final statement may also be made by a secretary of an embassy or legation, consul general, consul, vice consul, consular agent, or other officer in the foreign service of the United States stationed in the nation in which the writing is kept, authenticated by the seal of his office. If reasonable opportunity has been given to all parties to investigate the authenticity and accuracy of the docu-

ments, the court may, for good cause shown, (i) admit an attested copy without the final statement or (ii) permit the writing or entry in foreign custody to be evidenced by an attested summary with or without a final statement.

(b) The presumptions established by this section are presumptions affecting the burden of producing evidence.

LAW REVISION COMMISSION COMMENT

1965 Enactment

Section 1530 deals with three evidentiary problems. First, it is concerned with the problem of proving the content of an original writing by means of a copy, i.e., the best evidence rule. See Evidence Code § 1500. Second, it is concerned with authentication, for the copy must be authenticated as a copy of the original writing. Evidence Code § 1401. Finally, it is concerned with the hearsay rule, for a certification or attestation of authenticity is "a statement that was made other than by a witness while testifying at the hearing and that is offered to prove the truth of the matter stated." Evidence Code § 1200. Because this section is principally concerned with the use of a copy of a writing to prove the content of the original, it is located in the division relating to secondary evidence of writings.

Under existing California law, certain official records may be proved by copies purporting to have been published by official authority or by copies with attached certificates containing certain requisite seals and signatures. The rules are complex and detailed and appear for the most part in Article 2 (beginning with Section 1892) of Chapter 3, Title 2, Part IV of the Code of Civil Procedure.

Section 1530 substitutes for these rules a uniform rule that can be applied to all writings in official custody found within the United States and another rule applicable to all writings in official custody found outside the United States.

Subdivision (a)(1). Subdivision (a)(1) of Section 1530 provides that an official writing may be proved by a copy purporting to be published by official authority. Under Section 1918 of the Code of Civil Procedure, the acts and proceedings of the executive and legislature of any state, the United States, or a foreign government may be proved by documents and journals published by official authority. Subdivision (a)(1) in effect makes these provisions of Section 1918 applicable to all classes of official documents. This extension of the means of proving official documents will facilitate the proof of many official documents the authenticity of which is presumed (Evidence Code § 644) and is seldom subject to question.

Subdivision (a)(2) and (a)(3) generally. Paragraphs (2) and (3) of subdivision (a) of Section 1530 set forth the rules for proving the content of writings in official custody by attested or certified copies. A person who "attests" a writing merely affirms it to be true or genuine by his signature. Black, Law Dictionary (4th ed 1951). Existing California statutes require certain writings to be "certified." Section 1923 of the Code of Civil Procedure (superseded by Evidence Code Section 1531) provides that the certificate affixed to a certified copy must state that the copy is a correct copy of the original, must be signed by the certifying officer, and must be under his seal of office, if he has one. Thus, the only difference between the words "attested" and "certified" is that the existing statutory definition of "certified" requires the use of a seal, if the authenticating officer has one, whereas the definition of "attested" does not. Section 1530 eliminates the requirement of the seal by the use of the word "attested." However, Section 1530 retains, in addition, the word "certified" because it is the more familiar term in California practice.

Subdivision (a)(2). Under existing law, copies of many records of the United States government and of the governments of sister states may be proved by a copy certified or attested by the custodian alone. See, e.g., Code Civ.Proc. §§ 1901 and 1918(1), (2), (3), (9); Corp.Code § 6600. Yet, other official writings must be certified or attested not only by the custodian but also by a higher official certifying the authority and signature of the custodian. In order to provide a uniform rule for the proof of all domestic official writings, subdivision (a)(2) extends the simpler and more expeditious procedure to all official writings within the United States.

Subdivision (a)(3). Under existing law, some foreign official records may be proved by a copy certified or attested by the custodian alone. See Code Civ.Proc. §§ 1901 and 1918(4). Yet, other copies of foreign official writings must be accompanied by three certificates: one executed by the custodian, another by a higher official certifying the authority and signature of the custodian, and a third by still another official certifying the signature and official position of the second official. See Code Civ.Proc. §§ 1906 and 1918(8).

For these complex rules, subdivision (a)(3) of Section 1530 substitutes a relatively simple and uniform procedure that is applicable to all classes of foreign official writings. Subdivision (a)(3) is based on a proposed amendment to Rule 44 of the Federal Rules of Civil Procedure that has been prepared by the Advisory Committee on Civil Rules, the Commission and Advisory Committee on International Rules of Judicial Procedure, and the Columbia Law School Project on International Procedure, Proposed Amendments to Rules of Civil Procedure for the United States District Courts with Advisory Committee's Notes (mimeo., Feb. 25, 1964).

Subdivision (a)(3) requires that the copy be attested as a correct copy by "a person having authority to make the attestation." In some foreign countries, the person with authority to attest a copy of an official writing is not necessarily the person with legal custody of the writing.

See 2B Barron & Holtzoff, Federal Practice Procedure § 992 (Wright ed. 1961). In such a case, subdivision (a)(3) requires that the attester's signature and official position be certified by another official. If this is a United States foreign service officer stationed in the country, no further certificates are required. If a United States foreign service officer is not able to certify to the signature and official position of the attester, subdivision (a)(3) permits the attester's signature and official position to be certified by a higher foreign official, whose signature can in turn be certified by a still higher official. Such certifications can be continued in a chain until a foreign official is reached as to whom the United States foreign service officer has adequate information upon which to base his final certification. See, e.g., New York Life Ins. Co. v. Aronson, 38 F.Supp. 687 (W.D.Pa.1941).

Subdivision (b). Where evidence is introduced that is sufficient to sustain a finding that the copy is not a correct copy, the trier of fact is required to determine whether the copy is a correct copy without regard to the presumptions created by this section. See Evidence Code § 604 and the Comment thereto. [7 Cal.L.Rev.Comm. Reports 1 (1965)]

1970 Amendment

Section 1530 of the Evidence Code is concerned with the use of a copy of a writing in official custody to prove the content of the original. Section 1530 was deficient insofar as it prescribed, in subdivision (a) (3), the procedure for proof of foreign official writings. Subdivision (a) (3) requires that the copy of the foreign official record be attested as a correct copy by "a person having authority to make the attestation." The subdivision further requires that the first attester's signature and his official position be certified by a higher foreign official, whose signature can in turn be certified by a still higher official. Under the section as it formerly read, such certifications could be continued in a chain until a foreign official was reached as to whom a United States foreign service officer "stationed in the nation in which the writing is kept" had adequate information upon which to base his final certification. In other words, to prove a copy of a foreign official record, it was necessary to have a certificate of a United States foreign service officer stationed in the nation in which the writing was kept.

In some situations, it was impossible to satisfy the basic requirement of subdivision (a) (3) of Section 1530 because there were no United States foreign service officials in the particular foreign country (such as East Germany) and, hence, there was no one who could make the certificate required by subdivision (a) (3). As a result, in some situations, it was extremely difficult and expensive or even impossible to establish such matters as birth, legitimacy, marriage, death, or a will.

The problem described above was particularly troublesome in the case of a foreign will because Probate Code Section 361 was amended at the 1969 session to provide that a copy of a foreign will (and the related documents concerning the establishment of proof of the will in the foreign country) can be admitted in California "if such copy or other evidence satisfies the requirements of Article 2 (commencing with Section 1530) of Chapter 2 of Division 11 of the Evidence Code."

When Section 1530 of the Evidence Code was drafted in 1964, the Commission had the benefit of a proposed amendment to Rule 44 of the Federal Rules of Civil Procedure and based subdivision (a) (3) on that proposed amendment. After the Evidence Code was enacted in 1965, Rule 44 was revised (in 1966) to provide for proof of foreign official records. In the revision of Rule 44 in 1966, the defect pointed out above was discovered and provision was made in Rule 44 to cover the problem.

Rule 44 (as revised in 1966) includes the following provision to deal with the East Germany type of case:

If reasonable opportunity has been given to all parties to investigate the authenticity and accuracy of the documents, the court may, for good cause shown, (i) admit an attested copy without final certification or (ii) permit the foreign official record to be evidenced by an attested summary with or without a final certification.

The Note of the Advisory Committee regarding revised Rule 44 states:

Although the amended rule will generally facilitate proof of foreign official records, it is recognized that in some situations it may be difficult or even impossible to satisfy the basic requirements of the rule. There may be no United States consul in a particular foreign country; the foreign officials may not cooperate; peculiarities may exist or arise hereafter in the law or practice of a foreign country. See United States v. Grabina, 119 F.2d 863 (2d Cir.1941); and, generally, Jones, International Judicial Assistance: Procedural Chaos and a Program for Reform, 62 Yale L.J. 515, 548–49 (1953). Therefore the final sentence of subdivision (a) (2) provides the court with discretion to admit an attested copy of a record without a final certification, or an attested summary of a record with or without a final certification. See Rep. of Comm. on Comparative Civ.Proc. & Prac., Proc. A.B.A., Sec. Int'l & Comp. L. 123, 130–31 (1952); Model Code of Evidence §§ 517, 519 (1942). This relaxation should be permitted only when it is shown that the party has been unable to satisfy the basic requirements of the amended rule despite his reasonable efforts. Moreover it is specially provided that the parties must be given a reasonable opportunity in these cases to examine into the authenticity and accuracy of the copy or summary.

Senate Bill No. 266 [Stats.1970, c. 41] adds the substance of the sentence of Rule 44 quoted above, making only those changes needed to conform the language of that sentence to the language used in Section 1530. The bill also adopts the language of Rule 44 which specifies the officers who can make the final certificate. The change made by adopting this language is to restrict the United States foreign service officers who can make the final certificate to certain specified responsible officers and to liberalize the provision by permitting "a diplomatic or consular official of the foreign country assigned or accredited to the United States" to make the final certificate. This latter conforming change achieves desirable conformity with Rule 44 and liberalizes the rule but at the same time assures that a responsible official will make the final certificate. [10 Cal.L.Rev.Comm. Reports 1022 (1970)]

§ 1531. Certification of copy for evidence

For the purpose of evidence, whenever a copy of a writing is attested or certified, the attestation or certificate must state in substance that the copy is a correct copy of the original, or of a specified part thereof, as the case may be.

LAW REVISION COMMISSION COMMENT

Section 1531 is based on the provisions of Section 1923 of the Code of Civil Procedure. The language has been modified to define the process of attestation as well as the process of certification. Since Section 1530 permits a writing to be attested or certified for purposes of evidence without the attachment of an official seal, Section 1531 omits any requirement of a seal. [7 Cal.L.Rev.Comm. Reports 1 (1965)]

§ 1532. Official record of recorded writing

(a) The official record of a writing is prima facie evidence of the existence and content of the original recorded writing if:

(1) The record is in fact a record of an office of a public entity; and

(2) A statute authorized such a writing to be recorded in that office.

(b) The presumption established by this section is a presumption affecting the burden of producing evidence.

LAW REVISION COMMISSION COMMENT

Section 1530 authorizes the use of a copy of a writing in official custody to prove the content of that writing. When a writing has been recorded, Section 1530 merely permits a certified copy of the record to be used to prove the record, not the original recorded writing. Section 1532 permits the official record to be used to prove the content of the original recorded writing. However, under the provisions of Section 1401, the original recorded writing must be authenticated before the copy can be introduced. If the writing was executed by a public official, or if a certificate of acknowledgment or proof was attached to the writing, the original writing is presumed to be authentic and no further evidence of authenticity is required. Evidence Code §§ 1450, 1451, and 1453.

Where evidence is introduced that is sufficient to sustain a finding that the original writing is not authentic, the trier of fact is required to determine the authenticity of the original writing without regard to the presumption created by this section. See Evidence Code § 604 and the Comment thereto.

Code of Civil Procedure Section 1951 (superseded by Evidence Code Section 1600) is similar to Section 1532, but the Code of Civil Procedure section relates only to writings affecting property. Section 1532 extends the principle of the Code of Civil Procedure section to all recorded writings. There is no comparable provision in existing law. [7 Cal. L.Rev.Comm. Reports 1 (1965)]

ARTICLE 3. PHOTOGRAPHIC COPIES AND PRINTED REPRESENTATIONS OF WRITINGS

§ 1550. Photographic copies made as business records

Text of section prior to amendment by Stats.2002, c. 124 (A.B.2033), § 1.

A nonerasable optical image reproduction provided that additions, deletions, or changes to the original document are not permitted by the technology, a photostatic, microfilm, microcard, miniature photographic, or other photographic copy or reproduction, or an enlargement thereof, of a writing is as admissible as the writing itself if the copy or reproduction was made and preserved as a part of the records of a business (as defined by Section 1270) in the regular course of that business. The introduction of the copy, reproduction, or enlargement does not preclude admission of the original writing if it is still in existence. A court may require the introduction of a hard copy printout of the document.

§ 1550. Types of evidence as writing admissible as the writing itself

Text of section as amended by Stats.2002, c. 124 (A.B.2033), § 1.

(a) If made and preserved as a part of the records of a business, as defined in Section 1270, in the regular course of that business, the following types of evidence of a writing are as admissible as the writing itself:

(1) A nonerasable optical image reproduction or any other reproduction of a public record by a trusted system, as defined in Section 12168.7 of the Government Code, if additions, deletions, or changes to the original document are not permitted by the technology.

(2) A photostatic copy or reproduction.

(3) A microfilm, microcard, or miniature photographic copy, reprint, or enlargement.

(4) Any other photographic copy or reproduction, or an enlargement thereof.

(b) The introduction of evidence of a writing pursuant to subdivision (a) does not preclude admission of the original writing if it is still in existence. A court may require the introduction of a hard copy printout of the document.

For text of section prior to amendment by Stats.2002, c. 124 (A.B. 2033), § 1, see Evidence Code § 1550, ante.

OPERATIVE EFFECT

Stats.2002, c. 124 (A.B.2033), § 2, provides that this act shall become operative on the date the Secretary of State adopts uniform standards for storing and recording permanent and nonpermanent documents in electronic media as required by Government Code § 12168.7.

LAW REVISION COMMISSION COMMENT

Section 1550 continues in effect those provisions of the Uniform Photographic Copies of Business and Public Records as Evidence Act that are now found in Code of Civil Procedure Section 1953i.

Section 1550 omits the requirement, contained in Section 1953i of the Code of Civil Procedure, that the original writing be a business record. As long as the original writing is admissible under any exception to the hearsay rule, its trustworthiness is sufficiently assured; and the requirement that the photographic copy be made in the regular course of business sufficiently assures the trustworthiness of the copy. If the original is admissible not as an exception to the hearsay rule but as evidence of an ultimate fact in the case (e.g., a will or a contract), a photographic copy, the trustworthiness of which is sufficiently assured by the fact that it was made in the regular course of business, should be as admissible as the original. [7 Cal.L.Rev.Comm. Reports 1 (1965)]

§ 1551. Photographic copies where original destroyed or lost

A print, whether enlarged or not, from a photographic film (including a photographic plate, microphotographic film, photostatic negative, or similar reproduction) of an original writing destroyed or lost after such film was taken or a reproduction from an electronic recording of video images on magnetic surfaces is admissible as the original writing itself if, at the time of the taking of such film or electronic recording, the person under whose direction and control it was taken attached thereto, or to the sealed container in which it was placed and has been kept, or incorporated in the film or electronic recording, a certification complying with the provisions of Section 1531 and stating the date on which, and the fact that, it was so taken under his direction and control.

§ 1552. Printed representation of computer information or computer programs

(a) A printed representation of computer information or a computer program is presumed to be an accurate representation of the computer information or computer program that it purports to represent. This presumption is a presumption affecting the burden of producing evidence. If a party to an action introduces evidence that a printed representation of computer information or computer program is inaccurate or unreliable, the party introducing the printed representation into evidence has the burden of proving, by a preponderance of evidence, that the printed representation is an accurate representation of the existence and content of the computer information or computer program that it purports to represent.

(b) Subdivision (a) shall not apply to computer-generated official records certified in accordance with Section 452.5 or 1530.

LAW REVISION COMMISSION COMMENT

1998 Addition

Subdivision (a) of Section 1552 continues former Section 1500.5(c) without substantive change, except that the reference to "best available evidence" is changed to "an accurate representation," due to the replacement of the Best Evidence Rule with the Secondary Evidence Rule. See Section 1521 Comment. See also Section 255 (accurate printout of computer data is an "original").

Subdivision (b) continues former Section 1500.5(d) without substantive change. [26 Cal.L.Rev.Comm. Reports 369 (1996)].

§ 1533. Printed representation of images stored on a video or digital medium

A printed representation of images stored on a video or digital medium is presumed to be an accurate representation of the images it purports to represent. This presumption is a presumption affecting the burden of producing evidence. If a party to an action introduces evidence that a printed representation of images stored on a video or digital medium is inaccurate or unreliable, the party introducing the printed representation into evidence has the burden of proving, by a preponderance of evidence, that the printed representation is an accurate representation of the existence and content of the images that it purports to represent.

LAW REVISION COMMISSION COMMENT

1998 Addition

Section 1553 continues the last three sentences of the second paragraph of former Section 1500.6 without substantive change, except that the reference to "best available evidence" is changed to "an accurate representation," due to the replacement of the Best Evidence Rule with the Secondary Evidence Rule. See Section 1521 Comment. [26 Cal.L.Rev.Comm. Reports 369 (1996)].

LAW REVISION COMMISSION COMMENT

Section 1551 restates without substantive change the provisions of Code of Civil Procedure Section 1920b. [7 Cal.L.Rev.Comm. Reports 1 (1965)]

ARTICLE 4. PRODUCTION OF BUSINESS RECORDS

§ 1560. Compliance with subpoena duces tecum for business records

(a) As used in this article:

(1) "Business" includes every kind of business described in Section 1270.

(2) "Record" includes every kind of record maintained by such a business.

(b) Except as provided in Section 1564, when a subpoena duces tecum is served upon the custodian of records or other qualified witness of a business in an action in which the business is neither a party nor the place where any cause of action is alleged to have arisen, and the subpoena requires the production of all or any part of the records of the business, it is sufficient compliance therewith if the custodian or other qualified witness, within five days after the receipt of the subpoena in any criminal action or within the time agreed upon by the party who served the subpoena and the custodian or other qualified witness, or within 15 days after the receipt of the subpoena in any civil action or within the time agreed upon by the party who served the subpoena and the custodian or other qualified witness, delivers by mail or otherwise a true, legible, and durable copy of all the records described in the subpoena to the clerk of the court or to the judge if there be no clerk or to another person described in subdivision (c) of Section 2026 of the Code of Civil Procedure, together with the affidavit described in Section 1561.

(c) The copy of the records shall be separately enclosed in an inner envelope or wrapper, sealed, with the title and number of the action, name of witness, and date of subpoena clearly inscribed thereon; the sealed envelope or wrapper shall then be enclosed in an outer envelope or wrapper, sealed, and directed as follows:

(1) If the subpoena directs attendance in court, to the clerk of the court, or to the judge thereof if there be no clerk.

(2) If the subpoena directs attendance at a deposition, to the officer before whom the deposition is to be taken, at the place

designated in the subpoena for the taking of the deposition or at the officer's place of business.

(3) In other cases, to the officer, body, or tribunal conducting the hearing, at a like address.

(d) Unless the parties to the proceeding otherwise agree, or unless the sealed envelope or wrapper is returned to a witness who is to appear personally, the copy of the records shall remain sealed and shall be opened only at the time of trial, deposition, or other hearing, upon the direction of the judge, officer, body, or tribunal conducting the proceeding, in the presence of all parties who have appeared in person or by counsel at the trial, deposition, or hearing. Records which are original documents and which are not introduced in evidence or required as part of the record shall be returned to the person or entity from whom received. Records which are copies may be destroyed.

(e) As an alternative to the procedures described in subdivisions (b), (c), and (d), the subpoenaing party may direct the witness to make the records available for inspection or copying by the party's attorney, the attorney's representative, or deposition officer as described in paragraph (3) of subdivision (d) of Section 2020 of the Code of Civil Procedure, at the witness' business address under reasonable conditions during normal business hours. Normal business hours, as used in this subdivision, means those hours that the business of the witness is normally open for business to the public. When provided with at least five business days' advance notice by the party's attorney, attorney's representative, or deposition officer, the witness shall designate a time period of not less than six continuous hours on a date certain for copying of records subject to the subpoena by the party's attorney, attorney's representative or deposition officer. It shall be the responsibility of the attorney's representative to deliver any copy of the records as directed in the subpoena. Disobedience to the deposition subpoena issued pursuant to this subdivision is punishable as provided in subdivision (h) of section 2020 of the Code of Civil Procedure.

LAW REVISION COMMISSION COMMENT

Section 1560 is the same in substance as Code of Civil Procedure Section 1998, except for the clarifying definition of "hospital" added in subdivision (a). [7 Cal.L.Rev.Comm. Reports 1 (1965)]

§ 1561. Affidavit accompanying records

(a) The records shall be accompanied by the affidavit of the custodian or other qualified witness, stating in substance each of the following:

(1) The affiant is the duly authorized custodian of the records or other qualified witness and has authority to certify the records.

(2) The copy is a true copy of all the records described in the subpoena duces tecum, or pursuant to subdivision (e) of Section

1560 the records were delivered to the attorney, the attorney's representative or deposition officer for copying at the custodian's or witness' place of business, as the case may be.

(3) The records were prepared by the personnel of the business in the ordinary course of business at or near the time of the act, condition, or event.

(4) The identity of the records.

(5) A description of the mode of preparation of the records.

(b) If the business has none of the records described, or only part thereof, the custodian or other qualified witness shall so state in the affidavit, and deliver the affidavit and those records that are available in one of the manners provided in Section 1560.

(c) Where the records described in the subpoena were delivered to the attorney or his or her representative or deposition officer for copying at the custodian's or witness' place of business, in addition to the affidavit required by subdivision (a), the records shall be accompanied by an affidavit by the attorney or his or her representative or deposition officer stating that the copy is a true copy of all the records delivered to the attorney or his or her representative or deposition officer for copying.

LAW REVISION COMMISSION COMMENT

Section 1561 restates without substantive change the provisions of Code of Civil Procedure Section 1998.1. [7 Cal.L.Rev.Comm. Reports 1 (1965)]

§ 1562. Admissibility of affidavit and copy of records

If the original records would be admissible in evidence if the custodian or other qualified witness had been present and testified to the matters stated in the affidavit, and if the requirements of Section 1271 have been met, the copy of the records is admissible in evidence. The affidavit is admissible as evidence of the matters stated therein pursuant to Section 1561 and the matters so stated are presumed true. When more than one person has knowledge of the facts, more than one affidavit may be made. The presumption established by this section is a presumption affecting the burden of producing evidence.

§ 1563. One witness and mileage fee

(a) This article shall not be interpreted to require tender or payment of more than one witness fee and one mileage fee or other charge, to a witness or witness' business, unless there is an agreement to the contrary between the witness and the requesting party.

(b) All reasonable costs incurred in a civil proceeding by any witness which is not a party with respect to the production of all or any part of business records the production of which is requested pursuant to a subpoena duces tecum may be charged against the party serving the subpoena duces tecum.

(1) "Reasonable cost," as used in this section, shall include, but not be limited to, the following specific costs: ten cents ($0.10) per page for standard reproduction of documents of a size 8½ by 14 inches or less; twenty cents ($0.20) per page for copying of documents from microfilm; actual costs for the reproduction of oversize documents or the reproduction of documents requiring special processing which are made in response to a subpoena; reasonable clerical costs incurred in locating and making the records available to be billed at the maximum rate of twenty four dollars ($24) per hour per person, computed on the basis of six dollars ($6) per quarter hour or fraction thereof; actual postage charges; and the actual cost, if any, charged to the witness by a third person for the retrieval and return of records held offsite by that third person.

(2) The requesting party, or the requesting party's deposition officer shall not be required to pay those costs or any estimate thereof prior to the time the records are available for delivery pursuant to the subpoena, but the witness may demand payment of costs pursuant to this section simultaneous with actual delivery of the subpoenaed records, and until such time as payment is made, is under no obligation to deliver the records.

(3) The witness shall submit an itemized statement for the costs to the requesting party, or the requesting party's deposition officer, setting forth the reproduction and clerical costs incurred by the witness. Should the costs exceed those authorized in paragraph (1), or the witness refuses to produce an itemized statement of costs as required by paragraph (3) upon demand by the requesting party, or the requesting party's deposition officer, the witness shall furnish a statement setting forth the actions taken by the witness in justification of the costs.

(4) The requesting party may petition the court in which the action is pending to recover from the witness all or a part of the costs paid to the witness, or to reduce all or a part of the costs charged by the witness, pursuant to this subdivision, on the grounds that those costs were excessive. Upon the filing of the petition the court shall issue an order to show cause and from the time the order is served on the witness the court has jurisdiction over the witness. The court may hear testimony on the order to show cause and if it finds that the costs demanded and collected, or charged but not collected, exceed the amount authorized by this subdivision, it shall order the witness to remit to the requesting party, or reduce its charge to the requesting party by an amount equal to, the amount of the excess. In the event that the court finds the costs excessive and charged in bad faith by the witness, the court shall order the witness to remit the full amount of the costs demanded and collected, or excuse the requesting party from any payment of costs charged but not collected, and the court shall also order the witness to pay the

requesting party the amount of the reasonable expenses incurred in obtaining the order including attorney's fees. If the court finds the costs were not excessive, the court shall order the requesting party to pay the witness the amount of the reasonable expenses incurred in defending the petition, including attorney's fees.

(5) If a subpoena is served to compel the production of business records and is subsequently withdrawn, or is quashed, modified or limited on a motion made other than by the witness, the witness shall be entitled to reimbursement pursuant to paragraph (1) for all costs incurred in compliance with the subpoena to the time that the requesting party has notified the witness that the subpoena has been withdrawn or quashed, modified or limited. In the event the subpoena is withdrawn or quashed, if those costs are not paid within 30 days after demand therefor, the witness may file a motion in the court in which the action is pending for an order requiring payment, and the court shall award the payment of expenses and attorney's fees in the manner set forth in paragraph (4).

(6) Where the records are delivered to the attorney, the attorney's representative or the deposition officer for inspection or photocopying at the witness' place of business, the only fee for complying with the subpoena shall not exceed fifteen dollars ($15), plus the actual cost, if any, charged to the witness by that third person for retrieval and return of records held offsite by the third person. If the records are retrieved from microfilm, the reasonable cost, as defined in paragraph (1), shall also apply.

(c) When the personal attendance of the custodian of a record or other qualified witness is required pursuant to Section 1564, in a civil proceeding, he or she shall be entitled to the same witness fees and mileage permitted in a case where the subpoena requires the witness to attend and testify before a court in which the action or proceeding is pending and to any additional costs incurred as provided by subdivision (b).

(Stats.1965, c. 299, § 2, operative Jan. 1, 1967. Amended by Stats.1972, c. 396, p. 719, § 1; Stats.1981, c. 1014, p. 3913, § 2; Stats.1982, c. 452, p. 1825, § 3; Stats.1986, c. 603, § 8; Stats. 1987, c. 19, § 3, eff. May 12, 1987; Stats.1997, c. 442 (A.B.758), § 17.)

§ 1564. Personal attendance of custodian and production of original records

The personal attendance of the custodian or other qualified witness and the production of the original records is not required unless, at the discretion of the requesting party, the subpoena duces tecum contains a clause which reads:

"The personal attendance of the custodian or other qualified witness and the production of the original records are required by this subpoena.

The procedure authorized pursuant to subdivision (b) of Section 1560, and Sections 1561 and 1562, of the Evidence Code will not be deemed sufficient compliance with this subpoena."

LAW REVISION COMMISSION COMMENT

Section 1564 restates without substantive change the provisions of Code of Civil Procedure Section 1998.4. [7 Cal.L.Rev.Comm. Reports 1 (1965)]

§ 1565. Service of more than one subpoena duces tecum

If more than one subpoena duces tecum is served upon the custodian of records or other qualified witness and the personal attendance of the custodian or other qualified witness is required pursuant to Section 1564, the witness shall be deemed to be the witness of the party serving the first such subpoena duces tecum

LAW REVISION COMMISSION COMMENT

Section 1565 restates without substantive change the provisions of Code of Civil Procedure Section 1998.5. [7 Cal.L.Rev.Comm. Reports 1 (1965)]

§ 1566. Applicability of article

This article applies in any proceeding in which testimony can be compelled.

LAW REVISION COMMISSION COMMENT

This section has no counterpart in the portion of the Code of Civil Procedure from which this article is taken. Section 1566 is intended to preserve the original effect of Code of Civil Procedure Sections 1998–1998.5 by removing Sections 1560–1565 from the limiting provisions of Section 300. [7 Cal.L.Rev.Comm. Reports 1 (1965)]

§ 1567. Employee income and benefit information; forms completed by employer; support modification or termination proceedings

A completed form described in Section 3664 of the Family Code for income and benefit information provided by the employer may be admissible in a proceeding for modification or termination of an order for child, family, or spousal support if both of the following requirements are met:

(a) The completed form complies with Sections 1561 and 1562.

(b) A copy of the completed form and notice was served on the employee named therein pursuant to Section 3664 of the Family Code.

CHAPTER 3. OFFICIAL WRITINGS AFFECTING PROPERTY

§ 1600. Record of document affecting property interest

(a) The record of an instrument or other document purporting to establish or affect an interest in property is prima facie evidence of the existence and content of the original recorded document and its execution and delivery by each person by whom it purports to have been executed if:

(1) The record is in fact a record of an office of a public entity; and

(2) A statute authorized such a document to be recorded in that office.

(b) The presumption established by this section is a presumption affecting the burden of proof.

LAW REVISION COMMISSION COMMENT

1965 Enactment

The sections in this chapter all relate to official writings affecting property. The provisions of some sections provide hearsay exceptions; other sections provide exceptions to the best evidence rule; still others provide authentication procedures.

Section 1600 is based on Code of Civil Procedure Section 1951, which it supersedes. It is similar to Section 1532 of the Evidence Code, which applies to all recorded writings, but it gives an added effect to the writings covered by its provisions. Under Section 1600, as under existing law, if an instrument purporting to affect an interest in property is recorded, a presumption of execution and delivery of the instrument arises. Thomas v. Peterson, 213 Cal. 672, 3 P.2d 306 (1931). [7 Cal.L.Rev.Comm. Reports 1 (1965)]

1967 Amendment

One effect of making the official record "prima facie evidence" is to create a rebuttable presumption. See Evidence Code § 602 ("A statute providing that a fact or group of facts is prima facie evidence of another fact establishes a rebuttable presumption."). The classification of this presumption as one affecting the burden of proof is consistent with the prior case law. See Thomas v. Peterson, 213 Cal. 672, 3 P.2d 306 (1931); DuBois v. Larke, 175 Cal.App.2d 737, 346 P.2d 830 (1959); Osterberg v. Osterberg, 68 Cal.App.2d 254, 156 P.2d 46 (1945). Such a classification tends to support the record title to property by requiring that the record title be sustained unless the party attacking it can actually prove its invalidity. See Evidence Code § 606 and Comment thereto.

The word "official," which modified "record," has been deleted as unnecessary in light of the requirements of paragraphs (1) and (2) of subdivision (a).

Record of deed to regents of university as conclusive evidence, see Education Code § 23259. [8 Cal.L.Rev.Comm. Reports 1 (1965)]

§ 1601. Proof of content of lost official record affecting property

(a) Subject to subdivisions (b) and (c), when in any action it is desired to prove the contents of the official record of any writing lost or destroyed by conflagration or other public calamity, after proof of such loss or destruction, the following may, without further proof, be admitted in evidence to prove the contents of such record:

(1) Any abstract of title made and issued and certified as correct prior to such loss or destruction, and purporting to have been prepared and made in the ordinary course of business by any person engaged in the business of preparing and making abstracts of title prior to such loss or destruction; or

(2) Any abstract of title, or of any instrument affecting title, made, issued, and certified as correct by any person engaged in the business of insuring titles or issuing abstracts of title to real estate, whether the same was made, issued, or certified before or after such loss or destruction and whether the same was made from the original records or from abstract and notes, or either, taken from such records in the preparation and upkeeping of its plant in the ordinary course of its business.

(b) No proof of the loss of the original writing is required other than the fact that the original is not known to the party desiring to prove its contents to be in existence.

(c) Any party desiring to use evidence admissible under this section shall give reasonable notice in writing to all other parties to the action who have appeared therein, of his intention to use such evidence at the trial of the action, and shall give all such other parties a reasonable opportunity to inspect the evidence, and also the abstracts, memoranda, or notes from which it was compiled, and to take copies thereof.

LAW REVISION COMMISSION COMMENT

Section 1601 restates without substantive change the provisions of Section 1855a of the Code of Civil Procedure. [7 Cal.L.Rev.Comm. Reports 1 (1965)]

§ 1602. Repealed by Stats.1967, c. 650, p. 2008, § 10

§ 1603. Deed by officer in pursuance of court process

A deed of conveyance of real property, purporting to have been executed by a proper officer in pursuance of legal process of any of the courts of record of this state, acknowledged and recorded in the office of the recorder of the county wherein the real property therein described is situated, or the record of such deed, or a certified copy of such record, is prima facie evidence that the property or interest therein described was thereby conveyed to the grantee named in such deed. The presumption established by this section is a presumption affecting the burden of proof.

LAW REVISION COMMISSION COMMENT

1965 Enactment

Section 1603 restates without substantive change the provisions of Section 1928 of the Code of Civil Procedure. [7 Cal.L.Rev.Comm. Reports 1 (1965)]

1967 Amendment

One effect of Section 1603 is to create a rebuttable presumption. See Evidence Code § 602 ("A statute providing that a fact or group of facts is prima facie evidence of another fact establishes a rebuttable presumption.").

Prior to the enactment in 1911 of Code of Civil Procedure Section 1928 (upon which Section 1603 of the Evidence Code is based), the recitals in a sheriff's deed, made pursuant to legal process, could not be used as evidence of the judgment, the execution, and the sale upon which the deed was based. The existence of the prior proceedings were required to be proved with independent evidence. Heyman v. Babcock, 30 Cal. 367, 370 (1866); Hihn v. Peck, 30 Cal. 280, 287–288 (1966). The enactment of the predecessor of Evidence Code Section 1603 had two effects. First, it obviated the need for such independent proof. See, e.g., Oakes v. Fernandez, 108 Cal.App.2d 168, 238 P.2d 641 (1951); Wagnor v. Blume, 71 Cal.App.2d 94, 161 P.2d 1001 (1945). See also Basye, Clearing Land Titles § 41 (1953). Second, it obviated the need for proof of a chain of title prior to the execution of the need. Krug v. Warden, 57 Cal.App. 563, 207 Pac. 696 (1922).

The classification of the presumption in Section 1603 as a presumption affecting the burden of proof is consistent with the classification of the similar and overlapping presumptions contained in Evidence Code Sections 664 (official duty regularly performed) and 1600 (official record of document affecting property). Like the presumption in Section 1600, the presumption in Section 1603 serves the purpose of supporting the record chain of title. [8 Cal.L.Rev.Comm. Reports 101 (1967)]

§ 1604. Certificate of purchase or of location of lands

A certificate of purchase, or of location, of any lands in this state, issued or made in pursuance of any law of the United States or of this state, is prima facie evidence that the holder or assignee of such certificate is the owner of the land described therein; but this evidence may be overcome by proof that, at the time of the location, or time of filing a preemption claim on which the certificate may have been issued, the land was in the adverse possession of the adverse party, or those under whom he claims, or that the adverse party is holding the land for mining purposes.

LAW REVISION COMMISSION COMMENT

Section 1604 restates without substantive change the provisions of Section 1925 of the Code of Civil Procedure. [7 Cal.L.Rev.Comm. Reports 1 (1965)]

§ 1605. Authenticated Spanish title records

Duplicate copies and authenticated translations of original Spanish title papers relating to land claims in this state, derived from the Spanish or Mexican governments, prepared under the supervision of the Keeper of Archives, authenticated by the Surveyor–General or his successor and by the Keeper of Archives, and filed with a county recorder, in accordance with Chapter 281 of the Statutes of 1865–66, are admissible as evidence with like force and effect as the originals and without proving the execution of such originals.

LAW REVISION COMMISSION COMMENT

1965 Enactment

Section 1605 restates without substantive change the provisions of Section 1927.5 of the Code of Civil Procedure. [7 Cal.L.Rev.Comm. Reports 1 (1965)]

1967 Amendment

Chapter 281 of the Statutes of 1865–66 required the California Secretary of State to cause copies to be made of all of the original Spanish title papers relating to land claims in this state derived from the Spanish and Mexican governments that were on file in the office of the United States Surveyor–General for California. These copies, authenticated by the Surveyor–General and the Keeper of Archives in his office, were then required to be recorded in the offices of the county recorders of the concerned counties.

Section 5 of the 1865–66 statute, which is now codified as Section 1605 of the Evidence Code, provided that the recorded copies would be admissible "as prima facie evidence" without proving the execution of the originals. It is apparent that the original purpose of the section was to provide an exception to the best evidence rule—which would have required production of the original or an excuse for its nonproduction before the recorded copy could be admitted—and an exception to the rule, now expressed in Evidence Code Section 1401(b), requiring the authentication of the original document as a condition of the admissibility of the copy. Section 1605, therefore, has been revised to reflect this original purpose. [8 Cal.L.Rev.Comm. Reports 101 (1967)]

Appendix V

CASE LAW DIVERGENCE FROM THE FEDERAL RULES OF EVIDENCE

By Daniel J. Capra

Philip Reed Professor of Law, Fordham Law School

Reporter to the Judicial Conference Advisory Committee on Evidence Rules

I. Introduction

Assume that a lawyer is reading one of the Federal Rules of Evidence to determine whether a piece of evidence will be admissible at trial—for example, the lawyer wants to know whether a videotape can be admitted as a learned treatise. Obviously, the best place to start is with the text of the Federal Rules of Evidence. But if the lawyer thinks that the text of a particular rule plainly answers the question of admissibility, or simply leaves the question open for argument, that lawyer will often be wrong. That is because the case law has diverged from the text of the Federal Rules on many important points. Thus, in our example, the Rule admitting learned treatises does not on its face permit introduction of videotapes, and yet such tapes have been admitted under the case law.

The Advisory Committee on Evidence Rules, which this author currently serves as Reporter, has expressed concern that the divergence between case law and the text of the Rule might create a trap for the unwary. See generally Becker and Orenstein, *The Federal Rules of Evidence After Sixteen Years—The Effect of "Plain Meaning" Jurisprudence, the Need for an Advisory Committee on the Rules of Evidence, ans Suggestions for Selective Revision of the Rules,* 60 Geo.Wash.L.Rev. 857, 868 (1992) (noting the need to "resolve discrepancies between the plain text of the Federal Rules and the generally shared interpretation of the Rules deriving from preexisting common law traditions"). One way to correct this divergence might be to propose an amendment to the text of any Rule subject to divergent case law. But the Advisory Committee is acutely aware of the costs of amending an evidence rule. Amendments can lead to the disruption of settled expectations, and may create further problems of interpretation and divergence. The Advisory Committee resolved to take a less drastic course—a course that would not require an amendment of any rules and yet would highlight for lawyers and judges the existence of divergent case law. The Committee directed the Reporter to prepare this report in an effort to increase the awareness of counsel practicing in federal courts, as well as judges, about the possibility that case law has diverged from the text of some of the Federal Rules of

Evidence. This divergence comes in two forms: 1) where the case law (defined as case law in at least one circuit) is inconsistent with either the text of the Rule, the Advisory Committee Note explaining the text, or both; and 2) where the case law has provided significant development on a point that is not addressed by either the text of the Rule or the Committee Note.

This report highlights the major instances in which case law has diverged from an applicable Rule. Before proceeding to these illustrations, it is important to stress several qualifications on the scope of this report.

First, there is no intent to imply that any of the case law discussed herein is incorrect or "wrongly decided." The goal of this report is to point out the case law divergence from the Federal Rules of Evidence, without commenting on the merits of that divergence. Indeed, commentators have opined that much of the divergent case law is sensible and well-decided. See, e.g., Jonakait, *Text, Texts, or Ad Hoc Determinations: Interpretation of the Federal Rules of Evidence,* 71 Ind.L.J. 551, 571 (1996) ("Sometimes we must look beyond the words of the Rules to understand evidentiary doctrine. We must do so when the Rules are not definitive or ambiguous * * * but sometimes even when the text is clear.").

Second, there is no intent to imply that any of the Rules discussed herein are problematic or need to be amended. The fact that the case law diverges from the Rule might be relevant to the need for an amendment, but it is certainly not dispositive. Whether a particular Rule should be amended is a complex question that is well beyond the scope of this report.

Third, there is no attempt to be comprehensive in the treatment of the case law construing the Evidence Rules discussed herein. Divergent case law is defined as case law in at least one circuit that has diverged from the text of the particular rule. This report does not purport to provide a treatise-like discussion of all the pertinent case law, from all the circuits, construing a particular rule.The goal of this report is to raise "red flags" with lawyers and judges, by providing basic information about areas where case law can be found that diverges from the text of the Federal Rules of Evidence.

II. Examples of Case Law In Conflict With the Text of the Rule and/or Committee Note:

1. ***Rule 106:*** Rule 106 sets forth a rule of completeness, providing that when a party introduces a writing or recorded statement, the adversary may "require the introduction at that time of any other part or any other writing or recorded statement which ought in fairness to be considered contemporaneously with it." Rule 106 by its terms permits the adversary to introduce completing statements only where the proponent introduces a *written or recorded* statement. The language of the Rule does not on its face permit completing evidence when the proponent introduces an oral statement, such as a criminal defendant's oral confession. Some courts have found, however, that Rule 106, or at least the principle of completeness embodied therein, applies to require admission of omitted portions of an oral statement when necessary to correct a misimpression. See *United States v. Tarantino,* 846 F.2d 1384 (D.C. Cir. 1988) (prior oral statements of a government witness were properly offered on redirect examination since the defendant had used portions of the statements in cross-examination and the omitted portions placed the statements in context). See also the discussion in *United States v. Branch,* 91 F.3d 699 (5th Cir. 1996) (noting the case law permitting criminal defendants to offer omitted parts of statements they make to law enforcement officers that provide exculpatory information). Compare *United States v. Harvey,* 914 F.2d 966 (7th Cir. 1990) (Rule 106 does not apply to oral statements).

Moreover, some courts have held that Rule 106 can operate as a de facto hearsay exception when the opponent opens the door by creating a misimpression by offering only part of a statement. In other words, completing evidence is found admissible under Rule 106 even if it would otherwise be hearsay. See *United States v. Sutton,* 801 F.2d 1346, 1369 (D.C.Cir. 1986) ("Rule 106 can adequately fulfill its function only by permitting the admission of some otherwise inadmissible evidence when the court finds in fairness that that proffered evidence should be considered contemporaneously"). See also C. Wright & K. Graham, *Federal Practice and Procedure: Evidence* § 5078, at 376 (supporting this approach). Such a reading is not apparent from the text or Committee Note. See *United States v. Wilkerson,* 84 F.3d 692 (4th Cir. 1996) (interpreting Rule 106 as purely a timing device, not as a rule permitting the admission of otherwise inadmissible evidence).

2. ***Rule 403:*** Rule 403 provides that a trial judge may exclude proffered evidence if its probative value is substantially outweighed "by the danger of unfair prejudice, confusion of the issues, or misleading the jury, or by considerations of undue delay, waste of time, or needless presentation of cumulative evidence." Of the negative factors listed that would support exclusion, only one refers to the jury directly—the danger of "misleading the jury". This would seem to indicate that other negative factors mentioned in the Rule, specifically the danger of unfair prejudice and confusion of the issues, must be taken into account in a bench trial. Yet courts have held to the contrary, reasoning that unfair prejudice and confusing evidence will not have the same negative impact on the judge as it would have on the jury See, e.g., *Schultz v. Butcher,* 24 F.3d 626 (4th Cir. 1994) (trial court erred in excluding evidence in a bench trial on the ground of its prejudicial effect); *Gulf States Utils. v. Ecodyne Corp.,* 635 F.2d 517 (5th Cir. 1981) (the portion of Rule 40 referring to prejudicial effect "has no logical application in bench trials").

3. ***Rule 404(a):*** The Rule states that no party is permitted in the first instance to introduce character evidence to prove action in accordance with character, except for the "accused"—i.e., only the "accused" can open the door to circumstantial use of character evidence. Thus, the Rule seems explicit in prohibiting the circumstantial use of character evidence in civil cases. And the Advisory Committee Note confirms this exclusionary principle. Yet some courts have permitted civil defendants to use character evidence circumstantially "when the central issue in a civil case is by its nature criminal." *Palmquist v. Selvik,* 111 F.3d 1332, 1342 (7th Cir. 1997) (assuming that character evidence could be admissible in certain civil cases); *Perrin v. Anderson,* 784 F.2d 1040 (10th Cir. 1986) (police officers charged with excessive force are permitted to prove the decedent's character for violence).

4. ***Rule 407:*** Rule 407 prohibits the admission of actions taken after an injury or harm which, if taken previously, would have made the injury or harm less likely to occur, if the remedial measure is offered to prove negligence, culpable conduct, product defect, design defect, or failure to warn. The Rule by its terms would appear to preclude evidence of any action by *anyone* that would have made the injury or harm less likely to occur. Courts have held, however, that subsequent remedial measures are not excluded by Rule 407 if the measure is taken by someone *other than the defendant*, i.e., if it is a "third party repair." See, e.g., *TLT-Babcock, Inc. v. Emerson Elec. Co.,* 33 F.3d 397 (4th Cir. 1994) (design change not excluded by Rule 407 where the change was made by an entity that was not a party to the case); *Dixon v. International Harvester Co.,* 754 F.2d 573 (5th Cir. 1985) (repair by tractor owner after an accident not excluded when offered against tractor manufacturer).

Also, the Rule states that "impeachment" is a proper purpose for admitting subsequent remedial measures. Taken literally, this would mean that a plaintiff in a product liability case could offer proof of a subsequent remedial measure to "impeach" a defense witness' assertion that the product used by the plaintiff was safely designed. Yet courts have generally limited the use of subsequent remedial measures when offered for impeachment by way of contradiction. The fear is that this exception would swallow the rule of exclusion. See, e.g., *Harrison v. Sears, Roebuck & Co.,* 981 F.2d 25 (1st Cir. 1992) (a desire merely to undercut an expert's credibility cannot be sufficient to trigger the impeachment exception to Rule 407, or else the exception would swallow the rule of exclusion); *Kelly v. Crown Equip. Co.,* 970 F.2d 1273 (3d Cir. 1992) (subsequent remedial measure cannot be offered for simple contradiction of expert's statement that a design was safe). Thus, the "impeachment" permitted by the Rule has been limited to cases where defense witnesses have made extravagant claims of safety. See *Wood v. Morbark Indus.,* 70 F.3d 1202 (11th Cir. 1995) (post-accident design change admissible for impeachment where defense witness testified that the original design was the safest possible design); *Muzyka v. Remington Arms Co.,* 774 F.2d 1309 (5th Cir. 1985) (design change should have been admitted for impeachment where defense witnesses testified that the product was the best and safest product of its kind).

5. Rule 601: Rule 601 essentially states that all questions that had been treated previously as matters of competency are now matters of credibility for the factfinder. The Advisory Committee Note, elaborating on the Rule, indicates an intent to prohibit a trial judge from excluding a witness on grounds of incompetence. Yet courts have excluded witnesses who have been found incapable of testifying in a competent fashion. See, e.g., *United States v. Gates,* 10 F.3d 765, 766 (11th Cir. 1993) ("Notwithstanding Rule 601, a court has the power to rule that a witness is incapable of testifying, and in an appropriate case it has the duty to hold a hearing to determine that issue."); *United States v. Gutman,* 725 F.2d 417, 420 (7th Cir. 1984) (trial court retains the power, and sometimes the duty, to hold a hearing "to determine whether a witness should not be allowed to testify because insanity has made him incapable of testifying in a competent fashion.").

6. Rule 607: The Rule states categorically that a party can impeach any witness it calls. On its face, the Rule permits the following scenario: 1) in a criminal case, a witness would testify at trial that the defendant was not at the scene of the crime, yet having stated previously to a police officer that the defendant committed the crime; 2) the prior statement to the police officer could not be admitted as substantive evidence because it is hearsay; 3) but the prosecutor calls the witness, knowing he will give testimony favorable to the defendant, and then "impeaches" the witness with his prior statement to the police officer, on the ground that it is inconsistent with the witness' in-court testimony. Thus, Rule 607 by its terms permits the prosecutor to proffer prior inconsistent statements, not made under oath (and therefore not admissible for their truth under Rule 801(d)(1)(A)) in the guise of impeachment. Yet despite the affirmative and permissive language of the Rule, the courts have held that a prosecutor cannot call a witness solely to impeach that witness, because to allow this practice would undermine the hearsay rule. See, e.g., *United States v. Hogan,* 763 F.2d 697, 702 (5th Cir. 1985) ("The prosecution, however, may not call a witness it knows to be hostile for the primary purpose of eliciting otherwise inadmissible impeachment testimony, for such a scheme merely serves as a subterfuge to avoid the hearsay rule. The danger in this procedure is obvious."); *United States v. Morlang,* 531 F.2d 183 (4th Cir. 1975) (conviction reversed on the ground that the government should not have been permitted to call a witness for no other purpose than to impeach him). See generally Jonakait, *The Supreme Court, Plain Meaning, and the Changed Rules of Evidence,* 68 Tex. L. Rev. 745 (1990) (noting this and other situations where courts have felt compelled to diverge from the text of an Evidence Rule in order to reach a just result).

7. ***Rule 608(b):*** This Rule states that specific instances of the conduct of a witness, "for the purpose of attacking or supporting the witness' *credibility* * * * may not be proved by extrinsic evidence." Read literally, "the first sentence of (b) could bar extrinsic evidence for bias, competency and contradiction impeachment since they too deal with credibility." American Bar Association Section of Litigation, *Emerging Problems Under the Federal Rules of Evidence* 161 (3d ed. 1998). Yet courts have held that the Rule 608(b) extrinsic evidence ban is not applicable unless the sole reason for the impeachment is to attack the witness' character for veracity. See, e.g., *United States v. Winchenbach,* 197 F.3d 548 (1st Cir. 1999) (impeachment with proof of prior inconsistent statement is governed by the balancing process of Rule 403 rather than the absolute exclusion of Rule 608(b)); *United States v. Tarantino,* 846 F.2d 1384, 1409 (D.C.Cir. 1988) (admissibility of extrinsic evidence offered to contradict a witness is governed by Rules 402 and 403, not Rule 608(b)); *United States v. Lindemann,* 85 F.3d 1232 (7th Cir. 1996) (admissibility of extrinsic evidence of bias is governed by Rules 402 and 403, not by Rule 608(b)).

The Advisory Committee on Evidence Rules has proposed an amendment to Rule 608(b) that would codify this divergent case law. The amendment would clarify that the ban on extrinsic evidence applies only if it is offered to prove the witness' "*character for truthfulness*." The proposed Advisory Committee Note states that "[b]y limiting the application of the Rule to proof of a witness' character for truthfulness, the amendment leaves the admissibility of extrinsic evidence offered for other grounds of impeachment (such as contradiction, prior inconsistent statement, bias and mental capacity) to Rules 402 and 403." Barring any glitches in the rulemaking process, the amendment to Rule 608(b) will take effect on December 1, 2003. The full text of the amendment and the Committee Note can be found at http://ao.uscourts.gov.

8. ***Rule 613(b):*** The Rule and the Advisory Committee Note both indicate that it is not necessary to give a witness an opportunity to examine a prior inconsistent statement before that statement is admissible to impeach the witness. All that is necessary is that the witness be given an opportunity at some point in the trial to explain or deny the statement. The Rule thus rejects the common-law rule from Queen Caroline's case, under which the proponent was required to lay a foundation for the prior inconsistent statement at the time the witness testified. Despite the language of the Rule and Note, however, some courts have reverted to the common-law rule. See, e.g., *United States v. Sutton,* 41 F.3d 1257 (8th Cir. 1994) (trial judge properly excluded testimony as to inconsistent statements by a prosecution witness on the ground that the witness had not been given an opportunity to explain or deny the prior statement while cross-examined by defense counsel);

United States v. Marks, 816 F.2d 1207, 1211 (7th Cir. 1987) (trial judge is entitled despite the language of Rule 613(b) "to conclude that in particular circumstances the older approach should be used in order to avoid confusing witnesses and juries").

9. Rule 704(b): Rule 704(b) would seem to prohibit all expert witnesses from testifying that a criminal defendant either did or did not have the requisite mental state to commit the crime charged. It states that "[n]o expert witness ... may state an opinion or inference as to whether the defendant did or did not have the mental state or condition constituting an element of the crime charged or of a defense thereto." But some courts have held (and others have implied) that the rule is applicable only to mental health experts, and therefore does not prohibit intent-based testimony from law enforcement personnel such as narcotics agents. See, e.g., *United States v. Gastiaburo,* 16 F.3d 582 (4th Cir. 1994) (stating that Rule 704(b) does not apply to the testimony of an expert law enforcement agent); *United States v. Lipscomb,* 14 F.3d 1236 (7th Cir. 1994) (expressing sympathy with such a position, but finding it unnecessary to decide the matter). Other courts, while technically applying the Rule 704(b) limitation to all expert witnesses, have applied it in such a way as to nullify its impact—permitting, for example, an expert to opine as to the mental state of a hypothetical person whose fact situation mirrors the fact situation in issue. See, e.g., *United States v. Williams,* 980 F.2d 1463 (D.C.Cir. 1992) (permitting a law enforcement agent to testify that a hypothetical person carrying ziplock bags each containing small amounts of drugs was intending to distribute them; the hypothetical matched the facts of the case).

10. Rule 801(c) (Implied Assertions): Rule 801(c) defines hearsay as an out-of-court statement "offered in evidence to prove the truth of the matter asserted." The Committee Note states that "verbal conduct which is assertive but offered as a basis for inferring something other than the matter asserted" is excluded from the definition of hearsay "by the language of subdivision (c)". This would mean that a statement would be hearsay only if it were offered for the truth of the express assertion in the statement—offering it for any implied assertion would escape hearsay proscription. So for example, a statement "It is raining cats and dogs" would be admissible to prove it is raining—the statement would not be offered to prove the express assertion that cats and dogs were falling from the sky.

This highly constricted definition of hearsay generally has been rejected by the courts. The cases generally state that statements are hearsay if 1) they are offered for the truth of a matter *implied* in the statement and 2) the speaker *intended* to communicate that implication. See, e.g., *United States v. Reynolds,* 715 F.2d 99 (3rd Cir. 1983) (rejecting the government's suggestion that only a statement's express assertion should be considered in deciding whether it constitutes hearsay); *Lyle v. Koehler,* 720 F.2d 426, 433 (6th Cir. 1983) (concluding that letters were hearsay because "the inferences they necessarily invite form an integral part of the letters"; the reference to "matters asserted" in Rule 801(c) covers both express and implied assertions); *United States v. Jackson,* 88 F.3d 845, 848 (10th Cir. 1996) (stating that the important question under Rule 801(c) is whether the assertion, express or implied, "is intended"). See also Milich, *Re-examining Hearsay Under the Federal Rules: Some Method for the Madness,* 39 Kan. L.Rev. 893 (1991) (arguing for an intent-based test in determining whether implied assertions are hearsay).

11. Rule 801 Advisory Committee Note on Confrontation: The original Advisory Committee Note includes an extensive discussion of the law of confrontation as it existed at the time the Rules were proposed. This Note is quite outdated, since the Supreme Court has substantially developed and revised its interpretation of the Confrontation Clause since that time. For example, the Advisory Committee Note draws a fairly sharp distinction between the hearsay exceptions and the Confrontation Clause. But the recent jurisprudence leads to the conclusion that statements fitting within the Federal Rules hearsay exceptions will ordinarily satisfy the Confrontation Clause. Most of the major Federal Rules exceptions, have been found by federal courts to be "firmly rooted", which means that statements falling within these exceptions automatically satisfy the Confrontation Clause. And as to the exceptions not found firmly-rooted, the reliability requirements of those exceptions have been found congruent with those imposed by the Confrontation Clause. See generally *Ohio v. Roberts,* 448 U.S. 56 (1980); *Idaho v. Wright,* 497 U.S. 805 (1990); *White v. Illinois,* 502 U.S. 346 (1992). See the discussion of this case law in S. Saltzburg, M. Martin and D. Capra, *Federal Rules of Evidence Manual* 1702–5, 1852–4 (7th ed. 1998).

12. Rule 803(4): The Rule provides a hearsay exception for statements made for purposes of treatment or diagnosis when the statements deal with the "cause or external source" of the medical condition. The exception does not, by its terms, provide a hearsay exception for statements attributing fault. The Committee Note states that statements of fault "would not ordinarily qualify" under the exception, and distinguishes a statement "I was hit by a car" (admissible when made to medical personnel) from "I was hit by a car that ran a red light" (inadmissible). Yet in at least some classes of cases, statements attributing fault, when made to medical personnel, are admitted by the courts under Rule 803(4). The most common example is a statement from a child victim of sexual abuse, specifically identifying her attacker. See, e.g., *United States v. Renville,* 779 F.2d 430, 438 (8th Cir. 1985) (child's statement attributing fault is admissible under Rule 803(4) "where the physician makes clear to the victim that the inquiry into the identity of the abuser is important to diagnosis and treatment, and the victim manifests such an understanding"); *United States v. Joe,* 8 F.3d 1488,

1494 (10th Cir. 1993) ("[T]he domestic sexual abuser's identity is admissible under Rule 803(4) where the abuser has such an intimate relationship with the victim that the abuser's identity becomes reasonably pertinent to the victim's proper treatment.").

13. ***Rule 803(5):*** The Rule provides a hearsay exception for past recollection recorded: a record "containing a matter about which a witness once had knowledge but now has insufficient recollection to enable the witness to testify fully and accurately" where the record is "shown to have been made or adopted by the witness when the matter was fresh in the witness' memory and to reflect that knowledge correctly." What happens, however, when a person makes a statement to another person, and that other person is the one who writes it down? The exception by its terms does not seem to permit a "two-party voucher" system of proving past recollection recorded, since it states that the record must be shown to have been "made or adopted by the witness." Thus, the Rule does not envision that a person with personal knowledge might make a statement recorded by another, with the record being made admissible by calling both the reporter and the recorder. Despite the language of the Rule, however, cases can be found that permit two-party vouching under Rule 803(5). See, e.g., *United States v. Williams,* 951 F.2d 853 (7th Cir. 1993).

14. ***Rule 803(6):*** The Rule defines a business record as one "made at or near the time by, or from information transmitted by, a person with knowledge, if kept in the course of a regularly conducted activity." This language could be read as abrogating the common-law requirement that the person transmitting the information to the recorder must have a business duty to do so. It states only that the transmitting person must have "knowledge", not that the person must be reporting within the business structure. Yet despite the text, the courts have held that all those who report information included in a business record must be under a business duty to do so—or else the hearsay problem created from the report by an outsider must be satisfied in some other way. See *United States v. Turner,* 189 F.3d 712, 719–20 (8th Cir. 1999) ("[W]hen the source of information and the recorder of that information are not the same person, the business record contains hearsay upon hearsay. If both the source and recorder of the information were acting in the regular course of the organization's business, however, the hearsay upon hearsay problem may be excused by the business records exception to the rule against hearsay."); *Bemis v. Edwards,* 45 F.3d 1369 (9th Cir. 1995) (911 call was not admissible as a business record because the caller was not under any business duty to report, and the report did not independently satisfy any hearsay exception); *Cameron v. Otto Bock Orthopedic Indus. Inc.,* 43 F.3d 14 (1st Cir. 1994) (product failure reports submitted to the manufacturer after the plaintiff's accident were inadmissible; the reports were submitted by parties who had no business duty to report accurately to the manufacturer).

15. ***Rule 803(8)(B):*** Rule 803(8) provides a hearsay exception for public reports. But the Rule specifically excludes from its coverage public reports setting forth "matters observed by police officers and other law enforcement personnel" if such reports are offered "in criminal cases." Read literally, the Rule would not provide a hearsay exception for a forensic report prepared by the police that concluded that the defendant was innocent. Such a report would be offered by the defendant, but the exclusionary language of Rule 803(8)(B) covers all police reports offered in criminal cases. Yet some lower courts have refused to be bound by the plain meaning of the rule, reasoning that Congress intended to regulate only police reports that unfairly inculpate a criminal defendant, and that the exception should therefore apply to public reports offered by the accused. See, e.g., *United States v. Smith*, 521 F.2d 957 (D.C.Cir. 1975) (despite its exclusionary language, Rule 803(8)(B) should be read in light of Congress' intent to exclude police reports only when offered *against* a criminal defendant). But see *United States v. Sharpe,* 193 F.3d 852, 868 (5th Cir. 1999) (the defendant's reliance on Rule 803(8)(B) to admit an exculpatory police report was "misplaced" because the Rule does not grant admissibility for any such reports offered in criminal cases).

16. ***Rule 803(8)(B) and (C):*** Rule 803(8)(B) and (C) both contain language appearing to exclude from the hearsay exception all records prepared by law enforcement personnel, when such records are offered against a criminal defendant. Read literally, these provisions would prevent the government from introducing simple tabulations of non-adversarial information. For example, these subdivisions appear not to grant a hearsay exception for a routine printout from the Customs Service recording license plates of cars that crossed the border on a certain day, when offered in a criminal case. Courts have refused to apply the plain exclusionary language of these subdivisions literally, however. They reason that the language could not have been intended to cover reports that are ministerial in nature and prepared under non-adversarial circumstances; it is only adversarial, evaluative reports (such as crime scene reports) that carry the risk of fabrication that the exclusionary language was designed to regulate. See, e.g., *United States v. Orozco*, 590 F.2d 789 (9th Cir. 1979) (customs records of border crossings are admissible under Rule 803(8) because they are ministerial and not prepared under adversarial circumstances); *United States v. Grady*, 544 F.2d 598 (2d Cir. 1976) (reports concerning firearms' serial numbers were admissible because they were records of routine factual matters prepared in nonadversarial circumstances).

17. ***Rule 804(b)(1):*** The Rule provides a hearsay exception for prior testimony when offered against a party who either 1) had a similar motive and opportunity to develop the testimony at the time it was given, or 2) had a predecessor in interest with such a similar motive and opportunity at the time the testimony was given. Some courts have defined the term "predecessor in interest" as *anyone* who had a similar motive and opportunity to develop the testimony, at the time it was given, as the opponent would have at the instant trial; these courts do not require some legal relationship between the prior party and the party against whom the evidence is now offered. This construction collapses the term "predecessor in interest" with the term "similar motive". See, e.g., *Lloyd v. American Export Lines, Inc.*, 580 F.2d 1179 (3rd Cir. 1978) (prior testimony properly admitted against plaintiff, where prior party had a similar motive to develop the testimony as the plaintiff in the instant case would have were the declarant to testify at trial; Judge Stern, concurring, states that such an expansive definition of "predecessor in interest" effectively reads that term out of the Rule); *Horne v. Owens–Corning Fiberglass Corp.,* 4 F.3d 276 (4th Cir. 1993) (prior testimony from a different case properly admitted against the plaintiff, where the previous plaintiff, though not affiliated in any way with the plaintiff, had a similar motive to develop the testimony). Other courts have admitted such evidence not as prior testimony (for want of a predecessor in interest) but as residual hearsay. See *Dartez v. Fibreboard Corp.,* 765 F.2d 456 (5th Cir. 1985).

18. Rule 804(b)(3): The Rule provides that if a declaration against penal interest is offered to exculpate an accused, it is not admissible under this hearsay exception "unless corroborating circumstances clearly indicate the trustworthiness of the statement." On its face, the rule does not require a showing of corroborating circumstances for statements offered by the government that *inculpate* the accused. Yet many courts have required the government to establish corroborating circumstances for inculpatory statements offered under Rule 804(b)(3). See, e.g., *United States v. Barone,* 114 F.3d 1284 (1st Cir. 1997) (imposing a corroborating circumstances requirement for statements offered by the prosecution under Rule 804(b)(3), while acknowledging that the Rule does not explicitly require a showing of corroborating circumstances for such statements); *United States v. Garcia,* 897 F.2d 1413 (7th Cir. 1990) (requiring a showing of corroborating circumstances for inculpatory declarations against penal interest). Similarly, the corroborating circumstances requirement does not appear to apply when declarations against penal interest are offered in civil cases, since the requirement covers statements offered to exculpate the "accused." At least one court, however, has applied the corroborating circumstances requirement to declarations against penal interest offered in civil cases. See *American Automotive Accessories, Inc. v. Fishman,* 175 F.3d 534, 541 (7th Cir. 1999) (reasoning that it is important to have a "unitary standard" for declarations against penal interest, no matter in what case and no matter by whom they are offered).

19. Rule 805: The Rule states that hearsay within hearsay is not excluded if each part of the combined statement "conforms with an exception to the hearsay rule." However, admissions and certain prior statements of testifying witnesses are classified by Rule 801(d) as "not hearsay." Rule 805 could technically be read to preclude admissibility of multiple hearsay where one level of hearsay would be admissible under the Rule 801(d) exemptions, as opposed to an "exception" as is mentioned by Rule 805. But it has been held that the technical distinction between the Rule 801(d) category of "not hearsay" and the Rule 803, 804 and 807 categories of "hearsay subject to exception" cannot control the application of Rule 805's standard for admitting multiple levels of hearsay. See, e.g., *United States v. Dotson,* 821 F.2d 1034, 1035 (5th Cir. 1987) ("For the purposes of the hearsay-within-hearsay principle expressed in Rule 805, non-hearsay statements under Rule 801(d) * * * should be considered in analyzing a multiple-hearsay statement as the equivalent of a level of the combined statement that conforms with an exception to the hearsay rule.").

20. Rule 806: The Rule states that a hearsay declarant's credibility may be attacked "by any evidence which would be admissible" if the declarant had testified as a witness. The language raises a problem when the proponent wishes to attack the declarant by proffering specific bad acts to prove the witness' bad character for veracity. Rule 608(b) prohibits extrinsic proof of bad acts when offered to show the witness' character for untruthfulness. Rule 806 could therefore be read literally as prohibiting bad acts impeachment of a hearsay declarant—since the only way to introduce such acts without the witness being there to admit them would be to proffer extrinsic evidence in apparent violation of Rule 608(b). But courts have stated that extrinsic evidence of a bad act offered to prove a hearsay declarant's character for veracity is admissible (subject to Rule 403). The reasoning is that since the declarant is not available for cross-examination, extrinsic evidence is "the only means of presenting such evidence to the jury." *United States v. Friedman,* 854 F.2d 535, n.8 (2nd Cir. 1988). See the extensive discussion of this problem in Cordray, *Evidence Rule 806 and the Problem of the Nontestifying Declarant,* 56 Ohio State L.J. 495 (1995).

21. Rule 807: Rule 807 provides a "residual exception" to the hearsay rule, granting admissibility to trustworthy statements that are "not specifically covered by" other exceptions. There are at least two ways in which the case law diverges from the text and/or Committee Note to Rule 807. First, the Rule permits the admission of residual hearsay only if that hearsay is "not specifically covered" by another exception. This might seem to indicate that hearsay that "nearly misses" one of the established exceptions should not be admissible as residual hearsay—because it is specifically covered by, and yet not admissible under, another exception. In fact, however, most courts have construed the term "not specifically covered" by another hearsay exception to mean "not admissible under" another hearsay exception. See, e.g., *United States v. Fernandez,* 892 F.2d 976 (11th Cir. 1989) (grand jury statement is "not specifically covered" by another hearsay exception because it is not admissible under any such exception). Compare *United*

States v. Dent, 984 F.2d 1453 (7th Cir. 1993) (Easterbrook, J., concurring) (arguing that grand jury testimony can never be admissible as residual hearsay, since such testimony is specifically covered by, though not admissible under, the hearsay exception for prior testimony).

The second divergence between the case law and the text of the residual exception involves the notice requirement. The Rule states that "a statement may not be admitted" under this exception unless the proponent gives notice "sufficiently in advance of trial or hearing to provide the adverse party with a fair opportunity to prepare to meet it." Most courts have read the notice requirement far more flexibly than its language would seem to indicate. For example, most courts have held that the notice requirement can be satisfied by providing notice at trial, so long as the adversary is given sufficient time to prepare. See, e.g., *United States v. Baker,* 985 F.2d 1248 (4th Cir. 1993). Other courts have read a good cause exception into the notice requirement. See, e.g., *United States v. Lyon,* 567 F.2d 777 (8th Cir. 1977). But see *United States v. Ruffin,* 575 F.2d 346 (2d Cir. 1978) (rejecting a good cause exception as not permitted by the text of the Rule).

III. Examples of Case Law Development Where the Rules and Committee Note Are Silent

1. ***Rule 103:*** The Rule provides conditions for a party wishing to preserve a claim of evidentiary error for appeal. It states that a party must make a timely objection or motion to strike, stating the specific ground of objection if that ground is not apparent from the context. An amendment to Rule 103, effective December 1, 2000, further provides that if the trial court makes a definitive ruling on the record admitting or excluding evidence, either at or before trial, a party need not renew an objection or offer of proof to preserve a claim of error for appeal. But the Rule does not address the question whether a party can appeal an advance ruling holding evidence admissible, if the evidence is not actually admitted at trial. For example, assume that a criminal defendant moves in advance of trial to preclude the prosecution from impeaching him with his prior convictions. Assume further that the trial court rules definitively that the convictions are admissible impeachment evidence. Can the defendant decide not to testify at trial, and then argue on appeal that the trial court erred in its advance ruling?

While Rule 103 is silent on whether an appeal can be taken from a ruling holding evidence admissible where the evidence is not eventually admitted at trial, there is significant case law on this question. The Supreme Court, in *Luce v. United States,* 469 U.S. 38 (1984), specifically held that an accused must testify at trial in order to preserve a claim of error predicated upon a trial court's decision to admit the accused's prior convictions for impeachment. The *Luce* principle has been extended by many lower courts to other comparable situations. See *United States v. DiMatteo,* 759 F.2d 831 (11th Cir. 1985) (applying *Luce* where the defendant's witness would be impeached with evidence offered under Rule 608). See also *United States v. Goldman,* 41 F.3d 785, 788 (1st Cir. 1994) ("Although *Luce* involved impeachment by conviction under Rule 609, the reasons given by the Supreme Court for requiring the defendant to testify apply with full force to the kind of Rule 403 and 404 objections that are advanced by Goldman in this case."); *Palmieri v. DeFaria,* 88 F.3d 136 (2d Cir. 1996) (where the plaintiff decided to take an adverse judgment rather than challenge an advance ruling by putting on evidence at trial, the *in limine* ruling would not be reviewed on appeal); *United States v. Ortiz,* 857 F.2d 900 (2d Cir. 1988) (where uncharged misconduct is ruled admissible if the defendant pursues a certain defense, the defendant must actually pursue that defense at trial in order to preserve a claim of error on appeal); *United States v. Bond,* 87 F.3d 695 (5th Cir. 1996) (where the trial court rules *in limine* that the defendant would waive his fifth amendment privilege were he to testify, the defendant must take the stand and testify in order to challenge that ruling on appeal).

Rule 103 is also silent on whether a party who objects to evidence that the trial court definitively rules admissible, and who then offers the evidence to "remove the sting" of its anticipated prejudicial effect, thereby waives the right to appeal the trial court's ruling. Lower courts had been in conflict on this question. See, e.g., *Judd v. Rodman,* 105 F.3d 1339 (11th Cir. 1997) (an objection made *in limine* is sufficient to preserve a claim of error when the movant, as a matter of trial strategy, presents the objectionable evidence herself on direct examination to minimize its prejudicial effect); *Gill v. Thomas,* 83 F.3d 537, 540 (1st Cir. 1996) ("by offering the misdemeanor evidence himself, Gill waived his opportunity to object and thus did not preserve the issue for appeal"). The Supreme Court, in *Ohler v. United States,* 529 U.S. 753 (2000), resolved this question by holding that a party who introduces evidence of a prior conviction on direct examination waives any right to appeal an *in limine* ruling holding that the evidence would be admissible at trial. The Court, in an opinion by Chief Justice Rehnquist, recognized that Rule 103 was silent on this question. It refused to depart from the general common-law rule that "a party introducing evidence cannot complain on appeal that the evidence was erroneously admitted.".

*2. **Rule 104(a):*** This Rule states that preliminary questions "concerning the qualification of a person to be a witness, the existence of a privilege, or the admissibility of evidence shall be determined by the court * * * ." But the Rule is silent on who bears the burden of proof on admissibility questions, and it is also silent on what standard of proof is to be employed. A significant body of case law has been developed to answer these questions. Most importantly, in *Bourjaily v. United States,* 483 U.S. 171 (1987), the Court held that the party seeking to admit the evidence–the proponent–generally has the burden of proving that the admissibility requirements set forth in the Federal Rules are met.

Furthermore, the *Bourjaily* Court held that the burden of proving an admissibility requirement under Rule 104(a) is by a preponderance of the evidence. The specific holding in *Bourjaily* was that for a statement to be admissible under the coconspirator exception to the hearsay rule, the trial court must find that the prosecution has established by a preponderance of the evidence that the defendant and the hearsay declarant were members of the same conspiracy. The reasoning in *Bourjaily* has been extended to most other questions of admissibility under the Federal Rules of Evidence. See, e.g., *Daubert v. Merrell Dow Pharmaceuticals,* 509 U.S. 79 (1993) (proponent of expert testimony has the burden of showing it is more likely than not reliable). So for example, a proponent who proffers a hearsay statement under the excited utterance exception has the burden of showing it more likely than not that the declarant was under the influence of a startling event when he spoke. See *Miller v. Keating,* 754 F.2d 507 (3d Cir. 1985) (proponent must establish admissibility of an excited utterance by a preponderance of the evidence). One important exception arises with privileges. Because privilege rules operate to exclude relevant and reliable evidence, they are not favored. Therefore, the party seeking to *exclude* proffered evidence on the ground that it is privileged bears the burden of showing, by a preponderance of the evidence, that a privilege applies. See generally *United States v. Zolin*, 491 U.S. 554 (1989).

3. Rule 301: This Rule provides some guidance on the effect of a presumption. The Rule does not define the term "presumption"; it simply states that unless otherwise provided, "a presumption imposes on the party against whom it is directed the burden of going forward with evidence to rebut or meet the presumption, but does not shift to such party the burden of proof in the sense of the risk of nonpersuasion." The Rule specifically leaves it to substantive law to determine when proffered evidence establishes a presumption that a fact exists. Generally speaking, presumptions are based on one or more of the following rationales: (1) one party has superior access to proof; (2) social or economic policies warrant a presumption; (3) experience indicates the high probability of a given conclusion from a given set of facts; (4) a presumption will promote efficiency and convenience. So for example, it has been held that proof that a letter was mailed establishes a presumption that it was received. *Anderson v. United States,* 966 F.2d 487 (9th Cir. 1982) (in a taxpayer's suit for a refund, the Government failed to rebut the common-law presumption of receipt that arose from the taxpayer's proof of mailing her return).

Rule 301 is also silent on whether a party favored by a presumption is entitled to a peremptory instruction if the party against whom the presumption operates fails to offer any rebuttal evidence. For example, if a party proves that he mailed a letter, and the opponent provides no conflicting evidence, is the mailing party entitled to an instruction to the jury that the letter is to be deemed mailed? Courts have held that such an instruction must be given upon request. See, e.g., *A.C. Aukerman Co., v. R.L. Chaides Constr. Co.,* 960 F.2d 1020, 1037 (Fed.Cir. 1992) (where presumption applies, the presumed fact "must be inferred, absent rebuttal evidence."). See also C. Mueller & L. Kirkpatrick, *Evidence* at 137 (1st ed. 1995) ("[I]f the basic facts of a presumption are established, the presumption controls decision on the presumed fact unless there is counterproof that the presumed fact is not so. In jury-tried cases, the judge gives an appropriate instruction. In bench-tried cases, the judge must find the presumed fact.").

4. ***Rule 404(b):*** Rule 404(b) provides that a person's uncharged acts of misconduct can be offered to prove something other than a person's character, such as intent or motive. Rule 404(b) imposes a notice requirement on the prosecution in criminal cases, which is intended to protect the accused from unfair surprise; it provides that "upon request by the accused, the prosecution in a criminal case shall provide reasonable notice in advance of trial, or during trial if the court excuses pretrial notice on good cause shown, of the general nature of any such evidence it intends to introduce at trial."

What happens if the government gives pretrial notice of its intent to proffer a prior bad act, and then subsequently discovers a *different* bad act that it wants to use as well? Or what if the government responds to a defense request by stating that it does not intend to use Rule 404(b) evidence, and *then* uncovers a bad act committed by the defendant that it does intend to use? The notice requirement of Rule 404(b) does not state whether the prosecution has a continuing obligation to notify the defendant, should it discover Rule 404(b) evidence after an initial response to the defendant's request. But it has been held that the Rule imposes a continuing obligation of notice. See, e.g., *United States v. Barnes,* 49 F.3d 1144, 1148 (6th Cir. 1995) (declaring that Rule 404(b) requires "a continuing obligation on the government to comply with the notice requirement * * * whenever it discovers information that meets the previous defense request"; noting that a contrary reading "would force the defense to make numerous, periodic requests until the trial has been completed–surely a wasteful procedure.").

The notice requirement of Rule 404(b) is conditioned on a request by the accused. The Rule does not state how specific the request must be to trigger the government's notice obligation. For example, is an omnibus motion for discovery sufficient to trigger the notice requirement? Courts have held that an omnibus motion is not sufficient to trigger the government's obligation to notify under the Rule. Rather, a request for notification, "at a minimum, must be sufficiently clear and particular, in an objective sense, fairly to alert the prosecution that the defense is requesting pretrial notification of the general nature of any Rule 404(b) evidence the prosecution intends to introduce." *United States v. Tuesta–Toro,* 29 F.3d 771, 774 (1st Cir. 1994) (notice not required where defense demanded outright pretrial disclosure of statements in any form, referring to the defendant in any way, without regard to their admissibility or the government's intention to introduce them). Compare *United States v. Williams*, 792 F.Supp. 1120, 1133 (S.D.Ind.1992) (notification required in response to detailed request reciting text of Rule 404(b)); *United States v. Alex*, 791 F.Supp. 723, 728 (N.D.Ill.1992) (notification required in response to request specifically referencing Rule 404(b)).

5. ***Rule 410:*** Rule 410 provides certain protections to criminal defendants during the process of plea bargaining. Rule 410 is silent, however, on whether its protections can be waived by a criminal defendant. In *United States v. Mezzanatto,* 513 U.S. 196 (1995), during guilty plea negotiations the defendant agreed that he could be impeached with statements made during the negotiations if he ultimately went to trial and testified inconsistently with those statements. The Supreme Court upheld the agreement, finding that the defendant had knowingly and voluntarily waived his right to the protection of Rule 410. The Court refused to hold that the Rule's silence on the matter meant that its protections could not be waived. Instead the Court presumed that any statutory right could be waived in the absence of a specific provision to the contrary, so long as the waiver was knowing and voluntary. The facts of *Mezzanatto* involved a waiver permitting the use for impeachment purposes of statements made during guilty plea negotiations. Neither *Mezzanatto* nor Rule 410 itself says anything explicitly about whether a defendant can waive the protections of the Rule so as to provide that the prosecution can admit his statements during plea negotiations as substantive evidence at trial, i.e., as party-admissions admissible even if the defendant does not testify. At least one court has relied on the rationale of *Mezzanatto* to uphold a waiver of Rule 410 protections that permitted the government to use the defendant's statements as substantive evidence in its case-in-chief. See *United States v. Burch,* 156 F.3d 1315 (D.C.Cir. 1998).

6. ***Article VI:*** Article VI governs treatment of testifying witnesses. The Article is silent about many of the common forms of impeachment, such as bias, contradiction, and mental capacity. There is, of course, a significant amount of case law dealing with impeachment matters on which Article VI is silent. Case law generally regulates the forms of impeachment not specifically covered by Article VI by using principles derived from Evidence Rules 402 and 403–such impeachment is permitted unless the probative value of the impeachment evidence is substantially outweighed by the risks of prejudice, confusion and delay. See *United States v. Abel,* 469 U.S. 45 (1984) (impeachment for bias governed by Rule 403 principles). See generally S. Saltzburg, M. Martin and D. Capra, *Federal Rules of Evidence Manual* 939–970, 1139–1148; 3 C. Mueller & L. Kirkpatrick, *Federal Evidence* 109–207, 327–470 (2d ed. 1994). See also Imwinkelreid, *The Silence Speaks Volumes: A Brief Reflection on the Question of Whether It Is Necessary To Fill the Seeming Gaps In Article VI of the Federal Rules of Evidence, Governing the*

Admissibility of Evidence Logically Relevant to the Witness's Credibility, 1998 Univ. Ill. L.Rev. 1013, 1036 (noting that Article VI is silent about most matters of impeachment, but concluding that "as a general proposition, there is little to be gained and much to be lost by initiating the process of revising Article VI.").

7. ***Rule 615:*** Rule 615 provides that at the request of a party, and with some exceptions, "the court shall order witnesses excluded so that they cannot hear the testimony of other witnesses, and it may also make the order of its own motion." The Rule specifically provides only for exclusion of witnesses from the courtroom. It is silent about whether a trial judge can order witnesses not to talk to each other outside the courtroom; it says nothing about a judge's power to order a potential witness to refrain from obtaining access to certain information, such as newspaper articles, that might taint the witness' testimony. The courts have held, however, that the trial court retains its common-law power to fashion a more far-reaching sequestration order appropriate to the circumstances of the case .. See the extensive discussion in *United States v. Sepulveda,* 15 F.3d 1161, 1175 (1st Cir. 1993) (Rule 615 "demarcates a compact procedural heartland, but leaves appreciable room for judicial innovation beyond the perimeters of that which the rule explicitly requires"). This common-law power includes the discretion to sequester witnesses before, during, and after their testimony, see *Geders v. United States*, 425 U.S. 80 (1976), and to compel the parties to present witnesses in a prescribed sequence. *United States v. Machor*, 879 F.2d 945, 954 (1st Cir.1989). As the court in *Sepulveda* stated: "Rule 615 neither dictates when and how this case-management power ought to be used nor mandates any specific extra-courtroom prophylaxis, instead leaving the regulation of witness conduct outside the courtroom to the district judge's discretion."

8. ***Rule 801(d)(1)(B):*** This Rule provides that a statement is not excluded as hearsay if the witness is subject to cross-examination and the statement is "consistent with the declarant's testimony and is offered to rebut an express or implied charge of recent fabrication." The hearsay exemption for prior consistent statements does not specifically provide that the prior consistent statement must *precede* the existence of the alleged motive to falsify in order to be admissible. However, the Supreme Court in *Tome v. United States*, 513 U.S. 150 (1995), held that a statement is not admissible under Rule 801(d)(1)(B) unless it was made before the witness's alleged motive to falsify arose.

Rule 801(d)(1)(B) is also silent on whether prior consistent statements can be admitted independently of the Rule, not for their truth but rather to rehabilitate the credibility of the witness. The courts have held that a consistent statement could be probative and admissible for rehabilitation purposes even if it is not admissible under the hearsay exemption. See, e.g., *United States v. Brennan,* 798 F.2d 581, 587 (2nd Cir. 1986) (prior consistent statement was not admissible to rebut a charge of improper motive, but it was admissible to clarify an apparent inconsistency that had been brought out by defense counsel on cross-examination: "prior consistent statements may be admissible for rehabilitation even if not admissible under Rule 801(d)(1)(B)."). Accord *United States v. Parodi,* 703 F.2d 768 (4th Cir. 1983).

9. Rule 803(3): The Rule provides a hearsay exception for statements of a declarant's state of mind. The Rule is silent, however, on whether a declarant's statement of intent can be used to prove the subsequent conduct of someone other than the declarant. When the victim says, "I am going to meet Frank tonight", is the statement admissible to prove that Frank and the victim actually met? Or is the statement admissible only to prove the future conduct of the declarant? The Advisory Committee Note refers to the Rule as allowing "evidence of intention as tending to prove the act intended." The case law is conflicted. Some courts have refused to admit a statement that the declarant intended to meet with a third party as proof that they actually did meet. See, e.g., *Gual Morales v. Hernandez Vega*, 579 F.2d 677 (1st Cir. 1978); *United States v. Jenkins,* 579 F.2d 840 (4th Cir. 1978) (statements of intent can prove only the declarant's subsequent conduct). Other courts hold such statements admissible if the proponent provides corroborating evidence that the meeting took place. See, e.g., *United States v. Delvecchio,* 816 F.2d 59 (2nd Cir. 1987). See C. Mueller and L. Kirkpatrick, *Evidence* at 938 (1st ed. 1995) ("Some modern cases take the clearly correct position that the exception in its present form cannot justify use of statements of intent by themselves as proof of what others did. And yet a growing number of cases approve use of a statement to prove what the speaker and another did together if other evidence confirms what the statement suggests the other did.").

10. Rule 803(18): Rule 803(18) provides a hearsay exception for "statements contained in published treatises, periodicals, or pamphlets" if they are "established as a reliable authority" by the testimony or admission of an expert witness or by judicial notice. The Rule does not mention whether the learned treatise exception covers evidence presented in demonstrative form, such as a chart or film. But the Second Circuit has upheld the admission of an authoritative videotape under the learned treatise exception. See *Costantino v. Herzog,* 203 F.3d 164, 171 (2d Cir. 2000) (reasoning that it is "overly artificial to say that information that is sufficiently trustworthy to overcome the hearsay bar when presented in a printed learned treatise loses the badge of trustworthiness when presented in a videotape").

11. Rule 1101: Rule 1101 states that the Federal Rules of Evidence are generally applicable to all federal proceedings. Rule 1101(d) lists certain proceedings to which the Rules are inapplicable, including grand jury and bail proceedings. Courts have found that the Federal Rules are inapplicable to a number of proceedings that are not specifically mentioned as exempt in Rule 1101(d). Examples include suppression hearings, proceedings to obtain a temporary restraining order, and proceedings seeking release from psychiatric commitment. See, e.g., *United States v. Frazier,* 26 F.3d 110 (11th Cir. 1994) (Evidence Rules inapplicable in supervised release revocation proceedings); *United States v. Schaefer,* 87 F.3d 562 (1st Cir. 1996) (evidence rules inapplicable at suppression hearings); *United States v. Palesky,* 855 F.2d 34 (1st Cir. 1988) (Evidence Rules are not applicable in hearings held to determine whether a person will be committed to or released from a psychiatric facility). The courts establish these exemptions because they are within the spirit of Rule 1101(d)–exempting from the Rules those proceedings that are less formal than a trial and in which the judge is the finder of fact. See e.g., *Government of Virgin Islands in Interest of A.M.*, 34 F.3d 153, 161 (3rd Cir. 1994) (Evidence Rules do not apply in juvenile transfer proceedings, even though such proceedings are not specifically exempted in Rule 1101(d)(1); a juvenile transfer proceeding "is of a preliminary nature and is consequently not comparable to a civil or criminal trial.").

†

A. S.